(MCTS) Microsoft BizTalk Server (70-595) Certification and Assessment Guide

Second Edition

Including Microsoft Partner Network Technical Competency Assessment for Application Integration (BizTalk Server 2013) and Windows Azure BizTalk Services coverage

Johan Hedberg
Morten la Cour
Kent Weare

[PACKT] enterprise
PUBLISHING
professional expertise distilled

BIRMINGHAM - MUMBAI

(MCTS) Microsoft BizTalk Server (70-595) Certification and Assessment Guide

Second Edition

First published: June 2012

Second Edition: March 2014

Production Reference: 2280214

Published by Packt Publishing Ltd.
Livery Place
35 Livery Street
Birmingham B3 2PB, UK.

ISBN 978-1-78217-210-9

www.packtpub.com

Cover Image by Ankita Jha (ankitajha17@gmail.com)

Credits

Authors

Johan Hedberg

Morten la Cour

Kent Weare

Reviewers

Jan Eliasen

Mikael Håkansson

Todd Uhl

Steef-Jan Wiggers

Acquisition Editors

Nikhil Karkal

Mary Nadar

Content Development Editor

Vaibhav Pawar

Technical Editors

Shashank Desai

Rosmy George

Abhishek Kanade

Ankita Thakur

Copy Editors

Janbal Dharmaraj

Sayanee Mukherjee

Deepa Nambiar

Karuna Narayanan

Project Coordinator

Amey Sawant

Proofreaders

Bridget Braund

Mario Cecere

Indexer

Monica Ajmera Mehta

Graphics

Ronak Dhruv

Abhinash Sahu

Production Coordinator

Manu Joseph

Cover Work

Manu Joseph

About the Authors

Johan Hedberg is based in Stockholm, Sweden, where he does consultancy, solution architecture, training, mentoring, speaking, and authoring. Johan has 15 years of experience architecting and developing enterprise-grade solutions based on Microsoft technologies. He works closely with Microsoft as a Virtual Technology Solution Professional (V-TSP) and with the community as a Microsoft Most Valuable Professional (MVP), and is one of the founders of the BizTalk User Group Sweden. He blogs irregularly at `http://blogical.se/blogs/johan` and can be found as `@JoHed` on Twitter.

I would like to say thanks to the people at Microsoft for encouraging a second edition that would otherwise not have come to pass and to my fellow authors, Kent and Morten, for again sharing the work. A special thanks to my family, Maria and the boys, for their patience as work takes up weeknights and weekends and for keeping me balanced. To Max for the struggle still ahead.

Morten la Cour has worked with the MS BizTalk Server platform for nine years. Besides designing and developing Integration solution for customers, he has also worked on deployment and maintenance of BizTalk applications and BizTalk Server environments.

Starting in 2011, he is also working with Windows Azure, Azure Service Bus, and the new Windows Azure BizTalk Services.

He has taught several BizTalk Server courses in development, deployment, and management.

Besides working with MS BizTalk Server, Morten has 15 years of experience on the Microsoft development platform, including the .NET Framework and SQL Server. Other experiences include XML, XSLT, XPATH, and Oracle databases.

I would like to thank my daughter (Clara) and girlfriend (Daniela) for their patience during all the writing weekends, thus leading up to this book.

Kent Weare was born in Regina, Saskatchewan, Canada. He developed a love for ice hockey, football, and technology. He attended the University of Regina, where he obtained a Degree in Computer Science. After completing his undergraduate degree, he spent time in India completing a Post Graduate diploma in Object Oriented Technology. Recently, Kent has decided to pursue a Master's Degree in Information Management from Arizona State University. He currently lives in Calgary, Alberta, Canada but remains a die-hard Saskatchewan Roughrider football fan.

Kent began his career at a small Internet startup before taking on a junior role with the Saskatchewan Government. Since then, he has worked on projects for the Canadian Federal Government, a multinational bank in the United States, health care projects in Eastern and Western Canada, and has spent the last eight years employed in the Energy/Utilities sector in Calgary. Kent's current role as a senior enterprise architect involves setting the technical direction for the organization and is very involved in cross-domain disciplines such as Integration and Mobility.

During Kent's time at the Federal Government, he had an opportunity to participate in his first BizTalk project. Ten years later, he is still "hooked" on BizTalk, having worked with every BizTalk version released since then.

In 2008, Kent was awarded his first Microsoft MVP award for BizTalk Server. He continues to be active in the BizTalk community and recently, received his sixth consecutive MVP award. Kent maintains active blogs at http://kentweare. blogspot.com and http://www.MiddlewareInTheCloud.com. He may also be seen presenting BizTalk-related material at local and international user groups.

Recently, Kent has co-authored two BizTalk books: *Microsoft BizTalk 2010: Line of Business Systems Integration and (MCTS)* and *BizTalk Server 2010 (70-595) Certification Guide*.

Writing a book is a very demanding activity. Writing a book while working full time makes a person question his or her sanity. Writing a book while working full time and pursuing a Master's degree confirms one's sanity or lack thereof. I would not have been able to contribute to this book without the support of my wife, Melissa, and my two kids, Brooke and Paige. So, thank you for putting up with this activity once again. I can't say this will be the last time I do this but at least while pursuing a Master's degree, it will be.

During the period in which I contributed to this book, I also joined a new organization. While at this organization, I introduced BizTalk and could not have done so without the tremendous support from Nipa Chakravarti and Nguyen Tran. The two of you are true professionals, and I have benefitted so much by working with you.

Lastly, I want to thank the BizTalk community and more specifically, the Microsoft Integration MVPs. Never in my life have I been associated with such a quality group of individuals. Every time we meet up, it is like a family reunion, so SKOL to Mikael, Johan, Mick, Steef-Jan, Richard, Stephen, Saravana, Tord, Nino, Sandro, Michael, Dan, Ben, Leonid, Bill, Rick, Dwight, Jon, and Matt.

About the Reviewers

Jan Eliasen has a Master's degree in Computer Science and has nine years of experience using BizTalk Server, starting from BizTalk Server 2002. Jan is a five-time and current Microsoft MVP in BizTalk Server, and he has passed all the five existing exams in BizTalk.

Jan is a co-author of the *Microsoft BizTalk Server 2010 Unleashed* book.

Mikael Håkansson is employed by Breeze in Australia. He has a long-standing commitment to the community through the contribution of free software and components, such as BizTalk SFTP Adapter and BizTalk Benchmark Wizard. He has been recognized as a Microsoft Most Valuable Professional (MVP). Mikael maintains his blog at `http://blogical.se/blogs/mikael`, and you can also follow him on twitter at `@wmmihaa`.

Todd Uhl is an IT consultant with over 15 years of experience in Microsoft developer technologies. He has been working with all facets of BizTalk Server since its original launch. He currently works for a large software company supporting customers in all their endeavors with BizTalk.

> I would like to thank my beautiful wife, Mechelle, for always putting up with me and my two boys, Owen and Sebastian, for bringing a smile to my face every day.

Steef-Jan Wiggers has over 15 years of experience as a technical lead developer, application architect, and consultant, specializing in custom applications, enterprise application integration (BizTalk), web services, and Windows Azure. He works for SLTN in the Netherlands and is very active in the BizTalk community (`http://social.technet.microsoft.com/wiki/contents/articles/7141.user-page-steef-jan-wiggers-microsoft-biztalk-server-consultant-and-mvp.aspx`) as a blogger, Wiki author/editor on forums, writer, and public speaker in the Netherlands and Europe. For these efforts, Microsoft has recognized him as a Microsoft MVP for the past four years. On his personal blog (`http://soa-thoughts.blogspot.com/`) and BizTalk Administrators blog (`http://www.biztalkadminsblogging.com/`), he shares his knowledge around SOA, Azure (ServiceBus), BizTalk Services, and BizTalk.

In addition to consulting, Steef-Jan is also an author and technical editor for Packt Publishing. He has written the *BizTalk Server 2010 Cookbook* available through *Packt Publishing* and was a technical reviewer for the *BizTalk Server 2010 Patterns* book by *Dan Rosanova* and *(MCTS): Microsoft BizTalk Server 2010 (70-595) Certification Guide* by *Johan Hedberg, Morten la Cour,* and *Kent Weare.*

> The second edition of this book is an excellent guide for you to prepare for either the 2010 exam or 2013 assessment. It has been a joy reviewing it, and I like to thank the authors Johan Hedberg, Morten la Cour, and Kent Weare for giving me the opportunity. They have done an excellent job writing it.

www.PacktPub.com

Support files, eBooks, discount offers and more

You might want to visit www.PacktPub.com for support files and downloads related to your book.

Did you know that Packt offers eBook versions of every book published, with PDF and ePub files available? You can upgrade to the eBook version at www.PacktPub.com and as a print book customer, you are entitled to a discount on the eBook copy. Get in touch with us at service@packtpub.com for more details.

At www.PacktPub.com, you can also read a collection of free technical articles, sign up for a range of free newsletters and receive exclusive discounts and offers on Packt books and eBooks.

PACKTLIB

http://PacktLib.PacktPub.com

Do you need instant solutions to your IT questions? PacktLib is Packt's online digital book library. Here, you can access, read and search across Packt's entire library of books.

Why Subscribe?
- Fully searchable across every book published by Packt
- Copy and paste, print and bookmark content
- On demand and accessible via web browser

Free Access for Packt account holders

If you have an account with Packt at www.PacktPub.com, you can use this to access PacktLib today and view nine entirely free books. Simply use your login credentials for immediate access.

Instant Updates on New Packt Books

Get notified! Find out when new books are published by following @PacktEnterprise on Twitter, or the *Packt Enterprise* Facebook page.

Table of Contents

Preface

This book will give you all the information you need to pass the 70-595 TS: Developing Business Process and Integration Solutions exam using Microsoft BizTalk Server 2010. Additionally, this second edition of the book will also provide the information needed for Microsoft Partners to complete the Microsoft Partner Network Technical Assessment for Application Integration (BizTalk Server 2013).

The book's intent is to be as focused as possible on providing content for just what you need to know, while still providing context to allow you to understand rather than just remember. Coverage of additional topics that are not included in the exam has been filtered out to reduce the noise.

Included in this book are also close to 60 sample questions that help re-enforce what you need to know as well as let you practice the type and style of questions given in the exam itself.

At the same time, though the book is tailored for the tests, you will not find the actual words or questions of either in this book. This book was made to help you strengthen your knowledge of the product and allow you to focus your learning towards a goal. It is not a cheat sheet. However, if you understand the content of this book, you will be fully equipped to pass the exam as well as the assessment.

The book follows an outline similar to the exam to provide a mapping towards certification objectives. This helps you practice as well as better understand the certification objectives that you are strong in and those which may need development. The certification objectives are supplied at `http://www.microsoft.com/learning/en/us/exam.aspx?ID=70-595`.

The objectives of the assessment are included in these chapters, in this outline, and in the additional chapter dedicated to BizTalk Server on Azure and Windows Azure BizTalk Services.

What this book covers

Chapter 1, Configuring a Messaging Architecture, covers the core architecture of BizTalk, including publish/subscribe, context and content-based routing, Receive and Send Ports, and other administrative artifacts.

Chapter 2, Developing BizTalk Artifacts – Creating Schemas and Pipelines, covers creating rich and useful Schemas with restrictions and reusable types.

Chapter 3, Developing BizTalk Artifacts – Creating Maps, covers creating Maps and applying logic, such as conditional mapping, looping, scripting and external assemblies, and other map and Functoid logic.

Chapter 4, Developing BizTalk Artifacts – Creating Orchestrations, covers creating Orchestrations and working with messages, scopes, transactions, binding, correlation, and other shapes and processing logic.

Chapter 5, Testing, Debugging, and Exception Handling, covers handling exceptions in messaging and Orchestration scenarios and recovering from them using catch, compensation, and failed message routing.

Chapter 6, Deploying, Tracking, and Administrating a BizTalk Server 2010 Solution, covers performing administrative tasks, such as installing, configuring, tuning, deploying, maintaining, and troubleshooting BizTalk Server 2010 groups and solutions.

Chapter 7, Integrating Web Services and Windows Communication Foundation (WCF) Services, covers working with Web Services and WCF, exposing and consuming services, and applying custom configurations and behaviors.

Chapter 8, Implementing Extended Capabilities, covers using the additional features in BizTalk, such as Business Rules Engine (BRE), Electronic Data Interchange (EDI), and Business Activity Monitoring (BAM).

Chapter 9, Using Azure BizTalk Features, covers setting up and developing Windows Azure BizTalk Services (WABS) as well as using Windows Azure Virtual Machine Infrastructure as a Service (IaaS) capability for BizTalk Server.

Chapter 10, Test-taking – Tips and Tricks, covers additional resources for learning tips, tricks, and strategies for preparing for and taking the certification.

Appendix A, Sample Certification Test Questions, contains additional sample certification questions to reinforce what you learned and provide training on the certification format.

Appendix B, Sample Certification Test Question – Answers, contains the answers and short explanations to the sample certification questions in *Appendix A*.

Appendix C, Testing Your Knowledge – Answers, contains the answers and short explanations to the questions in the *Testing Your Knowledge* section contained in each chapter.

What you need for this book

This book comes with sample code to provide hands on and practical implementation of the theory provided in the book. In some cases, the code is meant to be viewed in Visual Studio, other times to be deployed to show the aspects of deployment, configuration, or runtime. For the second edition of the book, we have chosen to update all code samples to BizTalk Server 2013. All concepts and techniques shown are, however, equally usable for BizTalk Server 2010. To view, deploy, and run the code, the following requirements are needed:

- Windows Server 2012, Windows Server 2008 R2 SP1, Windows 8 or Windows 7 SP1
- IIS 8.0 or IIS 7.5
- .NET Framework 4.5
- SQL Server 2008 R2 SP1 or SQL Server 2012
- Visual Studio 2012 with Visual C#.NET and Visual Web Developer
- BizTalk Server 2013 Developer edition
- Excel 2013 or Excel 2010 (for business activity monitoring)

The first edition of the book has sample code that works with BizTalk Server 2010 and Visual Studio 2010

Who this book is for

This book is for anyone wanting to achieve the certification of Microsoft Certified Technology Specialist (MCTS): Microsoft BizTalk Server 2010 by passing the 70-595: TS: Developing Business Process and Integration Solutions exam using Microsoft BizTalk Server 2010 or a Microsoft Partner that wants to pass the Microsoft Partner Network Technical Assessment for Application Integration (BizTalk Server 2013) exam.

The target audience for this book is similar as for the exam. A typical reader is someone who works as a BizTalk developer today. You are familiar with the product and the technology in and around it, having had at least a year or so of exposure to developing BizTalk Server integration solutions primarily but perhaps not using all parts of the product.

Even senior BizTalk developers aiming to get certified will benefit from this book because of the refresh on important topics and targeted study that it provides.

This book is not for a beginner who wants to use it to learn the basics of BizTalk Server as it will start from a level and continue at a pace where you are assumed to be accustomed to those basics already.

The typical exam candidate listed on the certification web page suggests slightly more than the following message:

> *Candidates should have at least two years of experience developing, deploying, testing, troubleshooting and debugging BizTalk Server 2006 or later across multiple projects and have experience using the Microsoft .NET Framework, XML, Microsoft Visual Studio, Microsoft SQL Server, Web services, and WCF while developing BizTalk integration solutions.*

Conventions

In this book, you will find a number of styles of text that distinguish between different kinds of information. Here are some examples of these styles, and an explanation of their meaning.

Code words in text, database table names, folder names, filenames, file extensions, pathnames, dummy URLs, user input, and Twitter handles are shown as follows: "The state of a Receive Location is merely a flag inside the `Receive Location` table in the `Management` database of the BizTalk Group."

A block of code is set as follows:

```
<xs:schema xmlns="http://Chapter02_Example01.Schemas.
SimplifiedCar" xmlns:b="http://schemas.microsoft.com/BizTalk/2003"
targetNamespace="http://Chapter02_Example01.Schemas.SimplifiedCar"
xmlns:xs="http://www.w3.org/2001/XMLSchema">
  <xs:element name="Car">
    <xs:complexType>
      <xs:sequence>
        <xs:element name="RegistrationNo" type="xs:string" />
        <xs:element name="Make" type="xs:string" />
        <xs:element name="Model" type="xs:string" />
        <xs:element name="Color" type="xs:string" />
      </xs:sequence>
    </xs:complexType>
  </xs:element>
</xs:schema>
```

When we wish to draw your attention to a particular part of a code block, the relevant lines or items are set in bold:

```
<xs:annotation>
  <xs:appinfo>
    <b:schemaInfo is_envelope="yes" />
  </xs:appinfo>
  </xs:annotation>
  <xs:element name="ManufacturingReport">
  <xs:annotation>
  <xs:appinfo>
      <b:recordInfo body_XPath="/*[local-
name()='ManufacturingReport' and namespace-uri()='http://Chapter02_
Example03.Schemas.CarEnvelope']/*[local-name()='Cars' and namespace-
uri()='']" />
    </xs:appinfo>
  </xs:annotation>
```

Any command-line input or output is written as follows:

```
The 'RegistrationNo' element is invalid - The value 'RegistrationNo_0'
is invalid according to its datatype 'String' - The Pattern constraint
failed.

File 'Car02.xml' is not a valid instance of schema file 'Car02.xsd'.
```

New terms and **important words** are shown in bold. Words that you see on the screen, in menus or dialog boxes for example, appear in the text like this: "The **Group Hub** window gives the user an overview of what is currently going on inside BizTalk".

> Warnings or important notes appear in a box like this.

> Tips and tricks appear like this.

Reader feedback

Feedback from our readers is always welcome. Let us know what you think about this book—what you liked or may have disliked. Reader feedback is important for us to develop titles that you really get the most out of.

To send us general feedback, simply send an e-mail to feedback@packtpub.com, and mention the book title via the subject of your message.

If there is a topic that you have expertise in and you are interested in either writing or contributing to a book, see our author guide on www.packtpub.com/authors.

Customer support

Now that you are the proud owner of a Packt book, we have a number of things to help you to get the most from your purchase.

Downloading the example code

You can download the example code files for all Packt books you have purchased from your account at http://www.packtpub.com. If you purchased this book elsewhere, you can visit http://www.packtpub.com/support and register to have the files e-mailed directly to you.

Errata

Although we have taken every care to ensure the accuracy of our content, mistakes do happen. If you find a mistake in one of our books—maybe a mistake in the text or the code—we would be grateful if you would report this to us. By doing so, you can save other readers from frustration and help us improve subsequent versions of this book. If you find any errata, please report them by visiting http://www.packtpub.com/submit-errata, selecting your book, clicking on the **errata submission form** link, and entering the details of your errata. Once your errata are verified, your submission will be accepted and the errata will be uploaded on our website, or added to any list of existing errata, under the Errata section of that title. Any existing errata can be viewed by selecting your title from http://www.packtpub.com/support.

Piracy

Piracy of copyright material on the Internet is an ongoing problem across all media. At Packt, we take the protection of our copyright and licenses very seriously. If you come across any illegal copies of our works, in any form, on the Internet, please provide us with the location address or website name immediately so that we can pursue a remedy.

Please contact us at copyright@packtpub.com with a link to the suspected pirated material.

We appreciate your help in protecting our authors, and our ability to bring you valuable content.

Questions

You can contact us at questions@packtpub.com if you are having a problem with any aspect of the book, and we will do our best to address it.

1
Configuring a Messaging Architecture

This chapter covers the *Configuring a Messaging Architecture* part of the exam. It will introduce some of the basic concepts of the messaging architecture in BizTalk, and also give the reader an insight into configuring some of the core Adapters in BizTalk. Other areas in this chapter will be the publish/subscribe engine, port authentication, and some discussions about implementing messaging patterns.

In this chapter, the following topics will be covered:

- The publish/subscribe mechanism
- BizTalk Platform Settings
- Ports
- Core Adapters
- Messaging patterns
- Testing your knowledge

Understanding the publish or subscribe model

At its core, BizTalk is a publish/subscribe engine, nothing more nothing less. Whenever a message is received, BizTalk will look through all subscriptions and pass a copy of the message to all the subscribers, if any. The following are the three kinds of artifacts inside BizTalk that can subscribe to messages:

- Send Ports
- Orchestrations
- Request-Response Receive Ports

If messages, for some reason, cannot be sent to one or more of the subscribers, BizTalk will store the message for resuming or later analysis as to why the message could not be delivered. When all subscribers have processed their messages, BizTalk will no longer need to hold on to the message, and the message will be removed from BizTalk. A new subscriber will not be able to subscribe to messages that have already been processed and delivered inside BizTalk.

The following model shows how the BizTalk publish/subscribe mechanism works:

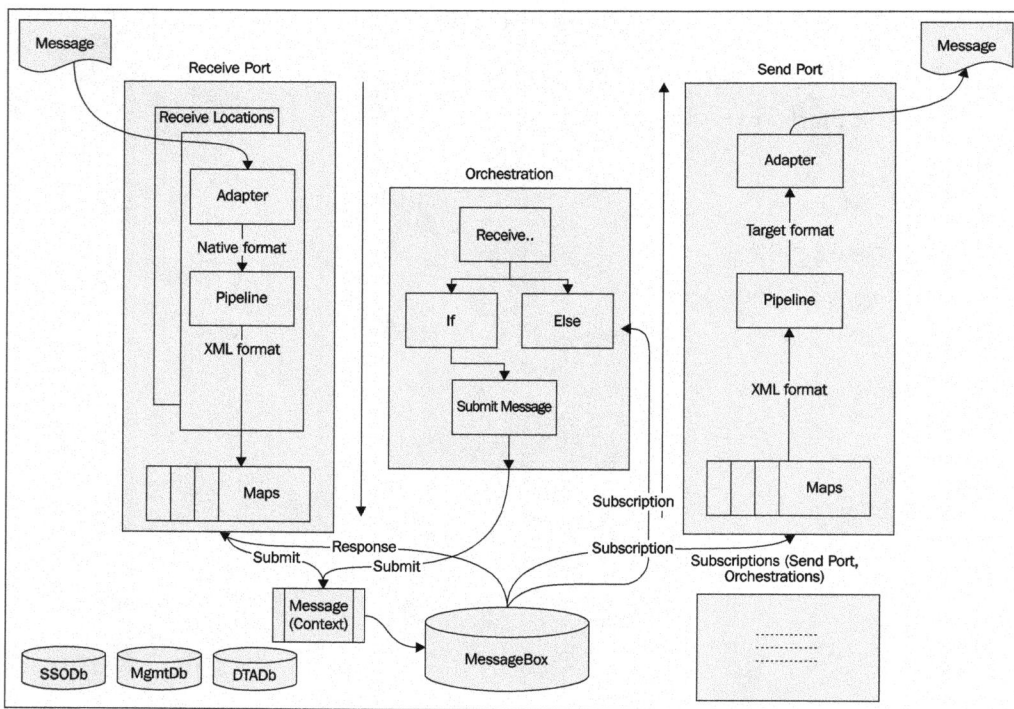

The previous diagram shows a BizTalk Server Group. The BizTalk Server Group consists of at least four databases, which are as follows:

- `SSODB`: This is used to store passwords and other configuration parameters that should be hidden from even administrators
- `BizTalkMgmtDb`: This is a management database that is used to store metadata about the BizTalk Server Group
- `BizTalkDTADb`: This is a `Tracking` database that is used to store tracking information and actual messages of what has passed through BizTalk
- `BizTalkMsgBoxDb`: This is used for storing message parts, message metadata, subscriptions, and so on, which will be covered in detail later

Receiving the message

First, BizTalk Server will receive a message through the Receive Port. A message is received in a Receive Port through one of the Receive Locations associated with the Port. A Receive Port contains one to many Receive Locations. Each Receive Location contains one Adapter and one Pipeline. Each Receive Port can hold any number of Maps, but no Map is required.

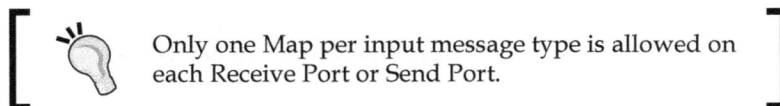

> Only one Map per input message type is allowed on each Receive Port or Send Port.

Adapter

The Adapter, responsible for communicating with the various applications/protocols needed, receives or picks up messages or batches of messages, writes metadata to the Context (message metadata) of the message, and sends the message to the Pipeline.

Some examples of Adapters are as follows:

- FILE
- FTP
- SQL
- HTTP
- Web Service (WCF)
- SAP
- Third party
- Custom build

Pipeline

The main purpose of the Pipeline, on the receive side, is to recognize the message type and transform the native format of the message into XML, if needed. Out of the box, two Receive Pipelines are available: **PassThruReceive** and **XMLReceive**. Of these two Pipelines, only **XMLReceive** will recognize the Message Type, whereas **PassThruReceive** will send the message onwards to the MessageBox as an unknown type.

Some examples of native formats are as follows:

- XML
- Flat Files (comma separated values, positional, and so on)
- EDI (X12, EDIFACT, and so on)
- Excel *
- PDF *

> * Not included in BizTalk, needs to be custom written or purchased from third-party vendors.

The Receive Pipeline will do parts or all of the following activities:

- Decrypt the message if needed
- Convert the native format into XML
- De-batch the message
- Promote properties (write metadata to the Context of the message)
- Validate the XML message to a Schema
- Resolve the sender of the message if signed (see more about this in *Chapter 2, Developing BizTalk Artifacts – Creating Schemas and Pipelines*)

Maps

Now, the message is evaluated with the Maps applied on the Receive Port (if any); if the message matches the source message type on a Map, the Map will be applied.

> If the output of the Map executed again matches the source of another Map on the Port, this Map will not be executed; only one Map can be applied to a message on a Port.

MessageBox

The MessageBox is a SQL Server database where all messages received by BizTalk are stored, evaluated with all subscriptions, and sent to matching subscriptions.

The main purposes of the MessageBox are as follows:

- Storing all subscriptions
- Storing all messages (both bodies and Context) entering BizTalk
- Storing all Host queues
- Evaluating subscriptions
- Distributing messages to the matching subscribers
- Storing failed and awaiting messages

Whenever a message is received by BizTalk, the receiving message agent will store the message in the MessageBox. During the publishing of the message, the agent will check all the subscriptions inside the MessageBox with the Context of the message, and all matching subscribers will get a reference to the actual message in their respective Host queues. When all subscribers have successfully processed their messages, the message is no longer required in the MessageBox and it will be removed. The MessageBox also consists of all the subscriptions inside the BizTalk Group. Subscriptions are primarily made by Send Ports and Orchestrations; they will be discussed in the following section.

Subscriptions

A subscription in BizTalk means that if certain parameters concerning the message are met, the subscriber will get a copy of that message.

A subscription could look something similar to the following pseudo code:

```
((Message Type = Order) and (Customer = HP)) or (Message Type =
Invoice)
```

This would result in the subscriber getting all invoices entering BizTalk and also all orders from HP.

Subscriptions are made by Send Ports, Orchestrations, or Request-Response Receive Ports. If a Send Port subscription is met, the message will be sent through the Send Port to the target system/location. If an Orchestration activation subscription is met, a new instance of that Orchestration type will be initialized (read more about Orchestrations in *Chapter 4, Developing BizTalk Artifacts – Creating Orchestrations*). All the matching subscriptions will get a copy of the message, so a one-way message entering the MessageBox can easily have more than one subscriber, and therefore, be replicated to multiple subscribers.

We will further look into Send Port subscriptions in the *Setting up a Send Port* section later in this chapter.

Message Context Properties

When subscribing, it is not possible to subscribe to any content of the actual messages entering BizTalk, but only to what information is stored in the Context of the message. The message metadata is called **Context Properties**; on receiving the message, the Adapter, Pipeline, and Map will possibly add information to the Context.

Context Properties can either be **Promoted** or **Not promoted**. Properties that are promoted can be used for subscribing to the message. However, **Not promoted** properties cannot be used for subscribing to the message.

Orchestrations

An Orchestration can receive messages from the MessageBox, based on its subscriptions. The subscriptions can either be an activating subscription (which will start a new Orchestration) or an instance subscription (which will deliver the message to an existing running Orchestration). If an Orchestration needs to send or receive messages during the execution, it will happen through the MessageBox, with the Orchestration submitting messages just as the Receive Ports and receiving messages similar to the Send Port.

Sending the message

When a message is sent to a Send Port, the process is almost reverse of what happened in the Receive Port, except that the location concept doesn't exist on a Send Port.

Maps

First, if Maps are applied to the Port, BizTalk will try to match the type of the message in hand with the source Message Type of the Map(s) on the Port; if a valid Map is found, it will be applied to the message.

> Just as Receive Ports, there will only be one Map executed on a Send Port.

Pipeline

Next, the Pipeline will typically do some or all of the following activities:

- Validate the message
- Convert the message from XML to the desired target format
- Encrypt and sign the message if needed

Adapter

Finally, the Adapter will transmit the message to the destination location.

Getting started with the BizTalk Platform Settings and Applications

This section talks about how the various BizTalk platform settings and Applications work and are configured.

BizTalk Administration Console

In this section, we will look at the BizTalk Administration Console, which is used for managing and configuring the BizTalk Server and to deploy, manage, monitor, and troubleshoot BizTalk Applications.

The Group Hub

The **Group Hub** window gives the user an overview of what is currently going on inside BizTalk.

To view the **Group Hub** window, open the BizTalk Administration Console and click on **BizTalk Group**.

A dashboard will appear where we get an overview of Applications that are currently running, how many running messages are currently in the `MessageBox`, and how many suspended messages there are.

An overview of the dashboard can be seen in the following screenshot:

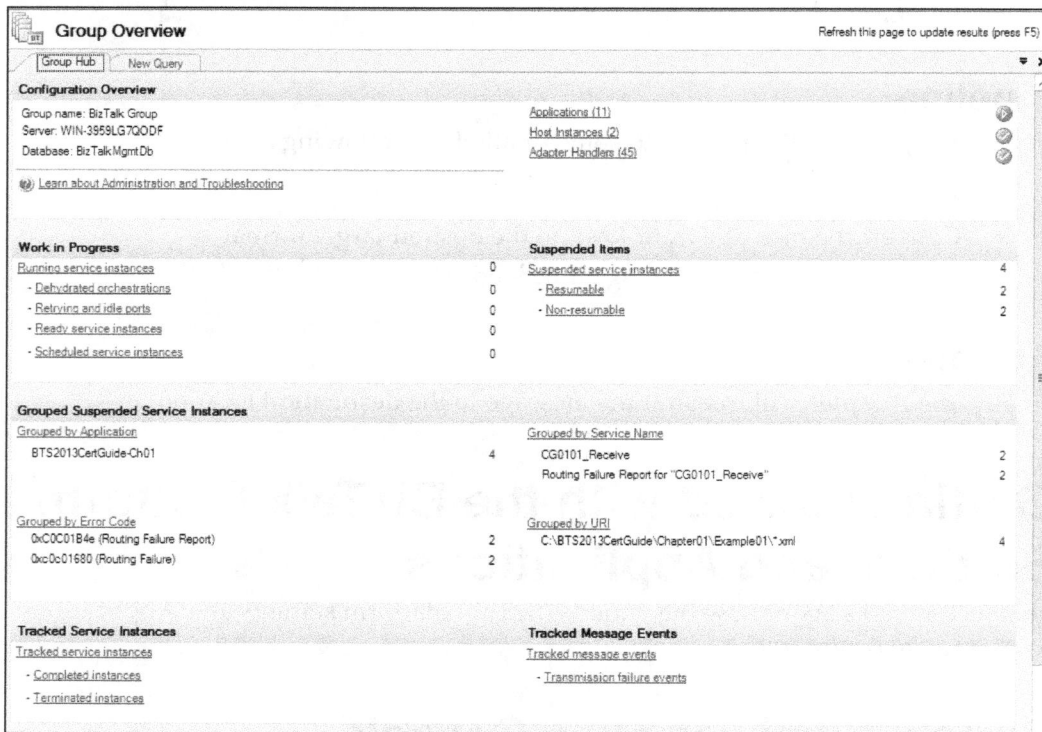

Work in progress should not be of any concern to us unless the amount of messages is large and keeps rising; in that case, we might have a bottleneck in one of the solutions that needs to be addressed.

Suspended Items, on the other hand, requires our attention, since they are messages that for some reason cannot be processed further.

Suspended Items fall into two categories:

- **Resumable**: This contains items that can be manually resumed.

- **Non-resumable**: This typically holds metadata and cannot be resumed. They will either disappear when the corresponding resumable instance is resumed, or in other cases they might need manual termination.

Hosts and Host Instances

For each BizTalk Group, multiple Hosts can be created. Creating a Host is merely creating a logical container where various BizTalk tasks can be assigned.

A Host can have a **Host Type** of either **In-Process** or **Isolated**.

The In-Process type is used for most BizTalk tasks and what *In-Process* means is that all the tasks performed in the Host will happen in an actual BizTalk process (Windows Service). The Isolated Host, on the other hand, will have its work done by someone other than BizTalk; for example, an IIS receiving service calls and processing the messages on its own. By using various BizTalk Modules, the IIS Host will run the received message through the same steps that would occur when using an In-Process BizTalk service, Adapter and Pipeline processing, and mapping and storing the message in the MessageBox.

Out of the box, the use of Isolated Hosts is limited to the following Adapters:

- HTTP Receive
- SOAP Receive
- WCF-BasicHttp Receive
- WCF-CustomIsolated Receive
- WCF-WebHttp Receive
- WCF-WSHttp Receive

What these Adapter Handlers have in common is that receiving the messages will happen through the IIS and not from a Windows Service (when BizTalk receives HTTP messages, the submitter will actually call a URL on an IIS residing on the BizTalk Server).

Each Host should have at least one corresponding Host Instance running. An In-Process Host Instance is nothing more than a Windows Service running on one or more BizTalk Servers and it performs the tasks assigned to the Host.

Creating a Host

Creating a Host can be done through the BizTalk Server Administration Console by navigating to **Platform settings | Hosts | New | Host**. The following screen should appear:

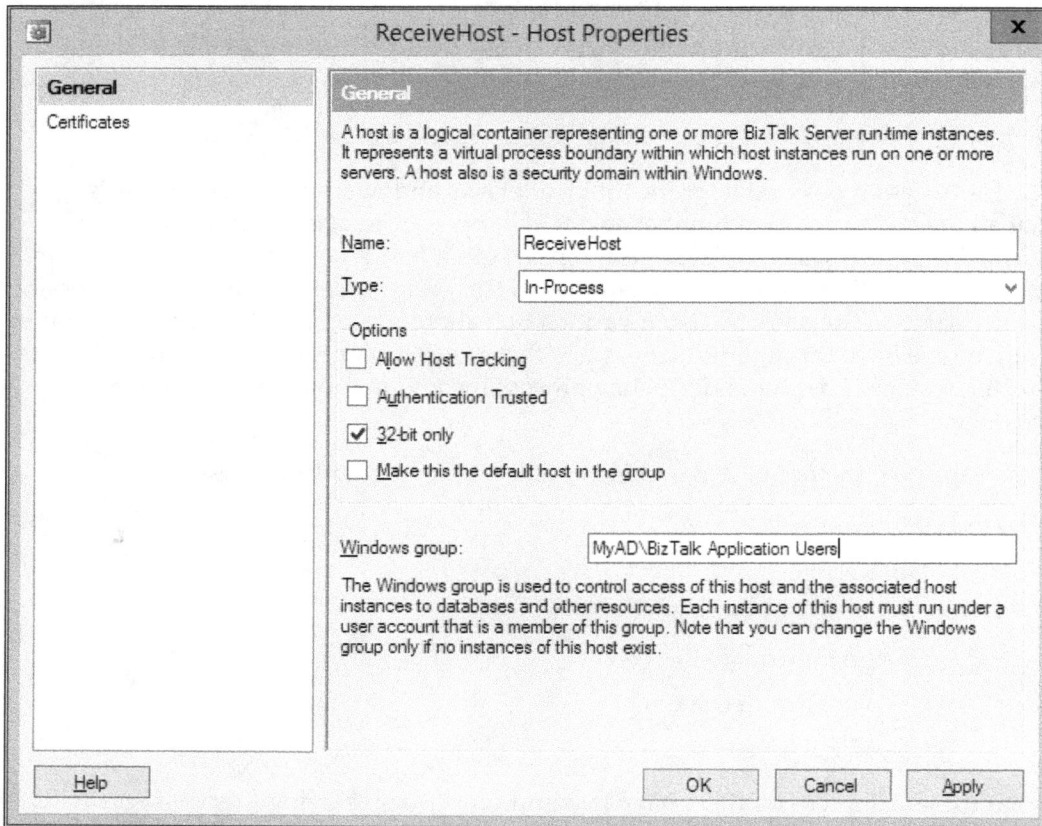

Creating a new Host will result in a new entry in the Host table inside the Management database, and also create a new Host Queue inside the MessageBox.

There are a few parameters on each Host that should be taken into consideration when creating Hosts. The parameters are as follows:

- **Name**: The name of the Host is not without importance. When moving a BizTalk Application from one environment to another by the use of Binding files, the naming of Hosts must be the same on each environment.

- **Type**: This is either **In-Process** or **Isolated**.

- **Allow Host Tracking**: This checkbox, if enabled, will allow the Host Instances associated with this Host to perform tracking tasks such as moving data from the `MessageBox` to the `Tracking` database. Only one Host per BizTalk Group should have this feature enabled.

- **Authentication Trusted**: When a Host is set to **Trusted**, the identification of the initial sender of a message will travel together with the message. If the identification needs to stay with the message until the Send Port (possibly for the use of **Single Sign-On** credential control on the Send Port), all Hosts from receive to send needs to be **Trusted**.

- **32-bit only**: This flag is enabled by default. If removed, the process will run as a 64-bit process, otherwise a 32-bit process.

- **Make this the default host in the group**: Any BizTalk Group will always have one default Host. If this checkbox is checked and disabled, the Host is already the default Host.

- **Windows Group**: This specifies a Windows Group that will be given access to all the Host queues tables created in the `MessageBox`. It is recommended that all users running Host Instances under this Host are members of this group.

There can be several reasons for creating multiple Hosts inside a BizTalk environment. There is no Host setup recommendation that will fit all environments and some considerations will need to be made based on the actual environment and the specific requirements.

Here are a few general guidelines that we must follow:

- As best practice, it is recommended to have at least five Hosts:
    - **A Receive Host**: This is used for all In-Process receiving.
    - **An Isolated Host**: This is used for all IIS receive.
    - **A Processing Host**: This is used for all Orchestrations.
    - **A Send Host**: This is used for sending of all messages.
    - **A Tracking Host**: This is a dedicated Host for moving data from the `MessageBox` to the `Tracking` and BAM databases. As this task can have a performance impact, the other Hosts should not be set to **Allow Host Tracking**.

- When using Adapters that must run in a 32-bit process, 32-bit Hosts may be needed to be created on receive and/or send side to host the 32-bit only Adapters. Another approach could be to have the Receive Hosts and Send Hosts running in the 32-bit mode. If 64-bit processing is required (typically when receiving large messages), a 64-bit Host can be created for handling the tasks where 64 bit is desired.

- Some Receive Adapters should not run in a multiserver environment such as FTP, POP3, and MSMQ. In these cases, a special Host for hosting these Receive Locations might be created and only run on one server. If High Availability is required, this Host should be clustered (see more about clustering Hosts in *Chapter 6, Deploying, Tracking, and Administrating a BizTalk Server 2010 Solution*).

- Don't just make too many Hosts. The advantages of multiple Host Instances (Windows Services) on each BizTalk Server are that they will use their own processes, have their own queue, and so on. However, each service will also consume resources (such as memory), thus creating too many Host Instances that can have a negative impact. Therefore, we need to find a balance. If we have a small BizTalk Solution with few messages running through the BizTalk environment, chances are that performance will be fine by just using one In-Process Host for everything.

Creating a Host Instance

Unlike creating a Host, creating a Host Instance will happen on both the BizTalk Server and the BizTalk databases. A new Host Instance will result in a new Windows Service running on a BizTalk Server. Only one Instance of a certain Host type can be created on each BizTalk Server in the BizTalk Group. When creating a new Host Instance, we are presented with the following screen:

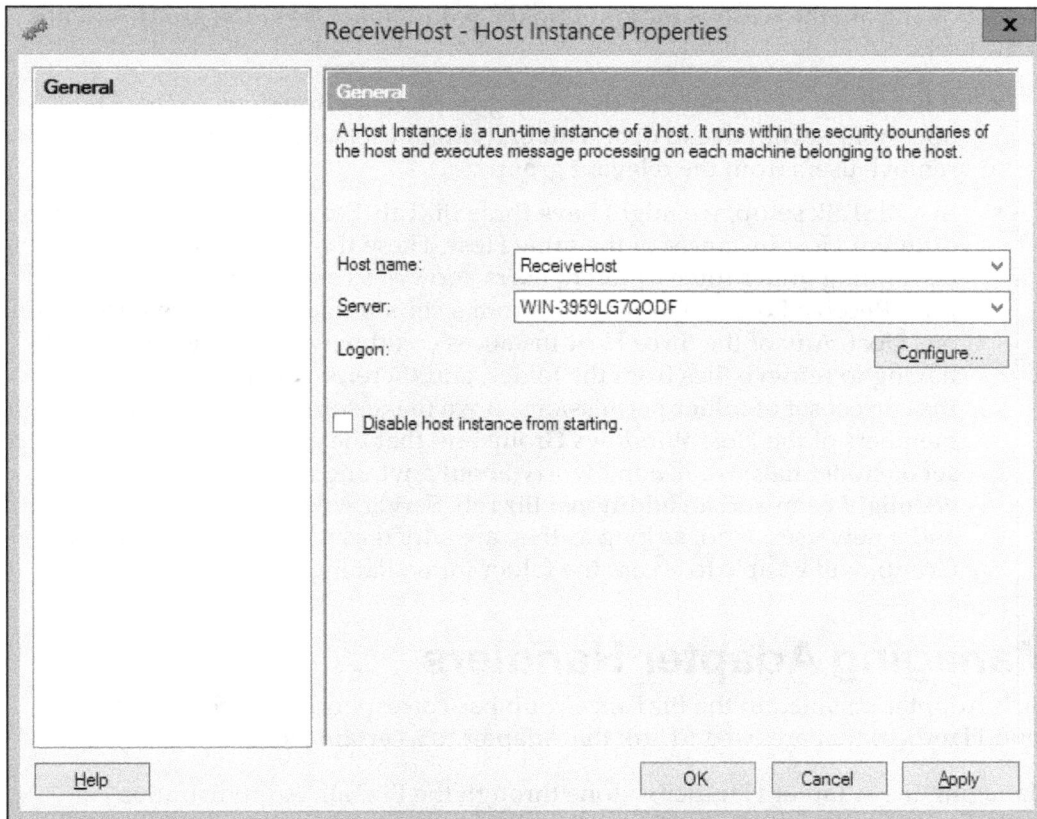

In the previous example, we are creating a new Host Instance of the Host type **ReceiveHost** on server **WIN-3959LG7QODF**.

After selecting the correct Host and server, click on **Configure** to specify which user the service should run as. This user will need access to the Host Queues/tables in the MessageBox, and the easiest way to grant the user these privileges is to add the user to the Windows Group that we associated with the Host when creating it.

If the recommendation of adding the user to the Host Windows Group is followed, the service will be able to do all the tasks needed towards communication with the MessageBox, but not necessarily with the outside world. The user running a Receive Location by using a FILE Adapter will be the user trying to access the source file folder, read the file, move/delete the file, and so on. When dealing with granting the BizTalk Host Instances access to various surrounding environments, the Host Windows Group and not the individual user should be used.

The following are the reasons for granting the required access to the group and not to the users:

- It is usually recommended that only groups get permissions so that IT operators never have to deal with individual users, but rather just add and remove users from the relevant groups.

- In a BizTalk setup, we might have three BizTalk Servers and therefore three different Host Instances of the same Host. These three Host Instances could be running under three different users. Now, let's say that we configure a FILE Receive Location to poll files from a certain folder and have it run under our Host. Any of the three Host Instances could now be getting the task of having to retrieve files from the folder, and therefore all three users need the correct set of folder permissions. If we make sure that all three users are members of the Host Windows Group and that the group is given the correct set of credentials, we needn't worry about anything else, and at some point, we might even add an additional BizTalk Server with a new Host Instance and a new user, who, as long as they are added as a member of the Host Group, will be able to access the folder immediately.

Managing Adapter Handlers

Each Adapter installed in the BizTalk Group has corresponding Receive and/or Send Handlers that are used to link the Adapter to a certain Host.

Managing the Adapter Handler is done through the BizTalk Administration Console, as shown in the following screenshot:

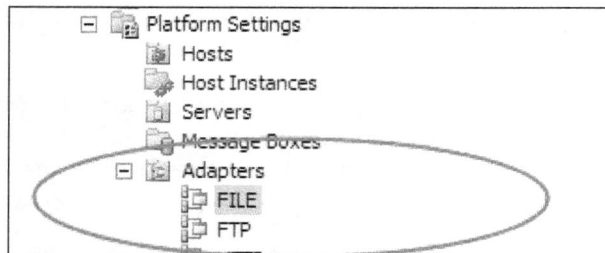

From BizTalk Administration Console, we can install new Adapters and add Receive or Send Handlers to Adapters.

In order to add a new Handler to an Adapter, click on **Adapter** and right-click somewhere in the blank space underneath the existing Handlers, or choose **Actions | [Adapter Name] | New** in the right pane of the window.

Each Handler will be the link between an Adapter and a Host. Only one Handler per Adapter and Host can be created, and only Hosts for which a Handler of the correct type exists can be chosen when choosing Adapters on either Receive Locations or Send Ports.

Some Handlers have the ability to have some basic properties configured that will be applied to all Adapter settings using that Host as default.

The SMTP Adapter is an example where we sometimes set up some basic configuration on the Handler level because these properties will often be the same for all Send Ports using the SMTP Adapter. These Handler properties can be overwritten on the specific Send Port if required, as shown in the following screenshot:

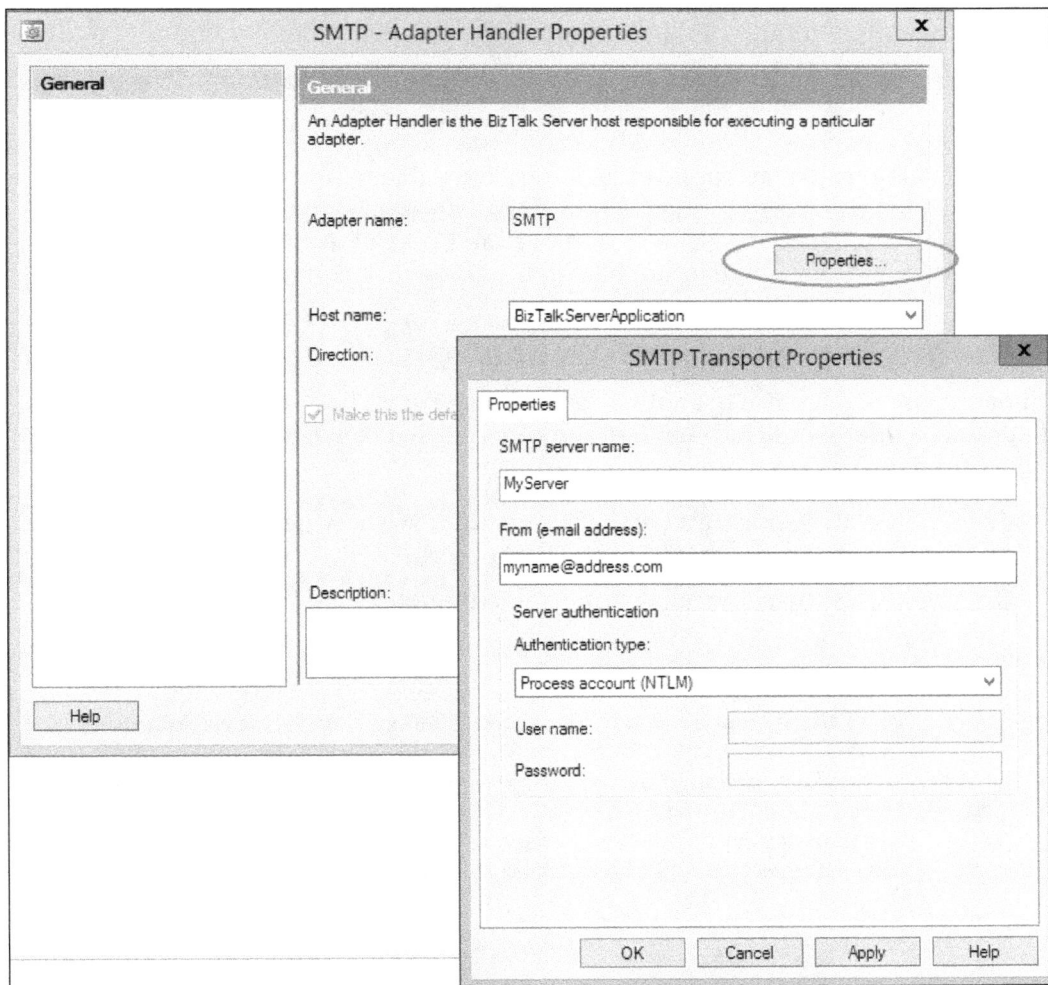

As shown in the previous screenshot, we can configure some general properties for all SMTP Adapter usage under the Host **BizTalkServerApplication**. For more information, see the *SMTP Adapter* section later in this chapter.

Applications

Applications are logical containers inside the BizTalk Server Administration Console, which allow us to group certain items together. The purpose of Applications is mainly to make planning, deployment, administration, and the general overview easier when working with BizTalk.

To create a new Application, perform the following steps:

1. Open the BizTalk Server Administration Console.
2. Right-click on **Applications** and choose **New | Application**.
3. Give the Application an appropriate name and click on **OK**.

When working inside an Application, we are only able to work directly with the other artifacts in that Application. For example, if we need to use a Pipeline in a Send Port, that Pipeline needs to be deployed in the same Application as the Port, or we need to make a reference to the Application which contains the Pipeline.

Referencing another Application

When making a reference to another Application, right-click on the Application that needs a reference to another Application, choose **Properties**, and perform the following steps:

1. Click on **Reference**, and then click on **Add**. We now get a list of all available Applications other than the current Application.
2. Choose the Application(s) you want to reference.
3. Click on **OK** twice.

> **BizTalk.System** is already referenced in all new Applications. As a result of this, we can work with several Pipelines as soon as the Application is created, even though these Pipelines are deployed in the **BizTalk.System** Application. The **BizTalk.System** Application is a read-only Application that can neither be deleted nor used for normal BizTalk activities, since no custom artifacts can be added to it.

Setting up and managing Ports

Inside BizTalk, we have both Receive and Send Ports. Ports are entry points and exit points in and out of BizTalk. All messages entering BizTalk will be received through a Receive Port and almost all messages exiting BizTalk will be through a Send Port. Even if it is possible to send out messages directly through code inside an Orchestration, this will not be the correct approach very often.

Receive Ports

Receive Ports are the entry points for messages that enter BizTalk. Each Receive Port contains one to many different Receive Locations (we can create Receive Ports without any Receive Locations, but that wouldn't make much sense since the Port would have no function).

To create a new Receive Port, perform the following steps:

1. Right-click on the **Receive Ports** folder in the Application where the Port should be created, and choose **New | One-way Receive Port** or **Request Response Receive Port**.

2. The same action can be performed in the **Actions** pane on the right when **Receive Ports** is selected.

3. In most routing scenarios, **One-Way Receive Ports** are used, and the use of **Request-Response Receive Ports** should be limited to flows where BizTalk exposes services, where an actual response message is required, or the consumer of the service needs to know if certain events have taken place before closing the connection to BizTalk. Read more about best practice later in this chapter in the *Implementing messaging patterns* section.

4. Next, we need to give a name to the Port, as shown in the following screenshot:

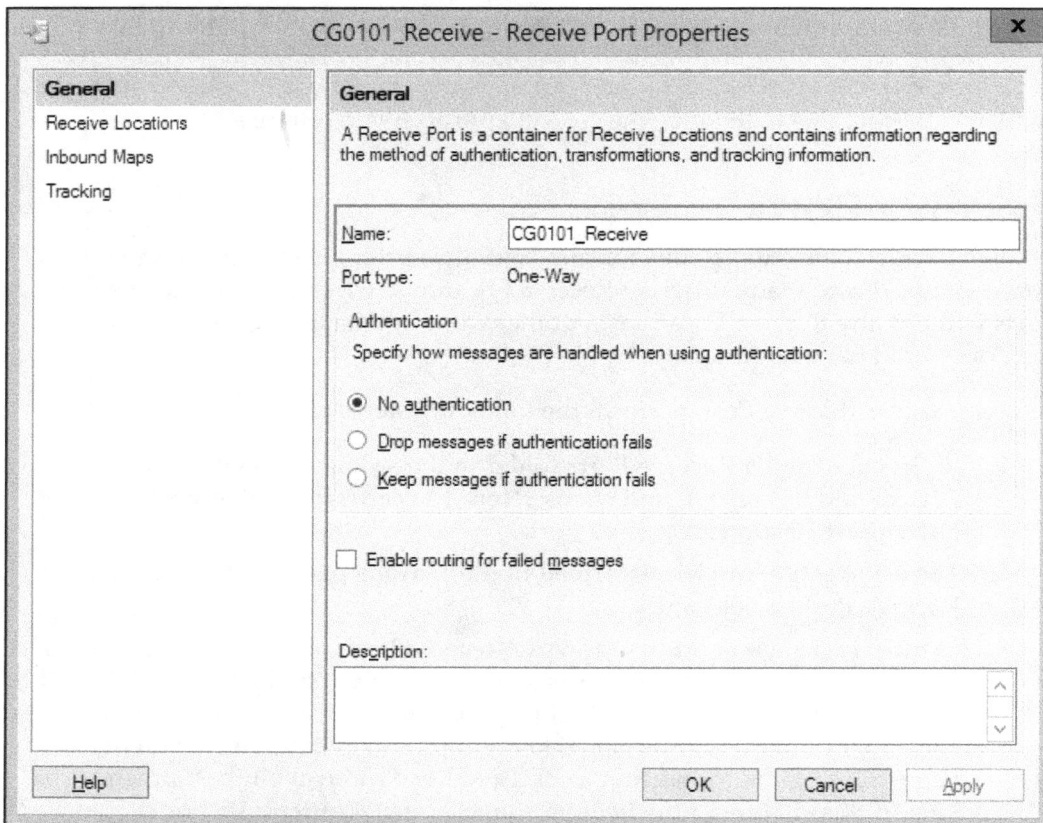

5. Next, click on **OK** to create the Receive Port.

> The names of the various Ports inside a BizTalk Group must be unique, not just per Application but for the whole Group.

Port Authentication

One way of making sure that only messages from known partners enter BizTalk is by using the **Authentication** feature available on Receive Ports, as seen in the following screenshot:

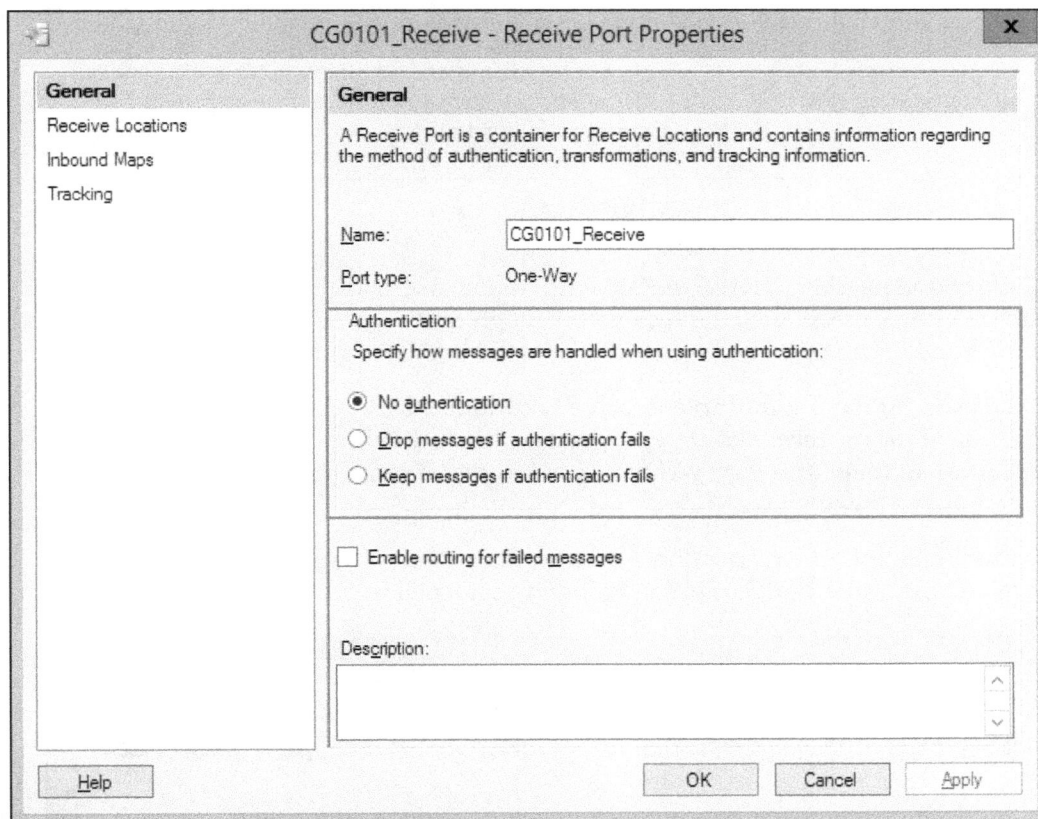

When using Receive Ports, we can set up filters so that only messages from known parties are allowed to pass through to the MessageBox. This will only work if messages are signed and we have the public certificates of the sending parties in store or if the Windows user who submitted the message can be located. There are three Authentication properties on each Receive Port:

Type	Description
No authentication (Default)	All messages will be let through to the MessageBox whether or not the party resolution inside the Pipeline finds a valid sender
Drop messages if authentication fails	If the party resolver does not match a valid sender from the message signature, the message will be thrown away and not submitted to the MessageBox

Type	Description
Keep messages if authentication fails	If the party resolver does not match a valid sender from the message signature, the message will be suspended inside the `MessageBox` and an error will be written to the Event Log

Receive Locations

As mentioned earlier, a Receive Port with no Receive Locations doesn't have any function. No messages can be received through that Port. So, for each Receive Port, at least one Receive Location should be created and configured.

The reason for having multiple Receive Locations inside one Receive Port is to have the ability to receive different messages from different locations and having BizTalk treat them as if they were received from the same place and/or had the same message type.

To make a new Receive Location, you can create it from within an already created Receive Port, as you can see in the following screenshot:

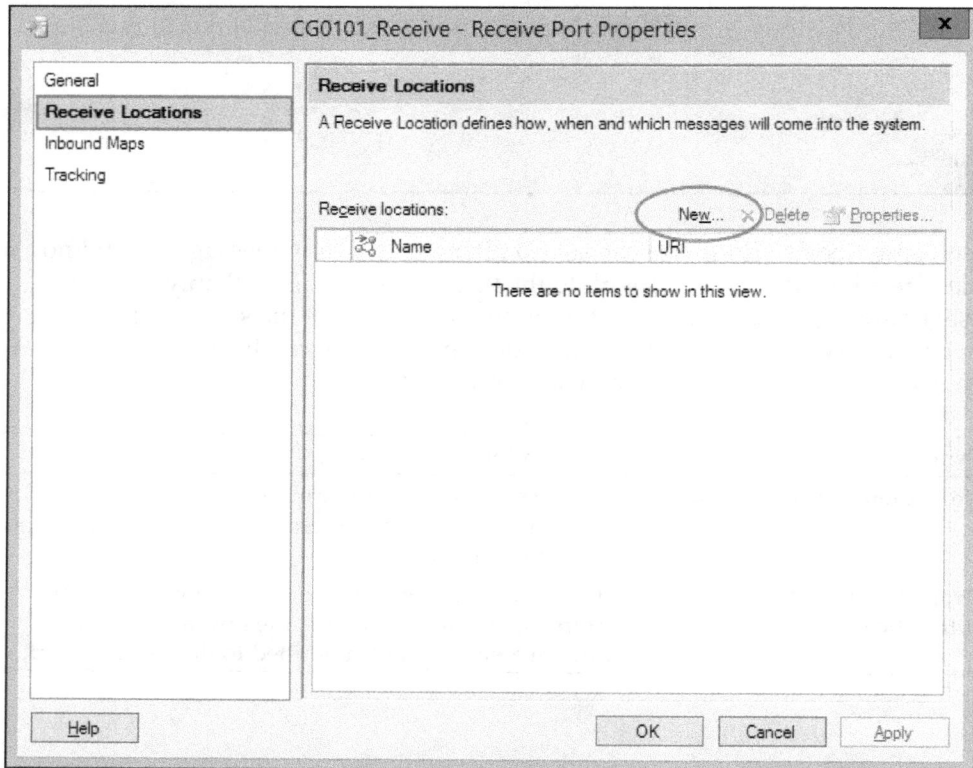

Another option is to right-click on the **Receive Locations** folder in the Application and choose **New | One-Way Receive Location** or **Request-Response Receive Location**. As for Receive Location types, only One-Way Receive Locations can be added to a One-Way Receive Port, and only Request-Response Locations to a Request-Response Port.

If a Receive Location is created directly, the console will prompt for a parent Receive Port before we can configure the location, since all locations must be a part of one specific Port.

Choose the appropriate Receive Port; click on **OK**, and the Receive Location configuration will appear.

Just as Receive Ports, Receive Locations need to be supplied with a name. Also, a type (Adapter) needs to be selected and configured, a Receive Handler (Host) needs to be selected, and finally, a Pipeline needs to be chosen. Read more about Pipelines in *Chapter 2*, *Developing BizTalk Artifacts – Creating Schemas and Pipelines*.

Service windows

Each Receive Location can be scheduled to only operate at certain times.

On the **Schedule** page inside the Receive Location, **Start date**, **Stop date**, and **Service Window** can be applied, as shown in the following screenshot:

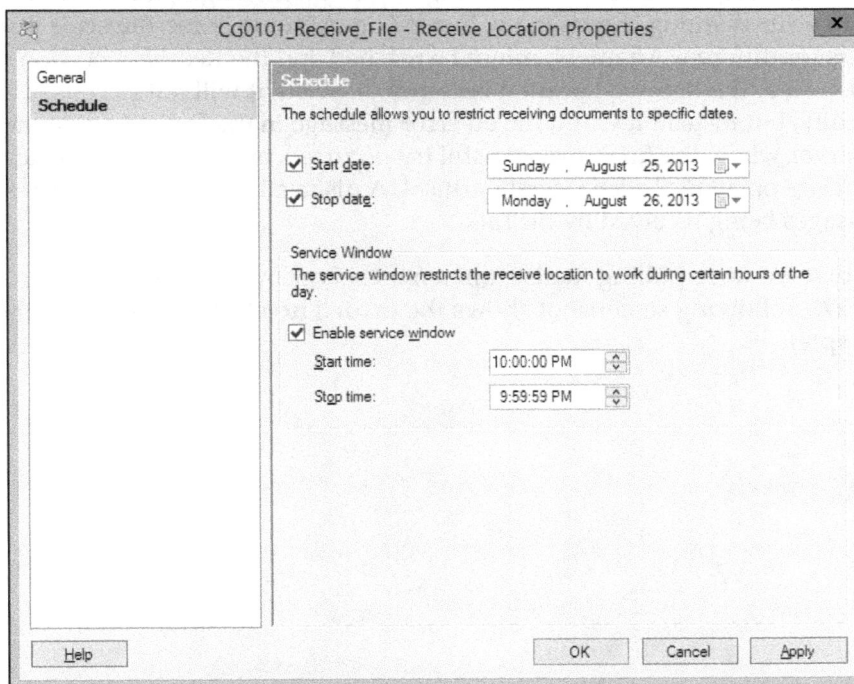

As seen in the previous screenshot, each of the three parameters can be enabled or disabled, and each enabled time period will limit the time the Receive Location is enabled for receiving messages.

Location states

A Receive Location can have two different states, **enabled** or **disabled**. If the location is enabled, it will receive any available messages; if disabled, no messages will be received.

Enabling a Receive Location can be done by right-clicking on it inside the BizTalk Administration Console and choosing **enable**. It can also be done through code script or PowerShell.

The state of a Receive Location is merely a flag inside the `Receive Location` table in the `Management` database of the BizTalk Group. It has nothing to do with whether or not the Host Instances (Windows Services) are running. Therefore, a Receive Location will only pick up messages if it is enabled, and at least one instance of the Host type it is using is running.

Error threshold

If errors occur in a Receive Location (for example, access denied in a file folder, logon failure to a database, and so on) when trying to pick up messages, the Host Instance will start to write warning entries in the Event Log. At some point, the error threshold (this differs for different Adapters) might be reached and the Receive Location will become disabled. If a Receive Location becomes disabled, it will not start itself again automatically, but instead it will write an error message in the Event Log on the BizTalk Server where the final unsuccessful try occurred, and therefore monitoring the Event Logs on all BizTalk Servers is critical. A disabled Receive Location results in no messages being received by BizTalk.

Let's say that we were polling mails from a mail server by using the POP3 Receive Adapter. The following screenshot shows the **Error Threshold** attribute for the POP3 Adapter:

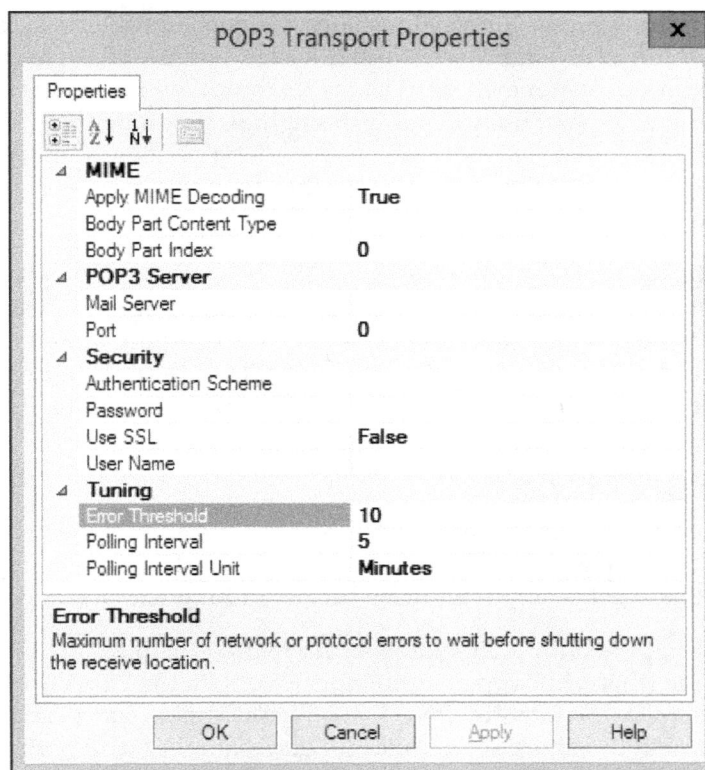

When setting up the Adapter, we are asked for the values of **Polling Interval** and **Error Threshold**. If set to **5** and **10**, as seen in the preceding screenshot, the following consequences would occur if the Receive Location started failing:

- BizTalk will poll mails every five minutes. At some point, the mail server becomes unavailable and the process of logging on and retrieving mails starts failing.

- The first time BizTalk unsuccessfully tries to access the mail server, it will write a warning in the Event Log stating that it wasn't able to connect to the mail server and that it will try again later.

- The second try will be five minutes later and unless the mail server becomes available again, this will go on for an additional seven times.

- When the last retry occurs, BizTalk will no longer retry and therefore it will stop the retrying scenario by disabling the Receive Location, writing an error to the Event Log stating that the number of retries were reached, and leave it to the administrators to fix the problem and enable the Receive Location again.

When configuring the various Receive Locations, we need to find a balance between how many retries (error threshold) we want. If we have an unstable environment, such as an FTP Server, residing somewhere outside our control with multiple unscheduled service windows and general unavailability, it might be tempting to increase the error threshold to 9,000 or similar. This way we can have long periods of unavailability, and when the FTP Server eventually comes back online, we don't risk the Receive Location having shut down.

This might not be the best of approaches, since it is likely that the people monitoring BizTalk will only look at errors and not warnings in the Event Log, so nobody will notice that we are not polling data from the source if something more critical happens (such as our password expiring). In that case, we will not be notified until all 9,000 attempts fail and the Receive Location, after possibly months, eventually shuts down.

Receive Port Maps

Receive Port Maps are applied to a message after the message leaves the Pipeline; at which point all messages should be in the format of XML. This is important, since Maps can only take XML as input and also because a Map will always output XML.

Maps can only be applied if the Pipeline has discovered the message type of the incoming message (this will happen automatically unless the **PassThruReceive** Pipeline or some other custom Pipeline with no Disassemble stage is used). For more information on Pipelines, see *Chapter 2, Developing BizTalk Artifacts – Creating Schemas and Pipelines*. If the message type is not known by the time the message leaves the Pipeline, no Map will be applied, even if a Map matching the message is present on the Port.

The matching of a Map works as follows:

If the message type was discovered and promoted by the Receiving Pipeline, BizTalk will look for a Map with a source type matching the message type. If such a Map is found, it will be executed and the source message will be mapped using that Map.

It is also worth mentioning that after a Map has been executed on a Receive Port, an XML Disassemble Pipeline Component is executed against the output XML. This is why we can promote properties on the destination Schema of a Map executed on the Receive Port and still have the properties promoted before the message is submitted to the MessageBox. Also, not more than one Map will be executed even if a map-chain exists. The following example will explain this:

On a Receive Port (PortA), we have applied three different Maps:

- MessageA_to_MessageU
- MessageB_to_MessageU
- MessageU_to MessageI

If we receive Message A (and the message type is discovered in the Pipeline), the message will be transformed to Message U. But after that, the message exits the Port, no additional Map discovery will be done, so even though we may want Message A to be transformed first into message U and then into message I, this will not happen. The same goes for Message B, and only if we submit a message U will the Map (MessageU_to_MessageI) be applied.

Maps are applied on Receive Ports by selecting **Properties** on the Port and then selecting **Inbound Maps**, as shown in the following screenshot:

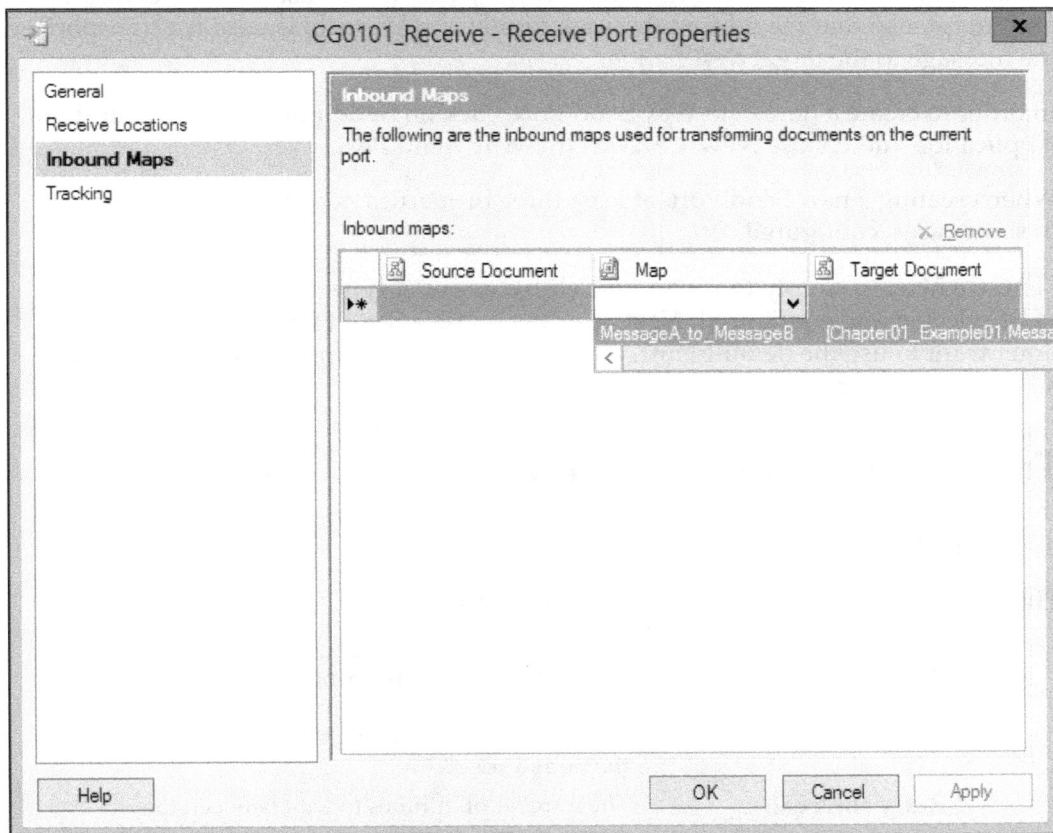

Under the **Map** section, use the drop-down list, then all Maps deployed in the Application (or Applications that are being referenced) should appear. Choose the Map(s) to be applied on the Receive Port; remember that multiple Maps can be selected.

> If many Maps are present in the Application and/or in the referenced Applications, it might be difficult to find the correct Map to apply. If the source or target document is known, it might help to first choose one of these, since this will limit the list of available Maps.

Send Ports

Unlike Receive Ports, Send Ports do not operate with locations. Each Send Port will point to a specific location, database, application, service, and so on, somewhere outside of BizTalk. Just as the Receive Location, a Send Port uses one Pipeline and one Adapter so that the desired message format and Protocol is used for transporting the message to the target destination.

In order to create a new One-Way Send Port, click on **Send Ports** inside the desired Application and choose **New | Static One-Way Send Port**.

When creating a new Send Port, at least three properties need to be selected and, in some cases, configured.

First, we need to supply the Send Port with a name. A type (Adapter) also needs to be selected and configured. Next, we can choose a Send Handler (Host) if we don't want to use the default Host. Finally, if the default Pipeline is not adequate, a Pipeline must be chosen and configured.

Transport Advanced Options

In **Transport Advanced Options**, several common parameters can be configured in the Send Port.

The transport options consist of three parameters:

Retry count	The number of tries the Send Port should try to resend the message on failure before giving up and suspending the message in the `MessageBox`
Retry interval	The number of minutes to wait between the retries in case of failure

Priority	The priority given to the Send Port subscription (**1** being the highest and **10** the lowest); the higher the priority, the faster the Send Port will get messages it has subscribed to from the Host Queue

Retry on a Send Port is a bit different from Receive Locations. First of all, the behavior is per message and the Port will never disable itself after any number of retries has been exhausted, but rather suspend the message.

What the Send Port does is try to send each message it receives the number of times specified in the **Retry count** parameter, with an interval specified in the **Retry interval** parameter. When the number of retries has been exhausted, the message will be suspended and an error will be written to the Event Log. (Just as the Receive Location, the first failure(s) results in warnings in the Event Log; only the final try, that also causes the suspension of the message, will result in an error).

Scheduling and service window

Each Send Port created can have a scheduled service window in which messages will be sent through the Port. The setup is done under **Transport Advanced Options**, which is shown in the following screenshot:

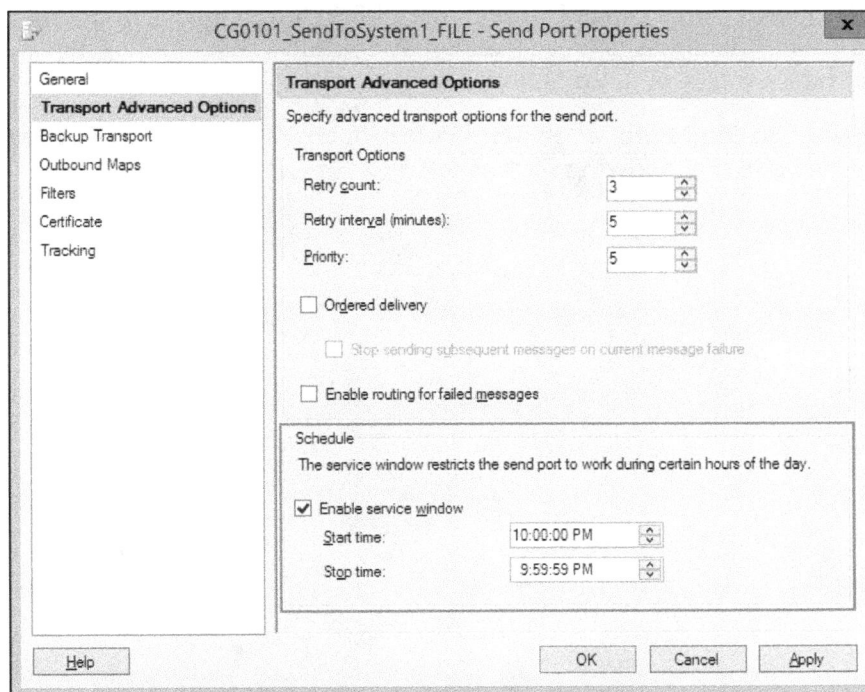

Similar to Receive Locations, certain operation periods can be set up on a Send Port. We can specify a period within the day, where messages should be sent through the Port. At all other times, all messages going to the Port will be queued up inside BizTalk, and when the **Operation Window** opens, all the queued-up messages will be sent.

The term service window might be a bit confusing. Normally, a service window is a time period where maintenance is going on, and therefore a period where no messages should be sent to the system. However, in this case, the service window is the time where messages are actually sent through the Send Port.

Backup transport

Each Send Port can have a backup transport configured, where an alternate Adapter and/or address can be selected so that if the primary target has exceeded its retry counts, the Send Port will try to send the message to an secondary location.

Send Port Maps

Just as Receive Ports, multiple Maps can be applied to the Send Ports in order to transform the messages being sent from the MessageBox to the target format requested by the target system or the format required for the Pipeline to proceed. Also, multiple Maps may be applied to the Send Port, but only one of them will be used, and only if the message type is known by BizTalk at the time the message is sent from the MessageBox to the Send Port.

To apply Maps to Send Ports, open **Send Port properties** and click on **Outbound Maps**, as shown in the following screenshot:

CG0101_SendToSystem1_FILE - Send Port Properties   ✕

General
Transport Advanced Options
Backup Transport
Outbound Maps
Filters
Certificate
Tracking

Outbound Maps

The following are the outbound maps used for transforming documents on the current port.

Outbound maps: ✕ Remove

	Source Document		Map		Target Document
▶✱					
			MessageA_to_MessageB		[Chapter01_Example01.Messa
			<		

Help   OK   Cancel   Apply

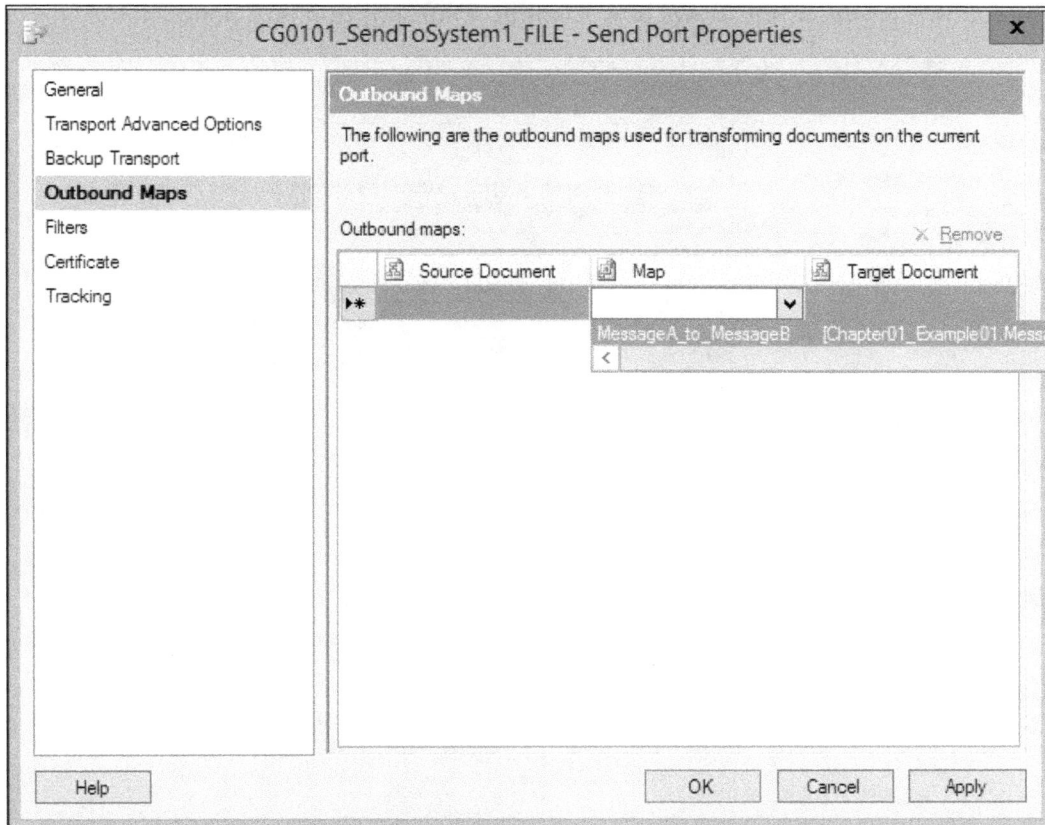

Configuring Filters (subscriptions)

Inside the **Filters** page, it is possible to set up subscriptions for the Send Port. The filters can be a combination of several Boolean expressions and include a combination of promoted properties, operators, and values. Only promoted properties deployed through Property Schemas in the BizTalk Server Group will be selectable in a filter.

The following screenshot shows how to set up a subscription on a Send Port:

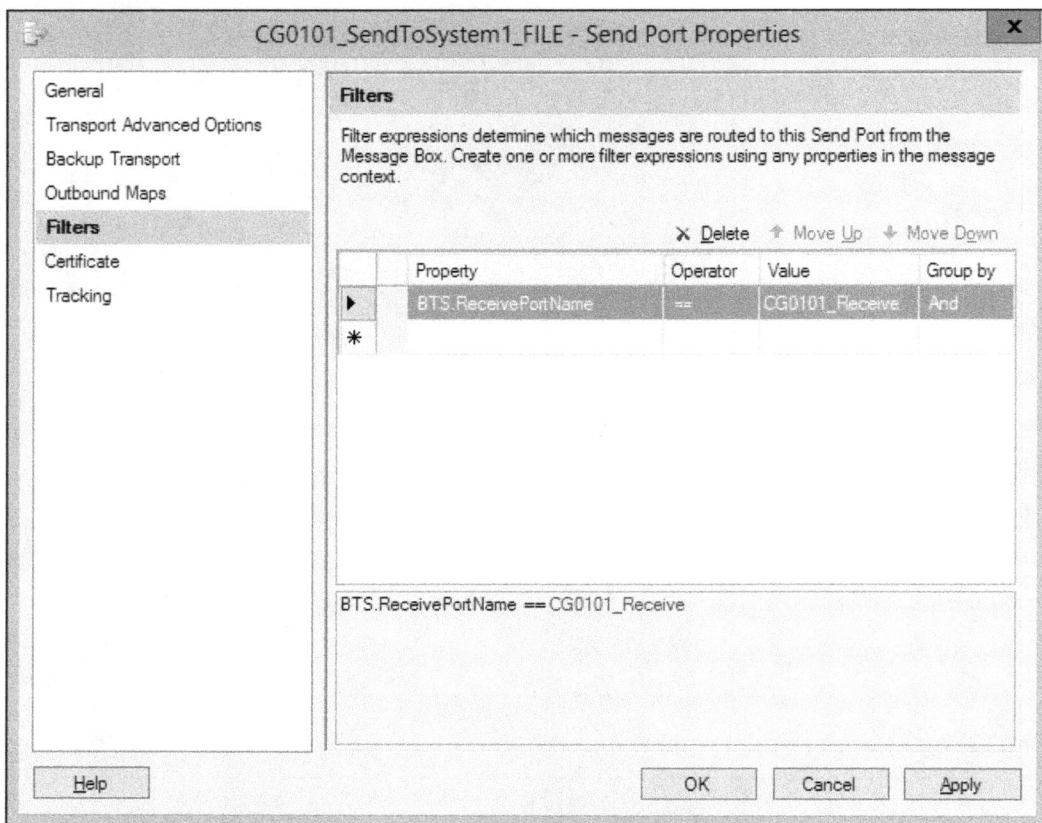

The example in the previous screenshot will subscribe to all messages that come from the Receive Port **CG0101_Receive**.

Port states

A Send Port can have the following states:

- **Started**: The Send Port will be getting messages that match its subscriptions and send them to the target system, if it is not outside the service window.

- **Stopped**: The Send Port will be getting messages that match its subscriptions, but the messages will reside in a Send Port queue inside the MessageBox and not be sent through the Send Port until it is started.

- **Unenlisted**: The Send Port does not subscribe to any messages and no messages will be sent through the Port. The Port will not be able to get messages that are already received in the `MessageBox` later on. This behavior is similar to the instance of the Port not being created all together.

Port states can be changed by right-clicking on the Port inside the Administration Console, as shown in the following screenshot:

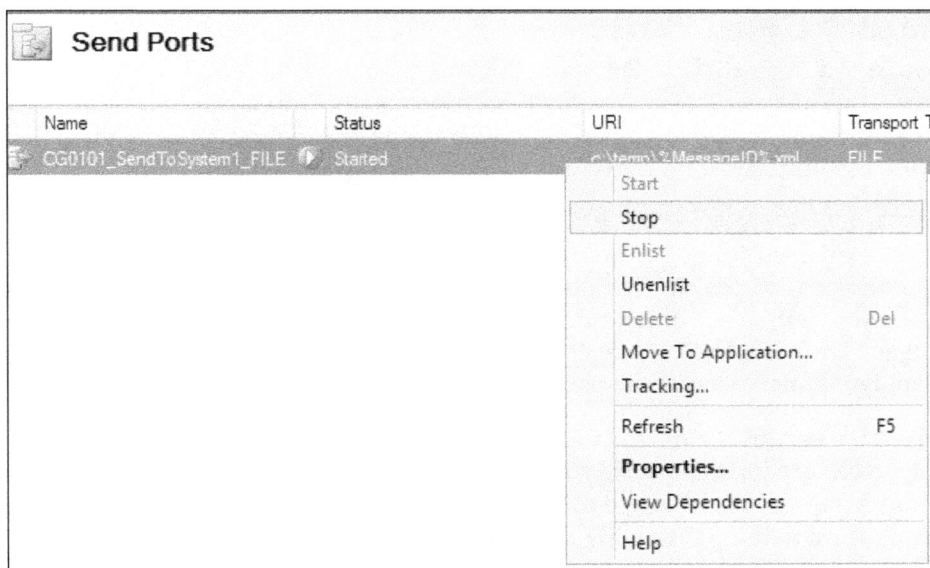

> Note that if we right-click on an **Unenlisted** Port, the state will be named **Enlist** and not **Stop** in the menu.

The **Stopped** state will queue up all messages for the Send Port, and when the Port is started again, all messages will be sent immediately through the Send Port (if no service window is configured). This might not always be what is desired, especially not if the Port was stopped due to some configuration error in BizTalk or on the target system, resulting in messages failing upon arrival at the target. In that case, sending 100 messages all at once, when we think the problem has been resolved, might not be the best approach.

If we just want to send one of the 100 messages currently lying in the `MessageBox` waiting for the Port to be started, we can go to the **Group Hub** window, find the 100 suspended messages, and resume just one of them while the Port is still in the **Stopped** state. This will force the one message to be sent through the Send Port even though the state is still set to **Stopped**; on acceptance that the problem is gone, we can then start the Port and the last 99 messages (or more if more messages have arrived in the `MessageBox`) will be sent automatically through the Port.

Dynamic Send Ports

Dynamic Send Ports differ from Static Ports as their Adapter and/or address is not configured and hardcoded on the Port. Both protocol (Adapter) and address can be set from inside BizTalk (from either Orchestrations or Pipeline components), and therefore, the Port can send messages to different locations using different protocols (SMTP, FTP, and so on).

They are often used for SMTP because an SMTP Send Port often requires sending mails to different addresses that might be located somewhere in the message. This is not possible with a static Send Port, which will always point to the same address (as well as all other static Ports using any type of Adapters). So, to solve this problem, Dynamic Ports can be used.

In BizTalk Server 2013, a new Handler configuration has become available. It is now possible to choose individual Handlers (Host) for each Adapter type, so even though the actual Adapter is not known at configuration time, potential Handlers can still be chosen, as shown in the following screenshot:

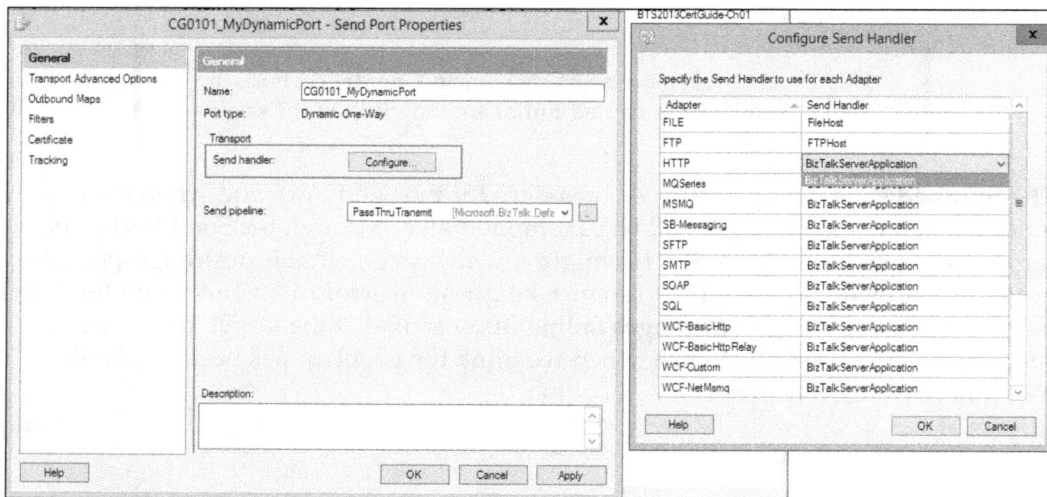

Dynamic Ports are usually combined with Orchestrations and will be discussed further in *Chapter 4, Developing BizTalk Artifacts – Creating Orchestrations*.

Send Port Groups

Send Port Groups are logical subscription containers, where one or more Send Port can join the subscription of the group. A Send Port can be a part of multiple Send Port Groups, and also have its own local subscription, and can therefore have multiple subscriptions.

Send Port Groups are created by right-clicking on the **Send Port Group** folder inside an Application and choosing **New | Send Port Group**. You are then presented with the following screen:

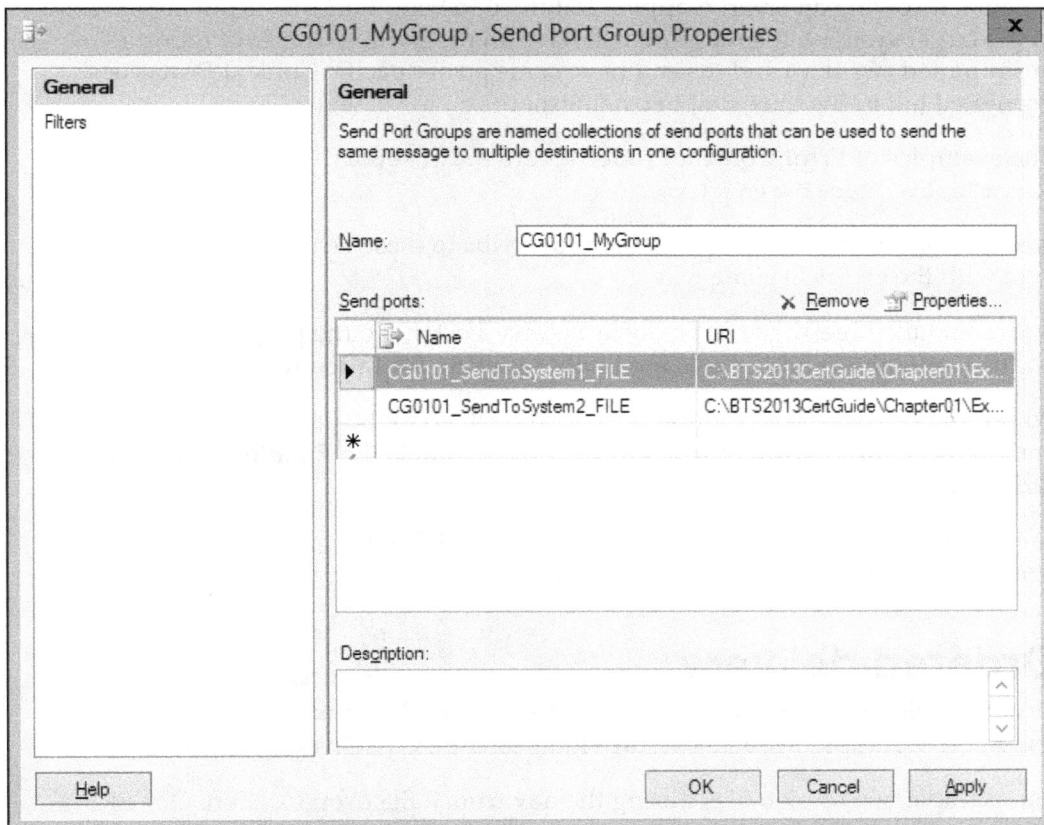

Inside the Send Port Group configuration, we can configure **Filter** and **Send Ports** that should be a part of the group subscription.

> A Send Port can be a part of many groups and have its own subscription (**Filter**) on the Port. The result could be that the same message submitted to the `MessageBox` can also be sent through the Port multiple times if more than one of these subscriptions match the Context of the message.

Failed message routing

It is possible to enable routing for failed messages on both Receive and Send Ports. What this will do is, in case of an error occurring in the Port (could be either the Pipeline throwing an error, mapping failure, or a Send Port that is not able to send to the target system), the message will have all the normal Context Properties unpromoted (written) and instead have some error-specific Context Properties promoted (all in the `ErrorReport` namespace).

The examples of Error Context Properties are `ErrorReport.ErrorType` and `ErrorReport.ReceivePortName`.

A Send Port or Orchestration can then subscribe to these error properties and deal with the errors in some way.

To set up failed message routing on a Receive Port, go to the properties of the Port, on the **General** tab, and enable the **Enable routing for failed messages** checkbox.

To set up failed message routing on a Send Port, go to the properties of the port and on the **Transport Advanced Options** page, enable the **Enable routing for failed messages** checkbox.

See more about Failed Message Routing in *Chapter 5*, *Testing, Debugging, and Exception Handling*.

Ordered delivery

Ordered delivery might not come as easy as one might think in BizTalk. Only a few Receive Adapters are able to provide true ordered delivery out of the box.

For example, we receive files during the day from a file drop location. Our ERP system has requested that it receives all files in the same order as they were submitted to the file folder, because receiving data in the wrong order could potentially cause inconsistent data.

Let's think of BizTalk as a post office. If one customer has asked the mailman to deliver today's letter in exactly the same way he received the letters in the mailbox on the street, the mailman immediately faces a problem. He can give the customer the letters in the same order that he got the letters out of the mailbox, but that is not necessarily the same order that they were put into the mailbox. The same is true for BizTalk. We are able to send messages through a Send Port or to an Orchestration in the same order as they were submitted to the MessageBox, but that order might not be the same order that the original submitter intended.

Let's consider the file drop example. The FILE Adapter, just as many other Adapters, might not submit the messages received in the same order as one might intend/ expect. The FILE Adapter doesn't look at timestamps, file sizes, or even filenames when choosing which file to process first. There could also be more than one Host Instance receiving batches of files at the same time from the same folder and submitting them in the same MessageBox. In other words, if BizTalk is started and two files are present at a certain file location, we have no way of knowing if the oldest file is taken first, and therefore have no certain way of making a total **first in first out** (**FIFO**) scenario using the FILE Receive Adapter. In fact, this is true for most of the BizTalk Receive Adapters, and out of the box, only the message queue Adapters (MSMQ, MQSeries, and WCF-NetMsmq) support true ordered delivery. Some database Adapters and WCF Service Adapters can be set up to implement ordered delivery, but only with certain limitations such as only one Host Instance.

Receive Locations

On the receive side, it is based on the different protocols (Adapters) if ordered delivery is supported or not. For the very few Adapters that do support it (mainly MQ), it can usually be enabled on the Receive Adapter.

Send Ports

Each Send Port can be set up to use ordered delivery. Setting a Send Port to ordered delivery means that all messages will be sent through that Port in the same order as they were received in the MessageBox. If messages are not received in the MessageBox in the order intended, which was discussed before, using ordered delivery on a Send Port might not have the desired result.

Using ordered delivery on a Send Port has some serious performance impacts, since only one thread can submit messages through the Port, and each message has to wait for the message ahead to complete before it can be processed. This can be both an advantage and a disadvantage. The disadvantage is obvious; BizTalk will perform slower when using ordered delivery.

In some cases, however, this might turn into an advantage. If, for instance, a Send Port calls a service that cannot handle multiple calls, we might experience a lot of messages going into a retry or even fail state, because the amount of messages being sent to the service is exceeding the amount of messages the service can handle. In this case, it could make sense to introduce ordered delivery to the Send Port, not because we necessarily need the messages to be sent in a certain order, but merely because this will result in BizTalk sending only one message at a time.

1. To set up ordered delivery on a Send Port, go to the properties of a Send Port (either by double-clicking on **Send Port** or right-clicking and choosing **Properties**).

2. Go to the **Transport Advanced Options** page and enable **Ordered delivery**, as shown in the following screenshot:

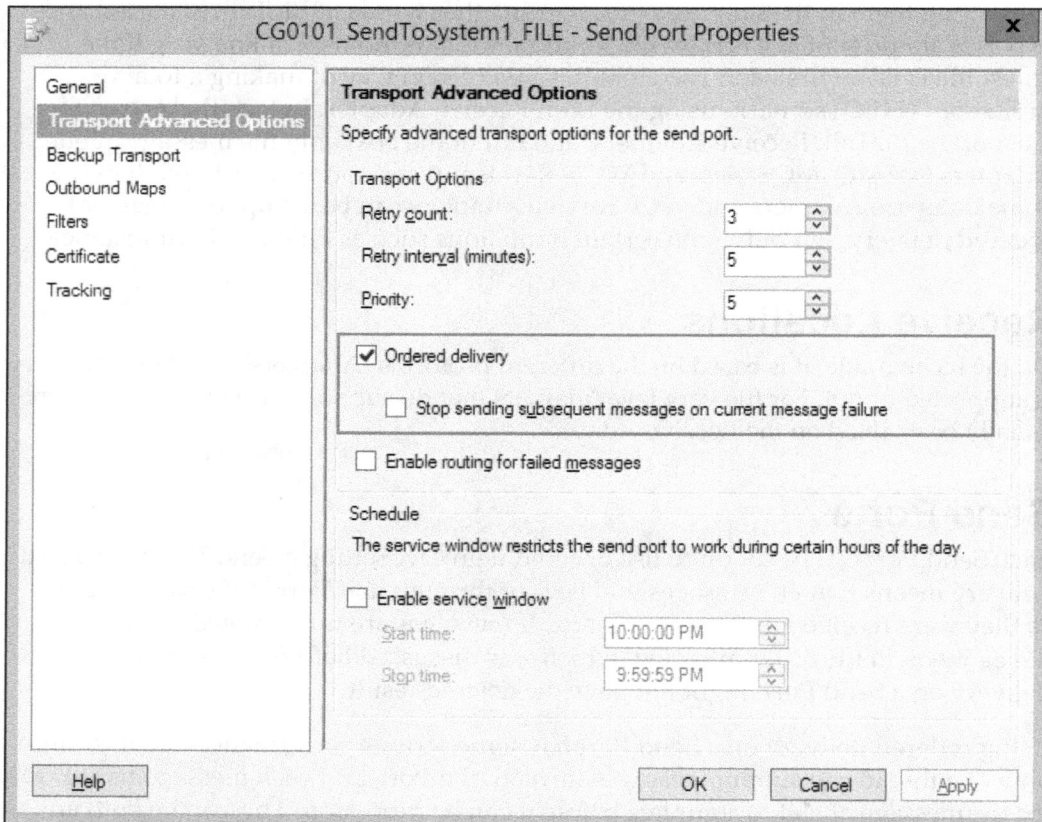

CG0101_SendToSystem1_FILE - Send Port Properties	X

Transport Advanced Options

Specify advanced transport options for the send port.

- General
- **Transport Advanced Options**
- Backup Transport
- Outbound Maps
- Filters
- Certificate
- Tracking

Transport Options

Retry count: 3

Retry interval (minutes): 5

Priority: 5

☑ Ordered delivery

☐ Stop sending subsequent messages on current message failure

☐ Enable routing for failed messages

Schedule

The service window restricts the send port to work during certain hours of the day.

☐ Enable service window

Start time: 10:00:00 PM

Stop time: 9:59:59 PM

Help   OK   Cancel   Apply

When enabling ordered delivery, an additional setting, **Stop sending subsequent messages on current message failure**, will become active. This means that if 10 messages are currently queued up to be sent through the Sent Port (message 1 to 10), and message 3 fails, the rest of the messages (4 to 10) will get suspended together with message 3. If true ordered delivery is required, this option should be enabled, simply because if it is not, the solution is not 100 percent ordered delivery. On the other hand, if ordered delivery is nice to have, but not vital for the solution, or we are simply using ordered delivery to slow down the Send Port, then the option should be disabled.

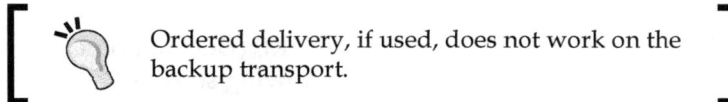

> Ordered delivery, if used, does not work on the backup transport.

Configuring core Adapters

When choosing an Adapter on both Receive Locations and Send Ports, the Adapters need to be configured. To do this, choose the **Configure** button, as shown in the following screenshot:

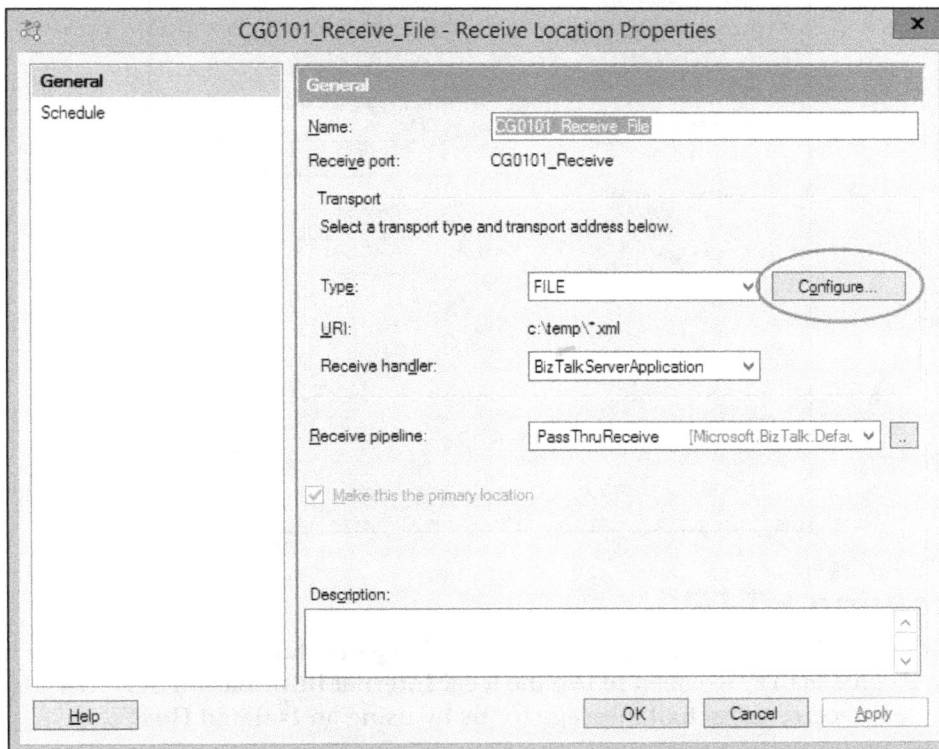

What will appear next depends on which type of Adapter was chosen. In this chapter, we will look at some of the core Adapters and how they are configured.

HTTP

The HTTP section will discuss the use of the HTTP Adapter in both receive and send scenarios.

Sending HTTP

When configuring the HTTP Send Adapter, the URL (Destination URL) of the target HTTP site needs to be configured. The following screenshot shows the basic configuration, and the Destination URL being configured:

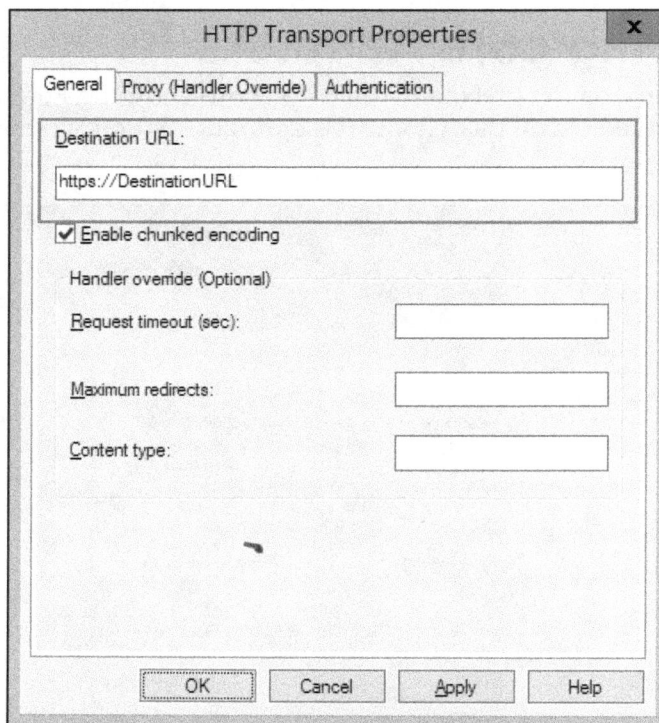

Receiving HTTP

Setting up BizTalk to receive HTTP requires more work than sending HTTP. To be able to receive HTTP, we need to use the local **Internet information Services (IIS)** and have it receive the actual message for us by using an **Isolated Host**.

First, we need to add `BTSHttpReceive.dll`. This file is found in the `%Program Files%\Microsoft BizTalk Server 2013\HttpReceive64` folder (`HttpReceive` folder if not using a 64-bit IIS). This DLL needs to be added as an extension inside the IIS. Open the IIS Manager by navigating to **Start | Administrative Tools | Internet Information Services(IIS) Manager**, click on the computer name and double-click on **Handler Mappings**. In the action pane on the right-hand side of the window, choose **Add Script Map**. The following screenshot shows the **Add Script Map** window:

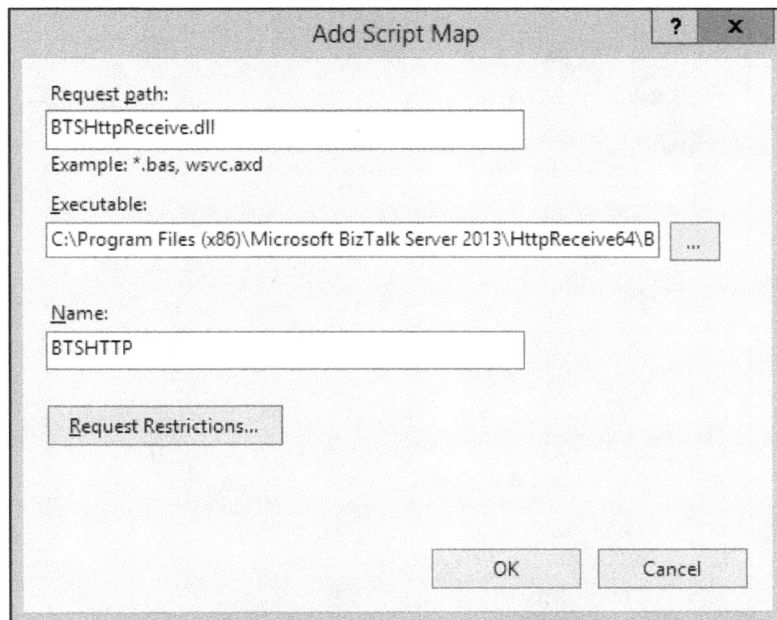

In the **Request path** field, type `BTSHttpReceive.dll`. In the **Executable** field, choose the `BTSHttpReceive.dll` file from within program files and give the mapping a proper name. Now click on **OK**.

Click on **Yes** in the **Add Script Map** dialog.

Now, we need to perform the following steps for creating a Virtual Directory containing `BTSHttpReceive.dll`, as mentioned earlier:

1. Right-click on the **Default Web Site** folder and select **Add Virtual Directory**.

2. Set the **Alias** property to the name we want the callers of our HTTP service to use in the URL (`http://servername/Alias/BTSHTTPReceive.dll`).

3. Under **Physical Path**, choose the folder where the `BTSHTTPReceive.dll` file is located (under `Program Files`) and click on **OK**.

Next, we need to set up an HTTP Receive Location. The HTTP flow we are receiving in BizTalk can be both One-Way or Request-Response (refer to the *Implementing messaging patterns* section).

When configuring the HTTP Receive Adapter, we need to specify the Virtual Directory and the DLL extension, as shown in the following screenshot:

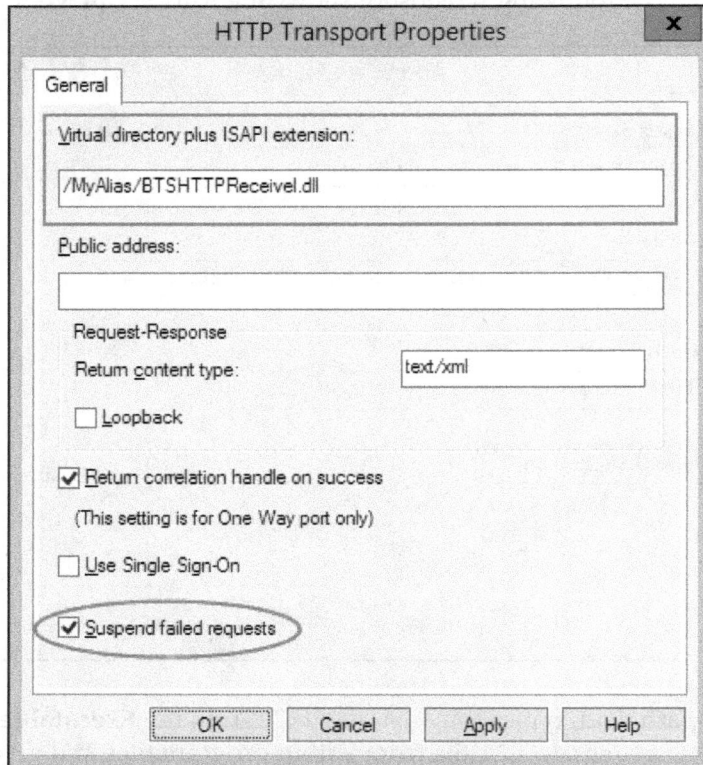

In most cases, the **Suspend failed requests** option should also be enabled. What this option does is gives BizTalk the responsibility of processing the message as soon as it has been submitted. If this option is not enabled (default), the caller will get an error back if the message could not be processed correctly (the Pipeline fails, no subscribers were found, and so on). This could be a valid setup, but in most situations it would make more sense to have the HTTP Receive Adapter handle errors the same way as a FILE Adapter, by taking responsibility for the message as soon as it is submitted, and not bother the caller with any problems inside BizTalk, but rather suspend the message and deal with the problems internally and let the caller believe that everything processed as expected. This is, of course, only the case of one-way HTTP calls.

POP3

The POP3 Adapter is used to receive e-mails. The Adapter is a receive-only Adapter because sending something through POP3 doesn't make any sense. The send equivalent of POP3 is usually SMTP, which we will look at in the next section.

> Under certain conditions, the POP3 Adapter will not run under a multiserver setup, and in these cases, the use of clustering Hosts might be needed. Read more about this at http://msdn. microsoft.com/en-us/library/gg634567.aspx.

The following screenshot shows the configuration of the POP3 Receive Adapter:

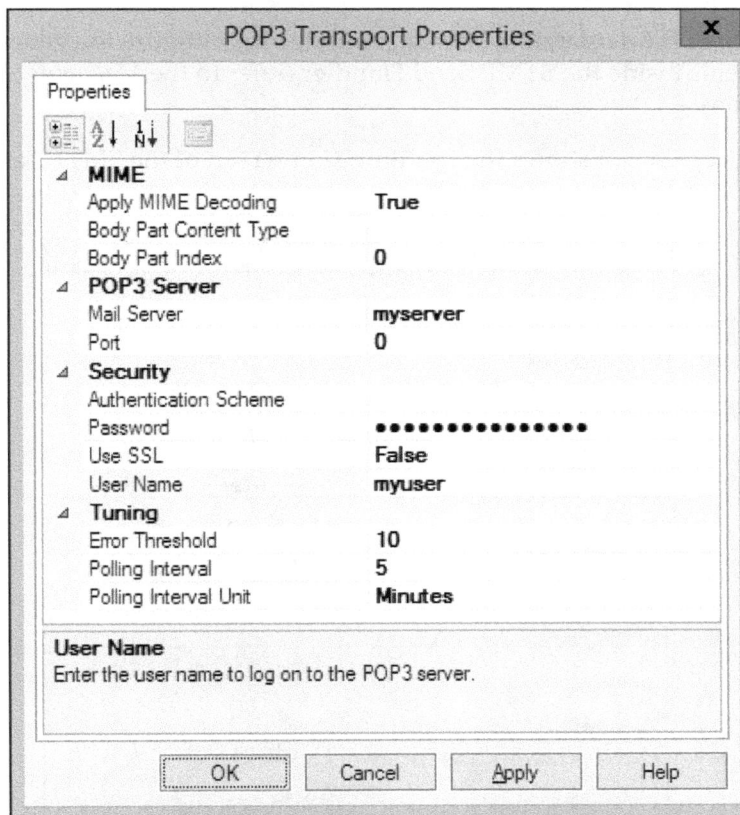

POP3 Transport Properties	X

Properties

⊿ **MIME**
Apply MIME Decoding	**True**
Body Part Content Type	
Body Part Index	**0**

⊿ **POP3 Server**
| Mail Server | **myserver** |
| Port | **0** |

⊿ **Security**
Authentication Scheme	
Password	••••••••••••••••
Use SSL	**False**
User Name	**myuser**

⊿ **Tuning**
Error Threshold	**10**
Polling Interval	**5**
Polling Interval Unit	**Minutes**

User Name
Enter the user name to log on to the POP3 server.

| OK | Cancel | Apply | Help |

We need to set up **Mail Server** (from which the messages can be retrieved), **User Name**, **Password**, and **Body Part Index**.

The **Body Part Index** attribute is used to choose what part of the mail will be considered as the actual message inside BizTalk. **0** is the message body, **1** is the first attachment, **2** is the second attachment, and so on.

> Note that if **Body Part Content Type** is set to a specific content type, the algorithm for choosing which part of the mail to use is a bit more complex. For further information, visit http://msdn.microsoft.com/en-us/library/aa560251(v=bts.80).aspx.

SMTP

The SMTP Adapter is used for sending e-mails.

To set up the SMTP Adapter, it is often a good idea to configure the general server credentials inside the STMP Send Handler (refer to the *Managing Adapter Handlers* section).

The following screenshot shows the configuration screen of the SMTP Send Handler Adapter:

SMTP Transport Properties   X

Properties

<u>S</u>MTP server name:

smtp.mail.com

<u>F</u>rom (e-mail address):

myaddress@domain.com

Server authentication

Authentication type:

Process account (NTLM) ∨

User name:

Password:

| OK | Cancel | <u>A</u>pply | Help |

On the Send Handler, the SMTP Server name and **From (e-mail address)** can be configured since they will likely be the same for all SMTP Send Ports. These parameters can be overwritten on a single Send Port, if required.

When configuring the actual SMTP Adapter on a Send Port, perform the following steps:

1. In the **General** tab, type the desired e-mail address in the **To: field**. Also, give a subject to the e-mail and, if needed, specify a CC address.

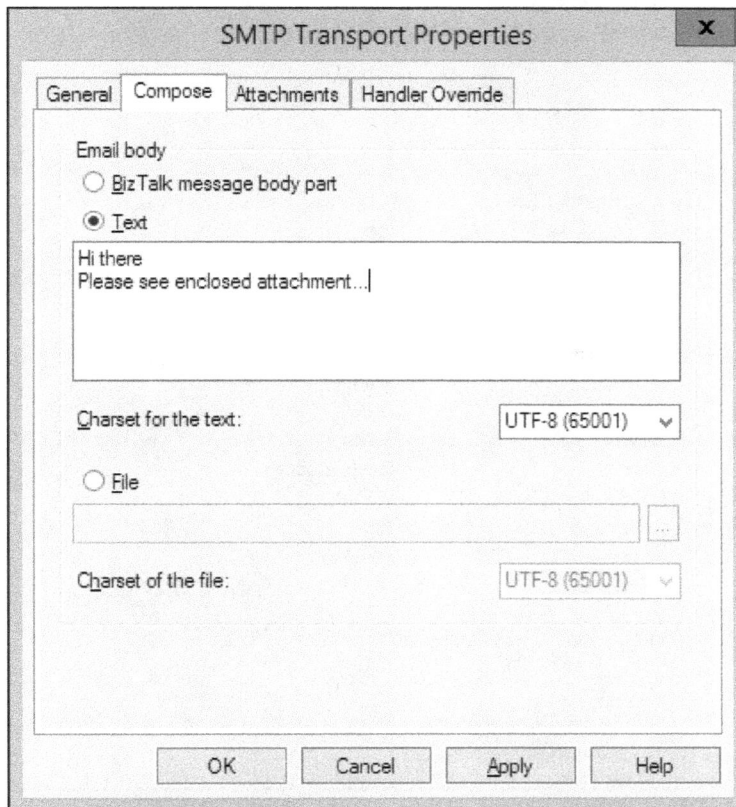

```
┌─────────────────────────────────────────────────────────┐
│           SMTP Transport Properties            [ X ]     │
├─────────────────────────────────────────────────────────┤
│ │General│ Compose │ Attachments │ Handler Override │     │
│                                                          │
│    Email body                                            │
│      ○ BizTalk message body part                         │
│      ⦿ Text                                              │
│     ┌──────────────────────────────────────────────┐    │
│     │ Hi there                                      │    │
│     │ Please see enclosed attachment...│            │    │
│     │                                               │    │
│     │                                               │    │
│     └──────────────────────────────────────────────┘    │
│    Charset for the text:            │UTF-8 (65001)  ∨│    │
│                                                          │
│      ○ File                                              │
│     ┌───────────────────────────────────────────┬──┐    │
│     │                                           │...│    │
│     └───────────────────────────────────────────┴──┘    │
│    Charset of the file:             │UTF-8 (65001)  ∨│    │
│                                                          │
│                                                          │
│        │  OK  │  │ Cancel │  │ Apply │  │ Help │         │
└─────────────────────────────────────────────────────────┘
```

2. In the **Compose** tab, choose either the **BizTalk message body part** option as the e-mail body or the **Text** option for standard text.
3. If a standard text is chosen, move to the **Attachments** tab.
4. Choose **Attach only body part** to have the actual message as an attachment.
5. Use the **Handler Override** options if the SMTP Server setup in the Adapter handler should be overwritten.

FTP

The FTP Adapter can be used for both receiving and sending messages in BizTalk. On the receive side, only single Host Instance server set up is allowed.

When configuring the FTP Adapter, there are some basic features that apply to both sending and receiving, as shown in the following screenshot:

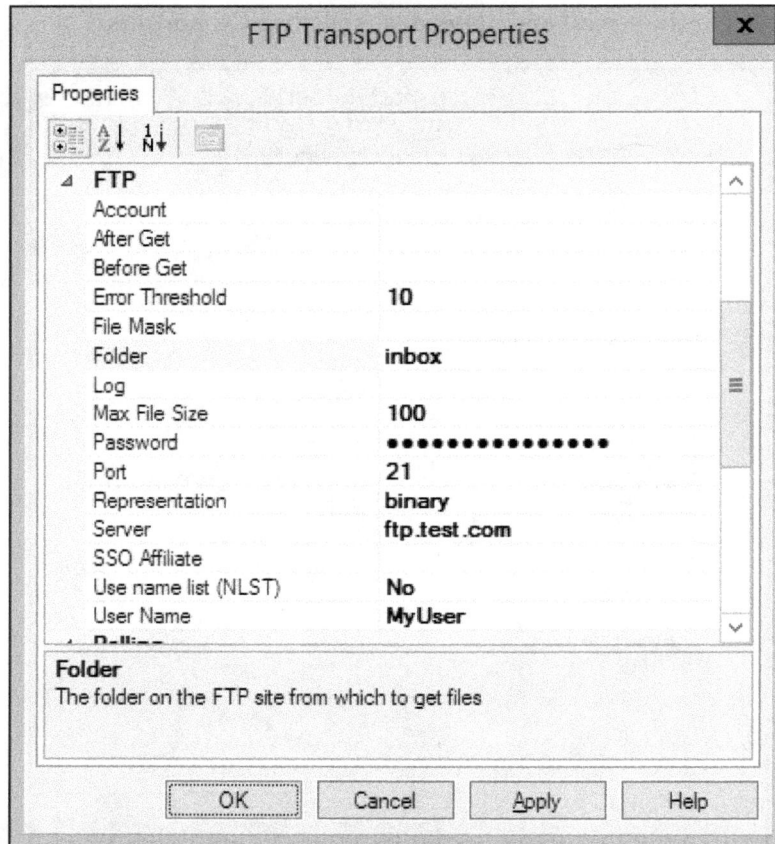

For all FTP configurations, at least the following four parameters should be configured:

- **Server**: This is the name or IP address of the FTP Server
- **User Name**: This is the user name of the user logging onto the FTP Server
- **Password**: This is the password for the user logging onto the server
- **Folder**: This is the folder to either download files from (receive) or upload files to (send)

Receiving FTP

When using basic configuration, the FTP Server will delete the files when they are processed so that the same files are not processed more than once.

However, this might not always be the desired functionality since we might not be allowed to delete the files. The server could be holding files that are not just for us, but published for many subscribers.

In order to overcome this issue, new polling features have been introduced in BizTalk Server 2010, and are still available in 2013, which are shown in the following screenshot:

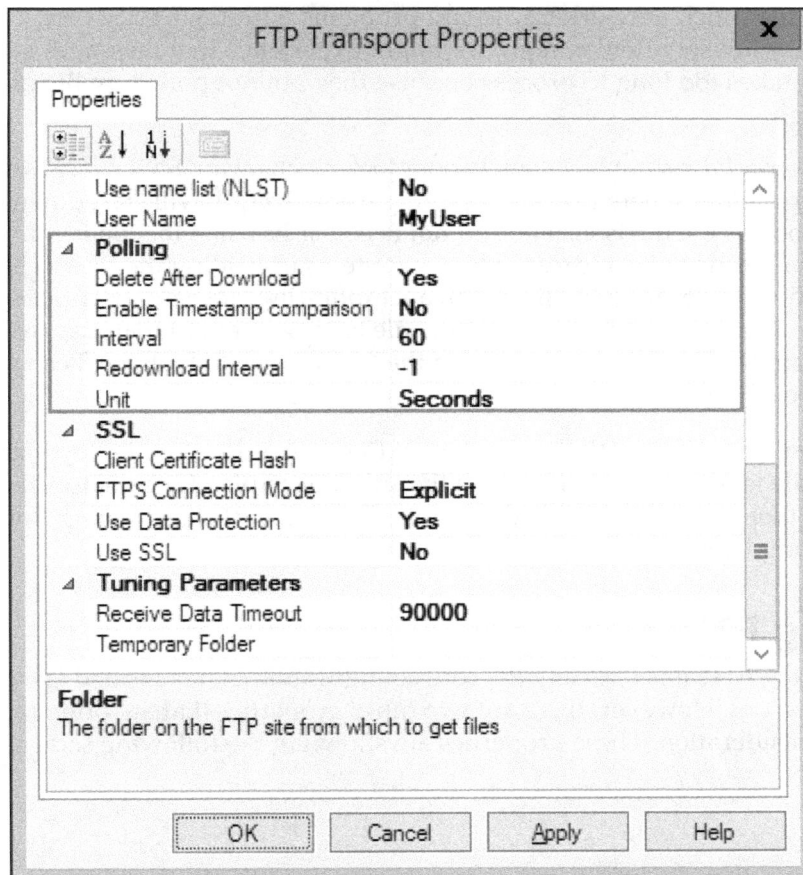

It is now possible to change the **Delete After Download** attribute on the FTP Receive Adapter from **Yes** to **No**. By doing this, BizTalk will keep track of which files have already been downloaded, and the same files will not be downloaded again even though they are still on the FTP Server. If existing files are edited and overwritten on the FTP Server, and we want a new copy when changes happen to the files, we should also set the **Enable Timestamp comparison** attribute to **Yes**. By doing this, we will not only get new files once, but also a fresh copy of any file that has been overwritten on the FTP Server.

The interval (60 seconds in the previous example) should also be taken into consideration when setting up the receive FTP. This is an indication of how often BizTalk will look in the FTP folder for new messages. If set too often, we might experience too much network traffic and problems with the FTP Server. On the other hand, if not set often enough, we might experience that messages submitted for BizTalk takes too long to process because they are not polled by BizTalk often enough.

The FTP protocol does not have any proper lock mechanism. So if a large file is being written to the folder where BizTalk is polling from, BizTalk will start downloading the file as soon as the file is visible, and not necessarily when the file is complete. This problem needs to be addressed by the systems uploading the files to BizTalk in the FTP folders by creating the files with a temporarily extension (`filename.xml.tmp`) and then removing the `.tmp` after the file is completed. In that case, we also need to set up the **File Mask** property on the FTP receive to look for files with the xml extension (`*.xml`).

Another way of dealing with the problem of files being downloaded by BizTalk before the file is fully written, is having the submitter upload the file to a temporary folder, and then moving it to the correct folder where BizTalk is polling from when the file is completed.

Sending FTP

When sending FTP, it is basically the core configuration that is needed (server, user name, and so on). However, there are two other properties that are often relevant to take into consideration. These properties are shown in the following screenshot:

FTP Transport Properties   **X**

Properties

Log	
Password	
Port	**21**
Representation	**binary**
Server	
SSO Affiliate	
Target File Name	**%MessageID%.xml**
User Name	
⊿ **SSL**	
Client Certificate Hash	
FTPS Connection Mode	**Explicit**
Use Data Protection	**Yes**
Use SSL	**No**
⊿ **Tuning Parameters**	
Connection Limit	**0**
Temporary Folder	

Account
Optional account name for the FTP Server

OK   Cancel   Apply   Help

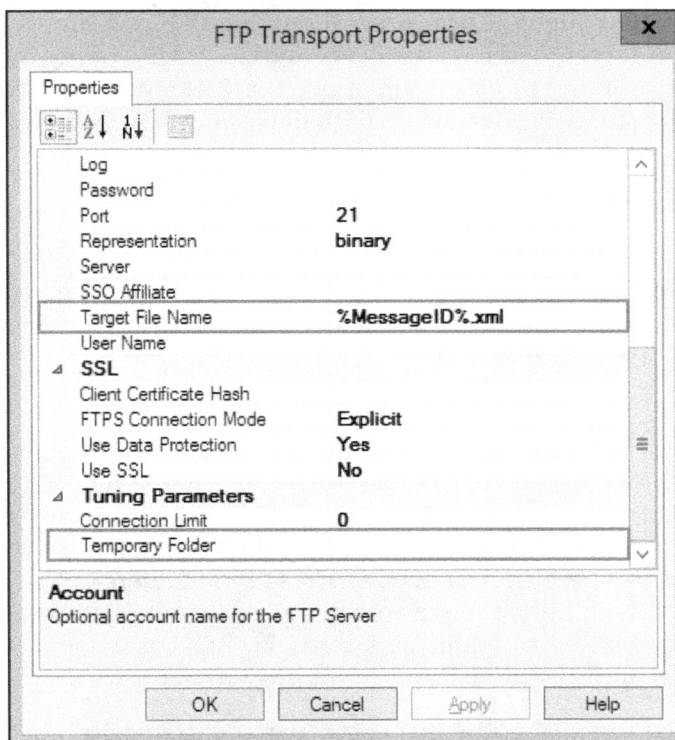

First, we will take a look at **Target File Name**. This is used to specify the name that BizTalk will give to the file written to the FTP Server. The default is `%MessageID%.xml`, where `%MessageID%` will be replaced with an internal GUID unique for each message so that no two files uploaded to an FTP Server from BizTalk will ever have the same name. The use of hardcoded name (such as `Order.xml`) is not recommended, as this will cause a failure on the send side if BizTalk tries to upload File with the same name twice and the first file has not been processed by the destination party yet. Depending on the FTP Server it might also result in the files just being overwritten. However, there is a property called **Append if exists** that can be set to **Yes**. This is seldom used and will only work for Flat Files and not for XML, since the latter requires one root element.

It is also possible to use `%SourceFileName%` as a file mask in **Target File Name**. This will give the file the same name as it had when submitted to BizTalk by either a file or FTP. Again, we need to take into consideration whether or not two files could end up with the same name, and therefore, cause the FTP Send Adapter to fail. Also, this will only work if all files sent through the FTP Adapter were in fact received into BizTalk by either the FILE or FTP Adapter (refer to the *Implementing messaging patterns* section).

Another property that might be useful when sending FTP is **Temporary Folder**. This enables the Adapter to upload the file to another folder, rather than to the one specified in the **Folder** property, and move the file to the correct folder when upload has completed. As we discussed with the receive FTP Adapter, this might be useful because FTP doesn't have any proper locking mechanism.

FILE

The FILE Adapter is one of the most used Adapters, both for testing/demo purposes and for communicating with several legacy systems where the only protocol supported is exporting and importing files.

Receiving files

Configuring the Receive FILE Adapter requires a path to the folder where BizTalk should pick up files (**Receive folder**) as well as a **File mask**, specifying which type of files and/or filenames should be received. This folder can either be local or located on a file server somewhere on the network. Using local folders is not recommended when working with multiserver environments since that would cause BizTalk to have more than one file entry-point. How many BizTalk Servers a BizTalk Group contains should be transparent to the surrounding environments.

When using a file server, be aware that using mapped drive letters in **Receive folder** might not work as intended (`z:\Inbox`), since it will use the mapped drives of the user running the Host Instance and not necessarily the mapped drives seen by the user configuring the Port. Therefore, UNC paths are recommended (`\\ServerName\Path\Inbox`). The following screenshot shows the general configuration properties for a Receive FILE Adapter:

FILE Transport Properties   ☒

General | Authentication | Batching

Receive folder:

C:\BTS2013CertGuide\Chapter01\Example01   Browse...

File mask: *.xml

Public address:

Network Failure

Retry count: 5

Retry interval (min):   5

Advanced settings...

OK   Cancel   Apply   Help

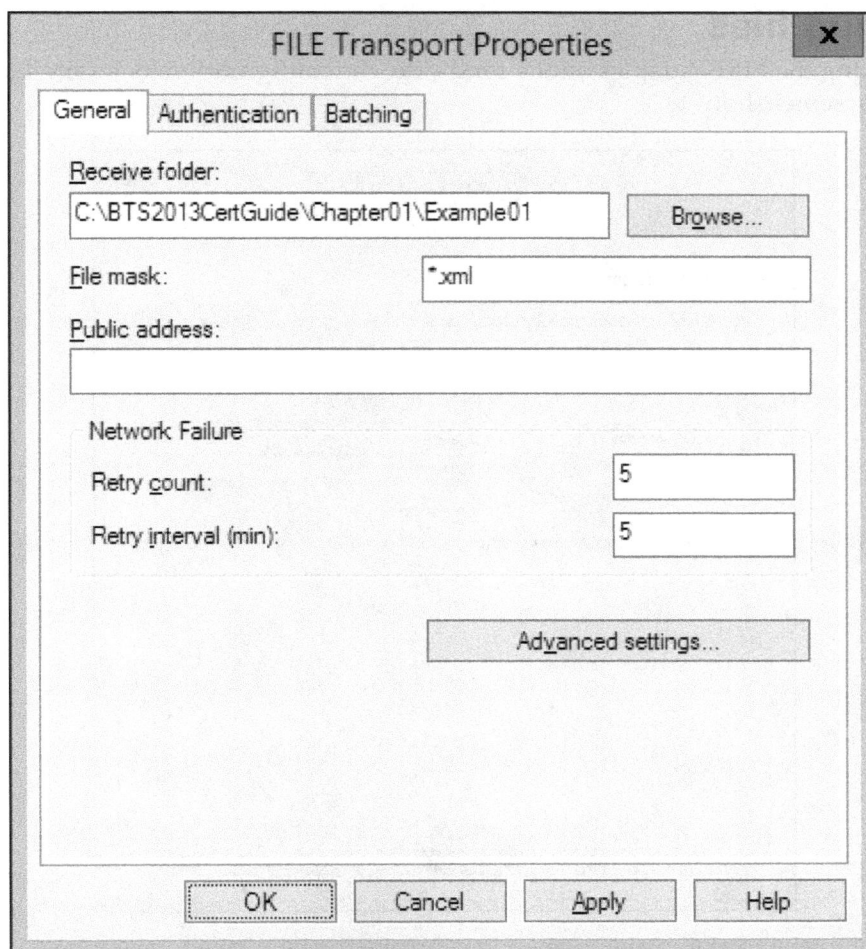

The **Receive folder** can only point to a single folder. It is not possible to have the same Receive Location probing in more than one folder. This limitation also includes subfolders.

When working on NTFS file systems, the FILE Adapter will work using **.NET File System Events**, so every time a file is submitted, BizTalk will be notified almost immediately and will start processing the file (except if service windows are implemented on the Receive Location).

Sending files

When using the FILE Adapter on the send side, the configuration looks similar to the following screenshot:

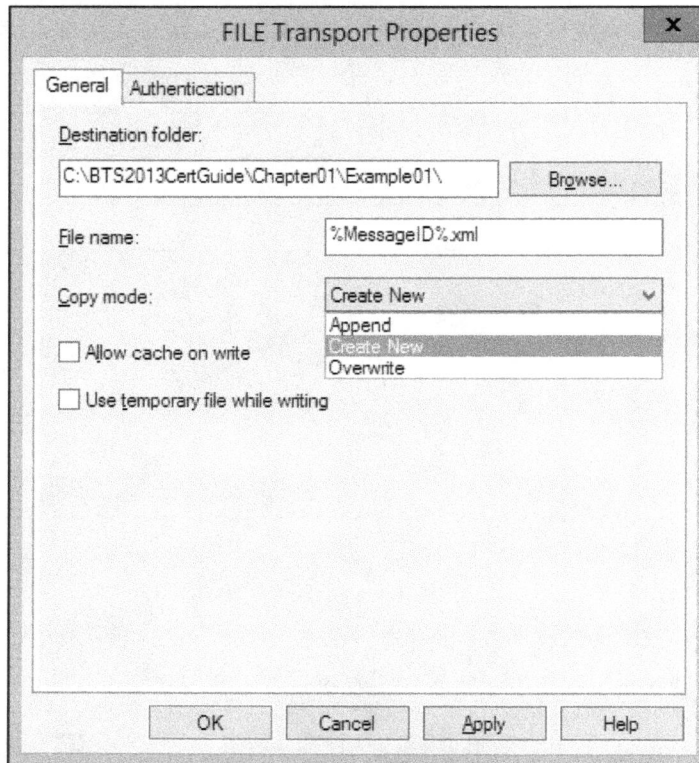

When sending files using the FILE Adapter, we need to specify the **Destination folder** and the **File name**. The default filename is %MessageID%.xml, which will give the filename a unique GUID to make sure no two files are given the same name.

Just as the FTP Adapter, %SourceFileName% can also be used on the FILE Adapter, but again we should use it with caution, since it will only work if the original message was received through either an FTP or FILE Adapter.

It is also possible to configure how the FILE Adapter should write the file to folder using the **Copy mode** option. The following are the three possible modes:

- **Append**: This will append the message into an existing file, if the file is already present. It is usually used for Flat Files (comma delimited, positional text files) and not for XML.

- **Create New** (default): This setting is the most commonly used setting. It will create, or try to create, a new file each time a message is sent to the Port. When using this setting, it is recommended that the filename is unique, which can be done by using the `%MessageID%` macro.

- **Overwrite**: This will overwrite any existing files that have the same name as the file currently being written to a file folder. This is often used when dealing with daily inventory reports and so on, where the old data is obsolete as soon as new data is present.

Credentials

If no credentials are specified in the FILE Adapter configuration, it will be the user running the Host Instance, which needs to have the correct amount of rights to the folder it is receiving from or sending to. If the user does not have the sufficient amount of credentials, we can supply another username and password for the FILE Adapter to use, as shown in the following screenshot:

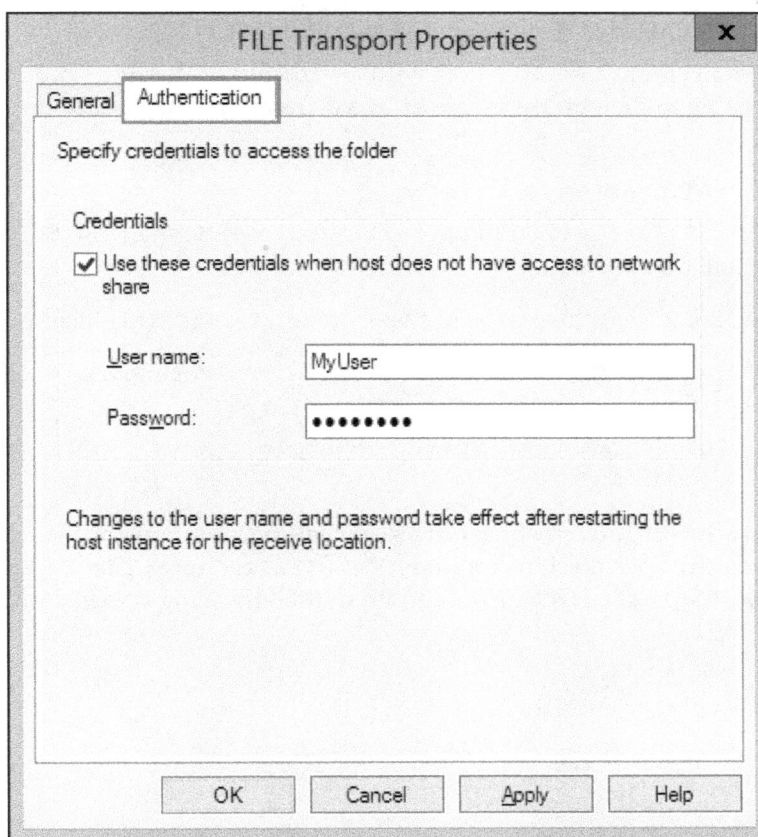

Click on the **Authentication** tab and specify a username and password. Now, this user will be used instead of the Host Instance User. This can be done for both receiving and sending files.

Configuring content-based routing

The following is a walk-through of a routing sample in BizTalk. The sample is done by using the FILE Adapter only, and coding is not done. The next chapter will introduce us to how to create various BizTalk artifacts inside Visual Studio, but for now, let's look at an example showing how BizTalk routes messages.

The setup is as follows:

- We receive files from both partner A and partner B in different file folders
- These files need to be routed to both System I and System II

Creating folders and Applications

The first step is to create a Receive Port with two different Receive Locations. We should be able to pick up messages at two different file locations:

- `C:\BTS2013CertGuide\Chapter01\Example01-Messaging\FileDrop\PartnerA\Inbox`
- `C:\BTS2013CertGuide\Chapter01\Example01-Messaging\FileDrop\PartnerB\Inbox`

We should be able to send messages to two different systems (file locations):

- `C:\BTS2013CertGuide\Chapter01\Example01-Messaging\FileDrop\SystemI\Outbox`
- `C:\BTS2013CertGuide\Chapter01\Example01-Messaging\FileDrop\SystemII\Outbox`

Make sure that the BizTalk Host user has sufficient permissions for the folders. Give the user **Full control** permissions on folder `C:\BTS2013CertGuide\Chapter01\Example01-Messaging\FileDrop`, as shown in the following screenshot:

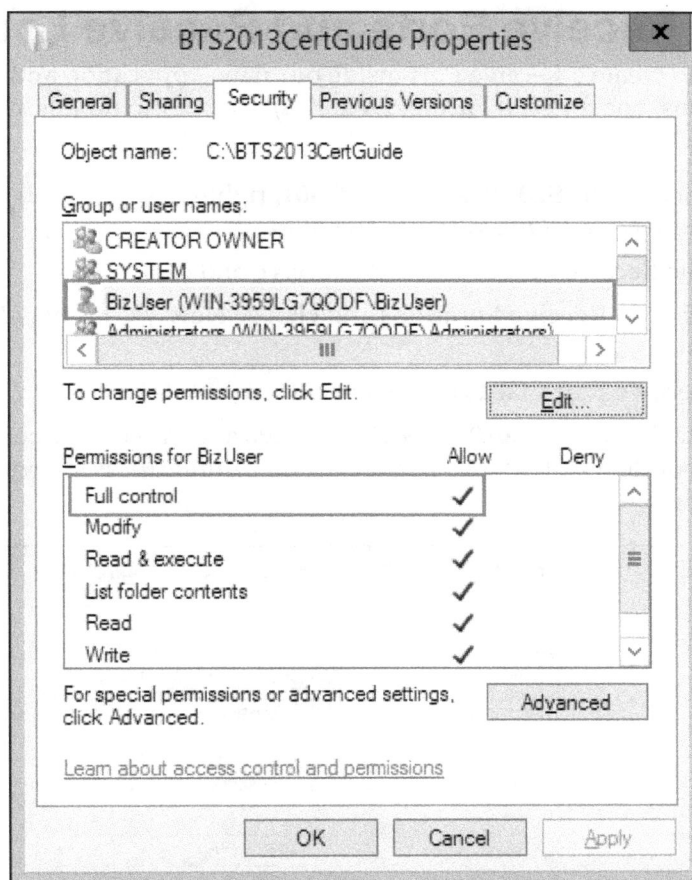

The user and/or group doesn't need **Full control**. It is sufficient to grant the **Delete subfolders and files** permission found under **advanced permissions**, along with read and write permissions.

Next, we need to create an Application called **BTS2013CertGuide-Ch01**. To do this, we need to perform the following steps:

1. Open **BizTalk Administration Console**.

2. Right-click on **Applications** and then choose **New | Application**.

3. Name the new Application **BTS2013CertGuide-Ch01** and click on **OK**.

Creating Receive Ports and Receive Locations

Now, we need to create a Receive Port inside our new Application and add two File Receive Locations, one for each Partner (A and B). In order to do this, carry out the following steps:

1. In Application **BTS2013CertGuide-Ch01**, right-click on **Receive Ports** and choose **New | One-way Receive Port**.

2. Name the Receive Port as **CG0101_Receive** and click on **OK**.

3. Right-click on **Receive Locations** and choose **New | One-Way Receive Location**.

4. Select Receive Port **CG0101_Receive** and click on **OK**.

5. Name the location **CG0101_ReceiveFromPartnerA_FILE**, choose **FILE** in **Transport Type** (Adapter), and click on **Configure**, as shown in the following screenshot:

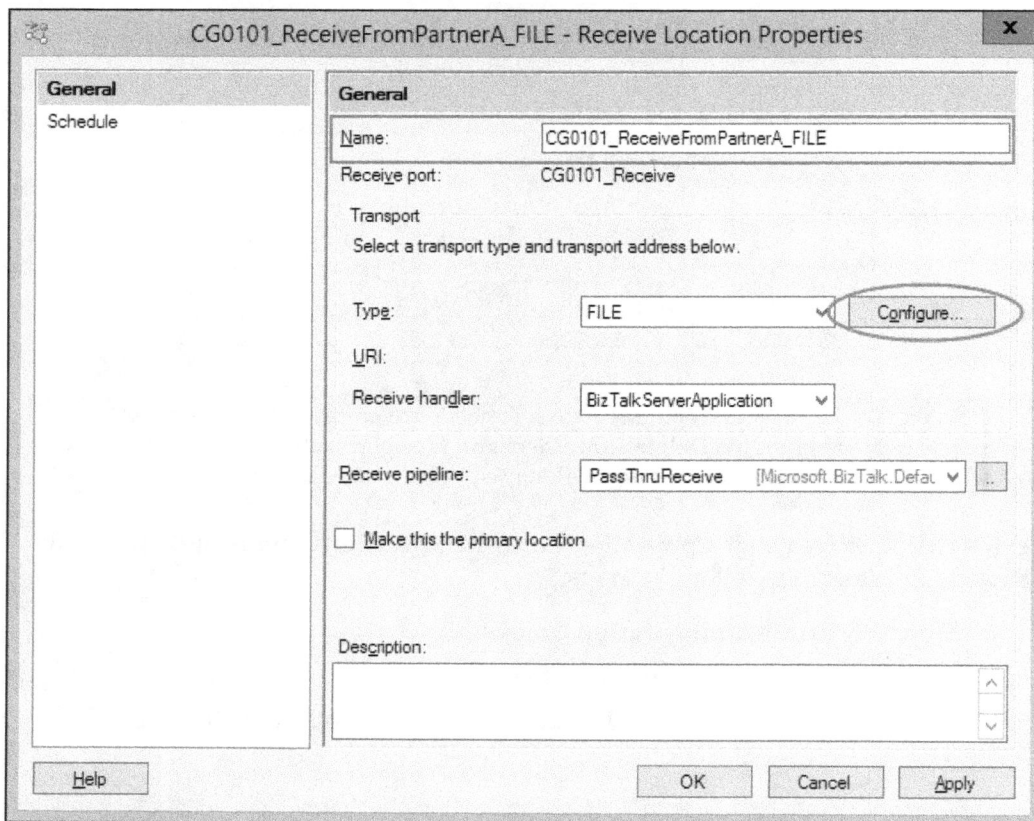

6. Configure the FILE Adapter, as shown in the following screenshot, and click on **OK** (the **Receive Folder** path is C:\BTS2013CertGuide\Chapter01\ Example01-Messaging\FileDrop\PartnerA\Inbox):

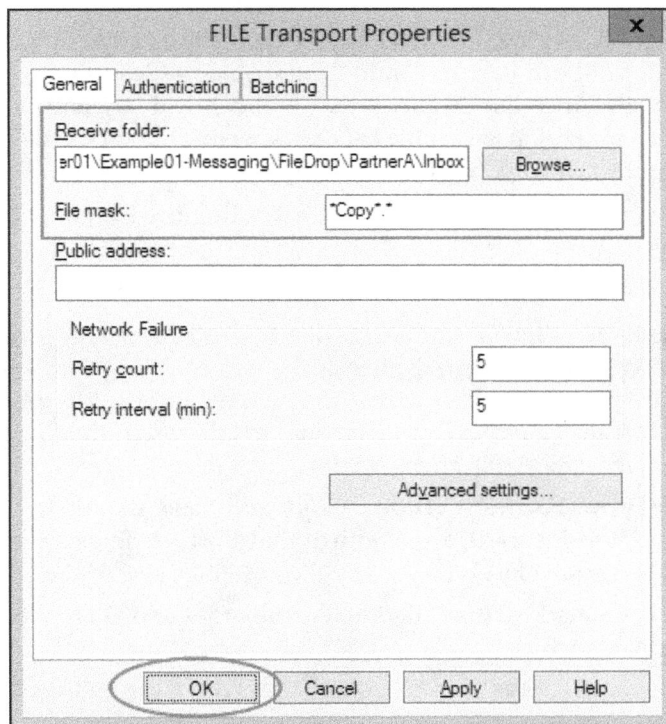

7. Click on **OK** again.

8. Make another Receive Location from steps 3 to 7. Name it **PartnerB** instead of **PartnerA** and choose **PartnerB** file folder instead of **PartnerA**.

In the Administration Console, our **Receive Locations** should now look similar to the following screenshot:

Testing the Receive Locations

Now, we need to see that everything is running as intended by testing the solution. In order to start testing, perform the following steps:

1. Create a small text file, fill it with a few characters, and copy the file into each inbox folder of both PartnerA and PartnerB. The files must consist of at least one character, since the FILE Adapter will throw away empty messages as they do not make sense in a BizTalk perspective. Do not give the files a name containing the word "Copy".

2. Verify that the BizTalk Host Instance executing the Receive Locations is running.

3. Right-click on each **Receive Location** and choose **Enable**.

4. Check the Event Viewer and verify that no BizTalk Server errors have been written to **Windows Logs/Application** when enabling the Receive Locations. If errors are present, examine them, since they are most likely caused by the BizTalk Host user not having sufficient permission in the folders (refer to the *Creating folders and Applications* section).

5. Go to **FileDrop\PartnerA\Inbox**. Copy and paste the file in the same folder so that a copy is inserted, and confirm that BizTalk deletes the file. It might be quick, so watch closely!

6. If the file is deleted by BizTalk, our **PartnerA** locations are working. Do the same test **PartnerB**.

Debugging the messages

Now, let's examine what happened to the messages we submitted to BizTalk.

1. Upon opening Event Viewer again, you should find four errors (two for each message submitted).

2. Open the last error submitted in Event Viewer, it should look something similar to the following screenshot:

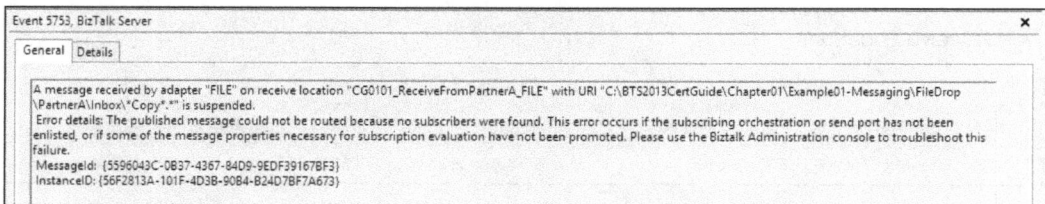

```
Event 5753, BizTalk Server                                                                              ×

 General  Details

A message received by adapter "FILE" on receive location "CG0101_ReceiveFromPartnerA_FILE" with URI "C:\BTS2013CertGuide\Chapter01\Example01-Messaging\FileDrop
\PartnerA\Inbox\*Copy*.*" is suspended.
Error details: The published message could not be routed because no subscribers were found. This error occurs if the subscribing orchestration or send port has not been
enlisted, or if some of the message properties necessary for subscription evaluation have not been promoted. Please use the BizTalk Administration console to troubleshoot this
failure.
MessageId: {5596043C-0B37-4367-84D9-9EDF39167BF3}
InstanceID: {56F2813A-101F-4D3B-90B4-B24D7BF7A673}
```

What BizTalk is telling us here is that even though the receive processing of the messages was successful, the messages could not be routed because there were no subscribers. In other words, neither Send Ports nor Orchestrations were created with a subscription matching the Context of the messages.

Now, we will examine the Context of one of the messages that failed to be routed:

1. Go to **Group Hub** by clicking on the **BizTalk Group** folder in the Administration Console, then press *F5* to refresh the dashboard showing in the right pane.

2. We should now see four suspended items:

Suspended Items	
Suspended service instances	4
- Resumable	2
- Non-resumable	2

3. Click on the **Resumable** link.

> The **Non-resumable** instances are primarily there for debugging purposes. They show the Context as it appeared after Port processing, whereas the **Resumable** instances show the message and the Context as it appeared before Port processing.
>
> In this example, the promoted properties are the same for both instances, and we can therefore use the **Resumable** instance. If properties had been added during Pipeline processing and/or mapping, we would need to examine the **Non-resumable** instance.
>
> Also, note that the **Non-resumable** instance will disappear by itself if the **Resumable** instance is resumed successfully.

4. Double-click on one of the suspended items.

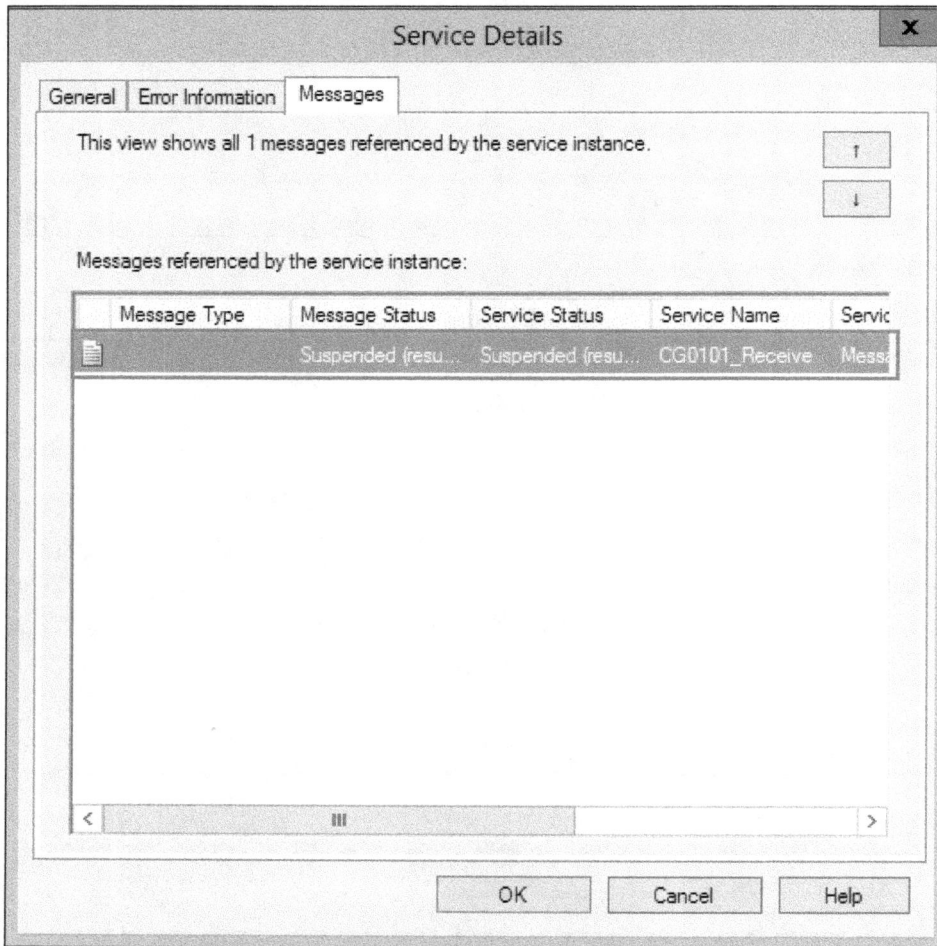

Service Details				X

General | Error Information | Messages

This view shows all 1 messages referenced by the service instance.

Messages referenced by the service instance:

Message Type	Message Status	Service Status	Service Name	Servic
	Suspended (resu...	Suspended (resu...	CG0101_Receive	Messa

OK | Cancel | Help

5. Choose the **Messages** tab, and double-click on the message.

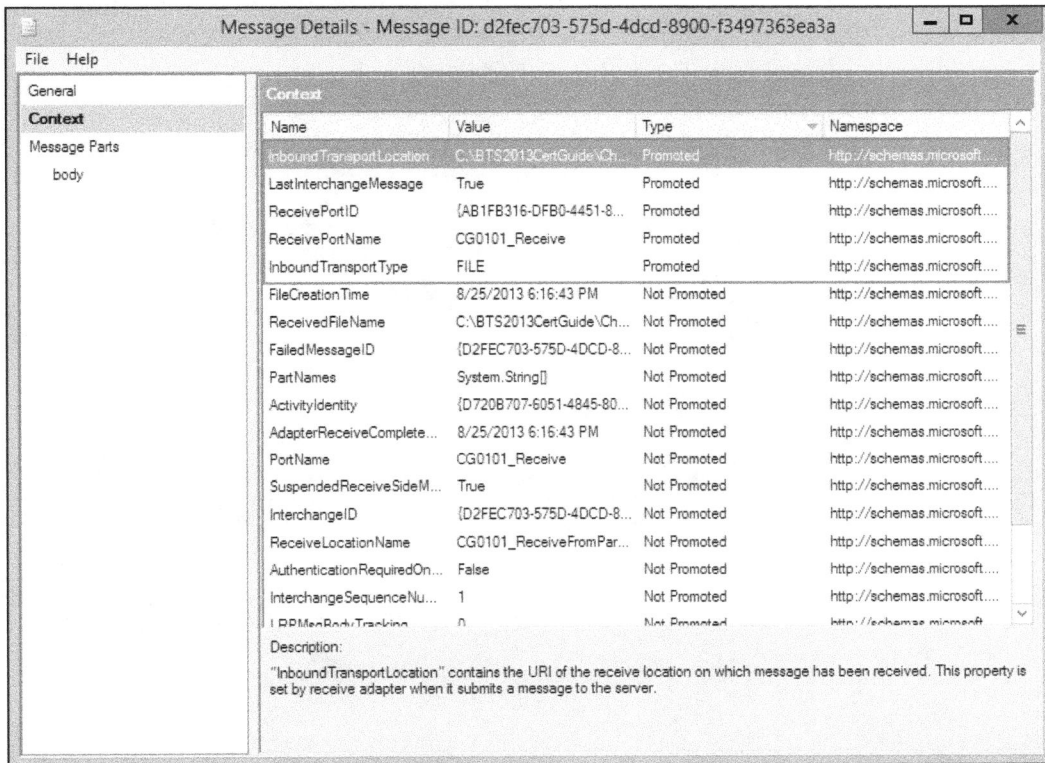

6. Choose **Context**, and click on **Type** twice so that the promoted properties are shown on top.

7. Examine the five promoted properties. These are the only properties we can use for subscription for now. The best candidate for subscription might be the **ReceivePortName** with the value of **CG0101_Receive**.

Setting up a Send Port

Now, we will perform the following steps for creating a Send Port that subscribes to all messages where **ReceivePortName** has the value of **CG0101_Receive** in its **Context**:

1. Create a new Send Port by right-clicking on the **Send Port** folder and navigating to **New | Static One-Way Send Port**.

2. Fill in **Name** and **Type**. Click on **Configure**.

3. Fill in the **Destination folder** path (C:\BTS2013CertGuide\Chapter01\
   Example01-Messaging\FileDrop\SystemI\Outbox) and the **File name**,
   as shown in the following screenshot, and click on **OK**:

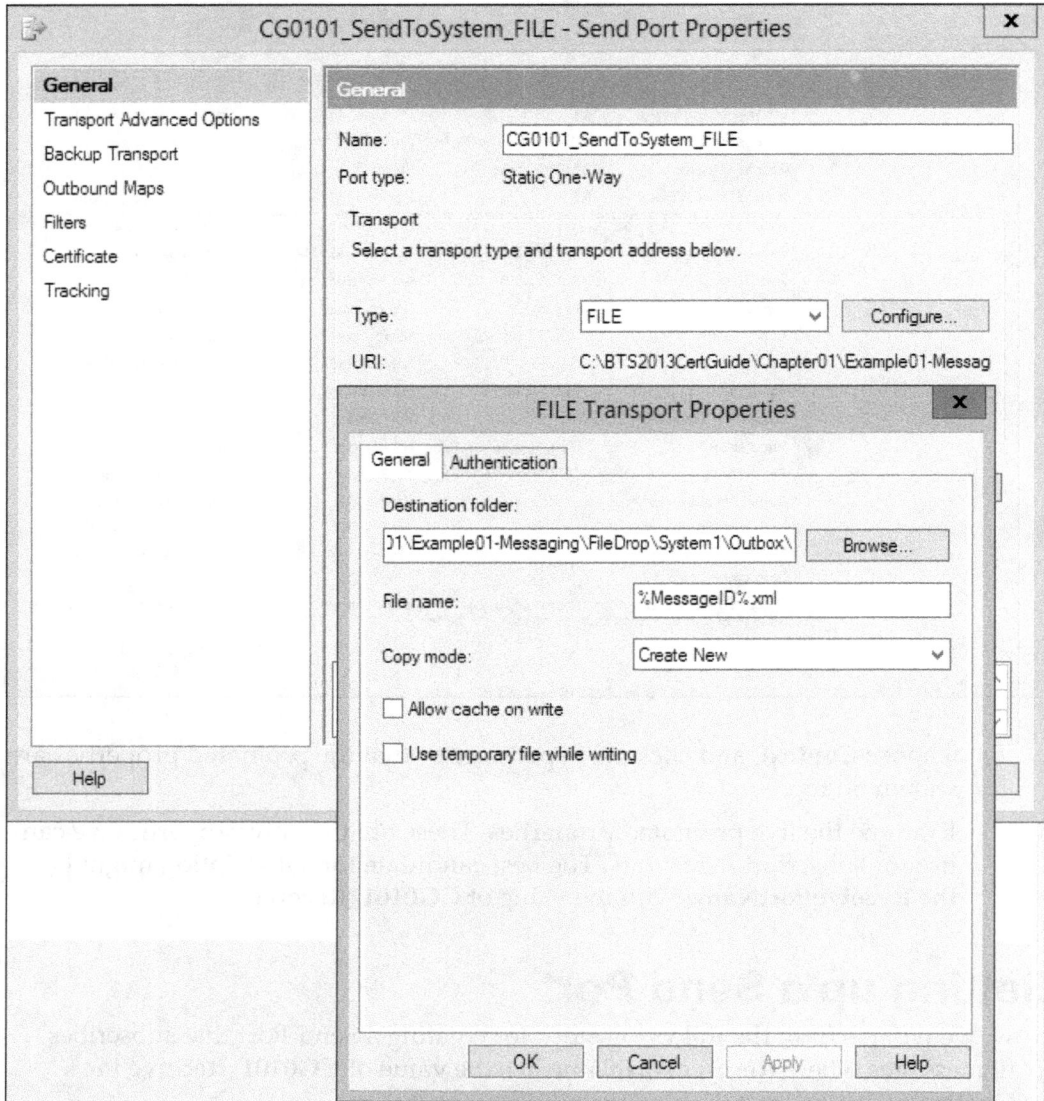

CG0101_SendToSystem_FILE - Send Port Properties ⊠

General
Transport Advanced Options
Backup Transport
Outbound Maps
Filters
Certificate
Tracking

General

Name: CG0101_SendToSystem_FILE

Port type: Static One-Way

Transport
Select a transport type and transport address below.

Type: FILE ∨ Configure...

URI: C:\BTS2013CertGuide\Chapter01\Example01-Messag

FILE Transport Properties ⊠

General | Authentication

Destination folder:
01\Example01-Messaging\FileDrop\System1\Outbox\ | Browse...

File name: %MessageID%.xml

Copy mode: Create New ∨

☐ Allow cache on write

☐ Use temporary file while writing

Help

OK | Cancel | Apply | Help

4. Choose the **Filters** page. Select **BTS.ReceivePortName** in the **Property** drop-down list. Leave **Operator** as **==** and type the Receive Port name in the **Value** textbox.

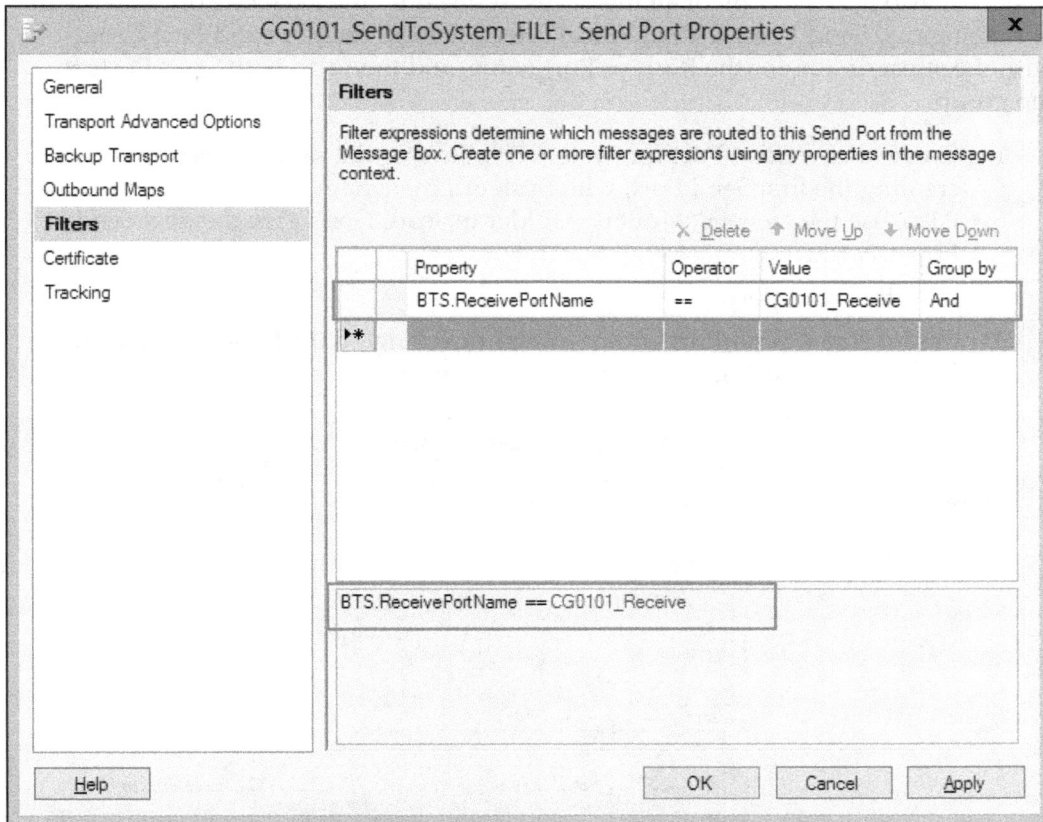

	CG0101_SendToSystem_FILE - Send Port Properties				x
General	**Filters**				
Transport Advanced Options	Filter expressions determine which messages are routed to this Send Port from the Message Box. Create one or more filter expressions using any properties in the message context.				
Backup Transport					
Outbound Maps					
Filters	X Delete ↑ Move Up ↓ Move Down				
Certificate		Property	Operator	Value	Group by
Tracking		BTS.ReceivePortName	==	CG0101_Receive	And
	▶*				
	BTS.ReceivePortName == CG0101_Receive				
Help			OK	Cancel	Apply

5. Click on **OK**.

6. Start the Send Port by right-clicking on it and choosing **Start**.

7. Submit a message from either Partner A or Partner B.

8. Check that System I gets a file in the `outbox` folder.

9. Go back to **Group Hub**, choose the two resumable suspended items, and right-click and choose **Resume Instances**. Click on **Yes**, and then click on **OK**.

10. Verify that the two additional files are now in the `System I` folder.

Setting up Send Port for System II and a Send Port Group

System II also needs a copy of all messages received by the Receive Port. So instead of making two Send Ports with identical filters, we will make a Send Port Group with the subscription for the Receive Port name, and then add both Send Ports to the group.

1. Create a new Send Port for System II following the same steps we did when creating the first Send Port, with SystemII in its name instead of SystemI. Also, use the `SystemII outbox` folder instead. Don't give the new Send Port any filter.

2. Start the Send Port.

3. Create a new Send Port Group by right-clicking on the **Send Port Group** folder and choosing **New | Send Port Group...**.

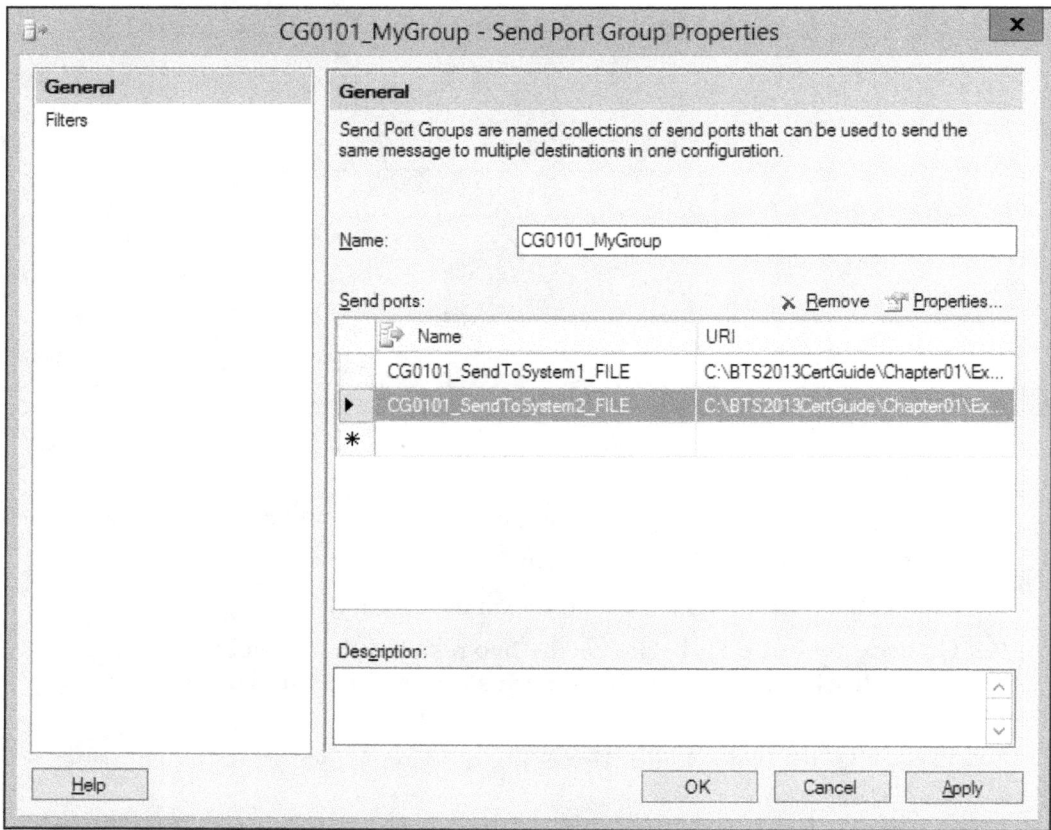

CG0101_MyGroup - Send Port Group Properties

General
Filters

General

Send Port Groups are named collections of send ports that can be used to send the same message to multiple destinations in one configuration.

Name: CG0101_MyGroup

Send ports: ✕ Remove   Properties...

	Name	URI
	CG0101_SendToSystem1_FILE	C:\BTS2013CertGuide\Chapter01\Ex...
▶	CG0101_SendToSystem2_FILE	C:\BTS2013CertGuide\Chapter01\Ex...
*		

Description:

Help   OK   Cancel   Apply

---

4. Give the group a name, as shown in the preceding screenshot, and add the two Send Ports to the group.

5. Give the group a filter with the Receive Port name, just as we did with the first Send Port.

6. Click on **OK**.

7. Right-click on the group and start it.

8. Submit a message from one of the partners.

9. Notice how System II got one message, but System I got two. This is because a Send Port inside a Send Port Group will have two subscriptions both its own subscription and the Group subscription. If both of them are met, the Port will receive the same message twice.

10. Go to the System I Send Port and remove the subscription inside the **Filter** page by pressing *Delete*. Click on **OK**.

11. Test again; this time System I should only get one copy.

Implementing messaging patterns

When working with BizTalk, the design considerations are very important. A bad design might result in poor performance, difficulty in changing the solution if the surrounding environment changes, and redundant code.

Working with canonical messages

One of the design patterns we should always try to meet (unless there is a good reason for doing otherwise) is the use of canonical messages inside BizTalk.

If BizTalk receives a message of type A and that message needs to be sent to another system and transformed to type B, we should make up our own internal message type instead of transforming directly from A to B. We do this, not by looking at the structure of either type A or B, but rather by making a type of the message that is independent of both types (type I).

This will require two transformations (Maps), one from type A to type I, and another from type I to type B.

We should also make sure that only canonical/internal messages hit the MessageBox, so Map A to I should be applied on the Receive Port, and Map I to B on the Send Port.

This pattern has the following advantages:

- If we receive messages from various partners/systems (type A1, A2, A3, and so on) and we map all of these different structures to a canonical type on the receive side, then the target system (type B) could change structure or format and we would only have to change the solution in one place, the transformation from the canonical type to B.

- If more subscribers are interested in the message, and we make transformations directly from Message Type A to all of the desired formats of the subscribers, and we start receiving the messages in other formats, we would again need to make transformations from the new format to each of the subscribers instead of just transforming the new format to the internal format.

This is also the case when working with Orchestrations. Try not to use the Adapter or trading partner-specific Schemas inside the Orchestrations. Use internal versions of the messages instead. Use these internal versions inside the Orchestrations and then map from and to the internal Schemas in the Receive and Send Ports. By doing this, we don't have to recompile (let alone recode) an Orchestration if a Message Type on a Send or Receive Port is changed, or if the Adapter on a Send Port changes. The structure of the XML sent and received from the old and new messages would be different, but if we are only dealing with internal messages in our Orchestrations, only the Maps on the Send and Receive Ports would need to be changed.

Debatching

Another pattern we should try to implement, for most solutions, is the use of singular messages inside BizTalk. If we receive batches, such as several messages inside the same file, we should debatch them into individual items on the receive side of BizTalk (the Receive Pipeline).

The rule of thumb is that the solution should act the same way if we receive one large file containing 10 orders, as it should if we receive 10 orders in 10 files (one in each file).

BizTalk cannot handle the items individually if they are kept as a batch through BizTalk Server. If we receive orders, and some subscribers are only interested in orders containing a specific customer number, we would have no means (at least not with normal content-based routing) of subscribing to just those messages if all of them were kept inside a batch message.

There are other cases where keeping multiple items inside a batch and not debatching them makes sense. If a solution picks up a large batch of products, because full inventory is done once a day, and all subscribers are interested in seeing these products as a whole inventory report, we should not try to debatch them. Also, note that although BizTalk comes with great debatching functionality on the receive side, there is no automatic way of batching these items again if some subscribers need the inventory report as it was received and others need them individually. In this case, we would need to keep the batch inside BizTalk and then do some extra code (possibly using Orchestrations) to make debatched copies.

In other words, a debatched message is not easily assembled again with the same items in the same order.

Using the correct flow

We often have a decision whether to use a One-Way or Request-Response flow. The following table describes some of the scenarios where it makes sense to use one over the other:

Direction	Type	Usage
Receive	Request-Response	Used only if the caller submitting messages to BizTalk needs an answer back, such as `GetNumberOfProductsInStock`, or if it is vital to the calling system to know that everything in the flow went well
Receive	One-Way	Used for cases other than the ones described in Request-Response
Send	Request-Response	Used if BizTalk calls a system and needs an answer back from that system
Send	One-Way	Used in all other cases

It is important to not use Request-Response when only One-Way is needed. If calling a Web Service on a Send Port, it does not provide us with more reliability if we use a Request-Response port, instead of a One-Way port. The One-Way Port will, just as in a Request-Response scenario, wait for the service to finish and acknowledge that everything went well until the message is removed from the `MessageBox`. Also, using Request-Response when not needed, will give us less performance and less flexibility, because a Request-Response message submitted to the `MessageBox` can only have one subscriber.

Adapter independence

When designing a BizTalk Solution, we should try, whenever possible, not to make it so that code and/or logic is dependent on messages being received or sent using specific Adapters.

It might seem like a good idea to send files to an FTP Server using the `%SourceFileName%` macro in the **Target File Name** property, because we want to give the target server the same filename as the file had when we received it either by FILE or FTP. If this is a requirement, then this is, of course, how the solution should be made. However, try always to focus on the idea that the solution should also work if we changed the Adapter. If we start receiving messages from both a file folder and an Oracle database tomorrow, the `%SourceFileName%` logic on our Send Ports will fail to work for the messages received from Oracle, simply because no original filename exists.

On the send side, people also tend to hardcode specific Adapter properties inside Orchestrations, which results in situations where changing the Adapter type requires us to change and recompile the Orchestrations.

Testing your knowledge

1. HWLC Motors is sending XML orders to a file server at our place using FTP and BizTalk picks up the messages using a FILE Adapter through a Receive Port named **ReceiveOrders**. The files are currently being sent through a Send Port (Send Port A) using an SMTP Adapter and by using the **Filter** BTS. `ReceivePortName == ReceiveOrders`. You realize that three other Send Ports also want to subscribe to these messages and want to do this with the least amount of effort. What should you do (choose all that apply)?

    a. Create three new Receive Ports.

    b. Create three new Send Ports with no filter.

    c. Create three new Send Ports with the **Filter** of `BTS.ReceivePortName == ReceiveOrders`.

    d. Create a Send Port Group and set the **Filter** of the Group to BTS. `ReceivePortName == ReceiveOrders`.

    e. Assign the three Receive Ports to the Send Port Group.

    f. Assign the three Send Ports to the Send Port Group.

2. We receive XML from several trading partners through Receive Port *RP1*. At times, the XML is not well formed, the **XMLReceive** Pipelines throw errors, and the messages are suspended. Our partner coordinator Brian has requested that the invalid XML be sent to him in an e-mail, instead of being suspended in BizTalk. How would you achieve this (choose all that apply)?

   a. Set up e-mail alerting on the server if errors occur in the Event Viewer with BizTalk Server as the source.

   b. Create a Send Port *SP1* using the SMTP Adapter and target it to Brian's e-mail address. Set up a filter on the Send Port in the **ErrorReport.ReceivePortName == RP1** format.

   c. Enable **routing for failed messages** on the Send Port *SP1*.

   d. Enable **routing for failed messages** on the Receive Port *RP1*.

   e. Create a Send Port *SP1* using the SMTP Adapter and target it to Brian's e-mail address. Set up a filter on the Send Port in the **BTS. ReceivePortName == RP1** format.

3. HWLC has several Send Ports that point to different internal systems, and many of the message types flowing processed by BizTalk have multiple Send Ports as subscribers. One of the Send Ports targets the company's ERP system. The Adapter used is an HTTP Adapter. The ERP administrator wants to take the system offline for the next 24 hours and no messages should be sent to the system during that time. They do, however, want all messages processed during those 24 hours once they are back online. How should we accomplish this without impacting on the other subscribers?

   a. Disable all Receive Locations so that no messages are received in BizTalk for the next 24 hours.

   b. Stop the ERP Send Port and start it again when the system comes back online.

   c. Unenlist the ERP Send Port and start it again when the system comes back online.

   d. Stop all in-process BizTalk Services.

4. You receive messages of type A from a Partner through a Receive Port and send it directly to your CRM system by using a Send Port. You want to transform the message to type C before it enters the `MessageBox`. What should you do (choose all correct answers)?

   a. Apply a Map (A to C) to the Receive Port.

   b. Apply two Maps to the Receive Port (A to B) and (B to C).

    c.   Apply a Map (A to C) to the Send Port.

    d.   Apply two Maps to the Receive Port (A to B) and (B to C).

5.   You are receiving messages from customers sending e-mails with one attachment through an Exchange Server. You want BizTalk to process the mail body as the message. How should you approach this?

    a.   Use the FTP Adapter to receive messages from the Exchange Server.

    b.   Use the FILE Adapter to receive messages from the Exchange Server.

    c.   Use the POP3 Adapter to receive messages from the Exchange Server, set the **Body Part Index** attribute to **0**.

    d.   Use the POP3 Adapter to receive messages from the Exchange Server, set the **Body Part Index** attribute to **1**.

Summary

This chapter has dealt with some of the basics of BizTalk Server 2013, looking at the subscription engine, Ports, and Adapters. You should now have a basic knowledge of how BizTalk works and how to navigate through the BizTalk Server Administration Console. Next, we will look at XML, Schemas, Pipelines, and start using Visual Studio for BizTalk.

2
Developing BizTalk Artifacts – Creating Schemas and Pipelines

This chapter maps to parts of the Developing BizTalk Artifacts section of the exam. It is not an introduction to developing BizTalk Artifacts, instead it will point out some of the most relevant areas where you should have a proven practice today in your BizTalk development; these in turn are areas that you need to know about when taking the exam.

This builds on and leverages the knowledge we acquired in the first chapter about how to compose messaging architectures by involving Schemas and Pipelines instead of just passing untyped messages. The objective of Developing BizTalk Artifacts is split into three logically coherent chapters of manageable size, so that you can focus your effort on the area where you most need to improve. This is the first, and it covers these main areas:

- Creating Schemas
- Creating Pipelines
- Testing your knowledge

The section in the certification skills measured, called Construct Messages, does not exist as a single self-contained section but instead is covered in different parts of this book.

After this chapter, we will have learned how to create clear reusable Schemas. We will practice encryption, decryption, signing, and validation of signatures. We will work with Schemas describing a single message as well as Schemas describing envelopes. We will work with batches and we will use Pipelines to validate Schemas and split batches into single messages.

Schemas and Pipelines explicitly targeting EDI and AS2 are excluded from this chapter. Information on EDI is included in *Chapter 8, Implementing Extended Capabilities*.

Creating Schemas

Creating Schemas is core to handling messages in BizTalk Server. It's not uncommon to come across poorly created Schemas, without namespaces, with only string types, with mandatory fields not specified and not followed, or simply with everything optional. To create truly usable and explanatory Schemas that promote re-use and coherence, we need to go further. This section helps with that.

Type of Schemas

Schemas are used in BizTalk Server for several purposes, these include:

- Describing, receiving, and parsing XML documents
- Describing, receiving, and parsing Flat Files (non-XML text files)
- Describing context properties (property Schemas)

XML Schemas

A Schema or XML Schema is a special kind of XML-formatted file that describes the format of another XML file, using a standardized form. XML Schemas are not only used to describe and parse XML documents. They also describe Flat File structures as well as context properties.

Envelope Schemas

An Envelope Schema is an XML Schema that has a very special purpose; it describes an XML document that serves as a container for one or more messages, and although it can be otherwise empty, it often contains header-like information. When you specify that a Schema is an Envelope Schema, you are saying that the body content is contained in a node within the Schema, at a set XPath location.

BizTalk is capable of both receiving and sending messages with envelopes. Envelope Schemas are covered in more depth later in the chapter.

Flat File Schemas

BizTalk Server uses the XML Schema standard of annotations to include information that helps to also explain what an instance of a Schema may look like if it were a Flat text file instead of a structured XML file.

Flat Files may be delimited as follows:

```
Car,ABC123,Audi,RS6,NurburgringBlue
```

```
Car,123ABC,Corvette,ZR1,DaytonaRed
```

Flat Files may also be positional as follows:

```
Car     ABC123     Audi        RS6      NurburgringBlue
```

```
Car     123ABC     Corvette    ZR1      DaytonaRed
```

They may also be a combination (which in some sense is often the case with positional files since rows of Flat Files are commonly delimited by some combination of carriage return and linefeed characters).

Header and Trailer Schemas

Instead of Envelope Schemas, Flat File Schemas can be configured to represent the format of text contained at the top or bottom of a text file. These are then called Header Schemas (the top) or Trailer Schemas (the bottom). Header Schemas are often used when text files contain information at the beginning, before a repeating record structure, where the format of a single record is defined in another Flat File Schema. Trailer Schemas can be used to, for example, validate that the entire intended message has indeed been received.

An example may look like the following:

```
CarBatchId1234
```

```
Car,ABC123,Audi,RS6,NurburgringBlue
```

```
Car,123ABC,Corvette,ZR1,DaytonaRed
```

```
CarBatchTotalCount2
```

Property Schemas

Property Schemas are a special type of XML Schema. These Schemas are not created to describe messages and instead describe context properties. They have multiple root nodes (in the form of elements) and no hierarchy. These root nodes represent so-called promoted properties, and you populate them by promoting values from non-repeating SimpleContent records, elements, or attributes of Message Schemas. The act of promotion creates associations between the fields of the Message Schema and the fields of the Property Schema. At runtime, BizTalk Server will identify these associations and promote the fields into the message context so that they can be used for routing.

Schema Identity

The identity of a Schema, and subsequently that of a message, is crucial to all message handling in BizTalk Server. There are a couple of different properties that are important when handling the identity of a Schema. Since BizTalk lives and operates in both the .NET and XML worlds, those identities also identify the Schema in both these worlds.

XML Identity

The XML identity of a Schema determines the identity of the Schema file and also the identity of a message instance based on the Schema as a separate entity. This is true regardless of whether the Schema is then made part of a .NET BizTalk component or not.

targetNamespace

Sometimes, there are entities that will occur multiple times within an integration solution. To make sure they are uniquely distinguished, you use the targetNamespace property. targetNamespace is to a Schema what a namespace is to a .NET object. Take for example the Color object in .NET. It exists in many different namespaces. The same thing might over time be true for objects in an integration solution. In Schemas, it is the root node that acts as the class name in this analogy. Perhaps a PurchaseOrder entity (root node) will be described in multiple Schemas with small variations in their structure based on, say, the vendor they belong to. Their targetNamespace property is then what separates them. You should never have a Schema without targetNamespace, if you can avoid it. There are proven Pipeline component examples of adding a namespace to a message being sent to BizTalk Server, if it does not have one arriving to BizTalk.

MessageType

In BizTalk Server, every message that is recognized and parsed by a disassembler has a MessageType. MessageType is a combination of `targetNamespace` and the root node. The MessageType determines what schema is used to disassemble the message. MessageType is also often involved in routing and can act as the sole filter expression in many solutions, especially in service or enterprise bus architectures. This is one of the primary reasons why you should make sure that you have a good `targetNamespace` and adequately named root node, so that the MessageType, represented as `targetNamespace#Rootnode`, is unique within your system. If it is not unique, then it will be a poor candidate for routing, and you will not be able to disassemble a message with that MessageType unless you specifically point out the Schema to be used.

Messages that do not have a MessageType can travel through Ports and Orchestrations, but as they are untyped, they can never be used as an input to a Map.

> BizTalk can route any type of message, even unknown binary messages, but to process or parse them it must be possible to disassemble them and discern their MessageType. Most commonly this is done with the help of an XML or Flat File Schema.

.NET Identity

As mentioned, a Schema also has a .NET class representation, and, as any .NET class, it has a namespace and a typename.

Namespace

The default namespace in a BizTalk project is that of the name of the project, but it can be changed to anything you want.

Typename

The typename is by default the same as the filename of the Schema (and not the root node), but again, it can be changed to anything you want.

Promoted property and distinguished fields

Promoting a node to a property field (or promoting a property for short) means to make a node value available in the context of a message. You will typically promote properties from a Schema that you want to use as part of your filter expression that forms the basis of your routing logic. Or for correlation, of which you can read more about in *Chapter 4, Developing BizTalk Artifacts – Creating Orchestrations*. You can promote only parts of a Schema that are not recurring (that have their Max Occurs value set to 1 or 0. 1 is the default if nothing is set). You may also feel tempted to promote properties, so that you can more easily access them in places such as Orchestrations or in Pipeline components. Don't. For easy access in Orchestrations, you use distinguished fields that allow you easy and familiar IntelliSense and dot notation in expressions. Other good reasons to promote a property is when there is information not contained in the body of the message, say header or envelope information that you want accessible later on. Also, when you set up correlation, which implicitly means setting up routing logic, the property that you wish to correlate on must be promoted.

> Not all context properties are promoted, and not all context properties come from Schemas. Many parts of the BizTalk infrastructure, such as adapters and Pipeline components, write to the context. One example of this is ReceivedFileName (http://schemas.microsoft.com/BizTalk/2003/file-properties#ReceivedFileName) or FILE.ReceivedFileName that the FILE adapter writes to the context. Another example is MessageType (http://schemas.microsoft.com/BizTalk/2003/system-properties#MessageType) or BTS.MessageType that the XML Disassembler promotes.

Promoting nodes as property fields

To promote a node as a property field, perform the following steps in Visual Studio:

1. Create or locate a Property Schema.

2. Create or identify the element in the Property Schema that you wish to promote a property to.

3. Open your Schema. In this case, we are using a SimplifiedCar Schema, as follows:

```
<xs:schema xmlns="http://Chapter02_Example01.Schemas.
SimplifiedCar" xmlns:b="http://schemas.microsoft.com/BizTalk/2003"
targetNamespace="http://Chapter02_Example01.Schemas.SimplifiedCar"
xmlns:xs="http://www.w3.org/2001/XMLSchema">
  <xs:element name="Car">
```

```
<xs:complexType>
  <xs:sequence>
    <xs:element name="RegistrationNo" type="xs:string" />
    <xs:element name="Make" type="xs:string" />
    <xs:element name="Model" type="xs:string" />
    <xs:element name="Color" type="xs:string" />
  </xs:sequence>
</xs:complexType>
</xs:element>
</xs:schema>
```

Downloading the example code

You can download the example code files for all Packt books you have purchased from your account at http://www.packtpub.com. If you purchased this book elsewhere, you can visit http://www.packtpub.com/support and register to have the files e-mailed directly to you.

4. Bring up the context menu for the Schema and select **Promote | Show Promotions...**, to bring up the **Promote Properties** dialog as shown in the following screenshot:

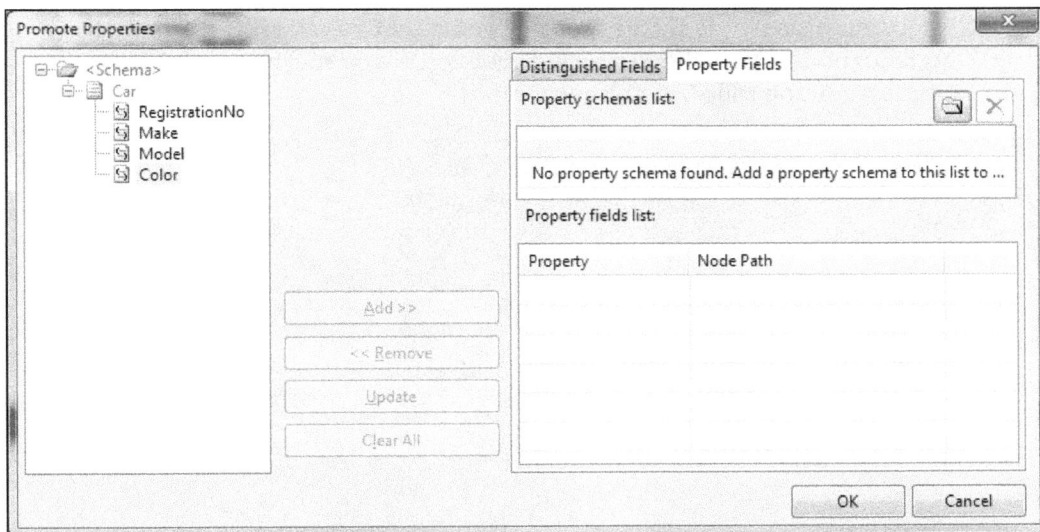

5. Select the **Property Fields** tab and click on the button that looks like a folder, to bring up **BizTalk Type Picker** as shown in the following screenshot:

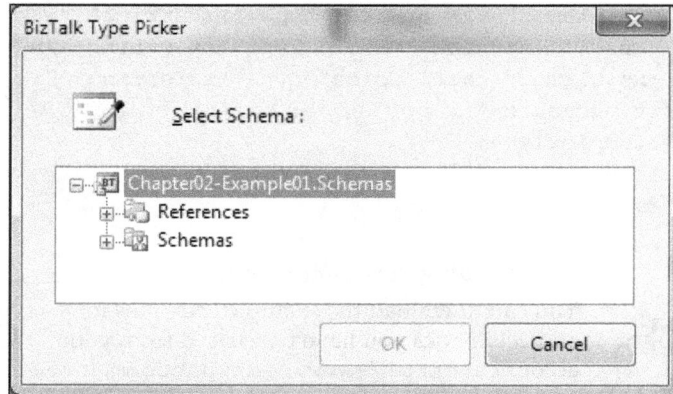

6. Locate your Property Schema. You need to have one already created that holds a property that you wish to promote the field to.

7. In the Schema view, on the left-hand side, in the **Promote Properties** dialog, select the (non-repeating) node in the Schema that you wish to promote.

8. Click on the **Add >>** button to promote the node as **Property Fields**.

9. Select the property in the Property Schema that you wish to promote the node to; in this case, the Property Schema has a property called **Color**, as shown in the following screenshot:

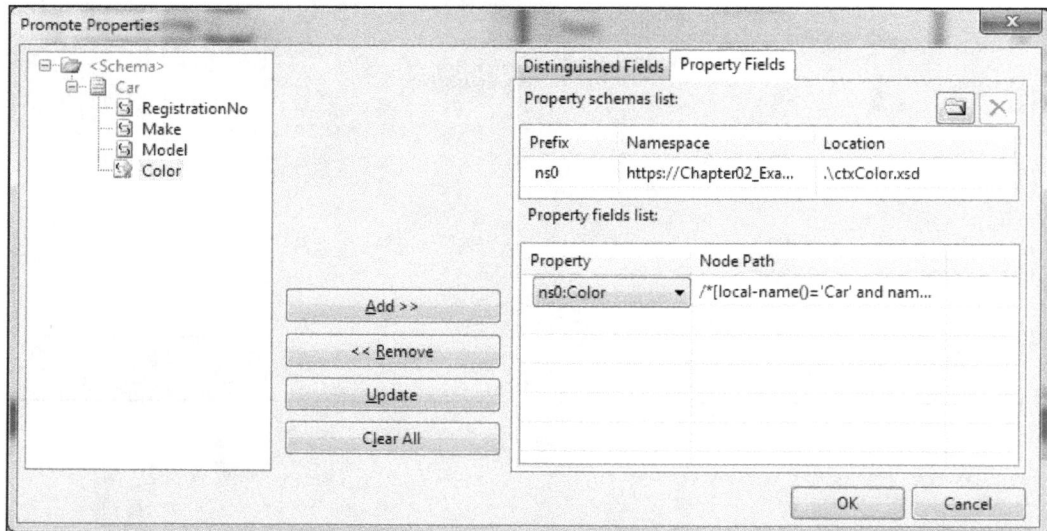

10. Complete the process by clicking on the **OK** button in the lower-right corner.

> All Schemas used in examples in this section can be found in the solution `C:\BTS2013CertGuide\Chapter02\Example01-SchemaConstructs\Chapter02-Example01\Chapter02-Example01.sln`.

Quick Promotion

The **Quick Promotion** option that is available, if we bring up the context menu for a selected node in the Schema Editor, is a faster way to promote properties, should you be ok with some default behavior. Choosing to Quick Promote a property will do the following:

1. Create a new Property Schema (if it does not already exist) in the `projects root` folder using the name specified on the Schema files properties in the `Default Property Schemas` property, which by default is `PropertySchema.xsd`.

2. Place a new property in that Property Schema, named the same as the node we are promoting (unless that property already exists in the Property Schema, in which case it will not create a new node, but instead assume that you meant to promote to the existing property).

3. Promote the field that you choose to quick promote to that property.

> When using Quick Promote, you will always get a node called `Property1` in the Property Schema with the first property you promote; you have to manually remove this or update it to a name and type you can use.

Promoting a node as distinguished field

Promoting a node in a Schema makes that node value appear as a promoted property and enables you to use it for routing whereas distinguishing a node does none of that. Instead, it enables you to use dot syntax (`root.subrecord.node`) to access the value of a node within an Orchestration. It is an alternative to using an XPath statement.

Had we made the `Color` property a distinguished field instead of a promoted property, it would have meant that we could have addressed it as `Car.Color`, which in turn would have aliased this XPath statement.

```
/*[local-name()='Car' and namespace-uri()='http://Chapter02_Example01.
Schemas.SimplifiedCar']/*[local-name()='Color' and namespace-uri()='']
```

Let's look at the process to do this. To promote a node to a distinguished field, you perform the following steps:

1. Open your Schema.

2. Bring up the context menu for the Schema and select **Promote | Show Promotions…** to bring up the **Promote Properties** dialog.

3. Select the **Distinguished Fields** tab.

4. In the Schema view, on the left-hand side in the **Promote Properties** dialog, select the (non-repeating) node in the Schema that you wish to promote.

5. Click on the **Add >>** button to promote the node as a **Distinguished Field** as shown in the following screenshot:

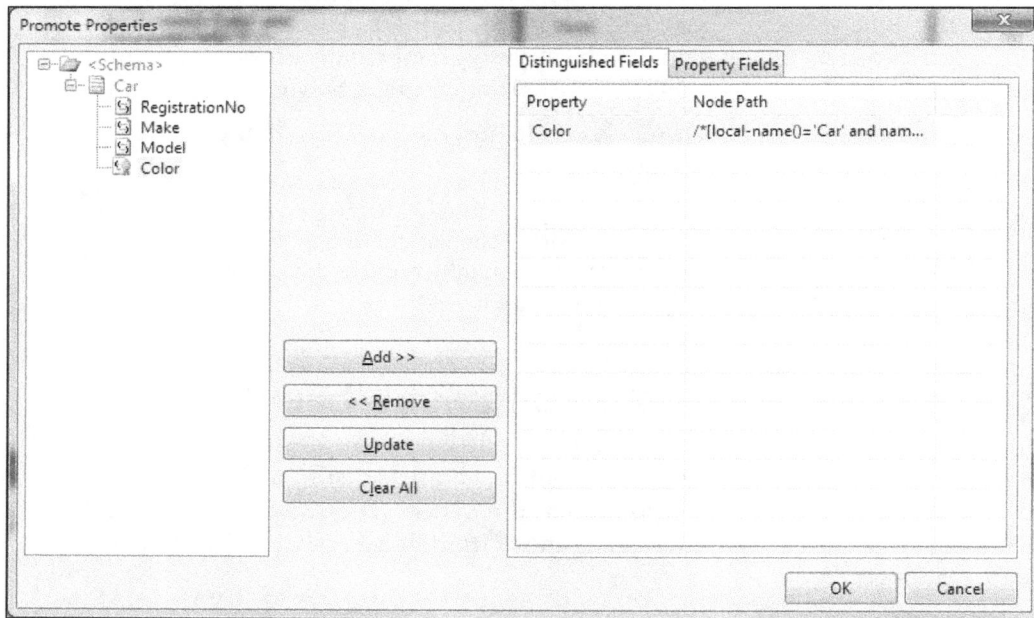

6. Complete the process by clicking on the **OK** button in the lower-right corner.

Creating the structure of a Schema

In BizTalk Server, Schemas are made up of records, elements, and attributes.

A sample structure may look like the following code:

```
RootNode
|
+-SubRecord1
|   @attribute1
|   element1
|
\-SubRecord2
    element2
```

As XML, it would look like the following code:

```
<RootNode>
  <SubRecord1 attribute1="">
    <element1 />
  </SubRecord1>
  <SubRecord2>
    <element2 />
  </SubRecord2>
</RootNode>
```

A record is a container node that can contain a collection of elements that are of one of the following types:

- **Complex types**: They include other records or groups (Sequence, Choice, or All)
- **Simple types**: They include strings and ints contained in child elements or attributes
- **Any node**: It is in the form of an Any element or an Any attribute
- **Attribute Groups**

Elements and attributes are, in contrast, simple types, such as string or int. There are a few things to consider when choosing whether to use an element or an attribute, such as max occurrence, sequence, length, and size of values. Another difference between them is how they are visually represented in a Schema or an XML document instance.

Here is a sample Schema shown in the BizTalk Schema Editor that uses a mix of records, elements, and attributes:

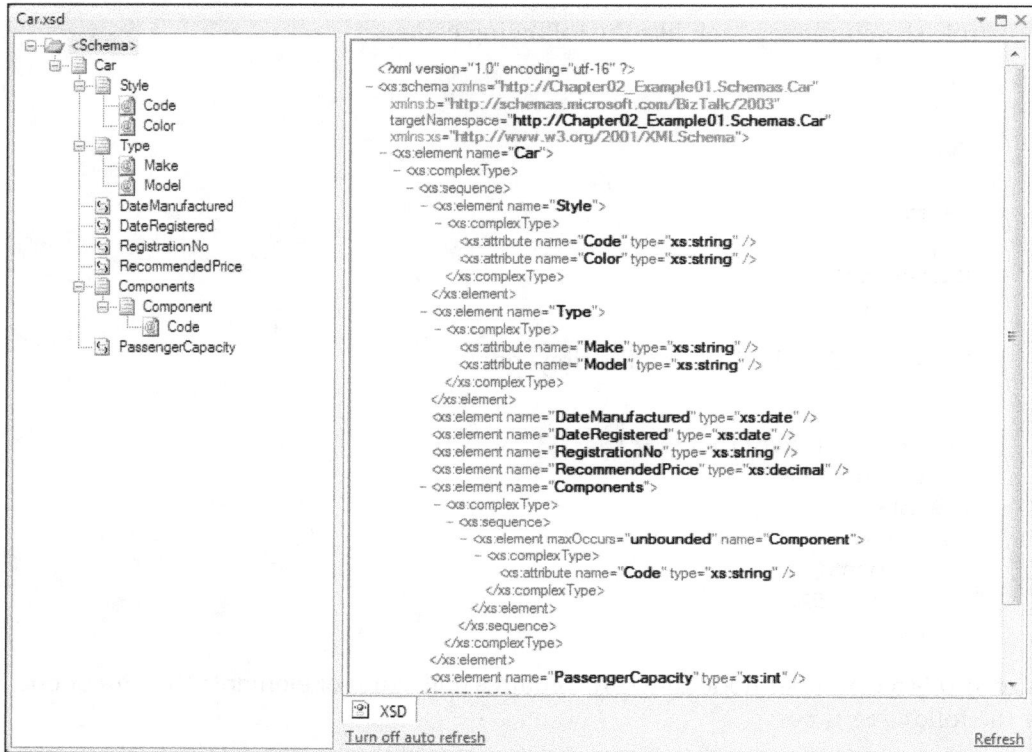

To best describe the format of a message, you will most likely combine records, elements, and attributes. You should also set their namespaces as well as define types, multiplicity, restrictions, and other properties, according to how they are used. This produces clear and usable Schemas that represent the actual rules applied to the content and not just the structure.

Creating recurring parts of a Schema

Often in Schemas, there are certain parts of it that need to occur more than once. Take for example Car, which is made up of multiple Component nodes, as shown in the following code:

```
<xs:schema xmlns="http://Chapter02_Example01.Schemas.
CarComponents" xmlns:b="http://schemas.microsoft.com/BizTalk/2003"
targetNamespace="http://Chapter02_Example01.Schemas.CarComponents"
xmlns:xs="http://www.w3.org/2001/XMLSchema">
```

```
<xs:element name="Car">
  <xs:complexType>
    <xs:sequence>
      <xs:element name="Components">
        <xs:complexType>
          <xs:sequence>
            <xs:element maxOccurs="unbounded" name="Component">
              <xs:complexType>
                <xs:attribute name="Code" type="xs:string" />
              </xs:complexType>
            </xs:element>
          </xs:sequence>
        </xs:complexType>
      </xs:element>
    </xs:sequence>
  </xs:complexType>
</xs:element>
</xs:schema>
```

In this case, the Component element has its maxOccurs property set to Unbounded (which can also be written as * in BizTalk server's Visual Studio Schema Editors). The XML document matching this Schema may look like the following:

```
<ns0:Car xmlns:ns0="http://Chapter02_Example01.Schemas.CarComponents">
  <Components>
    <Component Code="01" />
    <Component Code="02" />
    <Component Code="03" />
  </Components>
</ns0:Car>
```

There are also occasions where you may prefer to describe that the group of nodes beneath a record may appear multiple times, even though the node itself does not. The preceding Car XML document may as well have been created and will validate equally well against the following Schema:

```
<xs:schema xmlns="http://Chapter02_Example01.Schemas.
CarComponents" xmlns:b="http://schemas.microsoft.com/BizTalk/2003"
targetNamespace="http://Chapter02_Example01.Schemas.CarComponents"
xmlns:xs="http://www.w3.org/2001/XMLSchema">
  <xs:element name="Car">
    <xs:complexType>
      <xs:sequence>
        <xs:element name="Components">
          <xs:complexType>
```

```
<xs:sequence maxOccurs="unbounded">
  <xs:element name="Component">
    <xs:complexType>
      <xs:attribute name="Code" type="xs:string" />
    </xs:complexType>
  </xs:element>
</xs:sequence>
            </xs:complexType>
          </xs:element>
        </xs:sequence>
      </xs:complexType>
    </xs:element>
</xs:schema>
```

It's hard to give a clear example of when one is more preferable to the other. In any case, as XML is inheritably hierarchical, creating Hierarchical Schemas is preferable to keeping the structure flat.

Creating Envelope Schemas

Creating envelopes is not so much a part of creating the structure of a single message as it is about creating the structure of a batch of messages. When we create an envelope, we are saying that this Schema (the envelope) will contain one or more messages that are based on other Schemas.

The following steps are required to create an Envelope Schema, once you have a BizTalk project that you want to create in it:

1. Select **Add ... | New Item** from the context menu of the project, and choose to add a new Schema. Name it CarEnvelope.

2. Select the root node, and rename it ManufacturingReport.

3. Create an attribute below ManufacturingReport, call it BatchNo, and make it an int type.

4. Create a record below ManufacturingReport and call it Cars.

5. Create an Any element below Cars.

6. Now select the **Schema** node, and in the **Properties** window, change the value of the **Envelope** property to **Yes**.

7. Select the root node ManufacturingReport, and in the **Property** window, change the value of the **Body XPath** property to point to the Cars node. The finished Envelope Schema looks like the following screenshot:

Now we have created an Envelope Schema with an Any node. We can use it to send in any number of documents within it.

> The Envelope Schema we just created is available in the Chapter02-Example03 sample. This sample is expanded in the Pipeline section of this chapter to show the Pipeline configuration used with envelopes when splitting messages and configuring recoverable interchange processing.

> **Flat File Envelopes**
>
> Messages based on Flat File Schemas can be received in batches as well. The concepts of envelopes applies just as equally to Flat Files as it does to XML messages; however, it is configured slightly differently and instead includes configuring Header Schemas, Document Schemas, and Trailer Schemas. The preceding process applies to XML Schemas only.

Data types and formatting

To create a usable and descriptive Schema, it is important to not only create the correct structure, but also to describe the content of all nodes as best as possible.

One of the basics of describing a Schema field is to set the field's data type correctly. The default data type is `string`, which arguably is the most commonly used, but there are many different types to choose from, of which other commonly used ones are `int`, `decimal`, `date`, and `Boolean`. One of the first things to do is to make sure to select appropriate data types, as shown in the following screenshot:

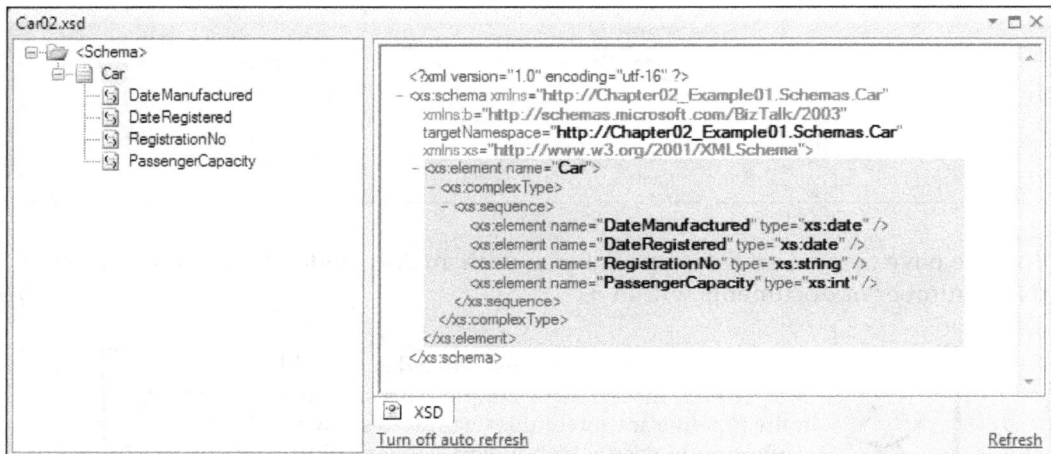

Specifying custom formatting restrictions

You may, and should, choose to apply additional restrictions or derivation of the basic data type, so that the Schema becomes really descriptive of what the expected content could look like.

Restricting string values

Say for example that we wanted to create a restriction on a registration for a car so that it matches the format of a Swedish license plate — three uppercase letters (A-Z) followed by three integers (0-9). This can be accomplished by the following steps:

1. Set **Base Data Type** to **xs:string**.
2. Set (leave the default) **Derived By** property to `Restriction`.
3. Set the **Pattern** property by adding a regular expression in a suitable pattern to the list of allowed patterns. In this case, a regular expression of ^[A-Z]{3}\d{3}$ would do the trick. This will produce the following Schema:

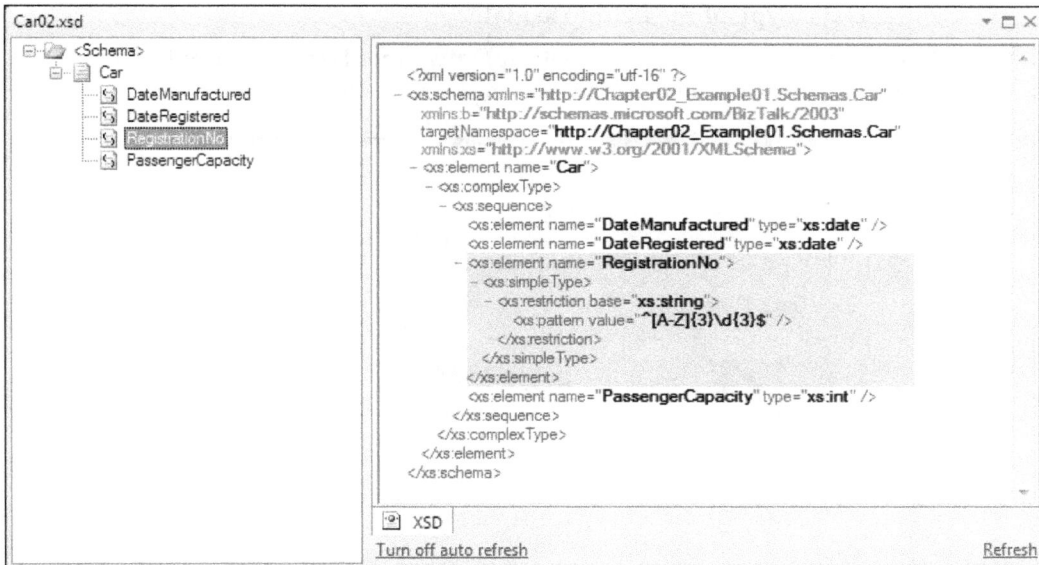

```
Car02.xsd                                                                    ▾ ☐ ✕

⊟ 🗁 <Schema>          | <?xml version="1.0" encoding="utf-16" ?>
  ⊟ 📄 Car            | - <xs:schema xmlns:b="http://Chapter02_Example01.Schemas.Car"
    🔲 DateManufactured|     xmlns:b="http://schemas.microsoft.com/BizTalk/2003"
    🔲 DateRegistered  |     targetNamespace="http://Chapter02_Example01.Schemas.Car"
    🔲 RegistrationNo  |     xmlns:xs="http://www.w3.org/2001/XMLSchema">
    🔲 PassengerCapacity| - <xs:element name="Car">
                       |   - <xs:complexType>
                       |     - <xs:sequence>
                       |         <xs:element name="DateManufactured" type="xs:date" />
                       |         <xs:element name="DateRegistered" type="xs:date" />
                       |       - <xs:element name="RegistrationNo">
                       |         - <xs:simpleType>
                       |           - <xs:restriction base="xs:string">
                       |               <xs:pattern value="^[A-Z]{3}\d{3}$" />
                       |             </xs:restriction>
                       |           </xs:simpleType>
                       |         </xs:element>
                       |         <xs:element name="PassengerCapacity" type="xs:int" />
                       |       </xs:sequence>
                       |     </xs:complexType>
                       |   </xs:element>
                       | </xs:schema>

                       | 🔲 XSD
                       | Turn off auto refresh                                 Refresh
```

When you try to validate a file that does not match the criteria, you will get something similar to the following exception inside Visual Studio (paths and filenames omitted for brevity):

```
The 'RegistrationNo' element is invalid - The value 'RegistrationNo_0'
is invalid according to its datatype 'String' - The Pattern constraint
failed.
File 'Car02.xml' is not a valid instance of schema file 'Car02.xsd'.
```

Controlling date formats

Say that we wanted to create a date format that matches the pattern **yyyyMMdd**, for example, 20110203 (February 3, 2011). In this case, you do not have much flexibility out of an XML file adhering to an XML Schema, and only the ISO 8601-derived format of CCYY-MM-DD is allowed. You can add a pattern to restrict what values you allow in these fields, but you cannot change the format. Should you use other date formats in XML, you must treat those fields as strings.

If you are accepting Flat Files on the other hand, more flexibility is given. Due to the inherent legacy nature of Flat Files, you can specify a **Custom Date/Time Format** when using a date or time data type in a Flat File Schema. The steps to do this are as follows:

1. Create a Schema with Flat File extensions.
2. Create an element or attribute field under the root node.

3. Set the **Data Type** of the field to **xs:date**.

4. Choose one of the values for **Custom Date/Time Format** out of the drop-down box or enter your own, which is shown as follows:

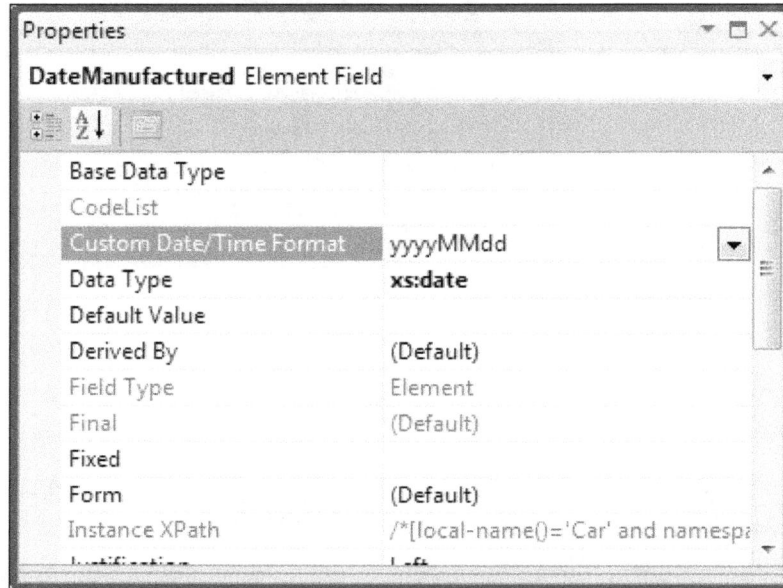

Properties	▼ ☐ ✕
DateManufactured Element Field	▼

⊟ A↓ 🖾	
Base Data Type	▲
CodeList	
Custom Date/Time Format	yyyyMMdd ▼
Data Type	**xs:date**
Default Value	
Derived By	(Default)
Field Type	Element
Final	(Default)
Fixed	
Form	(Default)
Instance XPath	/*[local-name()='Car' and namespa
	▼

> If you cannot see the **Custom Date/Time Format** property, remember that it is only available for Flat File Schemas.

Restricting integer formats

Say that we have an integer, such as the maximum number of allowed passengers in a car, and we want to illustrate in the Schema that (by an imaginary law) cars can have a minimum of zero passengers and a maximum of seven passengers, or else the vehicle is filed as a bus. One of the ways to do this would be to use the same procedure as described in the section about controlling registration numbers and to use a pattern restriction. Another option would be to take the following steps:

1. Set **Base Data Type** to **xs:int**.

2. Set **MinFacet Value** to **0**, and accept the default value of **Inclusive** for **MinFacet Type**, meaning that the allowed values must be greater than or equal to this value.

3. Set **MaxFacet Value** to **7**, and accept the default value of **Inclusive** for **MaxFacet Type**, as shown in the following screenshot:

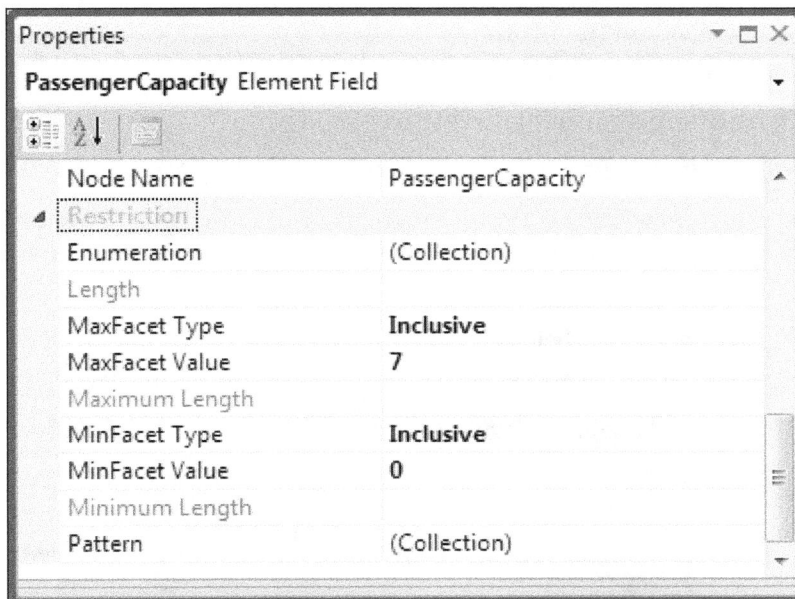

Properties	▼ □ ✕
PassengerCapacity Element Field	▼

Node Name	PassengerCapacity	▲
⊿ Restriction		
Enumeration	(Collection)	
Length		
MaxFacet Type	**Inclusive**	
MaxFacet Value	**7**	
Maximum Length		
MinFacet Type	**Inclusive**	
MinFacet Value	**0**	≡
Minimum Length		
Pattern	(Collection)	▼

> The **MinFacet** and **MaxFacet** properties are only available for data types that are value-based, that is, they are not available for the string data type, but they are also available to, for example, the date data type.

Creating reusable types

Often when you apply a pattern restriction to a node, that node is not alone in having those restrictions. If you, for example, have a Schema with several dates, say PurchaseDate and RegistrationDate, that need to conform to the same format, it makes sense to create that restriction once, instead of on each and every node. The same goes for if you have things that are more complex, say a customer and the customer's address; these are something that you want as reusable types, so that you can use them again in different constructs, in different Schemas.

Simple types

With `simpleType`, the way to create a reusable type is as follows:

1. Create an element (or attribute).
2. Select a **Base Data Type**.
3. Optionally apply meaningful restrictions to it.
4. Select the **Data Type** property, and enter a name for your new reusable type.

Doing this creates a new `simpleType` element at the bottom of the Schema; name it according to the naming convention you adopted, and set the current element to be of that type.

If you want to create a second element that has the same properties, all you have to do is create a new element and set its **Data Type** to be of the type you just created:

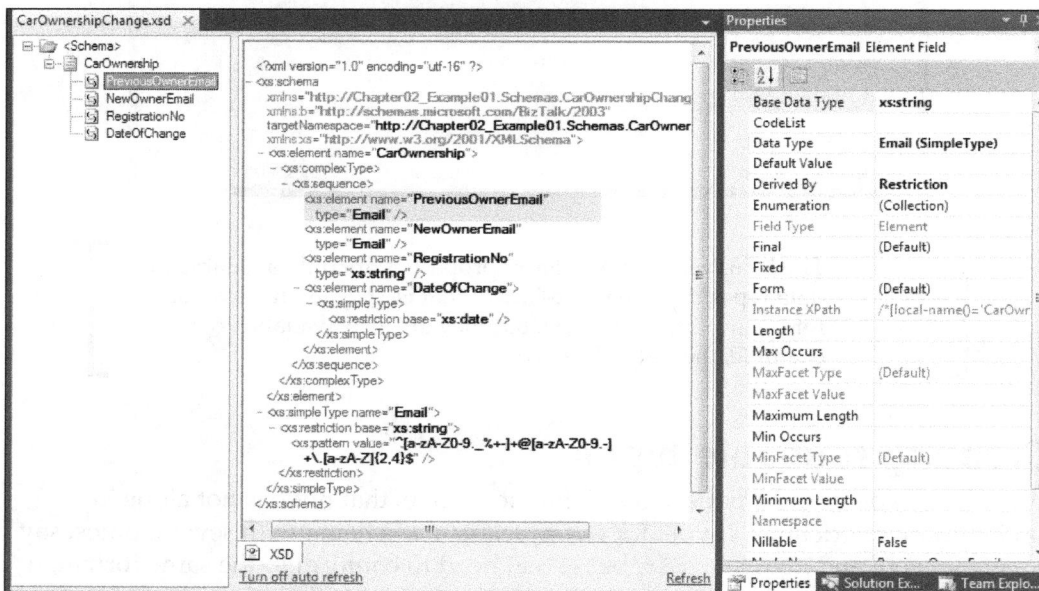

Alternatively, you could also select the second element's **Base Data Type**, and select the newly created type. You would do that if you are to apply further restrictions.

Complex types

With `complexType`, the procedure to create a reusable type is very similar, though not exactly the same as with `simpleType`:

1. Create a record.

2. Fill it with other records, elements, and attributes, so that it creates a reusable unit.

3. Select the **Data Structure Type** property, and enter a name for your new reusable type.

Doing this will create a new element named `complexType`, at the bottom of the Schema, and set the current record to be of that type. In the following example, I did this for the entire car definition:

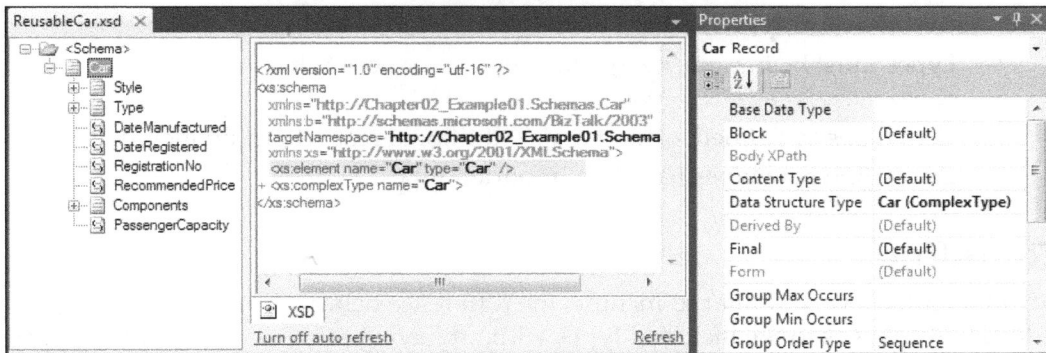

If you want to create a second record that has the same structure and content, all you have to do is create a new record and set its **Data Structure Type** to be of the type you just created. You could also select the second record's **Base Data Type** and select the newly created type. You would do that if you are to apply further restrictions.

Creating Schema hierarchies

While creating reusable types is useful, that re-use is limited if the scope is limited to a single Schema file. It is possible, both likely and common, and preferable that re-use of common types will be most useful when done across Schema files. For that reason, we have `import`, `include`, and `redefine` that allow us to do just that.

Import

XSD Import is arguably the most common re-use of a Schema. Import is often used when you want to build new Schemas that re-use already defined types:

- Allows use of types defined in another Schema
- Types must be in another `targetNamespace`
- Uses types as defined; cannot make additional restrictions on included types
- Can define new types based on imported types

Include

XSD Include is very similar to Import, the difference being the `targetNamespace` rules. Include is often used when you want to extend an existing Schema with new types.

- Allows use of types defined in another Schema
- Types must be in same `targetNamespace`, or both Schemas have no `targetNamespace`
- Uses types as defined; cannot make additional restrictions on included types
- Can define new types based on imported types

Redefine

XSD Redefine is very similar to Include, the difference being the ability to specify additional changes to the included types without having to create new derived types. Redefine is often used when you want to redefine existing types to suit your needs.

- Allows use of types defined in another Schema
- Types must be in the same `targetNamespace` or have no `targetNamespace`
- Uses types as defined, makes changes to them, or creates new types based on included types

Creating Flat File Schemas

Just like XML Schemas, Flat File Schemas can be created by manually building up records, elements, and attributes from scratch. Just like XML Schemas, this is not the most common of scenarios. While there are many different tools that allow you to generate XML Schemas, there is only one tool to generate a Flat File Schema. The Flat File Schema Wizard allows the generation of a BizTalk Flat File Schema from a Flat File message instance. The process below walks you through the creation of a Flat File Schema using the Flat File Schema Wizard.

1. Identify the Flat File message instance. In this case, we will use a simple file that represents a list of cars. We have shown it previously in this chapter. It looks like the following:

   ```
   Car,ABC123,Audi,RS6,NurburgringBlue
   ```

   ```
   Car,123ABC,Corvette,ZR1,DaytonaRed
   ```

2. On the BizTalk project, select **Add | New Item...**.

3. Choose **Flat File Schema Wizard** and name it `SimplifiedCarsFF.xsd`

4. Select the **Instance file** that contains the data mentioned previously, set the **Record name** to `Cars` and keep the defaults. This record will be the root record of the schema. This is shown in the following screenshot:

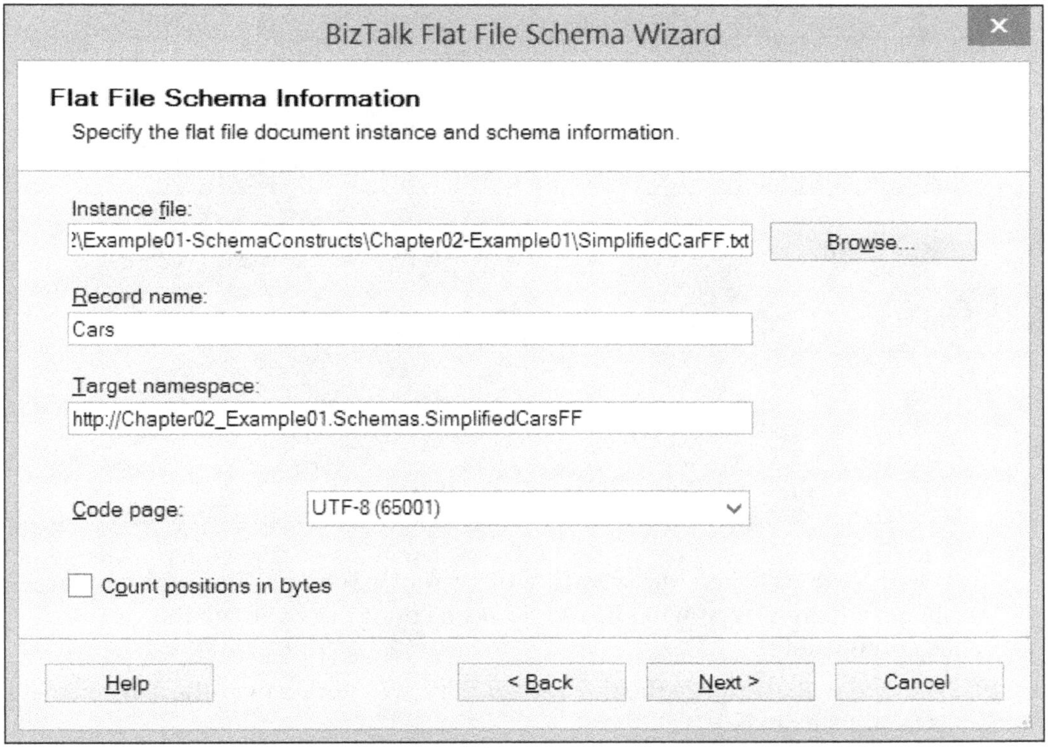

5. For the **Select Document Data** option, keep the defaults of `all text` selected.

6. For the **Select Record Format** screen, keep the default of **By delimiter symbol**.

7. For the **Delimited Record** screen, keep the default of {CR}{LF} as the delimiter without configuring a **Tag identifier**.

8. For the **Child Elements** screen, select the first row, set the **Element Name** to Car and set the **Element Type** to Repeating Record. Select the second row and set the **Element Type** to Ignore as shown in the following screenshot:

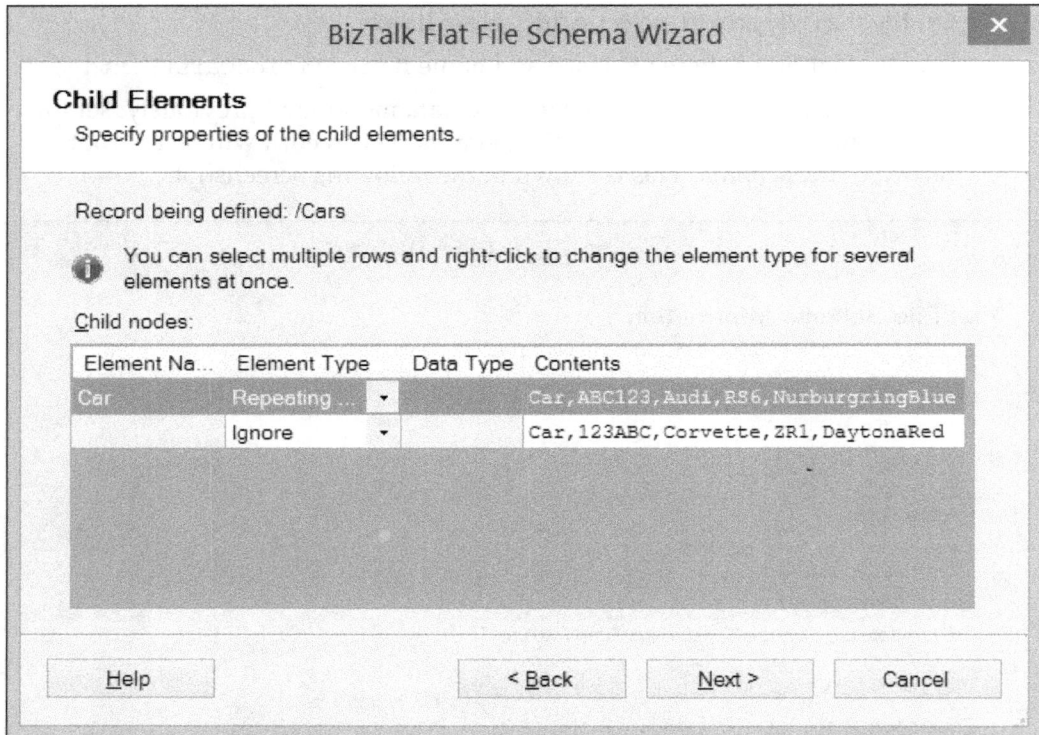

9. When **Next** is clicked, the wizard will present a **Schema View** screen that shows a hierarchy of what has so far been configured and what is next to be configured.

10. Next we will configure the Car record. This will iterate over the same screens as in steps from 6-9.

11. For the first two screens, **Select Document Data** and **Select Record Format**, keep the defaults.

12. On the **Delimited Record** screen, change **Child delimiter** to a comma, and select the **Record has a tag identifier** checkbox and configure **Tag** to be Car as shown in the following screenshot:

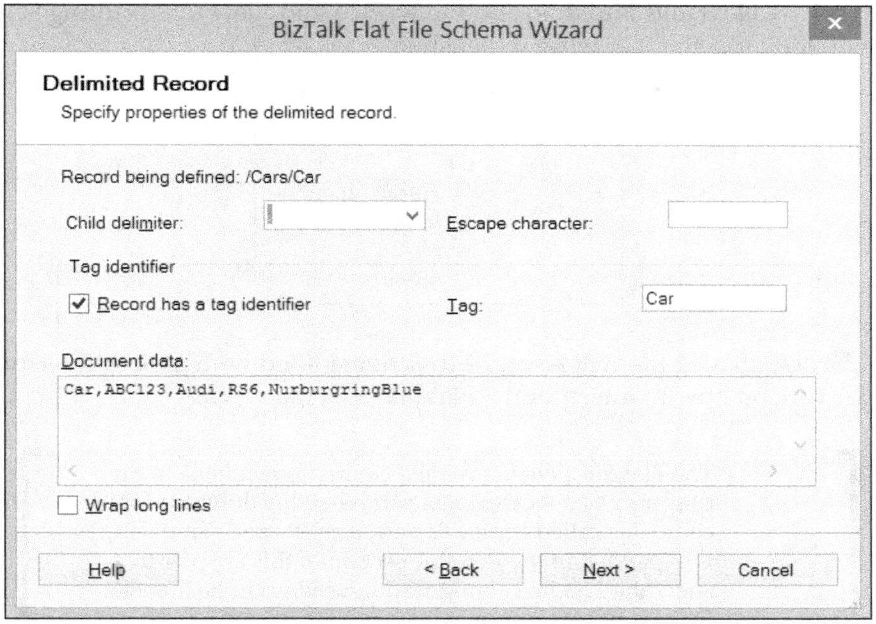

BizTalk Flat File Schema Wizard

Delimited Record

Specify properties of the delimited record.

Record being defined: /Cars/Car

Child delimiter: | Escape character:

Tag identifier

☑ Record has a tag identifier   Tag: Car

Document data:

```
Car,ABC123,Audi,RS6,NurburgringBlue
```

☐ Wrap long lines

Help   < Back   Next >   Cancel

13. On the **Child Elements** screen, configure the elements of the Car record as RegistrationNo, Make, Model, and Color as in the following screenshot:

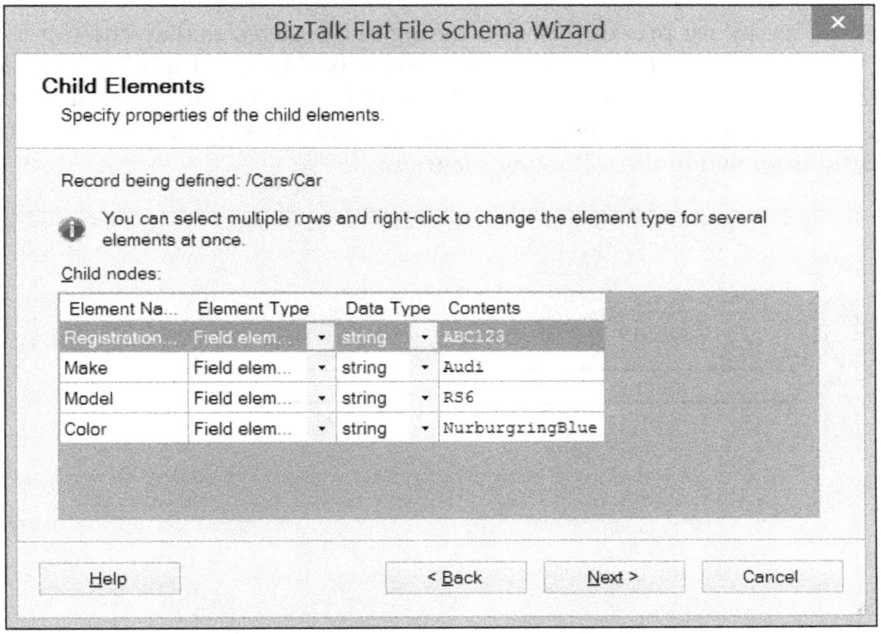

BizTalk Flat File Schema Wizard

Child Elements

Specify properties of the child elements.

Record being defined: /Cars/Car

ℹ You can select multiple rows and right-click to change the element type for several elements at once.

Child nodes:

Element Na...	Element Type	Data Type	Contents
Registration...	Field elem...	string	ABC123
Make	Field elem...	string	Audi
Model	Field elem...	string	RS6
Color	Field elem...	string	NurburgringBlue

Help   < Back   Next >   Cancel

14. Click on **Next** and **Finish** to end the wizard and view the resulting Schema. It will look like the following screenshot:

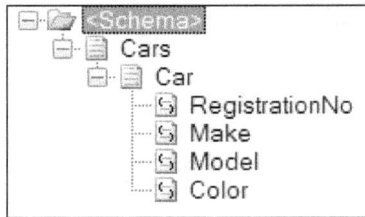

```
☐ 📂 <Schema>
   ☐ 📄 Cars
      ☐ 📄 Car
         📓 RegistrationNo
         📓 Make
         📓 Model
         📓 Color
```

15. The actual .xsd file will be an XML Schema filled with annotations for BizTalk on how to interpret the Flat File Schema.

> The Flat File Schema we just created is available in the Chapter02, Example01 sample of the downloadable code. It is called SimplifiedCarsFF.xsd. This sample is expanded in the Pipeline section of this chapter to show the Pipeline configuration used with the Flat File Disassembler component.

Creating Pipelines

Pipelines are meant for pre- or post-processing of messages as they enter or leave BizTalk Server. In special cases, they may also be used from within BizTalk Server Orchestrations to perform specialized tasks, such as splitting or aggregating a message. Pipelines execute between the **Adapter** and the **Map**, or vice versa for **Send Ports**, as shown in the following diagram:

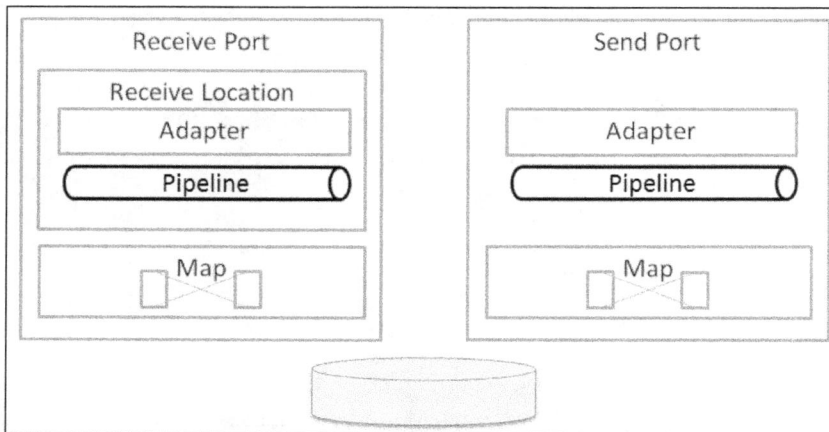

When receiving a message into BizTalk, the components displayed in the preceding diagram are triggered in the order **Receive Port, Receive Location, Adapter, Pipeline, Map** — MessageBox (- Subscription(s)) — Send Port, Map, Pipeline, Adapter.

There are two approaches to Pipelines in the BizTalk Server development; use the out of the box ones available when you install or create your own. Although the first approach will, and should be your starting point, you will often end up creating your own. When you do, it's important that you know which Pipeline components are available. Knowledge of Pipeline components and what possibilities the built-in ones provide, as well as the possibilities and limitations of creating custom Pipeline components, is key to creating a successful integration design and deciding which task is best performed where.

Pipeline Stages

A Pipeline is made up of a predetermined number of stages that differ between Receive and Send Pipelines. Stages put limitations on the type of Pipeline component that can be used there and on the execution of Pipeline components.

The Receive Pipeline has four stages: Decode, Disassemble, Validate, and Resolve Party. The Send Pipeline has three stages: Pre-Assemble, Assemble, and Encode.

A stage has three notable properties besides its name: Execution mode, Maximum components, and Minimum components.

The execution mode can be either All or FirstMatch. The All mode means that all Pipeline components are executed sequentially. The FirstMatch mode means that they are executed sequentially until a component is found that accepts the processing of a message, in which case, the chain stops and that component gets handed the message, and the next component to execute is the first component of the next stage.

All stages except the Disassemble stage have the execution mode All. The Disassemble stage is FirstMatch.

All stages take a minimum of zero components and a maximum of 255 components, except the Assemble stage that has a maximum of one.

Receive Pipelines

Receive Pipelines are meant for preprocessing the message such as parsing a Flat File or XML file, decrypting or verifying the signature of a message and validating full conformance to a Schema. They consist of four stages: **Decode**, **Disassemble**, **Validate**, and **ResolveParty**, as shown in the following diagram:

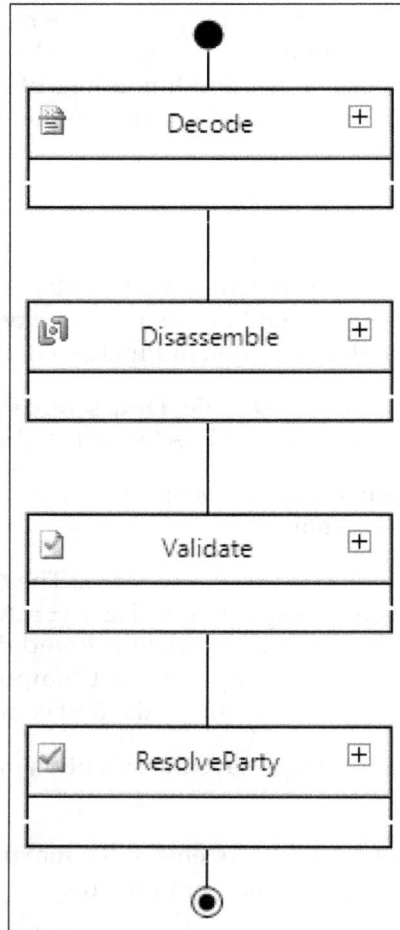

Decode

The Decode stage is meant for Pipeline components that perform decoding or decryption of the message, or verification. The MIME/SMIME decoder component fits this stage.

> The Decode stage can also be used by any custom component that needs to act on the message before it reaches the Disassemble stage. Examples of such processing could be adding an XML namespace or correcting known faulty data.

Disassemble

The Disassemble stage is meant for disassembling a message into XML. This stage can be resolved in more than one message being delivered to the next component. The components here can have a Probe method that looks at the message to determine whether the component is configured to parse the message or not. Only the first component that gives a true return to the Probe call will be executed. The components in this stage also handle property promotion and, optionally, message validation. The XML Disassembler or Flat File Disassembler components fit this stage.

Validate

This stage is used to validate the XML contents of the message; for example, to verify Schema conformance. The XML Validator Pipeline component fits this stage.

Resolve Party

This stage is meant for the Party Resolution Pipeline component, but it can also be used for any component that needs to run after the Validate stage.

Send Pipelines

Send Pipelines are meant for post-processing, for processing the message before it gets sent out by the adapter. The common scenarios include transforming XML into Flat File format, adding a signature, or encrypting the message. They consist of three stages: **Pre-Assemble**, **Assemble**, and **Encode**, as follows:

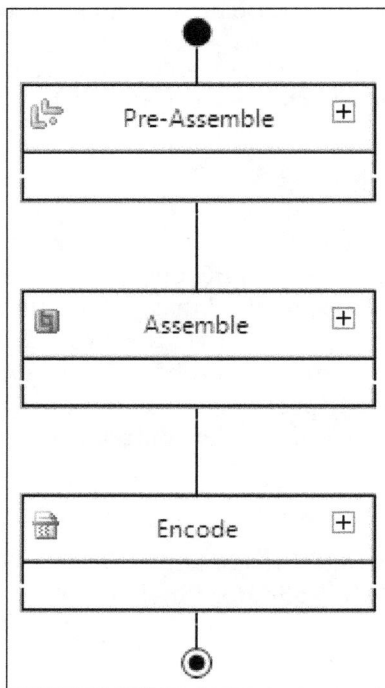

Pre-Assemble

This stage is meant for any component that needs to perform some form of processing on the message before it is assembled, such as inspecting or modifying the XML. This is the only step for which there are no out of the box Pipeline components to place in. It is meant for custom Pipeline components.

Assemble

This stage is meant for components that assemble or format the message, say by converting it to a Flat File. The XML Assembler and the Flat File Assembler components fit this stage.

Encode

This stage is meant for components that encode or encrypt the message, or to add a signature or do any other form of processing needed on the message after it is assembled. The MIME/SMIME encoder component fits this stage.

> By default, the Pipeline templates used by Visual Studio are empty. You can change them by altering the template files that are located in the `<BizTalk Install Folder>\Developer Tools\BizTalkProjectItems` folder. Pipelines have a file extension of BTP.

Default Pipelines

When you install BizTalk Server, you will get access to four Pipelines to use, two Receive and two Send. They are `PassThruReceive` and `XMLReceive` for Receive Pipelines, and `PassThruTransmit` and `XMLTransmit` for Send Pipelines. They are meant to get you started and to allow simple scenarios to be built without the need for any custom Pipeline development. If you have installed the EDI part of BizTalk, you will also have EDI and AS2 Pipelines. These are not covered in this chapter.

PassThruReceive

The `PassThruReceive` Pipeline has no components. It does no processing of the message and only passes it on to the `MessageBox` for transportation and/or for later processing in BizTalk Server.

> Although BizTalk Server can accept any message in any format, it can only transform or access data in messages that have been disassembled into XML. That includes messages that consist of XML. They must be disassembled using the XML Disassembler as well for them to be recognized by BizTalk.

XMLReceive

The `XMLReceive` Pipeline contains the XML Disassembler and the Party Resolution component.

PassThruTransmit

As with the `PassThruReceive` Pipeline, this has no components and performs no message processing before the message is sent out by the adapter.

XMLTransmit

The XMLTransmit Pipeline contains the XML Assembler component.

You do not need to use the XMLTransmit Pipeline just because you are sending out XML. Using PassThruTransmit for that is perfectly reasonable and in many cases, the best choice. Use XMLTransmit when you want further processing of the message, such as adding an envelope, influence encoding, demoting properties from the context into the message, or adding (InfoPath or other) processing instructions.

Custom Pipelines

Developing custom Pipelines is about adding Pipeline components to the Pipeline stages discussed earlier to form new Pipelines that conform to the capabilities you need out of your solution. You can use either the out of the box available components or custom Pipeline components.

You create custom Pipelines using Pipeline Designer inside Visual Studio. We can derive, from looking at the Default Pipelines, that all the Pipeline components installed with BizTalk are not included in the Default Pipelines.

The following is a list of the standard Pipeline components that are listed in the toolbox in Visual Studio that you can use to create a custom Pipeline:

Name	Pipeline Type	Target Stage	Short Description
BizTalk Framework Disassembler	Receive	Disassembler	The **BizTalk Framework (BTF)** is an approach to doing exactly one guaranteed delivery using HTTP or SMTP, mainly using acknowledgements. The components parse the BTF envelope and context properties and act according to BTF rules.

Name	Pipeline Type	Target Stage	Short Description
BizTalk Framework Assembler	Send	Assemble	The component is responsible for assembling BTF messages using envelope and context properties, and for resending messages should an acknowledgement not have arrived before timeout.
Flat File Disassembler	Receive	Disassemble	The component handles flat text file parsing, using Schema annotations to disassemble the message into XML.
Flat File Assembler	Send	Assemble	The component serializes an XML message into its Flat File format.
XML Disassembler	Receive	Disassemble	The component parses inbound XML messages.
XML Assembler	Send	Assemble	The component serializes outbound XML messages.

Name	Pipeline Type	Target Stage	Short Description
MIME/SMIME Decoder	Receive	Decode	The component is used to decrypt and verify signatures on inbound messages. It can also be used with the POP3 adapter to handle attachments.
MIME/SMIME Encoder	Send	Encode	The component is used to encrypt or sign outbound messages. It can also be used to send multipart messages.
XML Validator	Receive or Send	All except Assemble or Disassemble	The component validates that the message conforms to its Schema.
Party Resolution	Receive	Resolve Party	The component uses the sender's certificate or Security Identifier (SID) to resolve a BizTalk Party.

The XML Disassembler, the XML Assembler, the MIME/SMIME Decoder, and the MIME/SMIME Encoder will be covered in more depth later in this chapter.

EDI and AS2 add additional Pipeline components, namely EDI Disassembler, BatchMarker, AS2 Decoder, AS2 Disassembler, EDI Assembler, and AS2 Encoder. EDI will be covered later in the book, in *Chapter 8, Implementing Extended Capabilities*.

Configuring Pipelines and Pipeline components

Pipelines have two places where you can edit their configuration: BizTalk Server Pipeline Designer in Visual Studio or BizTalk Server Administration Console. The values entered in the **Properties** dialog of the Pipeline Designer act as your Pipeline's default settings, which are as follows:

RcvFF.btp ×			Properties	▾ ⫶ ×
			Flat file disassembler Pipeline Component properties	▾
	●		⫶⫶ ↓ ☐	
▤	Decode	⊟	(Name)	Flat file disassembler
			Assembly	Microsoft.BizTalk.Pipeline.Components,
	⎘ Drop Here!		Description	Streaming flat file disassembler compon.
			Document schema	Chapter02_Example02.Pipelines.DUMMY
			Header schema	(None)
			Managed	Yes
			Path	C:\WINDOWS\assembly\GAC_MSIL\Mic
▨	Disassemble	⊟	Preserve header	False
			Recoverable interchange processi	False
			Trailer schema	(None)
	▨ Flat file disassem...		Type	Microsoft.BizTalk.Component.FFDasmC
			Validate document structure	False
▱	Validate	⊟		
	⎘ Drop Here!			
☑	ResolveParty	⊟		
	⎘ Drop Here!			
	◉			

Once you deploy your Pipeline, you will be able to see it and select it among the available Pipelines when configuring a Send Port or Receive Location in the Administration Console, as shown in the following screenshot:

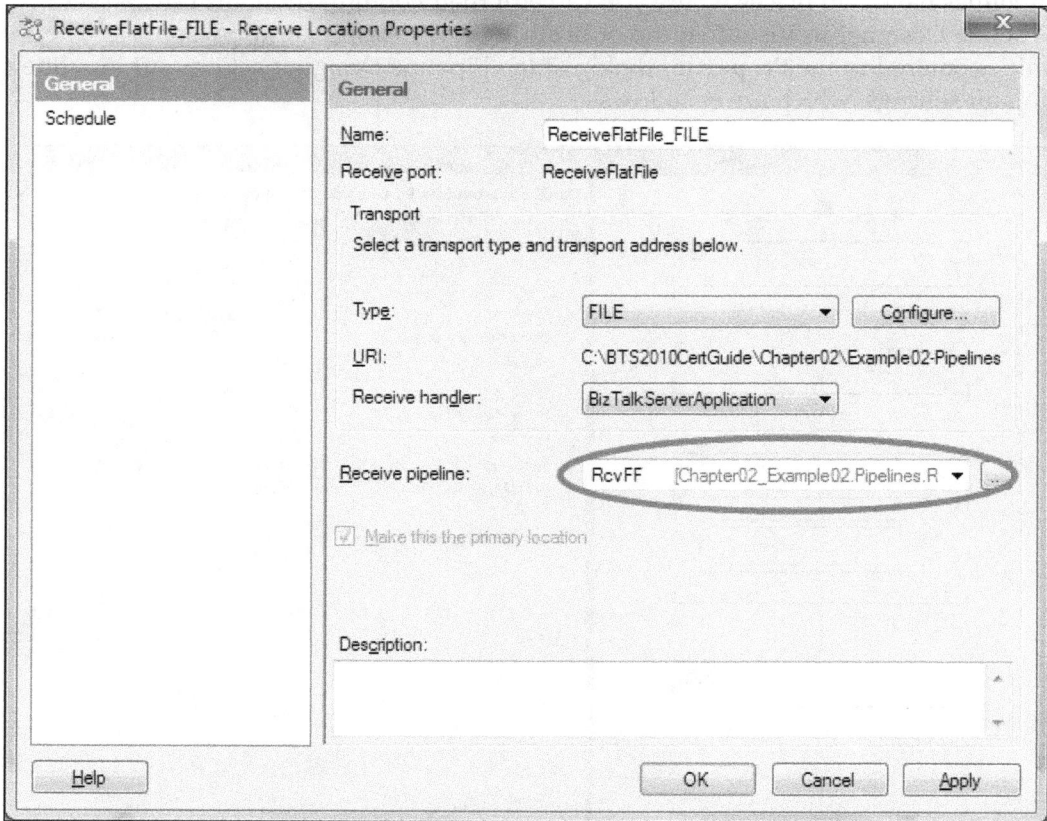

If you click on the ellipsis to the right of the drop-down box, this will bring up the **Configure Pipeline** dialog, where you have the option to override some or all of your default settings with new runtime settings. From a user interface perspective, those overridden runtime settings will then be shown in bold, as shown in the following screenshot:

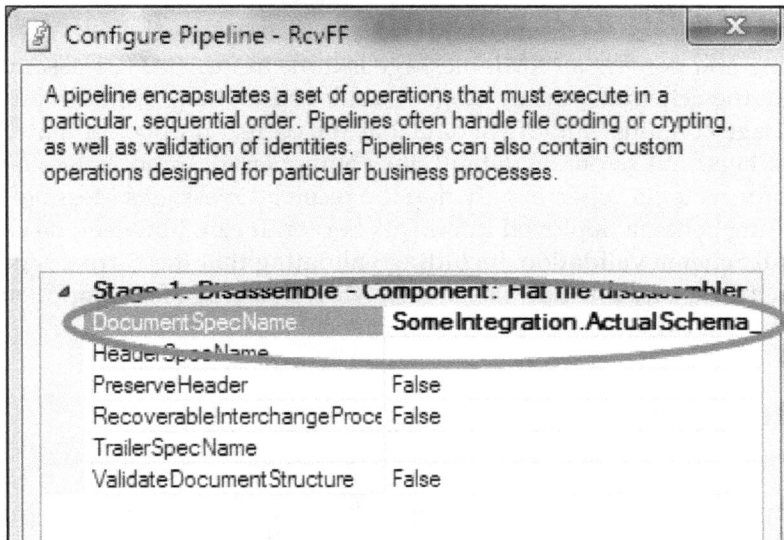

The alternative to overriding settings in runtime is creating additional Pipelines, which can result in many more Pipelines than actually needed.

> The RcvFF Pipeline that uses a dummy Schema as a default setting for the Flat File Disassembler component is available in `Chapter02-Example02`.

Working with XML messages

Working with XML messages is not always as easy as using the `XMLReceive` Pipeline, with default settings to receive the message and `PassThruTransmit` to send it out, although it could be. It's useful to know the capabilities of the components that process XML messages, among which we can find: XML Disassembler, XML Assembler, and XML Validator.

Disassembling and parsing

Disassembling and parsing an XML message is done in the XML Disassembler to ensure that the Schema of the message is deployed to the BizTalk Server and that the message contains valid XML data, has the correct number of matching start and end tags, and so on. By default, the component does not validate that the message conforms to its Schema, only that the received messages MessageType has a corresponding Schema deployed in BizTalk Server. It can, however, be configured to do do a full Schema validation, including validating that the correct type and number of elements and attributes exist. The XML Disassembler component has properties that are explained in the following sections.

Allow unrecognized messages

Default: False

This property allows you to accept messages that have an unrecognized format to pass through the disassembler. Setting this to True allows processing of messages that are recognized, for which we will get property promotion and so on, while still allowing unrecognized messages that do not conform to any deployed Schema to pass through.

Document Schemas

Default: Empty

The Empty option means that it is not limited to a specific Schema or Schemas and will accept messages matching any deployed Schema (or any message, depending on the setting of Allow unrecognized messages).

This property allows you to specify what Schemas are expected, and therefore authorized, to pass through this Pipeline.

Envelope Schemas

Default: Empty

The Empty option means that it will inspect the message for any deployed Schema marked as being an Envelope Schema and will try to remove the envelope if found.

This property allows you to specify which Envelope Schemas are expected, and therefore authorized to pass through this Pipeline.

Recoverable interchange processing

Default: `False`

This property is only interesting when the Disassemble stage forwards more than one message to the next stage, such as when an envelope is used and the message is split into several messages within the interchange. It allows you to indicate that the Pipeline is to use recoverable interchange processing.

If the value is set to `False`, the entire interchange is treated as a transactional unit against `MessageBox`. It will not recover (if that helps you remember) from an exception that occurs in the processing of any single message — if one of the split messages fail, the entire interchange fails.

If it is set to `True`, it means that each message within the interchange is treated in isolation and the interchange can recover and be processed completely even if any one or many messages get suspended.

Validate document structure

Default: `False`.

The `False` option means that there is no validation outside of the well-formed XML and that any received message with a MessageType that matches a deployed Schema will be accepted, regardless of whether the rest of the content matches the Schema or not.

`True` means that validation for Document and Envelope Schema conformance will be performed as applicable. If you set this property to `True`, you must also supply the Document Schemas that validation should be performed against.

Assembling and serializing

The XML Assembler has properties that are explained in the following sections.

Add processing instructions text, Add processing instructions, Processing instruction scope

These properties specify the processing instructions' text to Append (default), Create New (overwrite) or Ignore (clear) at the Envelope or Document (default) level.

Processing instructions are instructions directed at the application for processing of the XML document on how to interpret it, visualize it, authorize it, and so on. A closely related application that uses this is InfoPath.

Add XML declaration

Default: `True`.

Determines if an XML declaration, such as `<?xml version='1.0' encoding='UTF-8'>`, should be available in the outbound document.

Preserve Byte Order

Default: `True`.

This property determines whether a byte order mark should be prepended to the outbound message. A byte order mark is a Unicode character placed first in the stream to indicate which Unicode representation the text is encoded in.

Target charset

Default: `Empty`.

It allows you to define a specific character set to encode outbound messages.

Envelope Schemas

Default: `Empty`.

This property allows you to specify which Envelope Schemas are to be expected when assembling the document.

Working with XML envelopes is covered in more depth later in this chapter.

Document Schemas

Default: `Empty`.

This property allows you to specify which Schema the processed messages are expected to belong to. If left empty, it will accept any valid message that belongs to any deployed Schema.

Validating data

Sometimes, there are scenarios where you need to insert document validation without it being performed by the XML Disassembler; for example, the XML or Flat File Assemblers do not perform Schema validation. If you want to enable outbound message Schema validation, a suitable option is to place an XML Validator component in the Pre-Assemble stage of a Send Pipeline. It could also be placed in the Validate stage of a Receive Pipeline. This could be useful, say, when you want to validate the pieces of an interchange after it's been split into several messages.

The XML Validator only has two properties:

- **Document Schemas**: It indicates which Schemas are valid for messages. It also uses Schema information to validate messages against Schema for conformance. If left empty, messages matching any deployed Schema are valid to be processed through the Pipeline.

- **Recoverable Interchange Processing**: If the component is located in a Receive Pipeline and you set recoverable interchange processing to True on the XML Disassembler, you must also set recoverable interchange processing to True on this component, if you want them to follow the same pattern.

Working with XML envelopes

Working with envelopes is a common scenario that we are going to look at a bit more closely. We are going to use an Envelope Schema and, with the help of that Schema and a Pipeline, split an enveloped batch message into its part and send them through BizTalk. The Schema has the following structure:

```xml
<xs:schema xmlns="http://Chapter02_Example03.Schemas.CarEnvelope"
xmlns:b="http://schemas.microsoft.com/BizTalk/2003"
targetNamespace="http://Chapter02_Example03.Schemas.CarEnvelope"
xmlns:xs="http://www.w3.org/2001/XMLSchema">
  <xs:annotation>
    <xs:appinfo>
      <b:schemaInfo is_envelope="yes" />
    </xs:appinfo>
  </xs:annotation>
  <xs:element name="ManufacturingReport">
  <xs:annotation>
  <xs:appinfo>
      <b:recordInfo body_XPath="/*[local-
name()='ManufacturingReport' and namespace-uri()='http://Chapter02_
Example03.Schemas.CarEnvelope']/*[local-name()='Cars' and namespace-
uri()='']" />
    </xs:appinfo>
  </xs:annotation>
  <xs:complexType>
    <xs:sequence>
      <xs:element name="Cars">
        <xs:complexType>
          <xs:sequence>
            <xs:any maxOccurs="unbounded" />
          </xs:sequence>
```

```
            </xs:complexType>
          </xs:element>
        </xs:sequence>
        <xs:attribute name="BatchNo" type="xs:int" />
      </xs:complexType>
    </xs:element>
  </xs:schema>
```

Note the `recordInfo` annotation with its `body_XPath` attribute that contains an XPath that points out the Schema node that contains the message body.

To make sure we have a Schema to represent a message that we can send inside the envelope, a copy of the `SimplifiedCar` Schema created earlier in this chapter has been placed in the solution.

Let's examine what we must do to split the incoming envelope message into its document parts.

The following is the instance message we are sending through BizTalk:

```
<ns0:ManufacturingReport BatchNo="10" xmlns:ns0="http://Chapter02_
Example03.Schemas.CarEnvelope">
  <Cars>
    <ns0:Car xmlns:ns0="http://Chapter02_Example03.Schemas.
SimplifiedCar">
      <RegistrationNo>ABC123</RegistrationNo>
      <Make>Audi</Make>
      <Model>RS6</Model>
      <Color>NurburgringBlue</Color>
    </ns0:Car>
    <ns0:Car xmlns:ns0="http://Chapter02_Example03.Schemas.
SimplifiedCar">
      <RegistrationNo>XYZ789</RegistrationNo>
      <Make>Corvette</Make>
      <Model>ZR1</Model>
      <Color>DaytonaRed</Color>
    </ns0:Car>
  </Cars>
</ns0:ManufacturingReport>
```

No custom Pipelines are needed to complete this exercise – the Default Pipelines will do the job. These are the steps needed to configure the Pipelines to receive and split the message:

1. Make sure the project has a key file and a string name, and deploy it to BizTalk Server.

2. Configure a **Receive Port** and **Receive Location**.

3. In **Receive Location,** make sure you select `XMLReceive Pipeline`. No further configuration is needed.

4. Create a **Send Port** that has a **Filter** property that subscribes to messages from the **Receive Port**. No further configuration is needed on **Send Port**.

5. Enable **Receive Location** and start the **Send Port**.

6. Send the message.

The result is two messages sent from the Disassemble stage, on to the Send Port and out to the location we choose.

> This sample is available in the `C:\BTS2013CertGuide\`
> `Chapter02\Example02-Envelope\Chapter02-Example03\`
> `Chapter02-Example03.sln` solution, and the bindings are
> available in `C:\BTS2013CertGuide\Chapter02\Example03-`
> `Envelope\BTS2013CertGuide-Ch02-Envelope.XML file`.

> **Flat File Envelopes**
>
> Flat Files can be received in batches as well. The concept of envelopes applies just as equally to Flat Files as it does to XML messages. However, a Flat File is configured slightly differently and instead includes configuring Header Schemas, Document Schemas, and Trailer Schemas in the Flat File Disassembler component. Flat File Envelopes are not covered in this book. The Envelope Processing BizTalk Server sample is found in the `<BizTalkInstall>\ SDK\Samples\` `Pipelines\AssemblerDisassembler\EnvelopeProcessing` folder; the article at `http://msdn.microsoft.com/en-us/` `library/aa578216.aspx` discusses this further.

Working with Flat File messages

In an earlier section of this chapter titled *Creating Flat File Schemas*, we created a Schema that describes a Flat File with a combination of delimiters and tag identifiers. Now we will look at the next step to receive messages into BizTalk Server using this Schema — using the Flat File disassembler in a Receive Pipeline. The following steps walk you through this process:

1. In the BizTalk project, select **Add | New Item....**

2. Select **Receive Pipeline** and name it `RcvCars.btp`.

3. When **Pipeline Designer** is shown, open **Toolbox** and drop a **Flat File disassembler** component in the **Disassemble** stage.

4. In the **Document Schema** property of the **Flat File disassembler** component, select the `Chapter02_Example02.Pipelines.SimplifiedCarsFF` Schema.

5. **Build** and **Deploy** the project to BizTalk Server.

6. To be able to start receiving files using the Pipeline, in **BizTalk Server Administrator**, create a new **Receive Port** and **Receive Location**.

7. Configure **Receive Location** to use the `RcvCars` Pipeline. This will enable disassembling of Flat Files into their XML equivalent and further processing in BizTalk Server.

> The `SimplifiedCarsFF.xsd` Schema and the `RcvCars.btp` pipeline are available in the `C:\BTS2013CertGuide\Chapter02\Example02-Envelope\Chapter02-Example03\Chapter02-Example03.sln` solution and can be deployed, configured, and examined as needed.

Working with secure data

Sometimes there is a need to secure the conversation between BizTalk Server and the systems it uses to communicate. For those situations, you can use the MIME/SMIME Pipeline components in either Receive or Send Pipelines and take on the job of verifying digital signature and decrypting messages, and signing and encrypting messages.

> The following process assumes that you have certificates installed in the correct locations in Windows Certificate Store. Refer to `http://technet.microsoft.com/en-us/library/aa559322(v=bts.80).aspx` to learn how to set that infrastructure up or refer to `http://social.technet.microsoft.com/wiki/contents/articles/18846.biztalk-server-importing-certificates.aspx`.

Encryption and signing

To use the MIME/SMIME Pipeline component to encrypt a message, create a configuration along the following steps:

1. First, we need to create a custom Send Pipeline to contain the **MIME/SMIME encoder** component. All component properties are left at their defaults at this point, as shown in the following screenshot:

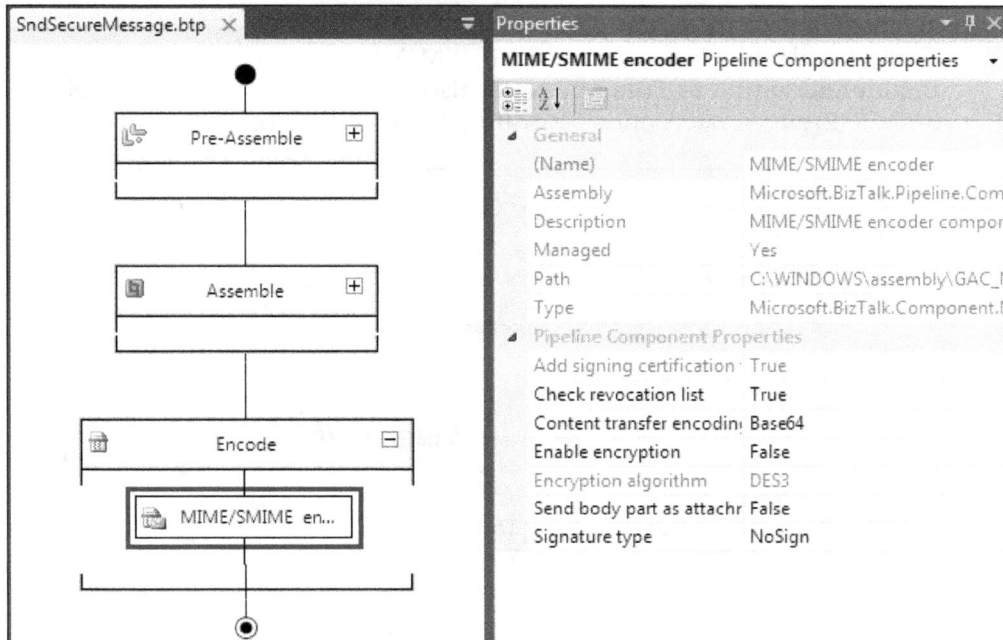

2. Next, we deploy the Pipeline to BizTalk Server.

3. Then, we need to create Receive Port to receive a cleartext message, just so that we have something to encrypt.

4. Create a **Send Port** that subscribes to the **Receive Port**.

5. Configure the Port with an **Encryption certificate** (the partner public key of the encryption certificate needs to be installed in the Local Computer\Other People store), as shown in the following screenshot:

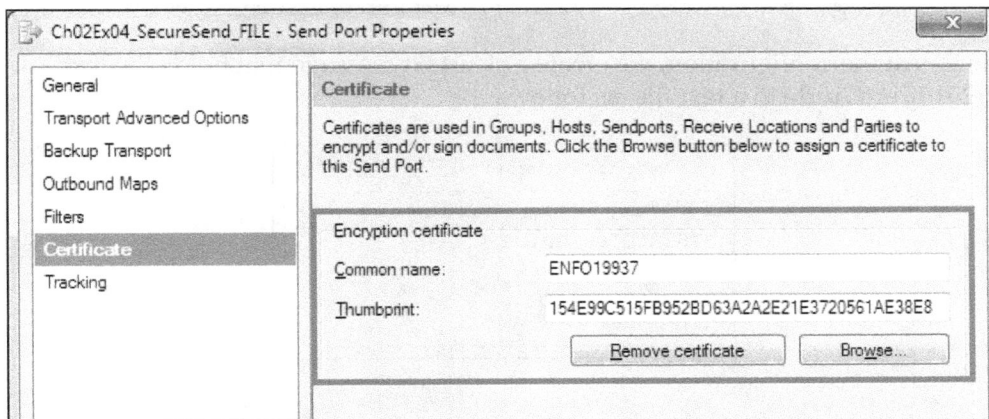

6. Configure the **Send Port** to use the **SndSecureMessage** Pipeline.

7. Configure the Pipeline and the MIME/SMIME component by setting **EnableEncryption** to **True**. We could also choose one of DES3 (0), DES (1), or RC2 (2) as our encryption algorithm. DES3 is default.

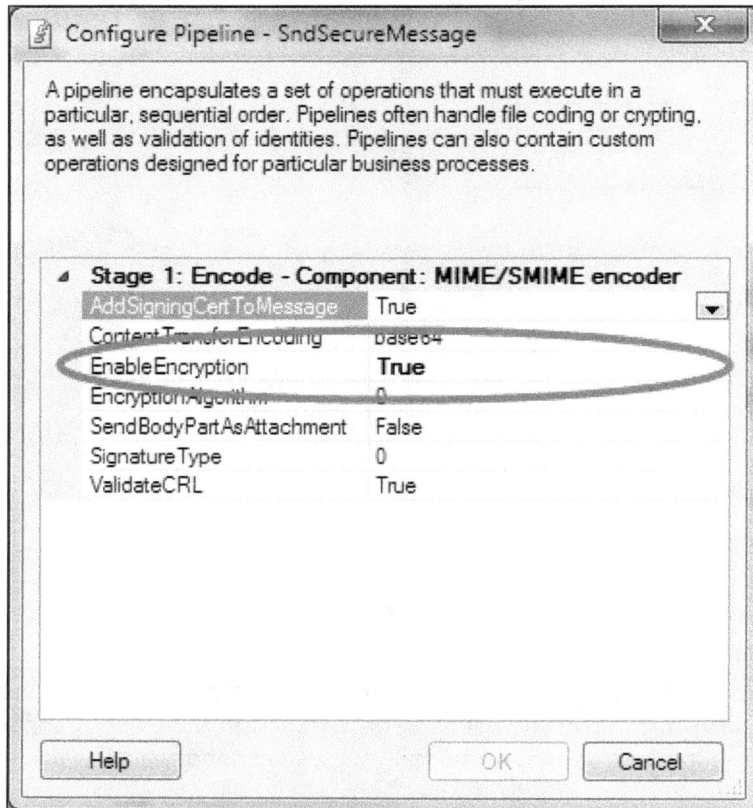

Now to test the configuration, we create a cleartext message that holds the text **BTS2010CertGuide** in a text file, as follows:

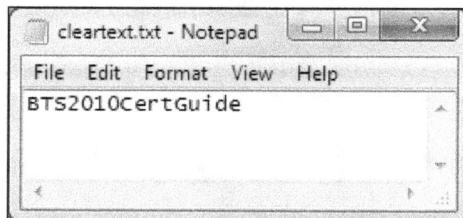

We make the Receive Port pick it up so that it gets routed to the Send Port and out comes an encrypted file, the content of which looks similar to the following screenshot:

```
encrypted.txt - Notepad

File  Edit  Format  View  Help

Content-ID: {CAC14259-652E-45CD-81EA-62E7B5C508AE}
BCC:
MIME-Version: 1.0
Content-type: application/x-pkcs7-mime; smime-type=enveloped-data; name="smime.p7m"
Content-Transfer-Encoding: base64

MIAGCSqGSIb3DQEHA6CAMIACAQAxggFEMIIBQAIBADAOMBQxEjAQBgNVBAMTCUVORk8xOTkwNwIQ
U2HjfN1B9qdKCp3TJGnTGjANBgkqhkiG9w0BAQEFAASCAQArvCkICBcFQQqCg2SfvrEh0+6cGysr
ygHe+absk2PCq4oeX4O31Y4vOR8IgBeI6G1wriUJL2imgf98hmyt4O9OOAg/o2agNXbEMRf5npxw
ZhoYw8v5EBUAjIUVlYRelJHs9qcPYBDsuWnyI/h5pVTDwySK6SEBDPrf3sgAuYyK0Q0sCC/a4LB9
z1hxHxrjKTwPOo6zQa0rMjvP61FEh18svgeVZFy/Nw8htlIu05cOL17owOjgwqkeZHdSXr1Xsmh7
plspupZNj/aXLD+7U41C25RdAReiKBRRya8exFc1U6gBy2yAOJzrNdoOftlRxvSDyZ5EAgz+yTR3
avhT2JGNMIAGCSqGSIb3DQEHATAUBggqhkiG9w0DBwQIruHYah3hmJeggARgLhpivwoPuouGF1rY
F43AiiwPe+a8+4VhSK4KY+hjIe8Dxh62TQi+p69/hcyvzUgIOTZTTYj5AS3GCRAmCWjjXcVOPx69
ZLcunWYo7HIKMq7DGhmvLj4TBwlR9TiNwamvAAAAAAAAAAAAA==
```

If instead we wanted to sign the message, we would change the configuration of the Send Pipeline and the MIME/SMIME component. The following is a screenshot of a possible configuration where we are using the **ClearSign (1)** option:

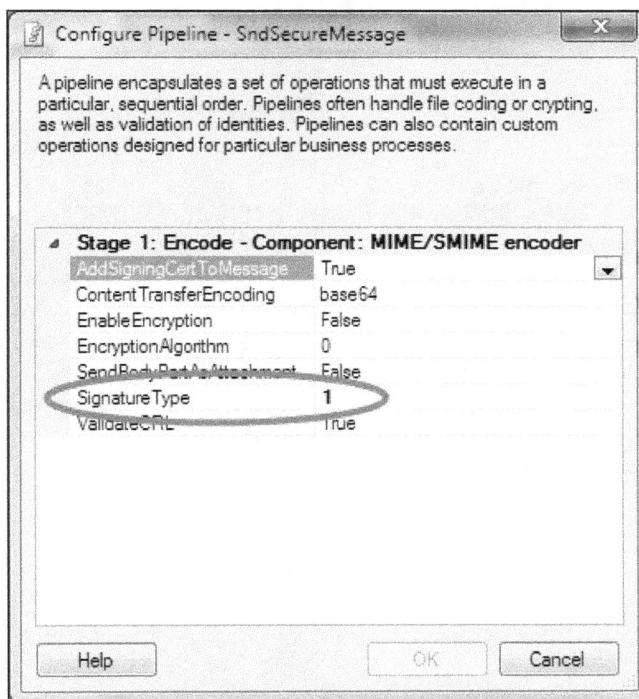

```
Configure Pipeline - SndSecureMessage

A pipeline encapsulates a set of operations that must execute in a
particular, sequential order. Pipelines often handle file coding or crypting,
as well as validation of identities. Pipelines can also contain custom
operations designed for particular business processes.


▲  Stage 1: Encode - Component: MIME/SMIME encoder
   AddSigningCertToMessage      True                        ▼
   ContentTransferEncoding      base64
   EnableEncryption             False
   EncryptionAlgorithm          0
   SendBodyPartAsAttachment     False
   SignatureType                1
   ValidateCRL                  True




      Help              OK        Cancel
```

It's also possible to both encrypt and sign, in which case the signature would be made using the **BlobSign (2)** option.

Signing requires our private key certificate to be in the `Host Instance User\ Personal` store and configured at the BizTalk Server Group level.

Now if we supply the same cleartext message, the output has a new look, as in the following screenshot:

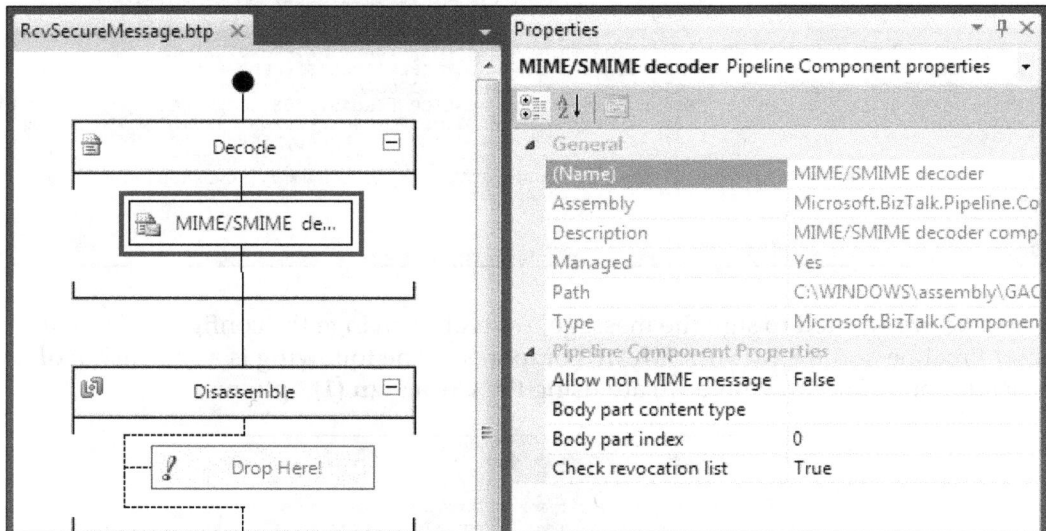

The sample `Chapter02\Example04-Security` contains a Send Pipeline configured with a MIME/SMIME Encoder named `SndSecureMessage`.

It also contains a Receive Port included in the bindings named `Ch02Ex04_ClearTextReceive`, as well as a Send Port named `Ch02Ex04_SecureSend_FILE` configured to use the `SndSecureMessage` Pipeline.

Please note that you need to create and deploy a certificate and update the sample with your own certificate's thumbprint, where applicable.

Decryption and signature verification

Now that we have encrypted and signed messages in the previous section, let's look at how to go about decrypting the message to get back to the cleartext representation:

1. First, we need to create a custom Receive Pipeline to contain the **MIME/ SMIME Decoder** component. All component properties are left at their defaults. In fact, there are no meaningful properties for us to change to affect either signature verification or decryption:

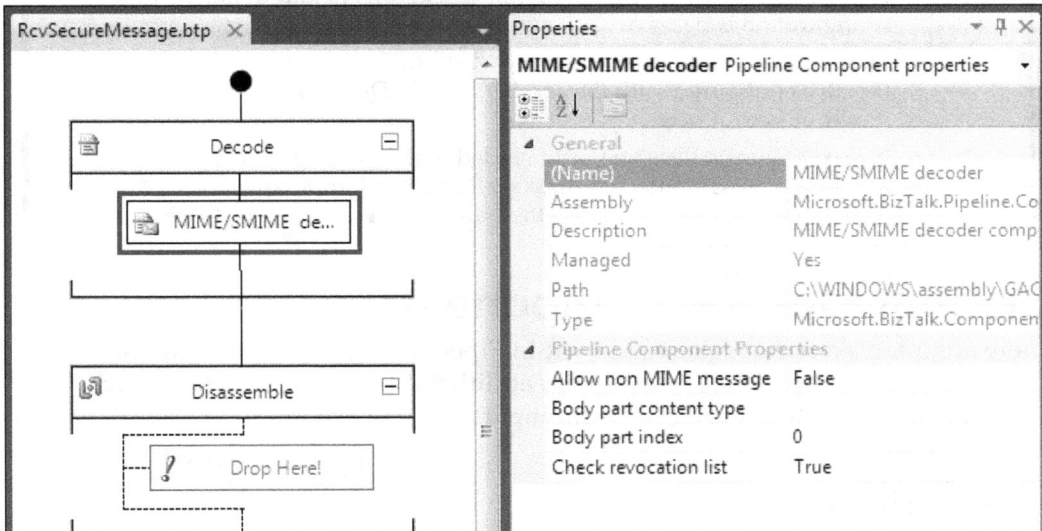

2. Next, we deploy the Pipeline to BizTalk Server.
3. Then, we need to create a **Receive Port** to receive secure messages.
4. We configure the **Receive Port** to use the **RcvSecureMessage** Pipeline.
5. Since we already established that the **MIME/SMIME Decoder** component had no properties we needed to alter to be able to receive encrypted or signed messages, we do not need to do any configuration.
6. We also create a **Send Port** that subscribes to the **Receive Port**, to be able to see the end result.

Now to test the configuration, we will send in the encrypted and signed messages we created in the previous section. It is sufficient to say that it will result in cleartext messages.

To decrypt encrypted messages, we need to configure our certificate to use at the Host level and have the private key installed in the `Host Instance User\Personal` store (the same store as when signing messages). For verifying signatures, we need to have the partner's public key deployed to the `Local Computer\Other People` store (the same store as when encrypting outbound messages). No additional BizTalk configuration is necessary.

The sample `Chapter02\Example04-Security` contains a Receive Pipeline configured with the MIME/SMIME Decoder named `RcvSecureMessage`.

It also contains a Receive Port included in the bindings named `Ch02Ex04_SecureReceive`, as well as a Send Port named `Ch02Ex04_ClearTextSend_FILE` using the `PassThruTransmit` Pipeline.

Custom Pipeline Components

There are many scenarios where the built-in Pipelines and Pipeline components are not enough. In this case BizTalk offers additional extensibility through the development of **Custom Pipeline Components**.

Developing

Pipelines components are developed using Visual Studio. There are four types of Pipeline components categorized based on the work they will perform. They are as follows:

- **General Pipeline Component**: This component can be used in the Decode, Validate, or Resolve Party stages of a Receive Pipeline or the Pre-Assemble or Encode stages of a Send Pipeline. This type of component receives a message and returns the same or another message to be passed to the next component.

- **Disassemble Pipeline Component**: This component can be used in the Disassemble Pipeline stage of a Receive Pipeline. This type of component receives a message and returns one or more messages.

- **Assemble Pipeline Component**: This component can be used in the Assemble Pipeline stage of a Send Pipeline. This type of component takes one or more messages as input and produces a single output.

- **Probing Pipeline Component**: If a Pipeline component intended for a `FirstMatch` Pipeline component stage needs to probe the message, they can implement the IProbeMessage interface to decide if they want to process the message or not.

BizTalk Server SDK's, and in particular the `Microsoft.BizTalk.Component` assembly, and the `Microsoft.BizTalk.Component.Interop` namespace contains a number of interfaces that you need to implement to create a Custom Pipeline Component. Those interfaces are as follows:

Name	Members	Short Description
IComponent	`IBaseMessage Execute(IPipelineContext pContext, IBaseMessage pInMsg)`	Contains the method that is triggered when a General Pipeline Component executes.
IBaseComponent	`Name Description Version`	Contains properties that expose information about the component.
IPersistPropertyBag	`GetClassID(...)  InitNew() Load(...)  Save(...)`	Contains methods for loading and saving configuration information.
IComponentUI	`IconValidate(...)`	Contains the Icon property to supply an icon for Visual Studio Toolbox and the Validate method where custom compilation validation can be implemented.
IDisassembler Component	`Disassemble(...) IBaseMessage GetNext(...)`	Contains methods to aid in disassembling the incoming message and outputting the resulting messages.
IAssembler Component	`AddDocument(...) IBaseMessage Assemble(...)`	Contains methods for adding one or more input message and assembling an output message.
IProbeMessage	`bool Probe(...)`	Contains a method for receiving a message and determining if it should be processed by the component or not.

Deploying

Once you have developed your Pipeline components and want to use them in your Custom Pipelines you need to deploy them to BizTalk Server. This is done by adding the component to the \Pipeline Components sub-folder of the BizTalk Server installation directory. The binary files must be present in this folder on all the servers where the component will be executed.

Testing your knowledge

1. Rob, a developer at HWLC motors, is working with a Schema that is to hold supplier contact details. Just the other week, the team finished work on a Customer Schema. Both have e-mail addresses. While working with the Customer Schema, they created an EmailAddress type with a restriction for e-mail addresses that he would like to reuse in the Supplier Schema. The Customer and Supplier Schemas are in different namespaces. What should he do?

    a. Import the Customer Schema to the Supplier Schema, and set the Data Type of all e-mail addresses in the Supplier Schema to the EmailAddress type defined in the Customer Schema.

    b. Include the Customer Schema in the Supplier Schema to be able to set the EmailAddress type as the Data Type of the e-mail addresses in the Supplier Schema.

    c. Import the Supplier Schema to the Customer Schema, and set the Data Type property of all e-mail addresses in the Supplier Schema to the EmailAddress type defined in the Customer Schema.

    d. Define a new Schema named EmailAddress, to hold the definition of the EmailAddress type.

2. You are configuring a secure communication with signed messages with a partner to ensure that messages are not tampered with while in transmission. You need to make sure that you can receive the messages and that the signature used is valid. What do you do?

    a. Create a Pipeline using the MIME/SMIME Encoder component. Install that partner's private key to the Certificate store of the computer, and configure the Host to use it.

    b. Create a Pipeline using the MIME/SMIME Decoder component. Install that partner's private key to the Certificate store of the computer, and configure the Host to use it.

c. Create a Pipeline using the MIME/SMIME Encoder component. Install that partner's public key to the Certificate store of the computer.

d. Create a Pipeline using the MIME/SMIME Decoder component. Install that partner's public key to the Certificate store of the computer.

Summary

In this chapter, we learned about Schemas and Pipelines. We looked at how to create Schemas. We created hierarchies in and between Schemas. We investigated how we can control the format for Schema nodes and how to re-use those formats as types. We looked at property promotion and discussed its use. We then continued to learn about creating Pipelines and how they can enable us to secure our interchanges and work with our messages in different ways. We also examined how to build Custom Pipelines and Custom Pipeline Components. In the next chapter, we will look at the *Developing BizTalk Artifacts – Creating Maps* section of the exam.

3
Developing BizTalk Artifacts – Creating Maps

This chapter will discuss how to transform messages between Schema formats using Maps. This chapter will cover the following main areas:

- Creating Maps
- Using Functoids
- Using Advanced Functoids
- Maps and Orchestrations
- Testing your knowledge

The sections on Functoids will include a closer look at how to use them to incorporate the conditional logic, to control looping behavior and external assemblies, and to include scripting of different sorts in our maps.

The chapter will conclude with a discussion on how Maps and Orchestrations work together to enable multipart Schemas as the source or destinations in Maps.

Creating Maps

Mapping is one of the areas that has got the biggest attention in BizTalk Server 2010 in terms of user interface. In BizTalk Server 2013, it was improved behind the scenes where the runtime was updated to use `XslCompiledTransform`, which increases the performance of Map execution.

Most integrations will use one or more maps as a part of processing the message. Being skilled at creating well-performing, change-friendly, and maintainable maps is therefore one of the most sought-after skills among the BizTalk developers.

Maps range from simple to very complex, where the user interface changes have really improved the usability around complex maps.

Simple maps may only include connecting a few elements together using simple direct links as shown in the following screenshot.

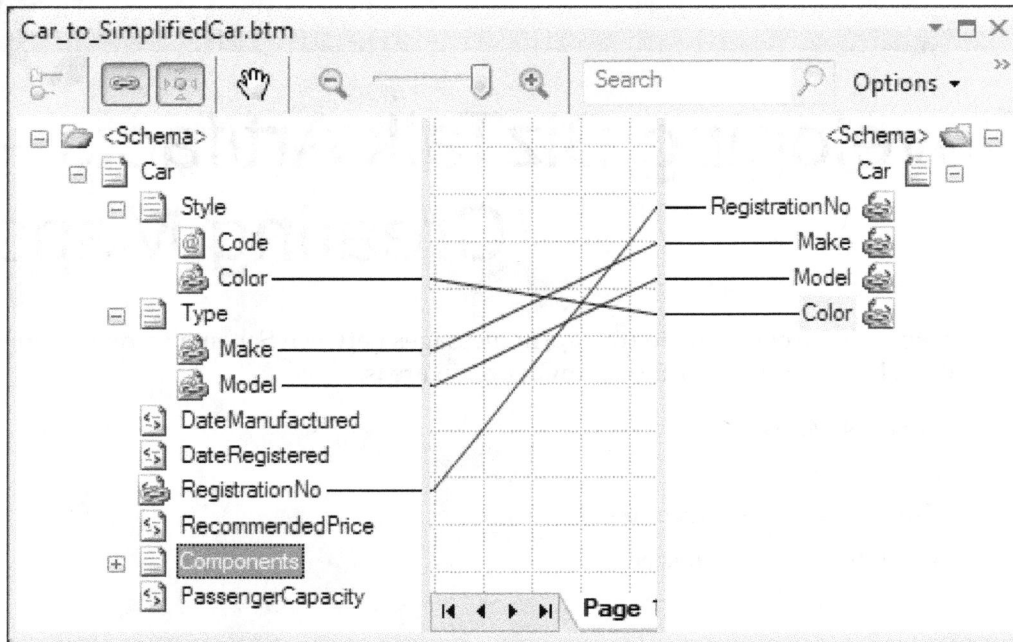

There are several ways a Map can be implemented:

- Links
- Functoids
- External XSLT script
- A combination of links, Functoids, and inline XSLT

All samples and Map images used throughout the this chapter can be found in the C:\BTS2013CertGuide\Chapter03\Example01-Mapping\Chapter03-Example01\Chapter03-Example01.sln solution.

Note that the sample code in this chapter is not built to be deployed, but only to illustrate the concepts, so there are no bindings.

More complex Maps may include a lot of Functoids and complex logic. The following screenshot is an example of a more complex Map from a real-life project (though far more complex and mapping-intense transformations than these are not uncommon):

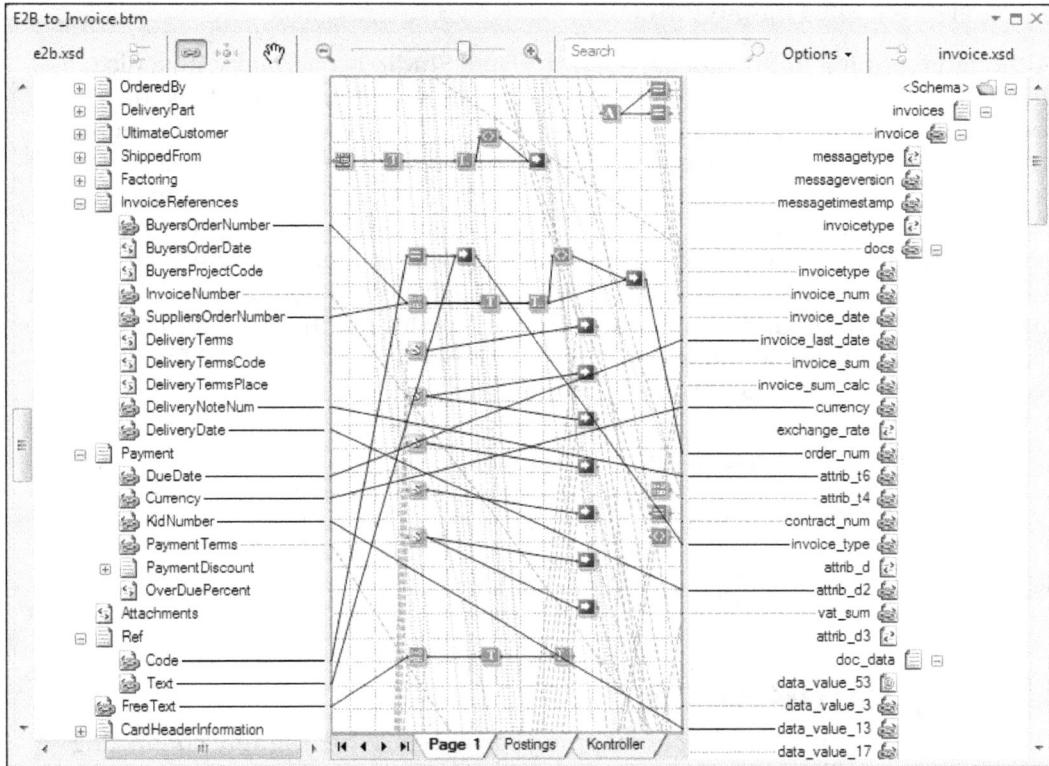

Making Maps maintainable is important and the designing and housekeeping of the mapping surface play into that.

Understanding why XSLT matters

XSLT (Extensible Stylesheet Language Transformations) is a declarative, XML-based language to describe the transformation of an input format to a different or the same output format.

Although mapping in BizTalk Server and Visual Studio is overlaid with a nice design to abstract you away from the fact, XSLT is something that forms the foundation of mapping in BizTalk. Maps are XSLT scripts or at least get compiled into them. Advanced Maps can contain parts that have pure XSLT (through the Scripting Functoid) or fully raw XSLT through the CustomXSLT property (where the mapping design surface is empty). Advanced troubleshooting will often mean running the Validate Map command in Visual Studio to look at, and sometimes debug the generated XSLT that represents the logic of the Map. Getting used to and understanding what kind of XSLT the designer creates in different situations can be really helpful in these situations, where experimenting with links and Functoids to reach the desired result is not quite enough.

> It is outside the scope of this book to cover details on XSLT. For a detailed walkthrough of XSLT, go to http://www.w3.org/TR/xslt.html.

We will look at some sample XSLT when we review the Scripting Functoid.

Using Functoids

Once you get past the simplest of mapping constructs, where simply connecting source and target Schemas using direct links is not enough, you will start using Functoids. Functoids are small reusable snippets of code that execute predefined logic based on parameters (inputs from source Schema or other Functoids in the Map). Referring to XSLT, Functoids will inject functions and function calls into the generated XSLT script. Functoids typically take zero to many inputs and deliver one output, with a few exceptions.

There are nine different categories of Functoids, which are as follows:

- Conversion
- Cumulative
- Database
- Date and Time
- Logical

- Mathematical
- Scientific
- String
- Advanced

As someone preparing to take the certification, you should be well aware of the available Functoids as they are important in the overall BizTalk and Map development. Most Functoids are however easy to use and quite self-explanatory, and an in-depth description of their use would be useless to the target audience of this book.

On top of the existing Functoids, custom Functoids can be created by developers extending the Functoid toolbox with the custom functionality.

Conversion Functoids

The Conversion Functoids do what the name says, that is, they convert between different formats. The available out of the box conversion Functoids are as follows:

- **Character to ASCII**: It converts a character to an ASCII value
- **ASCII to Character**: It converts an ASCII value to a character
- **Hexadecimal**: It converts a decimal number to a hexadecimal value
- **Octal**: It converts a decimal number to an octal value

Cumulative Functoids

All Cumulative Functoids accept the same two input parameters as follows:

- The source value to accumulate
- The scope of accumulation as follows:
    - ° 0 means entire message
    - ° 1 means values that have the same parent
    - ° 2 means values that have the same parent's parent
    - ° 3 means values that have the same parent's parent's parent, and so on

Except for the Cumulative String Functoid, all Cumulative Functoids accept only numeric values and will ignore any non-numeric values received. The following types of accumulations can be made:

- **Average**: It returns the average value of all the values
- **Concatenate**: It returns a string, that is, the concatenation of all the values
- **Maximum**: It returns the maximum value of all the values
- **Minimum**: It returns the minimum value of all the values
- **Sum**: It returns the accumulated sum of all the values

Database Functoids

The Database Functoids merit something of an explanation besides a list explaining their individual meaning. First, under the Database Functoids category, there are Functoids that are divided into two areas; Table Query and Lookup Functoids, and Cross Reference ID or Cross Reference Value Lookup Functoids.

Table Query Functoids

These Functoids enable us to query tables and supply lookup columns to look for an equally supplied value. The return is a single row from that table to extract the values. This is quite a limited database query functionality, and stored procedures cannot be called, as shown in the following table.

> If you are not careful using the Database Lookup Functoid, it can easily become a bottleneck in your process, especially if you handle large files that end up making tens of thousands of calls to the database.

Functoid	Input and output
Database Lookup	• **Input**: The following are the inputs: 　○　A lookup value 　○　A connection string 　○　Name of table 　○　Name of column • **Output**: The first row that matches the query (in an ADO recordset)
Value Extractor	• **Input**: The following are the inputs: 　○　A link from the Database Lookup Functoid—an ADO recordset—containing a row 　○　The name of the column to extract the value from • **Output**: The value from the configured column
Error Return	• **Input**: A link from the Database Lookup Functoid • **Output**: A string of the error that occurred, if any

Cross Referencing Data Functoids

The Cross Reference Functoids is one way by which you can fulfill the often-occurring requirement of cross-referencing the data, the need to translate values from one system identifier or value to another.

How it works is that you use either the BizTalk Server Cross Reference Import Tool (BTSXRefImport.exe) to import data defined in a series of XML files into your database or you use SQL statements to manipulate the tables directly. The tooling in this case is quite crude and if you are serious about using this built-in feature for data cross-referencing, you are often better off designing an alternative strategy. We are not going to cover the underlying database structures that data ends up in any depth.

Let us just assume that the data is in there and look at getting it out. To help in understanding the relationship between the data, let us look at the relationship between tables and the entities in play, as shown in the following diagram:

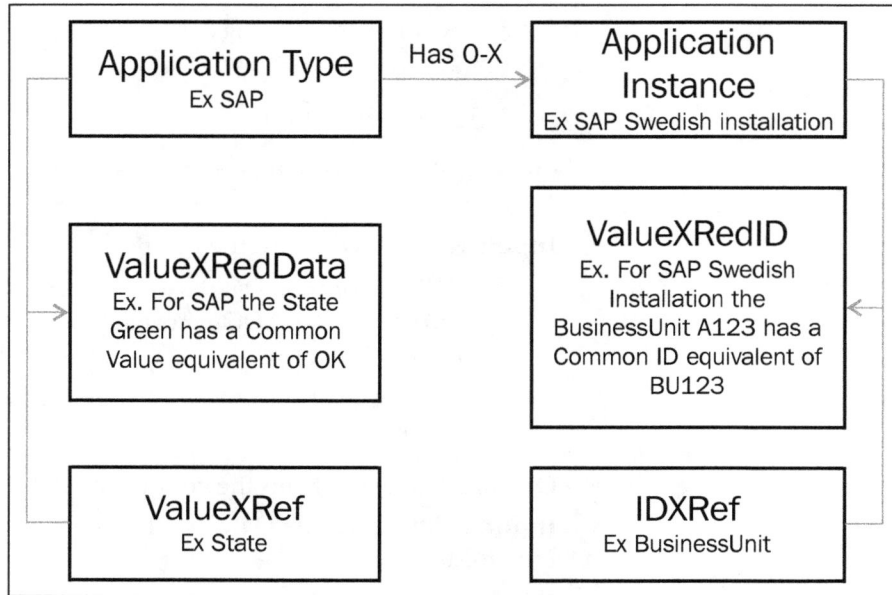

```
┌──────────────────────────────────────────────────────────────────┐
│  ┌───────────────────────┐  Has 0-X   ┌───────────────────────┐   │
│  │   Application Type     │ ─────────> │     Application        │   │
│  │      Ex SAP            │            │      Instance          │   │
│  └───────────────────────┘            │  Ex SAP Swedish        │   │
│                                        │     installation       │   │
│                                        └───────────────────────┘   │
│                                                                     │
│  ┌───────────────────────┐            ┌───────────────────────┐   │
│  │    ValueXRedData       │            │     ValueXRedID        │   │
│  │                        │            │  Ex. For SAP Swedish   │   │
│  │  Ex. For SAP the State │            │    Installation the    │   │
│  │  Green has a Common    │            │  BusinessUnit A123 has a│  │
│  │  Value equivalent of OK│            │  Common ID equivalent of│  │
│  │                        │            │        BU123           │   │
│  └───────────────────────┘            └───────────────────────┘   │
│                                                                     │
│  ┌───────────────────────┐            ┌───────────────────────┐   │
│  │     ValueXRef          │            │       IDXRef           │   │
│  │      Ex State          │            │   Ex BusinessUnit      │   │
│  └───────────────────────┘            └───────────────────────┘   │
└──────────────────────────────────────────────────────────────────┘
```

Working with application IDs

A part of Cross Referencing Functoids is about working with IDs that differ between application instances. They are unique identifiers in their respective application instances. These are often not IDs of things such as Order or Invoice but of something a bit more limited, say the ID of types, for example, BusinessUnit or CostCenter. Since they are IDs, they are suitable candidates for a one-to-one mapping relationship, that is, the ID of an application instance will always have (and map to) one and only one common ID. Similarly, one common ID will always map to one and only one application instance ID. Since it is moving data, a new BusinessUnit ID may appear at any given time. There is also logic available to handle new or removed IDs.

In the middle of cross-referencing of data between two applications, there is a common ID, which is something that you map to and from, to map between application instance IDs, as shown in the following table:

Functoid	Input and output

⊡ Get Common ID	• **Input**: The following are the inputs:
	  ◦ Type of object
	  ◦ The application instance we are mapping from
	  ◦ The application instance's ID
	
	• **Output**: The common ID equivalent to the application's ID

⊡ Get Application ID	• **Input**: The following are the inputs:
	  ◦ Type of object
	  ◦ The application instance we are mapping to
	  ◦ The common ID
	
	• **Output**: The application instance ID equivalent to the common ID

There are also ways for you to administer IDs in runtime when you find new IDs or find a situation that suggests you remove application IDs, which are as follows:

Functoid	Input and output

⊡ Set Common ID	• **Input**: The following are the inputs:
	  ◦ Type of object
	  ◦ The application instance we are mapping from
	  ◦ The application instance ID
	  ◦ An optional common ID, if this is not supplied then a new unique identifier is generated
	
	• **Output**: The common ID that is the same as parameter 4, or the generated ID

Functoid	Input and output

◄□ Remove Application ID	• **Input**: The following are the inputs
	   ° Type of object
	   ° The application instance we are mapping to
	   ° The common ID
	
	• **Output**: The application instance ID equivalent to the common ID; the application instance ID that is being removed

Working with application values

Application values stand in relation to the application type rather than the instance of an application. They are mostly used for values such as enumerations or other static values such as states or types that are steadier in their nature. Therefore, there are no Functoids available to add or remove values at runtime. It is a one-to-many mapping relationship; for example, one application can have the states as green, yellow, orange, and red, while another has only green, yellow, and red. In this case, both yellow and orange may result in a mapping to yellow. This is explained in the following table:

Functoid	Input and output

▦◄□ Set Common Value	• **Input**: The following are the inputs:
	   ° Type of object
	   ° The application type we are mapping from
	   ° The application value
	
	• **Output**: The common value

▦◄ Get Application Value	• **Input**: The following are the inputs:
	   ° Type of object
	   ° The application type we are mapping to
	   ° The common value
	
	• **Output**: The application value equivalent to the common value

Date/Time Functoids

The Date/Time Functoids help in determining the current date and time as well as providing some simple date calculation. They are as follows:

- **Add Days**: It either takes a `date` or `datetime` string and adds *X* number of days to it and returns the new date
- **Date**: It returns the current date
- **Date And Time**: It returns the current date and time
- **Time**: It returns the current time

> All dates are ISO 8601-compliant values, meaning that a date is represented as `YYYY-MM-DD`, time as a 24-hour `hh:mm:ss` format, and `datetime` as `YYYY-MM-DDThh:mm:ss`. Optionally, you can specify a timezone by suffixing either a Z for UTC or by adding a positive or negative time, such as `+hh:mm`. For example, `2011-11-10T14:02:02+02:00`.

Logical Functoids

The Logical Functoids category is arguably the most used and useful Functoid category. The Functoids in this category can take a wide variety of data types as input and even perform comparisons between parameters of different types in some cases. They all yield a Boolean output, representing whether or not the operation or comparison that the Functoid performed resulted in a `true` or `false` value. Since it is Boolean, the output should be used as input to other Functoids or nodes that can accept a Boolean value. It should not be used as an input to a Functoid or a destination node expecting to get a string such as `true`.

> While connecting the output of a Logical Functoid to a destination node, the result determines whether or not we can output that node, depending on the values being true or false. It is a very useful and common operation.

The following Functoids compare two input values to produce a Boolean result:

- Equal
- Not equal
- Greater than

- Greater than or equal to
- Less than
- Less than or equal to

The rest of the Functoids in the category are explained in the list that follows:

- **Logical Existence**: This Functoid must be connected to a source node and checks to see whether or not the message contains that node.

- **IsNil**: This Functoid can be used to inspect whether a node that exists is `nil`. A node that does not exist is not evaluated as `nil` since this Functoid checks if the node has an `xsi:nil` attribute set to `true`.

- **Logical String**: This Functoid evaluates whether or not a value can be interpreted as a string. This will return `false` if the value is `null`; for example, if the node does not exist or if the value is an empty string. This in the case of an empty node, that is, `<x></x>`.

- **Logical Numeric** and **Logical Date**: These Functoids basically work in the same way. The only difference is that they test to see whether the value can be interpreted as numeric or date respectively.

- **Logical AND**: These Functoids accept 2 to 100 inputs that are evaluated as either `true` or `false` and then combined to return a single Boolean value. An AND operation means that all values given must evaluate to `true` for a Boolean value of `true` to be returned. If only a single value is evaluated as `false`, then the value returned is `false`.

- **Logical OR**: This Functoid works in the opposite manner. It evaluates all inputs, and if at least one evaluates to `true`, the Functoid will return a Boolean value as `true`.

- **Logical NOT**: This Functoid is used to negate the input within it, that is, if it is given a value that is evaluated as `true`, it will return `false` and vice versa.

Mathematical Functoids

The Mathematical Functoids allow us to use some common mathematical operations on the data in our map. This ranges from what is extremely common, say addition or subtraction, to the lesser used ones such as square root. The full list of Mathematical Functoids supplied is as follows:

- **Addition**: This returns the result of adding between 1 and 100 inputs.

- **Subtraction**: This returns the result of subtracting 1 to 99 values from the first value. This works as P1-P2 [-P3...-Pn].

- **Multiplication**: This returns the result of multiplying 2 to 100 values.
- **Division**: This returns the result of dividing 2 values.
- **Absolute Value**: This returns the absolute value of the input. An absolute value is a positive value or a value with disregard for its sign; for example, input 7 will return 7 and input -7 will also return 7.
- **Integer**: This returns the integer portion of a decimal value without doing any rounding, for example, input 4.67 will return 4.
- **Modulo**: This returns the remainder of an integer division, a division that results in a non-decimal result; for example, inputs 5 and 2 will result in 1 (5 cannot be divided by 2 to produce an integer result, but 4 can, and so the remainder is 1).
- **Round**: This returns the rounded value as given by the first parameter, rounded to the number of decimals given in the second. The round to nearest, round to even (or banker rounding) is used, that is, if the second parameter is 0 or missing, 1.5 rounds to 2, while 4.5 rounds to 4.
- **Square Root**: This returns the square root of the supplied value.

Scientific Functoids

Using the Scientific Functoids built on mathematical concepts is basically the same as switching between the regular and scientific calculator in Windows. It adds a number of calculations that are considered outside the regular mathematical operations. They cover trigonometric, logarithmic, and exponential operations and are as follows:

- **10^n**: This returns 10 raised to the specified power
- **ArcTangentFunctoid**: This returns the arc tangent of a number
- **Base-specified Logarithm**: This returns the base-specified logarithm of a value
- **Common Logarithm**: This returns the base 10 logarithm of a value
- **Cosine**: It returns the cosine of an angle
- **Natural Exponential Function**: This returns e raised to the specified power
- **Natural Logarithm**: This returns the base e logarithm of a value
- **Sine**: This returns the sine of an angle
- **Tangent**: This returns the tangent of an angle
- **X^Y**: This returns the specified value, raised to the power of a specified second value

All Functoids take one argument with the exception of the Base-specified Logarithm and the X^Y Functoids, which take two.

String Functoids

The String Functoids are relatively simple but extremely useful string manipulation or exploratory Functoids. They are as follows:

- Lowercase
- Uppercase
- String Concatenate
- String Left
- String Right
- String Left Trim
- String Right Trim
- String Find
- String Extract
- Size

Most Functoids in this category map to the corresponding .NET functions such as `ToLower`, `ToUpper`, `Substring`, `TrimStart`, `TrimEnd`, `IndexOf,` and `Length`.

> String Functoids that refer to a position within the string will refer to the first character as position 1 and not 0.

Using Advanced Functoids

The Advanced Functoids help in five areas, which are as follows:

- Looping
- Conditional Mapping (which also makes use of the Logical Functoids)
- Copy-based Mapping
- Troubleshooting and Testing
- Scripting is done using external assemblies, inline code, or XSLT

In Visual Studio Toolbox, these Functoids are all under the Advanced Functoids category, there are no subcategories. In this book, we will use the preceding use cases to highlight some of the areas where these Functoids are valuable.

Looping

Most of the advanced Functoids deal with looping. In this subcategory, these Functoids exist as follows:

- Index
- Iteration
- Nil Value
- Record Count
- Looping
- Table Looping
- Table Extractor

Index

The Index Functoid will return a specific node in a looping node structure; for example, the second **Component** node in the **Components** structure is always the engine. The following Map gets the **Code** attribute of the **Component** record corresponding to Engine by supplying the **Code** attribute as the first parameter and 2 as the second parameter.

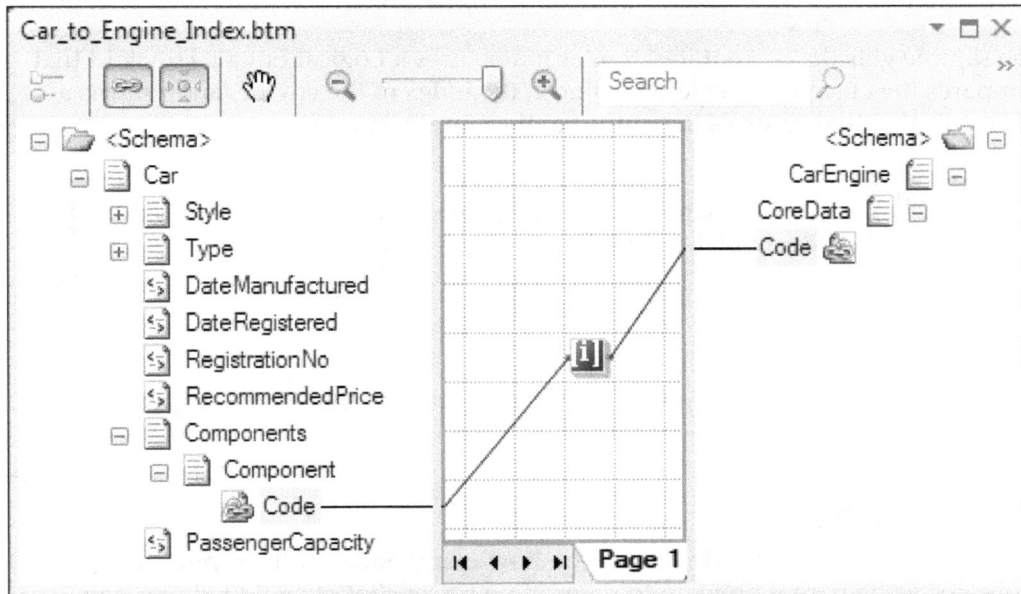

Iterator

The Iteration Functoid will tell you what the index of the current nodes is in a looping node structure. The same sample as the one in the preceding screenshot can be used to show a sample use of the Iteration Functoid, which is as follows:

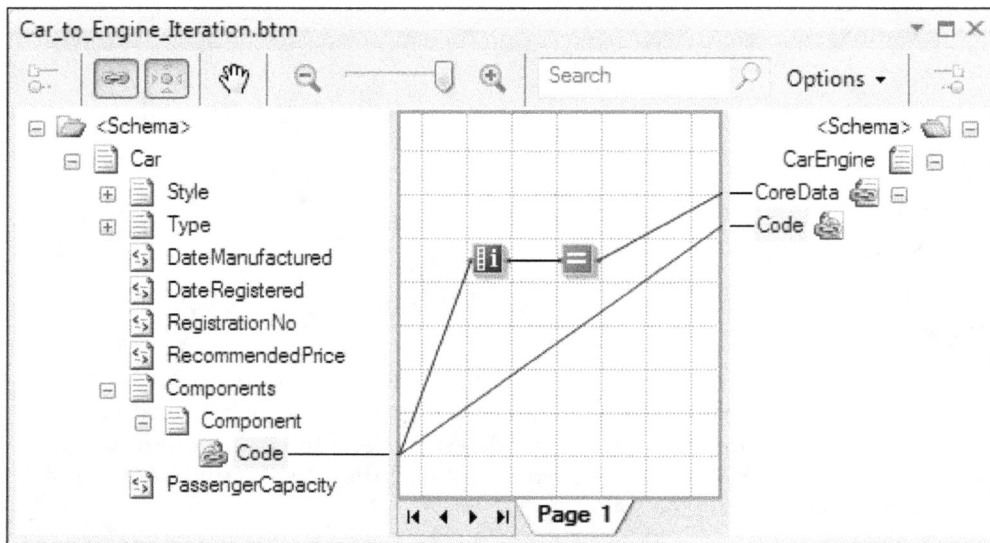

The sample gets the current iteration or index, uses a Logical Equals Functoid that compares the current index to the value 2, the index of the engine, and returns a Boolean value that controls the output of the **CoreData** node.

> All Functoids that return a Boolean value can be used this way to control the output.

Nil

The Nil Value Functoid will give a record a `null` value, that is, it will give it a `xsi:nil` attribute set to `true`.

Record Count

The Record Count Functoid will tell you how many nodes of the input type are under the same parent node. In the preceding screenshot, it could tell you how many **Component** nodes there are.

Looping

The Looping Functoid will help the mapper understand how you want looping to occur. The Mapper automatically understands that it needs to loop if you are mapping from one simple looping structure to another. It will automatically insert code to do the looping and extract the values. However, in cases where several loops are involved, it needs guidance. For example, if you want to combine multiple input elements into a single output element or loop over and combine multiple source looping structures while you create the output, you need to convey that instruction to the Mapper by using a Looping Functoid. The latter is shown in the following screenshot:

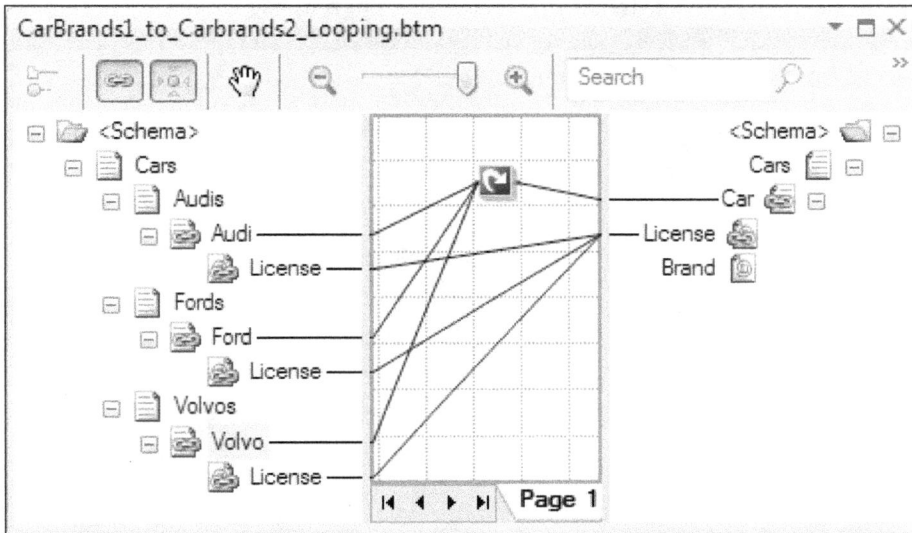

The previous example works only due to the use of the Looping Functoids. Had it not been for the Looping Functoids, only the **Audi** license would be outputted, and we would get a warning in our **Output** window in Visual Studio, which is as follows:

```
CarBrands1_to_Carbrands2_Looping.btm: warning btm1030: The destination
node "Car" has multiple source loop paths.
```

```
CarBrands1_to_Carbrands2_Looping.btm: warning btm1004: The destination
node "License" has multiple inputs. For a destination node to have
multiple inputs, one of its ancestors should be connected to a looping
functoid.
```

> You can create conditional looping logic by connecting a Logical Functoid to the same destination node as the Looping Functoid.

Table Looping

The Table Looping Functoid is another way of controlling the looping structures. It lets us configure an internal table and the columns within it and fills the rows of that table using data such as nodes from the input Schema, links from other Functoids, or constants.

It allows you to create multiple output rows from one input row.

Creating many output nodes from one input node can be done in many different ways. For example, if we map from Carbrands2 to Carbrands1 we can once again use Logical Functoids to control our output, as shown in the following screenshot:

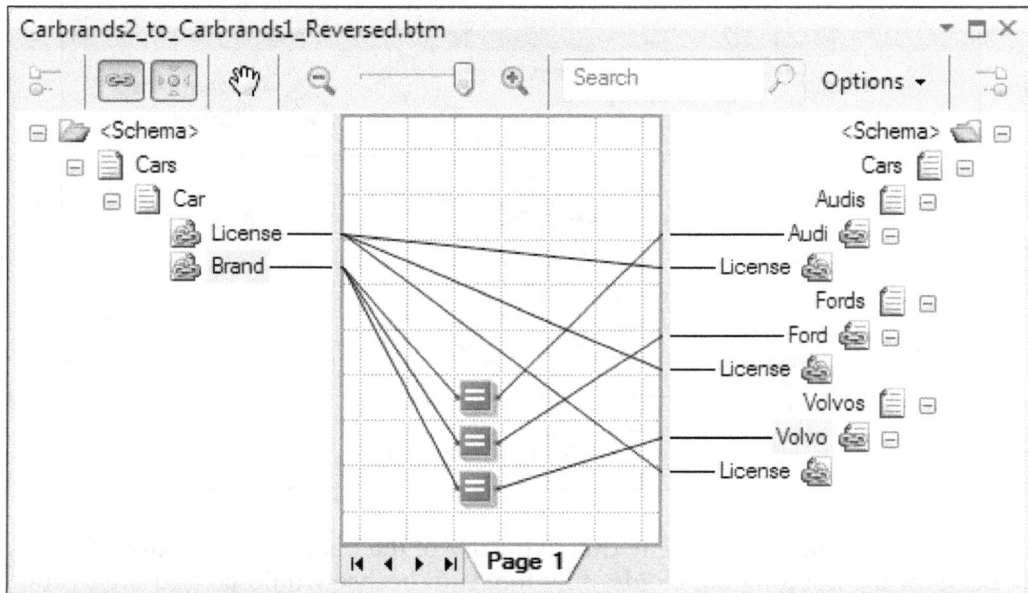

This will work fine. It is when you need to create two rows in the same destination structure based on only the single input that it gets difficult.

Let us look at a sample in which the use of Table Looping Functoid solves a mapping challenge. The car manufacturer HWLC Motors is selling directly to consumers as well as leasing firms and dealerships. As a part of the process for selling a car, HWLC needs to update the **customer relationship management (CRM)** system. It keeps information on cars sold, who the current owner is, and who the actual person using the car is (which is important for leasing, but not so for consumers).

In the case of a consumer, the buyer of the car will be both the owner and the user. Let us go through the steps to complete this Map:

1. Create a new Map with the appropriate Schemas, as shown in the following screenshot:

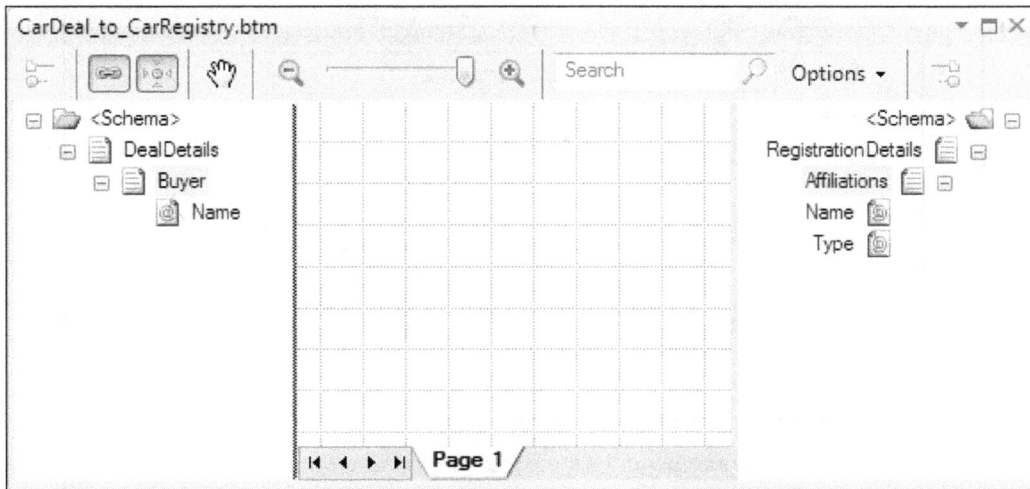

2. Drag-and-drop a **Table Looping** Functoid onto the mapping surface.
3. Link the **Buyer** node to the **Table Looping** Functoid to create a scoping link, and connect the **Table Looping** Functoid to the **Affiliations** destination node.
4. Right-click on the **Table Looping** Functoid, and select **Configure Functoid Inputs**.
5. Enter 2 as the second input for two columns.
6. Enter the string Owner as the value for the third parameter.
7. Create a fourth parameter, and enter the string User as the value.
8. Click on **OK** to close the Functoid configuration.
9. Link the **Name** column to the **Table Looping** Functoid.
10. Right-click on the **Table Looping** Functoid, and select **Configure Table Looping Grid**.

11. Create two rows, one with Name and Owner, and one with Name and User, as shown in the following screenshot:

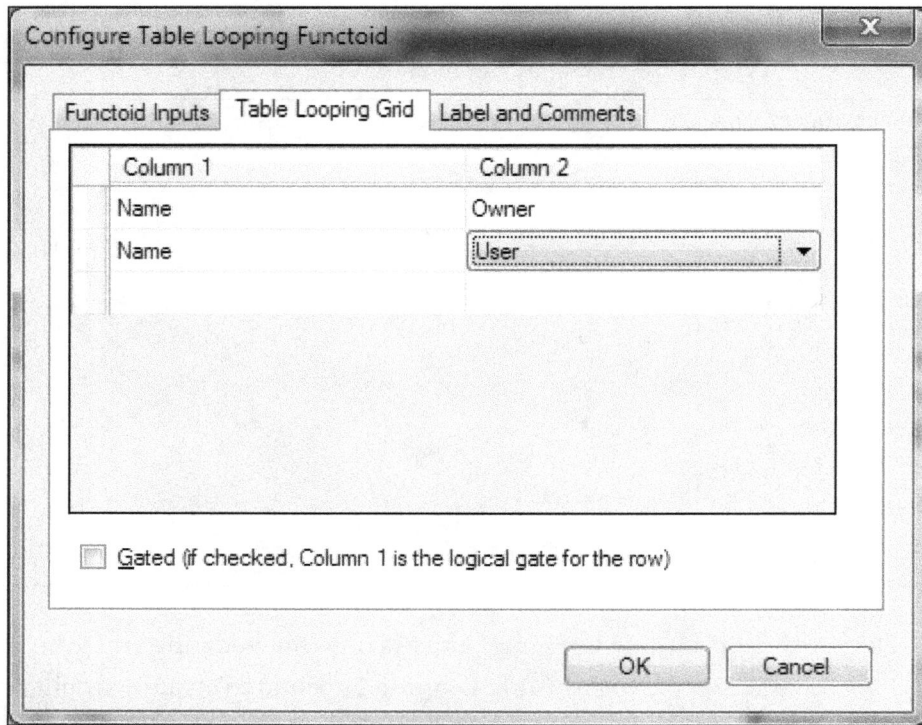

12. Click on OK to close the Functoid configuration.

    Next, to get anything out of the Table Looping Functoid, we need to use Table Extractor. It takes two inputs: the Table Looping Functoid and the number of columns to retrieve the value from. In this case, we need two Functoids, one for each of our columns.

13. Drop two **Table Extractor** Functoids onto the Mapper, and connect both of them to the **Table Looping** Functoid.

14. Configure the first Functoid to use **Column 1** and the second to use **Column 2**.

15. Connect them to **Name** and **Type** in the destination respectively.

16. The finished result should be similar to the following screenshot:

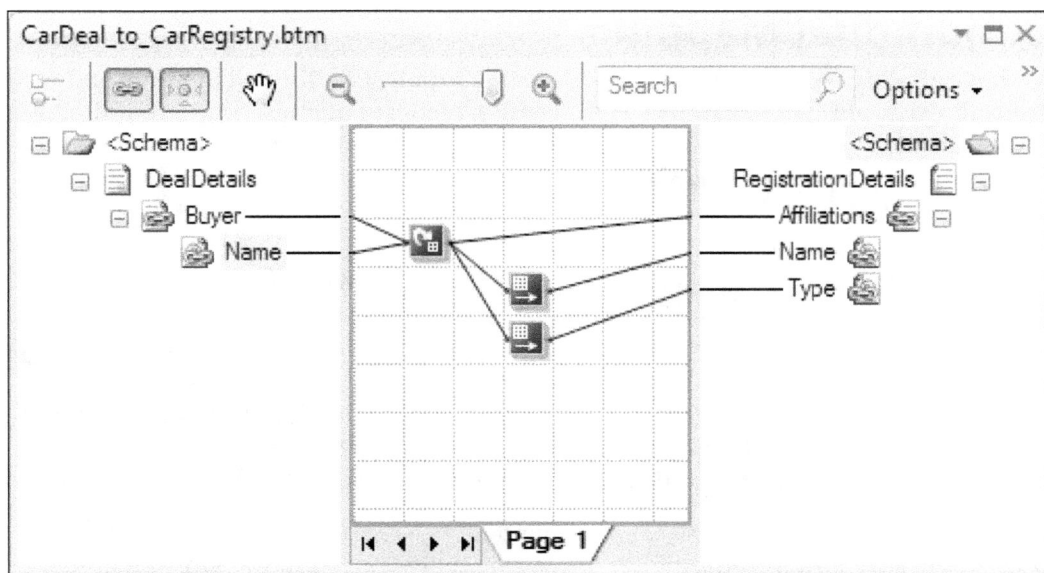

17. The input looks like the following code snippet:

```
<ns0:DealDetails
  MLns:ns0="http://Chapter03_Example01_Schemas.CarDeal">
<Buyer Name="Felix" />
</ns0:DealDetails>
```

18. We will have an output that looks like the following code snippet:

```
<ns0:RegistrationDetails
  XMLns:ns0=
  "http://Chapter03_Example01_Schemas.CarRegistry">
<Affiliations Name="Felix" Type="Owner"></Affiliations>
<Affiliations Name="Felix" Type="User"></Affiliations>
</ns0:RegistrationDetails>
```

Conditional Mapping

We have already seen samples of conditional mapping, conditional looping, and controlling output. These samples were using a Logical Functoid connected directly to the output. The Functoids that fall under Conditional Mapping Functoids in the advanced category are the Value Mapping Functoid and the Value Mapping (Flattening) Functoid.

> The Value Mapping Functoid is often used in conjunction with the Looping Functoid. The Value Mapping (Flattening) Functoid, on the other hand, should not be used in conjunction with the Looping Functoid.

The main difference between the two is that while the Value Mapping Functoid will create one output for each input row, the Value Mapping (Flattening) Functoid will flatten the input into a single output row, as you will see in the following example.

We will use the same `CarRegistry` Schema that we created in the Table Looping sample for input and for output. Let us assume that we need to transform that to a more typed registry, where the `Owner` and `User` of the car exist as nodes.

The input is as follows:

```
<ns0:RegistrationDetails
  XMLns:ns0="http://Chapter03_Example01_Schemas.CarRegistry">
<Affiliations Name="Felix" Type="Owner"></Affiliations>
<Affiliations Name="Felix" Type="User"></Affiliations>
</ns0:RegistrationDetails>
```

The Map used is shown in the following screenshot:

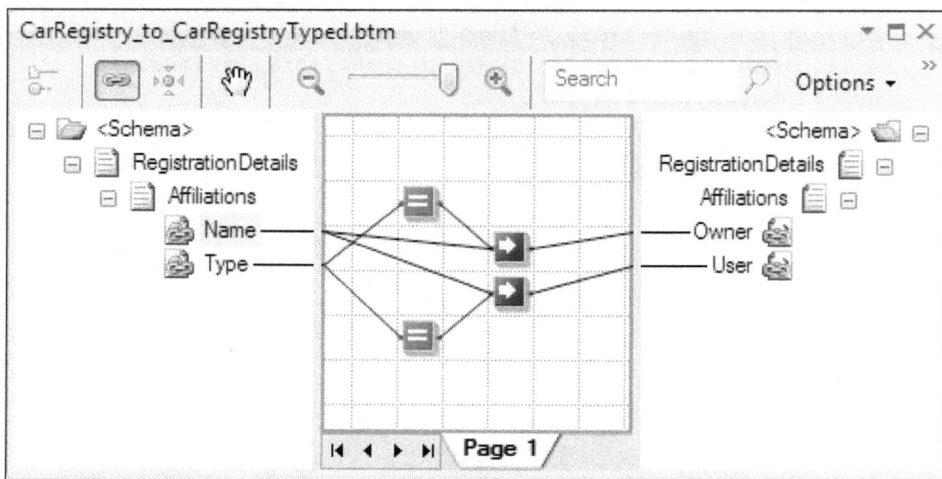

Using the Value Mapping Functoid, we will get the following output:

```
<ns0:RegistrationDetails
  XMLns:ns0=
  "http://Chapter03_Example01_Schemas.CarRegistryTyped1">
<Affiliations>
<Owner>Felix</Owner>
</Affiliations>
<Affiliations>
<User>Felix</User>
</Affiliations>
</ns0:RegistrationDetails>
```

Now on the other hand, if we create a new Map that looks exactly the same, with the only difference being that we replace the Value Mapping Functoid with the Value Mapping (Flattening) Functoid, we will get a different result. The Map is shown in the following screenshot:

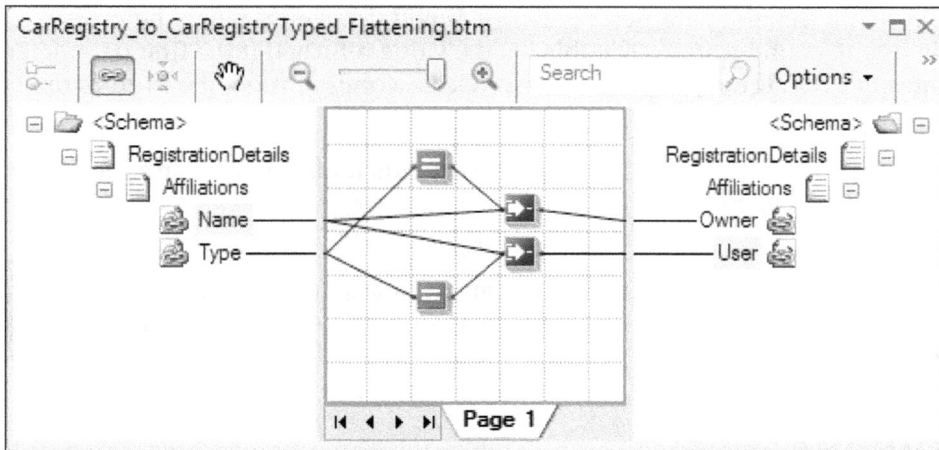

Our (flattened) output is as follows:

```
<ns0:RegistrationDetails
  XMLns:ns0=
  "http://Chapter03_Example01_Schemas.CarRegistryTyped1">
<Affiliations>
<Owner>Felix</Owner>
<User>Felix</User>
</Affiliations>
</ns0:RegistrationDetails>
```

As you can see, it no longer creates two rows for the output but instead compacts both of them into one.

Copy-based Mapping

The Copy-based messaging subcategory, or the simple mapping category as the BizTalk Server documentation calls it, consists of one single Functoid, that is, the Mass Copy Functoid. It does something very simple by recreating the linked input node and everything beneath it at the specified location in the output. It can simplify the Schema development, where only the parts of a large Schema structure that are used need to be defined. The rest can be hidden under an xs:any node as unknown content. It is also useful while mapping between two Schemas with the same structure, or even the same Schema when you want to do some small calculation or a similar small operation, yet do not want to relink all the nodes.

Troubleshooting

This category holds the Assert Functoid. It takes three parameters. The first is a Boolean value that indicates Error or Success. The second is the string thrown in an exception if the first parameter is false. It will do so only when the project is built in debug configuration. The third is the value returned if the first parameter evaluates to true. If the project is built in release configuration, the third parameter will always be returned.

Since the first parameter is Boolean, the Assert Functoids are often used together with the Logical Functoids.

> The Assert Functoid must still, like any other Functoid, be either directly or indirectly connected to an output node for it to trigger.

Scripting

The Scripting Functoid is the most advanced Functoid available. It gives you a multitude of options on how to extend and expand on the functionality of BizTalk Mapper. You have the following options:

- External Assembly (default)
- Inline C#
- Inline JScript
- Inline Visual Basic .NET
- Inline XSLT
- Inline XSLT Call Template

Most of the things, if not everything, that you can do with other Functoids, can be done with the Scripting Functoids. Through the use of external assemblies and inline code, you will be able to chain and make use of multiple Scripting Functoids that save values in internal .NET variables for inter-Functoid communication, and gain the access to the full array of the .NET functionality coupled with the full power of going directly to XSLT, when you need it. The Scripting Functoid really does offer endless possibilities.

> "With great power comes great responsibility". Even though you can use Scripting Functoids to do just about everything, you should not. Designing and developing a good maintainable Map is all about visibility and comprehension in your modeling. One of the unique selling points of BizTalk Mapper is the fact that it is a model. It is easy to change as it is all really visual. Over-using Scripting Functoids will seriously cripple that intention.

Using external assemblies

There are a lot of benefits of storing code outside your Map. The rule of thumb is that anything bigger than the editing window will benefit from being stored outside the Map. Placing the code in a library makes it easier to unit test, maintain and update, and debug, and also enables code sharing. It also gives you an extra component to deploy and manage. The bigger-than-editor-window rule is a bit crude, but if you follow regular common sense, it will usually be okay.

These are the steps required to call an external assembly using the Scripting Functoid:

1. Identify or create an external assembly that has a method that you would like to call. In this example, we are using a method that has the following signature:

```
public static string Reverse(string s)
{
  return new string(s.Reverse().ToArray());
}
```

2. Drop a Scripting Functoid onto the Map.

3. Configure the **Scripting** Functoid to use an **External Assembly**, and set
   Script assembly, **Script class**, and **Script method** according to your needs;
   for example, using a **HelperLibrary** assembly with a **CodeHelper** class and
   a **Reverse** method, as shown in the following screenshot:

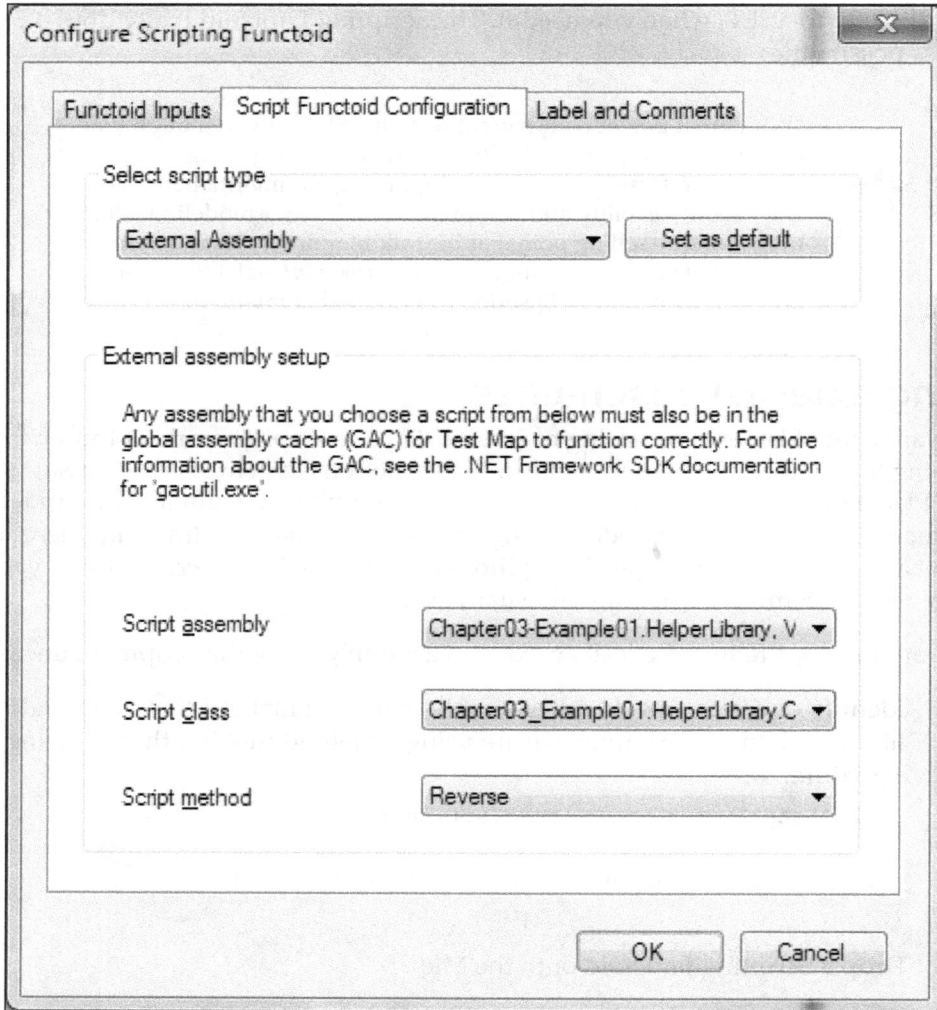

4. Click on **OK** and connect the **Scripting** Functoid according to the input
   parameters of the method and to a destination node in the output or a
   subsequent Functoid, as shown in the following screenshot:

SimplifiedCar_to_SimplfiedCar_Scripting.btm   ▾ ☐ ✕

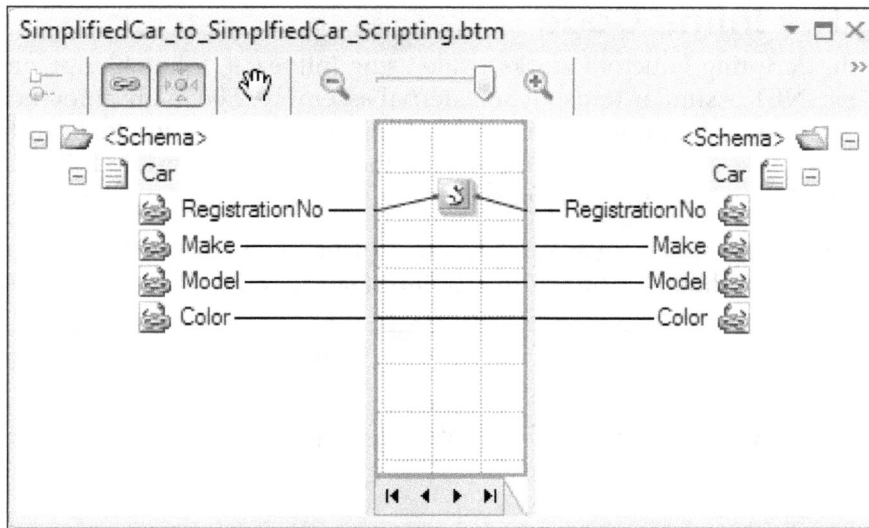

> Before we test the Map, we need to make sure that
> HelperLibrary is in the **Global Assembly Cache** (**GAC**).
> We can develop without it but cannot run Test Map.

5. We test the Map using the following input:

```
<ns0:Car
  XMLns:ns0=
  "http://Chapter03_Example01.Schemas.SimplifiedCar">
<RegistrationNo>RegistrationNo_0</RegistrationNo>
</ns0:Car>
```

6. We get the following output, that is, my external component has been called
and executed correctly:

```
<ns0:Car
  XMLns:ns0=
  "http://Chapter03_Example01.Schemas.SimplifiedCar">
<RegistrationNo>0_oNnoitartsigeR</RegistrationNo>
</ns0:Car>
```

Using the Inline Code

The way the Scripting Functoid works while using Inline C#, Inline JScript, or Inline Visual Basic .NET is similar to using an external assembly. The main difference is that the code is stored within the Map instead and the configuration looks different. You also don't have access to the full power of the .NET framework in Inline Code but are limited to only a few namespaces.

The following screenshot is an example of configuring the Scripting Functoid using **Inline C#** and a method that transforms an input string to uppercase:

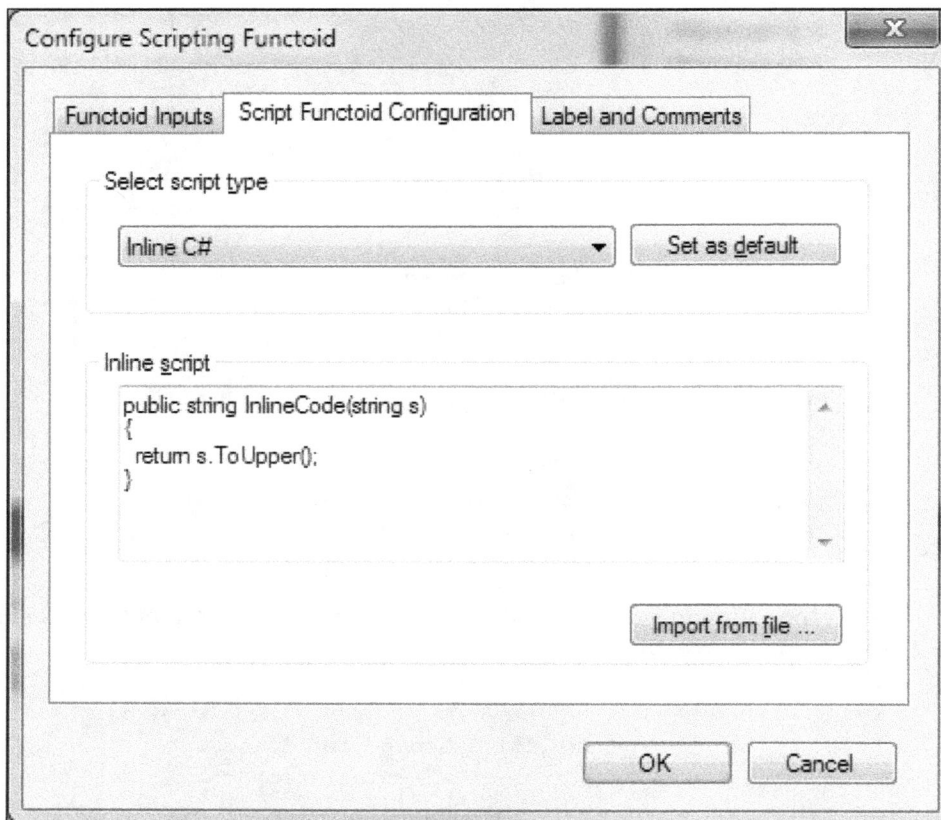

> The preceding example serves as an example of how to use the Scripting Functoid with Inline C# and at the same time serves as an anti-pattern that people fall into too often. You should not implement something with the Scripting Functoid that already exists. In this case, the Uppercase Functoid should have been used instead.

Besides the code contained within the method signature, choosing the inline code also allows us to declare global variables outside the method declaration. These are accessible throughout the Map from within all Inline Code Scripting Functoids.

Just like when it is configured to use an external assembly, the Scripting Functoid used with the inline code can take its input from several sources, such as input nodes or other Functoids, and its output may be linked to output nodes or to other Functoids similarly.

Using Inline XSLT

Using Inline XSLT allows us to use the power of XSLT directly. This gives us more freedom in accessing the full document in a way that other Functoids normally are not capable of doing.

Since we are running XSLT, the Scripting Functoid using any of the XSLT options can only be connected to an output node as it explicitly creates an XML structure.

The difference between the two options, that is, Inline XSLT and Inline XSLT Call Template, is that while the former is not allowed to take inputs, the latter is.

In advanced scenarios, XSLT Scripts may access global variables created in the inline code as well as call the inline code methods and external assemblies.

Let us look at a simple example of using XSLT inside a Map. In the following Inline XSLT sample, the XSLT has the same effect as a direct link, but XSLT can do so much more. Even if the example itself is simple, it does show one of XSLT's many powerful features: the ability to access any part of the source document regardless of the context. In this case, it finds the `RegistrationNo` node and outputs its value to the destination, as shown in the following screenshot:

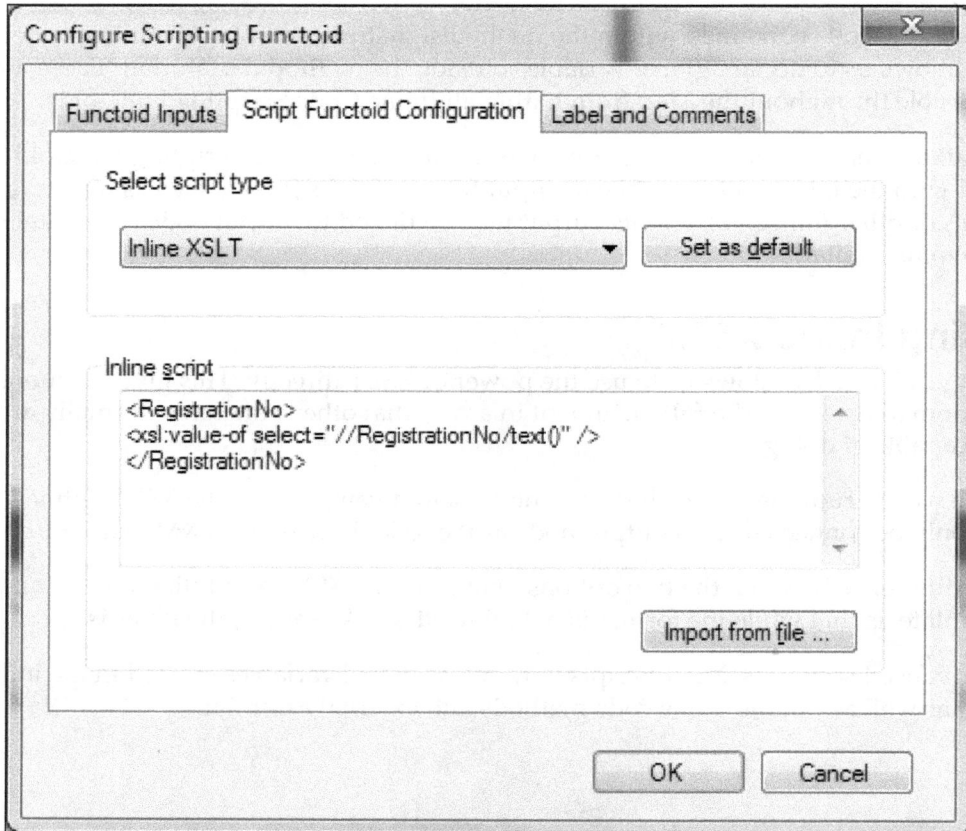

The Map looks similar to the following screenshot:

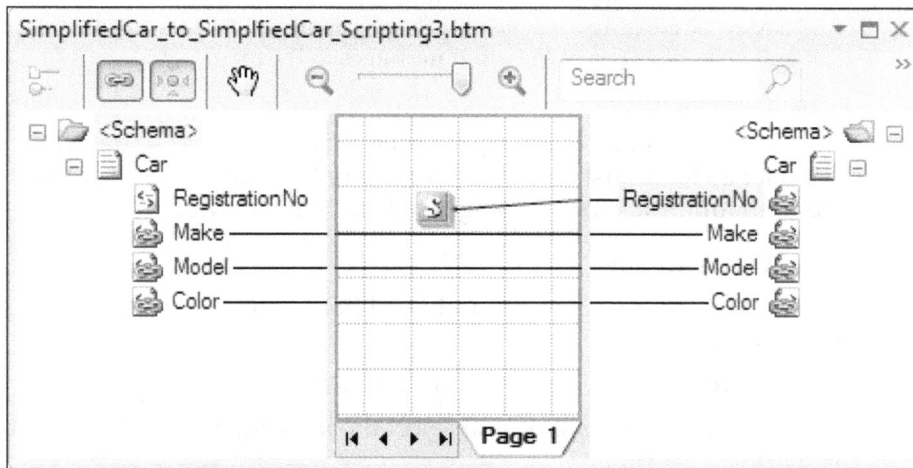

If we were to use an Inline XSLT Call Template instead, we would be able to take in a parameter but other than this, it behaves exactly the same and has the same benefits and limitations.

> There is also the possibility of sidestepping the BizTalk Mapper altogether by using the Custom XSLT property on a Map. It allows us to point to a file that contains a fully custom XSLT Script that is then responsible for the full Map. While opinions differ, it is generally agreed that this option should not be taken unless performance optimization or specific requirements such as sorting or grouping make it a much better and perhaps even the only option.

Maps and Orchestrations

Maps are normally configured to run in one of the three places: Receive Ports, Send Ports, or Orchestrations. There are some Maps that can only be created inside Orchestrations, specifically the Maps using multiple input messages to produce their output or though more uncommon, Maps that create multiple outputs.

XSLT only works with one input message and one output. The way Orchestration Designer works around this is by creating a temporary multipart message that is used as an input to the Map, where each of the parts contains the message details of the messages used. This is configured through the Transform shape. Should you need multiple outputs, the same concept will apply.

> You can also use the concept of multipart messages to pass parameters to a Map by creating a Schema for the parameter and a message to hold it and using it as one of the input messages to the map.

Orchestrations are covered in *Chapter 4, Developing BizTalk Artifacts – Creating Orchestrations*. So let us focus just on how to configure the Transform shape to perform a Map with multiple input messages, which is as follows:

1. Create an Orchestration.

2. Create the messages and Receive and Send Ports that you need to gather the information.

3. Drop a **Transform** shape into Orchestration Designer.

4. Configure the **Construct** shape and select the message that will be created by the map.

5. Open the **Transform** shape configuration, and select the messages that you need to use as input. Each message will become part of the multipart message, as shown in the following screenshot:

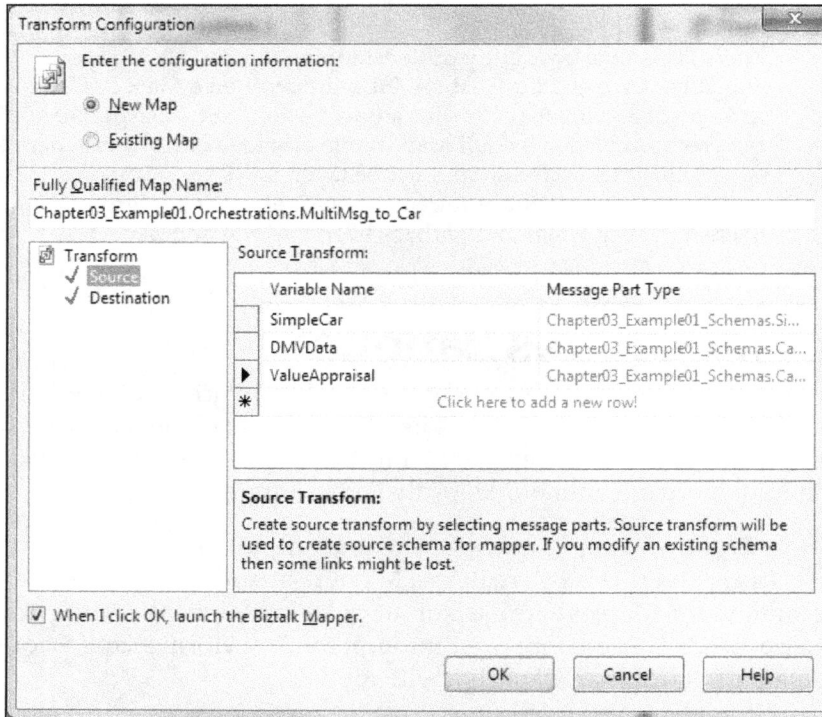

6. Click on **OK** to open the Mapper.

7. You can now see the multipart message; each selected message is contained within the parts; for example, messages such as **Car**, **DMVData**, and **CarValue** are shown in the following screenshot:

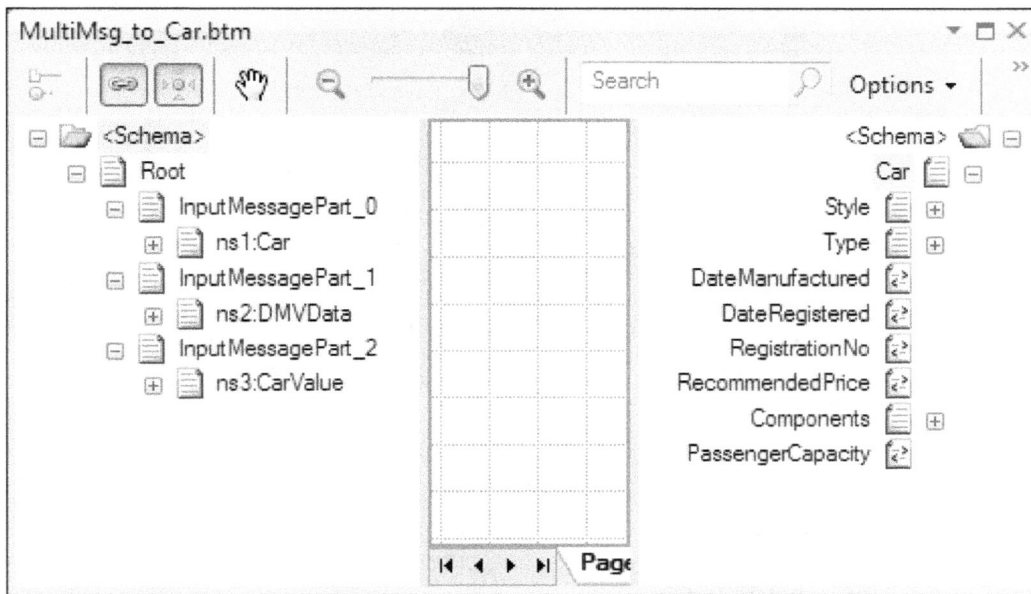

8. Complete the Map as shown in the following screenshot:

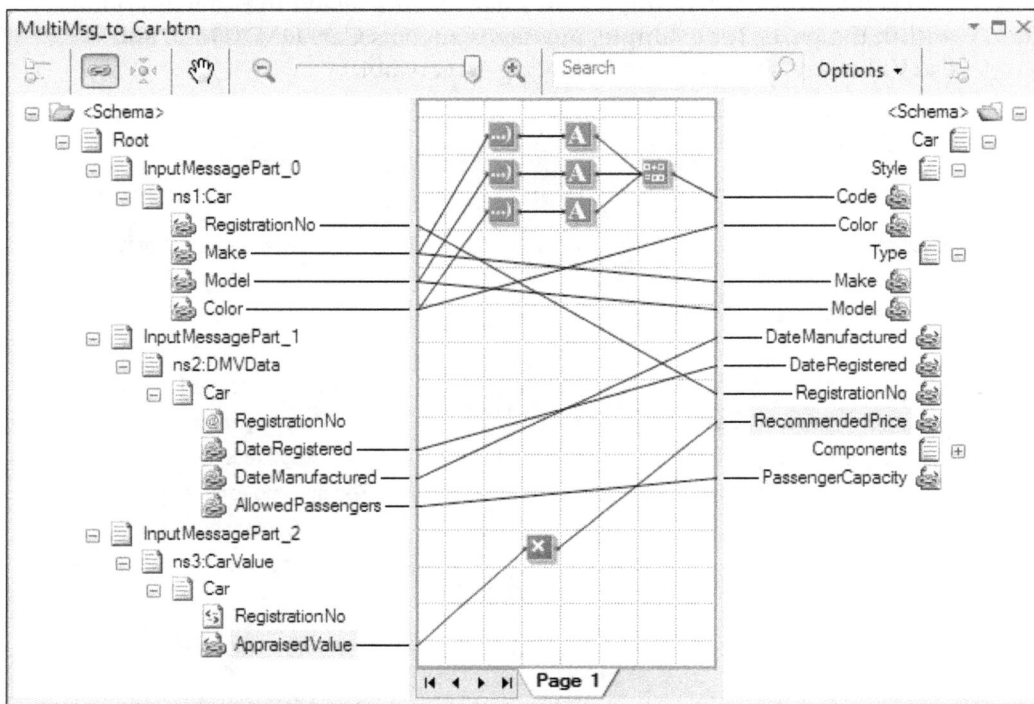

Testing your knowledge

Based upon what you have learned in this chapter, answer the following questions:

1. As part of a transformation, you need to re-use a piece of business logic previously defined in a method in a .NET component. You need to do this without writing any additional lines of code. What do you need to do to call the method from the transformation?

   a. Use the Expression shape and call the component using a XLANG statement.

   b. Use the Scripting Functoid, configure it to use Inline C#, and call the method using a C# statement.

   c. Use the Scripting Functoid, configure it to use an External Assembly, and call the method by pointing out the assembly, class and method.

    d. Drag-and-drop the activity created when you add a reference to the component to the mapping surface, and configure inputs and outputs.

2. HWLC Motors is starting a marketing campaign and wants to target strong customers that bought high-end cars. You are developing a Map that is going to process an input Schema that contains a list of customer nodes containing CustomerID and CarValue as child nodes. The output document is the same as the input document. You want to only include those customers whose cars had a value above $70,000 in the output. What do you need to do?

    a. Add an Equal Functoid. Link CarValue as the first input, and set the second input to 70000. Connect the output to the Customer node in the destination Schema.

    b. Add a Greater Than Functoid. Link the CarValue node as the first input, and set the second input to 70000. Connect the output to the Customer node in the destination Schema.

    c. Add a Less Than Functoid. Link the CarValue node as the first input, and set the second input to 70000. Connect the output to the Customer node in the destination Schema.

    d. Add a Value Mapping Functoid. Connect the CarValue node as the first input, and set the second input to 70000. Connect the output to the CarValue node in the destination Schema.

Summary

In this chapter, we learned about creating Maps and using Functoids. We took a closer look at connecting to a database as well as controlling looping, doing conditional mapping, and other advanced Functoids. The Scripting Functoid was examined closely and the options it enabled for integrating with external assemblies and writing XSLT Scripts. We also looked at using Maps from within Orchestrations to enable multipart Schema maps and talked about what options there are for testing the Maps. The next chapter is about developing the BizTalk artifacts—creating Orchestrations—as a part of the exam.

4
Developing BizTalk Artifacts – Creating Orchestrations

This chapter covers Orchestrations and Orchestration shapes and logic. It will provide an overview of all shapes and go into the details of a couple of them, such as using the Expression shapes to call additional logic in .NET components. It talks about how an Orchestration gets activated by subscribing to messages, getting called or started as well as dives deep into the port bindings that are available, and how to use them. We will also take a closer look at persistence, transactions, and scopes, though using scopes for exception handling and compensation will be covered in the next chapter. This chapter will cover the following:

- Developing Orchestrations
- Configuring Orchestration bindings
- Configuring correlation
- Testing your knowledge

Developing Orchestrations

Many integrations are based on pure messaging scenarios, that is, they do not need Orchestrations. They consist of receiving a message through an adapter, applying some form of transformations to the message, routing it to one or more subscribers, and sending them out again, using the same or another adapter. They might also require a response. In cases where that response is synchronous, and the ports are configured with the request-response message exchange pattern, this can be handled without an Orchestration. However, as soon as you require more control, you use an Orchestration. This could, for example, be when you want more control over exception handling or when an integration implies more than one logical step.

It is usually stated that Orchestrations exist to coordinate business processes. You could drop the word "business" from that. In a nutshell, the Orchestration engine is the workflow engine employed by BizTalk Server to allow you to handle various processes, whether they have their roots based in business or technology. Orchestrations are based on the C#-like language named **XLANG/s**. Though you sometimes resort to writing XLANG/s statements directly, you most often work with modeling your process using Orchestration shapes and setting properties.

Basic shapes and configuration

Orchestrations and the executable processes they implement are modeled using a sequence of shapes. Each shape has a distinct meaning and usage. The shapes can be divided into five areas, as follows:

- Message and data handling
- Containers
- Flow Control
- Orchestration nesting
- Other

The available shapes are the ones you have to work with. Orchestration shapes are not an area of extensibility. You do, however, like with the Scripting Functoid for Maps, have a way of writing code or calling external components to perform processing. In Orchestrations, this has the form of the Expression shape.

Message and data handling

Within this category, there are shapes that help to receive, send, construct, transform, or assign message variables as follows:

Shape	Description
Receive	Used to receive a message.
	A selection of its properties is as follows:
	• Activate
	• Initializing Correlation Sets
	• Following Correlation Sets
Send	Used to send a message.
	A selection of its properties is as follows:
	• Initializing Correlation Sets
	• Following Correlation Sets
Construct Message	Used as a parent container to any of the two message-constructing shapes.
	The possible nested shapes are as follows:
	• Message Assignment
	• Transform
	A selected property is as follows:
	• Messages Constructed
Message Assignment	Used to assign a value to a message or to part of a message; for example, assignment to a node through the use of a distinguished field. It is also used to assign values to context available as promoted properties as well as anything you can do in an Expression shape.
	A selected property is as follows:
	• Expression
Transform	Used to apply a Map to transform a message constructing a new message.
	A selection of its properties is as follows:
	• Input Messages
	• Output Messages
	• Map Name

Some shapes require nesting, such as the Assign and Transform shapes, which always need to be put into a Construct shape, as shown in the following diagram:

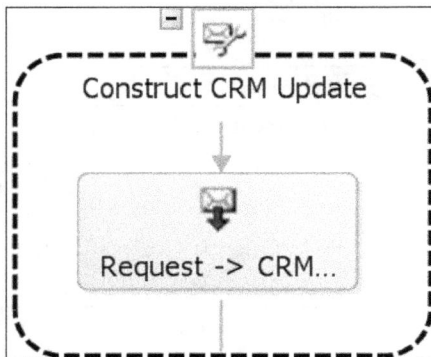

Containers

Containers are shapes that, either visually or technically, group other shapes, as follows:

Shape	Description
Group	Used to visually group shapes together and be able to expand and collapse that view in Orchestration Designer. These are also not part of the code at all (similar to a region in C#).
Scope	Used to divide logic into units of work or transactions that may make use of exception handling or compensation. Scopes are diversified and have many interesting properties. Scopes are similar to the combination of TransactionScope and a try/catch block in C#.

Flow control

Orchestrations are technical implementations of processes. The flow of information contained in messages is core to that implementation, and there are many shapes available to handle that flow, which are as follows:

Shape	Description
Decide	Used to create different branches of logic, based on `if`, `else if` (..., `else if`, ...), and `else` types of conditions. Each `if` branch takes an XLANG/s expression evaluating to `true` or `false`. Only one of the branches will execute.
Delay	Used to create a delay based on `TimeSpan` in your Orchestration. A selected property is as follows: • Delay allows you to create a new `TimeSpan` object to configure the delay.
Listen	Used to create different branches of logic, based on messages received or a timeout value. A Delay shape is used to configure the timeout. Only one of the branches will execute.
Loop	Used to create a looping logic similar to a `while` statement, where an XLANG/s statement that must be `true` before each execution of the contained logic is evaluated.
Parallel actions	Used to perform two or more independent branches of logic where all branches execute before continuing to the next shape after the Parallel shape.
Suspend	Used to suspend an Orchestration instance to allow administrative action to be taken. An administrator can then either resume or terminate the Orchestration instance. If `Resume` is chosen, execution will continue from the next shape. A selected property is as follows: • Error Message

Shape	Description
Terminate	Used to end the execution of the Orchestration instance. It is often used after handling an exception and possibly (although less often) while ending up in a branch of logic where no more work is required by the Orchestration. A selected property is as follows: • Error Message
Throw Exception	Used to forcefully throw an exception, for example, after evaluating data or some logical condition. A selected property is as follows: • Exception Object, referring to a variable of base type `Exception` caught within an exception block or created in an expression
Compensate	Used to call the compensation block of nested scopes. One compensation shape is required per nested compensation block to be called.

Orchestration nesting

Orchestrations can be nested and called from other Orchestrations, similar to methods in .NET. The shapes that control that are as follows:

Shape	Description
Call Orchestration	Allows to *synchronously* start another Orchestration and hold additional execution until it is completed. A selection of its properties is as follows: • Called Orchestration • Parameters (in and out)
Start Orchestration	Allows to *asynchronously* start another Orchestration. Processing in the calling Orchestration will continue to the next shape as soon as the Orchestration has been started and will not await the outcome. A selection of its properties are as follows: • Called Orchestration • Parameters (in only)

Other

These shapes are dynamic and either allow for advanced message processing, decision making, or actions through calling Business Rules, or allow for making arbitrary XLANG/s statements through calling .NET helper components. The shapes are as follows:

Shape	Description
Call Rules	Allows calling of Business Rules from within Orchestrations. Uses of Business Rules will be covered in a later chapter.
Expression	Allows to write XLANG/s statements that provide C#-syntax like inline coding capabilities. You can read message and context properties, read or write Orchestration variables, or access .NET class members. But you cannot do more complex statements or flow controlling logic such as if statements or for loops, unless inside a called .NET component.

> More information about the limitations and structure of the XLANG/s language can be found at http://msdn.microsoft.com/en-us/library/aa577463(v=BTS.70).aspx.

Orchestration activation

Orchestrations can be activated in one of two ways: by a message that matches the Orchestrations activation subscription or by the Orchestration that is called from another Orchestration. The Orchestrations activation subscription is created based on the configuration of the activating Receive Port. This activation process is not arbitrary. Instead, you need to determine how an Orchestration should be activated when you design it. The next section will examine this process closer.

Activating Receive

An activating **Receive** shape is used when the Orchestration is first constructed. It is fulfilled by a message publication matching the activation subscription. This port can be of any binding type. The two main differentiators from any other port in the Orchestration are as follows:

1. The port is triggered by an activation subscription, based on **design-time-determined** filter criteria.

2. The **Receive** shape connected to the port is marked with **Activate** set to **True**, as shown in the following screenshot:

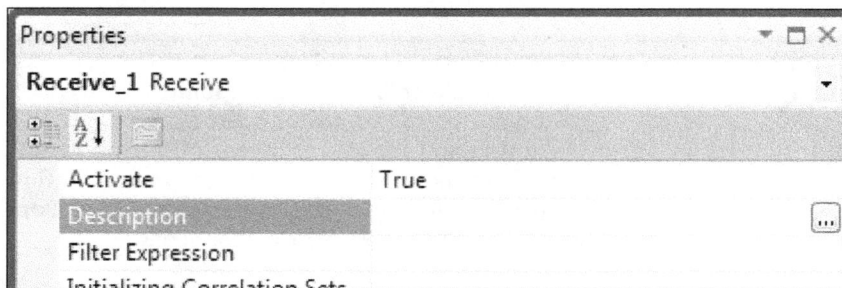

In this case, the **Filter** criteria for the subscription have not been set explicitly. We will examine when it is needed, and when it is not, later in this chapter, as we discuss port binding options. However, an activating **Receive** shape is the only shape that can include an explicit Filter expression.

Call and Start

Call or **Start** Orchestration is used when an Orchestration is used in the same way as a .NET method, that is, when it is called from another Orchestration directly using design-time coupling. Parameters are used to relay information. Such parameters might be variables, ports, messages, and so on.

Call is a direct **synchronous** instantiation that does not rely on message publication through the `MessageBox`. It waits for the called Orchestration to complete and then returns the control back to the caller. **Start** is a fire-and-forget style **asynchronous** instantiation that uses message publication through the `MessageBox`. A called Orchestration can return a response in the form of out or updated reference parameters, while a started Orchestration cannot return a result through parameters to its starter. However, it can use ports to receive a result.

Persistence

During the execution of an Orchestration, the state of the process is saved or persisted. This enables the Orchestration to recover from failures and retry or restart from a previous point of execution.

Persistence may occur at the following occasions:

- After the execution of a Send Port
- After the execution of a Start Orchestration shape
- After the successful execution (commit) of a transactional scope
- When the Orchestration instance is suspended
- When the Orchestration instance is completed
- When the Orchestration engine shuts down gracefully
- When a debugging breakpoint is hit
- When dehydration is determined appropriate by the engine

Persistence and **serialization** of the entire Orchestration, including all messages, variables, and state information, brings with it the requirement that everything used within an Orchestration must be serializable.

> If a class used within an Orchestration is not serializable, you must use it within a transactional scope marked as Atomic.

Dehydration and rehydration

Persistence also enables **dehydration** and **rehydration**, saving on precious processing resources by removing an Orchestration from active memory and serializing it to the database awaiting its next step (dehydration). For example, the correlation of a response message.

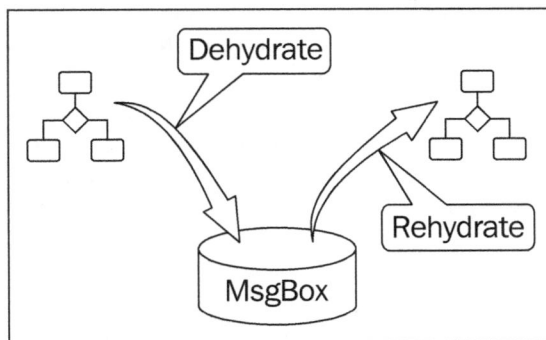

Once that event occurs, usually in the form of a message being published to the `MessageBox`, the Orchestration is rehydrated and the processing is continued.

The scenarios in which dehydration is considered by the engine are as follows:

- When the Orchestration instance is waiting for a response message
- When the Orchestration is listening for a message using the Listen shape
- When the Orchestration engine determines that it has reached an idle delay threshold

> The algorithm that the engine uses to determine dehydrations is based on the last 10 delays at that point in the Orchestration, and compared with a runtime calculated value that differs depending on available resources and other factors, but is between a configurable minimum and maximum time (that by default is 0 and 1800 seconds respectively).

Transactions

Orchestrations employ the use of transactions to compose operations in units or work, isolated from others, and to recover from failures.

Transactions in BizTalk Server can be either Long Running or Atomic.

Transaction types

Long Running transactions are Long Running units of work for which you want to have the ability to define custom compensating logic and exception handling, or those that need to serve as an **umbrella** for nested transactions. Long Running transactions persists state, and send operations are committed to the `MessageBox` and seen by subscribers immediately.

Atomic transactions are transactional and follow the **Atomicity, Consistency, Isolation**, and **Durability (ACID)** rules. Either everything within the transaction is correctly committed or none of it is. The persisted state of the Orchestration is either the state before the transaction began or the state after all operations are committed. The changes performed by any operation during the transaction, such as a message being published to the `MessageBox`, is not visible to anyone during the transaction but only after they are committed. Any changes, once committed, are persisted so that they are available, even if the system fails after the transaction is committed.

> Read more on the ACID rules of transactions at the following URL:
> http://en.wikipedia.org/wiki/ACID#Characteristics

Scopes

Scopes are the way to handle transactions within the Orchestrations.

All scopes have the following properties:

- Synchronized
- Transaction Type

Synchronized scopes ensures that the data being read is not simultaneously written to by other branches in a parallel shape. Scopes are, by default, not synchronized, though Atomic scopes are implicitly synchronized, regardless of the property value.

A scope can be marked as transactional by the **Transaction Type** property being set to either **Long Running** or **Atomic**. The third option for the **Transaction Type** property is **None**, as shown in the following screenshot:

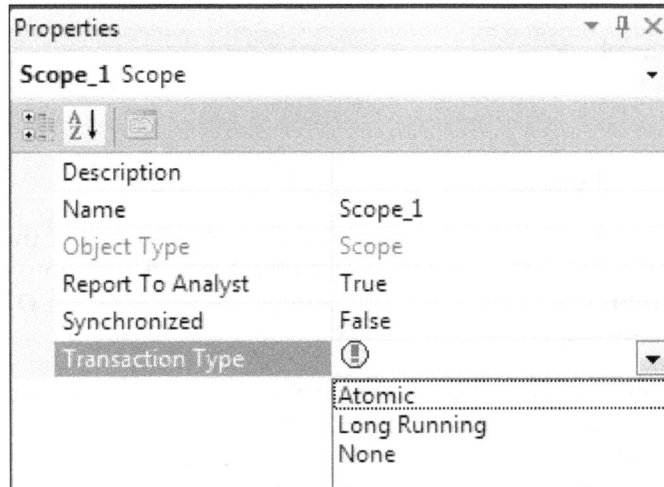

Properties	▼ ⁋ ✕
Scope_1 Scope	▼

Description	
Name	Scope_1
Object Type	Scope
Report To Analyst	True
Synchronized	False
Transaction Type	▣ ▼
	Atomic
	Long Running
	None

Long Running

While configuring the **Long Running** Transaction Type, the following additional properties (over a non-transactional scope) will become available:

- Compensation
- Timeout
- Transaction Identifier

Compensation can be **Default** or **Custom**. Setting it to **Custom** has the same effect as selecting to add a new Compensation Block to the scope. Compensation is covered further in *Chapter 5, Testing, Debugging, and Exception Handling*.

The Timeout property specifies the amount of time spent in the scope before TimeoutException is raised.

Atomic

While configuring the **Atomic** Transaction Type, the following additional properties (over a non-transactional scope) will become available:

- Compensation
- Isolation level
- Retry
- Timeout
- Transaction Identifier

For Atomic transaction, the Timeout value indicates the amount of time that passes before the transaction is marked as failed and is rolled back, but only if it was coordinated in a transaction together with another resource, by the **Distributed Transaction Coordinator** (DTC).

The Retry value indicates whether PersistenceException (caused by database connectivity issues) and RetryTransactionException (explicitly thrown in the Orchestration) should cause the transaction to be retried. Only these exceptions will be affected by the Retry flag. All other exceptions will cause the transaction to fail.

Isolation levels

Isolation levels control the locking levels used in the database by the engine while dealing with reads and writes for the actions performed by shapes in the scope. These transaction levels are available as follows:

- **Read Committed**: This reads only committed rows and prevents reading changes that are not yet committed by other transactions, but it does not prevent data it has read from being changed by other transactions before it is completed.

- **Repeatable Read**: This prevents updates to rows read by this scope until the transaction is completed.

- **Serializable**: This prevents data being committed by other transactions in such a way that queries used by this transaction would give a different result than when executed.

The default isolation level is `Serializable`.

Nesting

Long Running transactions can contain other transactions, either Long Running or Atomic. Atomic transactions can contain no other transactions.

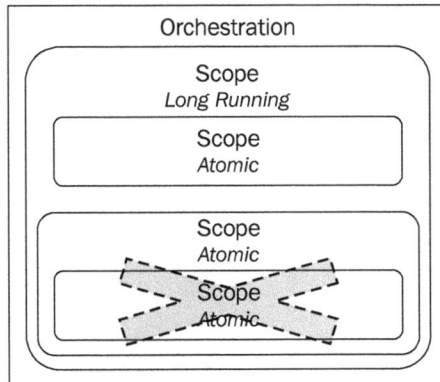

Conceptually, when it comes to transactions and nesting, you can look at the Orchestration level as a scope; that is, the Orchestration can be marked as a transaction in the same way as a scope. If you want to put an Atomic transactional scope directly inside the Orchestration, the Orchestration needs to be configured as Long Running.

Transaction reach

Another important concept about transactions in BizTalk Server is their reach. Transactions initiated in Orchestrations end in the MessageBox. This means that marking a scope as atomically transactional does not allow you to have a transactional conversation with the intended recipient of the message through the MessageBox from within the Orchestration. The reach of a transaction is depicted in the following diagram:

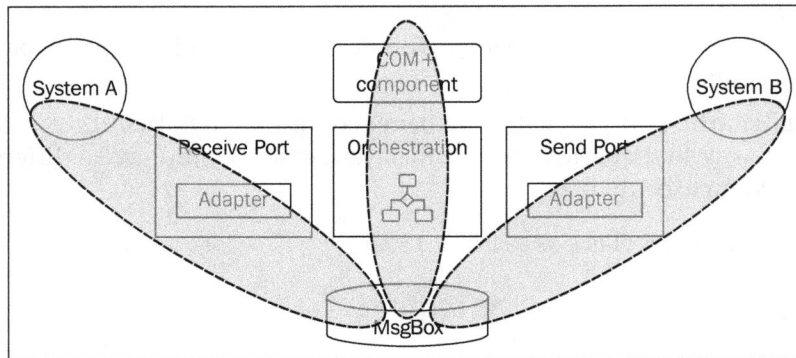

> As the diagram shows, it is possible to extend the reach of a transaction from an Orchestration to a COM+ (Enterprise Services-managed) component.

Storing configuration information

Many Orchestrations may rely on configuration parameters. There are different ways of supplying configuration to an Orchestration. We will examine some of these and look for the pros and cons.

Orchestration variables

Orchestration variables are a very static place to have configuration values. If variables point to a class, the default constructor of that class can be called automatically to instantiate the variable. If anything other than the default constructor is called, this would need to be done in an Expression shape. Also when Orchestrations are called or started, the caller can supply the initial values for parameters. However, they have to originate from somewhere.

Configuration placed in BTSNTSvc.exe.config

The BTSNTSvc.exe file is an executable file used by all BizTalk in-process Host Instances. As a .NET executable, it reads its configuration from the BTSNTSvc. exe.config file at startup. It is possible to place custom configuration into that file. The issue with this approach is that any addition or change to a configuration value requires the Host Instance to be restarted. Since the introduction of 64-bit processes, there is also a BTSNTSvc64.exe file with a corresponding configuration file. This requires configuration to be duplicated in two places (and on as many BizTalk Servers as there are in the group). Also, any configuration property supplied in this file is not available to the Isolated Hosts, though that is not an issue with Orchestrations since they only run in process. Accessing files under the Program Files folder might also be restricted in some organizations.

Configuration placed in web.config for Isolated Hosts

For Isolated Hosts, it is possible to place configuration in web.config, in the directory of the web service being called. In the end, this is just a bad practice resulting in many configuration duplications and maintenance challenges, not to mention configuration being overwritten and removed if the service is republished.

Configuration placed in machine.config

Configuration in machine.config solves the issue of having different places for in-process or Isolated Hosts. There is still the issue of whether to choose 32- or 64-bit, which will have their machine configs in C:\Windows\Microsoft.NET\ Framework\v4.0.30319\Config\machine.config and C:\Windows\Microsoft. NET\Framework64\v4.0.30319\Config\machine.config respectively. Also, as with BTSNTSvc.exe.config, if your BizTalk environment consists of more than one server, you will need to apply settings to all machines. The machine.config settings are also only read when the process is initiated, so this placement also requires Host restart for updates or new additions. Accessing the machine.config file is also often restricted in many organizations.

Some configuration can be placed on the Adapter Handlers

Specifically, WCF extension configuration can be placed in the Send and Receive Handlers for the WCF-Custom Adapter. This is detailed in *Chapter 7, Integrating Web Services and Windows Communication Foundation (WCF) Services*.

Through the message

Configuration values can be sent in as part of the message. It is not uncommon to determine the outcome of a process, based on the content of the message. However, sending in pure configuration values through the message is uncommon.

Through the message context

Configuration values can be part of the message context. A common place to configure values to be placed in the context is through the use of a custom Pipeline component, whose job is to write (or promote) the appropriate values to the context. Configuration can then be done in the Pipeline on a per-instance runtime configuration. The downside of this is that Orchestrations that can get their messages from more than one Receive Location must have those properties configured in all the locations. Also, more than one value (that is, either two Pipeline components or an untyped one) needs to be put into the context, where it is hard to keep track of the format for inputting configuration values.

> The ESB Toolkit uses a variation of this approach where the "itinerary" is included in the message context.

Business Rules

For configuration values that change often, or for those you would like an out of the box-versioned user interface for Business Rules are a good choice. They are centrally stored in the database, and as such are available on all machines to all types of Hosts. Business Rules can be, in some cases, a cumbersome addition to the solution just for the sake of configuration properties from some perspectives, but they are definitely a good viable option. There are also **Application Programming Interfaces** (**APIs**) available in the form of the Call Rules Orchestration shape that allows you to call Business Rules easily.

SSO

Single Sign-on (**SSO**) can be used as a centralized data store for configuration values. Besides storing user account mappings, it also stores custom configuration for adapters and can be used for secure storage of custom configuration for custom logic as well. Although there are no easy, out of the box options for using SSO this way, there are samples in the documentation and tooling available from BizTalk Community that makes this relatively easy.

Using a .NET helper component

If you decide to use a .NET helper component to store and retrieve your configuration, you can get the configuration from anywhere, say a file or a database. File storage will have its drawbacks, but it is certainly possible. In many cases, using a custom component may seem easy, but you should strive to use the built-in functionality and features wherever possible if you want to minimize maintenance costs.

Integrating with .NET assemblies

Sometimes there are methods or logic contained within .NET helper components that you would like to use from within an Orchestration. Even though there is no option to call an external assembly, such as with the Scripting Functoid, doing so is easy. It requires an assembly reference added to the project, a variable of that type, and an Expression shape. The following are the steps required to call a .NET assembly from an Orchestration:

1. Create a .NET assembly. In this sample, we will use a Helper component that uses directory services to find the full name of the sales representative that created a sales order for a car. The ADHelper class is contained in the Chapter04-Example01.ClassLibary project. The code looks as follows:

```
namespace Chapter04_Example01.ClassLibrary
{
  public class ADHelper
  {
    public static string GetFullname(string username)
    {
      // Lookup code goes here
      return "Max Mooremountain";
    }
  }
}
```

2. Create an Orchestration that will call the assembly. The Orchestration `SalesOrderProcess` is implemented in `Chapter04-Example01`. Orchestrations in `Chapter04-Example01.sln` for this sample look similar to the following screenshot:

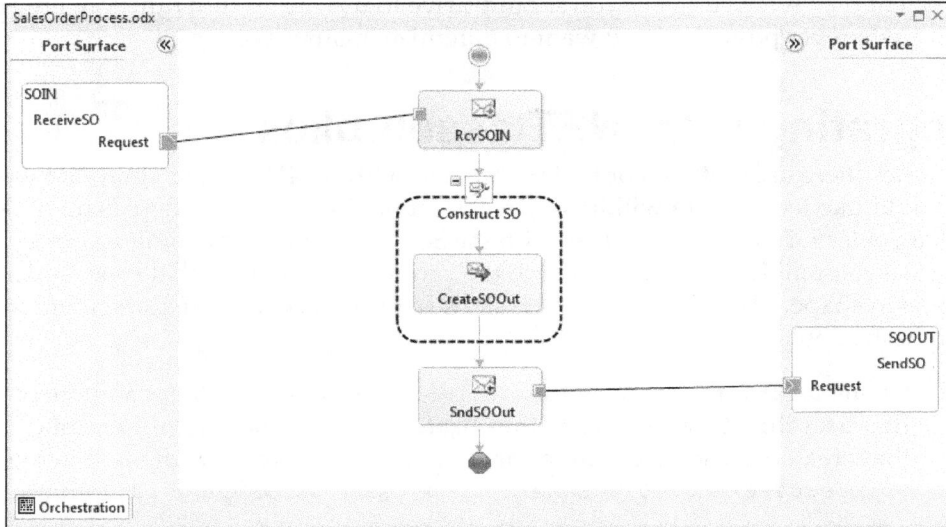

3. The expression in the `CreateSOOut` Message Assignment shape looks similar to that in the following screenshot:

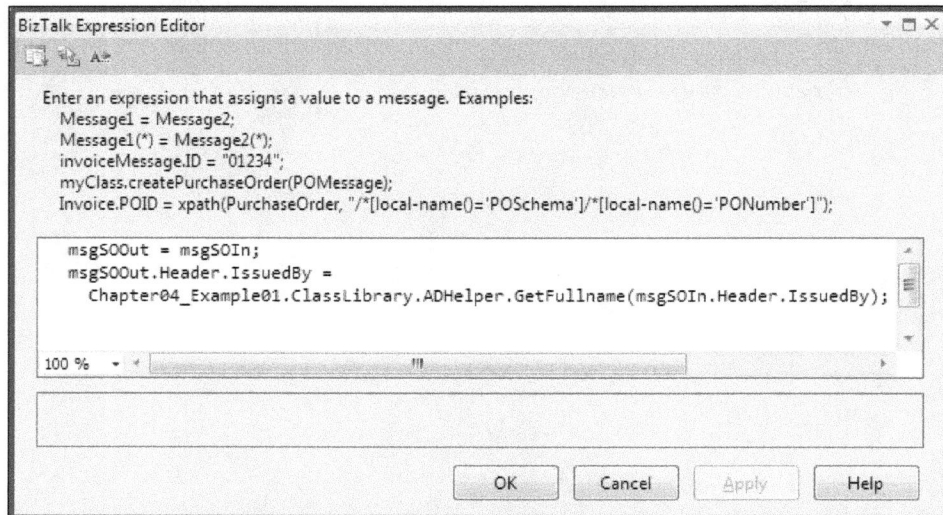

4. Build the solution.

5. Add the `Chapter04-Example01.ClassLibary` assembly to the **Global Assembly Cache (GAC)** so that it can be located and used from BizTalk Server.

6. Deploy the Orchestration.

7. Create ports. For simplicity, a Binding File is located at `C:\BTS2013CertGuide\Chapter04\Example01- Orchestrations\BTS2013CertGuide-Ch02- Orchestrations.xml`.

8. Configure the Orchestration.

9. Start and test the Orchestration.

> In step 2, the expression is using a static method. Therefore no variable of type `ADHelper` is required, and the method can be called outside an Atomic scope, even if the class is not marked as serializable.

Configuring Orchestration bindings

Orchestrations subscribe and publish messages to the `MessageBox`. They can do this in a number of different ways dependent on what messaging pattern the developer wants to use. Orchestrations can be bound directly to the `MessageBox`, bound to Receive and Send Ports or configured to route messages between Orchestration instances. The only time the `MessageBox` is not involved is when you use the Call Orchestration shape to initiate execution of another Orchestration, as explained earlier in this chapter. For the next few sections we are going to examine Orchestration Ports and Subscription patterns.

Ports versus Port Types

Ports in Orchestrations describe how the Orchestration will communicate with the `MessageBox` and the direction of that communication, inbound or outbound. Ports are based on Port Types. The Port Type describes the **Communication Pattern** (one-way or request-response) and `MessageType` communicated. A Port Type can have a one-to-many relationship with ports. Ports can be thought of as an instance of a Port Type. Ports define the **Communication Direction** and **Binding**, as well as define if the Port should use **Ordered Delivery**. Port Types can be re-used throughout a solution. For that purpose, Port Types has a `Type Modifier` property that controls the scope of the type, which are as follows:

- **Private**: Only ports in the same Orchestration may use it
- **Internal**: Only ports in Orchestrations in the same project may use it. This is the default
- **Public**: Any port in an Orchestration project that references this project or assembly may use it

Logical ports versus physical ports

Ports in Orchestration Designer are logical ports; they describe the logic of the operation and the direction of the communication to the `MessageBox`. Depending on the binding mode specified within the Orchestration (excluding Direct binding), the logical ports have to correlate to the physical ports (Receive and Send Ports). This process is also known as binding an Orchestration.

Using the Specify Now binding mode, you can also create the actual port configuration at the same time as you create the Orchestration, although that procedure is not recommended.

A selection of the properties of ports is as follows:

- Port Type
- Communication Direction
- Binding
- Ordered Delivery (on ports with Communication Direction Receive)
- Delivery Notification (on ports with Communication Direction Send)

There are more properties that become available depending on the binding option chosen.

Port binding options

There are several ways that logical ports can be bound to the MessageBox and physical ports. The most common are Specify Later or Direct (MessageBox).

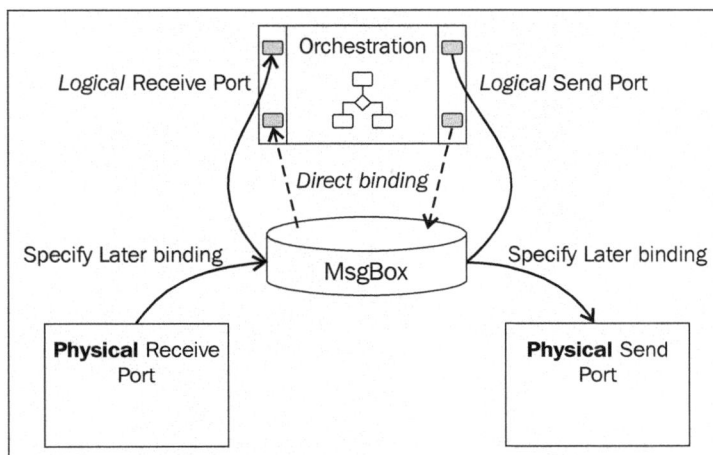

The complete list of available Port Binding options is as follows:

- Specify Now
- Specify Later
- Direct
    - MessageBox
    - Self Correlating
    - Partner Orchestration
- Dynamic (for Send Ports only)

While Specify Later and Direct MessageBox are both common, Self Correlating is not as widely used and understood, and Partner Orchestration is something that even experienced developers are often uncertain of how and when to use.

Specify Now

The **Specify Now** binding is utilized when the Receive or Send Port locations are defined at design time. This is typically not recommended.

The configuration interface has fewer options than the port configuration in the BizTalk Administration Console.

Using **Specify now** in the **Port Configuration Wizard** for a port with the **Receive Communication Pattern** allows the usage of adapters, **HTTP**, **SOAP**, and **FILE** as **Transport** and requires the **URI** and **Receive pipeline** to be specified, as shown in the following screenshot:

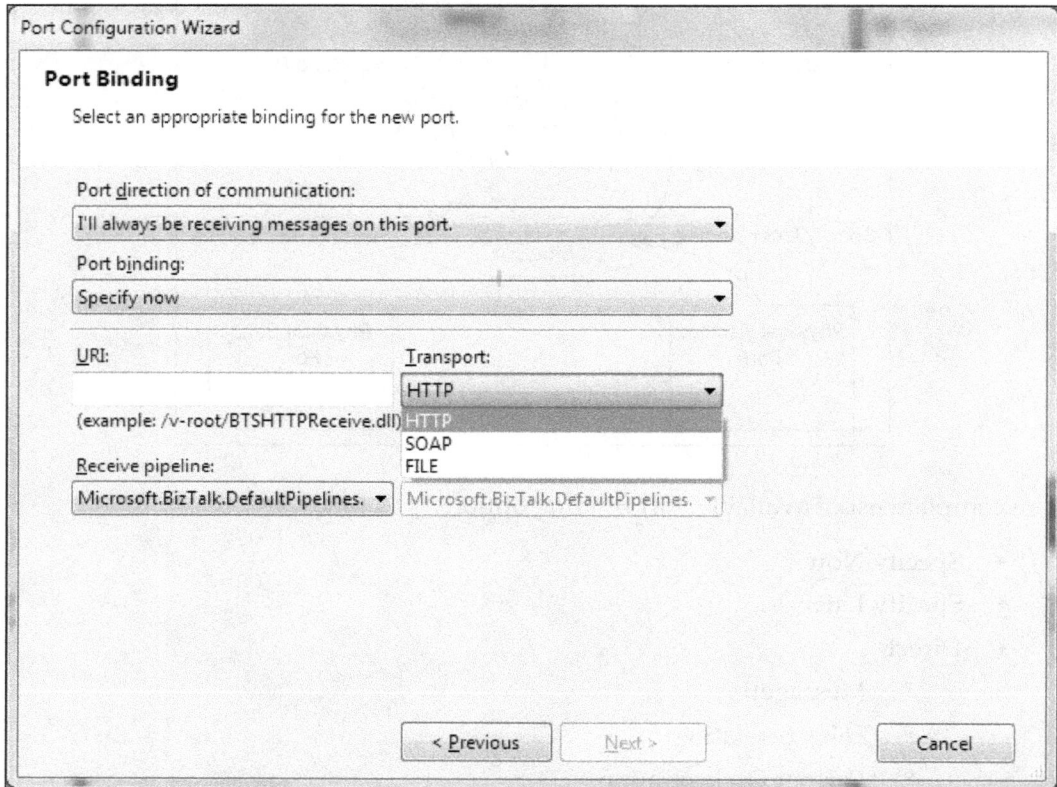

Using **Specify Now** in the **Port Configuration Wizard** for a port with a **Send Communication Pattern** allows the usage of **HTTP**, **FILE**, and **SMTP** as **Transport** and requires the **URI** and **Receive pipeline** to be specified, as shown in the following screenshot:

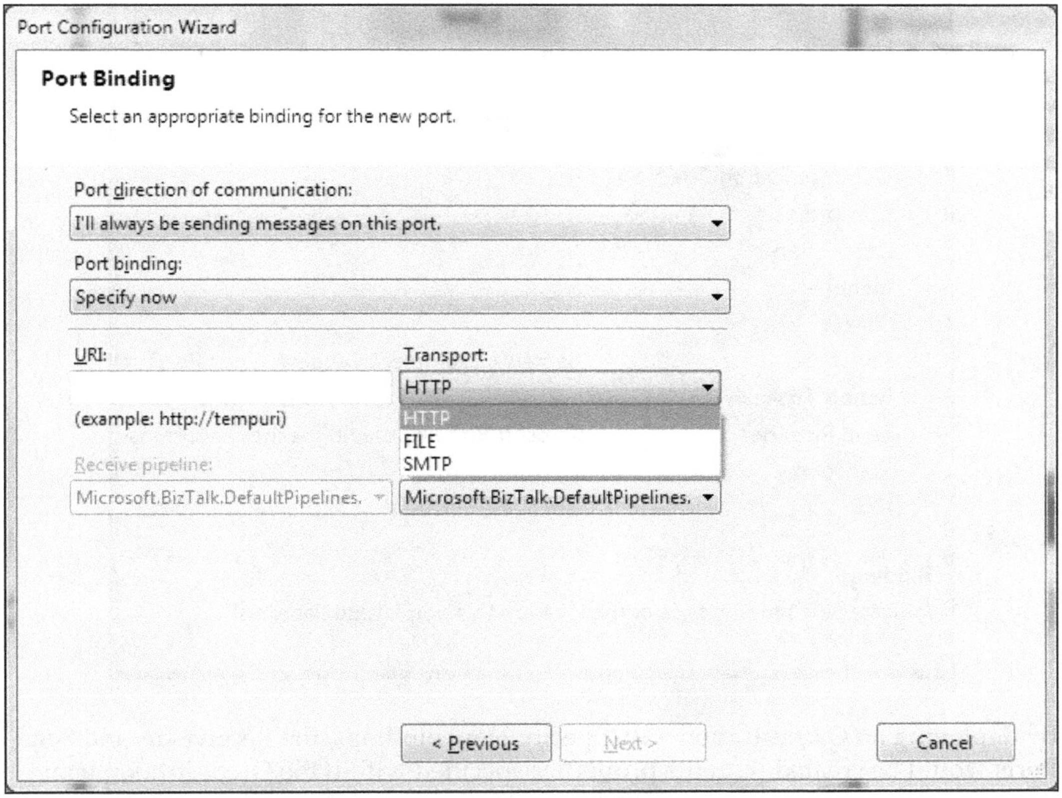

Regardless of what binding option you choose in the **Port Configuration Wizard**, the port can be reconfigured later during design time by going to **Port Properties**, as shown in the following screenshot:

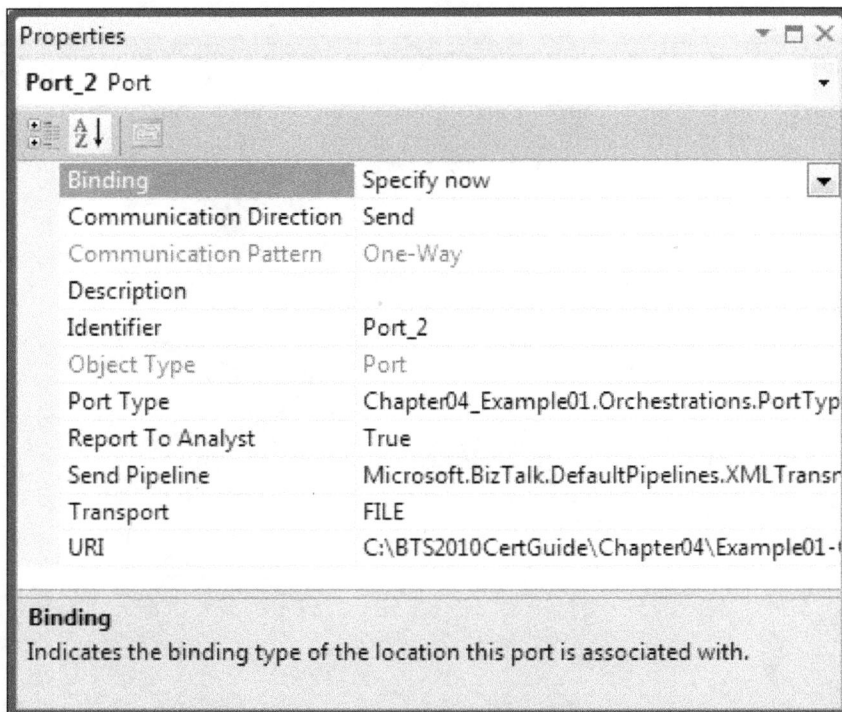

Properties	▾ ☐ ✕
Port_2 Port	▾

Binding	Specify now ▾
Communication Direction	Send
Communication Pattern	One-Way
Description	
Identifier	Port_2
Object Type	Port
Port Type	Chapter04_Example01.Orchestrations.PortTyp
Report To Analyst	True
Send Pipeline	Microsoft.BizTalk.DefaultPipelines.XMLTransr
Transport	FILE
URI	C:\BTS2010CertGuide\Chapter04\Example01-(

Binding
Indicates the binding type of the location this port is associated with.

By deploying an Orchestration with Specify Now bindings, the Receive or/and Send Ports would be created with the properties specified within the Orchestration using automatically generated names. The logical to physical port association, known as binding, would be deployed as well, as shown in the following screenshot:

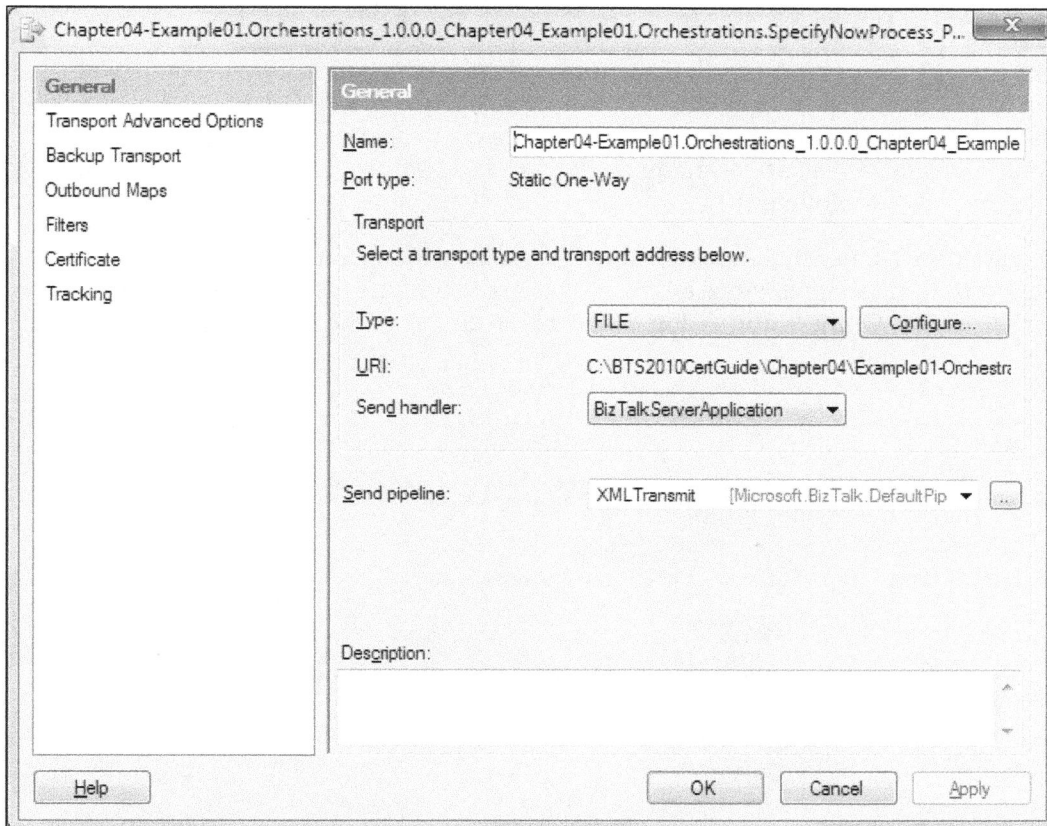

Chapter04-Example01.Orchestrations_1.0.0.0_Chapter04_Example01.Orchestrations.SpecifyNowProcess_P...

| General |
| Transport Advanced Options |
| Backup Transport |
| Outbound Maps |
| Filters |
| Certificate |
| Tracking |

General

Name: Chapter04-Example01.Orchestrations_1.0.0.0_Chapter04_Example

Port type: Static One-Way

Transport
Select a transport type and transport address below.

Type: FILE   Configure...

URI: C:\BTS2010CertGuide\Chapter04\Example01-Orchestra

Send handler: BizTalkServerApplication

Send pipeline: XMLTransmit   [Microsoft.BizTalk.DefaultPip

Description:

Help   OK   Cancel   Apply

Be careful while using this option since changes made to ports, once deployed, will be overwritten when the Orchestration is redeployed, as with reapplying a Binding File. You will also get less control over the settings such as **Handler**, which when deployed will be configured to use the default handler for the Adapter. If you want to keep your Orchestration Design and Deployment separate from your Port Configuration, using the **Specify Later** binding option is a better choice.

Specify Later

The **Specify Later** binding allows you to make the connection between a logical port and physical port once the Orchestration is deployed. You will need to create the physical port on your own as it will not be created for you during deployment. On the upside, any changes made to the port will be durable across Orchestration change and redeployment.

Using Specify Later makes no additional Port Configuration properties available in Orchestration Designer since all properties are configured on the physical port. Once deployed, the Orchestration's logical ports are bound to the physical ports.

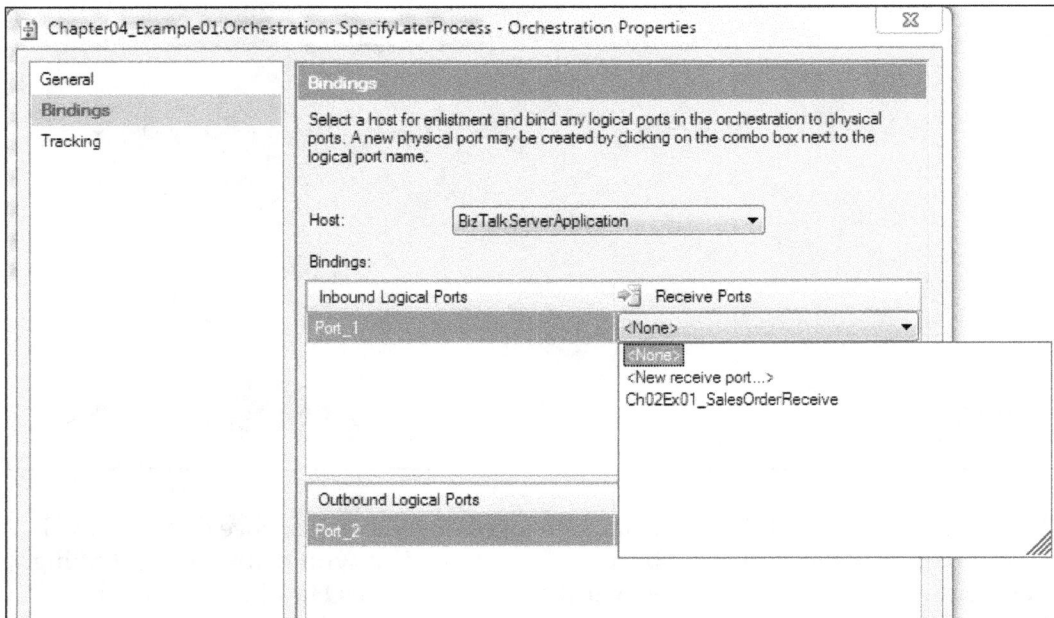

This still does not mean that messages bypass the `MessageBox`; it is just a shortcut to create very explicit subscriptions between Orchestration and its ports. Inspecting our Orchestration's subscription shows us that it is indeed activated by an explicitly identified Receive Port, as shown in the following screenshot:

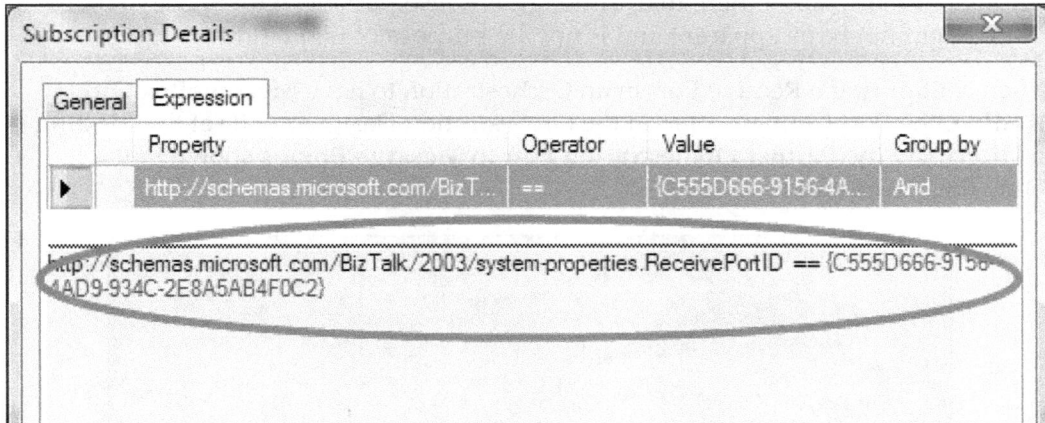

Direct

Direct Bound Ports are ports that are not configured to physical ports using the Administration Console Orchestration Binding GUI. Instead, they use the `MessageBox` and different kinds of pub or sub patterns and subscription filters to achieve their goal. Messages can be delivered to both ports and other Orchestrations. In fact, some binding types are directly aimed at Orchestration to Orchestration communication. The three types of Direct bindings that you have to choose from are as follows:

- MessageBox (filter-based)
- Self Correlating
- Partner Orchestration

On an activating Receive Port, the filter can be explicit, but for any other Receive instance, subscriptions are based on the message type and the correlation. We will take a closer look at correlations in the *Configuring correlation* section later in the chapter.

MessageBox (filter-based)

Direct Bound Ports are closest to the concept of pub or sub architecture. They allow you to deliver a message to the `MessageBox` without knowing the recipient and allow you to subscribe to messages without knowing the sender. There could be one recipient or many, something that, although it is also possible with Specify Later Ports, might not be as apparent and is not the purpose of that binding.

When configuring a Receive Port in an Orchestration to have **MessageBox Direct Binding**, the Port Configuration in the Orchestration Designer will set the **Binding** to **Direct** and the **Partner Orchestration Port** to **Message Box**, as shown in the following screenshot:

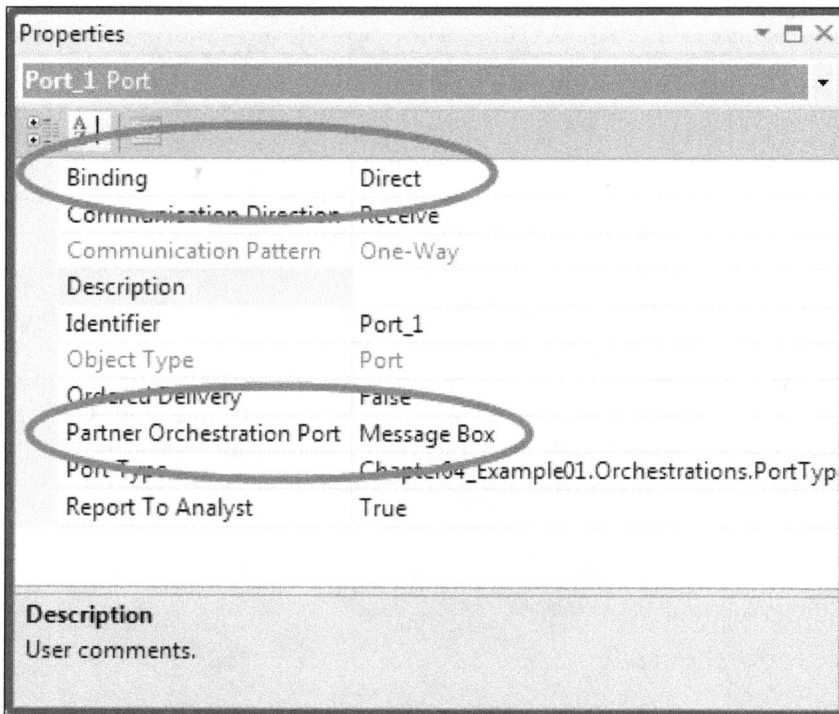

Properties	▾ □ ×
Port_1 Port	▾
Binding	Direct
Communication Direction	Receive
Communication Pattern	One-Way
Description	
Identifier	Port_1
Object Type	Port
Ordered Delivery	False
Partner Orchestration Port	Message Box
Port Type	Chapter04_Example01.Orchestrations.PortTyp
Report To Analyst	True

Description
User comments.

The configuration of an Orchestration Send Port will differ slightly as far as available properties go, but for these two properties they will look the same.

We should also specify a filter criterion on the Receive shape. If we do not, we will have created an Orchestration that subscribes to all messages that match the message type of the message that the Receive shape expects.

> Filters should be made as detailed as possible to avoid subscribing to unwanted messages.

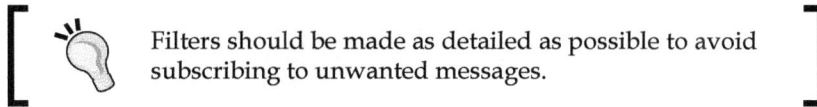

Once a `Direct MessageBox Port` is deployed, there will be no configuration of ports needed or possible. As the following screenshot shows, the only thing left to configure (if all ports are Direct) is **Host** under which the Orchestration should run:

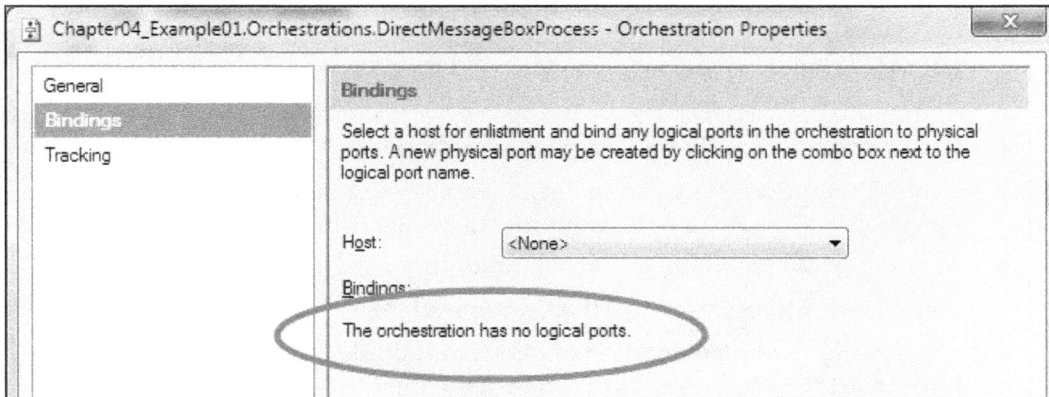

Self Correlating

By configuring a port with **Direct Self Correlating Direct** binding and passing it as a parameter to an Orchestration, you enable the Orchestration to send messages back to its caller without the use of a Correlation Set through the use of the Start Orchestration shape. The following diagram illustrates that process:

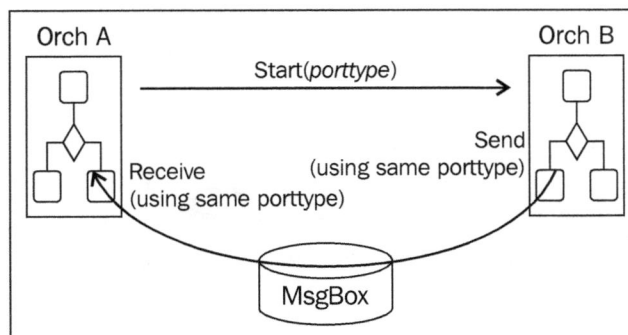

Instead, Self-correlated Ports generate an instance-specific (unique) correlation token, stored using the `PartnerService` promoted property. That property (among others) is then used to create a correlation.

> We will cover correlation later in this chapter. In short, a correlation token is required when you need to be able to get a response back to the correct Orchestration instance.

To use a Self-correlated Port, follow these steps:

1. Create and implement an Orchestration A.

2. Identify the use case in the processing logic to start another Orchestration asynchronously and generate a response.

3. In Orchestration A, create a new **Port** and **Port Type** and select **Direct** as **Binding** and **Self Correlating** as **Partner Orchestration**.

4. Create an Orchestration B designed to be started.

5. Add a **Configured Port Parameter**, select the previously created **Port Type** (in A), and select **Send** as **Communication Direction**.

6. Create the logic required in Orchestration B.

7. Send the result back through the Configured Port.

8. A very simple implementation of Orchestration B, named `DirectSelfCorrelatingChild.odx`, showing the concepts can be found in `Chapter04-Example01.sln`. The Orchestration can be seen in the following screenshot:

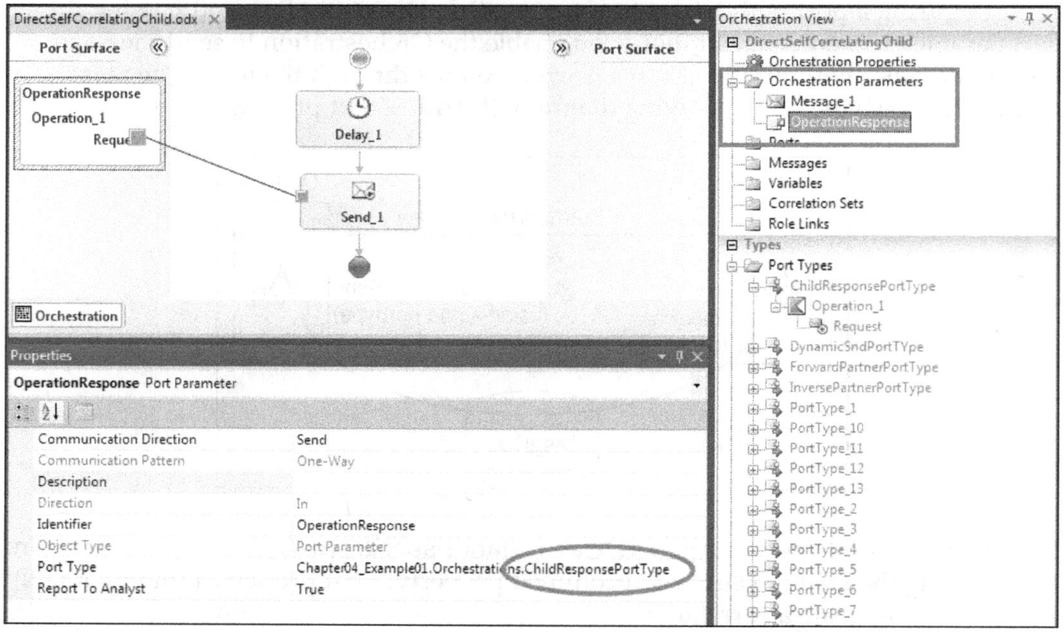

9. The preceding screenshot highlights the **OperationResponse Port Parameter**. Defining a Port Parameter places a port on the **Port Surface** of an Orchestration. In this case, the Orchestration also takes a Message Parameter, and all it does is send the same message back using the Port Parameter.

10. Use the **Start Orchestration** shape in A to call B, and supply the parameters needed including the port (**Port Type**).

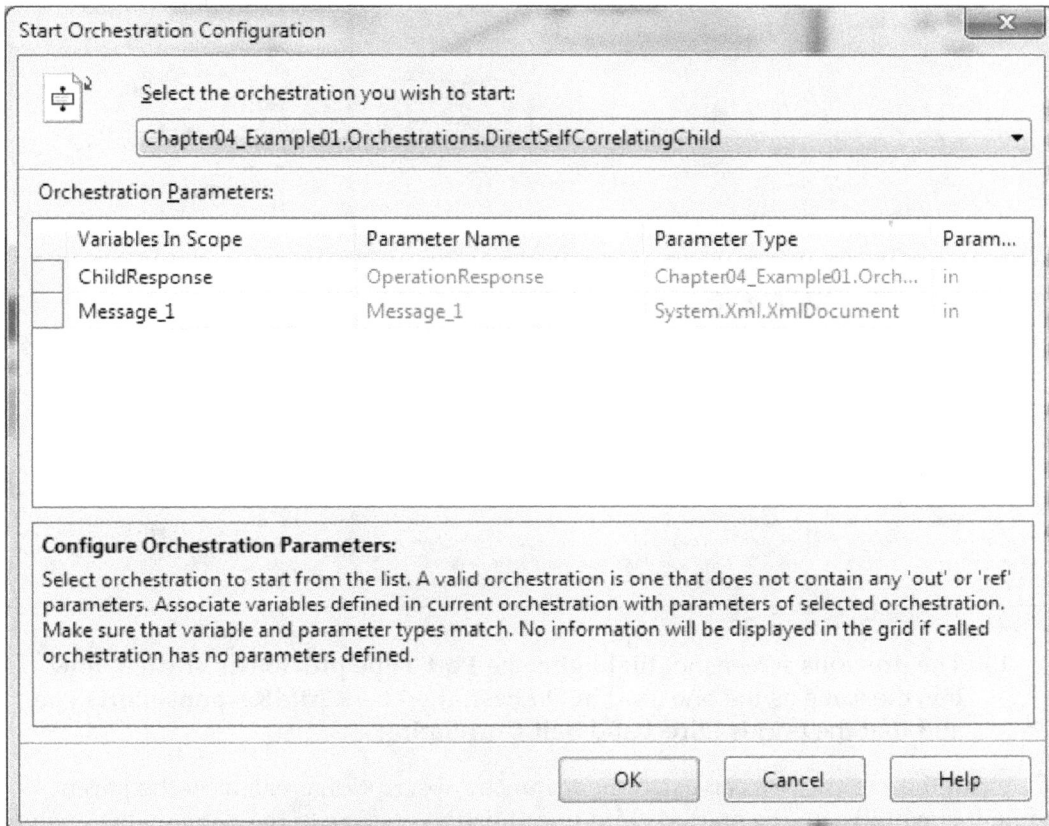

Start Orchestration Configuration   [x]

Select the orchestration you wish to start:

Chapter04_Example01.Orchestrations.DirectSelfCorrelatingChild   ▼

Orchestration Parameters:

Variables In Scope	Parameter Name	Parameter Type	Param...
ChildResponse	OperationResponse	Chapter04_Example01.Orch...	in
Message_1	Message_1	System.Xml.XmlDocument	in

Configure Orchestration Parameters:

Select orchestration to start from the list. A valid orchestration is one that does not contain any 'out' or 'ref' parameters. Associate variables defined in current orchestration with parameters of selected orchestration. Make sure that variable and parameter types match. No information will be displayed in the grid if called orchestration has no parameters defined.

OK   Cancel   Help

11. After starting the Orchestration, use a **Receive** shape to block the reception of the response from Orchestration B through the **Configured Receive Port**.

12. A very simple implementation of Orchestration A named `DirectSelfCorrelatingParent.odx` showing the concepts can be found in `Chapter01-Example04.sln`. The Orchestration can be seen in the following screenshot:

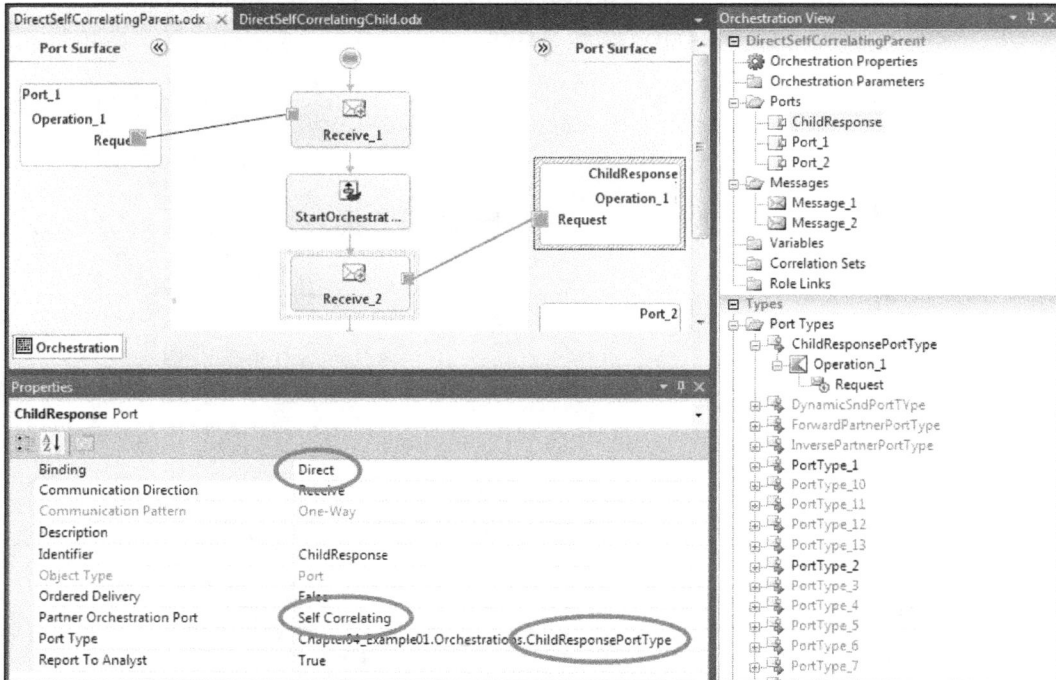

13. The previous screenshot highlights the **Port Type** previously created, how it is the same as the one used in Orchestration B—**ChildResponsePortType**, and that the port is **Direct** and **Self Correlating**.

If we run the sample, we can catch the instance subscription created by the parent while it is waiting for the started child to publish a message to the `MessageBox`, using the Self-correlated Port sent in as a parameter, as shown in the following screenshot:

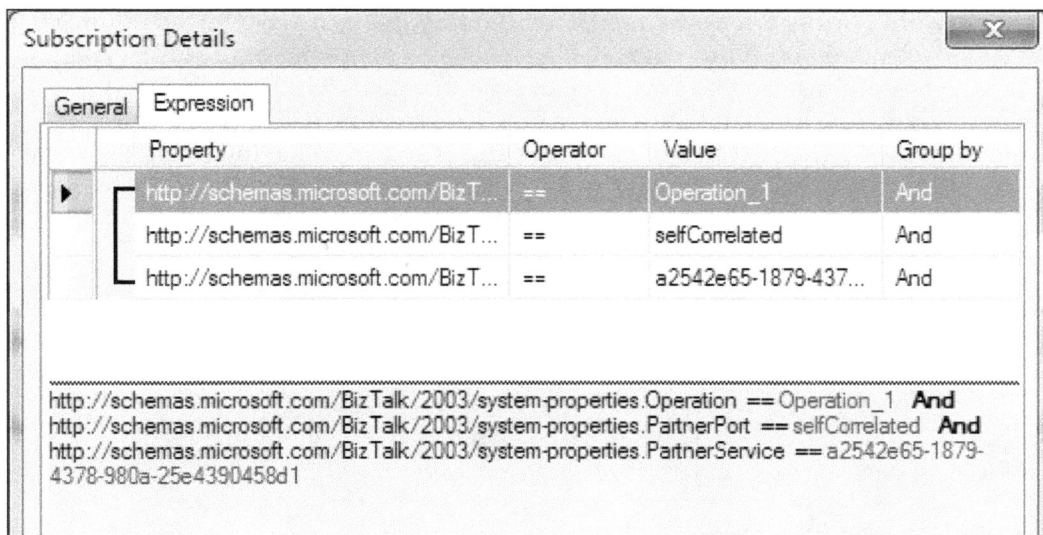

As you can see, it is based upon the unique `PartnerService` property, together with the `PartnerPort` property, which tell us `PartnerPort` is `selfCorrelated` and that the operation used is named as `Operation_1` (which is the default name given to the operation of the port by BizTalk).

Partner Orchestration

The **Partner Orchestration** option allows us to implement two patterns: **Forward Partner Orchestration Direct Binding** and **Inverse Partner Orchestration Direct Binding**. Basically, this means either receiving messages in one Orchestration from other Orchestrations or sending messages from one Orchestration to other Orchestrations.

One of the differences between using `Direct MessageBox` binding and using Direct Partner Orchestration binding is that, like with Self-correlated Ports, you use the Port Type to connect the Orchestrations together and one side sends the message and another side receives it. The main difference is that this is not solved through passing the port as a parameter in runtime; instead, it is a pure design-time configuration.

With Forward Partner Orchestration Direct Binding, the Receiver Orchestration can have many senders. With this pattern, the receiver is the owner of the Port Type. Other Orchestrations use that Port Type to send messages to the receiver.
The receiver has no forehand knowledge of who is sending it. This is the most commonly used pattern of the two methods and is shown in the following diagram:

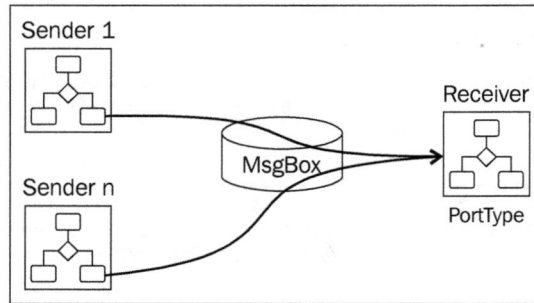

If we look at a sample subscription in a Receiver Orchestration, it looks similar to the following screenshot:

As you can see, the `PartnerService` property, as set by the sender(s), will have a direct binding with tight coupling to the receiver.

With Inverse Partner Orchestration Direct Binding, a single sender can have multiple receivers. With this pattern, the sender is the owner of the Port Type. Other Orchestrations connect to that Port Type to receive messages. The sender has no forehand knowledge of who the receivers are, as shown in the following diagram:

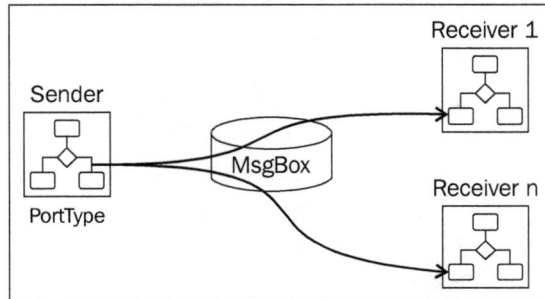

If we look again at a sample in one of the receivers connected to the sender, it looks similar to the following screenshot:

The big difference here is that the receiver is connected to the sender, and as such the sender owns the Port Type and the receiver is the one that has a direct binding with tight coupling to the sender.

Dynamic

A **Dynamic Send Port** is a port where you do not specify the address and transport type in the static configuration, as shown in the following screenshot:

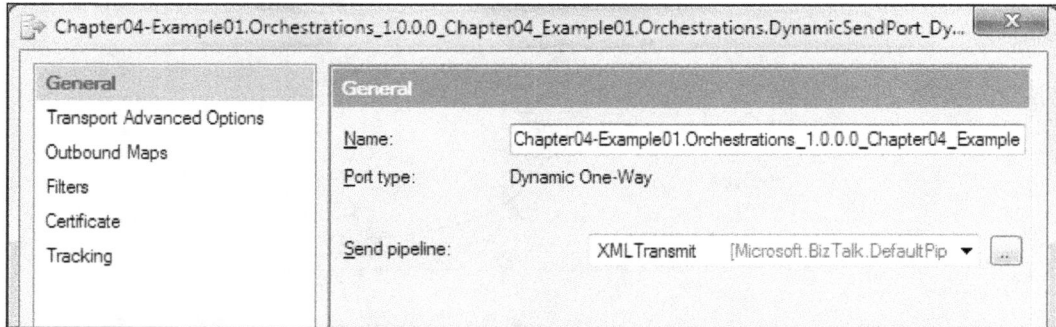

Instead, you are expected to supply it in runtime. This does not need to be through the use of an Orchestration, although it often is, when talking about the out of the box capabilities.

> You could easily use a Dynamic Send Port by populating the same properties through the use of Pipeline components — something that the ESB Toolkit relies heavily on.

To use a Dynamic Send Port in an Orchestration, these are the steps we need to follow:

1. Create a new logical Send Port using the **Port Configuration Wizard**.

2. When selecting **Port Binding**, select **Dynamic**, and select an appropriate Pipeline (you can always change this later in the **Properties** window for the port), as shown in the following screenshot:

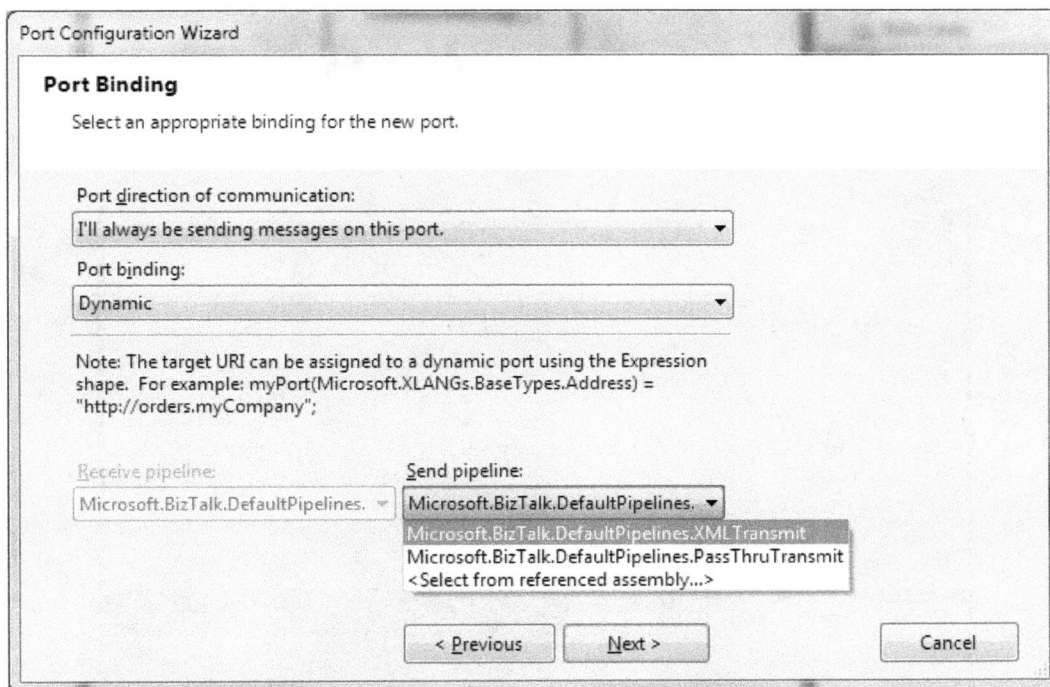

Port Configuration Wizard

Port Binding

Select an appropriate binding for the new port.

Port direction of communication:

I'll always be sending messages on this port.

Port binding:

Dynamic

Note: The target URI can be assigned to a dynamic port using the Expression shape. For example: myPort(Microsoft.XLANGs.BaseTypes.Address) = "http://orders.myCompany";

Receive pipeline:

Microsoft.BizTalk.DefaultPipelines.

Send pipeline:

Microsoft.BizTalk.DefaultPipelines.

Microsoft.BizTalk.DefaultPipelines.XMLTransmit
Microsoft.BizTalk.DefaultPipelines.PassThruTransmit
<Select from referenced assembly...>

< Previous   Next >   Cancel

3. In the Expression shape, set the `Microsoft.XLANGs.BaseTypes.Address` property of the port. For a file transport, this may be `C:\BTS2013CertGuide\Chapter04\Example01-Orchestrations\FileDrop\%MessageID%.xml`, as shown in the following screenshot:

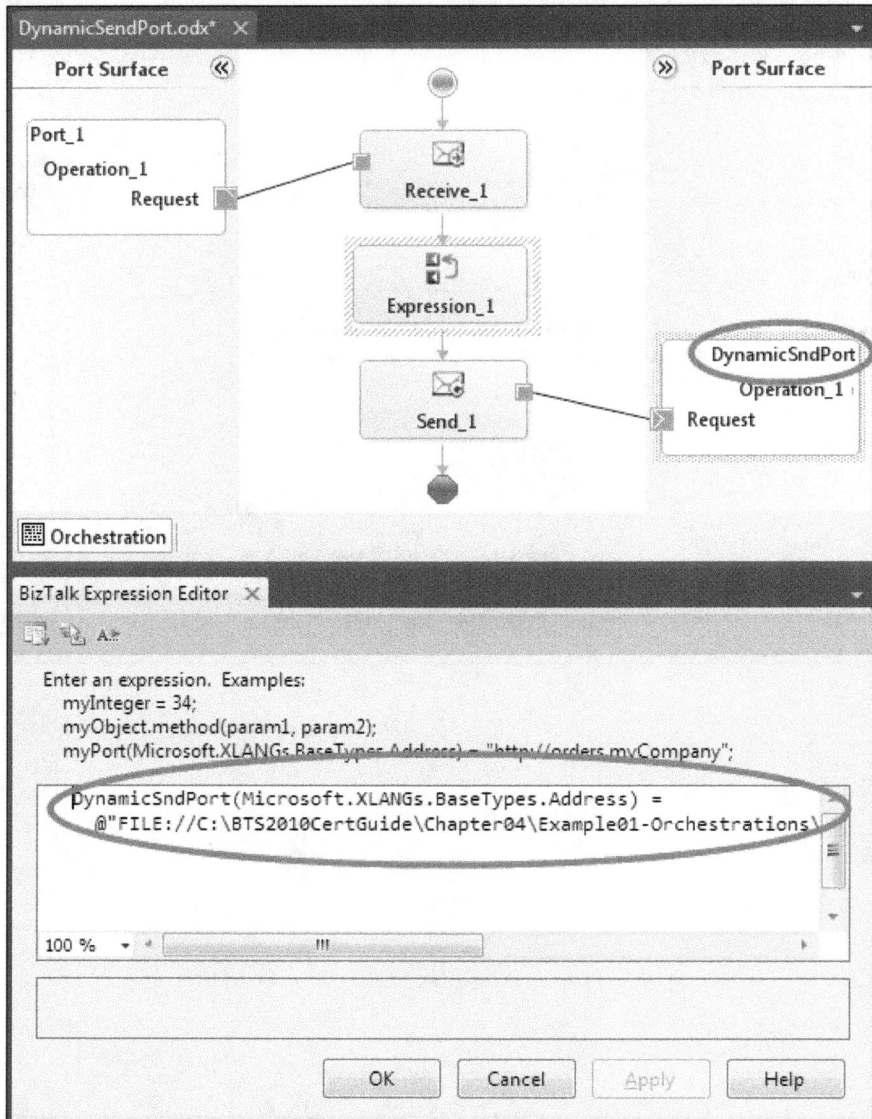

4. Use a **Send** shape, and connect it to the logical **Send Port** to send the message to `MessageBox` and the physical Dynamic Send Port.

The adapter BizTalk used in a Dynamic Send Port is chosen based on the first part of the address, `FILE://`. For some addresses and transport types, you may have to set additional properties; for example, if you use an HTTP address, you will have to specify `Microsoft.XLANGs.BaseTypes.TransportType` to ensure that BizTalk selects the adapter that you wanted, since the WCF-BasicHTTP, WCF-WsHTTP, WCF-Custom, and the HTTP adapter all handle HTTP addresses.

Also, some adapters may need additional configuration after that, such as for usernames, passwords, configuration, and binding information—everything that you would normally change from the defaults in the adapter configuration in the physical Send Port.

Once deployed, a Dynamic Port acts like a Specify Now Port, and a port is automatically created.

Configuring correlation

Correlation is used throughout BizTalk Server Messaging and Orchestration engines. In many cases, it is automatic and there is little or nothing you need to do to take advantage of it. BizTalk promotes the required properties for you without you having to explicitly configure which properties from which property schemas to use. Such examples are when using a Request-Response or Solicit-Response Port, when using a Self-correlated Binding or Partner Orchestration Binding. In these cases, correlations are created for you, in the engine, without you explicitly having to define the properties and the values of those properties needed to make sure that the second message gets routed back.

Correlation subscriptions are instance subscriptions, that is, they do not exist in sync with the status of an Orchestration (when it is Stopped or Started), and the Orchestration does not activate a new instance when met; instead, it exists only until it is fulfilled and the message gets back to the Orchestration instance that created the subscription.

The typical case is asynchronous responses, where we need to instruct BizTalk on how to route (by a separate Receive Port or Orchestration) the reply message published to the `MessageBox` back to the correct Orchestration instance. However, not all correlations are about receiving a response. Other common correlation uses are convoys.

Working with Correlation Types and Sets

Creating correlations in Orchestrations is based on **Correlation Types** that define the properties the correlation consists of. A Correlation Type is made up of one or more properties from Property Schemas, either out of the box BizTalk Property Schemas or your own. A Correlation Type is instantiated by creating a Correlation Set.

The following screenshot shows a simple Orchestration using correlation:

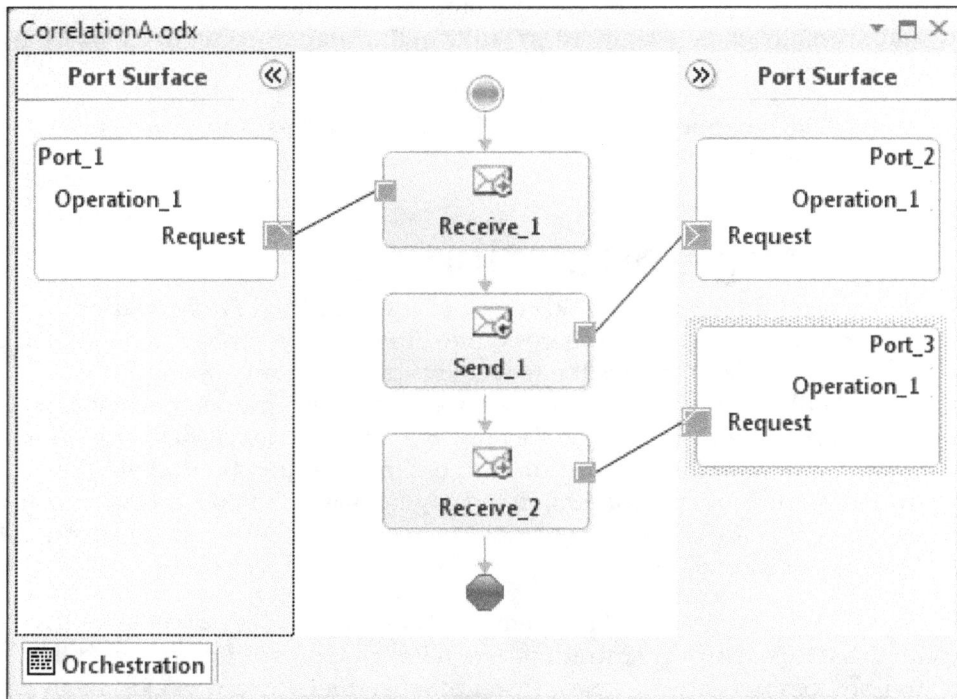

These instructions illustrate the relevant steps to enable correlation in an Orchestration:

1. Make sure that the message sent out as well as the one received back in have at least one promoted property that can be used for correlation. In this sample, we are using a `SalesOrder` Schema with an `OrderNo` node promoted to an `OrderNo` property in a Property Schema that we will use for correlation.

2. Choose to create a new Correlation Type and configure it by selecting the `OrderNo` property from our Property Schema and clicking on the **Add** button, as per the following screenshot:

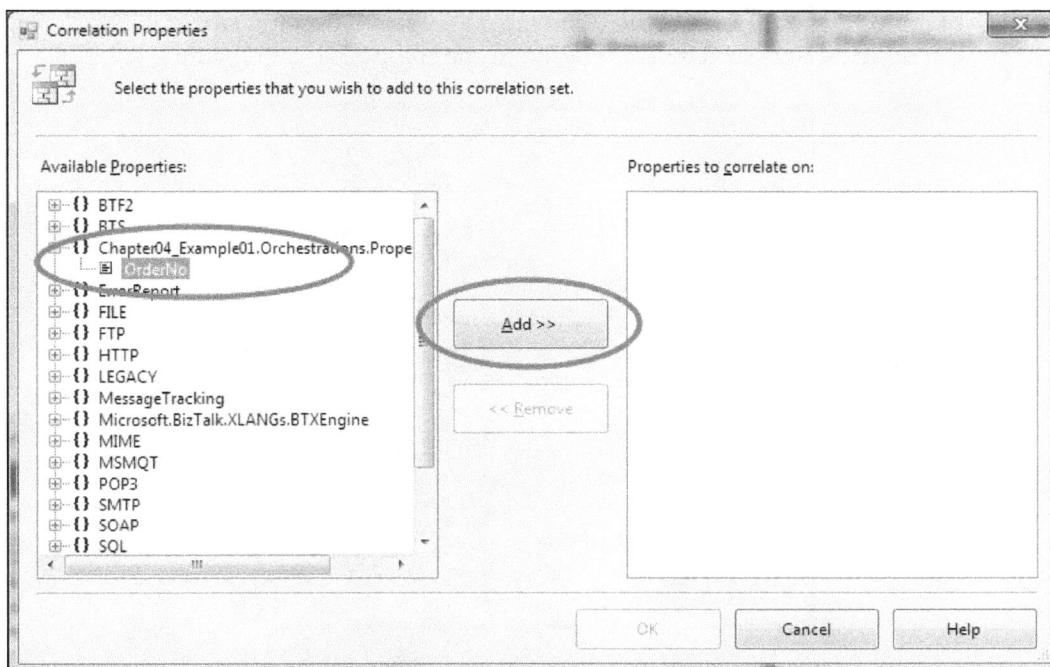

3. Create a new **Correlation Set** and configure it to be of the **Correlation Type** created in the preceding step, as shown in the following screenshot:

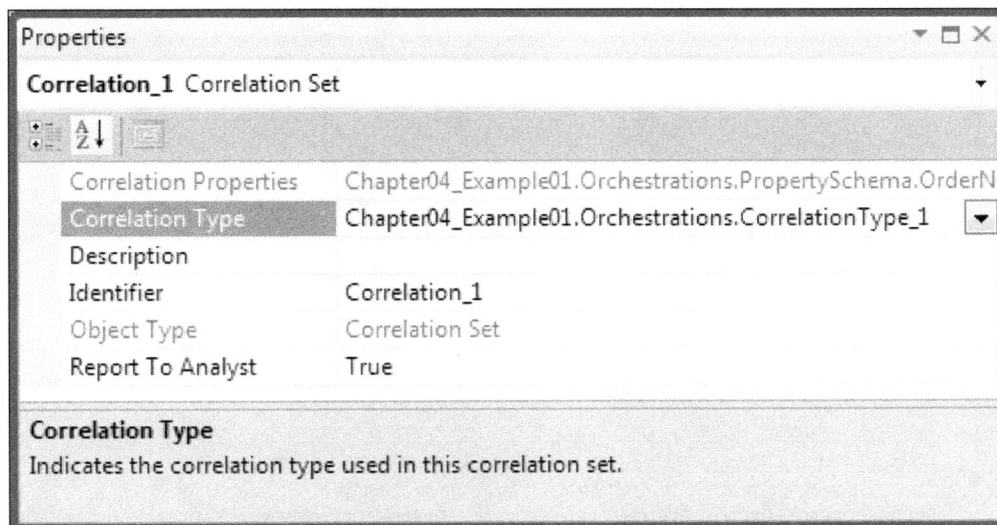

4. In the **Send** shape, select the Correlation Set created in the **Initializing Correlation Sets** property as shown in the following screenshot:

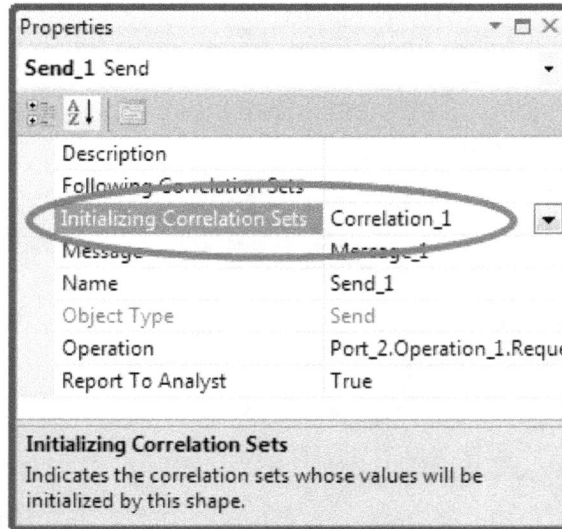

5. In the Receive shape following the Send shape, select the same Correlation Set as the **Following Correlation Sets** property instead.

Once the Orchestration is deployed, bound, and started, whenever it sends out a message through the Send Port, it will initiate an instance correlation waiting to receive the response and correlate the message back to the correct Orchestration instance. This instance subscription will look similar to the following screenshot:

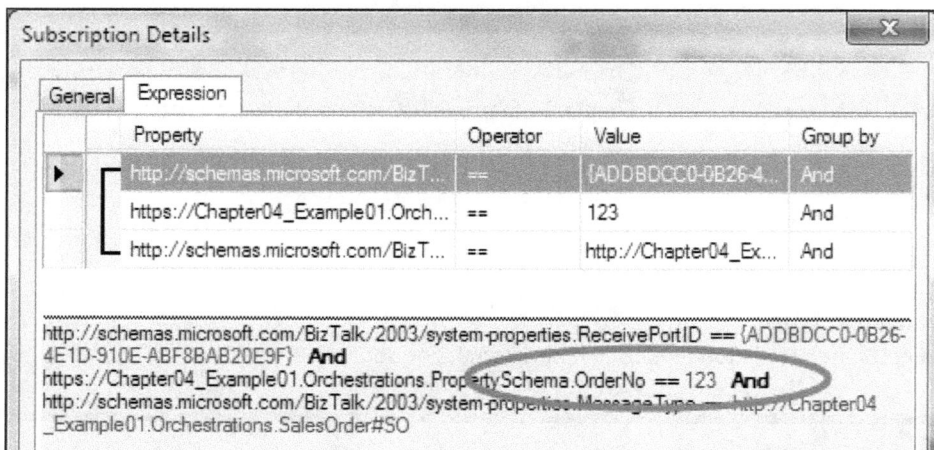

The ReceivePortID property is there only because the Port Binding used in this sample was Specify Later and the logical Orchestration Port is bound to a Receive Port. The MessageType is always there when working with typed messages in Orchestrations. The circled part is what we get from using the Correlation Set. That part defines the specific value that the OrderNo promoted property had when we sent the message. This same promoted property having that same value must be present in a received message to match the subscription of this particular Orchestration instance, which is what the preceding screenshot shows.

Had the receiver of a message been another Orchestration that would receive the message through the MessageBox, do some work, and then return a response (much like what a Self-correlated Port accomplishes, except through the MessageBox and not by using Start Orchestration), then that Orchestration would have defined a Correlation Type and Set that would have been configured in the Initializing Correlation Set on the Receive shape and in the Following Correlation Set on the Send shape.

Convoys

Convoys are about receiving multiple messages in sequence or in parallel to achieve a goal. There are two types of convoy scenarios that you can implement using Orchestrations:

- Sequential convoys
- Parallel convoys

Sequential convoys

A convoy is sequential when multiple messages must be received in a predetermined order. An out-of-context example is how, to enter a room, you must unlock three doors, one after another. A BizTalk example might be three orders that must be received in order, batched, and delivered to a backend store in a predetermined time.

The first Receive order is set to initialize the Correlation Set and the other Receive orders in the Convoy Set to follow that Correlation Set, as shown in the following diagram:

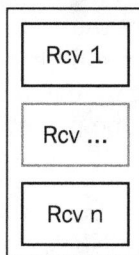

```
┌─────────────┐
│ ┌─────────┐ │
│ │  Rcv 1  │ │
│ └─────────┘ │
│ ┌─────────┐ │
│ │ Rcv ... │ │
│ └─────────┘ │
│ ┌─────────┐ │
│ │  Rcv n  │ │
│ └─────────┘ │
└─────────────┘
```

> For more information on Sequential Convoys, you can read further at the following URL:
>
> http://msdn.microsoft.com/en-us/library/
> aa561843(v=BTS.70).aspx

Parallel convoys

A convoy is parallel when multiple messages must be received to achieve a goal, but the order that they are received in is not important. An out-of-context example is how, to enter a room, you must unlock all three locks on its door, which you can do in any order. A BizTalk example might be that, when receiving scanned invoices, you will receive invoices both as scanned images as well as XML files describing the content. Both must be received before billing can be performed, as shown in the following diagram:

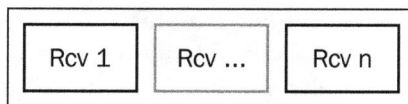

```
┌─────────┬─────────┬─────────┐
│  Rcv 1  │ Rcv ... │  Rcv n  │
└─────────┴─────────┴─────────┘
```

All the parallel Receive orders are set to initialize the Correlation Set.

> For more information on Parallel Convoys, you can read further at the following URL:
>
> http://msdn.microsoft.com/en-us/library/
> aa546782(v=BTS.70).aspx

Testing your knowledge

1. An Orchestration is currently configured with a Specify Later binding and is meant to be connected to a port that sends messages using the FILE Adapter. The requirements are that the folder and name of the file need to be specified at runtime, based on the data in the message. What should you do?

   a. Configure the port binding to be Dynamic, and in a Message Assignment shape, set the `Microsoft.XLANGs.BaseTypes.Address` field for the message to point to the correct folder and name of the file.

   b. Configure the port binding to be Dynamic, and in an Expression shape, set the `Microsoft.XLANGs.BaseTypes.Address` field for the message to point to the correct folder and name of the file.

   c. Configure the port binding to be Dynamic and in an Expression shape, set the `Microsoft.XLANGs.BaseTypes.Address` field for the port to point to the correct folder and name of the file.

   d. In a Message Assignment shape, set the `BTS.ReceivedFileName` context property of the message to point to the correct folder and filename. Leave the port binding as it is.

2. A big Orchestration contains a smaller part of the logic that either needs to succeed fully, or if something fails, nothing is to be committed to the `MessageBox`. The Orchestration has neither any transaction type nor any scope. What do you need to do?

   a. Configure the Orchestration as an Atomic transaction and set it to have a timeout of 90 seconds.

   b. Configure the Orchestration as a Long Running transaction. Use a scope configured as an Atomic transaction, and place the logic within the scope.

   c. Configure the Orchestration as a Long Running transaction. Use a scope configured as a Long Running transaction, and place the logic within the scope. Add a Compensation Block and an Exception Handler Block. If anything fails, call the code in the Compensation Block.

   d. Set the Synchronized property of all shapes included in the logic to `true`.

Summary

In this chapter, we learned about Orchestrations and focused on scopes, activating, nesting, and connecting Orchestrations, and using Call and Start shapes as well as bindings. We also learned core concepts, such as persistence and dehydration, and transaction support. We examined alternatives for storing configuration information and saw how to integrate with .NET assemblies.

In the next chapter, we will examine how we can handle errors as they occur throughout our solutions and messaging as well as Orchestration.

5

Testing, Debugging, and Exception Handling

This chapter maps to the debugging and exception handling parts of the exam, which include testing.

In the previous chapters, we have seen how to configure BizTalk Server to create a basic routing architecture and extended that architecture with identifying, transforming, orchestrating, and correlating requests and responses in that architecture. So far we have not discussed the errors that you might encounter while doing that or how you debug and troubleshoot the solution when that happens.

This chapter will cover the important concepts and topics that you need to know about to be able to efficiently debug and handle exceptions in your integration solution, while focusing on the areas in which you need to succeed in the exam.

This chapter covers the following main areas:

- Handling exceptions in Orchestrations
- Debugging Orchestrations
- Handling messaging errors
- Routing errors
- Validating and testing artifacts
- Testing your knowledge

After this chapter, we will have dived deeper into concepts introduced in the previous chapter, such as scopes, how to throw and handle exceptions, and how to do compensation. We will also handle exceptions outside of Orchestrations as they occur in our messaging architecture, and look at which ones are common and how we can handle them by routing them when they occur to enable programmatic handling instead of requiring administrative handling of suspended messages.

In order to examine why an exception occurred, we will also look at how we can do debugging, both of Orchestrations, and in the form of Schemas and Maps by validation and testing in Visual Studio.

Handling exceptions in Orchestrations

Following up from the last chapter where we dealt with developing Orchestrations, let's look at how to handle exceptions as they occur in Orchestrations.

Scopes

In the previous chapter, we looked at how we could use scopes to configure and use transactions, whether Long Running or Atomic. The other two major uses for the Scope shape are to handle exceptions and to trigger compensating logic. These two uses are in a way intertwined with the use of transactions.

A Scope shape configured with a Transaction Type of None or Long Running scope can have exception handling blocks added, but atomic scopes cannot. The rationale is that atomic scopes either complete, or they do not. If they do not, all state is reset to how it looked before the scope was initiated, and it is the initiator of the Atomic scope, usually a Long Running scope that should decide what action is to be performed.

A Scope shape configured as Atomic or Long Running can have Compensation blocks added, but scopes that are configured with no Transaction Type cannot. The rationale is that only transactional scopes that consider the steps performed to be part of a unit of work will need to compensate that work should it be required.

The following screenshot shows how exception handling and Compensation blocks can be added to Scopes with different Transaction Types:

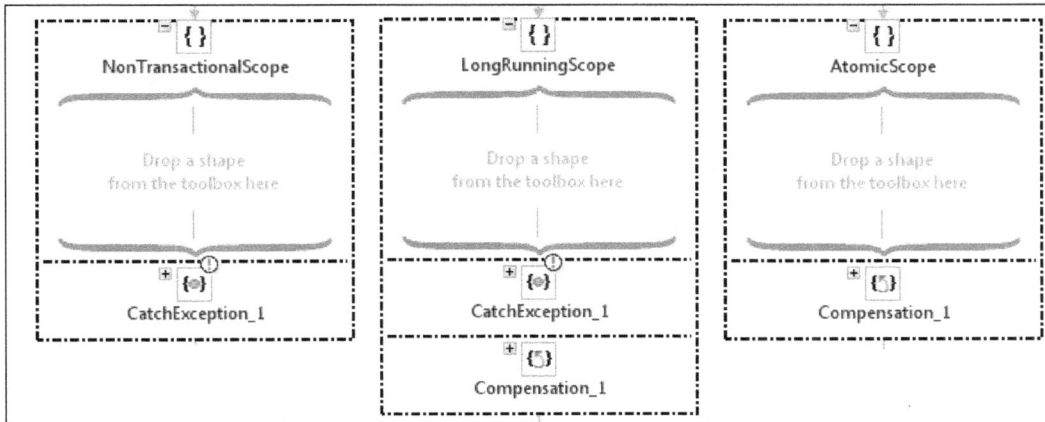

Throwing exceptions

Although the majority of all exception handling in BizTalk is about catching exceptions thrown by other parts in or outside BizTalk, sometimes you can also explicitly throw exceptions.

Throwing an exception may be a valid action, for example, in the following situations:

- When you reach a situation from which you cannot recover
- When a fatal error is relayed as part of a response rather than an exception
- When a Listen shape ends in a timeout
- When you discover an error situation in an atomic scope and want to make sure that the transaction is rolled back

In order to throw an exception, perform the following basic steps:

1. Define a variable with the type set to the exception class you wish to throw (in this example, the variable is called sysEx and is of the type System.Exception).
2. Instantiate it and set any value according to the error conditions.

3. Use the Throw Exception shape and configure it with the **Exception Object** (in the following screenshot, it is `sysEx`):

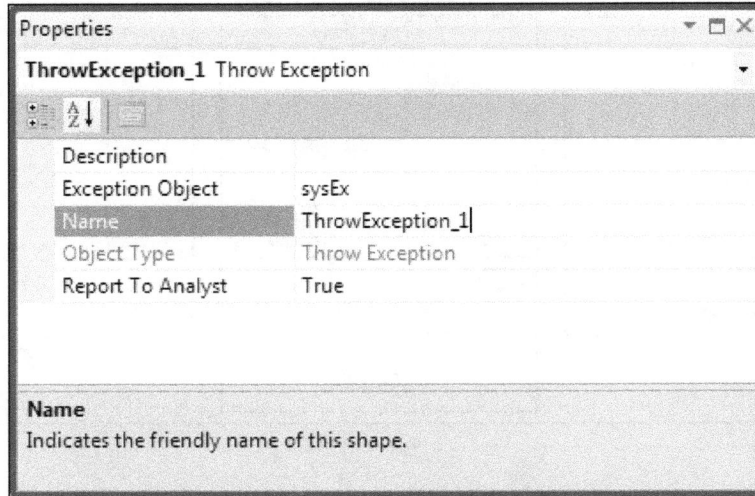

Properties	▾ ☐ ×
ThrowException_1 Throw Exception	▾

Description	
Exception Object	sysEx
Name	ThrowException_1
Object Type	Throw Exception
Report To Analyst	True

Name
Indicates the friendly name of this shape.

Catching exceptions

In order to catch an exception, you use an exception handling block. The exception block has two properties of interest, which are shown in the following screenshot:

- **Exception Object Name**
- **Exception Object Type**

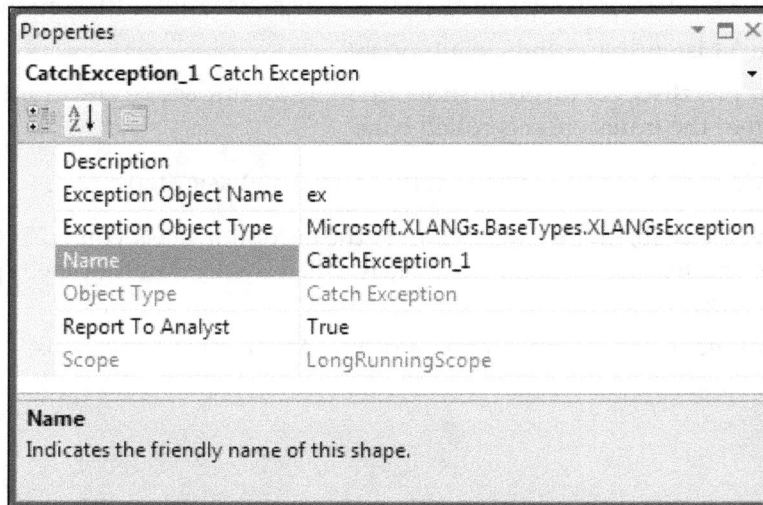

Properties	▾ ☐ ×
CatchException_1 Catch Exception	▾

Description	
Exception Object Name	ex
Exception Object Type	Microsoft.XLANGs.BaseTypes.XLANGsException
Name	CatchException_1
Object Type	Catch Exception
Report To Analyst	True
Scope	LongRunningScope

Name
Indicates the friendly name of this shape.

They allow you to define the type of exception to catch and a name by which you can access the caught exception. As far as exception handling goes, you can think of scopes and exception blocks in the same way that you would with the .NET equivalent; this is shown in the following code snippet:

```
try
{
  //code equivalent to shapes inside the scope goes here
}
catch (Microsoft.XLANGs.BaseTypes.XLANGsException ex)
{
  //code equivalent to shapes inside the
  //exception block goes here
}
catch (System.Exception exAll)
{
  //code to handle all .NET based exceptions goes here
}
```

When an exception is thrown, the engine will check for the closest exception handling block that can handle it. They are considered the way you would expect, that is, inside out, sequentially. Like in .NET, the exception handlers should be specified from the most detailed exception type to the least detailed, with `System.Exception` as the least detailed catch-all base type. When determining which exception handler to trigger it first checks the scope that the exception occurred in for an exception handling block. Then any parent scopes in the scope hierarchy. Then if the Orchestration was initiated though a Call Orchestration shape it checks the scope that contained the Call Orchestration shape, and so on up its scope hierarchy and calling Orchestration.

If an exception handler is found, processing will continue in that exception handling block. If no exception handler is found, the default exception handler is triggered. This means that the Compensation block for any nested scopes will be triggered, after which the exception is rethrown and the Orchestration will become suspended.

Also as in .NET, when an exception handling scope completes successfully, the Orchestration continues after the scope that held it, if nothing else is specified, such as ending the Orchestration using a Terminate shape or rethrowing the exception using a Throw Exception shape.

Compensation

If a transaction has completed (execution has left the scope) and an exception occurs in the Orchestration, the process might be in a state where, although technically coherent, it is logically incorrect. In such a situation, the actions performed in an already committed transactional scope might need to be compensated. This is done by adding a Compensation block.

> Adding a Compensation block is the same thing as setting up the **Compensation** property of a transactional scope to custom.

The Compensation block has no properties that control its behavior. It exists as a container for compensating logic. The following screenshot shows the **Properties** window for a Compensation block:

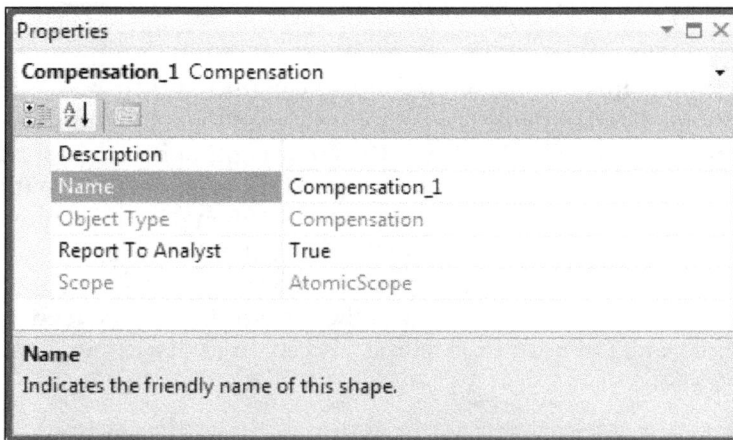

Properties	▾ ☐ ✕
Compensation_1 Compensation	▾

Description	
Name	Compensation_1
Object Type	Compensation
Report To Analyst	True
Scope	AtomicScope

Name
Indicates the friendly name of this shape.

> The **Report To Analyst** property exists on many shapes. Regardless of the value it is given, it has no effect on the behavior of your Orchestration. It is a property used to integrate with the **Orchestration Designer for Business Analysts (ODBA)** Visio plugin. If set to false, then that shape is considered a low-level detail that will not be visible in the Visio designer.

Although Atomic scopes do have the functionality of automatic rollback, if an exception occurs inside the scope, there is no such functionality once the scope has committed.

The default exception handler, if triggered, will initiate the compensation by calling the Compensation blocks for any nested scopes, but if you catch an exception in a custom exception handler, you must explicitly do the compensation. When you do explicit compensation, you need to use one or more **Compensate** shapes and configure them to compensate either the current scope or a selected nested scope.

The Compensate shape can only be used inside an exception handling or another Compensation block. When choosing to compensate the current scope, the Compensate shape will trigger the default compensation handler, and not the compensation code that may be defined by the scope (since the transaction will not be complete by then). Explicit use of the Compensate shape to compensate nested transactions allows us to specify the order in which to compensate transactions if the default order does not fit our logic. One Compensate shape is used to trigger one Compensation block, and thus the way to specify the order is by the use of multiple sequentially ordered compensate shapes.

If you have not added a custom Compensation block, default compensation will be performed. In the same way as the default exception handler, this will call the Compensation blocks of any nested scopes, starting with the most recently completed one and working its way back.

> Compensation blocks are possible in scopes that have their Transaction Type set to Long Running or Atomic. However, not for scopes that have their Transaction Type set to None. Such scopes cannot be compensated.

Although default compensation is triggered, if no Compensation blocks are added anywhere, nothing will be performed. Compensation is explicit; you must add the logic that compensates the actions performed, and you can use any shape you want inside the Compensation block to achieve this.

If the Orchestration is set to Long Running, you can also set Compensation to Custom on an Orchestration level. This will give you a Compensation block tab that is accessible at the bottom of the Orchestration window.

Regardless of whether you are handling Compensation at the scope or Orchestration level, the Compensation block can contain any Orchestration shape and perform any logic, without restriction.

Sample exception handling scenario

We are going to look at a scenario that incorporates the concepts of exception handling and compensation and see how they work in practice.

The completed sample is available in the `Chapter05-Example01` solution.

Let's start with a simple process. We will receive a `SimplifiedCar` Schema equipped with the `FuelTankCapacity`, `FuelConsumption`, and `OperationalRange` fields. The message will contain only the first two values and we need to calculate the last one. Inside a Scope, we will have a Send shape that sends the same message out again, for archival, and after that we will create a new message so that we can calculate and fill out the correct value for the `OperationalRange` field of the car. This is done by calling a .NET `helper` component that returns the value by dividing `FuelTankCapacity` by `FuelConsumption`. If the `FuelConsumption` field's value is 0, a divide by zero exception will occur. When we start out, no transactions are configured on the scope or on the Orchestration; the Transaction Type is None, which is the default.

> We are using a static method on the .NET component. Had we been using an instance method, the class would have to be instantiated and it would either have to be marked as serializable or used only from within an atomic scope (as no persistence is done while inside an atomic scope).

The Orchestration looks like the following screenshot:

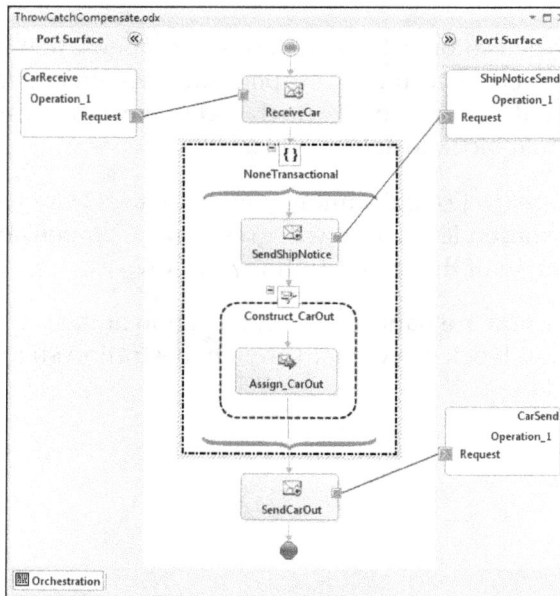

We could just as easily have done the simple division directly in the XLANG expression in the Message Assignment shape, but there is a lesson in doing it in a `helper` class — to show what we must do to handle the exceptions thrown by a .NET component.

The **Assign_CarOut** shape contains the code snippet that you can see in the following screenshot:

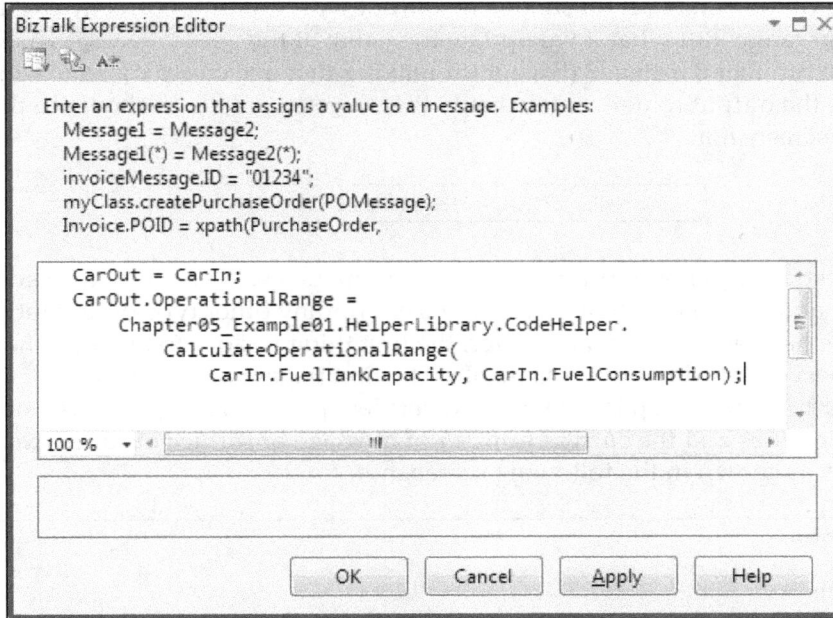

Let's run the following sample code. If you want to follow along, this state of the Orchestration is contained in the `ThrowCatchCompensate.odx` file. We will build upon this sample.

We will start by sending in a `SimplifiedCar` message that looks like the following code snippet:

```xml
<ns0:Car xmlns:ns0="http://Chapter05_Example01.Schemas.SimplifiedCar">
  <RegistrationNo>ABC123</RegistrationNo>
  <FuelTankCapacity>60</FuelTankCapacity>
  <FuelConsumption>0.7</FuelConsumption>
  <OperationalRange></OperationalRange>
</ns0:Car>
```

This will not cause an exception and we will get an output for both the **SendShipNotice** and **SendCarOut** sends respectively as shown in the following screenshot of the output folder:

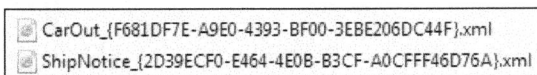

> CarOut_{F681DF7E-A9E0-4393-BF00-3EBE206DC44F}.xml
> ShipNotice_{2D39ECF0-E464-4E0B-B3CF-A0CFFF46D76A}.xml

In the case of the **SendCarOut** shape, the output will contain a correctly calculated operational range. But what if we update the value of the `FuelConsumption` field to hold the number 0 instead? (Except for making that one cheap car to drive). With this input, the output folder contains only the `ShipNotice` file as shown in the following screenshot:

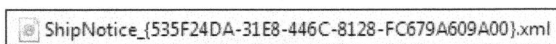

> ShipNotice_{535F24DA-31E8-446C-8128-FC679A609A00}.xml

The Orchestration is not outputting the **CarOut** message. When the expected output is missing and we suspect that a divide by zero (or any other type of) exception could have happened in BizTalk Server, the first thing to do is to open up the **BizTalk Server Administration Console**. The first page that comes up after you select your BizTalk Group is the **Group Overview** page. This page holds a number of default queries and the current number of message or service instances that match that query, as shown in the following screenshot:

Group Overview		Refresh this page to update results (press F5)
Group Hub		

Configuration Overview

Group name: BizTalk Group	Applications (16)	
Server: JEH8540	Host Instances (1)	
Database: BizTalkMgmtDb	Adapter Handlers (52)	

Learn about Administration and Troubleshooting

Work in Progress

		Suspended Items	
Running service instances	0	Suspended service instances	1
· Dehydrated orchestrations	0	· Resumable	1
· Retrying and idle ports	0	· Non-resumable	0
· Ready service instances	0		
· Scheduled service instances	0		

Grouped Suspended Service Instances

Grouped by Application		Grouped by Service Name	
BTS2013CertGuide-Ch05	1	Chapter05_Example01.Orchestrations.ThrowCatchCompensate. Cha...	1
Grouped by Error Code		Grouped by URI	
0xC0C01B52 (Orchestration Engine Error)	1	<URI is not available>	1

Tracked Service Instances

	Tracked Message Events
Tracked service instances	Tracked message events
· Completed instances	· Transmission failure events
· Terminated instances	

An example of such a query is **Suspended service instances**, which is marked red in the previous screenshot. Clicking on the **Suspended service instances** text executes the query and displays the results with more details as shown in the following screenshot:

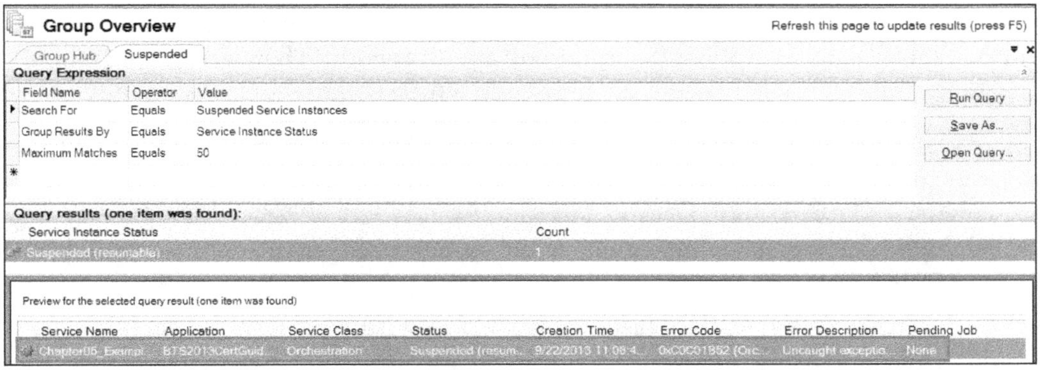

From here you can open the instance of the **Orchestration** that is **Suspended** and look at the **Error Information** tab as shown in the following screenshot:

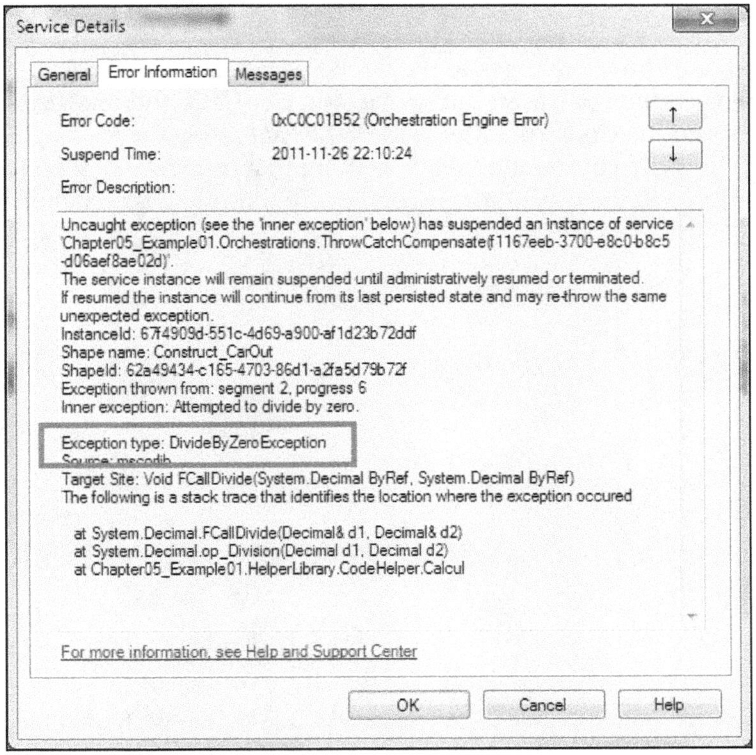

The Orchestration instance is resumable, but if we try to resume, it will continue from its last persistence point, which in this case is after the **SendShipNotice** shape, and all that will end up happening is that it will call the .NET `helper` component and get the same exception again. There is no fix to be made to the component to correct its behavior; it's the content of the messages that is creating the error. But, we can fix the code to check for the parameter being 0 (and for example return -1), compile the `helper` component, and deploy a new version. Then, when we resume the Orchestration, it will execute the new code which will execute successfully.

In this scenario, even though we got an exception, the Orchestration still created the `ShipNotice` file. This happens because the scope that contains the **SendShipNotice** Send shape and the **Assign_CarOut** Message Assignment shape, which makes the call to the .NET helper component, is not transactional. In order to make them succeed or fail, we need to set the Transaction Type of the scope to Atomic.

Once we do that no output will be created when the .NET `helper` component fails. This state of the Orchestration is contained in the `ThrowCatchCompensate1.odx` file.

> To be able to set the scopes' Transaction Type to Atomic, the Orchestration that contains it must have its Transaction Type set to Long Running.

Let's make two additional changes to the Orchestration. One, let's move the Construct shape outside of the atomic scope, and two, let's add another scope around both the scope and the Construct Message shape that holds the Message Assignment shape calling the .NET component. After making that outer scope a Long Running, the Orchestration will look like the one seen in the following screenshot:

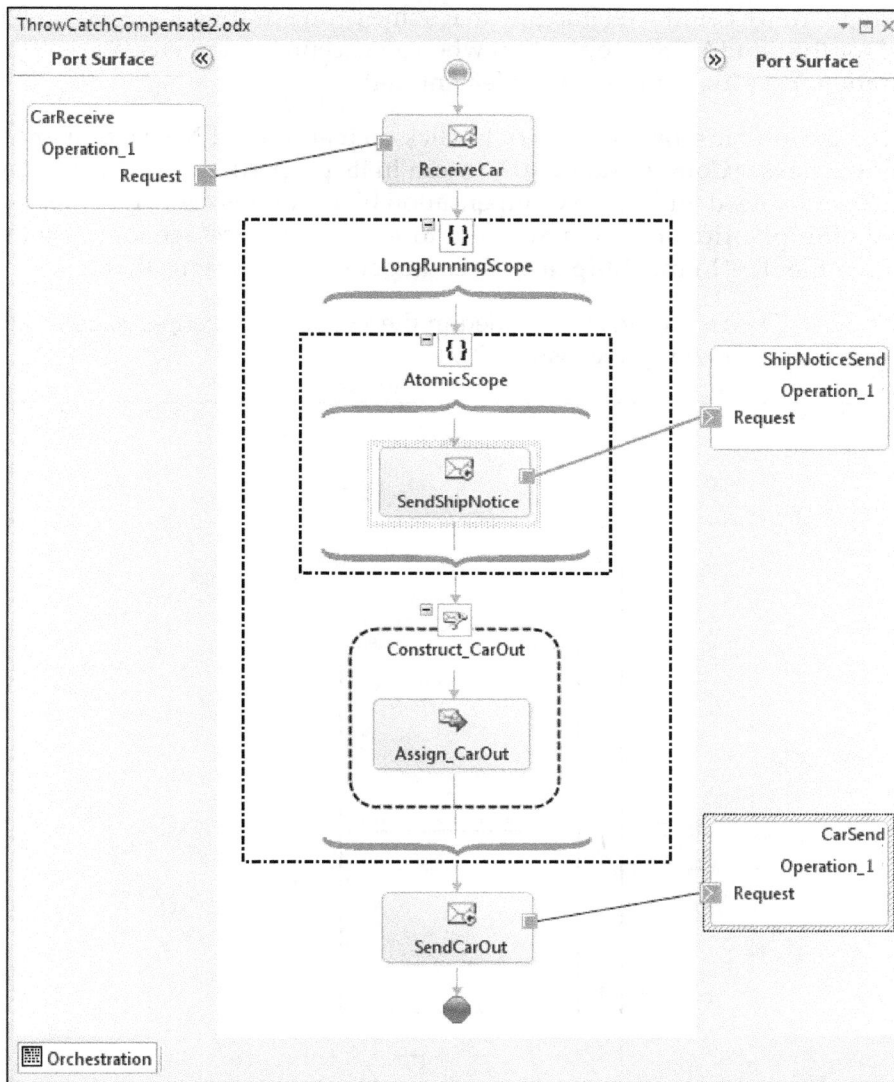

This state of the Orchestration is contained in the `ThrowCatchCompensate2.odx` file.

When we have done this, and run the sample, we will once again get the **SendShipNotice** shape outputted to disk because it is contained in an Atomic Scope that has been committed before the exception happens. The output folder will show an outputted file such as the one that can be seen in the following screenshot:

ShipNotice_{62C5A62D-7661-40FC-A8E3-3BF33612CD26}.xml

In this situation, we could well imagine that some compensating logic would be required for the **SendArchive** operation when an exception happens later in the Orchestration. Let's look at how to implement that.

If we select the atomic scope, we can right-click on it and select **New Compensation Block**, or we can set **Compensation** to **Custom** in its properties window. We can add any logic we need within the Compensation block. In this case, to compensate for the **SendShipNotice** operation, we need to send a new message to retract the ShipNotice file. The **RetractShipNotice** send operation represents that.

This state of the Orchestration is contained in the ThrowCatchCompensate3.odx file that is seen in the following screenshot:

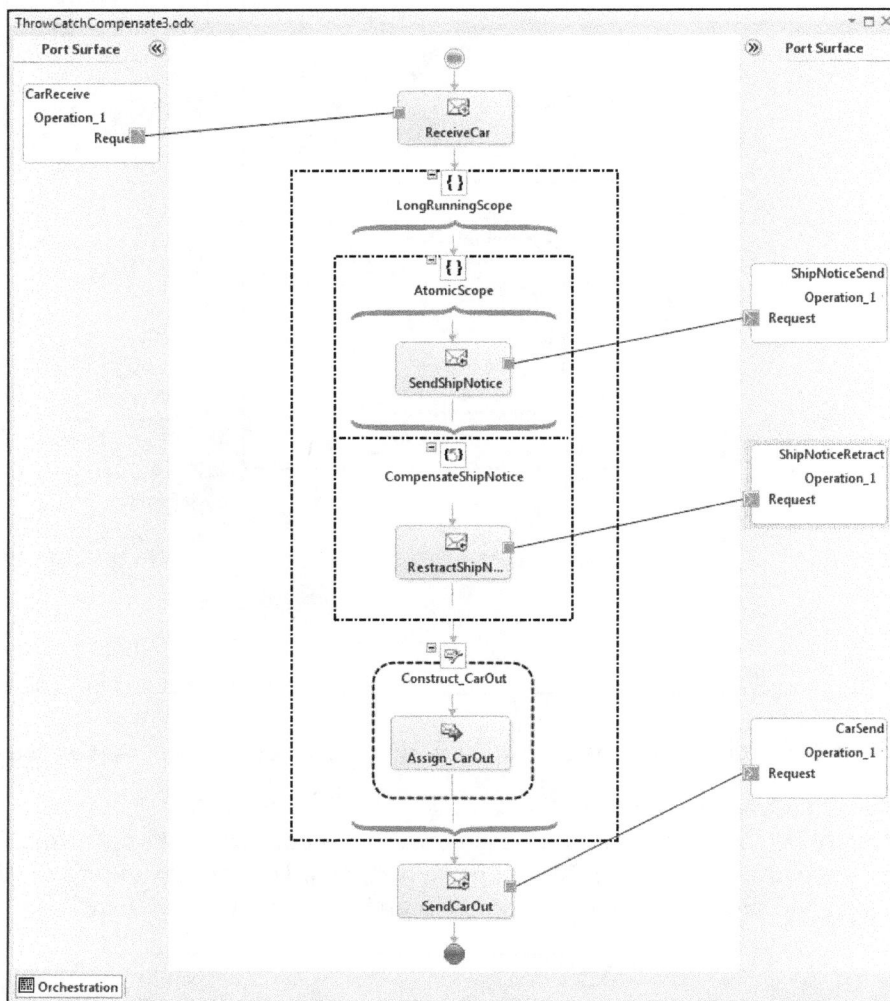

If we send the `SimplifiedCar.xml` message that does not contain an error, the messages outputted are a **CarOut** and a **ShipNotice** message.

What if we send the `CarSimplified_zero.xml` file that causes a divide by zero exception? The output will look like the one seen in the following screenshot:

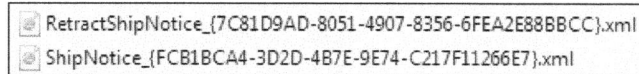

We get a **ShipNotice** message and then a **RetractShipNotice** message. Why?

The Atomic scope completes, thus sending out the **ShipNotice** message. Then an exception occurs. Remember, when we have no explicit exception handler that can handle the exception, the default exception handler kicks in. It automatically calls the Compensation blocks of any nested scopes that have completed; in this case, the **CompensateShipNotice** block that makes the **RetractShipNotice** send its message out. Then it rethrows the exception. In this case, it means that the Orchestration is suspended.

The next step is that when we get an exception, we want to notify a car shipment clerk by sending him/her a message about the car that failed shipment processing. That means implementing a custom exception handler. We do that by right-clicking on the Long Running shape and selecting **New Exception Block**.

We could be very specific in the exceptions we catch, which in this case means that if we suspect we could get a divide by zero exception, or any other exception that requires special handling, we could catch that specifically, as shown in the following screenshot:

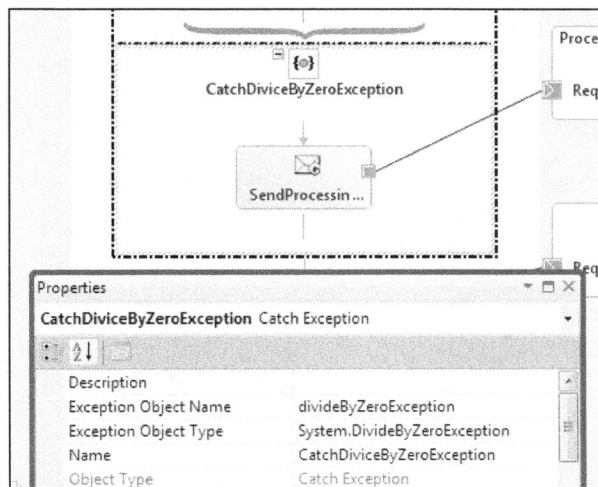

In this case, no exception requires special treatment. They should all result in a processing-error notification being sent; so, we'll create a catch-all exception handler as seen in the following screenshot:

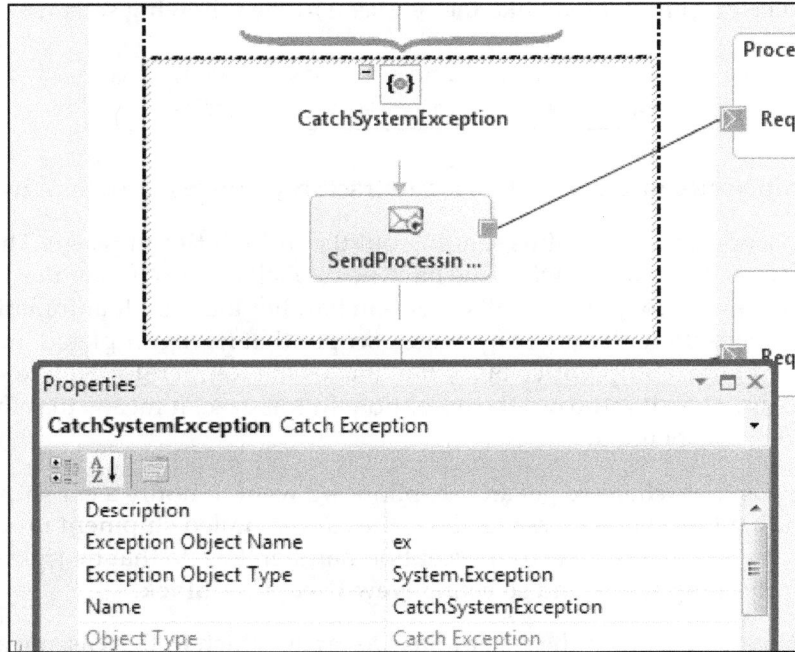

If we just leave it like that, we will now get an exception: **Use of unconstructed message 'CarOut'**. This is due to the fact that, as the logic stands, an exception could occur (and in our test of the exception handling it will occur) before the construction of the **CarOut** message. As we are now handling that exception, execution will continue to the **Send** shape after the scope that is configured to send the **CarOut** message, which in this case can potentially be unconstructed. We will solve this by moving the **SendCarOut** shape inside the Long Running.

This state of the Orchestration is contained in the ThrowCatchCompensate4.odx file that is seen in the following screenshot. As the Orchestration is now beginning to grow, the Construct shape has been minimized to save the space.

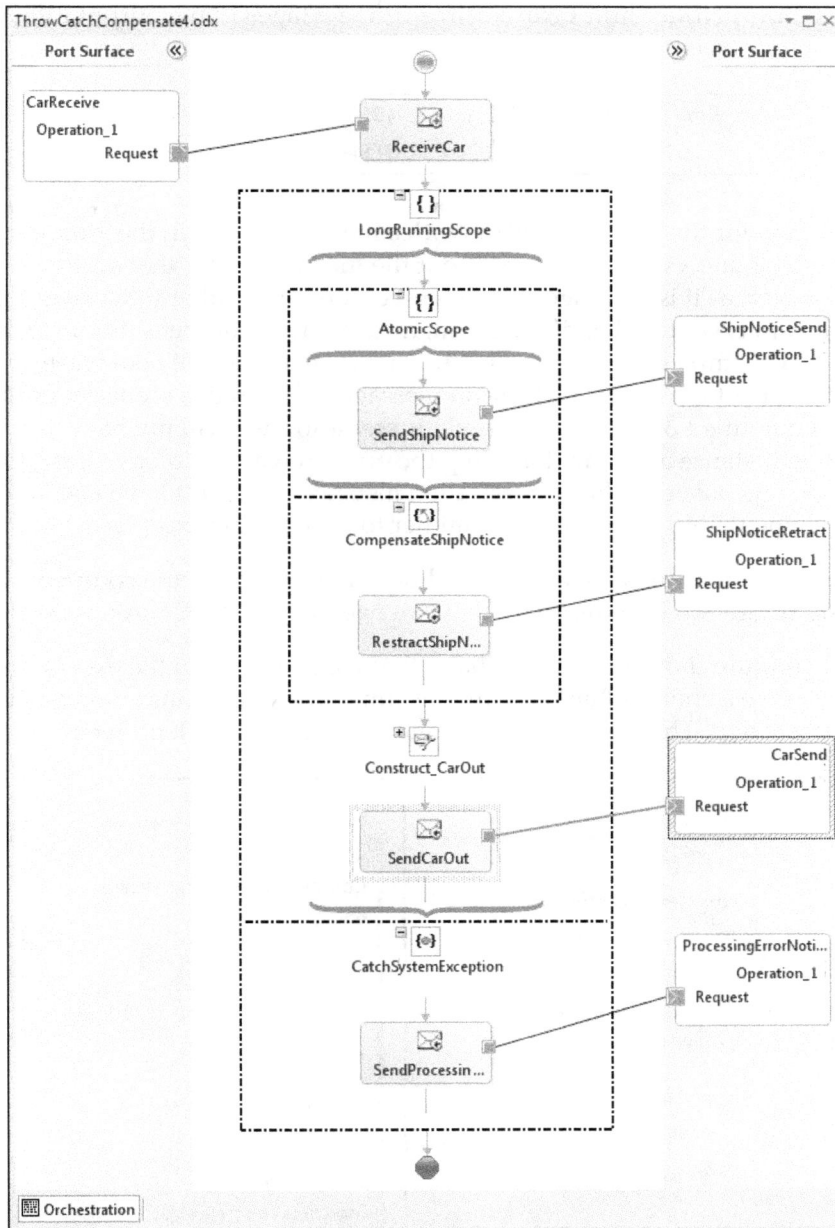

Now, let's deploy and test this scenario. A correct message will create the same two outputs as it always has: the **ShipNotification** and **CarOut** message. However, what about a message resulting in the divide by zero exception in the Construct/Message Assignment shape?

We will get a **ShipNotice** and **ErrorNotifcation** messages in the output folder as seen in the following screenshot:

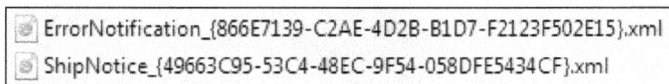

The explanation for this is that the **ShipNotice** message is sent in the atomic scope, which completes successfully and sends out the message. After that an exception occurs. However, as it is no longer the default exception handler that catches it, but our own custom exception handler instead, no automatic compensation will occur. Instead, the logic implemented by us in our custom handler will take place. In this case, the sending of the **ErrorNotification** message. Also, in this scenario, unlike when we have been notified of an error in previous scenarios, we will not have a suspended Orchestration instance as we are handling the error. If we would have liked to handle the exception and suspend the Orchestration instance, we could have used the Throw Exception shape within our exception handler to rethrow the exception.

As a final step in this scenario, we will add back logic to allow the compensation to be explicitly triggered. In order to do that, we need to use the Compensate shape.

When we configure the Compensate shape that we place inside the exception handler, we have a choice of either compensating an atomic transaction or the long running transaction. The following screenshot displays their identifiers:

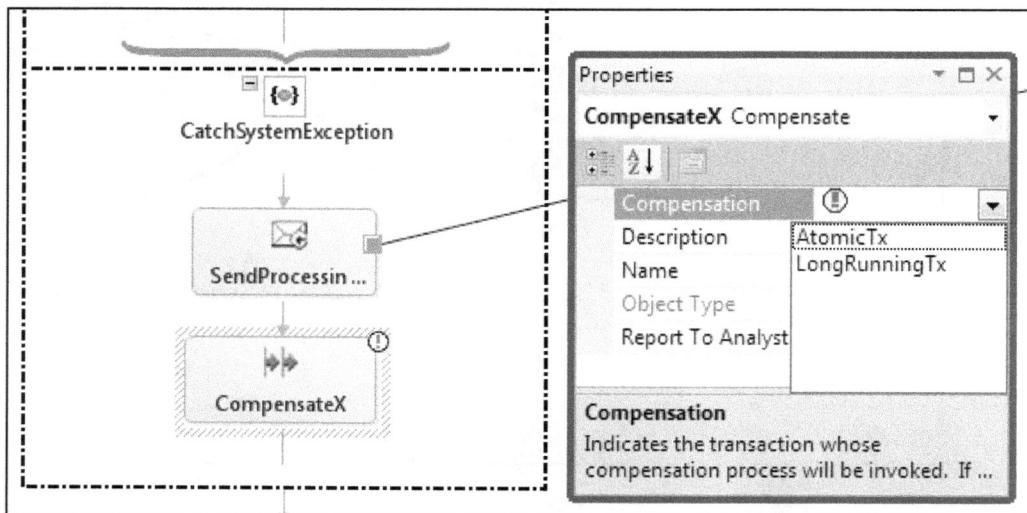

As we are in the long-running transaction's exception handler, choosing the **LongRunningTx** option, in this case, means compensating the current scope, which has a special meaning. This will automatically compensate for all nested transactions in a last-completed, first-compensated manner. If we want to choose the transactions we compensate, or dictate the order, we need to use Compensate shapes. Each **Compensate** shape can be configured to compensate for one transaction. This means we will execute the Scopes Compensation block. However, in this case, we will choose to compensate the current transaction and trigger the default compensation handling.

This state of the Orchestration is contained in the `ThrowCatchCompensate5.odx` file that is seen in the following screenshot. As the Orchestration has become larger than can be comfortably visualized in one page, the AtomicScope and Construct shapes have been minimized to save space.

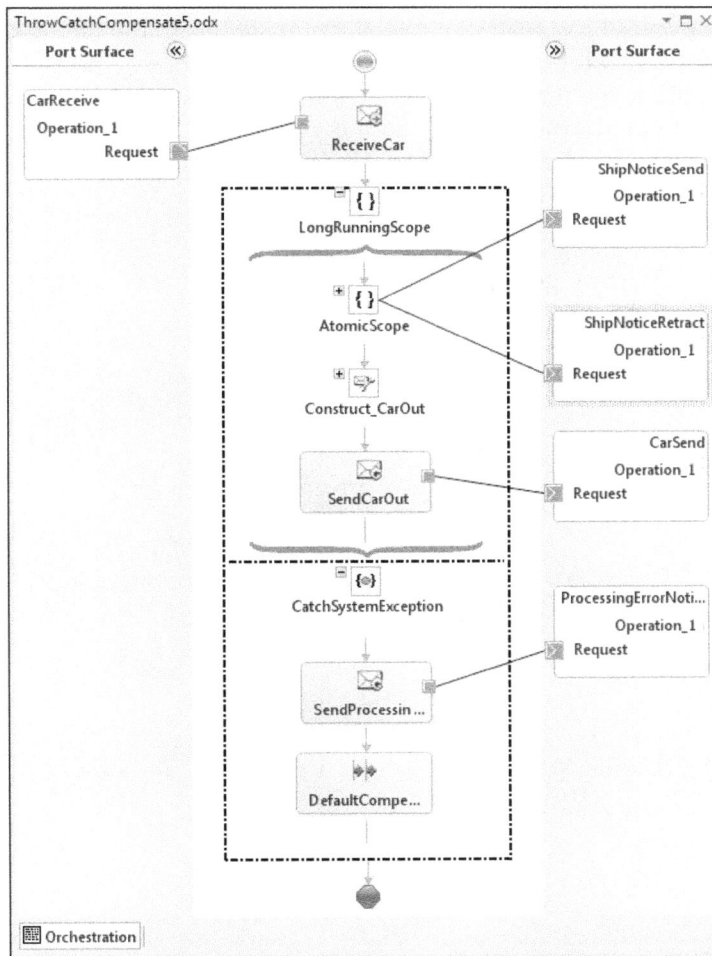

At this point, the output (in case of an exception in the Construct/Message Assignment shape) is the **ShipNotice**, **ErrorNotification**, and **RetractShipNotice** messages, in the chronological order as shown in the following screenshot:

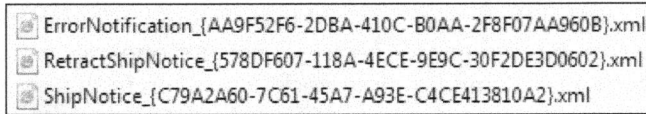

Delivery notification

BizTalk Server is built on a publish-subscribe architecture. Messages always go to the `MessageBox` before being delivered to a port. With a two-way port, a correlated response or another response aware pattern, you will potentially be aware of an error occurring somewhere after you sent the message from the Orchestration. With a one-way Send Port, you may not be aware when an exception occurs. This is true even for an Atomic scope that will happily complete even though the message may never reach its intended destination. This is because the transaction initiated by the atomic transaction scope commits to the `MessageBox`; the successful delivery by the intended Send Port is not included in the transaction.

We will use the Simple Orchestration contained in the `DeliveryNotification.odx` Orchestration as a starting point; it has the components needed for this illustration:

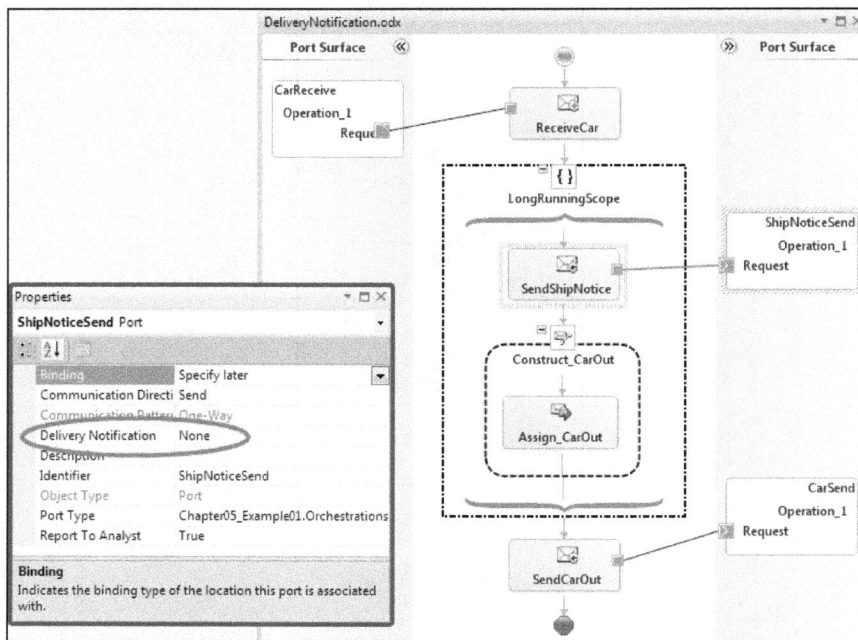

Without making any changes to the Orchestration, let's alter the
SendShipNotification physical port so that it sends message to an invalid location as
shown in the following screenshot:

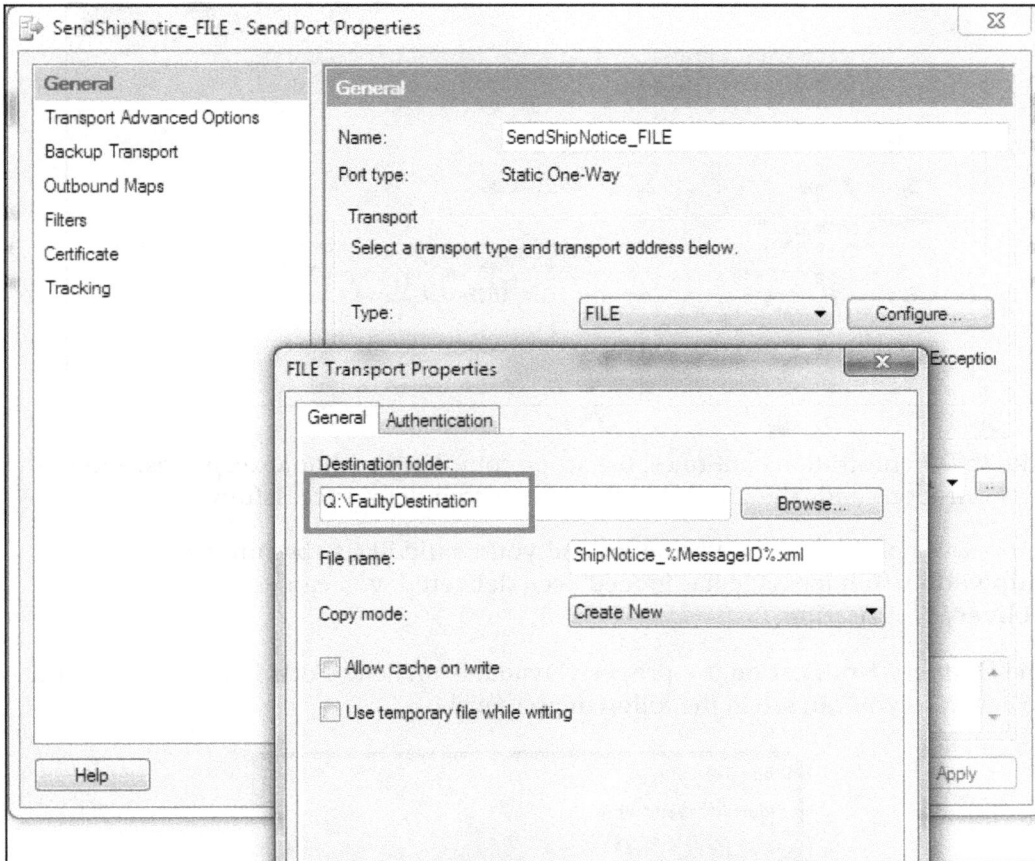

In other words, it is configured to fail. Now let's try the scenario. If you skipped the
previous section, the correct behavior should result in two messages: the **ShipNotice**
and **CarOut** messages in the chronological order. The output, however, looks like the
one seen in the following screenshot:

CarOut_{CF6FCDBD-1AF8-4E7C-97C3-5DF820A4F937}.xml

At the same time, we will have a suspended message on the **SendShipNotice_FILE** Send Port. As expected, it could not send out our message. The **Error Information** tab of the **Service Details** window is shown in the following screenshot:

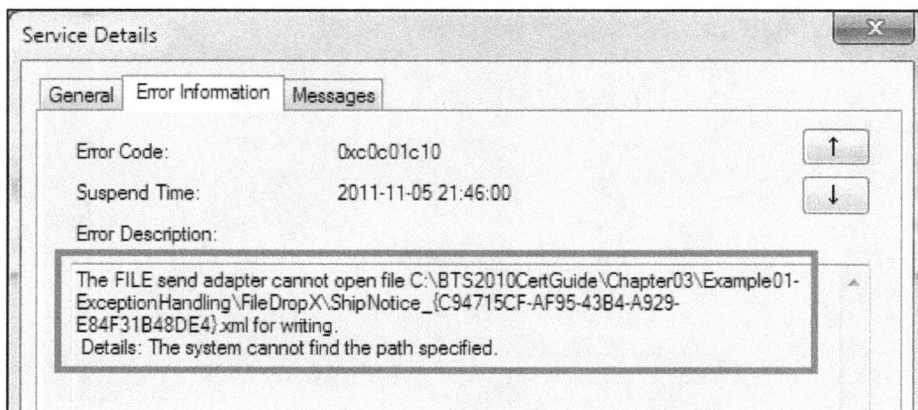

Still, the Orchestration continues, the scope completes without exceptions, and the Orchestration sends the **CarOut** message and completes successfully.

If this was not the intended behavior and you would like to be sure that the **ShipNotification** message has indeed been delivered, you can use the **Delivery Notification**.

The **Delivery Notification** is a property available on Send Ports in the Orchestration designer, as you can see in the following screenshot:

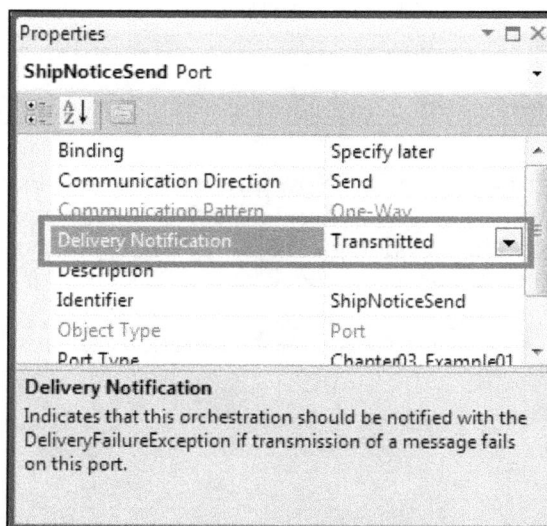

When set to **Transmitted**, the Orchestration waits for an acknowledgement from the physical Send Port before completing the scope. Should the Send Port not be successful, a `DeliveryFailureException` will be thrown that can be caught to handle the exception. An example of the properties of an exception handling block that handles such an exception is shown in the following screenshot:

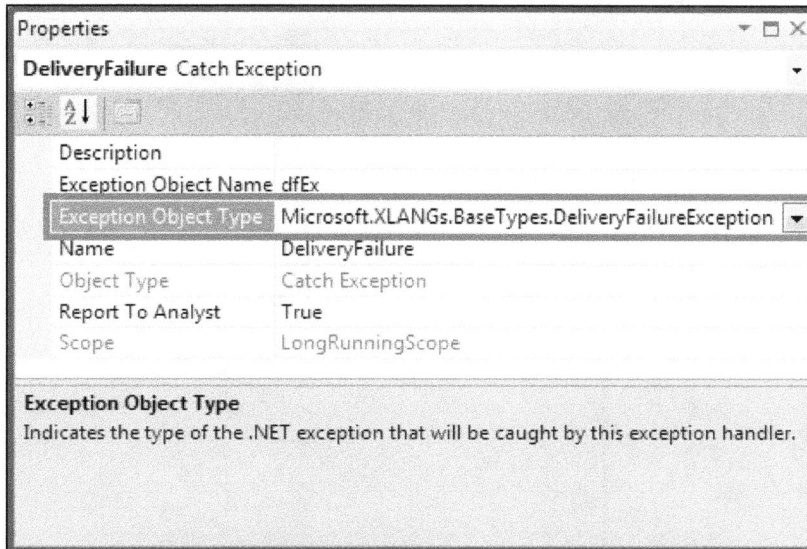

The `DeliveryFailureException` is thrown once all retries of a Send Port are exhausted.

> The **Delivery Notification** property can be used with atomic scopes as well, but as they cannot have exception handling blocks, the `DeliveryFailureException` exception would have to be caught in a parent scope. In order to simplify, we are using a Long Running directly in the previous sample.

This state of the Orchestration after configuring **Delivery Notification** to **Transmitted** and adding an exception handling block to handle the DeliveryFailureNotification is contained in the DeliveryNotification1.odx file that is seen in the following screenshot. We also moved the **SendCarOut** shape into the scope to avoid the use of unconstructed message build error as explained in the previous section on error handling.

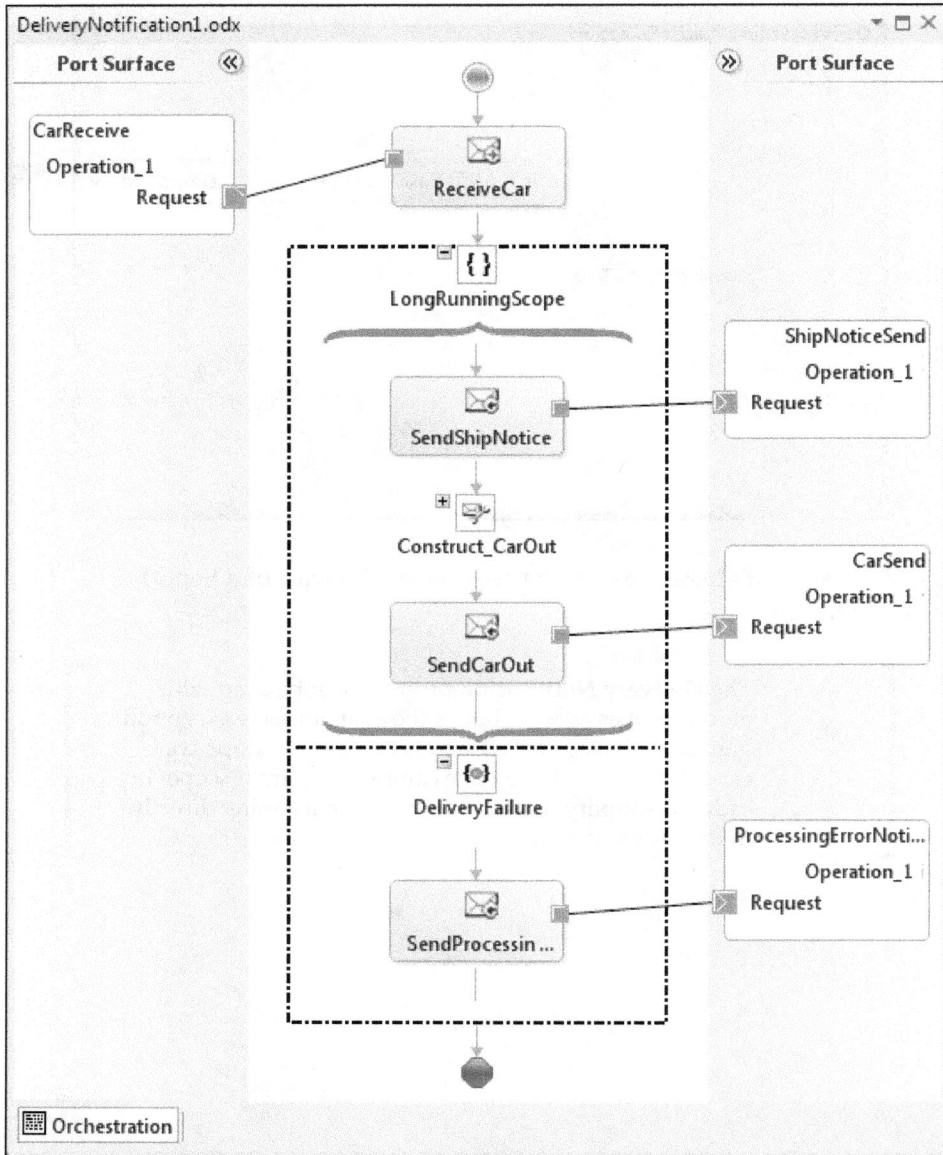

Now let's try out the scenario, with the same faulty configuration on the physical Send Port that the **ShipNoticeSend** Port is bound to.

This time we will get a single output again, but in the form of an **ErrorNotification** message sent from the exception handling block, as shown in the following screenshot:

ErrorNotification_{6BD58367-DB03-455A-A6E5-02BFB2E03836}.xml

Also, as the exception is handled, we will get no suspended Orchestration instances. You will however get a **Suspended Message Instance** on the Send Port.

> In order to get rid of that, you can use failed message routing, which we will discuss later in this chapter in the *Routing errors* section.

Debugging Orchestrations

When exceptions are thrown, it's useful and often an absolutely necessary pattern to handle them using exception handling blocks. For exception, we can anticipate and would like to handle separately. We apply the pattern of more detailed to less detailed exception catch blocks. But, we simply can't have exception handlers for each and every exception type that we can potentially get. For example, a divide by zero can happen in our Orchestration process in a place that we were not expecting. It's a runtime error, not a deterministic business error that we should have been able to anticipate and handle specifically. A divide by zero exception will then most likely end up in a catch-all exception handling block. The difficult part now is to find out exactly what and why it happened. We are going to take a look at some of the options you have for debugging Orchestration execution.

First, although probably well known for anyone looking to take the BizTalk Server 2010 certification or BizTalk 2013 assessment, let's get the simple yet long-time annoyance out of the way: You cannot debug Orchestrations using Visual Studio. At least, not in the traditional sense of stepping through the shapes of the designer and getting access to variables, messages, and the Orchestration state. There are things you can do with the generated C# classes, but those are out of the scope of this book and certification.

You need to use the BizTalk Server Administration Console. First, let's use the **Group Overview** window and create a new query to get some tracked service instances with service class of type Orchestration, as shown in the following screenshot:

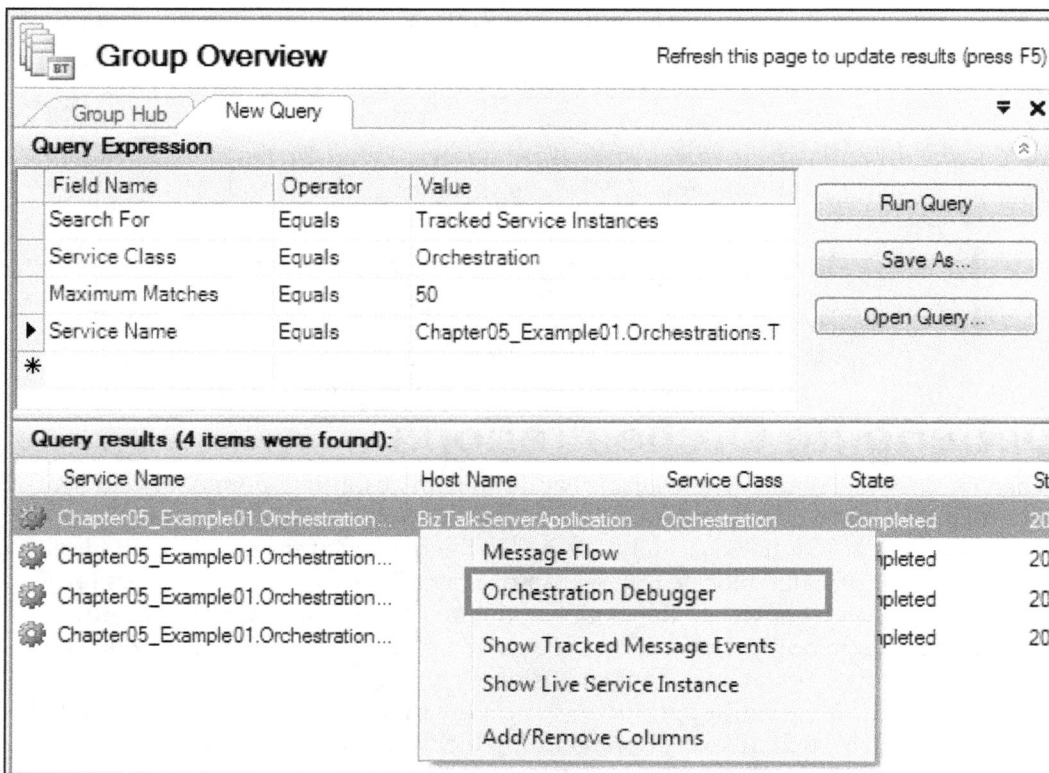

The Orchestration debugger is available through the context menu of any of the tracked Orchestration instances. Let's bring it up for the final state of the exception handling and compensation sample `ThrowCatchCompensate5.odx`, which we walked through in a previous section (if you have just read the section on **Delivery Notification**, for your information, the **SendShipNotice** port has been set back to its correct path).

Using the Orchestration debugger, we can step through the tracking that the Orchestration left behind, and see what happened. You can see exactly what shapes have been triggered and in what order. The numbers on the Orchestration surface in the following screenshot are an addition to aid the visualization in this book. They correlate to the numbers on the left-hand side. They are not there in the Orchestration debugger.

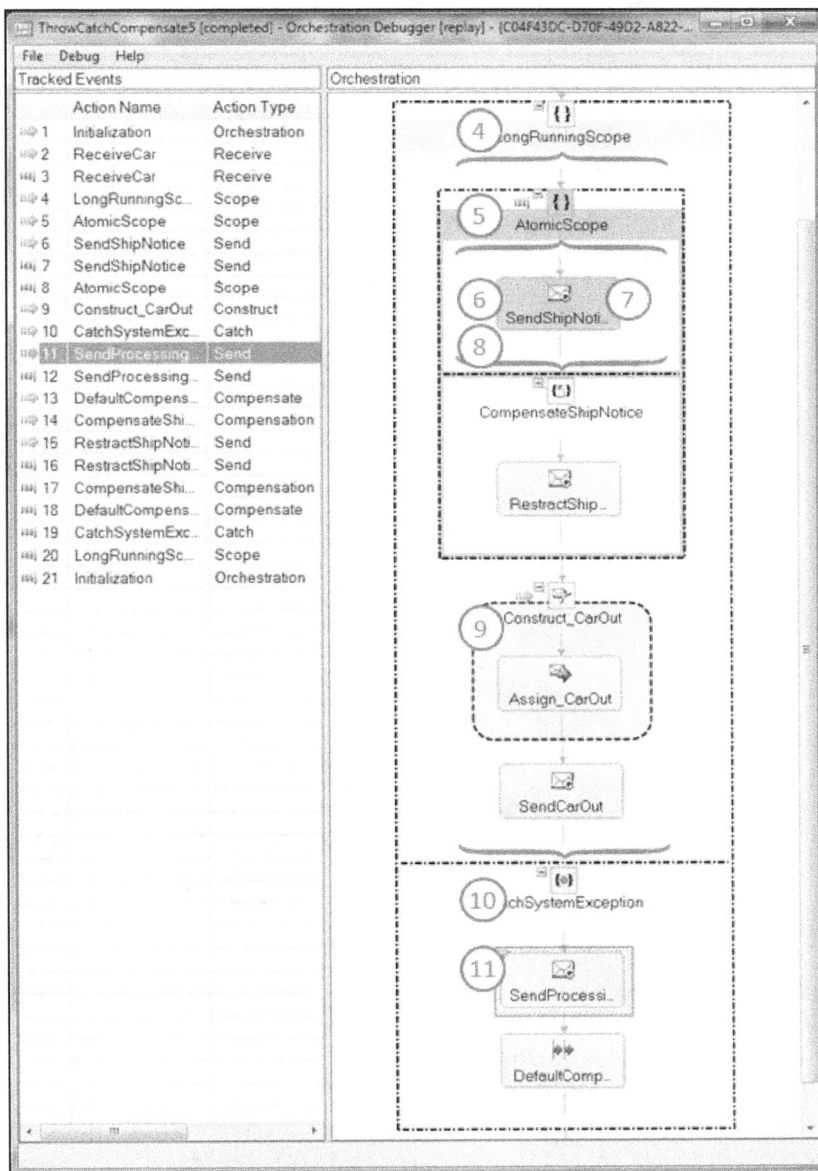

Using the Orchestration debugger in this after-the-fact manner can be very useful. In the **Tracked Events** pane, if you expand it to the right, you will also see the date and time of each event.

> The level of information available is dependent on the level of tracking configured. By default, only the Orchestration start and end, message send and receive, and shape start and end are configured.

You can also get access to any exception that has occurred by going to the **Debug** menu and choosing **Show Tracked Exceptions**, which brings up the exception dialog shown in the following screenshot:

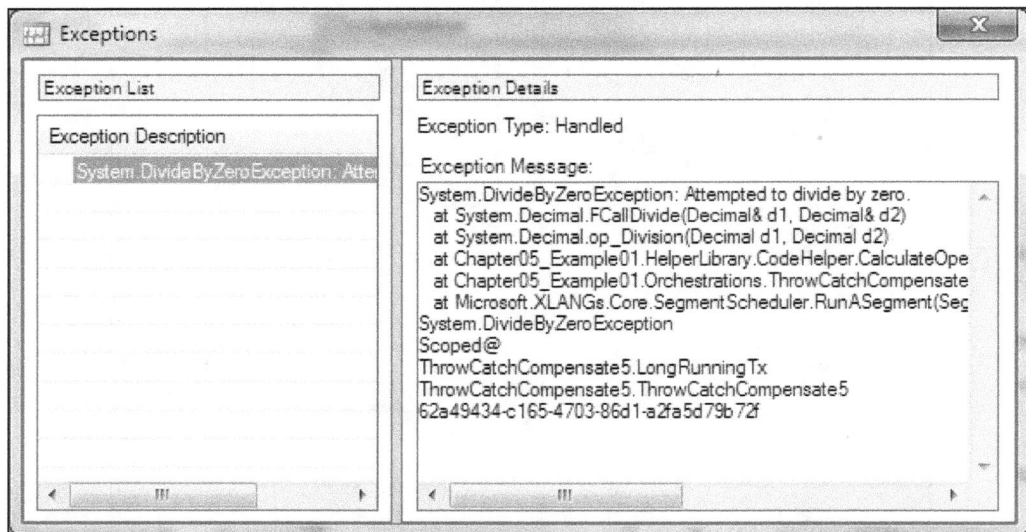

However, it does not give you access to the variables, messages, or state of the Orchestration as part of the tool experience. Hence, you can't really troubleshoot why it happened. Not even if you apply all the tracking possible (having done that, the information will be available to you through other queries, but that's beside the point for this walkthrough).

What you can do in the Orchestration debugger is to set a breakpoint. You do this by right-clicking on a shape and selecting **Set Breakpoint on Class**. After you have done this, you can close the **Orchestration Debugger** window. The next time an instance of the Orchestration runs, it will break on the spot you placed the breakpoint and the Orchestration instance will be in an **In Breakpoint (Active)** state as shown in the following screenshot:

If you launch the Orchestration debugger for this instance, you will have the option on the **Debug** menu to attach to the Orchestration instance. This will bring you to the breakpoint and you will have access to state, variables, and messages in the Orchestration.

From here you can step through the Orchestration and observe the changes as they occur. You can't really step through as you would have expected from a Visual Studio experience, but you can set new breakpoints (which are applied to that instance only) and choose to continue, which is the equivalent of *F5* or Run when you debug in Visual Studio. Execution will then halt once it reaches the next breakpoint.

Orchestrations will keep ending up **In Breakpoint (Active)** until you remove the breakpoint on the class level. You can only add and remove breakpoints to the class level when you are viewing an Orchestration while not attached.

Handling messaging errors

Now that we have looked at handling exceptions in Orchestrations, we are going to change focus to messaging solutions and examine some of the common exceptions that can occur and how we can eliminate or handle those exceptions through configuration.

Subscription errors

Failure in subscriptions usually comes from one of the following two main problem areas:

- Incorrectly configured subscribers, such as incorrect filters or an enlisted state
- Faulty messages or message handling resulting in the required promoted message context properties not being available

Regardless of this, the exception that occurs when the BizTalk Server cannot find a configured subscriber after evaluation of a message is: **The published message could not be routed because no subscribers were found**. This is shown in the following screenshot:

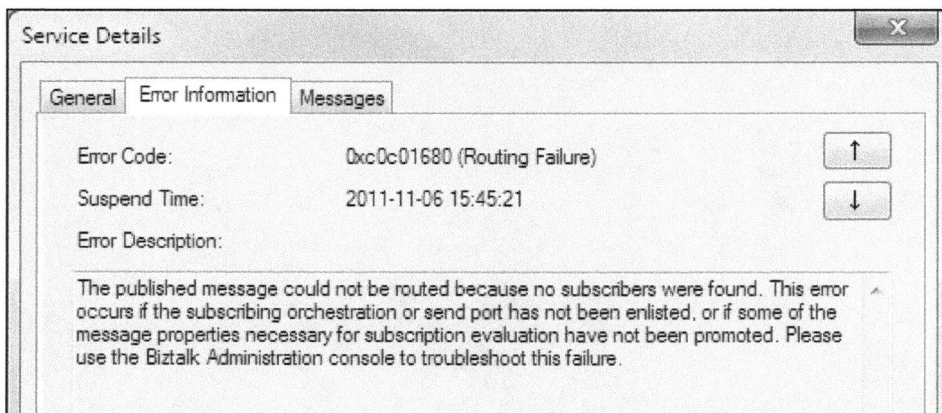

The message will (most of the time) be in a **Suspended (resumable)** state.

The problem with this **Suspended service instance** is that when an error occurs, BizTalk will always abort the current transaction and the message will have the form that it had before the operation was attempted. This means that you could have big difficulties in determining why the error occurred; since all states including the message context will also be reset to the state before the operation was attempted. For example, in a Receive Pipeline, many of the properties that will be used for routing, at least when that routing is based on any form of information that is the result of a disassembler component parsing the message, will not be available in that earlier form because what creates them has not yet occurred at that point. For this reason, BizTalk Server also creates another service instance, **Routing Failure Report**, in a **Suspended (not resumable)** state.

Group Overview			Refresh this page to update results (press F5)	

Group Hub / New Query (1)

Query Expression

Field Name	Operator	Value	
▶ Search For	Equals	Suspended Service Instances	Run Query
Maximum Matches	Equals	50	Save As...
∗			Open Query...

Query results (2 items were found):

!Service Name	Application	Service Class	Status	Error Description
⚙ ReceiveCar	BTS2010CertGui...	Messaging	Suspended (resumable)	The published m...
⚙ Routing Failure Report for "ReceiveCar"	BTS2010CertGui...	Routing Failure Report	Suspended (not resum...	This service insta...

This service instance allows you to review the state of the message and its context as it was when the messaging engine evaluated it against any subscribers.

You can use it to troubleshoot the reason the message was suspended and take necessary action. One such action could be to configure a Send Port with the correct filters to cause a subscription match. Such a subscription could be based on the **MessageType** property of the received message as shown in the following screenshot, or any other promoted properties:

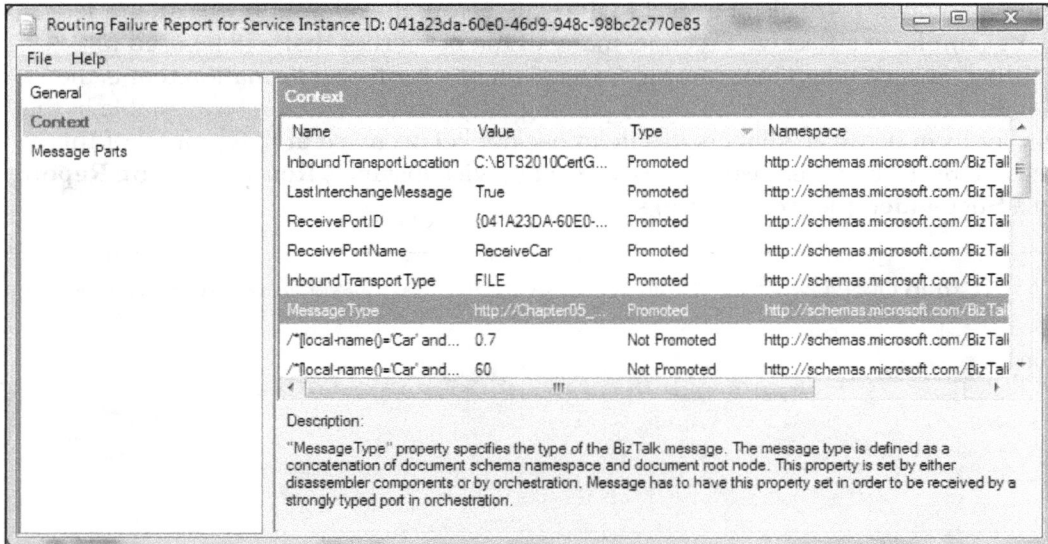

You could also use the **Routing Failure Report** instance to review the actual message, which could potentially be very different after the Receive Pipeline has triggered; especially, if the original message was a flat file or a Map was applied on the Receive Port.

Transmission errors

In transmission errors, all errors are included that are the result of a send adapter call failing and resulting in **Suspended service instance**. Transmission errors can occur under many different conditions, all depending on the adapter being used and the system or transport you wish to connect with. Common examples might be:

- A file share is unavailable or the BizTalk Host Instance user is not authorized
- A WCF call results in a Connection that was actively refused exception
- An application adapter gets a runtime exception from the system it connects to, for example, a SAP system
- A connection to an FTP Server cannot be made

Regardless of what the exception is, BizTalk Server has a built-in retry capability. By default, this will be configured to retry the operation three times with five minutes in between as the following screenshot shows:

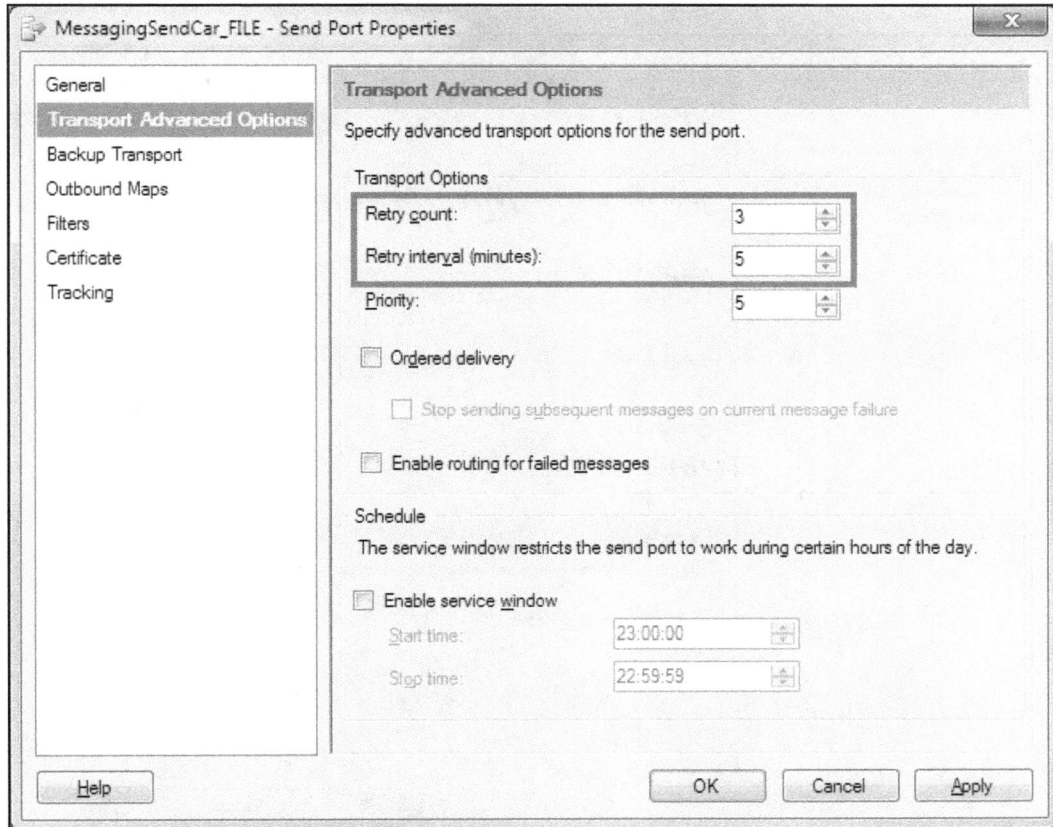

This configuration means that it will take 15 minutes before a message gets suspended.

> In a situation where the message needs to suspend or switch to the backup transport option (if configured) immediately, you should configure the **Retry count** option to **0**. This is also a suitable development setting.

Send Ports also have the possibility of configuring a backup transport that will trigger instead of the message being suspended once the retry attempts are exhausted. The **Backup Transport** tab has some of the same configuration as the primary transport has as can be seen in the following screenshot:

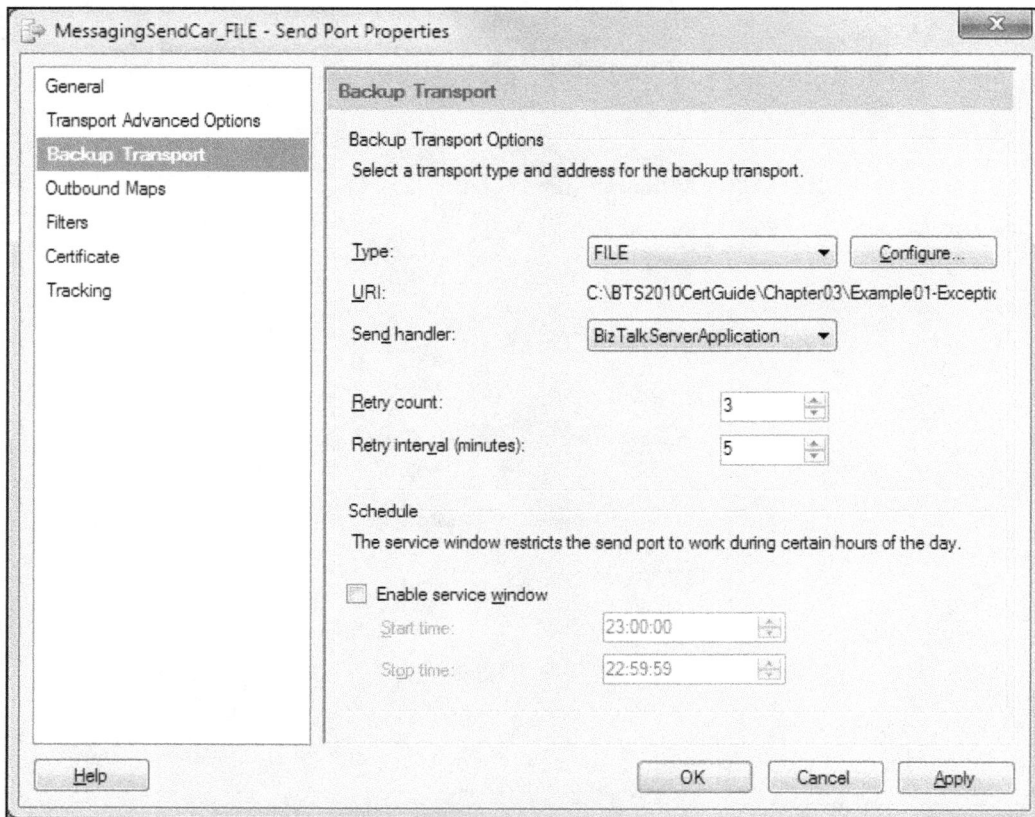

You can configure the backup transport with the same or another adapter, whichever suits your needs. You could even configure it against the same exact URI with different retry options if you wish to continue retrying, for example, once an hour for 12 hours if the initial retries fail.

Routing errors

Orchestrations allow for try, catch, and compensate patterns. For subscriptions, routing exceptions, failing adapters, handling exceptions that occur in interchanges with many parts, or in Maps or Schema validation, a feature known as **Failed Message Routing** is utilized.

When an exception occurs in a port, one of the following actions is performed by BizTalk Server Runtime:

- The port has retries left; so, it will wait to retry (only possible in Send Ports)
- The port has no retries configured but has a backup transport configured and will fall back to that (again, only possible in Send Ports)
- The service instance gets suspended
- Failed Message Routing kicks in

A message ends up in a suspended state when all retries and backup transport options have been evaluated and no Failed Message Routing has been implemented.

The Failed Message Routing option is available on both Receive and Send Ports. On Receive Ports, it is available on the **General** tab:

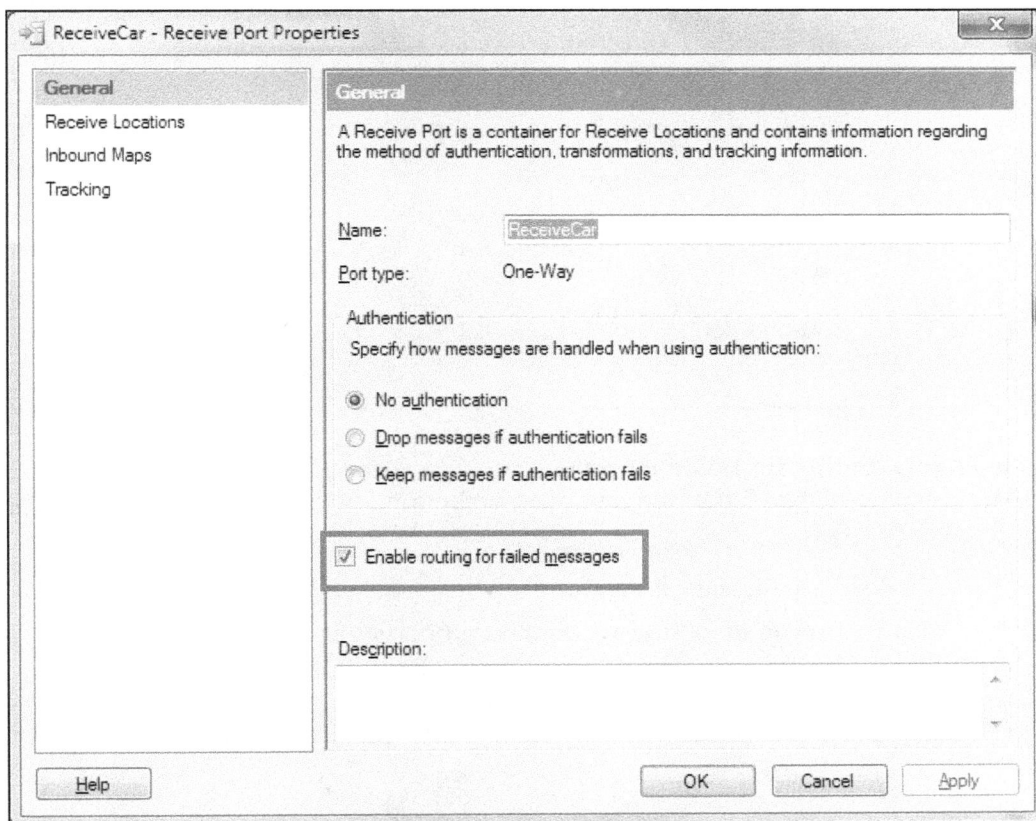

While on Send Ports, it is available on the **Transport Advanced Options** tab:

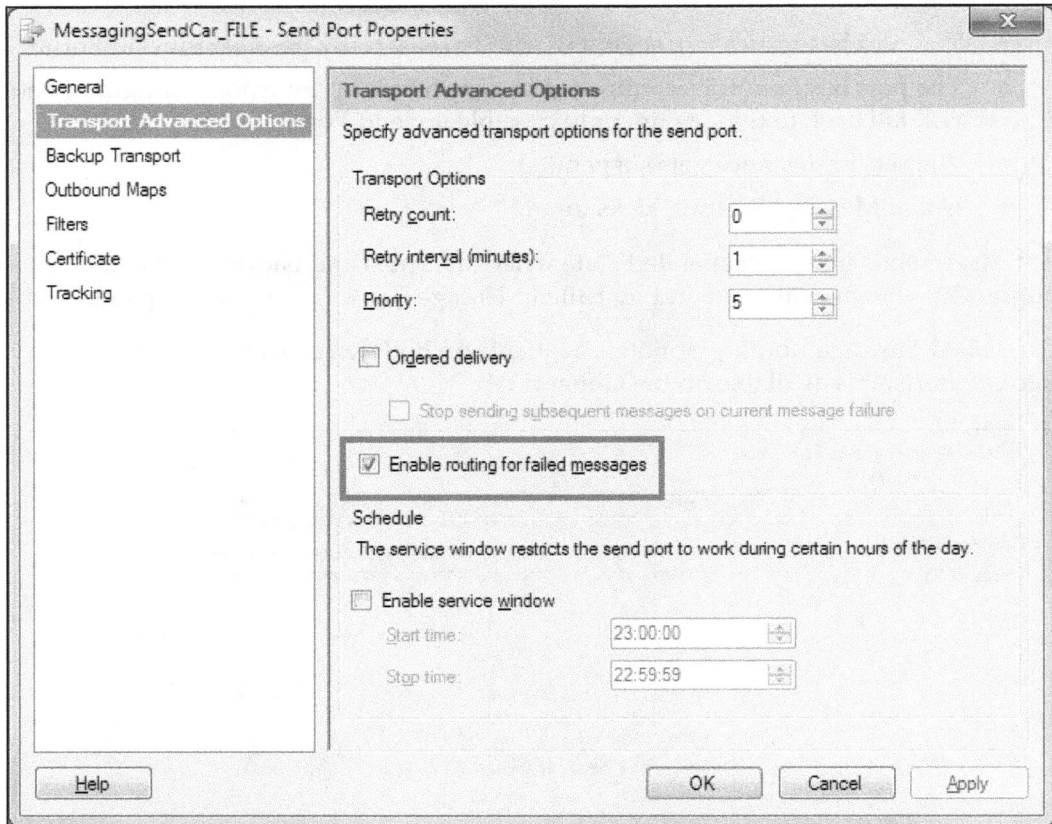

If the **Enable routing for failed messages** checkbox is checked, the service instance will not become suspended in the case of an exception. Instead, the following events will happen:

- A clone of the message is created
- All current promoted message context properties are demoted
- Additional properties describing the error condition are promoted to allow for routing of the error

The properties promoted from the `ErrorReport` namespace (`http://schemas.microsoft.com/BizTalk/2006/error-report`) are shown in the following table:

Name	Promoted	Description
FailureCode	Yes	A hexadecimal value. The same value that is visible in the Admin console if the message is suspended, for example, `0xC0C01680`.
FailureCategory	Yes	Not used, for example, (always) 0.
MessageType	Yes/No	Only available if known, for example, when an XML message fails on a Send Port such as `http://Chapter05_Example01.Schemas.SimplifiedCar#Car`.
ReceivePortName	Yes/No	Name of Receive Port. Promoted if exception occurred on a Receive Port, for example, **ReceiveCar**.
InboundTransportLocation	Yes/No	URI of Receive Location. Promoted if an exception occurred on a Receive Port, for example, `C:\BTS2013CertGuide\Chapter05\Example01-ExceptionHandling\FileDrop\*copy*`.
SendPortName	Yes/No	Name of Send Port. Available and promoted if exception occurred on a Send Port, for example, **MessagingSendCar_FILE**.
OutboundTransportLocation	Yes/No	URI of Send Port. Available and promoted if exception occurred on a Send Port, for example, `C:\BTS2013CertGuide\Chapter05\Example01-ExceptionHandling\FileDropX\MessagingCarOut_%MessageID%.xml`.
ErrorType	Yes	The type of message that the error contains, for example, (always) FailedMessage.
ProcessingServer	Yes	Name of the server where the error occurred, for example, `BTSSRV01`.

Additionally, the following properties are also available:

Name	Promoted	Description
Description	No	Error description. Also visible in the event log.
		For example, the published message could not be routed because no subscribers were found.
RoutingFailureReportID	No	Contains the ID of the routing failure report if the error occurred due to a routing failure, for example, Empty or a GUID.
FailureAdapter	No	Name of the adapter that failed, for example, FILE.
FailureInstanceID	No	ID (GUID) of the service that failed.
FailureMessageID	No	ID (GUID) of the message that failed.
FailureTime	No	The time of failure, for example, 2010-06-08 10:00:00.

Let's look at a scenario for using Failed Message Routing. For this scenario, we have a simple messaging integration. We will use a **ReceiveCar** Port and a **MessagingSendCar_FILE** Send Port connected by a simple **BTS.ReceivePortName** filter and see what happens when we experience errors on those and how we can route the exception that occurs. Both ports are configured with Failed Message Routing as per the previous screenshots.

We will begin looking at how we can handle an error on the Receive Port. When that error occurs, it will be routed instead of becoming suspended so we need to set up a port (or Orchestration) to handle the Failed Message Routing message (or we will get a routing failure for the Failed Message Routing message).

In order to receive failed messages from the Receive Port, we will configure an additional port to receive those messages with the filter shown in the following screenshot:

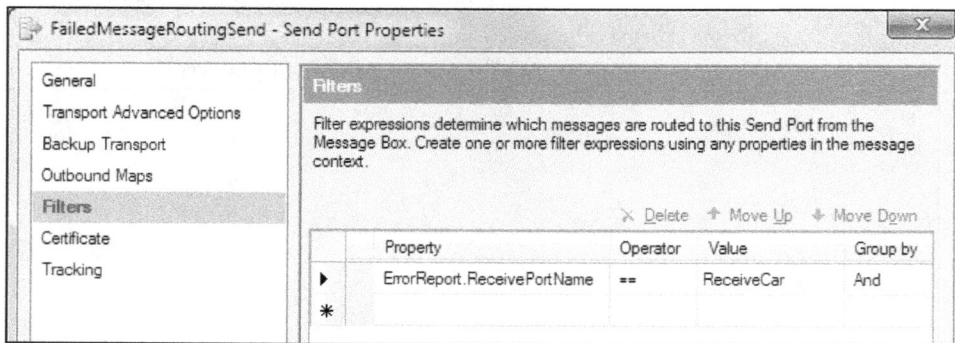

> We can use only the properties under the `ErrorReport`
> Schema as those are the only properties promoted.

What if the error occurred on a Send Port instead? The configuration is very similar. We will add an additional filter to the same port using an `Or` statement:

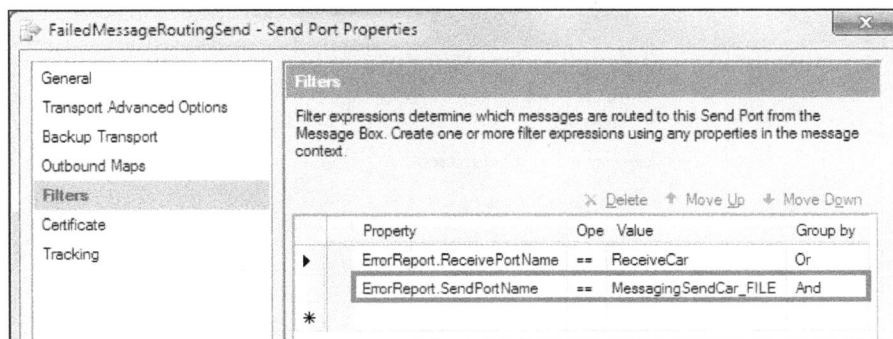

FailedMessageRoutingSend - Send Port Properties

	Property	Ope	Value	Group by
▶	ErrorReport.ReceivePortName	==	ReceiveCar	Or
	ErrorReport.SendPortName	==	MessagingSendCar_FILE	And
*				

General
Transport Advanced Options
Backup Transport
Outbound Maps
Filters
Certificate
Tracking

Filters

Filter expressions determine which messages are routed to this Send Port from the Message Box. Create one or more filter expressions using any properties in the message context.

✗ Delete ↑ Move Up ↓ Move Down

We could just as easily have used different ports for handling Receive and Send Port errors had we wished to.

Earlier in this chapter, we had an Orchestration that had *Delivery Notification = Transmitted configured*. In that case, the Orchestration handled the exception that resulted in no suspended Orchestration instances. Yet, the suspended Send Port remained even though the exception was handled. The way to get rid of it is to use Failed Message Routing as explained earlier. You can select any of the promoted properties under the `ErrorReport` Schema to configure a filter on a Send Port you wish to send the failed messages to.

Recoverable interchange processing

In *Chapter 2, Developing BizTalk Artifacts – Creating Schemas and Pipelines*, we looked at how to create an Envelope Schema, and how to configure a Pipeline to accept a message that contains an envelope and split the contained message into its parts.

This sample builds on what we learned by looking at what happens if one of the messages contained within the envelope is incorrect.

Let's start by setting the stage. The code for this sample is contained in the `Chapter05-Example01` solution within the `Chapter05-Example01.Schemas` project.

The project contains the following Envelope Schema:

```
CarEnvelope.xsd                                                          ▾ ☐ ✕
⊟ 📂 <Schema>           <?xml version="1.0" encoding="utf-16" ?>
  ⊟ 📄 CarEnvelope    - <xs:schema xmlns="http://Chapter05_Example01.Schemas.CarEnvelope"
    ⊟ 📄 Cars             xmlns:b="http://schemas.microsoft.com/BizTalk/2003"
      └ 📄 <Any>          targetNamespace="http://Chapter05_Example01.Schemas.CarEnvelope"
                          xmlns:xs="http://www.w3.org/2001/XMLSchema">
                        - <xs:annotation>
                          - <xs:appinfo>
                              <b:schemaInfo is_envelope="yes"
                                xmlns:b="http://schemas.microsoft.com/BizTalk/2003" />
                            </xs:appinfo>
                          </xs:annotation>
                        - <xs:element name="CarEnvelope">
                          - <xs:annotation>
                            - <xs:appinfo>
                                <b:recordInfo body_xpath="/*[local-name()='CarEnvelope' and
                                  namespace-uri()
                                  ='http://Chapter05_Example01.Schemas.CarEnvelope']/*
                                  [local-name()='Cars' and namespace-uri()='']" />
                              </xs:appinfo>
                            </xs:annotation>
                          - <xs:complexType>
                            - <xs:sequence>
                              - <xs:element name="Cars">
                                - <xs:complexType>
                                  - <xs:sequence>
                                      <xs:any maxOccurs="unbounded" />
                                    </xs:sequence>
                                  </xs:complexType>
                                </xs:element>
                              </xs:sequence>
                            </xs:complexType>
                          </xs:element>
                        </xs:schema>

  💿 XSD
  Turn off auto refresh                                                  Refresh
```

Where the **Envelope** property on the <Schema> node is set to Yes, and the **Body XPath** property on the CarEnvelope node is set to the XPath of the Cars node.

```
/*[local-name()='CarEnvelope' and namespace-uri()='http://Chapter05_
Example01.Schemas.CarEnvelope']/*[local-name()='Cars' and namespace-
uri()='']
```

It also contains the `SimplifiedCar` Schema that we have worked with in many previous samples:

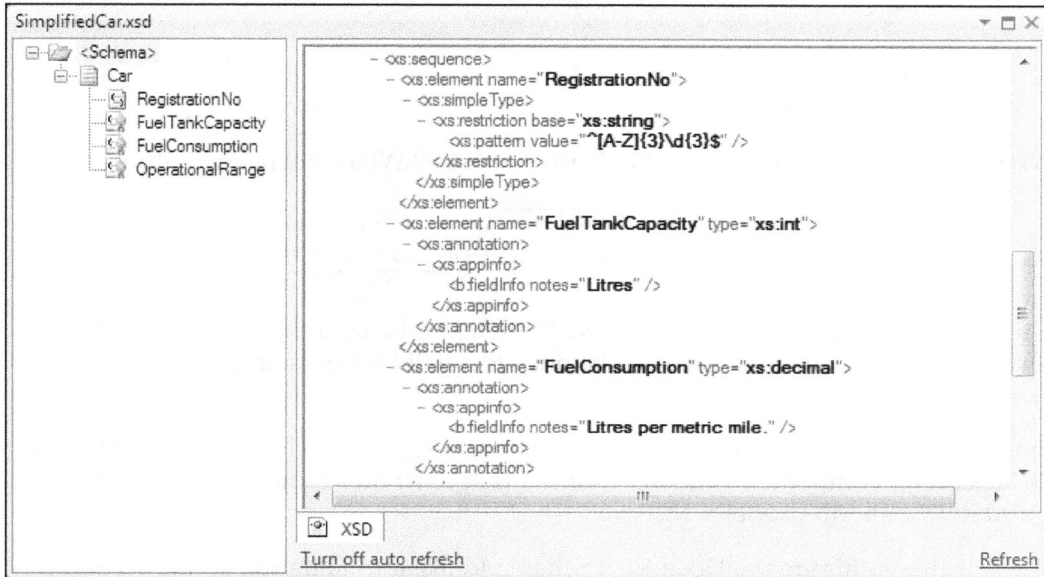

```
SimplifiedCar.xsd                                                          ▾ ☐ ✕
  ⊟ 🗁 <Schema>                    │  ─ <xs:sequence>                              ▲
    ⊟ 📄 Car                       │    ─ <xs:element name="RegistrationNo">
      ── 🔩 RegistrationNo         │      ─ <xs:simpleType>
      ── 🔩 FuelTankCapacity       │        ─ <xs:restriction base="xs:string">
      ── 🔩 FuelConsumption        │            <xs:pattern value="^[A-Z]{3}\d{3}$" />
      ── 🔩 OperationalRange       │          </xs:restriction>
                                   │        </xs:simpleType>
                                   │      </xs:element>
                                   │    ─ <xs:element name="FuelTankCapacity" type="xs:int">
                                   │      ─ <xs:annotation>
                                   │        ─ <xs:appinfo>
                                   │            <b:fieldInfo notes="Litres" />
                                   │          </xs:appinfo>                        ≡
                                   │        </xs:annotation>
                                   │      </xs:element>
                                   │    ─ <xs:element name="FuelConsumption" type="xs:decimal">
                                   │      ─ <xs:annotation>
                                   │        ─ <xs:appinfo>
                                   │            <b:fieldInfo notes="Litres per metric mile." />
                                   │          </xs:appinfo>
                                   │        </xs:annotation>                       ▾
                                   │  ◄                  ⠿                    ►
                                   │  🖭 XSD
                                   │  Turn off auto refresh              Refresh
```

In *Chapter 2, Developing BizTalk Artifacts – Creating Schemas and Pipelines*, we established that when sending in an envelope message using the `XmlReceive` Pipeline, it was split into its containing parts automatically by the XML Disassembler, without us having to do any custom configuration. This time though, we are going to send in a message that does not match one of the element types specified in the Schema.

The following code snippet is the instance envelope message we are sending through BizTalk:

```
<ns0:CarEnvelope xmlns:ns0="http://Chapter05_Example01.Schemas.
CarEnvelope">
  <Cars>
    <ns0:Car xmlns:ns0="http://Chapter05_Example01.Schemas.
SimplifiedCar">
      <RegistrationNo>ABC123</RegistrationNo>
      <FuelTankCapacity>60</FuelTankCapacity>
      <FuelConsumption>0.7</FuelConsumption>
      <OperationalRange>86</OperationalRange>
    </ns0:Car>
    <ns0:Car xmlns:ns0="http://Chapter05_Example01.Schemas.
SimplifiedCar">
```

```
            <RegistrationNo>XYZ789</RegistrationNo>
            <FuelTankCapacity>70</FuelTankCapacity>
            <FuelConsumption>ERROR</FuelConsumption>
            <OperationalRange>88</OperationalRange>
        </ns0:Car>
    </Cars>
</ns0:CarEnvelope>
```

What will happen if we send in this faulty message? What will be the output?

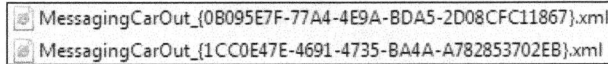

The output will be two messages. Why? Remember, by default no Schema validation is performed, only that the message belongs to a valid Schema and is of a well-formed XML.

In order to enable Schema validation in the XMLReceive Pipeline and make the **XML disassembler** component validate documents against their Schemas, we must set the **ValidateDocument** property to **True**.

We will also configure the Document Schema to use for validation as shown in the following screenshot:

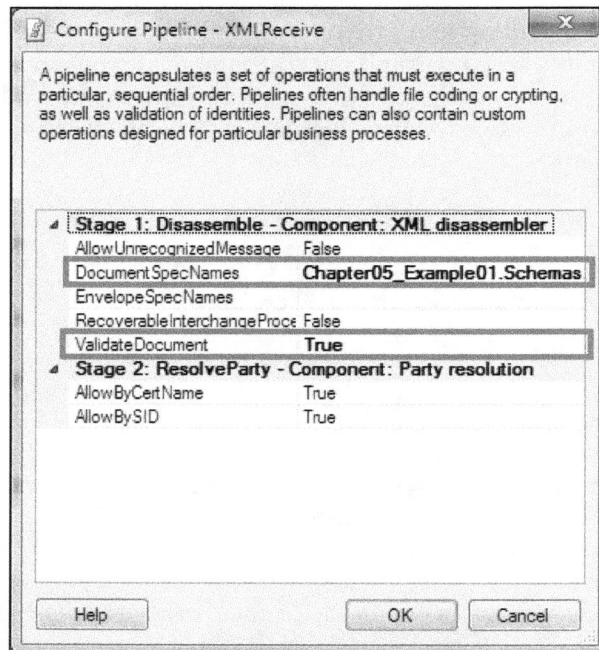

Now, if we send in the messages again, we will get no output! If we inspect our suspended messages, we will see that the entire interchange has failed with error information that says, **The Messaging Engine encountered an error during the processing of one or more inbound messages**.

In order to enable the successful delivery of the correct message, we need to enable **RecoverableInterchangeProcessing** as shown in the following screenshot:

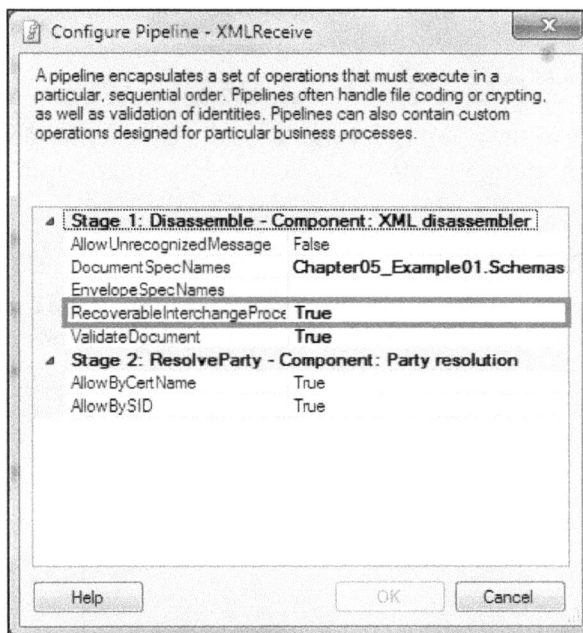

Now, with recoverable interchange processing enabled, if we submit our message once again, one of the two included body documents will be sent through the Send Port.

The other will become suspended with error information as follows:

An output message of the component "Unknown" in receive pipeline "Microsoft. BizTalk.DefaultPipelines.XMLReceive, Microsoft.BizTalk.DefaultPipelines, Version=3.0.1.0, Culture=neutral, PublicKeyToken=31bf3856ad364e35" is suspended due to the following error:

The 'FuelConsumption' element has an invalid value according to its data type.

The sequence number of the suspended message is 2.

Referring back to our sample instance message, this is the second car that had the text ERROR in its FuelConsumption element.

This message does not need to be suspended. Instead, Failed Message Routing could be configured to route the failing messages for further processing as described previously in this chapter.

Validating and testing artifacts

This section will look at how you can validate and test Schemas and Maps using the Visual Studio user interface and make a brief introduction to unit testing.

Validating Schemas and Message Instances

In Visual Studio, when you develop Schema artifacts, you have three options to test or validate this Schema through the UI. They are available through the context menu of a Schema in the Visual Studio Solution Explorer.

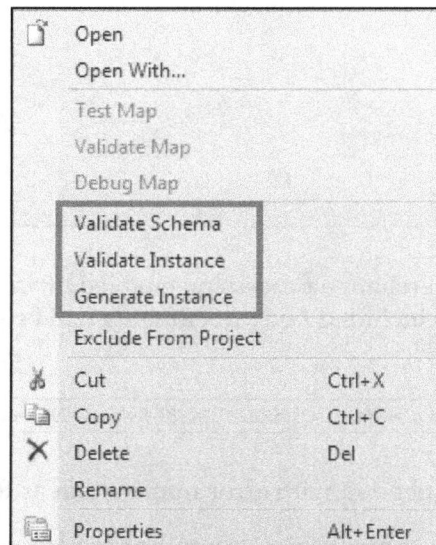

The options are as follows:

- Validate Schema
- Validate Instance
- Generate Instance

Validate Schema

The **Validate Schema** option can be useful; for example, if you receive a Schema from a third-party or after you have completed work on a Schema that you built yourself. It will validate that the structure and implementation of the Schema is correct.

Validate Instance

The **Validate Instance** option allows you to validate a sample input message against the Schema. This is a very useful option; for example, in situations where messages fail the disassemble stage in a production environment and it is not entirely clear why that is or where the error in the input is, more so for flat files than XML files, which input message to use is configured through the properties of the Schema.

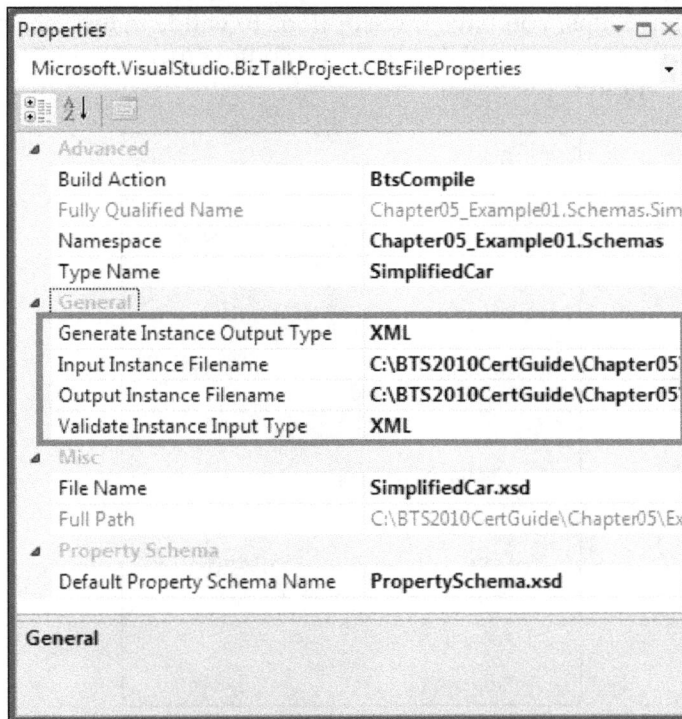

These properties also allow you to specify where to place a message that you generate from the Schema.

By default, Visual Studio will want to validate an XML file. To validate a flat file, the **Validate Input Instance Type** property must be set to **Native**.

Generate Instance

When you generate an instance, if you do not specify a location to place the instance to generate in, it will be placed in the current user's temp folder. The instance generation procedure is not very advanced, so it may well produce outputs that will not validate, especially if you have put restrictions in the form of patterns on your fields. The data that it fills the instance with will be sample data that does not necessarily adhere to the rules of the field.

By default, Visual Studio will generate an XML message. To generate a flat file, the property **Output Instance Type** must be set to **Native**.

Validating, testing, and debugging Maps

When you develop Maps, you have three options to validate, test, or debug this Map using the UI. These are available from the context menu of a Map in the Visual Studio Solution Explorer.

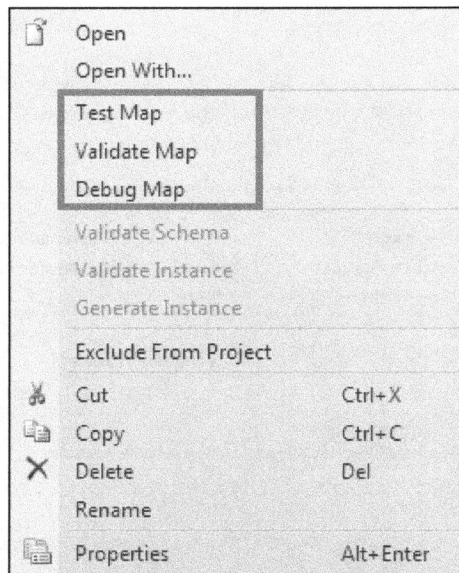

The options are as follows:

- Test Map
- Validate Map
- Debug Map

Test Map

The **Test Map** option allows you to supply an input and let Visual Studio run the Map and produce an output. This allows you to test and validate that your mapping logic is doing what you expect. It is a good way to test common input files and edge cases while developing. Both input and output messages can be (and are by default) validated against their Schemas. Note that this is a feature offered by Visual Studio only. In runtime, message instances are not validated against their Schemas as part of Map processing.

Validate Map

The **Validate Map** option, on top of validating the links and Functoid configuration of the Map, creates the resulting XSLT script and makes it available for viewing. Looking at the generated XSLT, it can teach you a thing or two about how the BizTalk Mapper works. It also helps you understand why your sequence of Functoids is not resulting in the output you expect. Validation does not execute the Map and no input is needed and no output created (apart from the XSLT file).

Debug Map

The **Debug Map** option combines the **Validate Map** and **Test Map** options. It gives you the possibility to debug the creation of the output by stepping through the XSLT script and viewing the input file getting processed and the output file getting built element by element. You can also set breakpoints. Debugging the Map is useful for more advanced troubleshooting scenarios.

Although all of these are highly useful and should be on your *To Learn* list, if you do not master them fully, it is outside of the scope of this book to go into any more detailed depth on any of these.

Testing Pipelines

There are several options available for testing Pipelines, and testing Pipeline Components. But, for Pipelines, Visual Studio provides no test methods equal to those available for Schemas or Maps. You do, however, have access to unit testing, covered later in this chapter, or the Pipeline test tools. These tools are located in the BizTalk Server SDK and allow you to perform command line testing of Pipelines. The next section will examine these tools in a little more detail.

Pipeline test tools

The following table lists tools that are available in the `\SDK\Utilities\PipelineTools` subfolder of BizTalk Servers installation directory that aids in testing Pipelines:

Name	Purpose
FFAsm.exe	It invokes the Flat File Assembler to create a Flat File message from one or more XML messages
FFDasm.exe	It invokes the Flat File Disassembler to create one or more XML messages from a Flat File message
XMLAsm.exe	It invokes the XML Assembler to create an XML message from one or more XML messages.
XMLDasm.exe	It invokes the XML Disassembler to create one or more XML messages from an XML message
Pipeline.exe	It runs a specified Pipeline, received or sent, to create one or more output documents given one or more input documents, and specified Schemas

There is also `DSDump.exe` that helps troubleshooting parsing errors, but it does not test a Pipeline.

> None of these tools require the Pipeline to be deployed to BizTalk Server.

Unit testing

If you are serious about testing in your BizTalk projects, as you should be, then doing manual tests through the UI isn't really sufficient. You want automated tests and tests that can be run during nightly builds using **Team Foundation Server** (**TFS**) or tests you can trigger when the solution has undergone some rework. Such testing is done by implementing unit tests.

In the case of BizTalk Server, the units that you can test are as follows:

- Schemas
- Maps
- Pipelines

This section will describe what is needed to unit test these artifacts.

Unit testing Schemas

When you unit test a Schema, you use the `ValidateInstance` method and supply it with the path to an input XML (or a flat file) document and you specify which one of those you have supplied, as shown in the following code snippet:

```
[TestMethod()]
public void ValidateSimplifiedCarInstanceTest()
{
    SimplifiedCar target = new SimplifiedCar();
    bool success = target.ValidateInstance(
        @"C:\BTS2013CertGuide\Chapter05\Example02-UnitTesting\
SimplifiedCar.xml",
        Microsoft.BizTalk.TestTools.Schema.OutputInstanceType.XML);
    Assert.IsTrue(success);
}
```

For the `ValidateInstance` method to be available, you must set **Enable Unit Testing** to **True** on the project that the Schema belongs to:

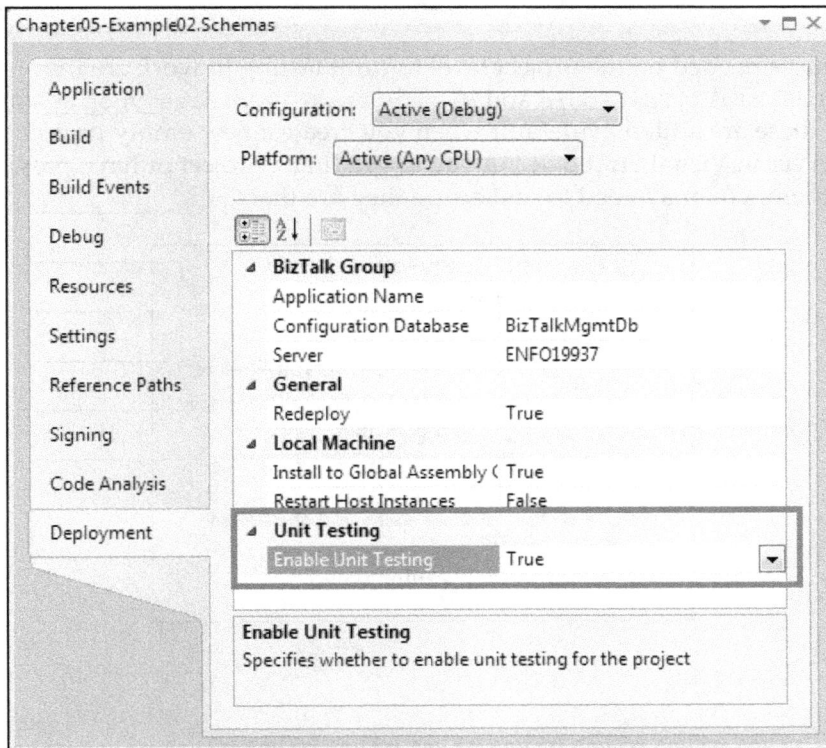

When you set this property to **True**, another base class will be injected in the inheritance hierarchy of the Schema, the `TestableSchemaBase` class that holds the `ValidateInstance` method.

The references needed on the project level for unit testing to work are the `Microsoft.BizTalk.TestTools` and `Microsoft.XLANGs.BaseTypes` assemblies. However, these are added by default when you create a new empty project for BizTalk Server in Visual Studio. If you are upgrading a project or have previously removed them, you may need to make sure they are there.

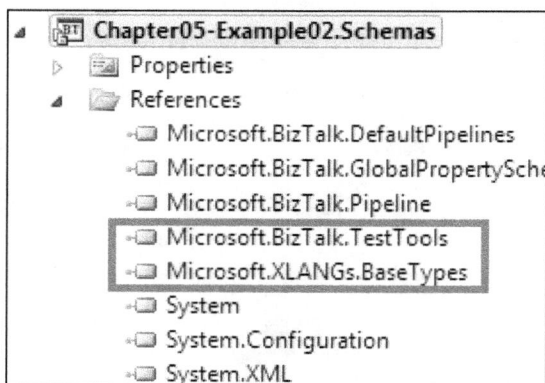

Unit testing Maps

Similarly, as when testing Schemas, testing Maps is done using a method that becomes available when you set **Enable Unit Testing** to **True** on the project that holds the Map. For Maps, this method is called `TestMap`. A sample usage is seen in the following code snippet:

```
[TestMethod()]
public void Map1OutputTest()
{
    Map1 target = new Map1();
    string input = @"C:\BTS2013CertGuide\Chapter05\Example02-
UnitTesting\SimplifiedCar.xml";
    string output = @"C:\BTS2013CertGuide\Chapter05\Example02-
UnitTesting\SimplifiedCar_MapOut.xml";
    target.TestMap(
        input,
        Microsoft.BizTalk.TestTools.Schema.InputInstanceType.Xml,
        output,
        Microsoft.BizTalk.TestTools.Schema.OutputInstanceType.XML);
    Assert.IsTrue(File.Exists(output));
}
```

Unlike the `ValidateSchema` method, the `TestMap` method has a void return. The way to validate that the Map executed successfully is to validate that the output was created. After that you will usually have a series of tests on the content of the output file to validate that the mapping logic did what we expected, given the input is provided.

As with Schemas, enabling unit tests injects a new base class into the inheritance hierarchy of the Map, the `TestableMapBase` class that contains the `TestMap` method.

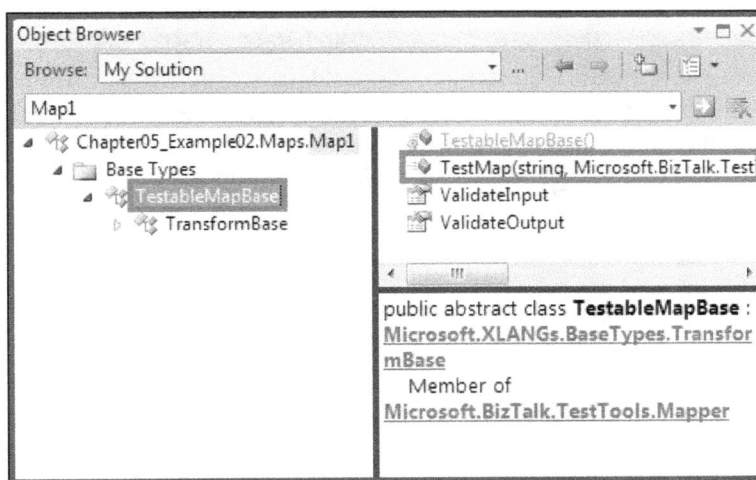

The same two references for testing Schemas are needed: `Microsoft.BizTalk.TestTools` and `Microsoft.XLANGs.BaseTypes`. No additional references are needed to test Maps.

Unit testing Pipelines

For Pipelines, the `TestPipeline` method is available on the `TestableReceivePipeline` or `TestableSendPipeline` classes. Your Pipelines will inherit from these when you enable unit testing in the property pages of a BizTalk project. It allows you to execute a Pipeline, supplying input and produce output, from the code. The following code snippet shows a sample test method for a Receive Pipeline called `RcvCar`:

```
[TestMethod()]
public void RcvCarTest()
{
RcvCar target = new RcvCar();
target.TestPipeline(
    new StringCollection() { "SimplifiedCar.xml" }, // documents
    new StringCollection(), // parts
    new Dictionary<string, string>()
        { { "Chapter05_Example02.Schemas.SimplifiedCar",
"SimplifiedCard.xsd" } } ); // schemas
Assert.IsTrue(Directory.GetFiles(testContextInstance.TestDir +
    "\\out", "Message*.out").Length > 0);
}
```

Like when testing Maps and using the `TestMap` method, using the `TestPipeline` method has a return type of void. The code calls the method by supplying the input document, any additional message parts (in addition to the body part) that the pipeline needs and a dictionary list over which Schema files to use. Note that the example code is simplified in that it does not supply full paths to files, which is typically needed in any working code. After having called the method, the code checks whether the output was produced. You could, and should, then check to make sure that the output is the expected, for example, by validating it against its Schema using the `ValidateInstance` method. This was left out of the code for brevity.

Testing your knowledge

1. HWLC Motors is having problems with a .NET component developed to calculate a car's fuel efficiency. Sometimes the component throws an exception. The class used from the component is marked as serializable. The Orchestration has no scopes configured. What two things must you do to be able to catch and handle the exception that occurs?

    a. Set the Orchestrations **Compensation** property to **Custom**.

    b. Add a scope shape to the Orchestration and move the call to the .NET component within the scope. Set Transaction Type to None.

    c. Configure the Orchestrations Transaction Type to Long Running.

    d. Add an exception block to the scope and handle the exception there.

    e. Add a scope shape to the Orchestration and move the call to the .NET component within the scope. Set Transaction Type to Atomic.

    f. Add a Compensation block to the scope and add logic to compensate for exceptions that occur.

2. HWLC Motors are developing a BizTalk Server solution to handle order fulfillment. As part of the Orchestration is a piece of logic that places an order to the factory to start construction on a new car, the logic is placed in an atomic scope. The Orchestration has no other scopes. Later in the solution, the customer is billed a down-payment for the car. HWLC has experienced problems with the customer having insufficient funds, which causes exceptions. What must you do to make sure that if that happens, a cancellation is sent to the factory?

    a. Set the **Compensation** property to **Custom** for the scope and implement logic to send a cancellation.

    b. Add a new scope and place the existing scope inside the new scope. Add a Compensation block to the new scope and implement logic to send a cancellation.

    c. Configure the Transaction Type of the Orchestration to be Long Running and implement logic to send a cancellation in the Orchestrations' Compensation block.

    d. Add a new scope and place the existing scope inside the new scope. Add an exception handling block to the new scope and implement logic to send a cancellation.

3. As part of a BizTalk Server solution for customer services, HWLC Motors have implemented an Orchestration that submits a warranty claim to a subcontractor through a logical one-way port configured to use a **Specify Later** binding. The send is placed inside a Long Running. You need to make sure that the warranty claim has been successfully sent before the Orchestration continues processing. What must you do?

   a. Do nothing. As the logical port is configured with a binding of **Specify Later**, the physical port is synchronously called by the Orchestration and processing will not continue until port processing is done.

   b. Configure the physical port to use failed message routing.

   c. Configure the logical ports' **Delivery Notification** property to **Transmitted** and add **Exception Handler** to the scope to catch `DeliveryFailureException`.

   d. Set the scopes' **Synchronized** property to **True**.

4. HWLC Motors are monitoring insurance claims. As soon as a claim arrives that is above $10,000, it must immediately be sent to the claims department for priority assessment. The claims department uses a mainframe that receives files through a file share. If the Send Port fails to deliver the message to the primary file share, the port must immediately fail over to a secondary share. What should you do to enable this scenario?

   a. Configure the port with a backup transport. Set the **Retry Count** option of the backup transport to **0**.

   b. Configure the port with a backup transport. Set the **Retry Count** option of the **Transport Advanced Options** tab to **0**.

   c. Configure the port with a backup transport. Set the **Priority** option of the backup transport to **1**.

   d. Configure the port for **Ordered Delivery** and to stop sending subsequent messages on current message failure.

5. HWLC Motors has a BizTalk Server solution developed to route orders from a partner to an in-house system based on a filter on the **MessageType** property of the message. When the solution is deployed and messages start to arrive, they get suspended with the error information: **The published message could not be routed because no subscribers were found**. This error occurs if the subscribing Orchestration or Send Port has not been enlisted, or if some of the message properties necessary for subscription evaluation have not been promoted. You should use the BizTalk Administration console to troubleshoot this failure. What must you do?

   a. Configure the Send Port to filter on `ErrorReport.ReceivePortName`.

   b. Configure the Send Port to use the `XmlTransmit` Pipeline.

   c. Configure the Receive Location to use the `XmlReceive` Pipeline.

   d. Use the BizTalk Server Administration console to edit the message context and then resume it.

Summary

In this chapter, we have looked at handling errors and exceptions, both in Orchestrations and in messaging solutions. We have also examined how we can compensate committed transactions in Orchestrations by adding Compensation blocks. We have seen how compensation is triggered, either automatically or explicitly. We have also looked at utilizing the **Delivery Notification** property. For messaging solutions, we have looked at common sources of errors, why they occur, and how we can handle them using failed message routing. Finally, we looked at recoverable interchange processing for recovering from errors in debatched messages and discussed what options are available to validate and test during development to mitigate errors occurring in runtime.

In the next chapter, we will cover administrative concepts and tasks such as installation and configuration, application state and deployment, message, port, Orchestration tracking, and other uses of the administration console.

6
Deploying, Tracking, and Administrating a BizTalk Server 2010 Solution

In the previous chapter, we discussed how to debug your BizTalk applications and how to manage exceptions. In this chapter, we are going to change gears and focus on administrating our BizTalk applications.

Managing and maintaining a BizTalk Solution requires the same diligence as developing BizTalk applications. Administering these solutions can sometimes be a challenging endeavor if the developer has not provided sufficient documentation or has implemented questionable design patterns.

BizTalk Server is often used to support mission-critical integration processes, which means there are often high-pressure situations when things do not go as planned. These situations may include BizTalk entering a throttled state or dependent systems being unavailable. Understanding the tools that BizTalk Administration Console provides gives BizTalk Administrators an edge when these support issues occur. In some cases, using the BizTalk Administration Console correctly may prevent issues from occurring in the first place.

The goal of this chapter is to review the features and tools that aid a BizTalk Administrator in ensuring that their BizTalk environment is supportable, maintainable, and performs well.

The topics that are included in this chapter are as follows:

- Installing and configuring a multiserver BizTalk environment
- Deploying BizTalk applications
- BizTalk application states (started, partially started, stopped)
- Configuring tracking
- Managing BizTalk Solutions using Administration Console
- BizTalk Settings Dashboard
- Testing your knowledge

Installing and configuring a multiserver BizTalk environment

For BizTalk Administrators that are used for single server deployments, installing BizTalk in a multiserver environment can lead to some confusion. Many BizTalk resources are familiar with setting up a single node environment, such as a local desktop. Introducing multiple nodes may include complex infrastructure components, such as Clustering and Load Balancing. The following sections will reduce some of this confusion and give you insight into some of the decisions that you need to make while building a multiserver environment.

High Availability

Every BizTalk Server that you would like to participate in this BizTalk Group requires the BizTalk Runtime to be installed. Each of these BizTalk Servers will also require the Enterprise Single Sign-on Service to be installed and configured. As a result, we need to designate a Master Secret Server, preferably the one that provides redundancy through Microsoft Windows Clustering. It is generally recommended to have the Master Secret Server hosted on the same cluster that the SQL Server is running on when High Availability is required. The last major component we need to address is a common SQL Server backend that all BizTalk Servers will use as `MessageBox`, tracking, and configuration databases.

The following diagram shows a typical two-node BizTalk environment with a Clustered SQL Server backend. In each of our BizTalk Servers, we are going to install BizTalk Runtime, the Administration Console, and Enterprise Single Sign-on. In the event we have requirements to host WCF or Web Services, we will also require **Internet Information Services (IIS)** to be installed. If one of our BizTalk Servers suffers a catastrophic failure, the remaining node(s) will pick up the work of the problematic server, provided the required Host Instances exist on the healthy server.

In order to have a redundant data store, we need to leverage Windows Clustering Services to host a SQL Server instance, Enterprise Single Sign-on Service, which will act as our Master Secret Server, and **Microsoft Distributed Transaction Coordinator (MSDTC)**. In the event of a catastrophic failure in our database tier, a passive node will be able to host these database services with little disruption to BizTalk.

Due to its role as a Master Secret Server, configuring Enterprise Single Sign-on for High Availability is very important since the Single Sign-On database contains passwords and other sensitive data.

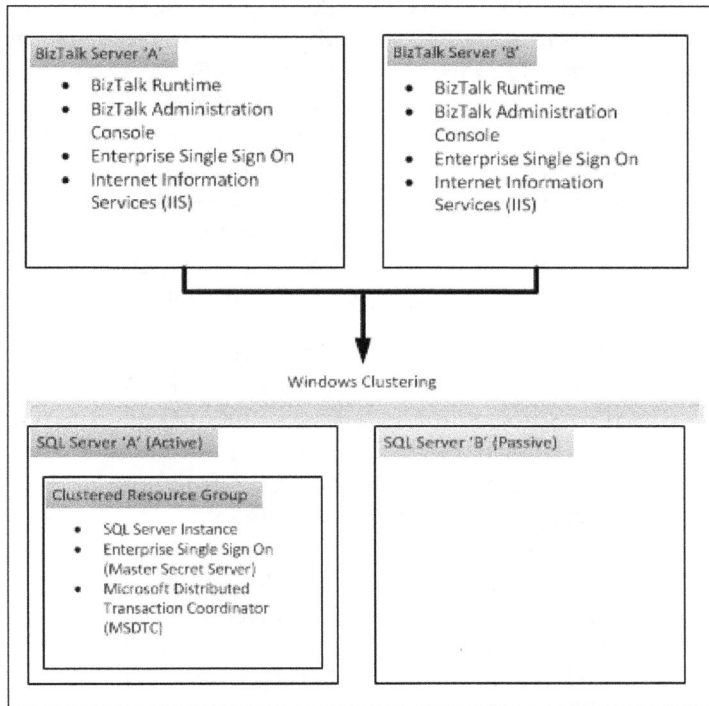

An excellent post-configuration Database Optimization guide exists on MSDN at:

http://msdn.microsoft.com/en-us/library/ ee377048(v=bts.70).aspx

This article provides advice on how to get better performance out of your SQL Server environment.

Role of Host and Host Instances in High Availability

A BizTalk Host may be defined as a logical container where our BizTalk artifacts will run. We can then think of Host Instances as the physical implementation of those logical containers. More specifically, a Host Instance is a Windows Service that will run our In-process BizTalk Services and act as a work process for our applications.

In the previous section, we discussed what is required from an infrastructure perspective in order to support High Availability. From a BizTalk perspective, we need to configure a server in such a way that we can take advantage of our redundant infrastructure. More specifically, if we have two BizTalk Servers that are going to run our applications, then we need to ensure that we have created the appropriate Host and Host Instances on these servers. A prerequisite for High Availability to be realized is to create a Host Instance on each BizTalk Server that our application will be running on. For instance, if we have two servers called Server A and Server B and we subsequently create a host called Process Host, we need to create a Process Host and Host Instance on both Server A and Server B. This will allow our application to run on both servers, and therefore, we will achieve High Availability.

In some situations, we may have a need to cluster a BizTalk Host Instance. Clustering a BizTalk Host Instance is not a prerequisite in order to achieve High Availability. However, it is required by some adapters to ensure the processes that are relying upon these adapters, as they do have High Availability but do not process duplicate messages. Consider a situation such as receiving a file from an FTP Server. If you have two BizTalk Servers, where each server contains a Host Instance that is supporting a BizTalk application receiving a file, you run the risk of processing duplicate files. The FTP/SFTP adapters, in particular, are prone to this symptom. In order to address this situation, Microsoft Clustering can be used to support a BizTalk Clustered Host. Clustering a BizTalk Host ensures that only one instance of the Host is online at any particular time. In the event that the server that is actively hosting this Host Instance goes offline, an active instance will appear on the other node within the Windows Cluster.

Multiple MessageBox databases

Scaling out with BizTalk Server is relatively easy as we can continue to add new BizTalk Servers to our group. At some point, the amount of Servers participating in the BizTalk farm will exceed the capabilities of a single `MessageBox`, and our Database Server now becomes a bottleneck. In the event that this occurs, we do have the ability to introduce multiple `MessageBox` databases in order to increase throughput in our database tier.

Configuring multiple `MessageBox` databases is outside the scope of this book, but it should be a concept that we are aware of in order to increase the performance of our BizTalk environment. For further information, please refer to the following MSDN article at `http://blogs.msdn.com/b/biztalknotes/archive/2013/08/06/how-to-add-multiple-message-box-database-in-an-existing-biztalk-group.aspx`.

Installation setup

The order and method in which we install and configure our BizTalk Servers is very important. As with many server products by Microsoft, installing BizTalk is a two-step process, as follows:

- Installation
- Configuration

Installation

The first step that we need to take is to install BizTalk prerequisites, BizTalk Runtime, and related components on the chosen BizTalk Server(s). This software can be installed even without the existence of an SQL Server. A detailed installation guide, which includes a list of prerequisite components, may be found at:

`http://www.microsoft.com/download/en/details.aspx?id=11503`

Configuration

Configuring a multinode BizTalk Group will involve making some decisions that we do not need to make in a single-node deployment. Some of these decisions include which server(s) will support our BizTalk Databases and Single Sign-On (SSO) System.

While configuring a multinode BizTalk Group, we need to select **Custom configuration** in the **Microsoft BizTalk Server 2010 Configuration** wizard, as shown in the following screenshot:

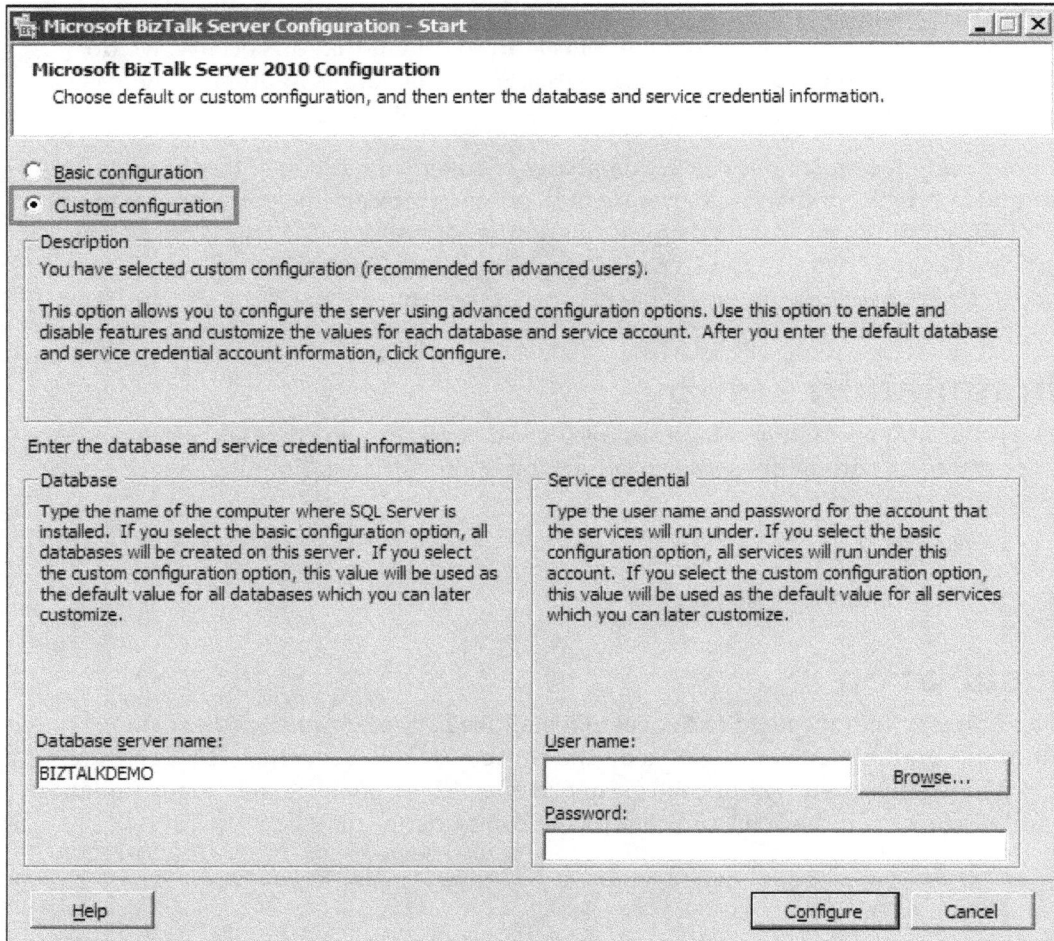

Configuring SSO

The configuration aspect of establishing a BizTalk environment requires a little more planning. Only one BizTalk node should be configured at a time. For the first node that is being configured, we will select **Create a new SSO system**. For any subsequent nodes, we should select **Join an existing SSO system**, as shown in the following screenshot:

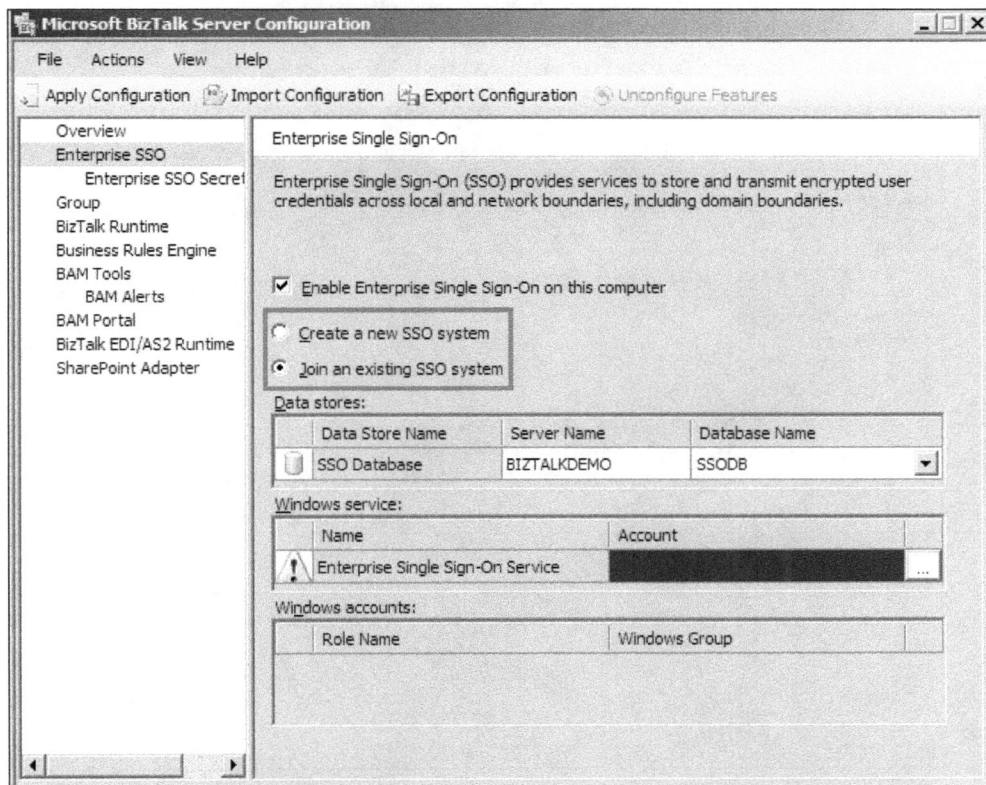

Setting up a BizTalk Group

Configuring a BizTalk Group is very similar to configuring an SSO System. The reason for this is that the first node that is being configured will select **Create a new BizTalk Group**, whereas the subsequent nodes will select **Join an existing BizTalk Group**, as shown in the following screenshot:

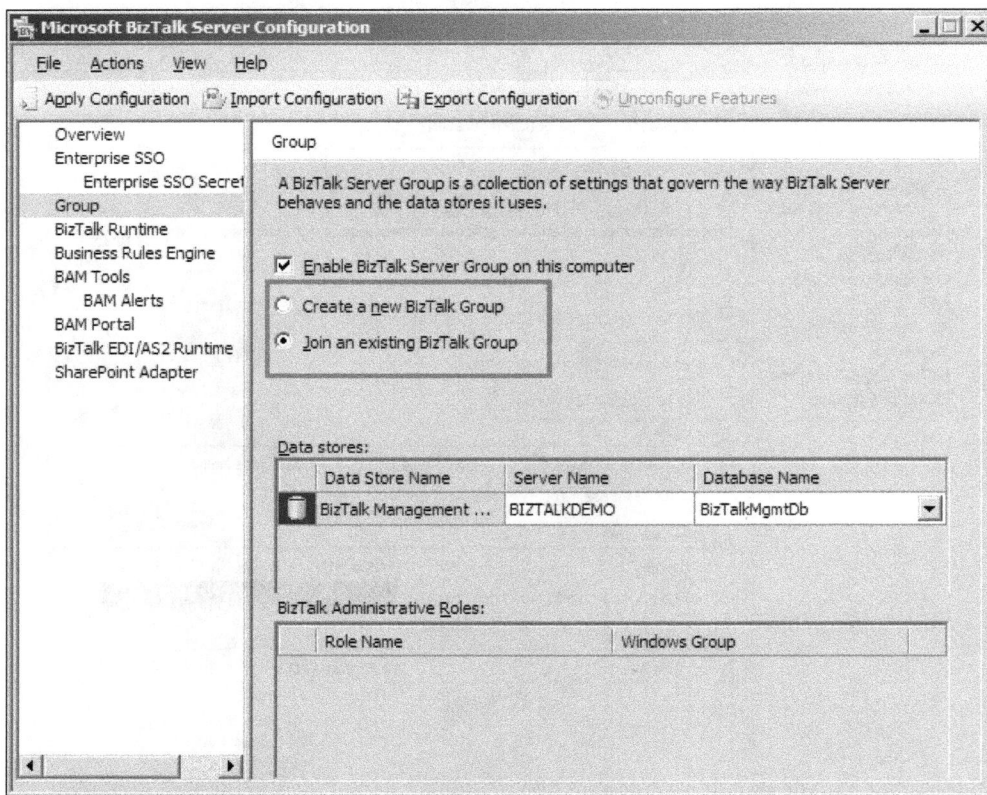

Configuring Runtime settings

When it comes to the **BizTalk Runtime** screen, we have the ability to create default In-process and Isolated Hosts and specify the accounts and groups that will support these Hosts. If we are installing BizTalk on a 64-bit system, we will have the opportunity to specify whether we want to create our default Hosts as 32-bit or 64-bit Hosts.

We also have the ability to specify whether or not to mark these Hosts as **Trusted**. **Trusted** Hosts are used to establish a trusted relationship between `MessageBox` and consuming services for authorization and outbound party-resolution purposes. For the purpose of this chapter, we will use the default settings and create Non-trusted Hosts.

If we would like to re-use this existing configuration in another environment or server, we have the ability to export our configuration by clicking on the **Export Configuration** button. If we decide to use this feature, then we will need to set our passwords in the new environment as these details are not included in the exported XML file, as shown in the following screenshot:

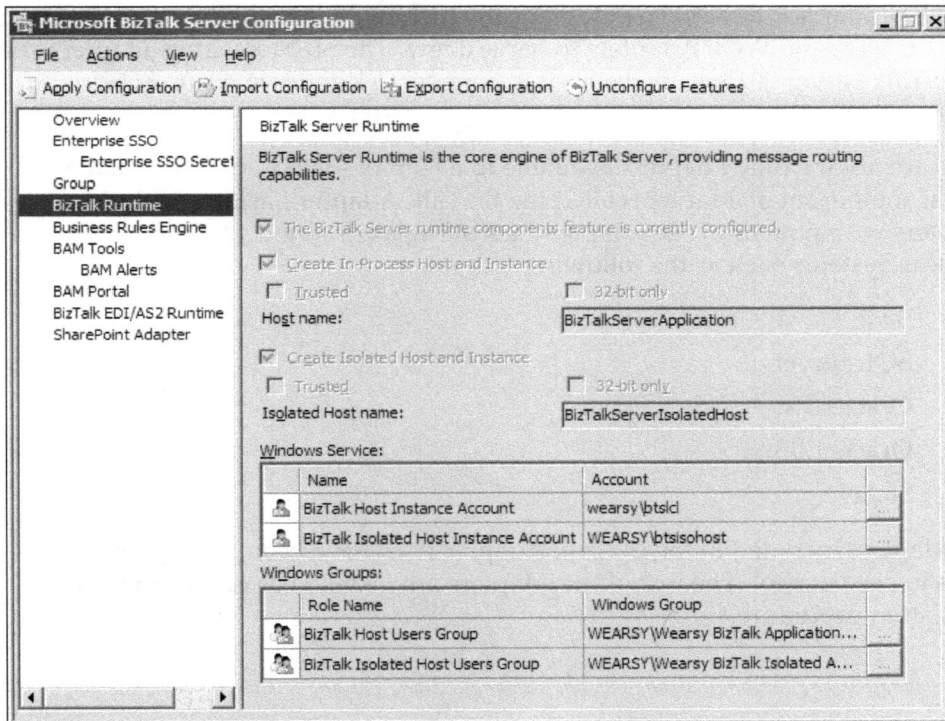

> The remaining screens in the configuration wizard pertain to non-core components and therefore, are out of the scope of this chapter. For more information pertaining to installing BizTalk in a multiserver environment, please refer to the Microsoft installation guide, which can be found at:
>
> `http://www.microsoft.com/download/en/details.`
> `aspx?id=11503`

Adapters

After we have installed and configured BizTalk, we will discover that a variety of out of the box adapters have been automatically included for us. These adapters include the FILE, FTP, and WCF Adapters to name a few. The SB-Messaging adapter is new for BizTalk Server 2013. It can be used to connect to Windows Azure Service Bus Queues and Topics.

These are not the only adapters available to us out of the box. On the installation media, another set of adapters called the BizTalk Adapter Pack are included. Adapters within the BizTalk Adapter Pack allow us to connect to Line of Business Systems such as the following:

- SAP
- SQL Server
- Oracle DB
- Oracle EBS
- Siebel

The adapters included in the BizTalk Adapter Pack have been highlighted in the following screenshot. The rest of the adapters are installed as part of the default installation procedure.

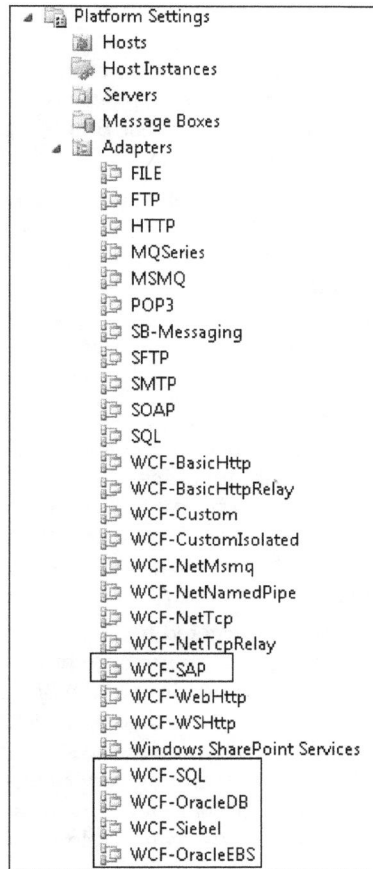

Active Directory Groups and Users

When establishing a multiserver BizTalk environment, Active Directory Users and Groups must be used. The following table lists the necessary groups and a brief description of each group function. If you would like to see a more detailed explanation of these various roles, please refer to the following MSDN web page:

```
http://msdn.microsoft.com/en-us/library/aa577661.aspx
```

Group	Group Description
SSO Administrators	This group has sufficient permissions to administer the Enterprise Single Sign-on Service. The account on which we plan to run our Enterprise Single Sign-on Service(s) needs to be a member of this group.
SSO Affiliate Administrators	An SSO Affiliate application is used to provide credential mapping for Single Sign-on Services. Since we can have many different systems involved in Single Sign-on scenarios, we have the ability to create Affiliate applications. This allows for some segregation of administration between different subsystems. We can use this group to add administrators for these different affiliate applications.
BizTalk Server Administrators	This group represents one of the more powerful groups in the BizTalk Platform. Having membership in this group provides us with the ability to install and manage applications, perform a message inspection and resolution activities in Group Hub, and manipulate Send and Receive Handlers for adapters. Members of this group must also be a part of the SSO Affiliate Administrators Group.
BizTalk Server Operators	This group is targeted towards people with administration-like responsibilities that do not require the same level of permissions that are needed by those in the BizTalk Server Administrators Group. Some of these activities include stopping and starting applications, viewing service state and message flow, and terminating or resuming service instances. This group does not have the ability to view message context or content and manipulate an application's configuration.
BizTalk Application Users	This is the default name of the BizTalk Host Group that the user for the BizTalk Server Application Host Instance needs to belong to. Microsoft recommends that for each Host that you create, you should also create a related Active Directory BizTalk Host Group.
BizTalk Isolated Host Users	Similar to BizTalk Application Users, this group is the default Host Group for accounts that run the BizTalk Server Isolated Host Instance(s). An example of using an Isolated Host would include a solution that has exposed a WCF Service through IIS. In our Receive Location for this WCF Service, we would specify an Isolated Host.
EDI Subsystem Users	Users within this group have access to the EDI database.
BAM	Portal Users
BizTalk SharePoint	Adapter Enabled Hosts
BizTalk B2B	Operators Group

Members of this group have access to the BAM Portal website. However, it is important to note that even though these users can access the BAM Portal website, it does not mean that these users have access to all views within the BAM Portal. Those permissions still need to be provided through the BAM "bm" command-line tool.

Users within this group have access to the Windows SharePoint Services Adapter Web Service.

A new BizTalk role, which has been created in BizTalk 2010, allows members to perform all party-management operations.

Deploying BizTalk applications

In this section, we are going to discuss how to deploy BizTalk applications. There are several ways to deploy BizTalk applications, including the following:

- Deploying from Visual Studio
- Building a **Microsoft Installer (MSI)** package that can be exported or imported between environments
- Using command line-based tools, such as MSBuild and BtsTask
- Leveraging community frameworks, such as BizTalk Deployment Framework and NANT

Using command-line or third party-based deployment tools are out of the scope of both the exam and this chapter, so we are not going to go into any detail in these areas. Instead, we will focus on deploying BizTalk applications from Visual Studio and using MSI packages.

Sample deployment through Visual Studio

In order to walk properly through the deployment scenarios, we need a sample solution. A sample solution called Example01-Deployment.sln can be found in the C:\BTS2013CertGuide\Chapter06\ Example01-Deployment folder. The business process behind this sample is that we have a business partner who has signed a contract to use some of our parts in the production of their vehicles. The name of this fictitious company is MBW Motors. When our company, HWLC Motors, discovers a recall, we require our partner companies, such as MBW Motors, to request replacement parts for the related recall.

Our simple solution will receive a recall request from MBW and transform it into a format that our recall system can support, as shown in the following diagram. We will then deliver this message to a file's folder that our recall system can access.

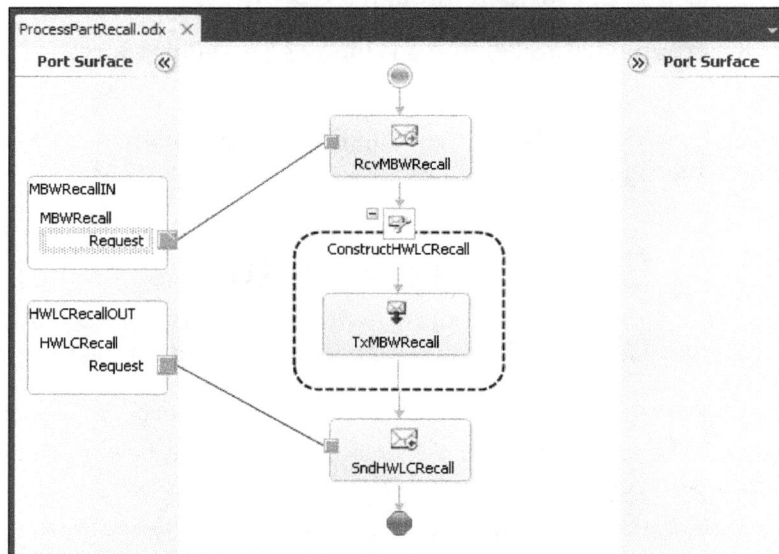

Preparing the solution

In order to deploy a BizTalk application from Visual Studio, there are a few things that we need to take care of first. They are as follows:

1. Right-click on our **BizTalk Project** and select **Properties**.

2. Click on the **Signing** label and then select **<New…>**, as shown in the following screenshot:

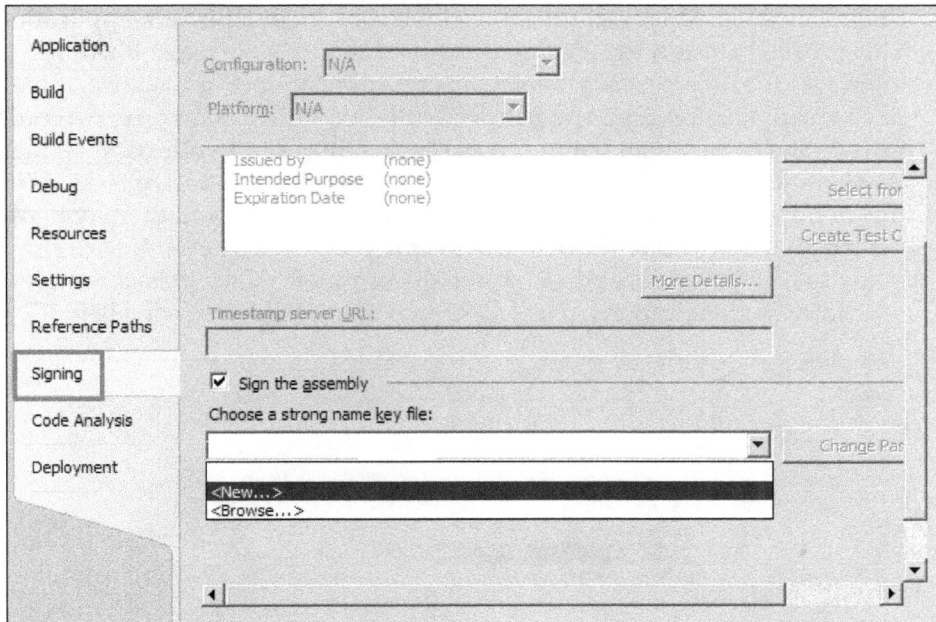

3. When prompted, provide the name, Example01-Deployment.snk, and clear the **Protect my key file with a password** checkbox, as shown in the following screenshot:

All BizTalk assemblies and helper assemblies that may be called from BizTalk must be deployed to the **Global Assembly Cache (GAC)**. In order to allow assemblies to be installed in the GAC, they must have Strong Name keys. Strong Name keys may be created from Visual Studio or through the sn-k<strongname>.snk command-line statement.

4. In BizTalk 2006, Microsoft introduced the concept of a BizTalk application. This is based around the idea that it would be nice to manage BizTalk interfaces that are logically related as one application. For instance, if we have an application for a specific department within a company, we could include the department name as a part of the BizTalk **Application Name**. We can then easily identify it when performing administrative tasks. With this in mind, we need to click on the **Deployment** label and then look for the **Application Name** textbox. For the purpose of this book, we are simply going to call our application **Chapter06-Example01**. Once this is complete, we can close this Property page, as shown in the following screenshot:

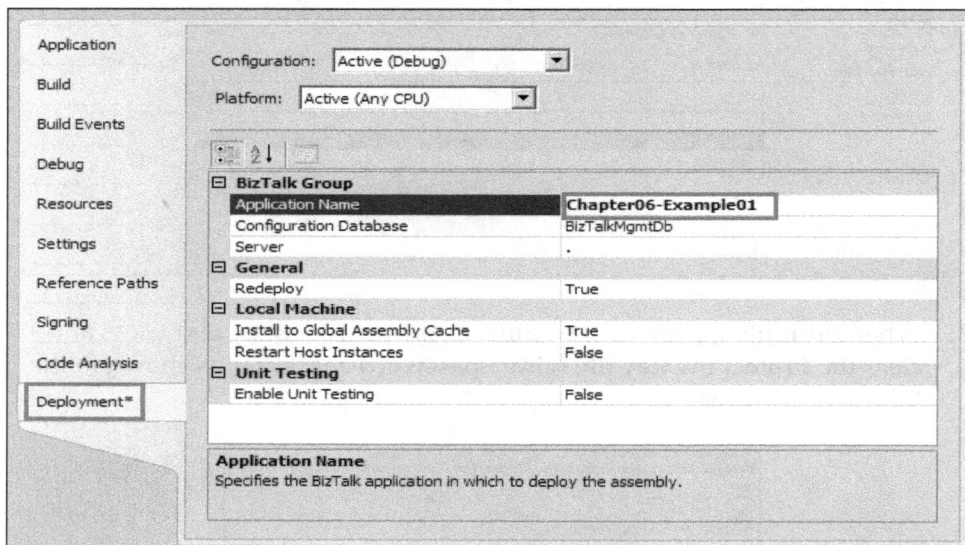

5. In the event we want to deploy our BizTalk application to a system other than the current local system, we do have the ability to provide an alternative Server Name in the Server field. In order to perform this action, we need to ensure that we have the appropriate level of permissions on that server for the account under which we are currently running Visual Studio.

6. We are now ready to deploy our application and can do so by right-clicking on our **Visual Studio Solution** and then clicking on **Deploy Solution**, as shown in the following screenshot:

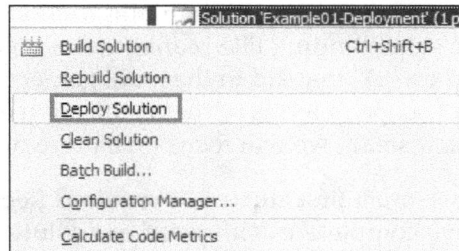

7. Provided our application has been deployed successfully, we can now launch BizTalk Administration Console and discover if our application exists. If the application exists, we will realize that it is pretty empty. We will discover our Orchestration in the **Orchestrations** folder, but we will not have any **Receive Ports**, **Receive Locations**, or **Send Ports**, as shown in the following screenshot:

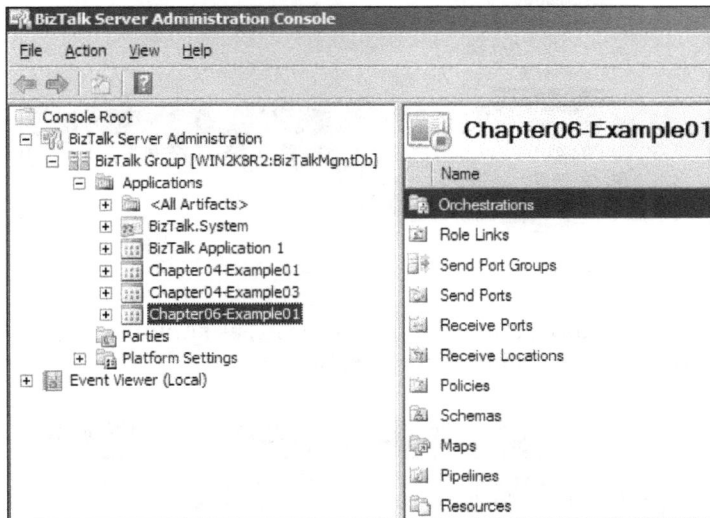

Binding Files

Binding Files are extremely important artifacts that can sometimes be difficult to manage. The Files provide BizTalk Solutions with a lot of portability and bind all of the major components together. Within a Binding File, we will be able to link our logical and physical Send Ports and Receive Ports to our Orchestrations. We can also include our URIs and other information required to connect to remote systems. Binding Files also allow us to move our BizTalk applications between the Development, Test, Quality Assurance, and Production environments with a reduced need for manual configuration.

There are many ways to manage Binding Files. In this section, we will discuss one of the methods. There are some Binding File Management Solutions, such as the BizTalk Deployment Framework, that aid in the management of Binding Files. Since third-party tools are out of scope in terms of the certification exam, we will not be discussing these methods. Instead, we will focus on a more manual approach.

To create a Binding File, we must first create our required Receive Location(s) and Send Port(s). Once we have completely configured our solution, we can export our configuration as a Binding File. Here are the steps that we need to perform:

1. Launch the BizTalk Administration Console and expand the **Chapter06-Example01** application.

2. On the **Receive Ports** label, right-click and navigate to **New | One-way Receive Port...**, as shown in the following screenshot:

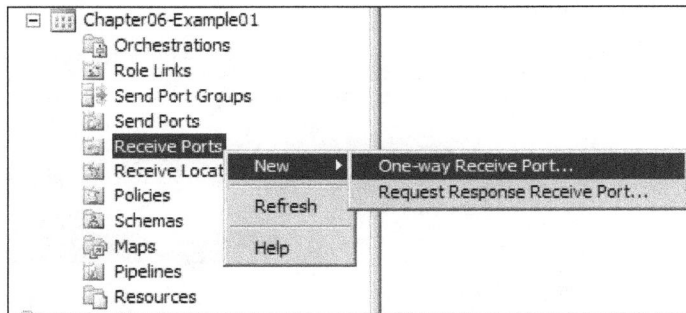

3. In the **Name:** textbox, enter ReceiveRecall, as shown in the following screenshot, and then click on the **OK** button:

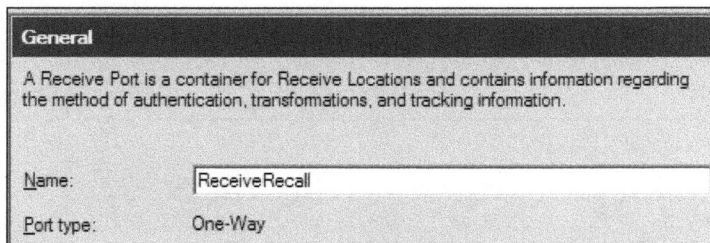

4. We now need to add a **Receive Location** by right-clicking on the **Receive Locations** label and navigating to **New | One-way Receive Location...**, as shown in the following screenshot:

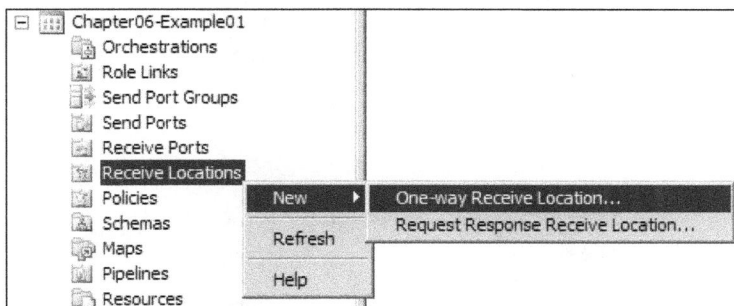

5. When prompted, click on the **ReceiveRecall** Receive Port and then on the **OK** button.

6. Provide a **Name:** ReceiveRecallMBWRecall, **Type:** of **FILE** under **Transport**, a **URI:** of C:\BTS2013CertGuide\Chapter06\FileDrop\DEV\MBW*. Copy. xml, a **Receive handler:** of **BizTalkServerApplication** and a **Receive Pipeline:** of XMLReceive. Once this information has been populated, as shown in the following screenshot, we can click on the **OK** button:

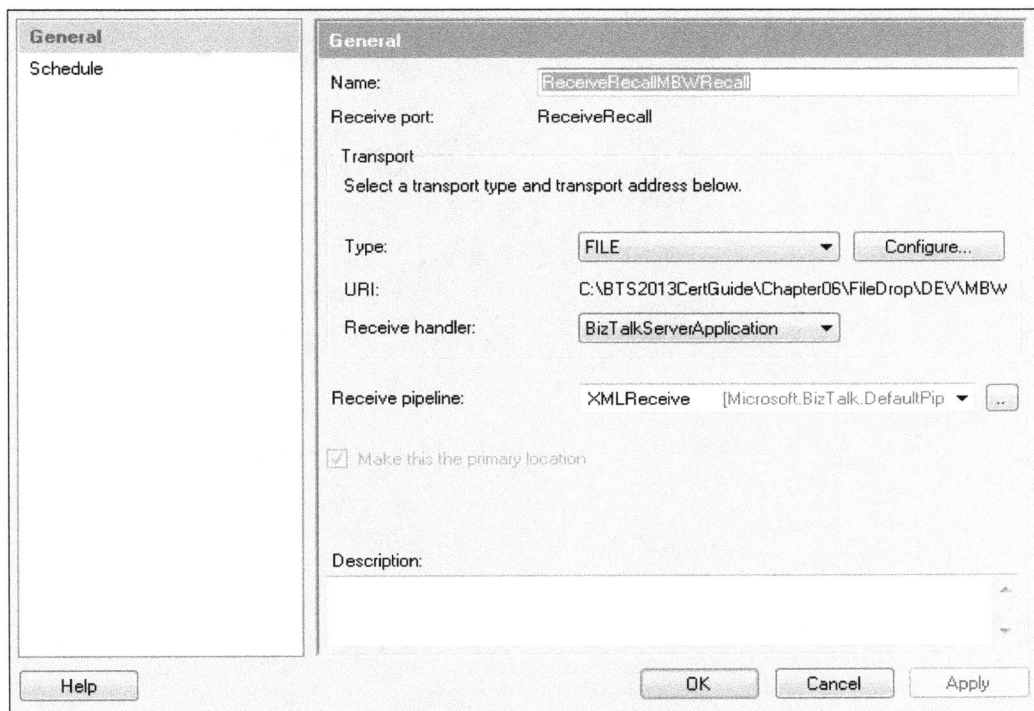

7. We now need to configure a Send Port. To do so, navigate to **Send Ports |
   New | Static One-way Send Port...**, as shown in the following screenshot:

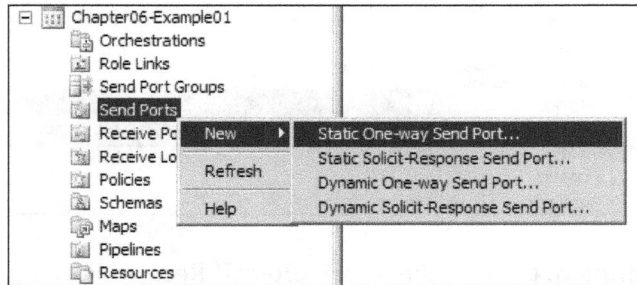

8. Provide a **Name:** of SendRecallToHWLC, a **Transport Type:** of
   FILE, a **URI:** of C:\BTS2013CertGuide\Chapter06\FileDrop\
   DEV\HWLCRecall%MessageID%.xml, a **Send handler:** of
   BizTalkServerApplication, and a **Send pipeline** of **PassThruTransmit**.
   Once this information has been populated, as shown in the following
   screenshot, we can click on the **OK** button:

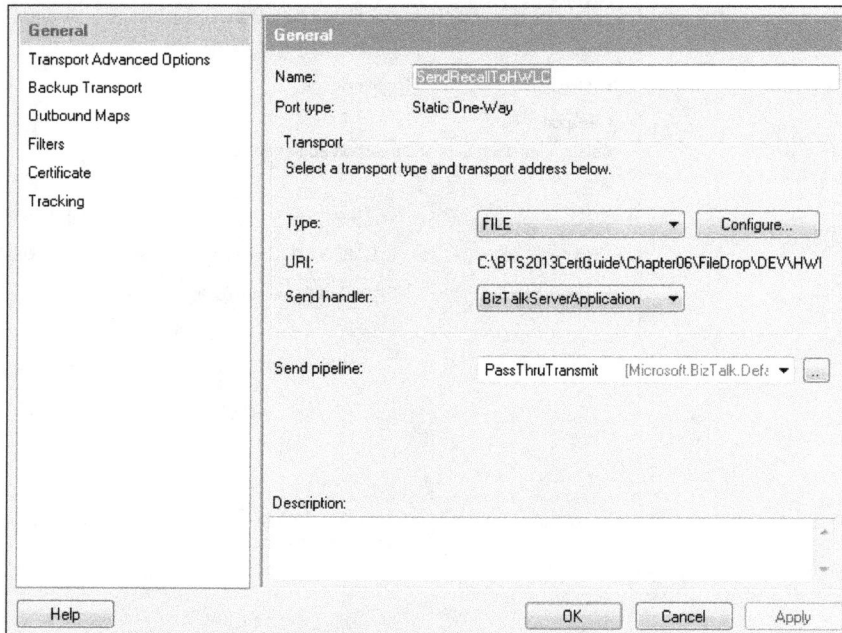

9. We now need to bind our Orchestration to our Receive and Send Ports. We can do so by double-clicking on **Orchestrations**, right-clicking on **Orchestrations**, and then clicking on **Properties...**, as shown in the following screenshot:

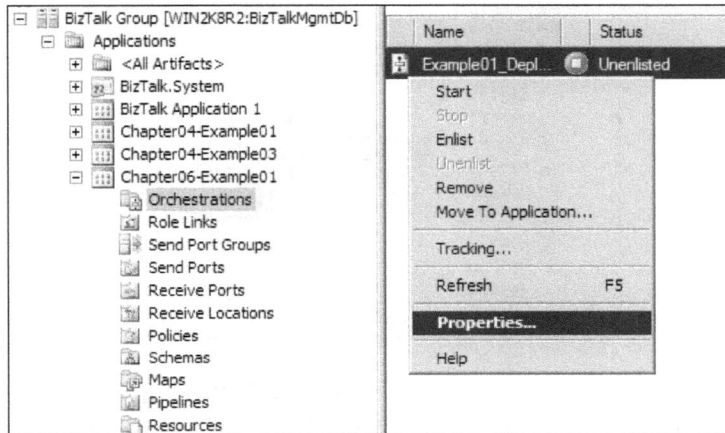

10. To finish binding our Orchestration to our ports, click on the **Bindings** label. Next, we need to set our **Host:** to **BizTalkServerApplication**, **MBWRecallIN** to **ReceiveRecall**, and **HWLCRecallOUT** to **SendRecallToHWLC**, as shown in the following screenshot:

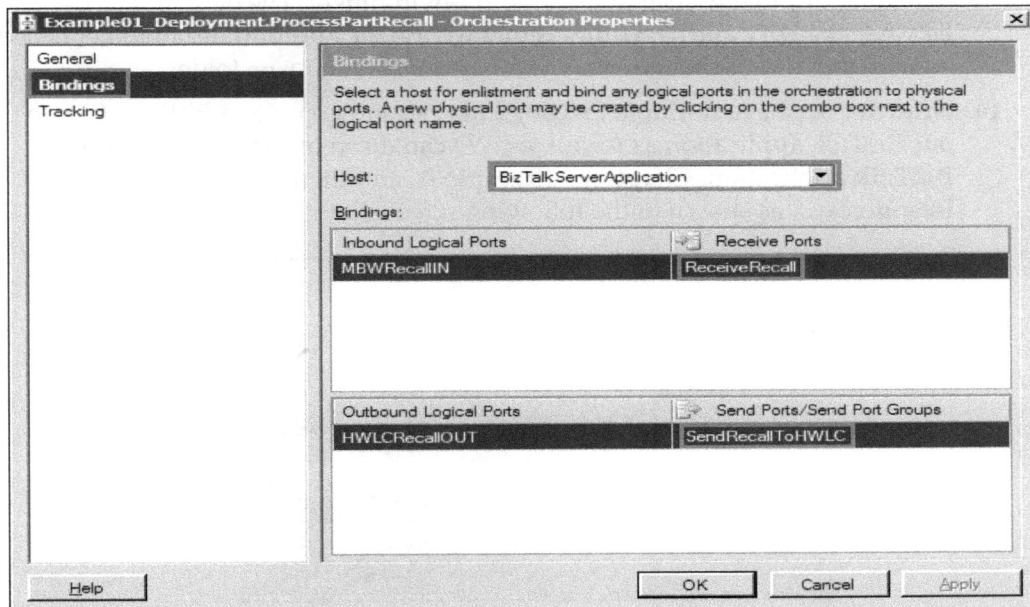

11. At this point, we have configured the application and are now in a position to export our configuration to a Binding File. To do so, we will simply right-click on the name of our BizTalk application, **Chapter06-Example01**, and navigate to **Export | Bindings...**, as shown in the following screenshot:

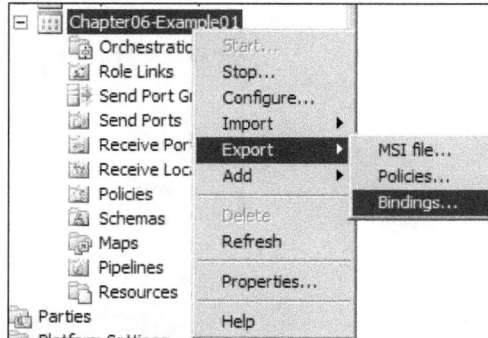

12. When prompted, we will navigate to **Export | Bindings...** from the current application and save our file as C:\BTS2013CertGuide\Chapter06\ Bindings\Chapter06-Example01.DEV.Binding.xml.

13. The Binding File that we just created represents a Binding File that could be used in a Development environment. For convenience, Test Binding File called Chapter06-Example01.TEST.Binding.xml.has also been provided in the C:\ BTS2013CertGuide\Chapter06\Bindings\ folder. This new file represents a Binding File that we can use in a TEST environment. The only difference between the DEV and TEST files is that we use the appropriate subfolder called Test in the C:\BTS2013CertGuide\Chapter06\FileDrop folder.

14. Now that we have multiple Binding Files, we are going to add these files to our BizTalk application as resources. We can do so by right-clicking on our **BizTalk** application, **Chapter06-Example01**, and then navigating to **Add | Resources...**, as shown in the following screenshot:

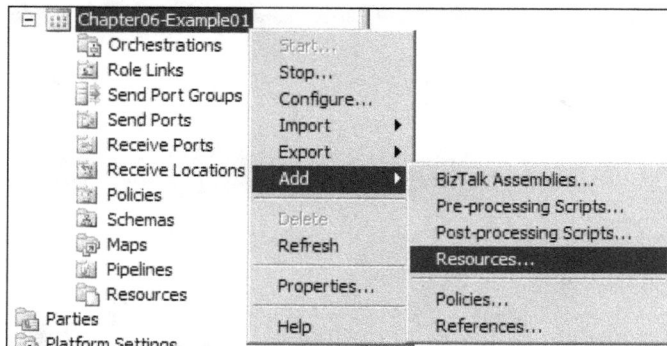

15. In the **Add Resources** dialog, we want to add both of our Binding Files
    that can be found in the C:\BTS2013CertGuide\Chapter06\Bindings
    folder of this chapter's sample code. We now want to specify which Target
    Environment each of these Binding Files belongs to. So, we can select the
    first file, **Chapter06-Example01.DEV.Binding.xml**, and then specify a
    Target Environment: of **DEV**. We want to perform this same action with
    our **Chapter06-Example01.TEST.Binding.xml** file, providing a **Target
    Environment** of **TEST** this time. Optionally, we can specify the **Overwrite
    all** checkbox in the event we have added these resources to our BizTalk
    application previously, as shown in the following screenshot:

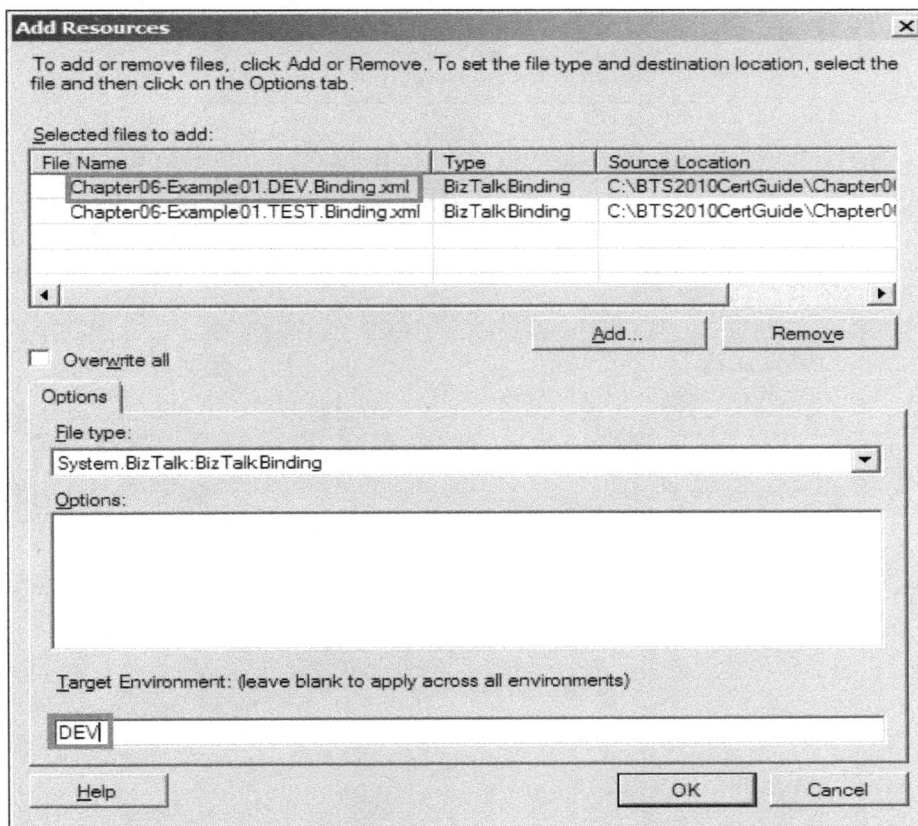

16. Now that we have added our Binding Files to our BizTalk application as resources, we can export our application as an MSI file. To do so, we need to right-click on our BizTalk application, **Chapter06-Example01**, and then navigate to **Export | MSI file...**, as shown in the following screenshot:

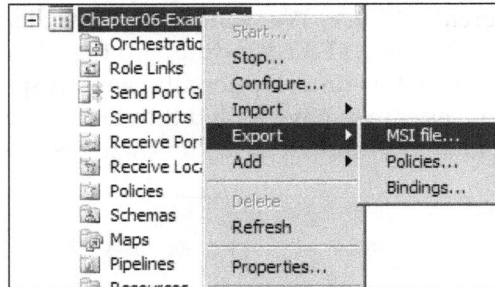

17. On the **Welcome** screen, click on **Next** to proceed to the next screen.

18. When prompted, we want to ensure that all of the artifacts we are interested in, including the ones in our MSI package, are checked. This includes our BizTalk assembly and Binding Files, as shown in the following screenshot:

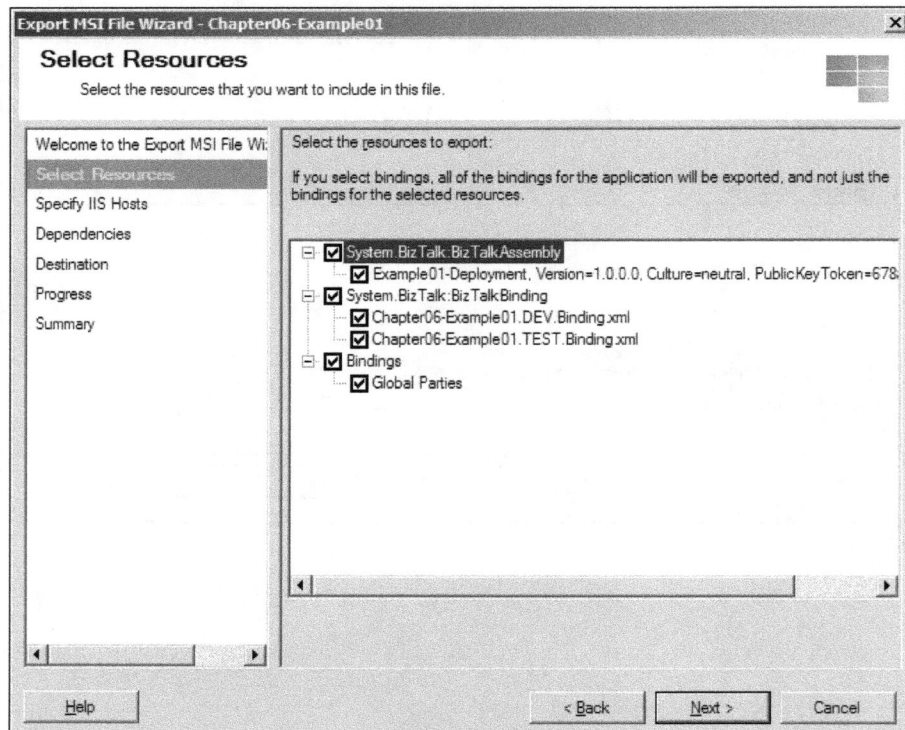

> Our sample application does not use Trading Partner Management and Global Parties. If our application did, we could include Global Parties in our MSI package.

19. Since we are not hosting any Web or WCF Services, we can skip the **Specify IIS Hosts** screen by clicking on **Next**.

20. On the **Dependencies** screen, click on **Next** to proceed. In the Destination screen, provide a **Destination application name:** of `Chapter06-Example01`. In the **MSI file to generate:** textbox, enter `C:\BTS2013CertGuide\Chapter06\MSI\Chapter06-Example01.msi`. Finally, click on the **Export** button to write the MSI file to the disk, as shown in the following screenshot:

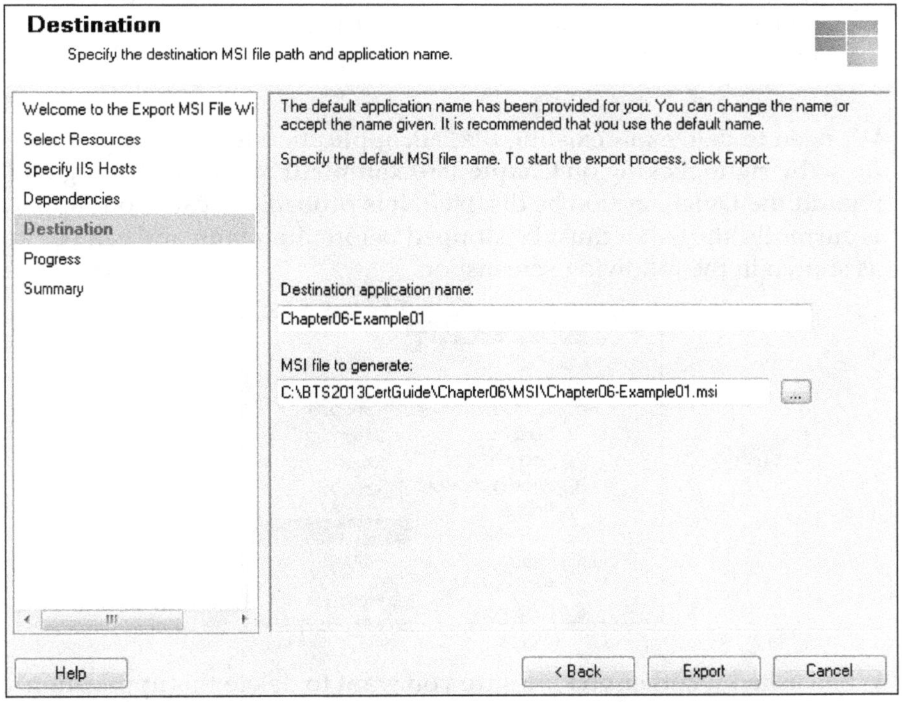

Destination

Specify the destination MSI file path and application name.

Welcome to the Export MSI File Wi
Select Resources
Specify IIS Hosts
Dependencies
Destination
Progress
Summary

The default application name has been provided for you. You can change the name or accept the name given. It is recommended that you use the default name.

Specify the default MSI file name. To start the export process, click Export.

Destination application name:

Chapter06-Example01

MSI file to generate:

C:\BTS2013CertGuide\Chapter06\MSI\Chapter06-Example01.msi

Help   < Back   Export   Cancel

21. Click on the **Finish** button to close the **Summary** screen.

Sample deployment through an MSI package

When the time comes to deploy our application to a different environment, we will have an MSI package that contains multiple Binding Files. For this purpose, in the next section, we are going to pretend that we are deploying our MSI package to a TEST environment, and we will, therefore, use the TEST Binding File when prompted. To keep things simple, we will just re-use our existing BizTalk environment and delete our existing BizTalk application, as follows:

> The following section requires that the `C:\BTS2013CertGuide\Chapter06\FileDrop\TEST` folder exist. If you have extracted the sample source code that has been provided with this book, then this folder exists on your machine. If you have not extracted the source code, please create this folder to ensure this sample functions correctly.

1. We need to delete our existing BizTalk application for this chapter and can do so by right-clicking on **Chapter06-Example01** and then clicking on **Delete**. Should the **Delete** option be disabled, it is probably because our application is currently started; it must be stopped before this command can be executed, as shown in the following screenshot:

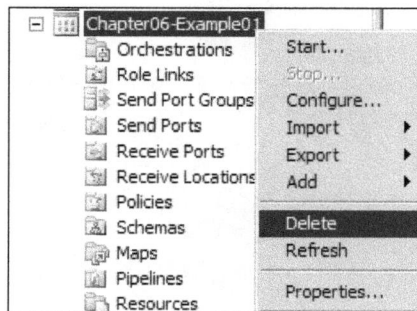

2. When asked whether you are sure you want to delete this application, click on the **Yes** button.

3. Deploying a BizTalk application, in most cases, is a two-step process. The first step is to run the MSI package, which will register the application with the Windows Operating System, from Windows and then load any related assemblies in the **Global Assembly Cache** (**GAC**). To do this, we want to find our MSI package in the `C:\BTS2013CertGuide\Chapter06\MSI` folder, right-click on it, and then select **Install**, as shown in the following screenshot:

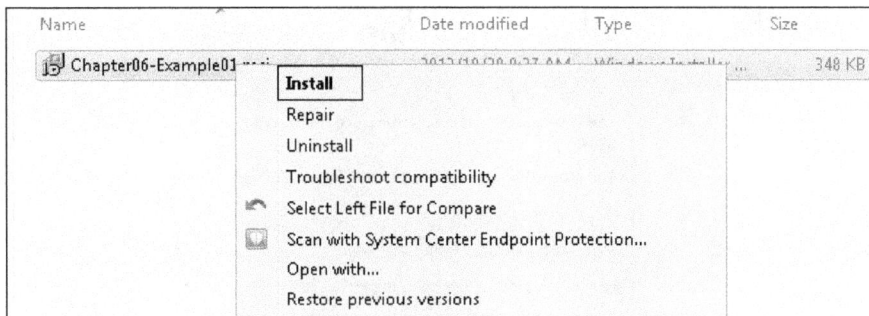

4. The installation wizard is straightforward, and we can simply accept the defaults.

5. Once we have completed the MSI package installation, we still need to import this MSI package in BizTalk Administration Console. At this point, the Windows Operating System is aware of our BizTalk application but BizTalk itself is not. To import our MSI package, we can right-click on the **Applications** label and then navigate to **Import | MSI file...**, as shown in the following screenshot:

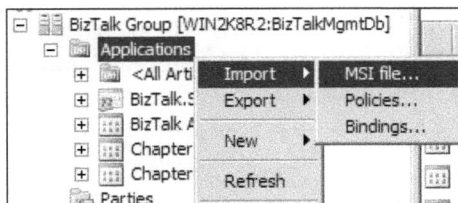

6. We now need to provide the location of our MSI package to the **Import MSI Wizard**. We can find our MSI package in the C:\BTS2013CertGuide\ Chapter06\MSI folder, as shown in the following screenshot:

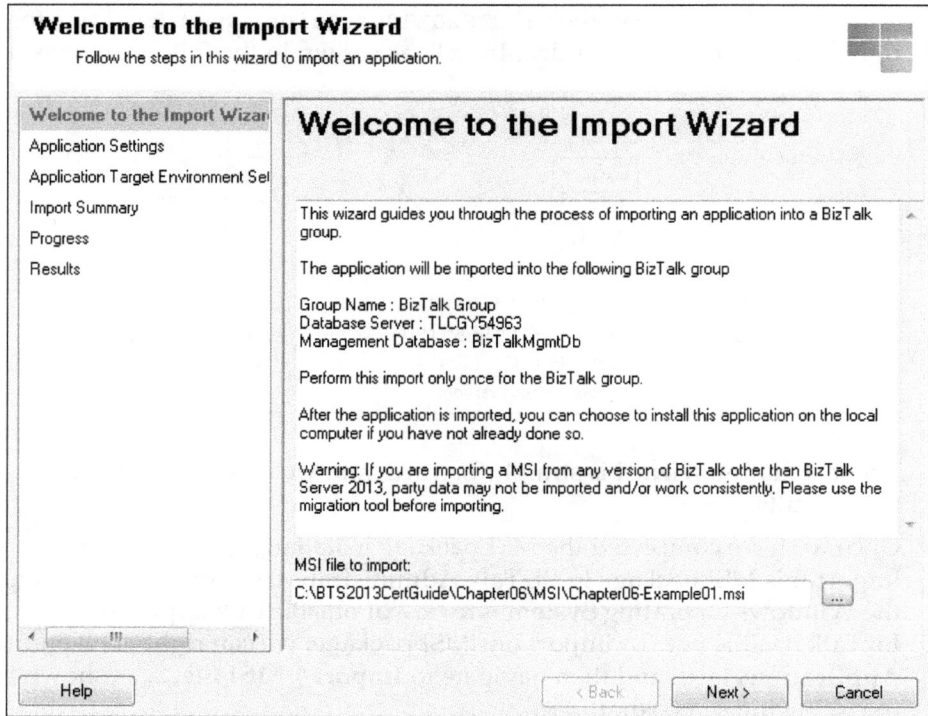

7. We now have the opportunity to provide an **Application name**. We will just accept the default value, which is **Chapter06-Example01**, as shown in the following screenshot:

Application Settings

Select the application name and add references.

Welcome to the Import Wizard
Application Settings
Application Target Environment Sel
Import Summary
Progress
Results

Application name:

Chapter06-Example01

Application References and Resources:

- References
  - BizTalk.System
- Resources
  - Example01-Deployment, Version=1.0.0.0, Culture=neutral, PublicKey
  - Chapter06-Example01.DEV.Binding.xml
  - Chapter06-Example01.TEST.Binding.xml

Available applications to add references to:

- ☑ BizTalk.System
- ☐ BizTalk Application 1
- ☐ BizTalk.EnterpriseApplication
- ☐ Microsoft.Practices.ESB
- ☐ Microsoft.Practices.JMS
- ☐ TransAlta.MOC

☐ Overwrite resources

(Bindings in the MSI file always overwrite those in the application.)

Help		< Back	Next >	Cancel

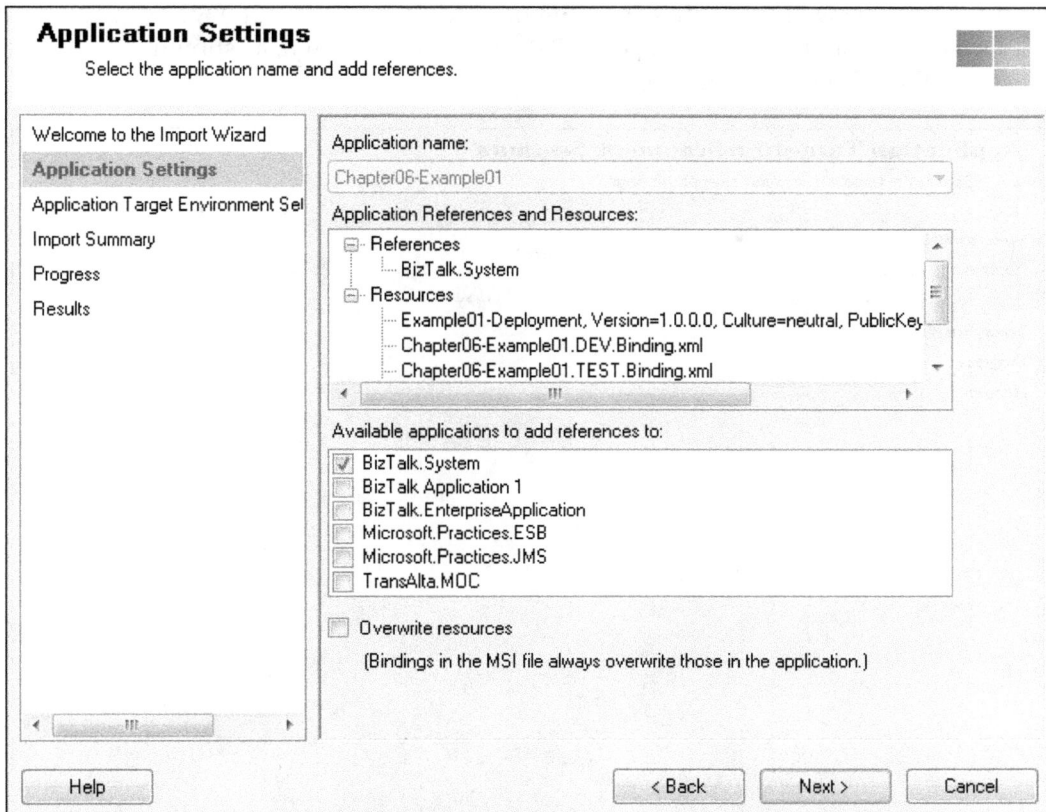

> If we were redeploying an application, we would want
> to select **Overwrite resources**, but since we deleted our
> application prior to running the **Import MSI Wizard**, it
> is not required.

8. We now have the opportunity to specify our **Target Staging Environment**.

9. Since this walkthrough is focusing on a deployment to our **TEST** environment, we will select **TEST** from the drop-down, as shown in the following screenshot:

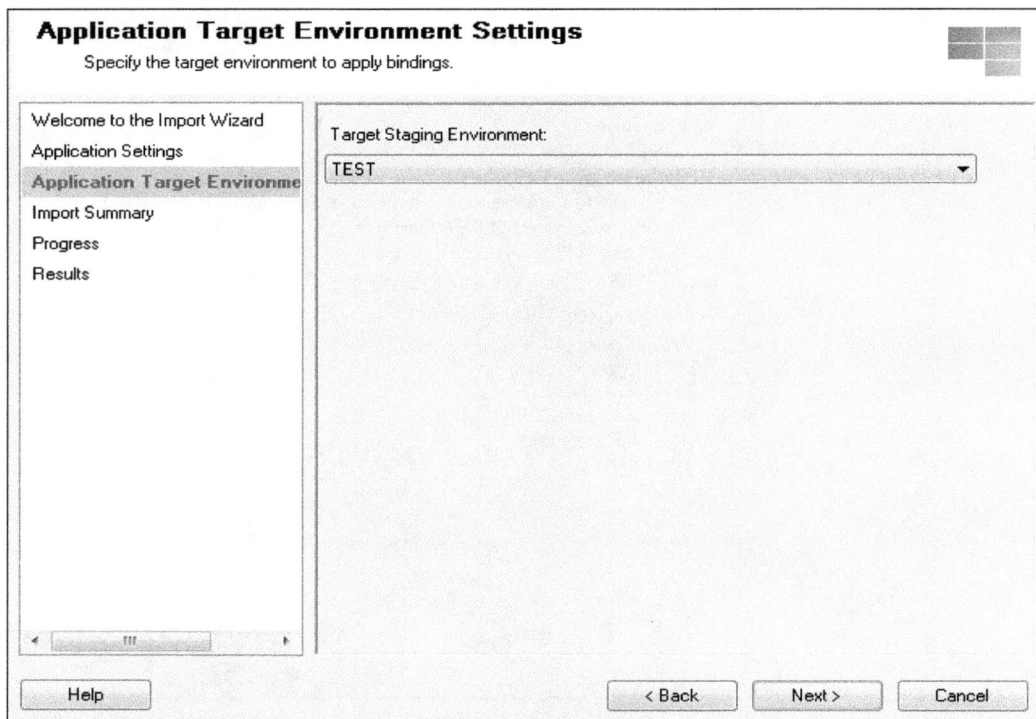

Application Target Environment Settings

Specify the target environment to apply bindings.

Welcome to the Import Wizard

Application Settings

Application Target Environme

Import Summary

Progress

Results

Target Staging Environment:

TEST

| Help | | < Back | Next > | Cancel |

> When we added Binding Files as resources in the previous section, we specified a Target environment. If we did not provide a Target environment, then we would want to select **Default** in this previous screen. A Binding File that does not have a Target environment will be used when **Default** is selected as the **Target Staging Environment**, when importing an MSI file.

10. On the **Import Summary** screen, select **Import** and once that is done, click on the **Finish** button. We will now discover that our application has been successfully imported.

It is important to note that for each server on which we would like our BizTalk application to run, we need to install this MSI package on each Server, where a Host Instance exists for this BizTalk Application. For example, if our application will be using a Host called Process Host and this Host has instances on Server A and Server B, then we need to install this MSI package on both Server A and Server B. The reason for this is that our BizTalk assemblies must be installed in the **Global Assembly Cache (GAC)** on each server where our application will run. This is in addition to the MSI package being imported via BizTalk Administration Console, which will subsequently update our BizTalk Management database.

Binding File dependencies

When importing Binding Files into a BizTalk environment, it is very important to ensure that any assemblies and artifacts that the Binding File is referencing exist. For instance, if we try to import a Binding File that references a particular Host, that Host must exist for the import to be successful.

Another area to be cautious about is specifying a Host within a Send Port configuration within our Binding File. A Host that is specified in a Send Port or Receive Location for that matter, must also exist in the handler configuration of an adapter. The following screenshot shows how this configuration should be set up. Suppose we have a Send Port that is going to use the **FILE** Adapter and will use a Host called **HWLCSend**. In order to configure this correctly, we need to navigate to the **Platform Settings** node and then expand the **Adapters** node. We can now right-click on the **FILE** Adapter and click on **New Send Handler**. We now have the ability to specify **HWLCSend** as a **Send Handler**. The next time we import a Binding File that is going to use the **HWLCSend** Host in a Send Port that uses the **FILE** Adapter (as shown in the following screenshot), we will not receive any errors:

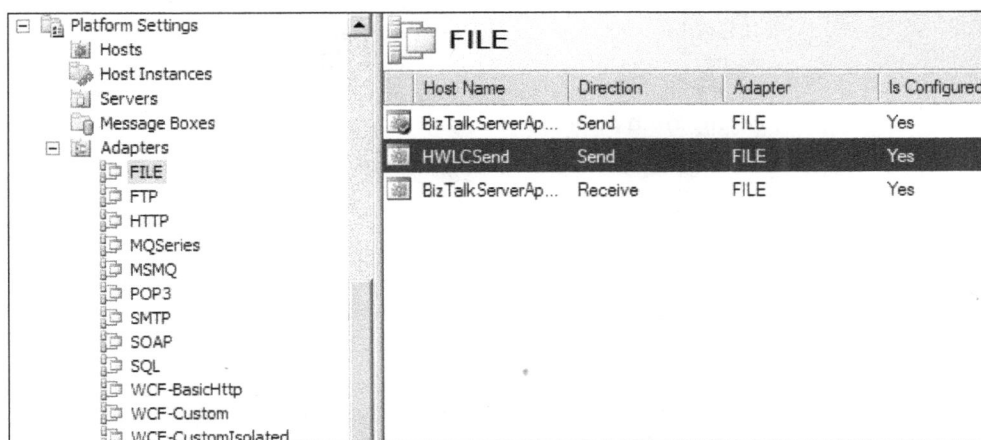

BizTalk Application states

BizTalk has many different application states. Understanding these states can be the difference between being a genius and a scapegoat. Modification of a BizTalk state is usually the result of an action that has taken place. In many cases, altering these states is due to an upcoming deployment, and we need to ensure that we allow messages that are currently being processed to complete without letting new messages into the BizTalk application. I am sure there are many horror stories out there about an inexperienced admin who accidently terminated some inflight messages because they did not understand these states.

Runtime Application states

There are three Runtime Application states. Setting these states is usually based upon explicit actions by an administrator, but can also occur if system resource(s), such as a source system, is not available. Do note that the following states do not account for Host Instances being online or offline. We can have an application that is started, but if we have Host Instances that are offline, this application will not function properly.

The following table describes these Runtime states in more detail:

State	Description
Started	In this state, all BizTalk application artifacts are enabled and ready to perform processing.
Partially Started	When an application is Partially Started, it means that some of the application artifacts and resources are online. An application may be placed into this state either explicitly by an administrator, or it may be the result of some dependent system resource(s) being offline. Consider a situation where we have a Receive Location that uses the FILE Adapter to connect to a network file system that is currently offline. In this situation, we will have a Receive Location that automatically gets disabled, and therefore, the state of our application will flip from Started to Partially Started.
We may have another situation where we have been asked to hold or queue messages because a destination system is either down or currently under maintenance. In this case, we want to stop the related Send Port, but leave the Send Port enlisted. This will allow BizTalk to queue these messages without sending them. It also results in the application state flipping to Partially Started.
Stopped	The final state is when an application is completely offline. This means we have no Receive Locations, Orchestrations, or Send Ports enlisted or capable of processing messages. An application enters this state through the actions of an administrator.

The following screenshot shows the working of these Runtime states:

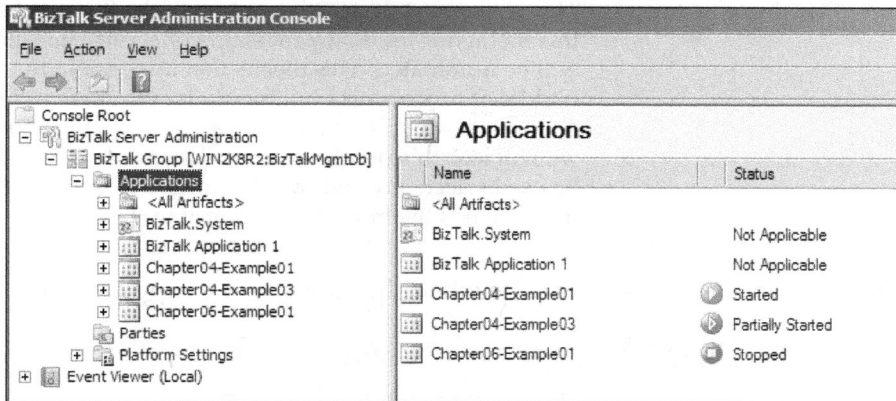

When stopping an application, BizTalk provides us with some options that allow us to control how the application will be stopped. Much like the Runtime states, stopping an application will affect the state of a Host. The following table will further explain each option when shutting down an application:

State	Description
Partial Stop - Allow running instances to continue	This option is ideal when you have inflight messages that have a short duration. By stopping an application that is using this mode, we will have all of our Receive Locations disabled. Meanwhile, our Orchestration(s) and Send Port(s) will continue to function. This allows us to drain our application. No new messages can enter the application, but messages that are currently in flight have the opportunity to complete.
Partial Stop - Suspend running instances	When we select Partial Stop - Suspend running instances, it is like pressing the pause button on the application. We cannot receive any new messages, and any Messages/Service instances that are currently being processed will be suspended. These messages/ service instances may be resumed if we attempt to start our application. Using this option is ideal when we have some Long Running processes, and it may not be feasible to wait for any active instances to complete.

State	Description
Full Stop - Terminate instances	This is the most destructive option of the three. When this method is used, any messages or service instances, will be terminated. This means that if we are in the middle of processing a million-dollar purchase order and we choose to stop an application using this mode, we will lose this purchase order. This method needs to be used selectively and by an administrator who clearly understands the impact of performing this action.

The following screenshot shows options when shutting down an application:

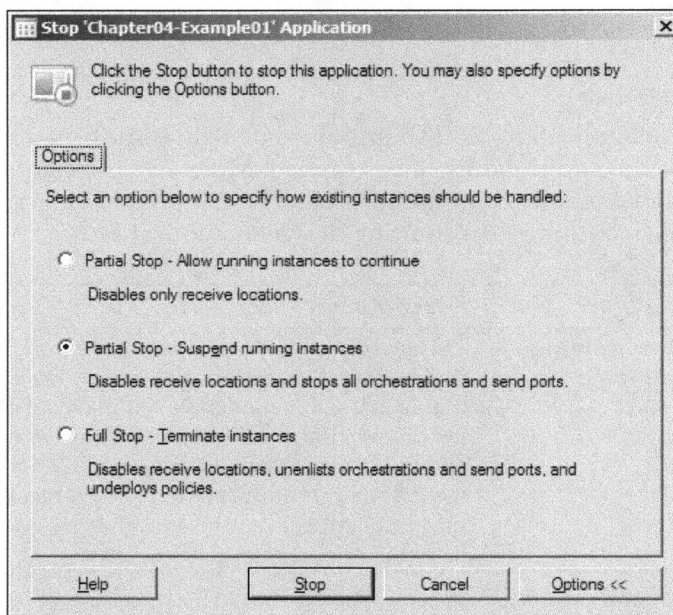

Tracking events in BizTalk Server

Tracking events in BizTalk Server can be an expensive but valuable endeavor. This activity is expensive as BizTalk will now need to look for specific properties or message bodies within Message or Orchestration instances and record this data. This activity can reduce the throughput of BizTalk Server but can become extremely beneficial in support scenarios. If you have ever participated in a BizTalk Project that involved multiple teams, you will inevitably have been asked "What happened with message XYZ?" The tracking capabilities of BizTalk allow you to solve the mystery much more easily.

In this section, we are going to discuss some of the different ways in which a BizTalk Administrator can track events as they occur inside BizTalk.

Tracking Receive Ports

We can enable our tracking properties on a Receive Port by right-clicking on the **Receive Port** and then selecting **Properties**. Once you go into the **Property** screen of the **Receive Port**, we need to click on the **Tracking** label.

We will discover the properties that we can set. The following table will elaborate on each of these properties and its purpose:

Property	Description
Track Message Bodies	These options are related to saving a copy of the message that has been received at two different stages.
Request message before port processing	When enabled, the content of the message will be saved before passing through any Pipeline.
Request message after port processing	Enable this option when you want to save the content of an inbound message after the message has passed through a Pipeline.
Track Message Properties	Use this option to track promoted properties at two different stages of receiving a message.
Request message before port processing	Setting this property allows us to track a promoted property when a message has been received and before the message enters a Pipeline.
Request message after port processing	When enabled, promoted properties will be tracked after a message has been through a Pipeline. This option is very beneficial in situations where a custom Pipeline component has promoted a property inside a custom Pipeline.

The following screenshot shows the properties:

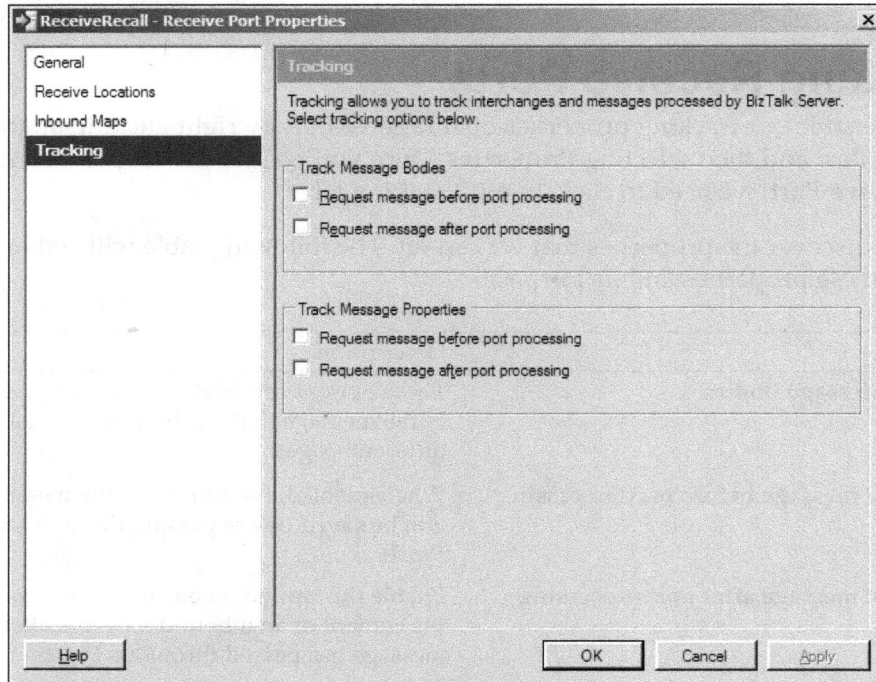

Tracking Orchestrations

Tracking an Orchestration is very similar to tracking a Receive Port. Much like a Receive Port, each Orchestration has its own tracking properties. To enable tracking on an Orchestration, right-click on it and then select **Properties**. Once you see this **Property** screen, click on the **Tracking** label.

However, we have a few more options that we can set; they are further discussed in the following table:

Property	Description
Track Events	These options are set by default and aid in identifying the Orchestration events so that we can query these events in the BizTalk Administration Console.
Orchestration start and end	Having this setting allows us to identify when an Orchestration started and finished inside the BizTalk Administration Console.

Property	Description
Message send and receive	If we want to be able to record the time when a message was sent or received, then we need to enable this option.
Shape start and end	When enabled, this setting can help troubleshoot performance bottlenecks. When we are debugging an Orchestration, we will be able to determine the amount of time each shape took to execute.
Track Message Bodies	These properties are very similar to the properties that exist in a Receive or Send Port. It allows us to save a copy of the message content as messages are making their way through our Orchestration.
Before Orchestration processing	This property and the remaining ones are only enabled if Message send and receive—Track Event is enabled. When enabled, the message content will be saved prior to it, thus entering an Orchestration. This property becomes extremely useful in situations where we are using Direct Bound Ports and have not received a message through a traditional Receive Port.
After Orchestration processing	The content of a message, after it has been processed by an Orchestration, will be saved when this option is enabled. Once again, this property is very useful in Direct Bound Port situations. Otherwise, we would not have a Physical Send Port that we could enable message body tracking on.
Track Message Properties	Much like Receive Ports, we can track promoted properties for both incoming and outgoing messages. This time around, properties are tracked when a message enters or exits an Orchestration.
Incoming messages	When this option is enabled, the properties will be promoted when a message enters an Orchestration.
Outgoing messages	When this option is enabled, we are able to track promoted properties after a message has left an Orchestration.

The following screenshot shows the **Tracking** properties:

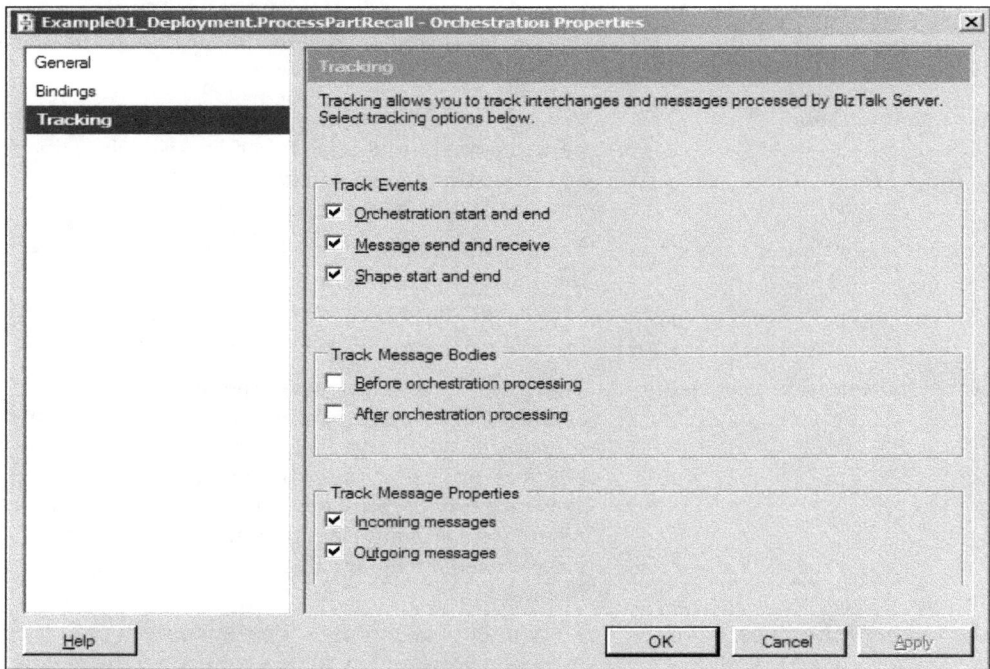

As you can see, there are a lot of events that can be tracked within a BizTalk Orchestration. These events can be aggregated when we view the Orchestration Debugger for an articular Service Instance. As we proceed from one step to another, we can see exactly when the event began and concluded. While the list of tracking events may seem to be comprehensive, there is one area that is lacking and that is in the area of tracking how long it takes for a Map to execute. We do have visibility into how long a message takes to construct, but if we have multiple events occurring within a Construct Message shape, then we lose some granularity, as depicted in the following screenshot:

Tracking Send Ports

Tracking Send Ports works the same way as Tracking Receive Ports, the difference being Tracking Send Ports will track messages entering and exiting a Send Port as opposed to a Receive Port. The following table describes our tracking properties in more detail:

Property	Description
Track Message Bodies	These options are related to saving a copy of the message that is about to be sent at two different stages.
Request message before port processing	When this option is enabled, the content of the message will be saved before passing through any Pipeline.
Request message after port processing	Enable this option when you want to save the content of an outbound message after the message has passed through a Pipeline.
Track Message Properties	Use these options to track promoted properties at two different stages of sending a message.

Property	Description
Request message before port processing	Setting this property allows us to track a promoted property when a message is about to be sent, but before the message enters a Pipeline.
Request message after port processing	When enabled, promoted properties will be tracked after a message has been through a Pipeline.

The following screenshot shows **Tracking** properties:

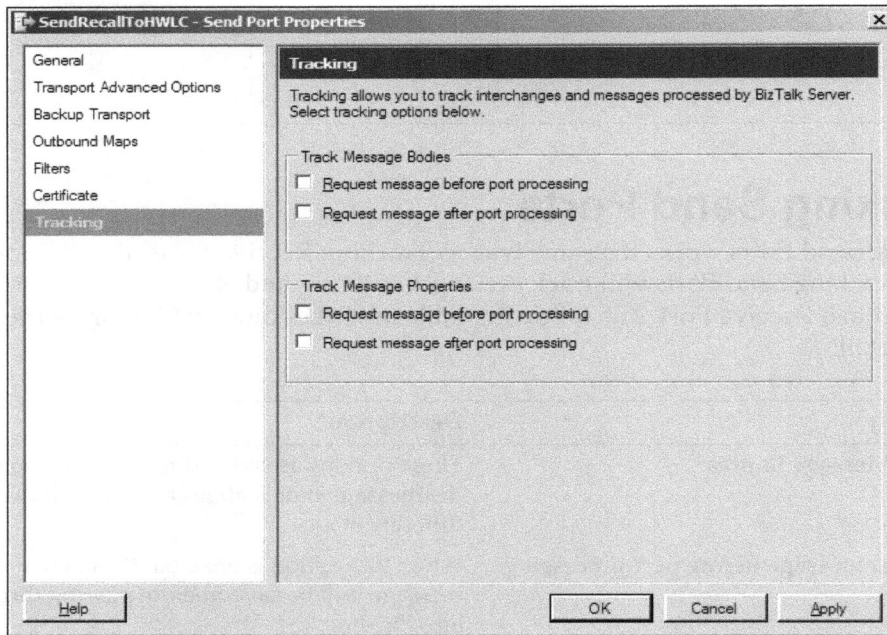

Tracking Promoted Properties

We also have the ability to track promoted properties and subsequently query instances that match our criteria. In order to track a promoted property, we need to select our Property Schema from within our Schemas folder that is within our BizTalk application. We then need to view its properties and check the promoted property that we are interested in tracking. This feature will be very beneficial in content-based routing situations, where we are interested in messages that contain a specific value, for example an Order Number, a location or a unique identifier. The following screenshot shows where we can enable tracking of promoted properties:

Provided we have promoted properties before deploying our application, we can enable and disable these tracking properties as required. However, we cannot retroactively obtain details about an Orchestration or message if we do not have the tracking settings enabled. By setting these tracking options, any message or Orchestration processed, going forward, will be tracked.

Managing BizTalk applications using BizTalk Administration Console

The BizTalk Administration Console is a very rich tool that allows us to manage all aspects of our BizTalk applications. We have already touched upon some of its capabilities, including managing Binding Files and MSI packages, in addition to managing Hosts and adapter Handlers. This section is going to focus more on the tools that allow us to determine the real-time health of our applications.

This section has been broken down into the following six sections:

- Configuration Overview
- Work in Progress
- Suspended Items
- Grouped Service Instances
- Tracked Service Instances
- Tracked Message Events

Each of these functions is a core component of what is referred to as the BizTalk Group Hub. When testing a BizTalk Application, if we do not get the outcome that we expect, checking the BizTalk Group Hub is the preferred destination when looking at troubleshooting the issue. The BizTalk Group Hub provides the broadest level of coverage for our BizTalk Solutions.

Within the BizTalk Administration Console, each of these different sections provides links to queries that we can run against our MessageBox and Tracking databases. We also have the ability to create our own queries and save them so that we can re-use them at a later time.

Configuration overview

In this section of **Group Hub**, we will discover our **Group name**, the name of our **Server**, and the name of our management **Database**. More importantly, we get a quick overview of the health of our BizTalk environment. We can see how many **Applications** have been installed and the summary of their health. There are three different states that are represented by icons. If all of our applications are stopped, this icon will be red. If we have some applications started and some partially started or stopped, the icon will be blue. If all applications are started, the icon will be green.

The next area to dive into is the Host Instances state view. If all of our Host Instances are stopped, then this icon will be red. If we have some Host Instances started and some stopped, then we will see an icon with a red exclamation mark (!). Finally, if all Host Instances are online, the icon will be a green check mark, as shown in the following screenshot:

Group Hub	New Query

Configuration Overview

Group name: BizTalk Group
Server: WIN2K8R2
Database: BizTalk Mgmt Db

Applications (5)
Host Instances (3)
Adapter Handlers (34)

(?) Learn about Administration and Troubleshooting

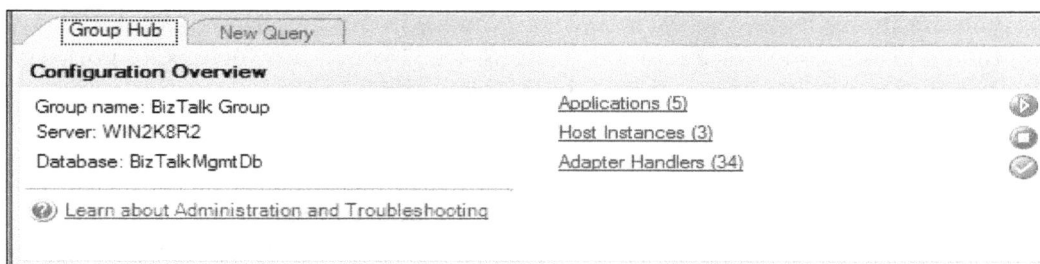

> In the event that your environment contains Clustered Host Instances, the BizTalk Administration Console is smart enough to detect this situation and will correctly display the state of our Host Instances, taking into account Active or Passive Host Instances.

Work in Progress

This area deals with active processes that have not entered an exception or suspended state. The **Running service instances** link provides a query that will display the total amount of running instances.

Dehydrated orchestrations refer to Orchestrations that are currently sitting idle. These Orchestrations may have just sent out a message to a destination system and may now be waiting for a response back.

The messages that were not successfully sent to a downstream system and have their Send Port configured to Retry will show up in the **Retrying and idle ports** link.

A message that has been found by a subscription but cannot be sent out due to a Host Instance being offline will end up as **Ready service instances**. For instance, suppose we have a message that was received through a ReceiveMessages Host Instance. The Send Port that subscribes to this message uses a Host Instance called SendMessages, but this Host Instance is currently offline. This message will remain in this **Ready service instances** state until the SendMessages Host Instance comes back online.

The last state that we are going to discuss is called **Scheduled service instances**.

In some situations, we may want to save our messages until a certain part of the day, and then release them. We can do so by setting a service window on a Send Port. The number of messages that are currently in this state will be reflected here, as shown in the following screenshot:

> Setting a service window is not limited to Send Ports. We can also set a service window on Receive Locations that prevents BizTalk from receiving messages during a specific timeframe.

Work in Progress	
Running service instances	3
- Dehydrated orchestrations	0
- Retrying and idle ports	1
- Ready service instances	2
- Scheduled service instances	0

Suspended Items

At the top of the **Suspended Items** section, we will discover a summary of all of the different **Suspended service instances**. There are two different types of **Suspended service instances**: **Resumable** and **Non-resumable**. **Resumable** instances can be restarted by a BizTalk Administrator. Messages may enter this state for a variety of reasons, but a frequent way in which messages enter this state is when Retry Thresholds of a Send Port have been exceeded.

Message Instances that cannot be restarted will remain in a **Non-resumable** state. Messages may enter this state for many reasons, including whether a message is experiencing a routing failure or whether an Orchestration has encountered a catastrophic failure.

In the event that an Orchestration has encountered an unhandled exception, we can expect our service instance to be in our **Suspended service instances** list, as shown in the following screenshot:

Suspended Items	
Suspended service instances	3
- Resumable	2
- Non-resumable	1

Group Suspended Service Instances

Within this section, we will discover four different links to queries. Each link will take us to a Query Results view, but the information will be grouped depending upon the link we clicked on.

The first link is called **Grouped by Application**. When selected, this link will take us to a Query Results page that will group all of the Suspended Instances based upon the BizTalk application they belong to. This feature becomes very useful if we are only concerned with errors that belong to a specific application. It also declutters some unrelated Suspended Messages that you may not immediately be interested in.

The second Suspended Instance Group that we are interested in is **Grouped by Error Code**. When this link is clicked, we will see all Suspended Instances grouped by their Error Code, regardless of which application they belong to. This type of query is good when you are trying to troubleshoot the issue, whether or not an underlying shared component is causing an issue.

When the **Grouped by Service Name** link is clicked upon, it will display all Suspended Instances that are grouped by their Service Name. A Service Name may include the name of a Receive Port, Orchestration, Send Port, or as in the following example, a Routing Failure.

The **Grouped by URI** link will take us to a Query Results screen that will group our exceptions by the URI that it is related to, as shown in the following screenshot. This may be a Universal Naming Convention (UNC) path, Web Service URL, or even a Database Connection String, Tracked Service Instances, and so on.

Grouped Suspended Service Instances			
Grouped by Application		Grouped by Service Name	
Chapter06-Example01	3	ReceiveRecall	1
		Routing Failure Report for "Re...	1
		Click on header to see all results	
Grouped by Error Code		Grouped by URI	
0xc0c01680 (Routing Failure)	1	C:\BTS2010CertGuide\Chapt...	2
0xC0C01B4e (Routing Failure ...	1	C:\BTS2010CertGuide\Chapt...	1
Click on header to see all results			

Tracked Service Instances

Tracked Service Instances is a good way to search for particular service instances that may have been successful or terminated. Service Instance includes messages that were received, sent, or Orchestrations. If we want to search for both these conditions, we can click on **Completed instances**, whereas if we want to only find Terminated Instances, we can click on the **Terminated instances** link, as shown in the following screenshot:

Tracked Service Instances

Tracked service instances

- Completed instances

- Terminated instances

Tracked Message Events

If we are just interested in Message Events, we can click on the **Tracked Message Events** link. Message Events include Send and Receive Events. If we are only interested in **Transmission failure events**, we can click on this link. An example of a Transmission failure could include a Message Instance that has exceeded the threshold of a Send Port. The following screenshot shows the **Tracked Message Events** list:

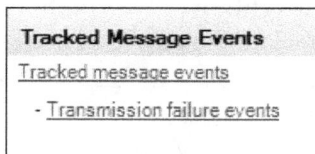

Tracked Message Events

Tracked message events

- Transmission failure events

As you have seen, every time we click on one of these links, it runs a query in the background. We also have the ability to create our own queries. Manually recreating these queries each time can become a tedious and labor-intensive endeavor. In order to reduce the manual effort, we do have the ability to save our queries. If we decide to save our queries in a central location, teammates can also take advantage of these queries and become more productive.

BizTalk Settings Dashboard

A common complaint with the earlier versions of BizTalk included a lack of consistency when carrying out performance tuning. Tuning performance in these earlier versions of BizTalk usually involved tweaking the registry settings, configuration files, and modifying settings in the BizTalk Administration Console.

Another common complaint was that modified settings were often applied to the entire BizTalk Group instead of more granular artifacts, such as Hosts. Microsoft. made some significant enhancements to their performance-tuning story in BizTalk 2010. We do not need to visit as many locations to tweak performance any longer. Instead, we will find a BizTalk Settings Dashboard that will allow us to make performance tweaks to our BizTalk Group and Hosts from a central location. Another beneficial feature is the ability to import and export our settings, which allows for better consistency and portability across our BizTalk environments.

Viewing and modifying performance-tuning settings

In order to view and modify the BizTalk Settings Dashboard, we need to perform the following steps:

1. Within the BizTalk Administration Console, right-click on our **BizTalk Group** and then select **Settings**, as shown in the following screenshot:

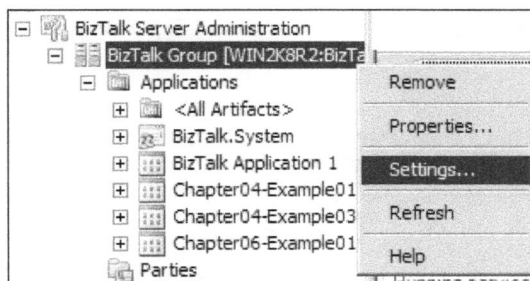

2. Within this BizTalk Settings Dashboard, we have settings related to our BizTalk Group, our Hosts, and our Host Instances. Going through each of these individual settings in detail is not within the scope of this chapter or the exam. We will concentrate on some of the more frequently used settings.

3. In the **Group** section of this dashboard, we will find global settings pertaining to our BizTalk Group. Some of the more important settings are shown in the following table:

Property	Description
Configuration refresh interval	Every time we make a change to our messaging configuration, there is always a delay before it takes effect. The default value is 60 seconds, which means if we make a change to a Receive Location, these changes will not take effect for these many seconds. Often, administrators get frustrated when they make a change to a configuration setting and become impatient. They then start performing unnecessary actions such as restarting Host Instances thinking that these actions have resolved their issue. Instead, they just need to wait for the next Configuration refresh interval.
Large message size	In BizTalk 2006, Microsoft introduced a streaming approach to transform large messages. This threshold will determine whether to try and transform complete messages or break the message up into a series of batches.

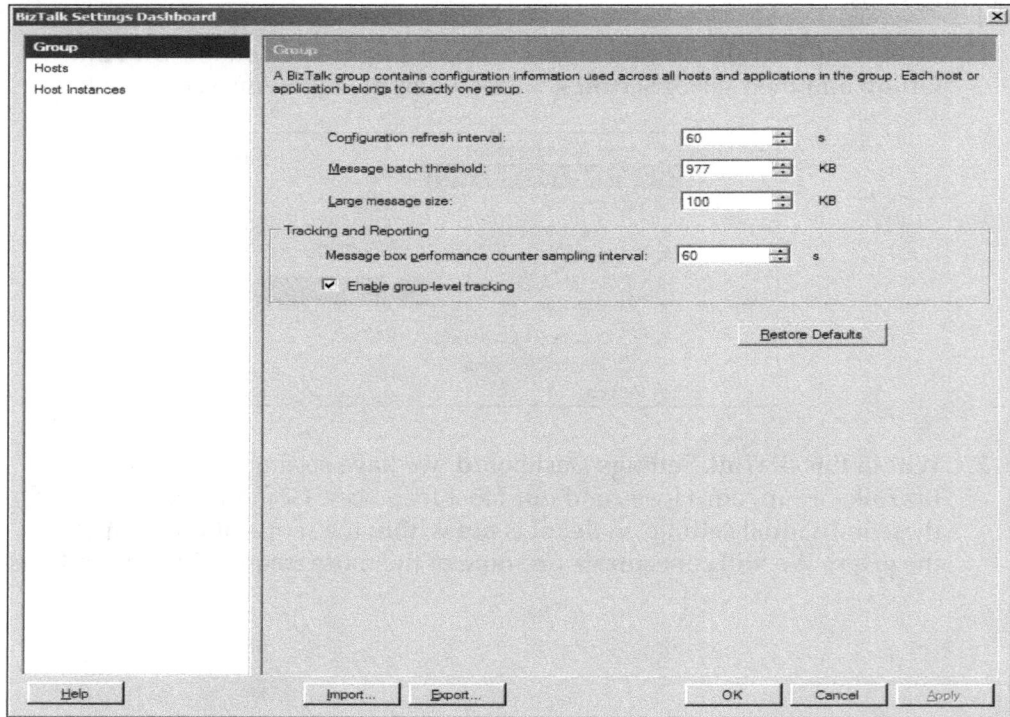

4. In the **Hosts** section of the Dashboard, we have the ability to isolate settings on a per-host basis. We have the ability to specify different configurations for each Host that we have configured in our BizTalk Group. We can isolate a Host by selecting our Host from the **Host:** drop-down, as shown in the following screenshot:

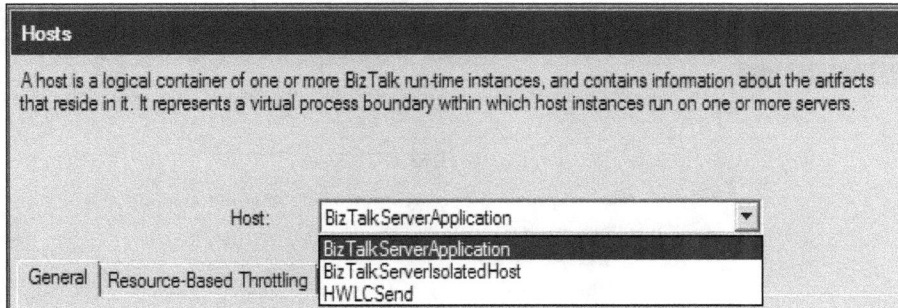

5. Once we have selected the Host that we want to manipulate, we have many different tabs where we can apply these settings, including the following:

   ° General
   ° Resource-based Throttling
   ° Rate-based Throttling
   ° Orchestration Throttling

6. The most compelling settings can be found on the **General** tab. On this tab, we will find the **Polling Intervals** section. One of the strengths of BizTalk is its ability to provide durable messaging. This means that while BizTalk is processing messages, they will be published to our BizTalk MessageBox.

7. When this publishing occurs, BizTalk Subscriptions are evaluated. If a subscription is determined, the subscriber will pick up the Message Instance during its next Poll cycle. Both Orchestrations and Messaging, such as Send Ports, can pick up these messages from a Host Work Queue. While this type of architecture is very reliable, it does come at a cost. The default Polling Intervals are set for 500 milliseconds (ms), which means that if we have a Send Port that wants to send out a message, a check will be made twice a second to see whether a message is available to be sent. For many organizations, checking a Host Work Queue twice a second more than satisfies their performance requirements. However, for some, this is just not fast enough. For these organizations, we can tune the Hosts that have more demanding performance requirements which need to be checked more often than the default settings permit. However, you do need to be careful in these situations since polling more frequently can also put more stress on your SQL Servers.

8. The opposite scenario also applies. Consider we have a batch that runs infrequently, perhaps outside of the core business hours. In this situation, there is no point checking our Host Work Queue so often. So, we can actually tune our BizTalk Host to check less frequently than the default setting, as shown in the following screenshot:

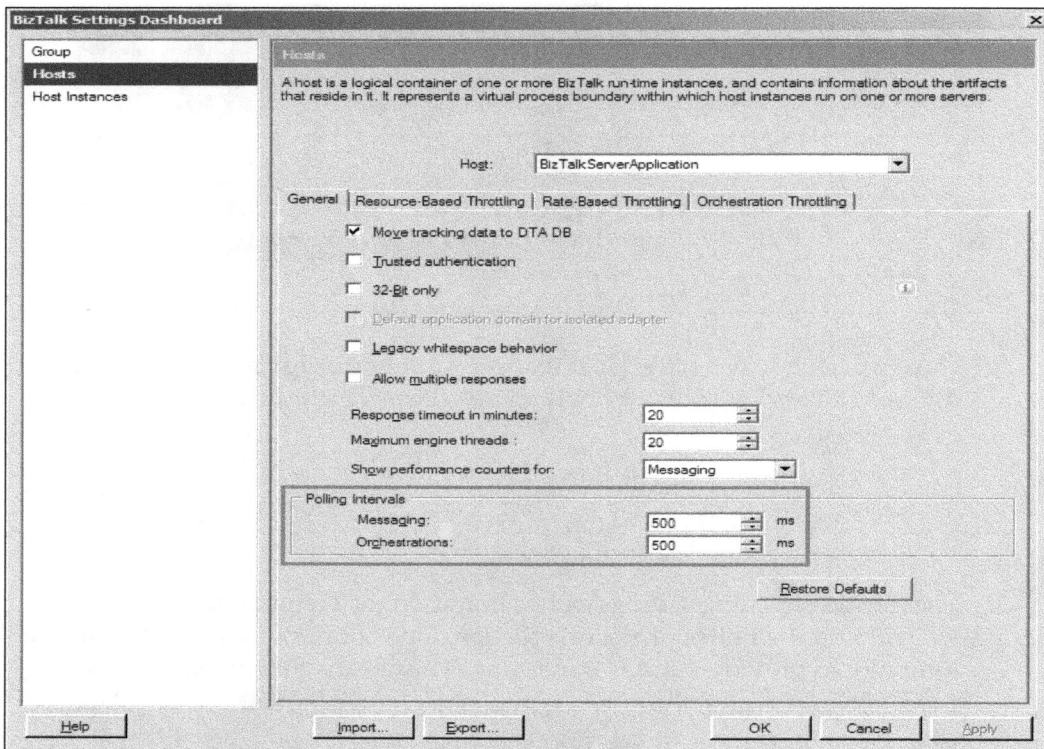

9. The final screen that we are going to discuss is the Host Instances screen. In the previous screen, we had the ability to specify Host-specific settings. We now have the opportunity to get even more granular by specifying a particular Host Instance setting. We can choose which Host Instance we want to manipulate and on which server we want to manipulate it by selecting it from the **Host Instance:** drop-down list.

10. So, why would we want to change settings at the Host Instance level? Perhaps we have different sets of hardware within our BizTalk Group. Consider having a Host called **BizTalkServerApplication** that has Host Instances on two nodes: A and B. Node A has more memory than Node B, so we may want to tune Node B differently due to the differences in the memory foot print, as shown in the following screenshot:

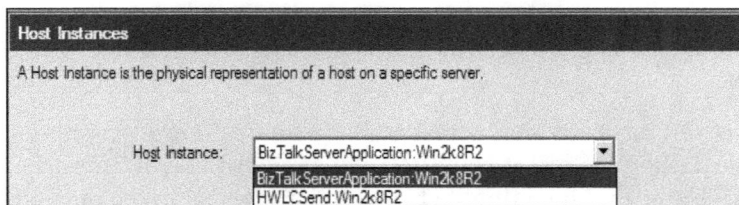

11. Once we have chosen our Host Instance, we now have the ability to modify the settings related to the following, as shown in the following screenshot:

   ° .NET CLR

   ° Orchestration Memory Throttling

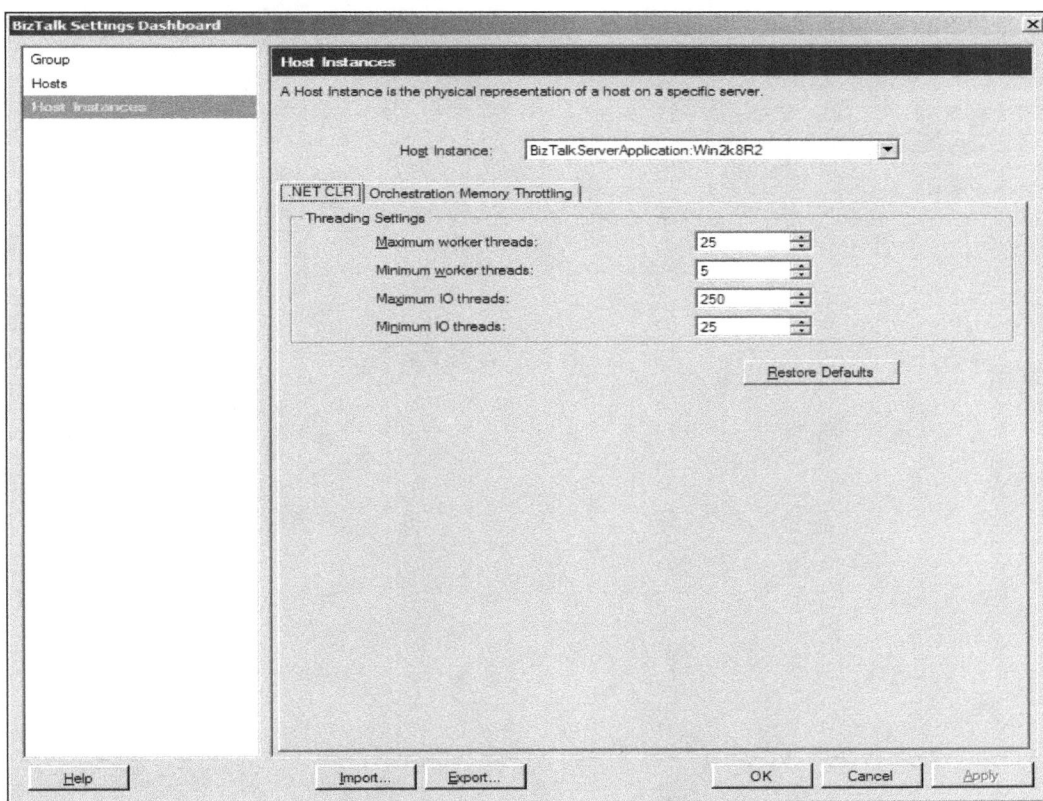

For more information related to performance tuning for BizTalk, please visit the following link: http://msdn.microsoft.com/en-us/library/ff629706.aspx.

Exporting and importing performance tuning settings

Now that Microsoft has provided access to Performance Tuning Settings from a single dashboard, they have also provided a convenient way to import and export these settings. This is a really valuable feature. It allows us to make changes to our BizTalk Group in a **Quality Assurance (QA)** or TEST environment. Once we have tested our application and are happy, we can export these settings from this QA or TEST environment and promote them to a Production environment.

To export our BizTalk Dashboard Settings, we need to perform the following steps:

1. While in the **BizTalk Settings Dashboard**, click on the **Export** button from the **Group**, **Host**, or **Host Instance** screen and then click on the **OK** button, as shown in the following screenshot:

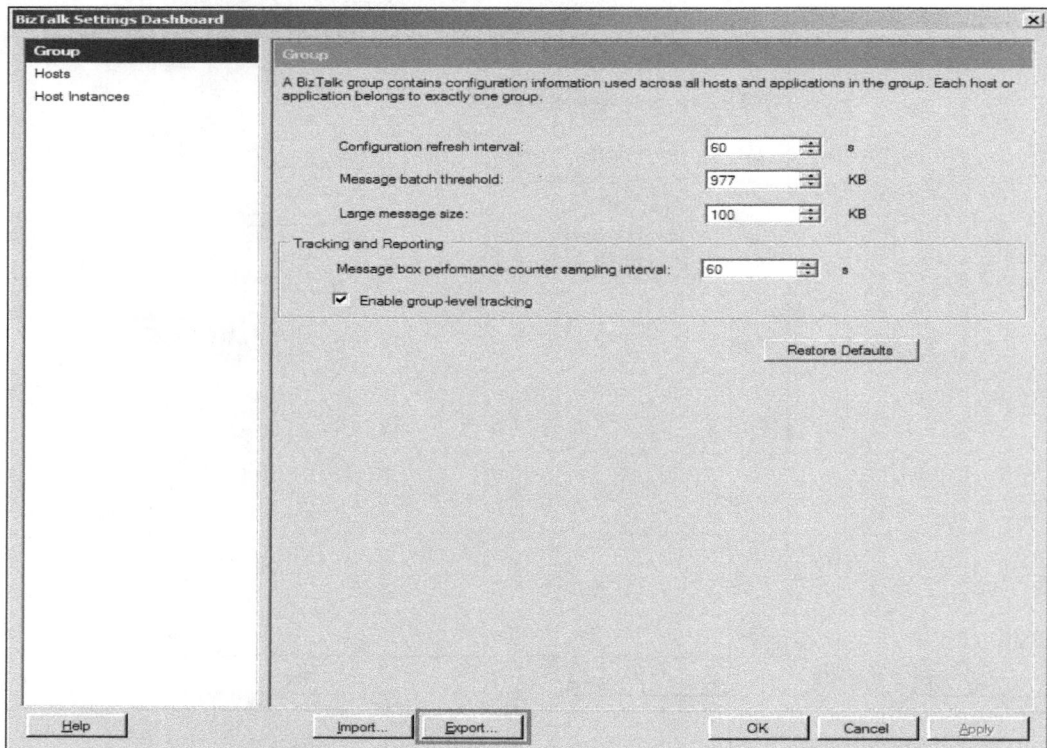

2. We are now prompted to provide a folder and a filename for our configuration to be stored in. Once we have provided this information, we should see a confirmation similar to the one in the following screenshot:

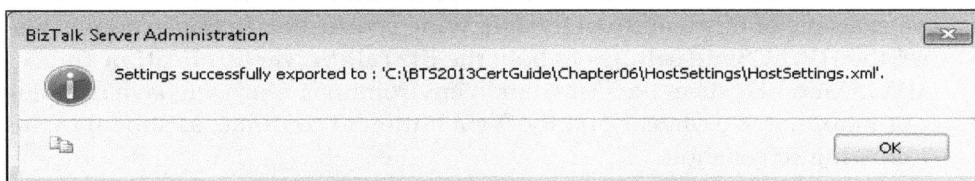

3. We now have an export of our settings from our current environment. If we want to import these settings to another environment, we can launch the **BizTalk Settings Dashboard** and click on the **Import** button, as shown in the following screenshot:

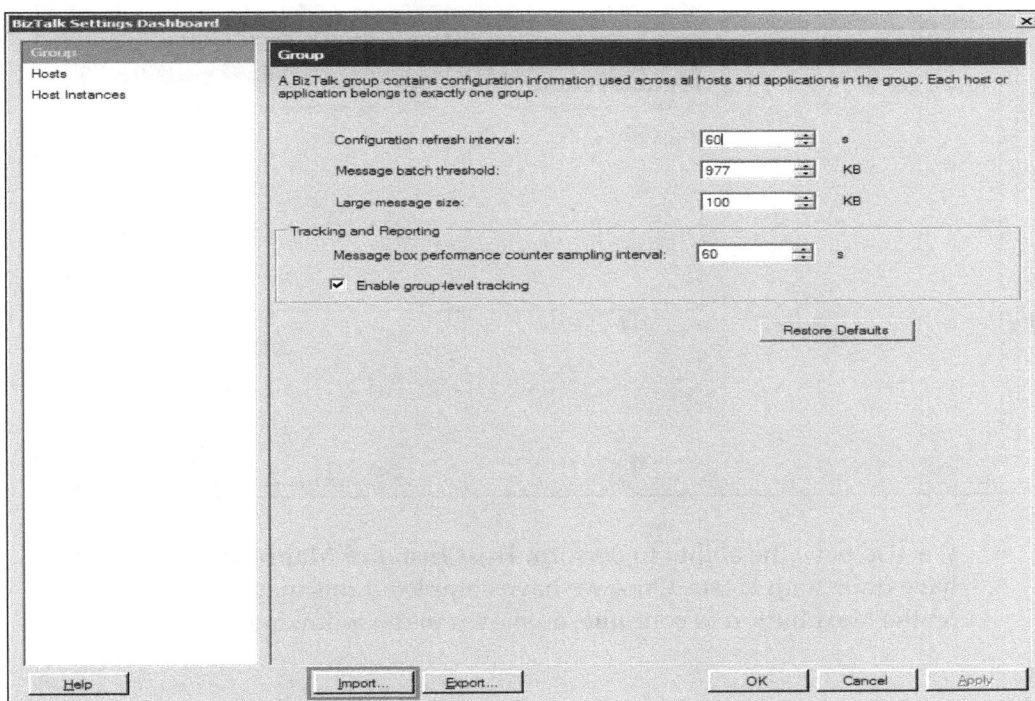

4. Upon clicking on the **Import** button, we are prompted for the location of our file that contains our settings from our previous environment. Once we have provided our file, we can click on the **Next** button to continue.

5. In the event that the environment where we generated our settings file is not an exact match to our Destination environment, BizTalk provides us with a Host Mapping tool. This tool will allow us to copy settings from any Host in our source file and map it to a Destination Host. We can find an example of this feature in the following screenshot. In this example, we set the **HWLCSend** settings to both the **BizTalkServerApplication** and **HWLCSend** Hosts in the Destination environment. Once we have completed our mapping, we can click on the **Next** button to continue, as shown in the following screenshot:

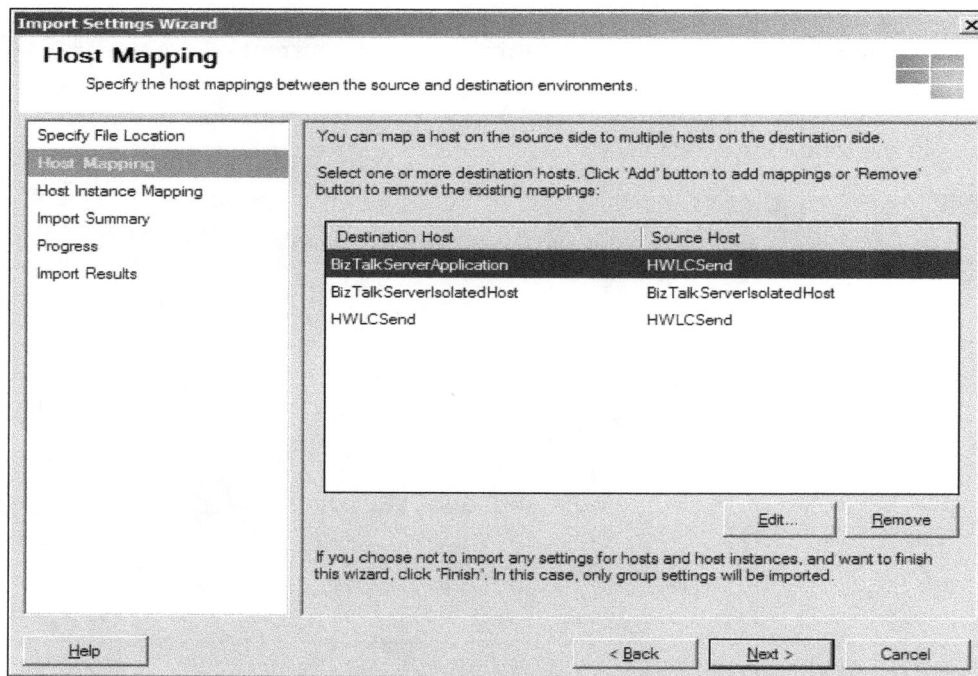

6. We also have the ability to perform **Host Instance Mapping** much like we have done with Hosts. Once we have completed this mapping, we can click on the **Next** button to continue, as shown in the following screenshot:

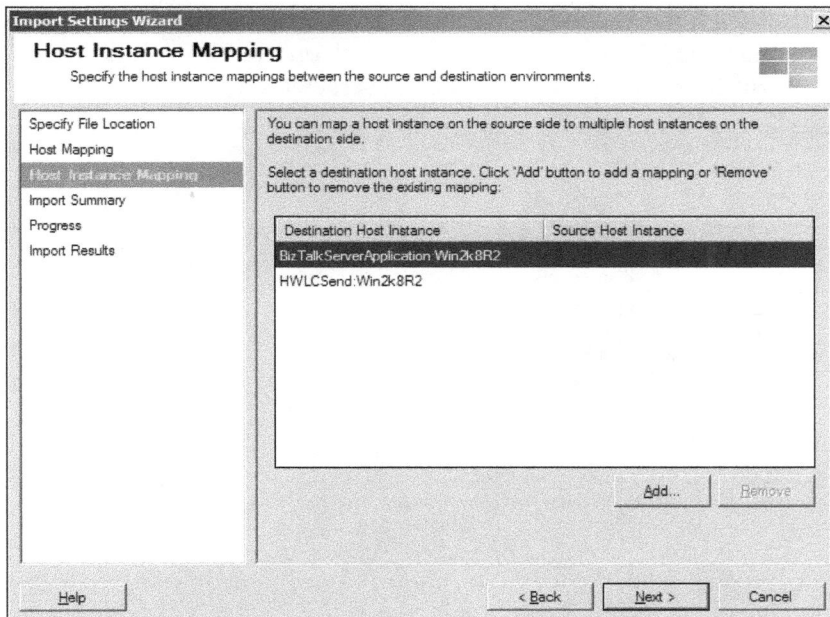

7. We now have an opportunity to review our settings. Once we are happy with them, we can click on the **Import** button to have these settings applied in our **Destination** environment, as shown in the following screenshot:

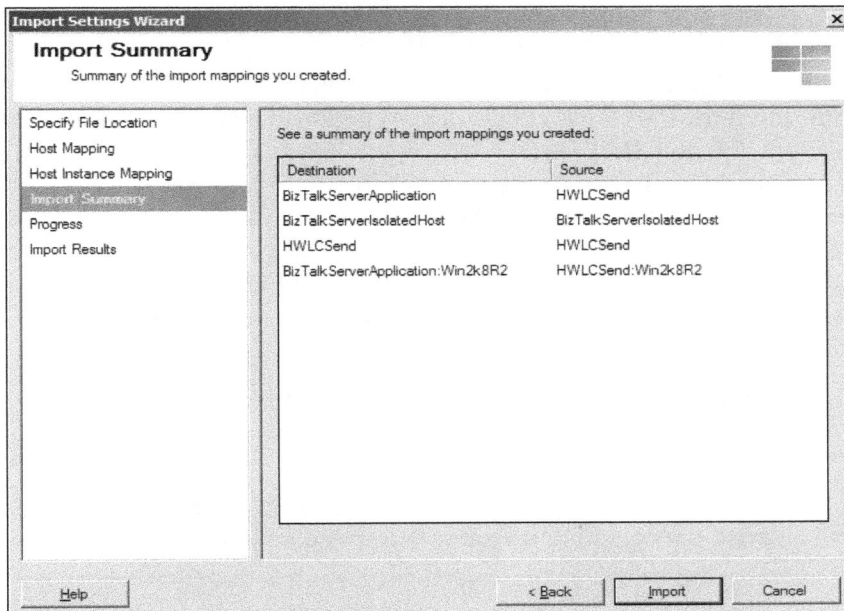

8. Once BizTalk has finished importing our settings, we will be prompted with a Summary Report. We can now click on the **Finish** button to close this wizard, as shown in the following screenshot:

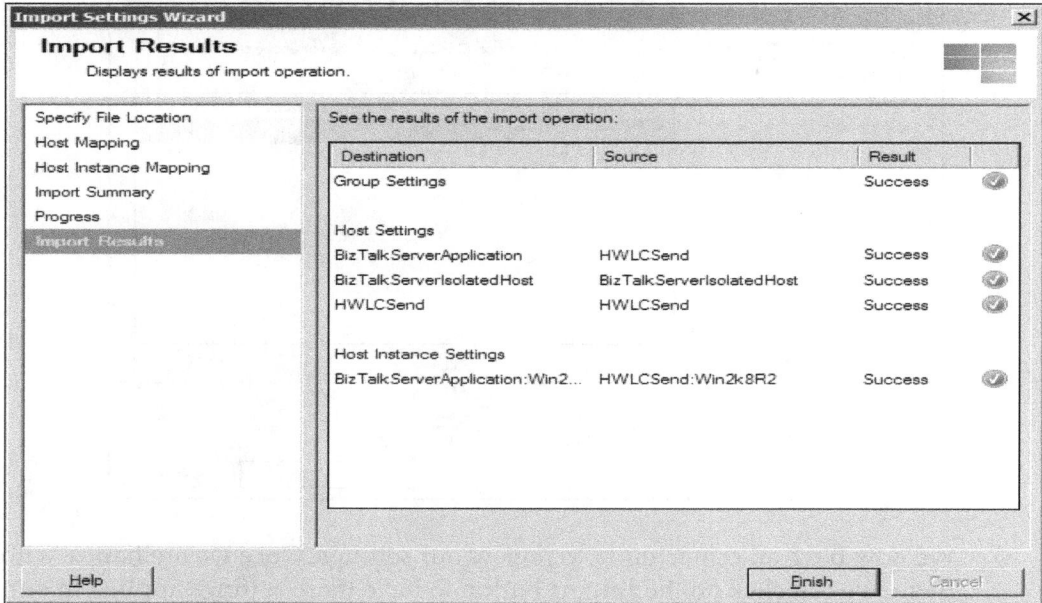

Testing your knowledge

1. Yossi, a BizTalk Server Administrator at HWLC Motors, has been asked to shut down the Part Recall BizTalk application at 12 a.m. He is not supposed to allow any new Part Recall requests into the system after 12 am but needs to ensure that any messages from the previous day are completed before completely turning off the application. Upon launching the BizTalk Administration Console, he discovers that there are five messages that are currently being processed that were received at 11:59 p.m. from the previous day. What should Yossi do to prevent losing these five messages while not allowing any new messages into the system?

   a. Stop the BizTalkServer Application Host Instance(s).

   b. Stop the Part Recall Application with the option Partial Stop—Suspend running instances.

   c. Stop all Receive Locations and then immediately stop the application with the option Full Stop—Terminate instances.

   d. Stop all Receive Locations, wait for the active instances to complete, and perform Full Stop—Terminate instances.

2. A new version of the HWLC Motors—Part Recall Application has been built by a new developer named Mick. Mick has added the functionality to receive Part Recall requests from another automobile manufacturer named MGC. Since MGC will be sending in Flat File versions of the requests, Mick has instructed Brooke, a BizTalk Administrator, to track only message bodies for the Flat File versions of the inbound messages. How should Brooke configure tracking to support this scenario?

   a. In the tracking settings for this Orchestration that processes these Recall requests, enable Track Message Bodies—Before Orchestration processing.

   b. In the Receive Port that supports receiving these Recall requests, enable Track Message Bodies—Request message before port processing.

   c. Brooke does not need to perform any action. All Receive Ports have message body tracking enabled by default.

   d. In the tracking settings for the Orchestration that processes these Recall requests, enable Track Message Bodies—After Orchestration processing.

3. HWLC Motors has just successfully tested a new Credit Application System in their QA environment. Paige, a BizTalk Administrator with HWLC Motors has updated a copy of the existing QA Binding File with the new URIs for both Receive Locations and Send Ports. BizTalk will communicate with all of these URIs using the FILE Adapter. Within the QA Binding File, all Receive Locations and Send Ports were configured to use a Host called HWLCSendReceive. Paige has gone ahead and created these Host and Host Instance(s) in the Production environment. However, when she goes to import the updated Binding File, she gets an error and is unable to complete the operation. What could be wrong?

   a. The user account that the HWLCSendReceive Host Instance(s) uses/ use does not have appropriate access to the URIs that the Receive Locations and Send Port are trying to access.

   b. The FILE Adapter's Send and Receive Handlers have not been configured to use the HWLCSendReceive Host.

   c. When Paige imported the BizTalk Dashboard Settings from the QA environment, she must have made a mistake when performing the Host Mapping.

   d. The default Host, BizTalkServer Application, has not been added to the FILE Adapter's Send and Receive Handlers.

4. The Credit Application System that was recently deployed to production consumes a third-party web service. During some high volume periods, there are some warnings in the Event Viewer indicating that the web service is not currently available. Winson, a BizTalk Administrator at HWLC Motors, has determined that during these situations, BizTalk is unable to submit all messages to this server in its first try. To ensure that messages are not suspended, Winson has increased the Retry Count in the Send Port that communicates with this Web Service. Winson's boss, Steef-Jan, has asked him how many messages are currently being processed and were not successfully submitted on the first attempt. What steps should Winson take in order to provide his boss with the correct answer?

    a. In the BizTalk Group Hub, Winson should click on the Suspended service instances — Non-resumable link.

    b. In the BizTalk Group Hub, Winson should click on the Running service instances — Ready service instances link.

    c. In the BizTalk Group Hub, Winson should click on the Running service instances — Retrying and idle ports link.

    d. In the BizTalk Group hub, Winson should click on the Running service instances — Scheduled service instances link.

5. Saravana, a BizTalk developer at HWLC Motors, needs to prepare an MSI package for the BizTalk Administration team so that they can deploy the MSI package in production. Saravana needs to include a proper Binding File in this MSI package. When he added his Binding File as a resource to his application, he forgot to include a Target environment. When the administrator installed the MSI package, there was not a Binding File that had a Target environment of production. The administrator just installed it using the <Default> Target Staging environment and default settings. What can Saravana expect his BizTalk application to look like after the administrator completes its activities?:

    a. Saravana's BizTalk application will be deployed but will not have any Receive Locations, Send Ports, or bound Orchestrations.

    b. Saravana's application assemblies will be found in the Global Assembly Cache, but there will not be a BizTalk Application found in the BizTalk Administration Console.

    c. The default BizTalk application has been updated to include all of Saravana's Receive Locations and Send Ports that he specified in his Binding File.

    d. Saravana's BizTalk application will exist and will have been configured using the settings that he provided in his Binding File, which was added as a resource to his BizTalk application.

Summary

In this chapter, we discussed many topics related to administrating a BizTalk environment. Some of these concepts were new to BizTalk 2010, such as the BizTalk Settings Dashboard. Others, such as adding Hosts to Send and Receive Handlers for a particular adapter, go back to the older versions.

In the exam, you can expect around 16 percent of the questions to pertain to BizTalk Server 2010 Administration. A thorough understanding of the content in this chapter should put you in a good position to do well in this section in the exam.

In the 2013 Partner Assessment exam, you can also expect a similar proportion of questions related to BizTalk Administration activities.

We are now going to switch gears and get into a more developer-focused topic: "Integrating Web Services and Windows Communication Foundation (WCF) Services". In this chapter, we will learn how to expose and consume WCF Services.

7
Integrating Web Services and Windows Communication Foundation (WCF) Services

In the previous chapter, we were focused on administration concepts that allow us to deploy and manage our applications. In this chapter, we are going to focus on integrating Web Services and **Windows Communication Foundation (WCF)** services.

Service Oriented Architecture-based solutions (SOA) have been increasing in popularity over the past decade. In the Microsoft technology stack, WCF has played an important role in SOA solutions. With this in mind, an entire section has been included in the Microsoft BizTalk Server 2010 exam that deals specifically with WCF.

The WCF framework is very rich and supports many different integration scenarios, including synchronous and asynchronous messaging, encryption, reliability, interoperability with other Web Service platforms, transactions, message durability, and extensibility.

The extensibility features of WCF create many opportunities for both BizTalk and non-BizTalk applications that leverage WCF. As WCF continues to evolve, these new investments that Microsoft makes in the technology suddenly are made available to BizTalk without massive rework or invasive software upgrades. An example of this is the ability to communicate with Azure Service Bus. When Microsoft added capabilities to WCF in order to support this communication, BizTalk benefitted as well.

Starting with BizTalk Server 2006 R2, Microsoft shipped BizTalk with a set of WCF-based adapters for communicating with WCF-based applications and traditional Web Service-based applications.

Now that we have established some base information about WCF Adapters, it is time to take a deeper dive into other WCF topics:

- Out of the box WCF Adapters
- Configuring a WCF Adapter
- Custom behaviors
- Exposing Schemas and Orchestrations by using publishing wizard
- Consuming WCF Services
- Handling web exceptions
- Testing your knowledge

Out of the box WCF Adapters

In BizTalk 2010, Microsoft shipped five physical adapters that have preconfigured bindings, including BasicHttpBinding, WsHttpBinding, NetTcpBinding, NetNamedPipeBinding, and NetMsmqBinding. Two custom adapters are also included: one is called WCF-Custom, which is an in-process adapter and WCF-CustomIsolated, which is an out-of-process Adapter.

The following table includes a brief description of each of these adapters:

Adapter name	Adapter description
BasicHttpBinding	This adapter conforms to the **WS-Interoperability (WS-I)** basic profile. It is one of the more interoperable bindings that allows communication with WCF and traditional Web Services.
WsHttpBinding	This adapter provides more security-related features than other adapters. It conforms to the WS-Security and WS-Transaction specifications while supporting both text and **Message Transmission Optimization Mechanism (MTOM)** encoding.
NetTcpBinding	The NetTcpBinding adapter supports both WS-Security and WS-Transaction specifications such as WsHttpBinding. The difference being that NetTcpBinding does so over the TCP protocol and uses Binary message encoding.

Adapter name	Adapter description
NetNamedPipeBinding	This adapter provides a cross-process communication in a secure and optimized manner. Transport security is used for the security model, named pipes for message delivery, and Binary for message encoding such as NetTcpBinding.
NetMsmqBinding	This adapter provides the ability to connect to MSMQ queues from a BizTalk Server so that we can build loosely coupled solutions and address disconnected client scenarios.
WCF-Custom	The WCF-Custom adapter takes advantage of WCF extensibility features by allowing us to plug in custom bindings. If you are familiar with the BizTalk Adapter Pack, this is how Microsoft has provided WCF-based adapters for connecting to Line of Business systems such as SAP, Oracle, and SQL Server.
WCF-Custom Isolated	This adapter allows us to use the extensibility features of WCF in an Isolated Host such as **Internet Information Services (IIS)**.

> If you are interested in learning more about the WCF-Custom Adapter and how you can leverage the BizTalk Adapter Pack to communicate with Line of Business Systems, please see http://www.packtpub.com/microsoft-biztalk-2010-line-of-business-systems-integration/book for more details.

Configuring a WCF Adapter

In this section, we are going to discuss how to configure the WCF-BasicHttp Adapter and then, how to configure the WCF-Custom Adapter that will use wsHttpBinding. When we configure the WCF-Custom adapter to use wsHttpBinding, we will discover some of the extensibility features that were discussed in the previous section.

Using out of the box WCF-BasicHttp Send Adapter

In this example, we are going to create a new Send Port that will use the WCF-BasicHttp Adapter and then, we will explore the various configurations provided in the adapter. In order to do so, there are a few steps that we need to follow:

1. Create a BizTalk Application and then, add a Send Port by navigating to **Send Ports | New | Static Solicit-Response Send Port**, as shown in the following screenshot:

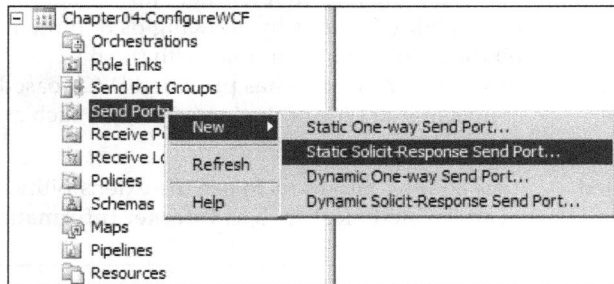

2. From the **Type** drop-down list, select **WCF-BasicHttp** and then, click on the **Configure** button.

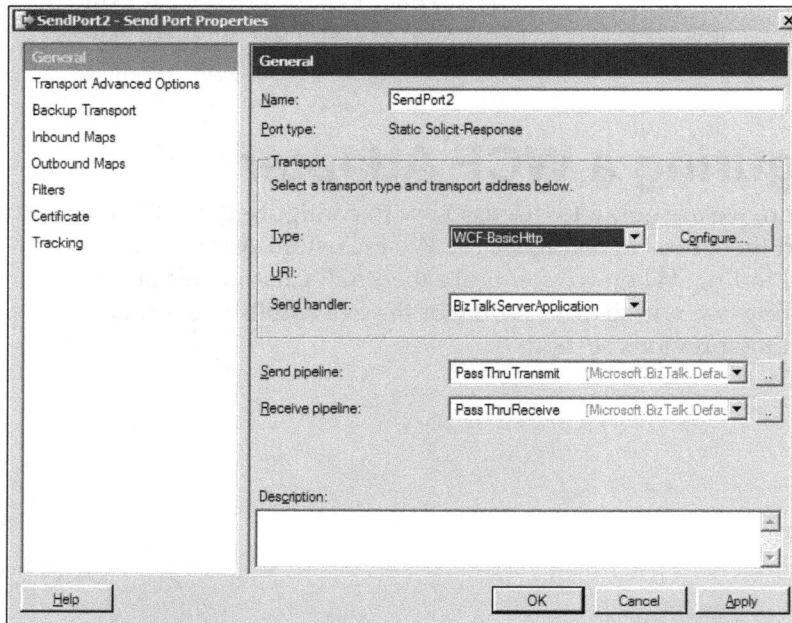

3. The first area that we want to configure is the **Address (URI)** textbox. In this textbox, we need to provide the location of the Web Service endpoint that we are going to be communicating with. The URI depicted in the next screenshot represents a fictitious Credit Check service.

4. The second area that we want to focus on is the **SOAP Action header**. The purpose of this text area is to provide a mapping between the name of the operation in our logical Send Port within an Orchestration and the **BTS Operation** property so that we can submit the right message to the Web method.

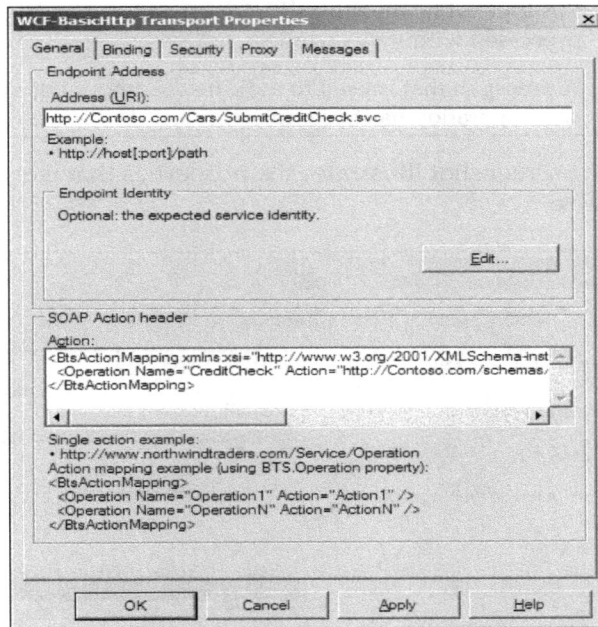

It is important to note that when we consume WCF Services and import the Binding Files, which are generated by the wizard, the **SOAP Action header** values in the Binding File match the value that exists in the Logical Port that was also generated for us. If we change the name of the operation in our logical **Send Port**, we will have a mismatch between our new value and the value that exists in the Binding File. If we make a change to the operation name in our Orchestration, then we will also have to make a change to our **Send Port** to ensure we do not have unexpected run-time errors. If you are interested in reading more on this topic please refer to the following URL: http://blogs.msdn.com/b/ adapters/archive/2007/12/26/ why-does-the-adapter-say- action-is-not-understood- even-though-i-am-using-the- binding-file-generated-by- the-consume-adapter-service- wizard.aspx

5. The next tab that we want to explore is the **Binding** tab. Some properties of interest include the timeout settings and are explained in the following table:

Property name	Property description
Open timeout	This property represents the amount of time a channel open operation has to complete.
Send timeout	Use this property to set the amount of time that a send operation has to complete. When used as part of a solicit-response scenario, this value encompasses the total amount of time for the interaction to complete. If we are sending a large message, we may need to increase this timeout to allow for the request and response messages to be processed within this window.
Close timeout	A timespan that is used to indicate the amount of time that a channel close operation has to complete.

The following screenshot illustrates the properties that were discussed in the preceding table:

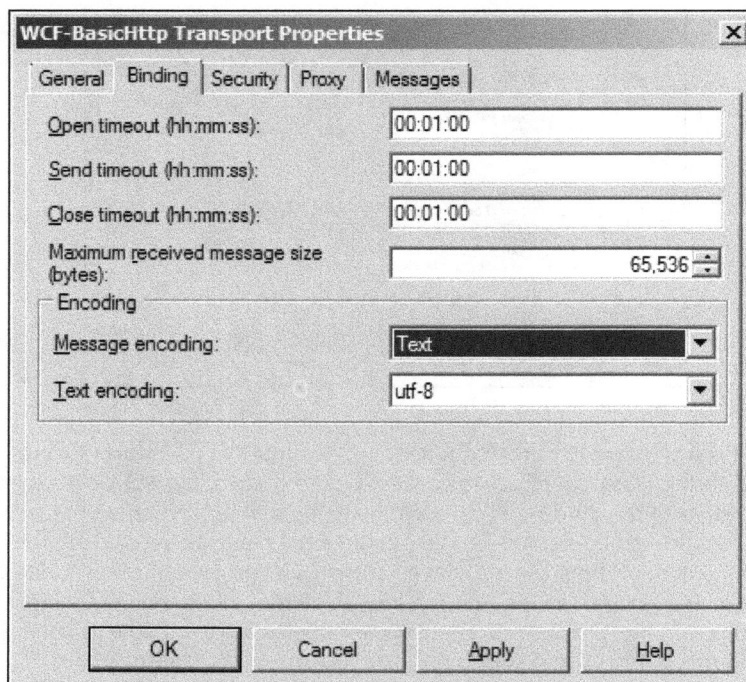

6. The next tab is the **Security** tab. Within this tab, we have many different security modes that we can utilize. These are shown in the following table:

Security mode	Description
None	No credentials will be passed. This is the equivalent of providing anonymous credentials.
Transport	Secures the transport (communication) for the mutual authentication and the message protection. Messages will not be secure from an end-to-end perspective if there are any hops in between the source and destination systems.
Message	Uses the WS-Security specification to secure messages. Each message is self-contained to allow for the contents to be confidential while being able to be authenticated. Message level security allows messages to remain secure across network hops that may exist between source and destination systems.
TransportWithMessageCredential	This mode is only available with some bindings including BasicHttpBinding, WSFederationHttpBinding, NetPeerTCPBinding, and WSHttpBinding. It provides the performance benefits of using the Transport Mode with the flexibility that the Message Security Mode provides. This allows a message(s) to be secure including hops between the source and destination systems.
TransportCredentialsOnly	This security mode will provide credentials to a WCF Service but does not provide protection when sending these credentials. In order to securely pass credentials across service calls, another means is required such as using **Internet Protocol Security (IPsec)**.

The following screenshot illustrates the properties that were discussed in the preceding table:

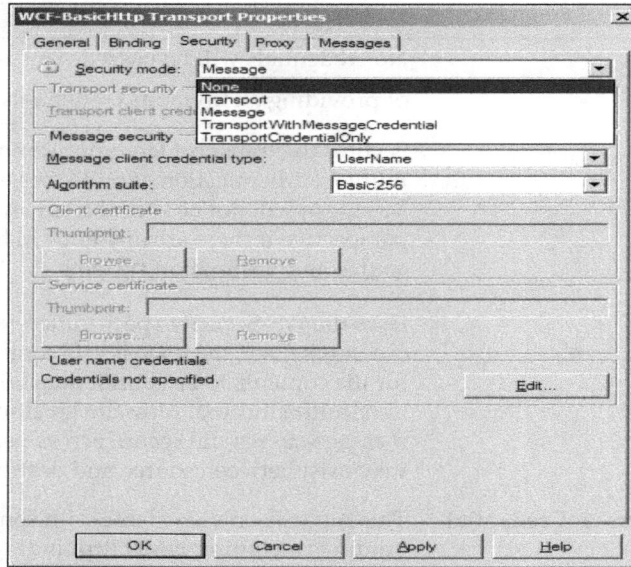

7. The **Proxy** tab is used to provide configuration information related to a Proxy Server. Some organizations implement Proxy Servers that filter out HTTP requests based upon a URL. Chances are if you work for a large organization, your web browser is configured to use a Proxy Server. From my experience, this tab is not used very often but is definitely beneficial should your organization implement Proxy Servers that filter outbound traffic.

Proxy settings	Setting description
Use send handler proxy settings	For a particular send handler or Adapter, we have the ability to specify a global value that will be used for any Send Port that uses this default value. If the send handler does not have a value populated, then no proxy server will be used.
Do not use proxy	In the event we have populated a send handler to include Proxy Server information, and if we do not want to use a Proxy Server for this particular interface, we can override this global value by specifying do not use proxy.
Use proxy	Use this option if you need to provide a proxy setting and want to override the value that exists in the send handler.

The following screenshot illustrates the properties that were discussed in the preceding table:

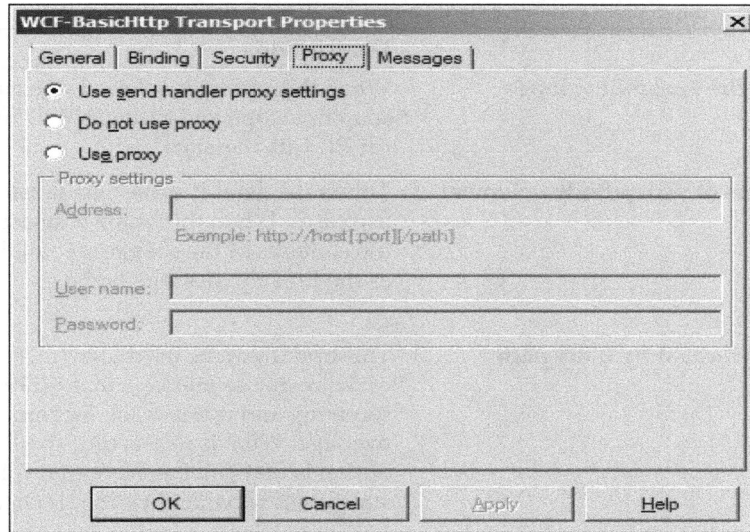

WCF-BasicHttp Transport Properties

General | Binding | Security | Proxy | Messages

○ Use send handler proxy settings
○ Do not use proxy
○ Use proxy

Proxy settings

Address: [   ]
Example: http://host[:port][/path]

User name: [   ]
Password: [   ]

OK | Cancel | Apply | Help

8. The last tab that we want to focus on is the **Messages** tab. In the Outbound WCF message body section, we have two options with two different behaviors. The following table describes the differences between these two options:

Option	Description
Body — BizTalk request message body	This is the default option and is usually sufficient in most use cases. When this option is selected, BizTalk will use the message body that has been passed to the Port as the message body of the outgoing SOAP message.
Template — content specified by template	This option can be used to add XML nodes that wrap around our BizTalk message. For instance, if we needed to wrap our BizTalk message in a new root node, create a standard message body or provide a namespace; we can do so by selecting this option.

9. In the Inbound BizTalk message body section, we have a few options when it comes to receiving the inbound message for a Solicit Response Send Port. The following table will describe these three options:

Option	Description
Envelope--entire <soap:Envelope>	When this option is selected, the entire soap:Envelope and contents will be used as the BizTalk message body.
Body--contents of <soap:Body> element	This is the default value and satisfies most use cases. When this value is selected, only the contents of the soap:Body will be used as the BizTalk Message Body.
Path--content located by body path	This option can be used to extract a portion of the response message that BizTalk is receiving and use it as the incoming BizTalk message. What is interesting about this option is that you can have multiple Xpath statements separated by the '|' character.

10. The last section that we are going to explore is **Error handling**. If we select the **Propagate fault message** checkbox, this fault message will be published to subscribing applications. If we do not enable this feature, any fault messages will end up being suspended and are available in the BizTalk Administration Console:

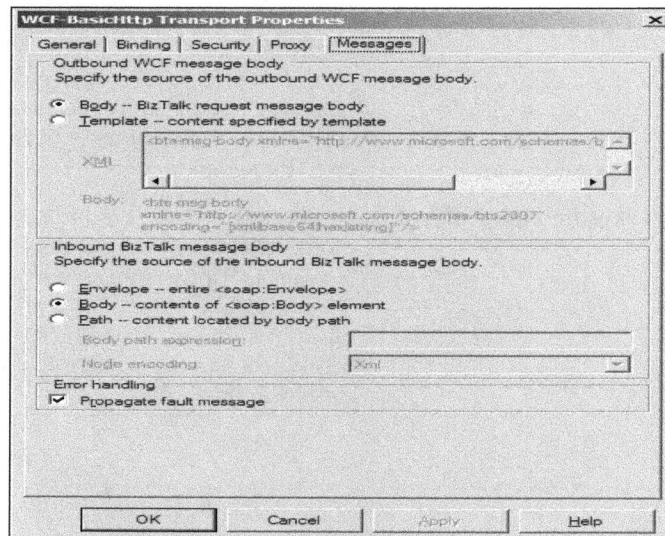

Using out of the box WCF-BasicHttp Receive Adapter

This chapter would not be complete if we only focused on the Send Port Adapter. However, you will discover that the Receive and Send Adapters share some common properties. Properties that have already been covered in the Send Port have been omitted unless the behavior is different in Receive scenarios. We will further investigate some of these common properties:

1. In the initial screen of our Receive Location, we will select the WCF-BasicHttp Transport Type. In this case, we will select the default BizTalkServerIsolatedHost Receive handler. What is important to understand about this handler is that it is running out of process, which means it is a process that BizTalk does not control. In this case, the Host is **Internet Information Services (IIS)**. For our Pipelines, we want to select **XMLReceive** as our Receive Pipeline, so the necessary properties can be used in the subscription evaluation process. Since we do not have any special processing when providing a response, we will stick with the **PassThruTransmit** in the **Send Pipeline** field.

2. In order to further explore the remaining settings, we need to click on the **Configure** button:

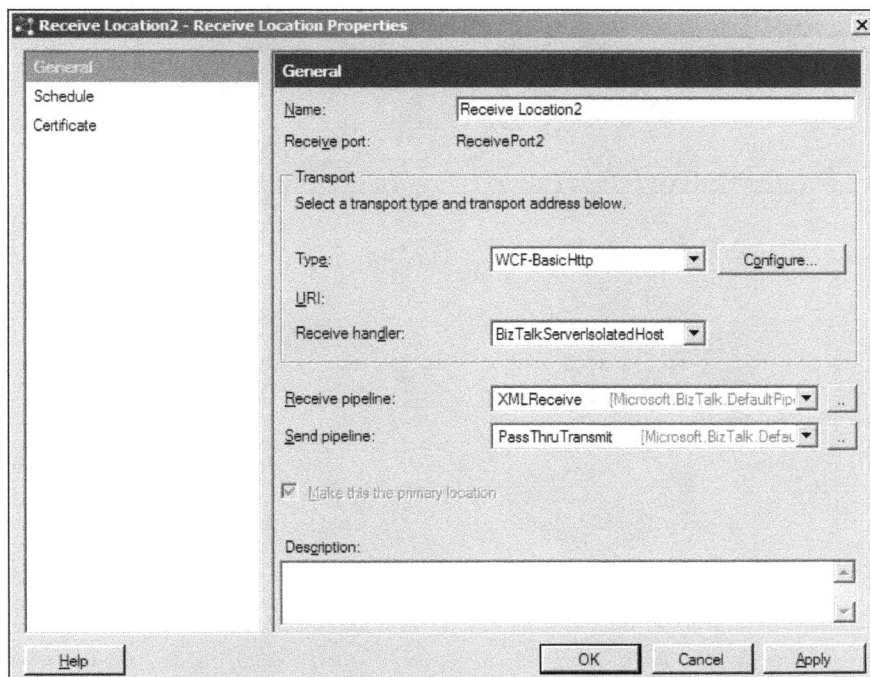

3. Once we have clicked on the **Configure** button, we will discover that a new dialog appears with four tabs. The first tab that we are going to discuss is the **General** tab. The primary configuration that needs to be made on this tab is providing the local address of the web service in the **Address (URI):** textbox. In this case, we do not need to provide the name of the server or protocol (`http://`). The address is relative to the default website that exists in IIS.

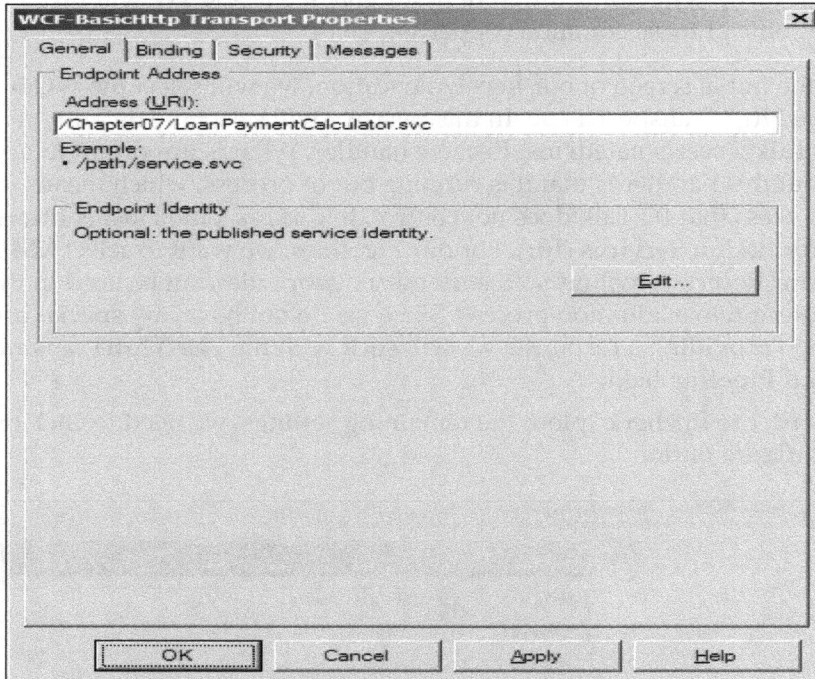

4. On the **Binding** tab, we have the ability to specify the following properties:

Property	Description
Open timeout	This property represents the amount of time that a channel open operation has to complete.
Send timeout	Use this property to set the amount of time that a send operation has to complete. When used as part of a solicit-response scenario, this value encompasses the total amount of time for the interaction to complete. If we are sending a large message, we may need to increase this timeout to allow for the request and response messages to be processed within this window.
Close timeout	A timespan is used to indicate the amount of time that a channel close operation has to complete.
Maximum received message size (bytes)	This is the default value for the maximum size a message can be in order to be processed. In some scenarios, where you will be receiving larger messages, this value will need to be increased.
Message encoding	Within this dropdown, we have the ability to specify whether or not we will use Text or MTOM for our Message encoding. Services that involve receiving XML should use the Text value whereas if we need to receive any binary data such as images or PDFs, you will want to use MTOM.
Text encoding	Provided we have chosen Text as our Message encoding type, we have the ability to specify how that text should be encoded. Our options include utf-8, utf-16, or utf-16BE.
Maximum concurrent calls	Indicates the maximum number of service calls being processed across a Service Host object.

The following screenshot illustrates the properties that were discussed in the preceding table:

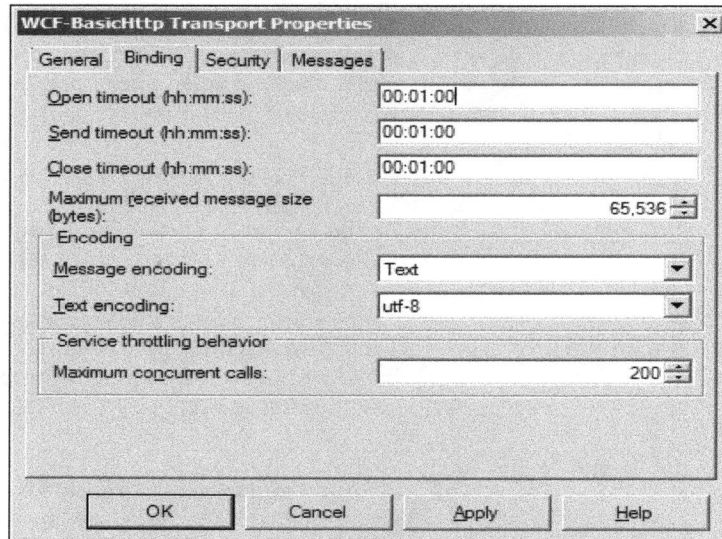

5. In the **Security** tab, we will discover options that are very similar to those exposed in the WCF Send Ports. As we have already discussed many of those options, we will focus on an option that is not included in the Send Port configuration.

6. When a **Security mode**, other than **None** is selected, the **Use Single Sign-On** checkbox will become visible/enabled. By enabling this checkbox, the WCF Adapter can now issue an SSO ticket. The WCF Adapter requires credentials that will be associated with the ticket. Using this feature allows user context to be passed from source applications to destination. This then allows BizTalk to execute operations on other systems on behalf of this user.

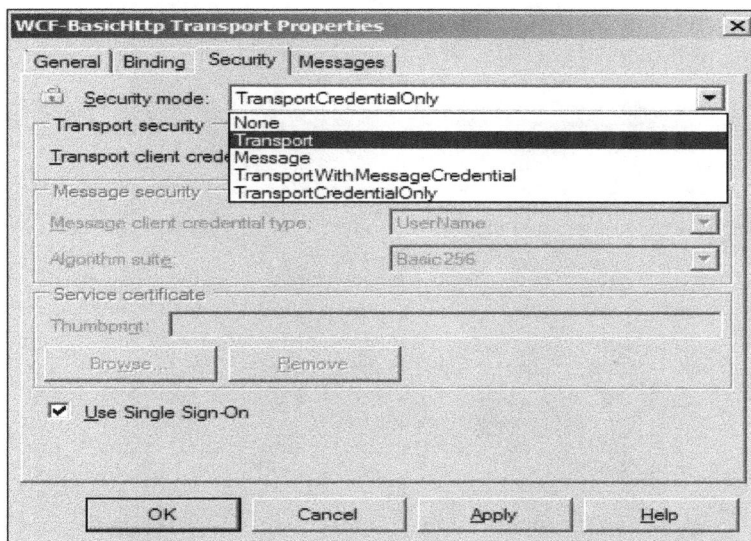

7. The final tab that we will discuss is the **Messages** tab. Once again, this tab is very similar to the **Messages** tab that exists on WCF Send Ports. We will focus on the properties that have not already been covered in this chapter.

8. The area we are going to focus on is the **Error handling** section. Within this section, we have the ability to enable the following options:

Property	Description
Suspend request message on failure	When enabled, if there is a Receive Pipeline error or routing failure, BizTalk will suspend the incoming message, and it will be available in the BizTalk Administration Console. The client will consider the transmission of this message to be successful but will not receive an exception message back by default.
Include exception detail in faults	If the client does require exception information to be passed back, then this property needs to be checked. The end result is that a SOAP fault will be returned back to the caller.

The following screenshot illustrates the properties that were discussed in the preceding table:

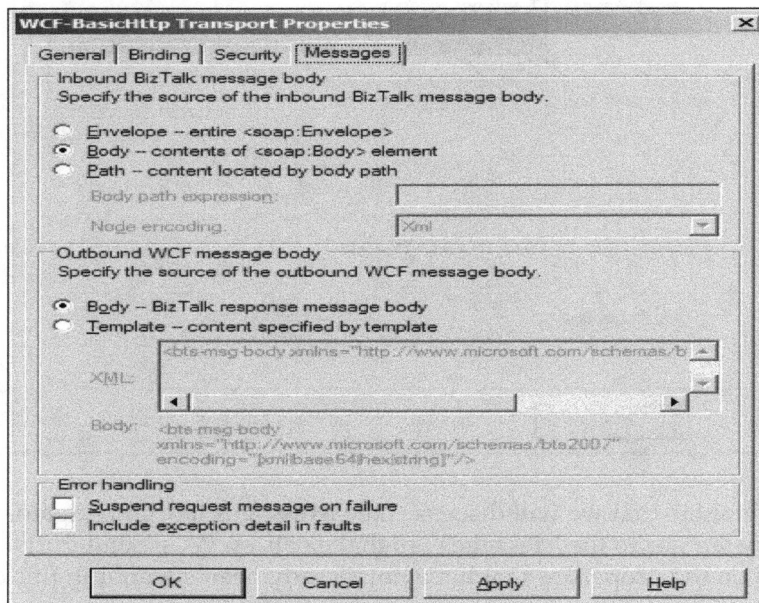

Understanding Custom behaviors

One of the benefits of using the WCF-Custom or WCF-CustomIsolated Adapters is the ability to specify a Custom behavior. A Custom behavior acts as an interceptor and can be used in both Receive and Send scenarios. If you are not familiar with custom behaviors, you are probably wondering why they exist since we have BizTalk Pipelines. Remember, WCF is not a technology that is exclusively used by BizTalk. WCF can be used outside of BizTalk and therefore Custom behaviors benefit non-BizTalk Solutions as well. The ability to intercept messages as they are being received or sent is something that other Web Service technologies do not provide. So having this capability is one reason to use WCF Adapters over the classic SOAP Adapter.

Once you have compiled a custom behavior and placed it in the **Global Assembly Cache (GAC)**, it now needs to be registered. In WCF applications that do not involve BizTalk, Custom behaviors need to be registered inside the server's `machine.config` file. You can generally find the `machine.config` file here `c:\<windows>\ Microsoft. NET\Framework\<version>\config\machine.config`. Another option that we have when registering Custom behaviors is to do so in the adapter's handler configuration.

To register a Custom behavior in a handler's configuration, go through the following steps:

1. Navigate to **Adapters** and then, select WCF-Custom as shown in the following screenshot:

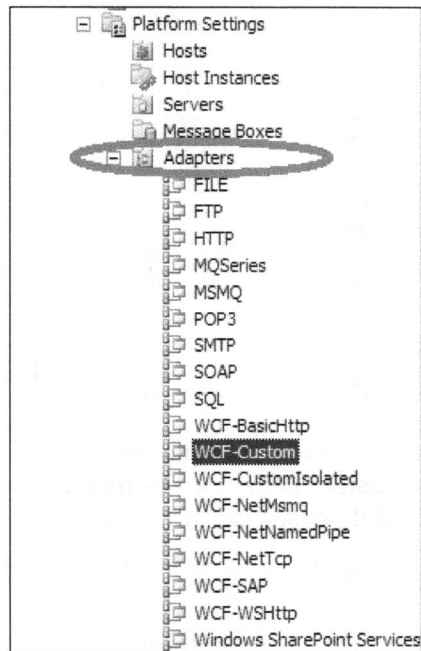

2. In the center pane, you should see all of the available handlers available for this adapter. Double-click on the **Send** or **Receive** handler of the BizTalkServerApplication.

3. Now click on the **Properties** button.

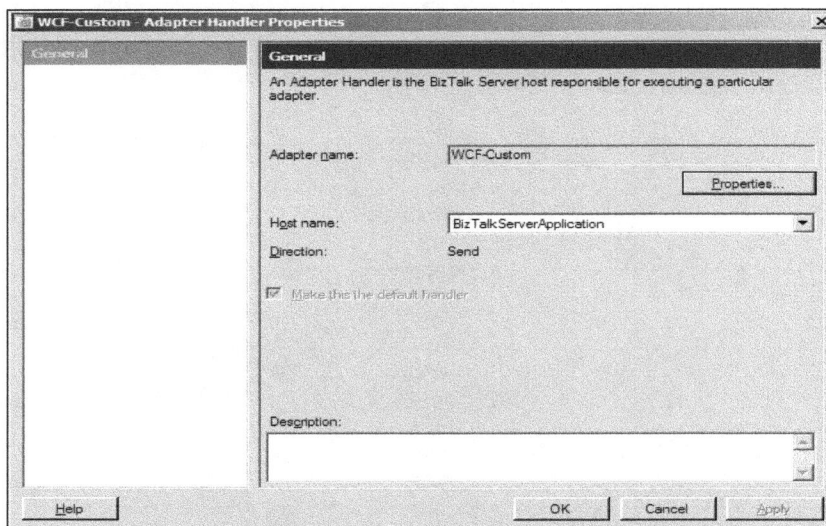

4. We now have the ability to import a file that contains our registration information for our Custom behavior assembly. We can do so by clicking on the **Import** button and then, select our configuration file.

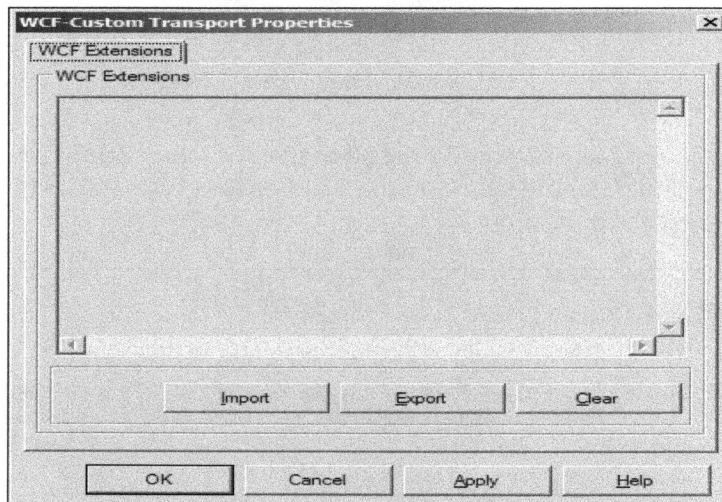

So which location is a better place to store Custom behavior registrations? In many situations, it is a personal preference, but it is important to understand that you can have the configuration of a custom behavior in only one location.

If you have a mixture of Custom WCF and BizTalk, then perhaps using the `machine.config` file is a better place to store this configuration as it will all be in one place. If you do not have a mixture of Custom WCF and BizTalk, perhaps you would want to store your Custom behavior configuration in BizTalk. In the event that you have multiple BizTalk Servers, storing this information inside your BizTalk configuration may also reduce maintenance complexity.

> Some organizations have restrictions on editing files that exist underneath the `C:\Windows` folder. In these situations, you can leverage the adapter's handler configuration instead.

Exposing Schemas and Orchestrations as WCF Services

In this section, we are going to move away from some of the theoretical aspects of WCF and actually expose a BizTalk process as a WCF Service so that it can be consumed by client applications. When it comes to exposing BizTalk Services, we have two options to exhibit BizTalk processes as WCF Services:

- Schemas
- Orchestrations

There are a few subtle differences between these two operations:

- Exposing Schemas can be used in message-only solutions and processes that include Orchestrations. A few additional steps, including naming Web Method operations and manually selecting Schemas is required, but you get more control in return.

- Exposing Orchestrations gives you less flexibility when naming your Web Method operations and automatically selects the Schemas that will be used in our WSDL contract. This method speeds up the process of exposing a BizTalk process as a service but provides us with less flexibility.

In order to demonstrate this functionality, a solution has been provided in this chapter's sample code called `Example01-ExposeWCFService`. The purpose of this sample is to determine whether or not a customer is eligible for financing from our car dealership. In order to keep things simple, we will keep all our business logic that will determine their eligibility in BizTalk as opposed to a database or Business Rules Engine.

The focus of this example is discussing how to expose a WCF Service, so we will not go into extensive details around other aspects of the BizTalk Solution.

Within our solution, we will find three different BizTalk Projects: one that will be used to include our Maps, another for our Orchestration, and finally one for our Schemas. Here are some additional details about the artifacts that make up our solution:

Artifact name	Artifact description
`FinanceRequest_to_DealerFinanceApprovedResponse.btm`	This map will perform the transformation when a customer's credit rating has been approved.
`FinanceRequest_to_DealerFinanceRejectedResponse.btm`	This map will perform the transformation when a customer's credit rating has been rejected.
`processCustomerFinanceRequests.odx`	The BizTalk Orchestration that will manage our business process.
`CustomerFinanceRequest.xsd`	The Schema for the message that we are expecting from a client application.
`CustomerFinanceResponse.xsd`	The Schema for the message we will be providing back to our client once we have determined whether our client has been approved for financing.

The following screenshot illustrates the BizTalk Solution that was discussed in the preceding table:

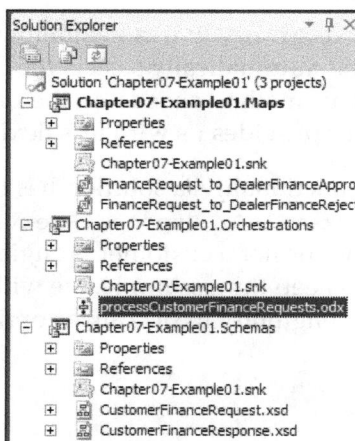

If we further examine our BizTalk Orchestration, we will discover the following logic:

1. Receiving an instance of our `CustomerFinanceRequest.xsd` message through a Logical Port that has been configured to receive a request and send a response.

2. A Decide shape will determine whether this customer's finance request will be approved. The business rule is if the customer has a Credit Score that is greater than five and had a greater income than the loan amount, they will be approved. In order to easily facilitate this logic, some of the elements included in the `CustomerFinanceRequest.xsd` message have been marked as distinguished fields.

3. If the customer has acceptable credit, then we will call the `FinanceRequest_to_DealerFinanceApprovedResponse.btm` map.

4. Should the customer not have acceptable credit then we need to call the `FinanceRequest_to_DealerFinanceRejectedResponse.btm` map.

5. Finally, we need to send an instance of our `CustomerFinanceResponse.xsd` message back to the calling client.

The following screenshot illustrates the steps that were previously described:

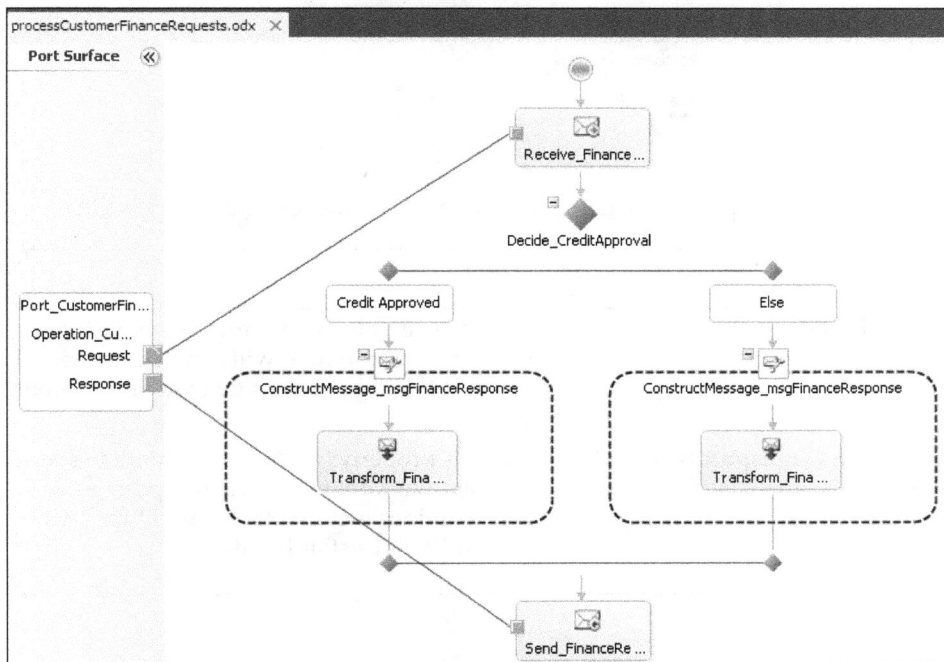

At this point, we can deploy our application into an application called Chapter07-Example01. Once our deployment is complete, we can focus on our second activity, which is exposing our two Schemas as WCF Services. Choosing to expose our Schemas, as opposed to Orchestrations, gives us more flexibility into how our artifacts are named and also gives us more flexibility should we need to modify our Schemas in the future.

In order to expose our Schemas as a WCF Service, we need to perform the following steps:

1. From the **Tools** menu in Visual Studio, click on **BizTalk WCF Service Publishing Wizard**, as shown in the following screenshot:

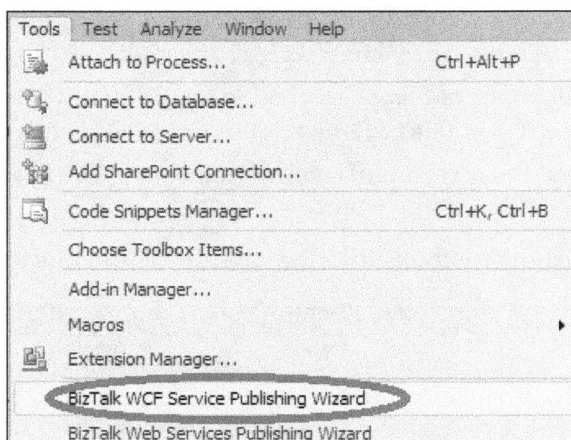

2. Within this step of the wizard, we have a few options that we need to consider:

Feature	Description
Service endpoint	Select this value if you are interested in exposing a service. When you do so, it will enable the three following additional properties that we can manipulate.
Adapter name (Transport type)	By setting this property, we have the ability to specify which adapter we want to use when exposing this service. The options include WCF-BasicHttp, WCF-WSHttp, and WCF-CustomIsolated.

Feature	Description
Enable metadata endpoint	If we want to expose metadata so that the client code can be generated through tools such as `ServiceUtil.exe`, we need to enable this property.
Create BizTalk receive locations in the following application	By enabling this feature and specifying a BizTalk Application, this wizard will automatically create a Receive Port and Receive Location in the application that we specify. This is part of the reason why we previously deployed our BizTalk Application so that we would have an application available during this part of the wizard.
Metadata only endpoint (MEX)	If we were only interested in exposing metadata, then we would select this property.

The following screenshot illustrates the properties that were discussed in the preceding table:

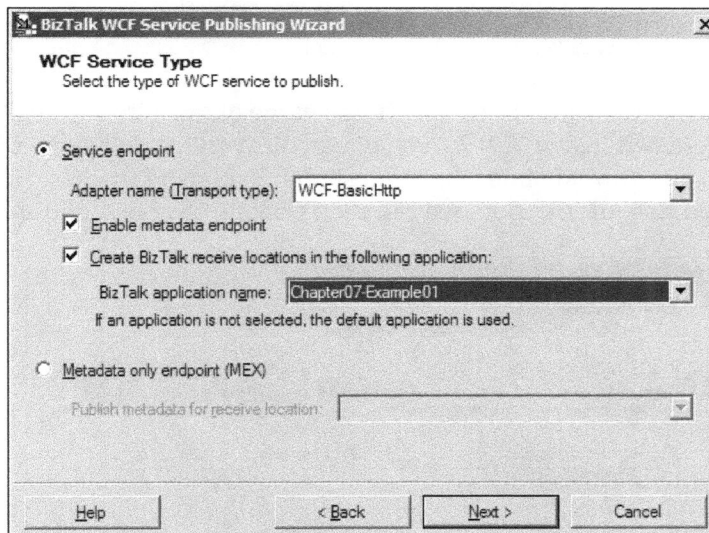

If we decide that we want to change the adapter for this service after we have published our WCF Service, the only way to do so is to run this wizard again and republish our service using the adapter that we would like to use.

Since we want to publish Schemas as a WCF Service, we can execute the following steps:

1. Select **Publish schemas as WCF Service** and then, click on the **Next** button.

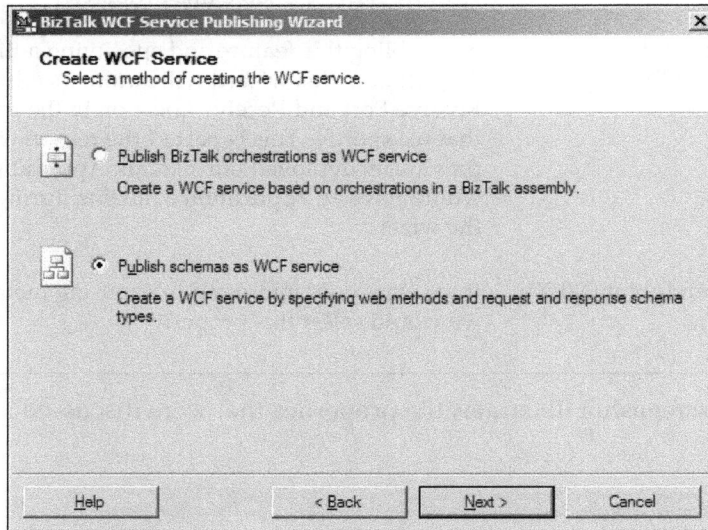

2. We now have the ability to specify the name of our virtual directory that will be created inside of IIS, the name of our Service, the name of our Web Method and provide both the request and response Schemas. After we have provided this information, we can then click on the **Next** button.

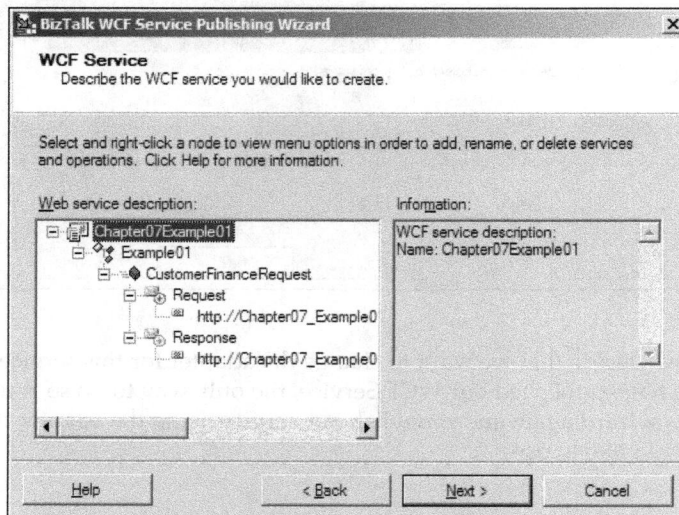

3. The next property that we have the ability to manipulate is the **Target namespace of WCF Service**. In our solution, we will provide `http://Chapter07.Example01/` and then, click on the **Next** button.

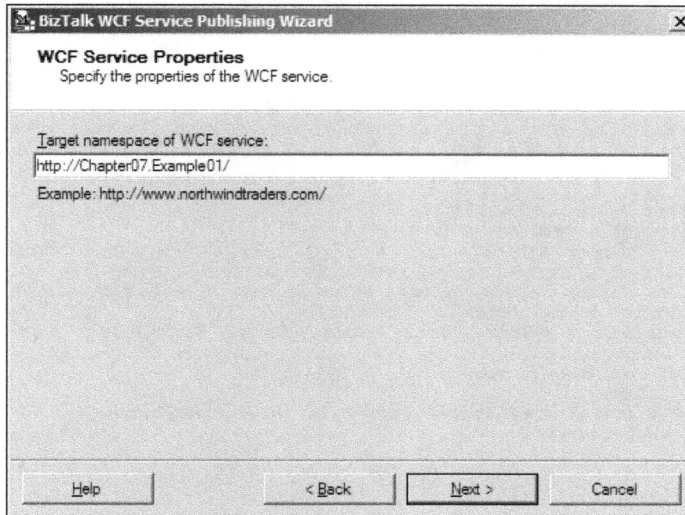

4. We now need to provide the location or URL for our service that will be deployed to the local machine. What we will discover later on is that a virtual directory called `Chapter07Example01` will be added to our default website in IIS. The other property we can manipulate is called **Allow anonymous access to WCF Service**. For the purpose of this demonstration, we will enable this property and click on the **Next** button:

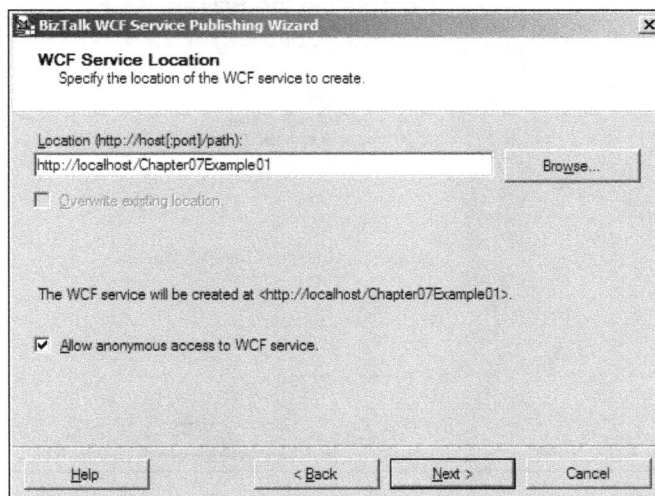

5. Our last step to complete is to review our metadata that is about to be exposed and then, click on the **Create** button provided we are satisfied.

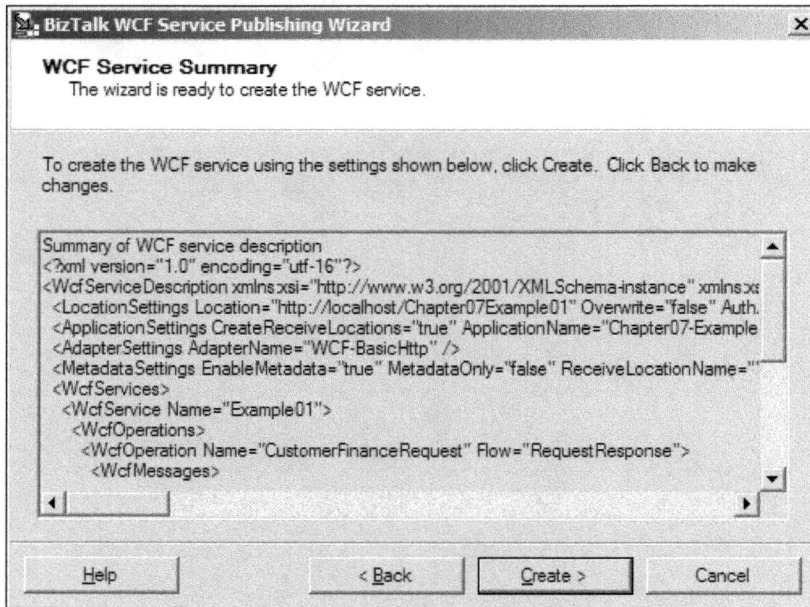

6. Provided everything executes correctly, we should see the confirmation message indicating that our service has been created successfully.

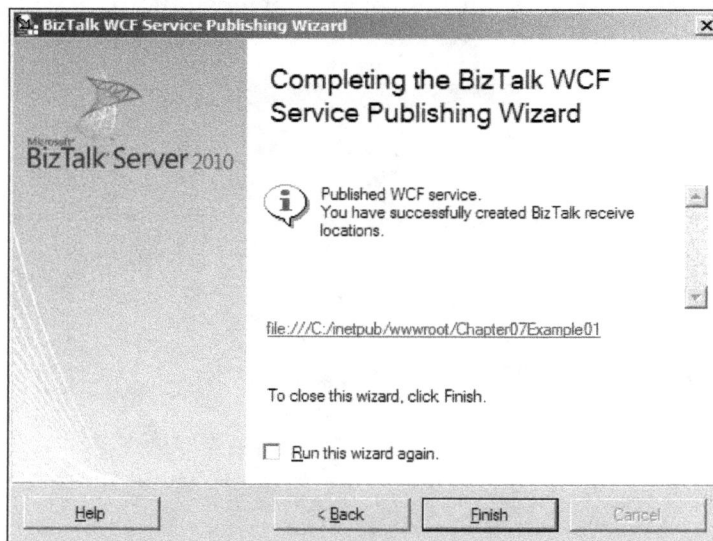

7. If we launch IIS now, we will discover that our WCF Service has been created, and we now have our `Example01.svc` and `Web.config` files, as shown in the following screenshot:

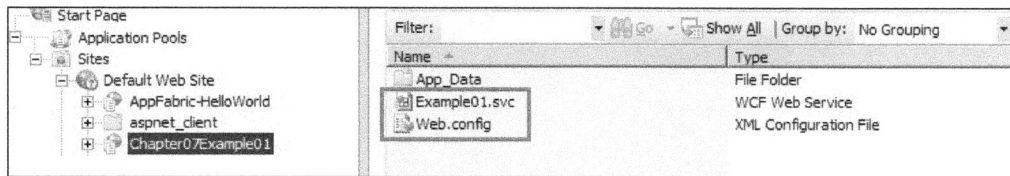

> By default, when this virtual directory is created, it will use the Default Application Pool identity to run this web application. By default, this Application Pool identity will not have the access to BizTalk resources and therefore, you will get an error when you try to browse this service via a web browser. In order to fix this issue, create an Application Pool that has an identity of the BizTalk Isolated Host Instance user and then, configure this web application to use this newly created Application Pool.

Testing our WCF Service

Before we can test our application, we need to ensure that we have our application fully configured, started, and that we have a Host Instance enabled for our Orchestration.

In order to simplify our test, we are going to leverage a tool called WCFTestClient, which is available as part of our Visual Studio installation. For 64-bit systems, we can find the application here `C:\Program Files (x86)\Microsoft Visual Studio 10.0\Common7\IDE\ WcfTestClient.exe`.

For 32-bit systems, we can find it here `C:\Program Files\Microsoft Visual Studio 10.0\Common7\IDE\ WcfTestClient.exe`.

With our WCFTestClient application open, we need to perform the following steps:

1. Right-click on **My Service Projects** and then, click on **Add Service** as shown in the following screenshot:

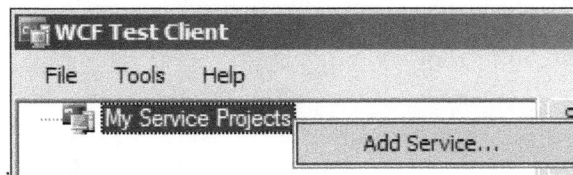

2. Now we need to specify our WCF Service URI, which in this case happens to be `http://localhost/Chapter07Example01/Example01.svc`, and click on the **OK** button.

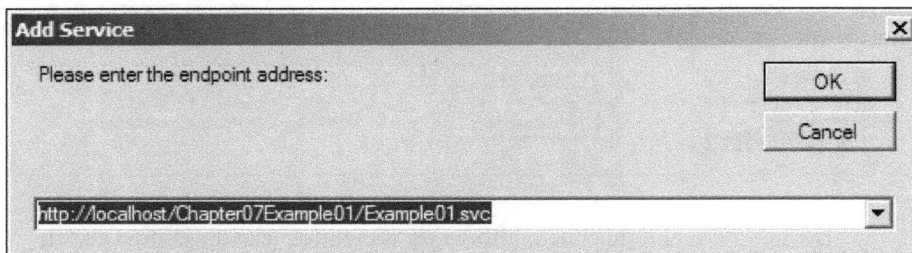

3. Our Request message needs to be populated and then, we can click on the **Invoke** button. After a few seconds, we should receive a reply and have it displayed in our Response section.

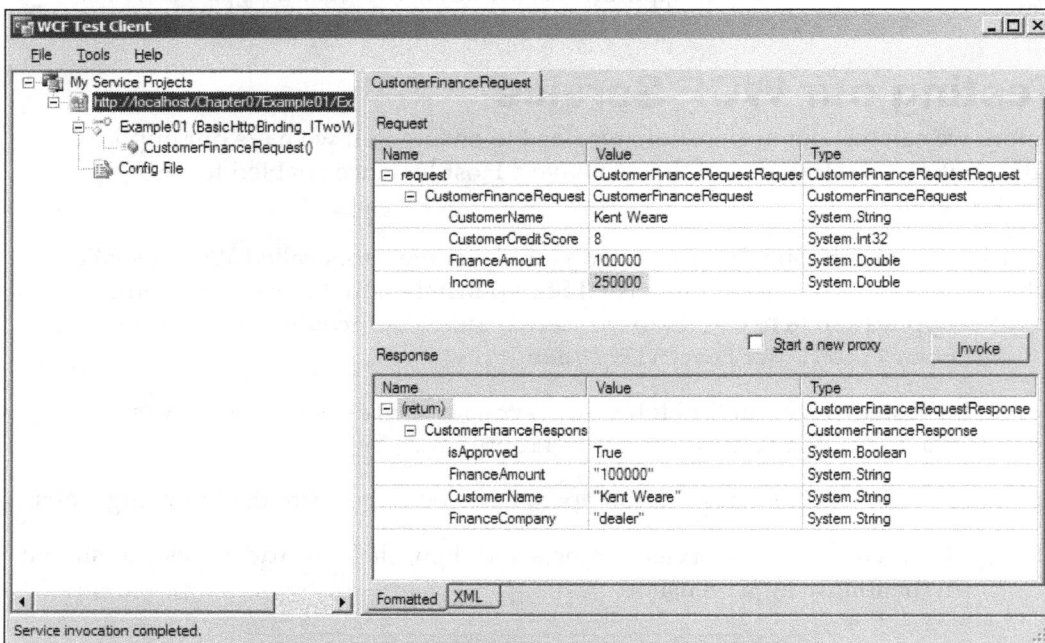

Exposing WCF Services to Windows Azure Service Bus

The ability to expose BizTalk endpoints to **Windows Azure Service Bus** was introduced in BizTalk Server 2010 as a feature add-in. In BizTalk Server 2013, the ability to expose endpoints to Windows Azure Service Bus is an out of the box feature.

To enable this feature, we continue to use the BizTalk WCF Service Publishing Wizard much like we did for the previous example. The difference is that a few new screens have been introduced.

After we have selected the adapter that we would like to use to support our WCF Service, we have the opportunity to use the **Add a Service Bus endpoint** option as illustrated in the following screenshot:

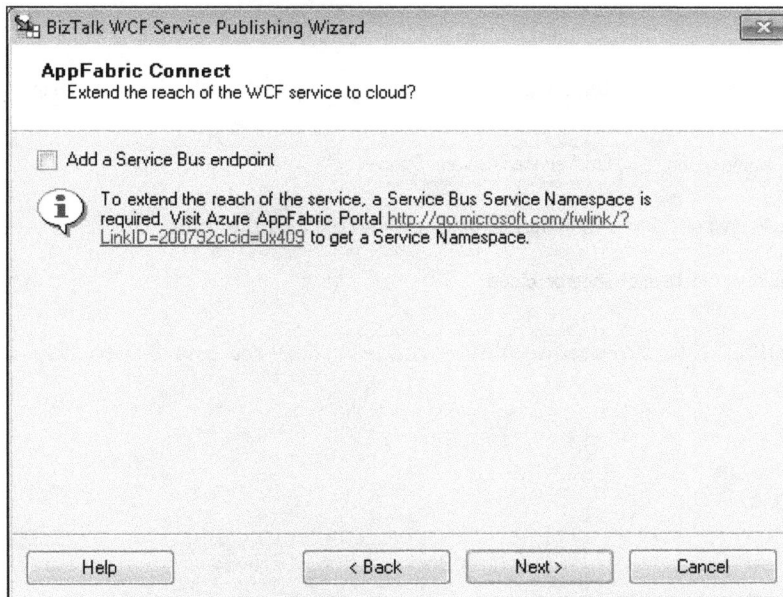

After we have chosen to **Add a Service Bus endpoint**, we will go through the regular process of choosing between exposing an Orchestration or Schema as a WCF Service. We also need to name our Service and Operation and select the appropriate Orchestration or Schema that we would like to expose.

Another new screen that has been introduced into this wizard is the **Service Bus Endpoint Configuration**. The first configuration option we have to choose is the appropriate **Relay Binding**. We can choose between **NetTcpRelayBinding**, **BasicHttpRelayBinding**, or **WS2007HttpRelayBinding**. The next area that we need to populate is our **Service Namespace** and indicate whether we want to allow our endpoint to be discoverable and whether we want to include a metadata exchange on the cloud.

Our Service Namespace is something that we need to create in the Windows Azure Portal. The portal is available at `http://www.windowsazure.com`. We have the ability to provide any name that we like, provided it is not already in use. The following screenshot illustrates how we can populate this screen:

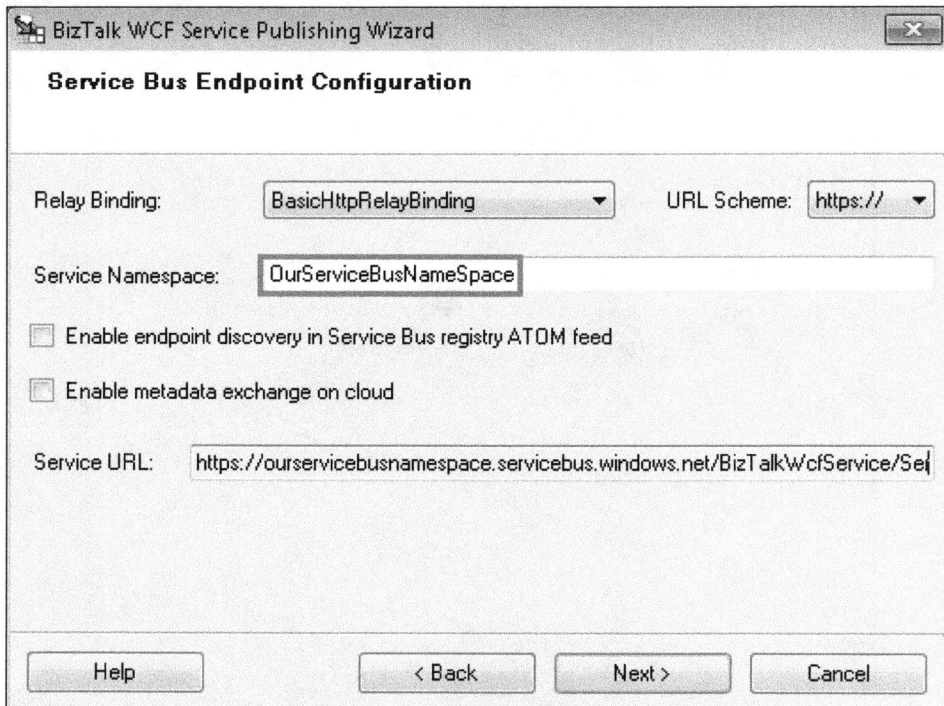

A core concept within Azure Service Bus is the idea of an **Issuer Name** and **Issuer Key**. These two properties act as our credentials when accessing Windows Azure Service Bus. Once again, we will be able to retrieve these values from the Windows Azure portal. Once we have them, we need to populate the fields that are shown in the following screenshot. Within this screen, we also have the ability to enforce a client to provide credentials when accessing our service and whether we want clients to provide credentials when accessing the metadata exchange.

Once we have provided our credentials to access the Service Bus, we can complete the wizard in the same manner that we did earlier in this chapter.

> When exposing endpoints to outside parties, it is important to consider interoperability. Not every organization that consumes your service is running on a Windows platform. For instance, if you are expected to expose an endpoint that conforms to the WS-I Basic Profile 1.1, then we want to ensure that we select the WCF-BasicHTTPRelay Adapter as it conforms to this standard.

Exposing only Service Metadata

Consider a situation where we have a service that has already been exposed. In this case, it is an in-process service that does not rely upon IIS to host the endpoint. An example of this situation may be a NetTCP endpoint hosted by BizTalk. In this case, how can we provide a service contract to a consuming application that it could use in order to conform to the message formats we are expecting? The answer can be found in the **BizTalk WCF Service Publishing Wizard**!

When we launch the BizTalk WCF Service Publishing Wizard, we have the opportunity to create an endpoint or we have the ability to publish **metadata exchange (MEX)** endpoint. Utilizing this process will allow us to select an existing Receive Location and then generate a MEX endpoint for that Receive Location. The following screenshot provides an illustration of the screen that we will use to generate this metadata. Once the metadata endpoint has been published, we can provide this endpoint to our consuming application. They would use this endpoint to generate their Schemas but would send messages to our in-process endpoint which could be a NetTCP endpoint.

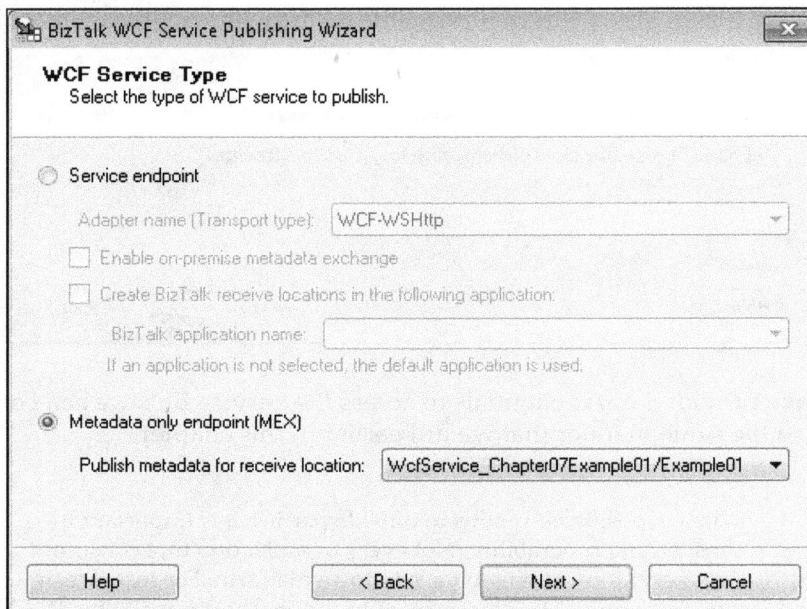

Consuming WCF Services from BizTalk Server

In the previous section, we discussed how BizTalk can expose WCF Services that can be consumed by client applications. In this section, we are going to turn our previous scenario around and have BizTalk be the client and consume a WCF Service.

Our business process in our previous example was a finance service that a car manufacturer provides to its customers. This car manufacturer has some strict financing rules that require the customer to have a Credit Score that is greater than five and an income that is greater than the loan amount. As the car manufacturer wants to sell more cars but does not want to take on additional financing risks, they have established an agreement with a third-party financing agency. So, if a customer does not fit the financing criteria of the car manufacturer, they can try to get the credit from this third-party agency. The third-party agency has looser requirements than the car manufacturer but in turn charges more interest.

Consume Sample WCF Service

In order for the third-party agency to facilitate financing requests, they have exposed a WCF Service that can be called from the car manufacturer's BizTalk Server. This WCF Service is included in this chapter's sample code in the folder: `C:\BTS2013CertGuide\Chapter07\Example02-ConsumeWCFService\Example02-ThirdPartyFinanceService`

In the `ThirdPartyFinanceService.cs` file, we will discover our interface called `IThirdPartyFinanceService`, which contains one operation called `ThirdPartyFinanceApproval`. This operation requires that a business object of type `FinanceRequest` is provided and in turn, a business object of type `FinanceResponse` will be returned. Both of these business objects are defined in the following code:

```
namespace Example02_ThirdPartyFinanceService
{

    [ServiceContract]
    public interface IThirdPartyFinanceService
    {
        [OperationContract]
        FinanceResponse ThirdPartyFinanceApproval
            (FinanceRequest fRequest);
    }


    [DataContract]
    public class FinanceRequest
    {
        string customerName ="";
        int customerCreditScore = 0;
        double financeAmount = 0;
        double income = 0;
```

```
    [DataMember]
    public string CustomerName
    {
        get { return customerName; }
        set { customerName = value; }
    }
    [DataMember]
    public int CustomerCreditScore
    {
        get { return customerCreditScore; }
        set { customerCreditScore = value; }
    }
    [DataMember]
    public double FinanceAmount
    {
        get { return financeAmount; }
        set { financeAmount = value; }
    }
    [DataMember]
    public double Income
    {
        get { return income; }
        set { income = value; }
    }
}

[DataContract]
public class FinanceResponse
{
    bool isApproved = false;
    double financeAmount = 0;
    string customerName = "";
    string financeCompany = "";

    [DataMember]
    public bool IsApproved
    {
        get { return isApproved; }
        set { isApproved = value; }
    }

    [DataMember]
    public double FinanceAmount
    {
        get { return financeAmount; }
```

```
            set { financeAmount = value; }
        }
        [DataMember]
        public string CustomerName
        {
            get { return customerName; }
            set { customerName = value; }
        }
        [DataMember]
        public string FinanceCompany
        {
            get { return financeCompany; }
            set { financeCompany = value; }
        }
    }
}
```

In the `ThirdPartyFinanceService.svc.cs` file, we will find the implementation of the `ThirdPartyFinanceApproval` operation that was declared in the previous code listing. This operation may be found inside the `ThirdPartyFinanceService` class, which implements our interface called `IThirdPartyFinanceService`.

The `ThirdPartyFinanceService` class has less restrictive financing requirements than the car manufacturer's BizTalk Solution. In this service, a customer's financing will be approved if their Credit Score is greater than two and they have an income that is greater than $10,000:

```
namespace Example02_ThirdPartyFinanceService
{

    public class ThirdPartyFinanceService :
      IThirdPartyFinanceService
    {

        public FinanceResponse
          ThirdPartyFinanceApproval(FinanceReque st fRequest)
        {

            FinanceResponse fResponse = new FinanceResponse();

            fResponse.CustomerName = fRequest.CustomerName;
            fResponse.FinanceCompany = "Wearsy Inc.";
            fResponse.FinanceAmount = fRequest.FinanceAmount;

            if (fRequest.CustomerCreditScore > 2 &&
              fRequest.Income > 10000)
```

```
        {
            fResponse.IsApproved = true;
        }
        else
        {
            fResponse.IsApproved = false;
        }
        return fResponse;
    }
    }
}
```

Consuming our WCF Service from BizTalk

We need a published endpoint that we can consume from our BizTalk Solution inside of Visual Studio in order to generate our required Schemas and Logical Port. The following steps will allow us to consume the **Third Party Finance WCF Service** that is available in this chapter's source code:

1. One way to publish this WCF Service is to simply start the debugger in our **C# - WCF Service Project**. In order to do this, we simply press the *F5* key or click on the green arrow as shown in the following screenshot:

2. Once we have pressed the *F5* key or clicked on the green arrow, we will discover that a local development server instance has been initialized. We now need to double-click on the yellow icon as shown in the following screenshot:

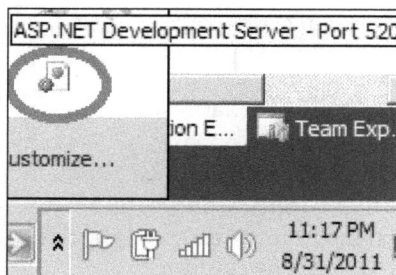

3. After we have clicked on this icon, the following dialog will be displayed. Click on the hyperlink shown in the dialog to display the contents of this directory:

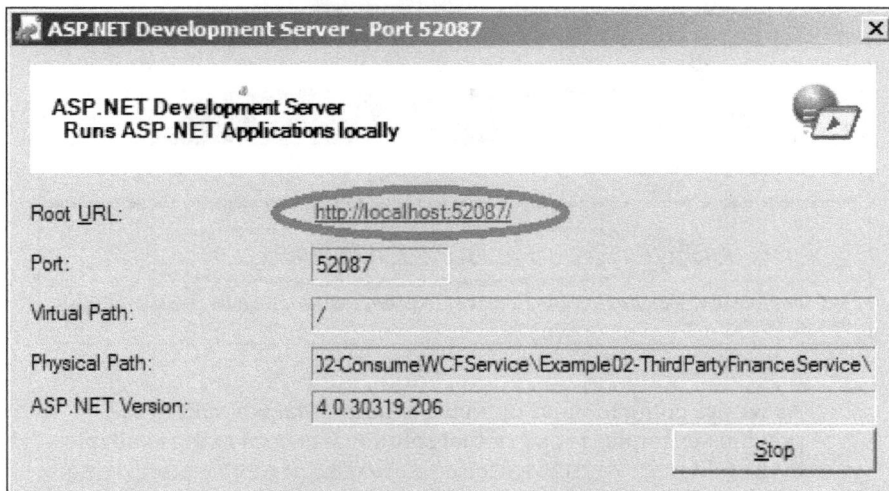

4. In this directory listing, we will discover our service called `ThirdPartyFinanceService.svc`. If we click on this link, we will launch the landing page for our service.

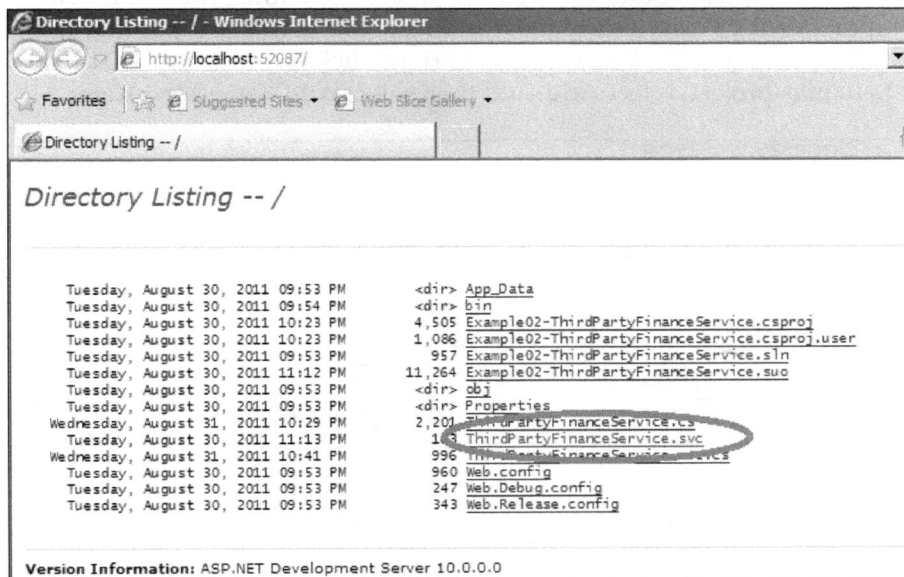

5. We now have a URL that we can use from within our BizTalk Solution.

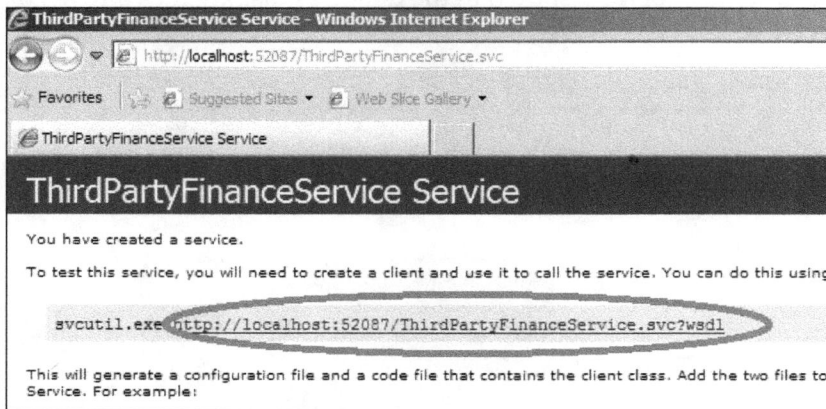

> As we are going to build upon the solution that we built in the previous example, a copy of that solution has been made available in the folder: `C:\BTS2013CertGuide\Chapter07\Example02-ConsumeWCFService\Example02-ConsumeWCFService`. This will allow us to simply redeploy our application that will contain the changes we are about to make without forcing us to republish our WCF Service that we built in the previous example.

6. From our BizTalk Solution, we now need to generate Schemas that are based upon our WCF Service's request and response message types that we just built. In order to do this, we need to right-click on our **Chapter04-Example01. Schemas** project, select **Add**, and then select **Add Generated Items**.

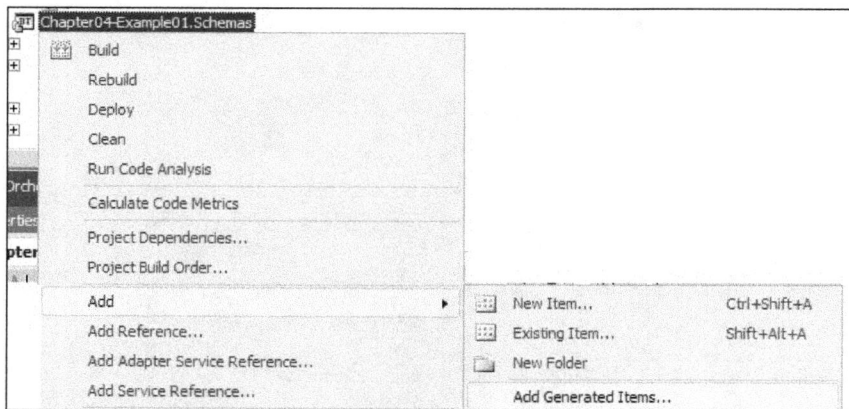

7. We will now select the **Consume WCF Service** label, click on the **Consume WCF Service** label, and click on the **Add** button:

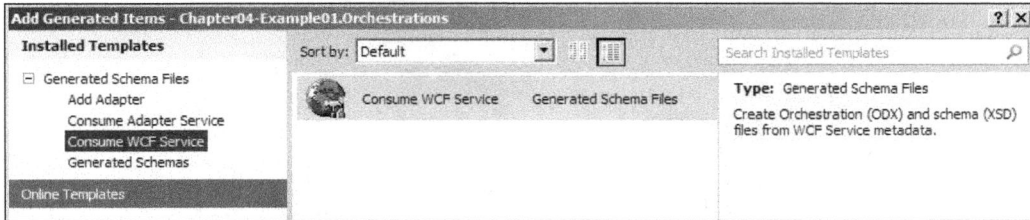

8. The **Welcome to the BizTalk WCF Service Consuming Wizard** dialog should now appear. Click on the **Next** button to proceed.

9. We will now select **Metadata Exchange (MEX) endpoint** and click on the **Next** button. This will allow us to provide the URL of the third-party financing service that we just launched.

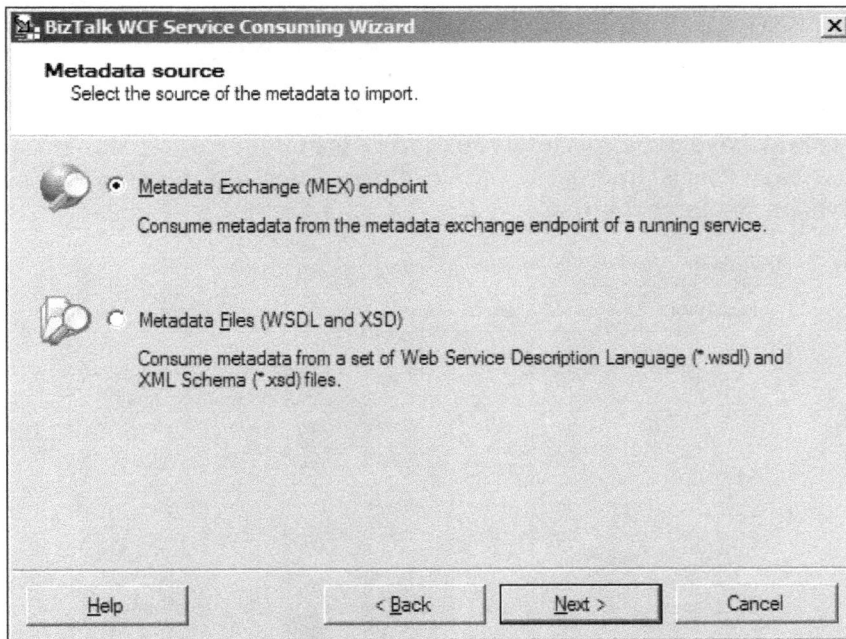

10. We will now provide the Metadata URL that we discovered in step 5. Next, we will need to click on the **Get** button, and we will discover that our **Service Description** page will load within this dialog. Now, we click on the **Next** button to continue.

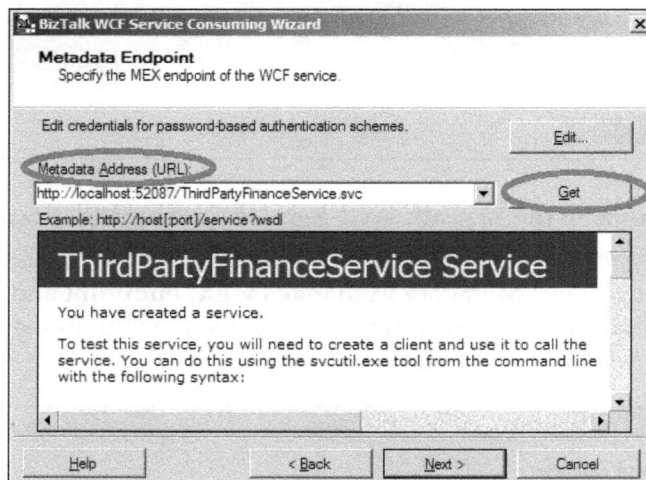

11. We now have the opportunity to modify the target namespace, but we will just leave it as is. In order to import the Schemas of our service, we need to click on the **Import** button.

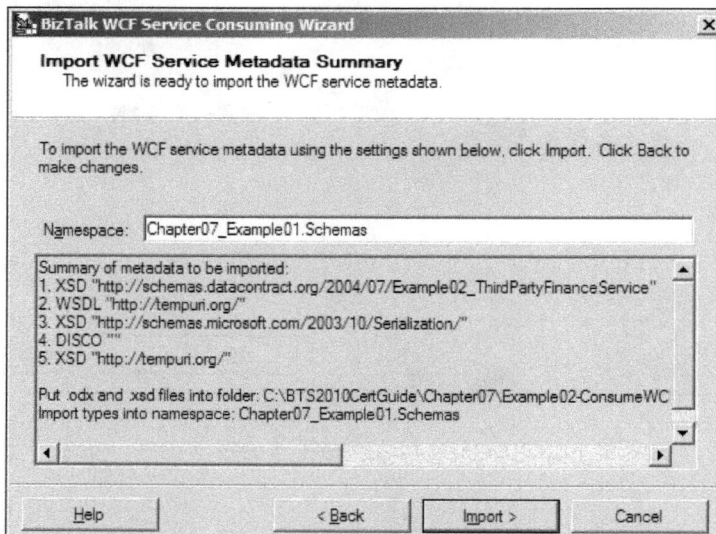

12. We can now click on the **Finish** button to complete the wizard.

Configuring generated WCF Service artifacts

In the previous section, we consumed a WCF Service. The result of this action is that we now have several artifacts in our BizTalk Solution including an Orchestration, Schemas, and Binding Files. We now need to configure these artifacts by performing the following steps:

1. If we examine our Schemas Project, we will discover several new artifacts have been added to our solution including:

    °   A Binding File, called `ThirdPartyFinanceService.BindingInfo.` `xml` that includes a Send Port based upon the WCF-BasicHttp Adapter. We can import this Binding File into our Application within the BizTalk Administration Console.

    °   A Binding File, called `thirdPartyFinanceService_Custom.` `BindingInfo.xml` that includes a Send Port based upon the WCF-Custom Adapter. We can import this Binding File into our application within the BizTalk Administration Console.

    °   An Orchestration that contains a preconfigured logical port type and multipart messages that we can leverage to call this third-party service.

    °   Schemas that represent the structures we can expect to send and receive.

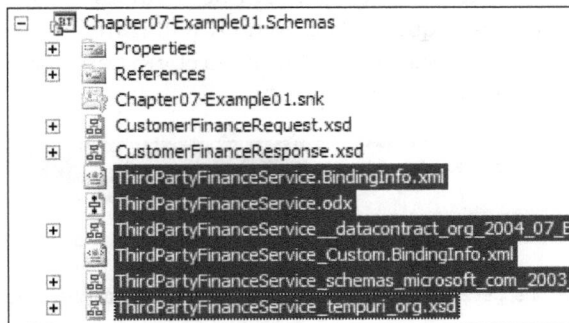

2. We now need to recompile our Schemas project so that the Orchestrations project will be able to access these newly added artifacts.

3. Once we have compiled our Schemas project, we should be able to create a new **Multi-part Message Type** in our `processCustomerFinanceRequests.odx` Orchestration based upon our Schemas that were added to our Schemas project.

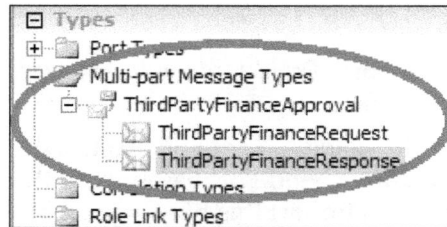

4. With our multipart messages created, we now need to create a request and response message based upon these new multipart types.

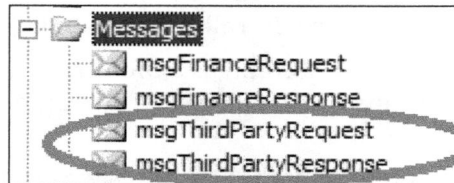

5. Next, we need to add a map called `FinanceRequest_to_ThirdPartyFinanceRequest.btm`, which will transform our incoming `CustomerFinanceRequest` into a `ThirdPartyFinanceApproval` request that we can send to our third-party agency.

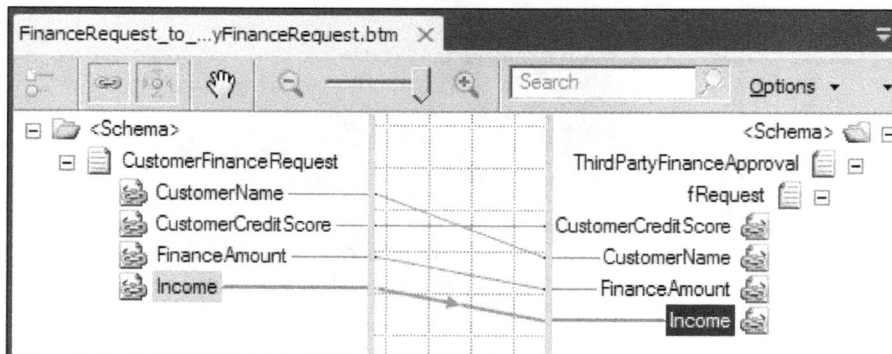

6. We also want to add a map that will deal with the responses generated from the third-party financing company called `ThirdPartyFinanceResponse_to_FinanceResponse.btm`.

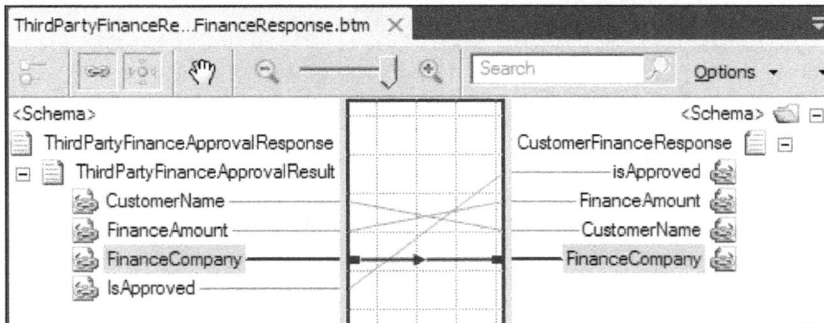

7. In order for our Orchestration project to access these new maps, we need to recompile our Maps project.

8. Since we are going to leverage a third-party finance service for customers who do not qualify for dealer financing, we can remove the `ConstructMessage_msgFinanceResponse` shape.

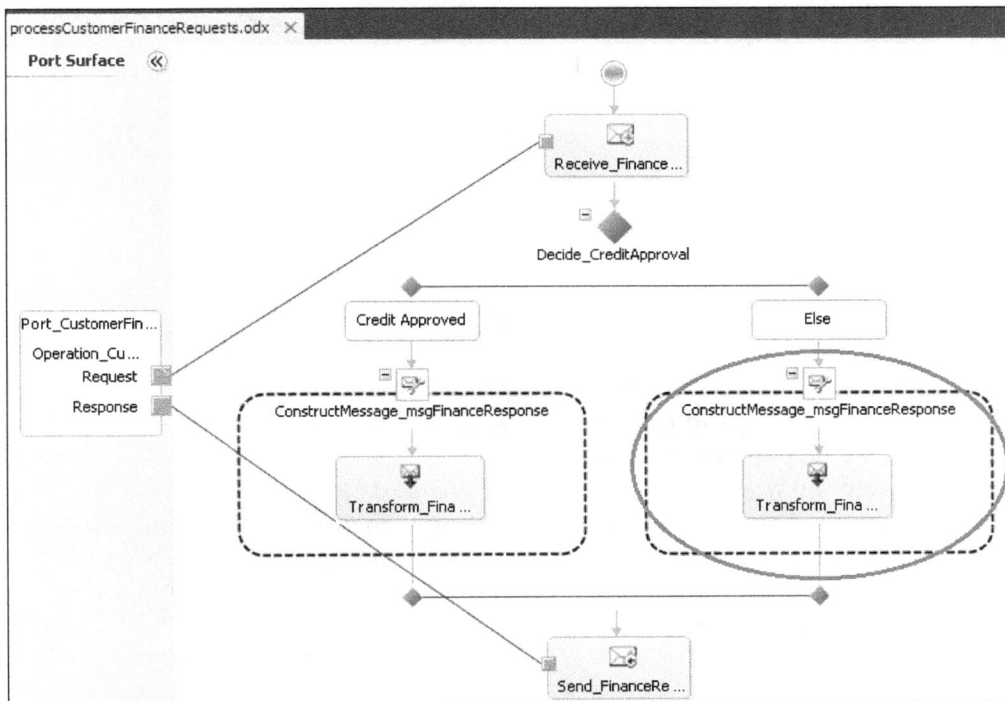

9. We now want to insert the `FinanceRequest_to_ThirdPartyFinanceRequest. btm` map that we created in step 5 of this section in the **Else** branch.

10. After inserting this map, we need to add both Send and Receive shapes. In the Send shape, we want to specify `msgThirdPartyRequest` and in the Receive shape, we want to specify `msgThirdPartyResponse`.

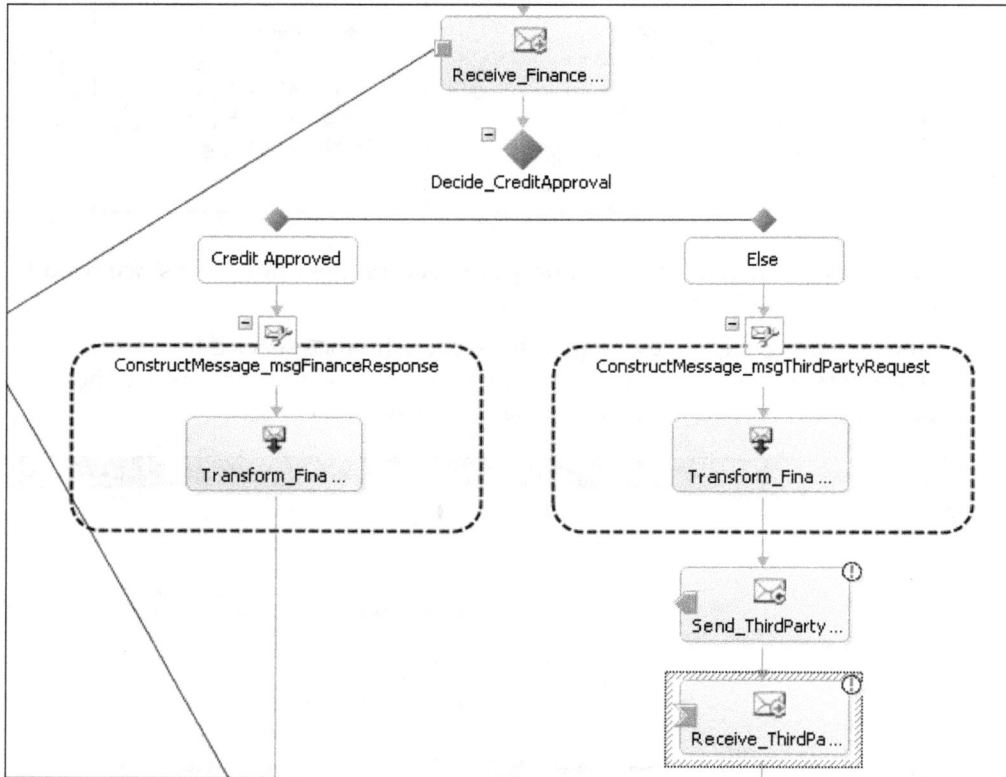

11. The next item that we need to address is adding a logical port that will support sending and receiving messages to and from the WCF Service. In this case, we want to leverage the logical Port Type that was created for us when we used the wizard to consume our third-party service. However, since we specified our Schemas project when we ran this wizard, we now have an Orchestration in our Schemas project. Even though we have a reference from our Orchestration project to our Schemas project, we cannot access this logical Port Type by default. By default, the Type Modifier is set to Internal. If we want to use this logical Port Type in our Orchestration project, we need to set our Type Modifier to be `Public`.

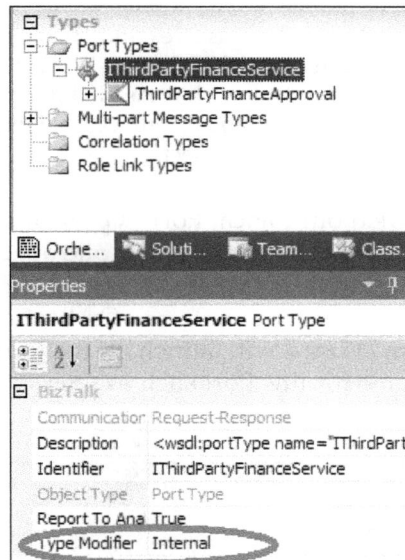

Also pay attention to the `Type Modifier` property when exposing Orchestrations as WCF Services. You cannot expose an Orchestration unless the `Type Modifier` property has been set to `Public`.

12. We also need to modify our Multi-part Message Types so that they also have a Type Modifer of Public. By doing so, our Port Type is available to other Orchestrations within our project.

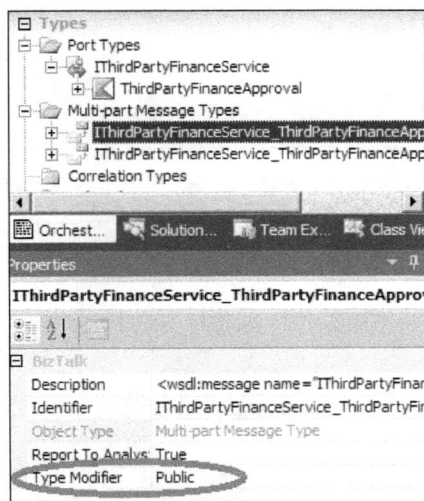

> Another option that we have is to exclude this Orchestration that was generated by the Consume WCF Service Wizard and add it to our Orchestration project. Once we have added it to our Orchestration project, we would need to modify our .NET Namespace so that it is conformed to the rest of the project.

13. Once we have modified our logical Port Type so that it can be accessed from other projects, we now want to recompile our Schemas project so that we can access this logical Port Type by dragging a Port shape onto our `processCustomerFinanceRequests.odx` Orchestration. When we do this, a **Port Configuration Wizard** will launch. In the **Port Configuration Wizard** dialog, provide a name for this Port such as `Port_ThirdPartyService` and then, click on the **Next** button.

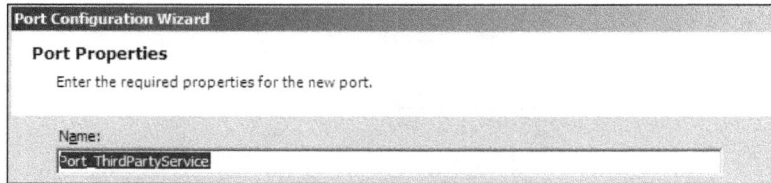

14. When prompted to select a **Port Type**, choose **Use an existing Port Type**, and then, select our **ThirdPartyFinanceService** Port Type:

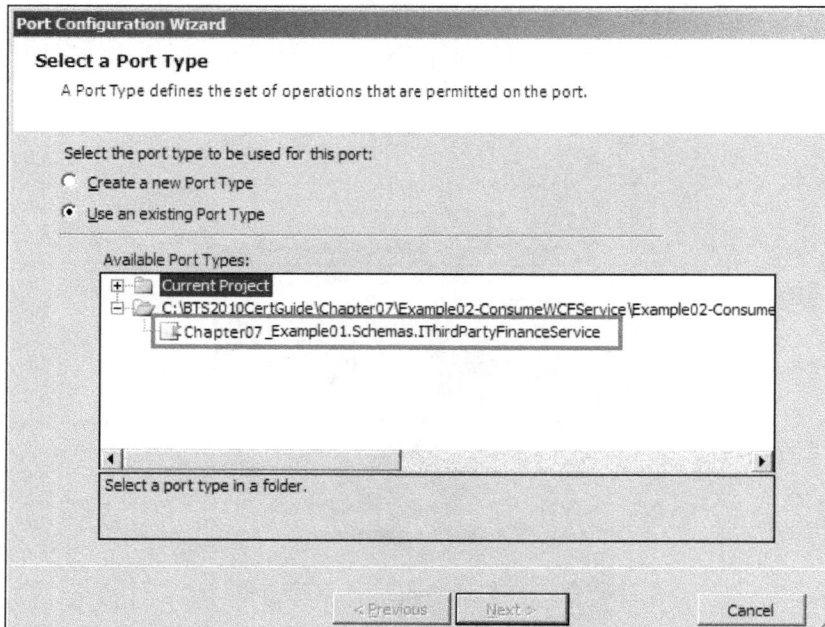

15. When prompted to select a **Port direction of communication,** choose **I'll be sending a request and receiving a response.** The type of **Port binding** that we need to choose is **Specify later.**

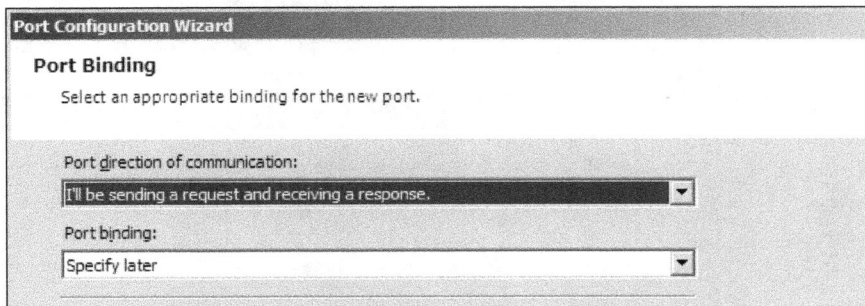

16. Click on **Finish** to complete the wizard and then, drag lines from our newly added Send and Receive shapes to this new logical Port.

17. We now need to add our `ThirdPartyFinanceResponse_to_FinanceResponse.btm` map that we created in step 6 of this section so that we can transform our response from our third-party service into the response type that we return back to our calling client.

18. The end result is that our **Else** branch will look similar to the following screenshot:

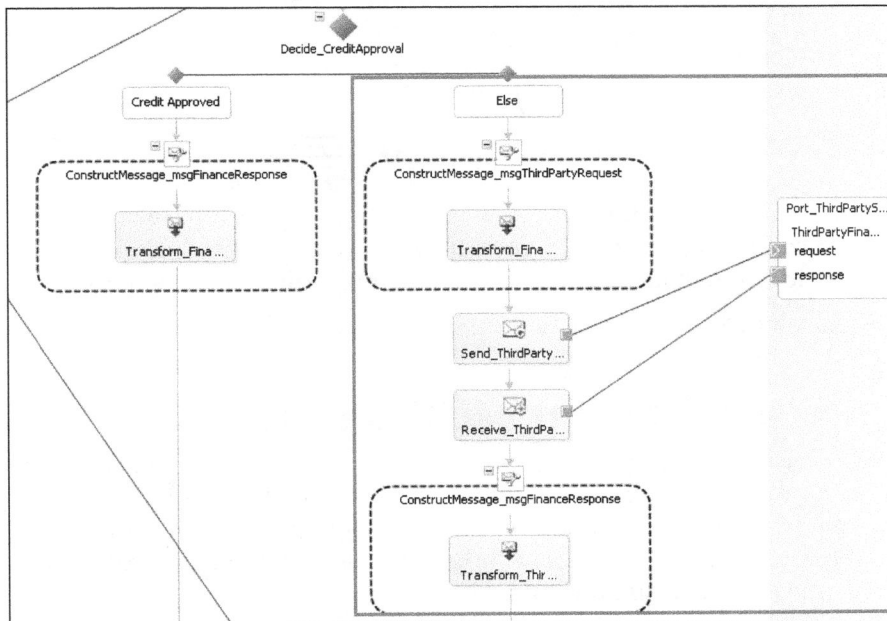

19. We can now deploy our application and then, import the
    `ThirdPartyFinanceService.BindingInfo.xml` Binding File that was
    generated by the Consume WCF Service Wizard. Once we have imported this
    Binding File, we will discover that the following Send Port has been created.

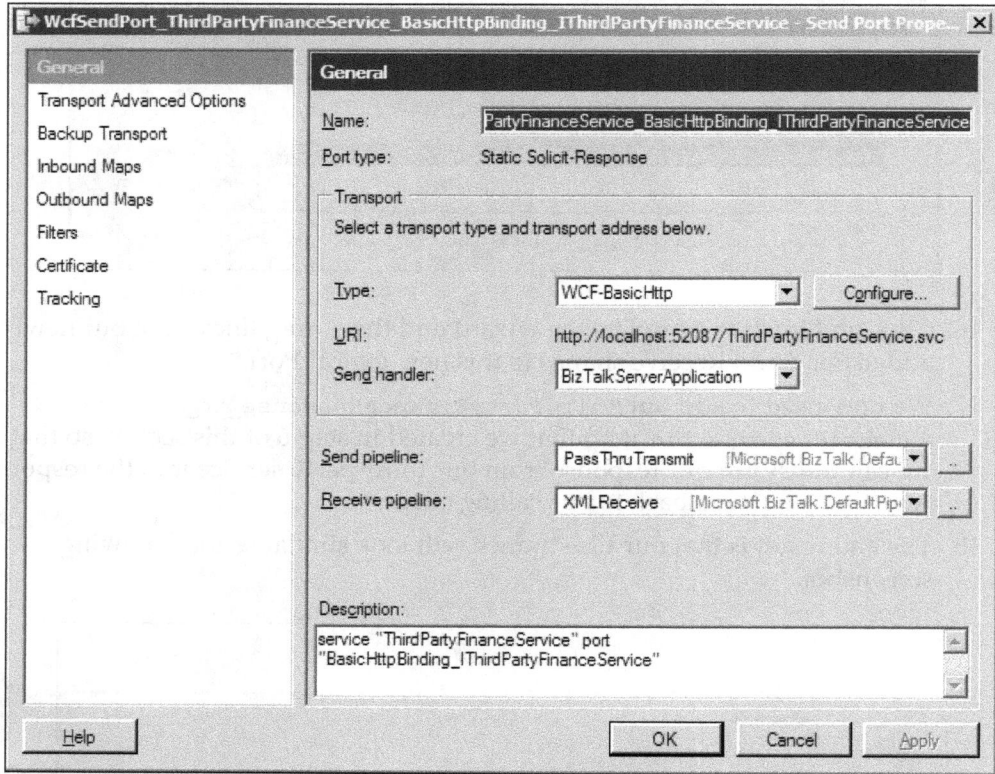

20. In preparation of testing our new application, we need to restart the Host
    Instance that supports our Orchestration and messaging processes. In this
    scenario, we will use the BizTalkServerApplication Host Instance.

21. We also need to bind and start our application.

Testing our Custom WCF Service

Once again we are going to leverage the WCF Test tool as our client application. This
time we are going to send a message into BizTalk that will not satisfy the dealer's
financing requirements but will satisfy our third-party financing requirements. This
means that our customer Credit Score should be less than five, but greater than two
and our income should be greater than $10,000.

In our response document, the **FinanceCompany** being returned should be **Wearsy Inc.**, which indicates that it was our third-party service responding, as shown in the following screenshot:

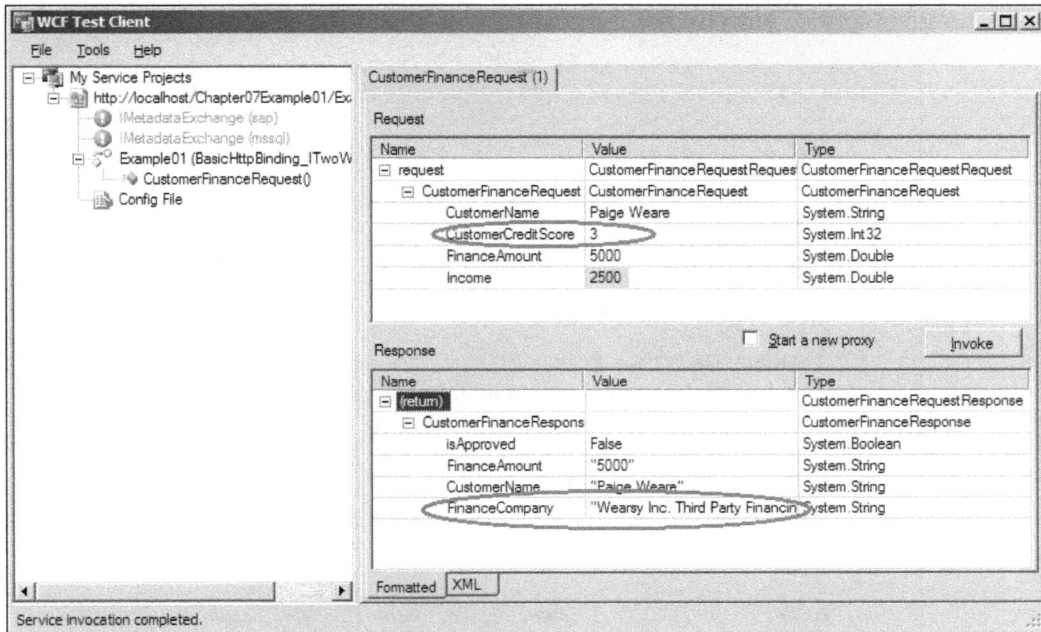

Manually importing WSDL files

In the previous example, we were able to generate artifacts required to support calling a WCF Service by consuming a WSDL, or metadata exchange endpoint by specifying the URL for these artifacts. In some situations, this may not be possible if we are integrating with another party and network boundaries prevent us from accessing their service during the early development phase(s). When this situation arises, we do have the ability to import a WSDL file manually without having the access to the service.

In the previous example, when we were presented with the following screen, we chose to select **Metadata Exchange (MEX) endpoint**. If we want to select a WSDL file that has been provided to us via email or some other means, we can select **Metadata Files (WSDL and XSD)** instead. This will allow us to generate the required artifacts to call another service without having real-time access to the service.

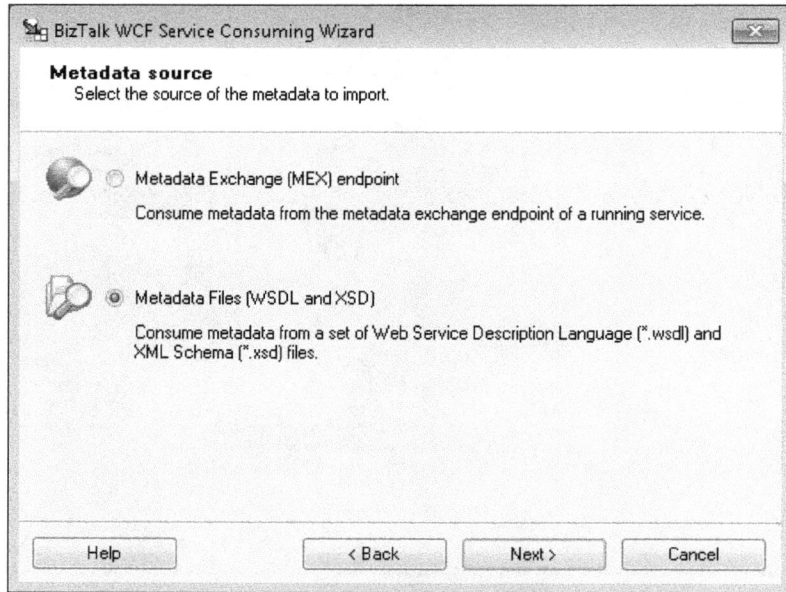

Handling web exceptions

When BizTalk consumes WCF Services, the opportunity exists for exceptions to be thrown. When this event occurs, we need to catch these exceptions and deal with them gracefully. If we do not handle them properly, we can expect suspended-service instances inside the BizTalk Administration Console.

The scenario that we are about to walk through will demonstrate how BizTalk can handle Typed Exceptions that have been thrown from a Custom WCF Service. The business scenario is that some customers at our car dealership may want to have custom paint applied to their new or used car. The car dealership will leverage an external **Autobody** shop to perform this work. However, some cars and colors are not valid to have this work done. This service will validate whether the car can have custom paint applied to it. In situations where a desired color has not been passed in, the WCF Service will throw a typed exception called **PaintServiceException**.

The source code for this demonstration can be found in the `C:\BTS2013CertGuide\Chapter07\Example03-Exceptions`, which is part of this book's sample code download. Within this folder, we will discover a folder called `Example03-CustomPaintService`. This folder contains our Custom WCF Service project called `Example03-CustomPaintService.csproj`. If we open this project, we will discover the following:

1. We are storing our operation and data contracts in a file called `ICustomPaintService.cs`. Within this file, we will discover that we have an operation contract called `CheckCustomPaintAvailability`. This method has been decorated with `FaultContract` that is of the type `PaintServiceException`:

```
namespace Example03_CustomPaintService
{
    [ServiceContract(Namespace="http://Chapter07-
    Example03")] public interface ICustomPaintService
    {
      //Our Web Method that contains a Fault Contract
        attribute
        [OperationContract]
        [FaultContract(typeof(PaintServiceException))]
        CarResponse CheckCustomPaintAvailability(Car car);
    }
```

2. Our first data contract represents our request object, which happens to be a car. Within this object, we have three properties including a car model, car year, and a desired color:

```
[DataContract]
public class Car
{
    string carModel = "";
    int carYear = 0;
    string desiredColor = "";

    [DataMember]
    public string CarModel
    {
        get { return carModel; }
        set { carModel = value; }
    }
    [DataMember]
    public string DesiredColor
    {
```

```
            get { return desiredColor; }
            set { desiredColor = value; }
        }
        [DataMember]
        public int CarYear
        {
            get { return carYear; }
            set { carYear = value; }
        }
}
```

3. Our response object is called `CarResponse` and has two properties including whether the service request is valid, from a business perspective, and the desired color being returned:

```
[DataContract]
public class CarResponse
{
    bool isValid = false;
    string desiredColor = "";

    [DataMember]
    public bool IsValid
    {
        get { return isValid; }
        set { isValid = value; }
    }


    [DataMember]
    public string DesiredColor
    {
        get { return desiredColor; }
        set { desiredColor = value; }
    }
}
```

4. The last data contract that we need to deal with is the one that represents our Typed Exception. We are calling this typed exception `PaintServiceException`, and it has three properties including an error code, error message, and details:

```
[DataContract]
public class PaintServiceException
{
```

```
            int errorcode=0;
            string errormessage="";
            string details="";
            public PaintServiceException()
            {

            }
            [DataMember]
            public int ErrorCode
            {
                get { return errorcode; }
                set { errorcode = value; }
            }

            [DataMember]
            public string ErrorMessage
            {
                get { return errormessage; }
                set { errormessage = value; }
            }
            [DataMember]
            public string Details
            {
                get { return details; }
                set { details = value; }
            }
        }
    }
```

5. The next file that we want to look at is called `CustomPaintService.svc.cs`. Within this file, we will discover our Web Method that we declared in the previous steps. An area that we want to focus on is where we determine the following code line is: `car.DesiredColor == null || car.DesiredColor==""`. If either of these situations exists, we want to populate our Typed Fault Exception object called `pse` and then, throw a new `FaultException`, passing in our `pse` object. Otherwise, if all information has been processed, we will construct a `CarResponse` object and indicate whether this is a valid scenario:

```
namespace Example03_CustomPaintService
{

    public class CustomPaintService : ICustomPaintService
    {
```

```
public CarResponse CheckCustomPaintAvailability
  (Car car)
{
    try
    {
        CarResponse carResponse = new
          CarResponse();

        if (car.DesiredColor == null
            ||car.DesiredColor =="")
        {
            PaintServiceException pse =
              new PaintServiceException();
            pse.ErrorCode = 123;
            pse.ErrorMessage = "A Desired Color
              must be provided";
            pse.Details =
              "CheckCustomPaintAvailability
            Method is missing a required
              parameter";
            throw new FaultException
                <PaintServiceException>
                    (pse,new FaultReason
                    ("CheckCustomPaintAvailability
                    Method raised an Exception"));
        }

    if (car.CarYear > 2010 && car.DesiredColor
      != "Hot Pink")
        {
    carResponse.DesiredColor=car.DesiredColor;
    carResponse.IsValid = true;
        }
```

```
            else
            {
        carResponse.DesiredColor =
          car.DesiredColor;
        carResponse.IsValid = false;
            }
            return carResponse;
        }
        catch (Exception ex)
        {
            throw ex;
        }
        }
    }
}
```

6. Once we have built our Custom WCF Service, we will need to consume it from BizTalk much like we did earlier in this chapter. You can find a BizTalk Solution called `Chapter07-Example03.sln` in the `C:\BTS2013CertGuide\Chapter07\Example03-Exceptions` folder that has this step already completed.

7. When we consume our WCF Service this time, we will discover a difference. This time around we will add a **Configured** Port to our Orchestration that will include a `PaintServiceExceptionFault` operation:

8. We will not connect this operation to a Send or Receive shape. Instead, we need to wrap our Send/Receive shapes that communicate with our WCF Service around a Scope so that we can add an Exception Handler. For the purpose of our scenario, this Scope shape can have its Transaction Type set to None:

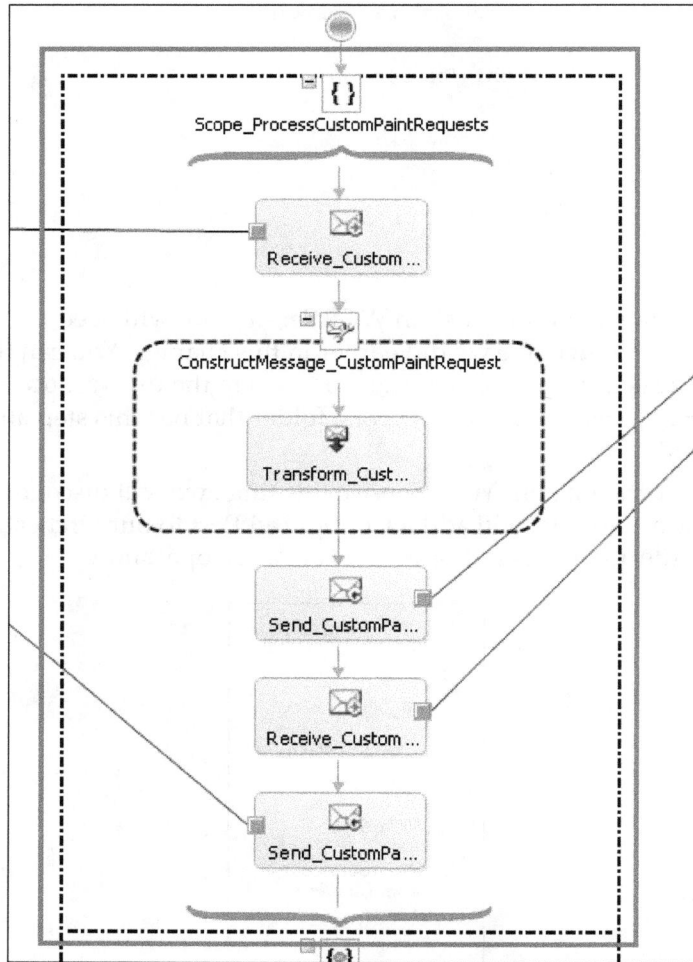

9. When we go to configure our Exception Handler, we can actually use this **PaintServiceExceptionFault** operation as our Exception type:

Properties   ▼ 🔲

CatchException_PaintServiceException Catch Exception

⊟ **BizTalk**	
Description	
Exception Object Name	pse
Exception Object Type	.equest.CheckCustomPaintAvailability.PaintServiceExceptionFault
Name	<.NET Exception...>
Object Type	General Exception
Report To Analyst	Port_SendCustomPaintRequest.CheckCustomPaintAvailability.Pain
Scope	

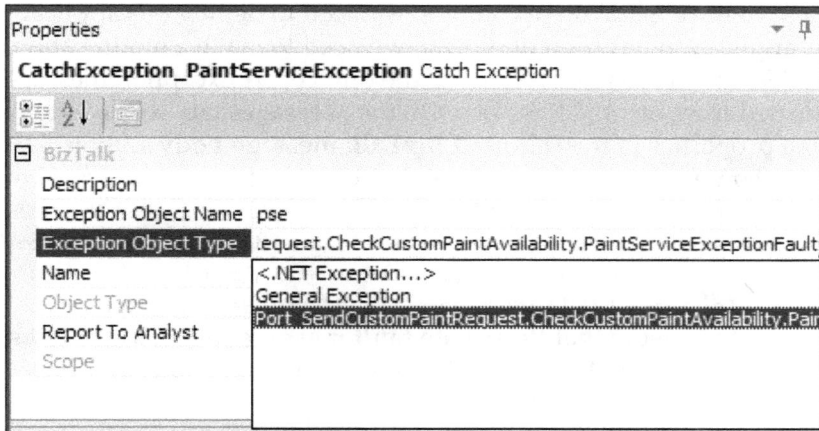

10. If an exception is raised, the Exception Handler will catch it and process it. In this case, we want to simply write out the result to a File Drop. It is important to note that when a typed exception is caught, we will have an instance of the Exception Object that we configured in our Exception Handler. If we want to actually send that message, we need to assign this object to an instance of our **PaintServiceExceptionFault** message:

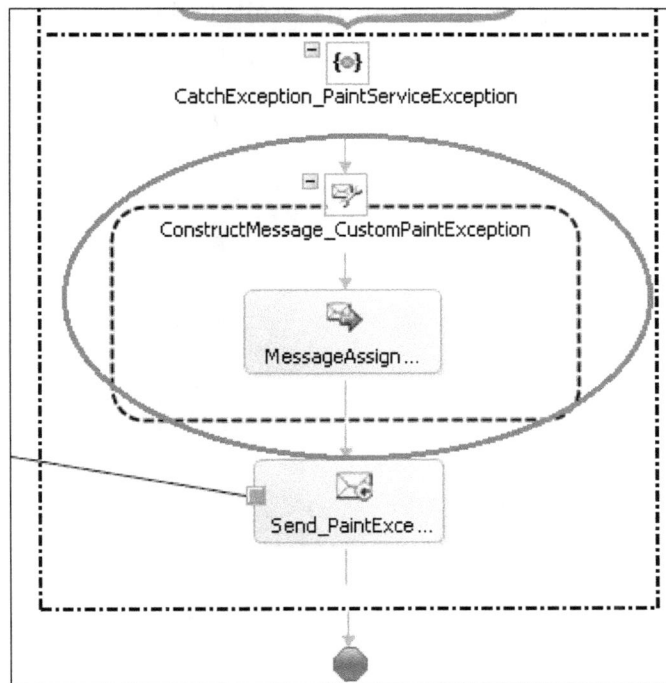

11. Once we have made these changes, we need to deploy our application. Once our application has been deployed, we need to make a modification to our WCF Send Port so that we can handle our Typed Exception message being returned from our WCF Service. On the **Messages** tab, we need to modify some properties in the **Inbound BizTalk message body** section. Select the **Path – content located by body path** radio button. Then, we need to modify the **Body path expression** and set it to `/*[local-name()='CheckCus tomPaintAvailabilityResponse'` and `namespace-uri()='http:// Chapter07- Example03']|/*[local-name()='Fault']/*[local-name()='detail']/*[local-nam e()='PaintServiceException']`. We also need to ensure that **Propagate fault message** remains enabled so that our application will be aware when faults have been raised.

> By specifying an Xpath expression, we have the ability to receive either a valid response or a typed exception from the WCF Service. While somewhat discrete, BizTalk does support the ability to provide multiple Xpath statements by separating them using a delimiter.

12. Sample files exist in the `C:\BTS2013CertGuide\Chapter07\Example03- Exceptions\FileDrop` folder that allows us to test both the successful and unsuccessful scenarios. In the case of our unsuccessful scenario, BizTalk will catch a typed exception and write the results to disk.

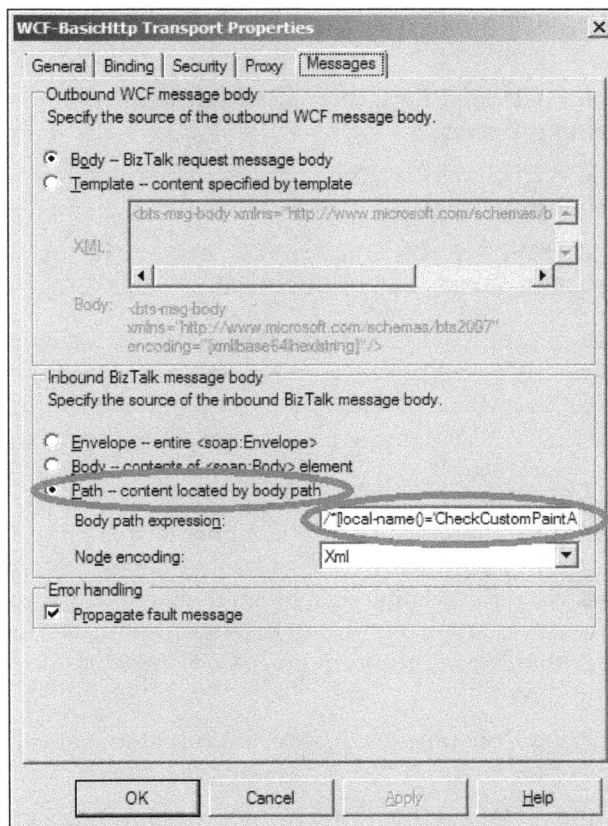

Testing your knowledge

The following questions will test your knowledge of Web Services and WCF Services Integration. These questions will reinforce the concepts that were previously discussed in this chapter:

1. A car manufacturer, HWLC Motors, has outfitted its **Sport Utility Vehicle (SUV)** lineup with FireBridge tires. Unfortunately, this line of FireBridge tires had a factory recall on them due to factory defects. The FireBridge Company has exposed a WCF Service that car manufacturers can use to order replacement tires. Due to the popularity of these FireBridge tires, their WCF Service is very busy and service requests are taking longer to complete. HWLC Motors is using BizTalk and have noticed that they are receiving some client-side timeouts as a result of the increase in service execution time. What should HWLC do to their BizTalk configuration?

    a. In the WCF Send Port, they should increase the Open timeout property.

    b. In the WCF Send Port, they should decrease the Send timeout property.

    c. In the WCF Send Port, they should increase the Send timeout property.

    d. In the `BTSNTSvc.exe.config` file, the `ServiceCallTimeOut` property value should be increased.

2. Tom, a developer for HWLC Motors, has been given strict BizTalk naming conventions by his boss Mikael. Tom has just consumed the third-party financing WCF Service in BizTalk using the WCF-BasicHttp Binding. In order to comply with Mikael's naming convention, Tom renames the operation on the logical port used to communicate with the WCF Service, from `ThirdPartyFinanceApproval` to `External_ ThirdPartyFinanceApproval`. Tom then compiles/deploys his application and then, imports the Binding File that was generated during the Consume WCF Service Wizard. Upon running the service for the first time, Tom discovers a runtime error and attributes it to the mismatch between his logical port naming and the SOAP Action header that is configured in his WCF Send Port. What must he do to resolve the problem?

    a. Rerun the Consume WCF Service Wizard and specify an operation name of `External_ ThirdPartyFinanceApproval`.

    b. Ask the makers of the third-party financing service to add the `UseCustomOperation` property to the services' `web.config`.

    c. In the WCF Send Port, remove the SOAP Action header entirely. BizTalk will then rely upon its Pub/Sub architecture to route the message.

    d. Update the WCF Send Port's SOAP Action header and change the operation name to `External_ ThirdPartyFinanceApproval`.

3. Richard, another developer at HWLC Motors has consumed the Custom Paint Service from his BizTalk Orchestration using the WCF-BasicHttp Binding. He has configured this application to catch Typed Exceptions from the Paint Service. However, when a Paint Service exception is thrown, it ends up getting suspended inside the BizTalk Administration Console and never makes it back into his BizTalk Application. How should he fix it?

    a. In the WCF Send Port, he should enable the Propagate fault message property.

    b. He should change his WCF Send Port to use the WCF-Custom Adapter instead due to its additional exception handling capabilities.

    c. In his WCF Send Port, he should modify the Outbound WCF message body to use a template. In this template, he will provide the name of the Paint Service Exception he expects to receive back from the service.

    d. He needs to run the Consume WCF Adapter Wizard again this time enabling the Use Custom Exceptions feature.

4. Tom has exposed an Orchestration as a WCF Service and has chosen to use the WCF-BasicHttp Adapter when running the BizTalk WCF Service Publishing Wizard. He has successfully deployed and configured his application. Mikael, his boss, has decided he would like to use the WCF-WSHttp Adapter instead due to the additional security features that are available. What must Tom do in order to successfully use the WCF-WSHttp Adapter?

    a. In the BizTalk Administration Console, Tom needs to modify his WCF Receive Location to use the WCF-WSHttp Adapter instead.

    b. Run the BizTalk WCF Service Publishing Wizard again, this time selecting the WCF-WSHttp Adapter.

    c. In the BizTalk Administration Console, Tom needs to modify his WCF Receive Location to use the WCF-Custom Adapter. Inside the Receive Location's configuration, he must set the binding to WsHttpBinding.

    d. No change is required. The WCF-BasicHttp Adapter can also leverage the WCF-WSHttp security features.

5. HWLC has changed its policy around processing orders from individual dealerships. Dealerships used to be able to submit order requests throughout the day. Now dealerships are being asked to submit orders once a day. It is expected that some busy dealerships may be sending messages that are more than 10,48,576 bytes (1 MB). What setting(s) needs to be changed inside of HWLC's WCF two-way Receive Location?

a. WCF two-way Receive Locations cannot accept messages that large. Instead, a one-way Receive Location and a one-way Send Port should be used instead.

b. The Open timeout needs to be increased to satisfy these new requirements.

c. The Maximum received message size needs to be increased to satisfy these new requirements.

d. All dealerships must increase the Send timeout in their client applications in order to satisfy these new requirements.

Summary

In this chapter, we were introduced to some of the concepts involved with WCF and WCF Adapters. We then covered Exposing and Consuming WCF and Web Services. As you have probably noticed, WCF is an extremely large and complicated topic. Luckily for BizTalk developers, Microsoft has provided wizards and the BizTalk Administration Console to reduce the complexities involved in building and consuming these types of services.

On the exam, you can expect around 14 percent of the questions to be centered around WCF and Web Services. A thorough understanding of this chapter will put you in a good position to do well in the examination.

In the next chapter, we will investigate a set of diverse technologies including **Business Activity Monitoring (BAM)**, **Business Rules Engine (BRE)**, **Radio Frequency Identification (RFID)**, and **Electronic Data Interchange (EDI)**. These technologies make up *Chapter 8, Implementing Extended Capabilities*, which aligns to the same set of competencies that will be tested in the exam.

8
Implementing Extended Capabilities

In this chapter, we will look at additional features that come with the BizTalk Server Product and also other products that ship with the BizTalk License.

Along with the BizTalk Server, several other features are available with the BizTalk Server License. The **Business Rules Engine** (**BRE**) helps implementing and maintaining complex business rules in both BizTalk and other applications. **Electronic Data Interchange** (**EDI**) is a BizTalk feature that allows receiving and sending EDI messages, and **Business Activity Monitoring** (**BAM**) is used both in BizTalk and other applications to collect data and present them to business users.

In this chapter, we will discuss the following topics:

- Business Rules Engine
- Electronic Data Interchange
- Business Activity Monitoring
- Testing your knowledge

Business Rules Engine

The Business Rules Engine is an engine used for controlling and maintaining rules for both BizTalk and other applications. It is mainly used for ever changing rules that need to be deployed without having to alter an existing BizTalk (or .NET) application.

Creating a BizTalk Solution with rules

In the following example, we will create a small BizTalk Solution and have it call rules inside the BRE, and based on the rules and content of messages, either approve or deny a loan application.

The first step will be to add a **Policy** determining if a loan application is approved.

We will need a Schema that represents the loan application entering BizTalk and the BRE.

Creating a Schema

To create a Schema, you will need to complete the following steps:

1. Create a Solution named `Chapter08.Example01`.

2. Create a Project named `Chapter08.Example01.Schemas` and a Schema named **LoanApp.xsd**.

3. Make the Schema look similar to the following screenshot, set the **Data Type** of **LoanAmount** to **xs:int**, and make the **Status** element distinguished as shown in the following screenshot:

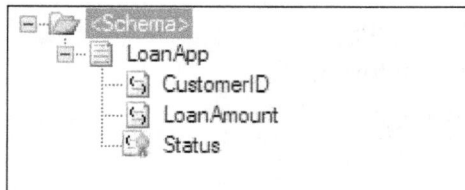

4. Build the Project.

Now, we need to set up a Policy in BRE for approving loan applications. We want to look at the **LoanAmount** element and set the **Status** element to **Approved**, if the loan is approved.

Creating a Policy

To create a Policy, you will need to complete the following steps:

1. Open the **Microsoft Business Rule Composer**.

2. In the **Policy Explorer**, right-click on **Policies**, and choose **Add New Policy**.

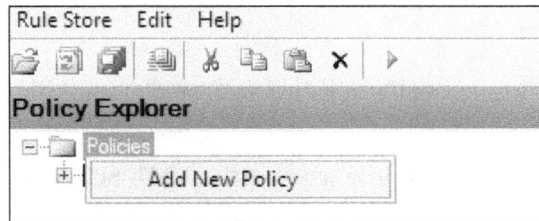

3. Name the Policy `Chapter08.Example01.ApproveLoan`.

4. Right-click on **Version 1.0 (not saved)**, and select **Add New Rule**.

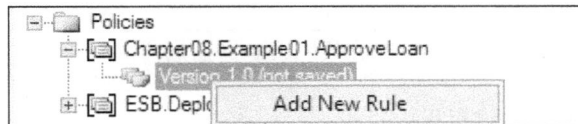

5. Name the rule **Rule ApprovedByAmount**.

6. On the right-hand side, right-click on **Conditions**, and select **Predicates->LessThan**.

7. We now need to make a condition saying that if the **LoanAmount** on the Loan Application is less than 100, then we will automatically approve the loan. Click on **argument2**, and type in `100`.

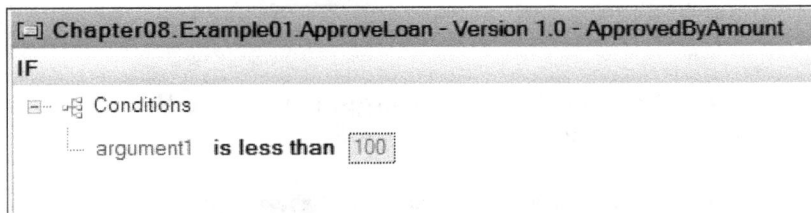

8. To insert **argument1**, we need the Composer to be familiar with the **LoanApp** Schema.

Import a Schema as facts into the Rule Composer

When working with the BRE, there are three types of sources that can be imported, which are as follows:

- XML Schemas
- Databases
- .NET classes

To import a Schema into the Business Rule Composer, you will need to complete the following steps:

1. In the **Facts Explorer** window, choose the **XML Schemas** tab.
2. Right-click on **Schemas**, and choose **Browse**.
3. Locate the **LoanApp.xsd** file created previously in Visual Studio.
4. Choose the Schema, and click on **Open**.
5. Expand the **LoanApp** Schema.

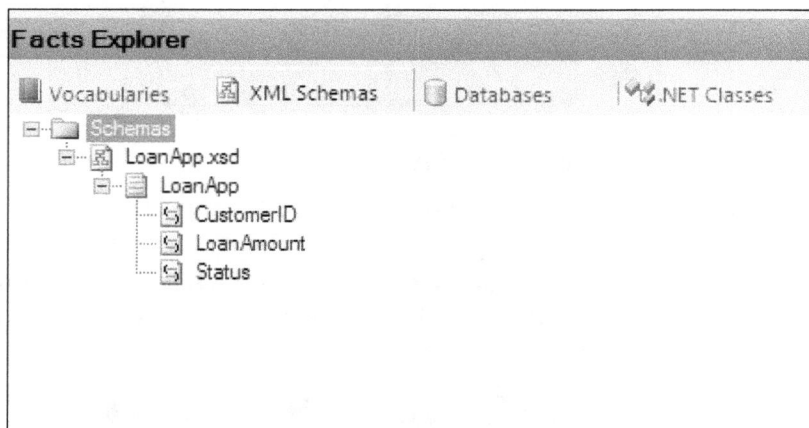

6. Drag the **LoanAmount** element into **argument1** in the **IF** window as seen in the following screenshot:

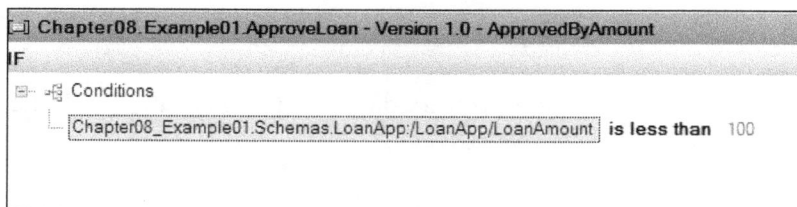

As you may be considering, this statement is not very readable because the **LoanAmount** element contains a long XPath expression. Since the Rule Composer is supposed to be used by other than IT people, we will later look at how to make it appear more human readable.

For now, let us keep the condition as it is, and tell the engine what to do with the **Status** element, if the condition is met.

Adding an Action

Now that we have specified a condition, we need to add the action(s) that will occur when the condition is met. In order to do this, perform the following steps:

1. Drag the **Status** element from the Schema onto **Actions** under **THEN**.

2. Click on **<enter a value>** and type **Approved**. Again, this does not look very readable and contains XPath expressions, but we will deal with that later.

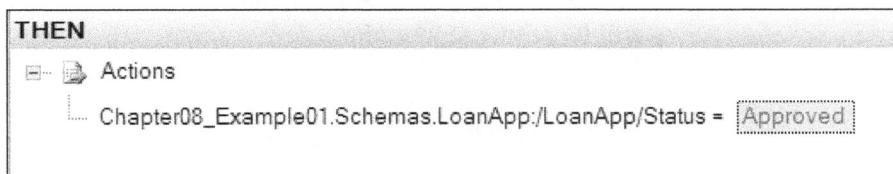

```
THEN
  ⊟   Actions
          Chapter08_Example01.Schemas.LoanApp:/LoanApp/Status =  Approved
```

3. Save the Policy by right-clicking on **Version 1.0(not saved)** and selecting **Save**.

Testing the Policy

Now, we will test the Policy we have created with both a **LoanApp** instance where the condition is met (approved) and another where the condition is not met (not approved) as follows:

1. Generated from the Schema, create two XML instances of type **LoanApp**. Give both of them `<Status>New</Status>`, and give one of them `<LoanAmount>200</LoanAmount>` and the other `<LoanAmount>20</LoanAmount>`.

2. Place them in an easily accessible file folder, and test that they are both valid XML instances by viewing them in Internet Explorer.

3. Right-click on **Chapter08.Example01.ApproveLoan | Version 1.0** inside the Composer, and select **Test Policy**.

4. Under XML Documents, select the **Schema**, and choose **Add instance**.

5. Locate the document with a loan amount of **20**, and select it.

6. Click on **Test**. A large trace will now be shown in the Composer. This has to do with the Rule Engine using the **Rete algorithm**, where everything is analyzed in a special kind of network. This book will not dig deeper into this behavior.

7. Open the XML file tested, and verify that **Status** was changed to **Approved**. Change it back to **New**.

8. Test the other XML document with **Amount** set to **200** by selecting the other document. Remove the old instance before clicking on **Test**.

9. Verify that this time the **Status** did not change since the condition was not met.

10. Publish the Policy by right-clicking on **Version 1.0**, and selecting **Publish**.

Publishing the policy will allow us to work with it outside the Composer. From here it will be immutable, meaning that after it has been published, it cannot be altered. If we need to change it, we will be required to make a new version.

> The Rule Composer does not hold any ELSE logic that allows us to set **Status** to **Denied**, if the condition is not met. If we were to do that, we would need to create a new Rule, and negate the first one (in this case, greater than or equal to 100). This is because of the way the Rete algorithm is executed.

So, with the Policy working, we will now build a small Orchestration inside BizTalk that can test it.

Creating an Orchestration

We will not go into detail about how to create Orchestrations. For a more detailed Orchestration description, refer to *Chapter 4, Developing BizTalk Artifacts – Creating Orchestrations*. Let's perform the following steps to create an Orchestration:

1. Create an Orchestration that resembles the following screenshot:

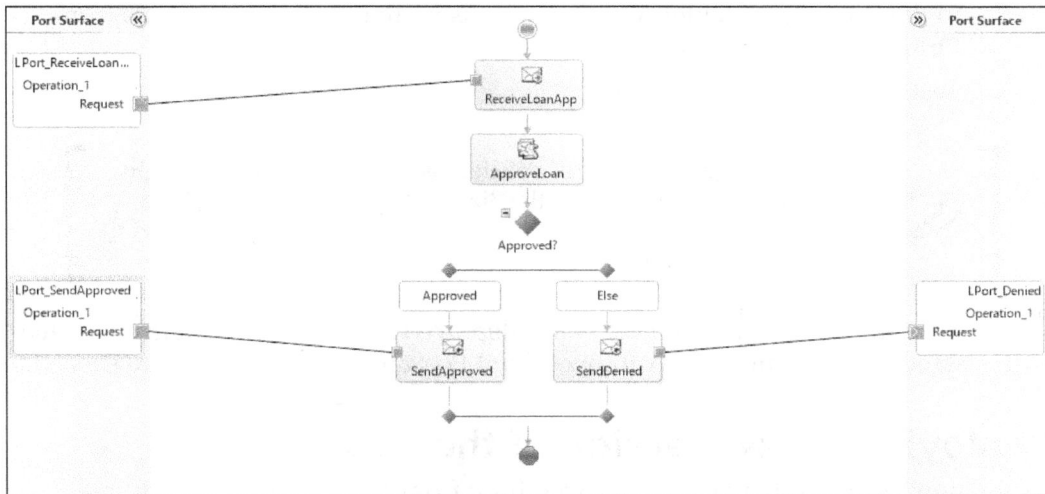

2. The Orchestration must have the following features:

   a. Receives a **LoanApp** instance.

      The Approved decide shape uses the Boolean expression:
      LoanAppMessage.Status == "Approved"

3. Double-click on the **ApproveLoan** (Call Rules) shape, and select the Policy **ApproveLoan**.

4. In **Parameter Name**, select the **LoanApp** message received in the **ReceiveLoanApp** Receive shape.

5. Deploy the Orchestration, create and bind all the required ports.

Deploying the Policy and testing

We now need to deploy the Policy in order to test that the Orchestration can use the Policy. In order to do this, perform the following steps:

1. Test the solution by submitting one of the XML documents previously created to the Orchestration.

2. Check the Event Viewer. The error **No versions of rule set "Chapter08. Example01.ApproveLoan" are deployed** should appear. This is because a rule called from an Orchestration must be deployed. The error message also shows that the Orchestrations do not call a specific version of the rule set but rather the deployed version with the highest version number.

3. In the Composer, deploy **Version 1.0**, ensure that the status changes from **Published** to **Deployed**.

4. Test the flow again.

> When changing the state of policies inside the Composer, it might be necessary to restart both the BizTalk Host Instance(s) and the `RuleEngineUpdateService.exe` because all of these services caches information.

The Orchestration combined with the Policy deployed should now result in one of the XML instances being sent to the Approved Send Port and another one sent to Denied.

Deploying a new version of the Policy

We are now asked to change the approved limit from 100 to 1000 (in which case both XML documents will be approved). As we discussed earlier, we cannot change an existing version of a Policy already published; so, in order to meet the new requirement, we must create a new version of the Policy. If we create Version 1.1 of the Policy and deploy it, the Orchestration will automatically start using the new and higher version. Let's carry out the following steps to deploy a new version of the Policy:

1. In the Rule Composer, right-click on **Chapter08.Example01.ApproveLoan Policy**, and choose **Add New Version**.

2. A red Version 1.1 should now appear as shown in the following screenshot:

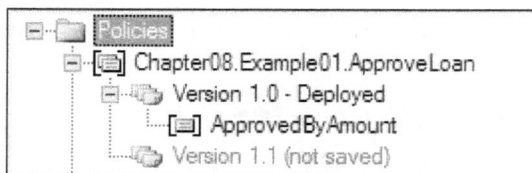

```
⊟ 📁 Policies
   ⊟ 📧 Chapter08.Example01.ApproveLoan
      ⊟ 📑 Version 1.0 - Deployed
           📧 ApprovedByAmount
        📑 Version 1.1 (not saved)
```

3. Right-click on **Version 1.0 | ApprovedByAmount** and select **Copy**.
4. Right-click on **Version 1.1 (not saved)**, and select **Paste**.
5. In the new **ApprovedByAmount** element, change 100 to 1000.
6. Publish and deploy **Version 1.1**.
7. Restart Hosts and the Rule service.
8. Test the documents.

Now, both of the test documents should be approved.

Adding a Vocabulary

As we discussed previously, we can make the conditions and actions appear more human readable in the Composer, so that it becomes easier for non-IT personnel to create and change rules.

To do this, we use **Vocabulary**. In this exercise, we will create a better name for the **LoanAmount** and **Status** fields as follows:

1. Under **Vocabularies**, right-click on **Vocabularies**, and select **Add New Vocabulary**.

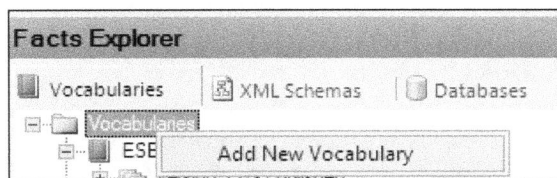

2. Name the new Vocabulary as **Loan**.
3. Right-click on **Version 1.0**, and choose **Add new definition**.
4. Choose **XML Document Element or Attribute** and click on **Next**.
5. Click on the **Browse** button.
6. Locate the **LoanApp** Schema and click on **Open**.
7. Expand the Schema, select **LoanAmount** and click on **OK**.
8. Name the definition **Total Loan Amount**.
9. Choose **Perform "Get" operation**, and set **Display name** to **Total Loan Amount**.
10. Click on **Finish**.
11. Make a new version of the **ApproveLoan** Policy, and copy and paste the old **ApprovedByAmount** to the new version.
12. Delete the left-hand side of the condition by selecting it and pressing *Delete* so that **argument1** appears again.
13. Publish **Version 1.0** of the Loan Vocabulary (note that **Vocabularies** do not need to be deployed but must be published before they can be used in a Policy).
14. Drag **Total Loan Amount** to **argument1**.

Now, we have a better appearance of the condition, and it will be easier for non-IT personnel to make Rule changes in the Composer, especially if the rules become more complex.

Electronic Data Interchange

Since BizTalk Server 2006 R2, Microsoft has implemented out of the box EDI capabilities in BizTalk.

EDI documents are like Flat Files, which we discussed in an earlier chapter. However, there are two major differences, which are as follows:

- EDI is standardized, the Schemas are already created
- EDI deals with the header information not found in the actual message (Schema) but must be configured using Parties and Agreements

Out of the box, BizTalk ships with numerous Schemas for the following EDI standards:

- X12
- EDIFACT
- HIPAA
- EANCOM

In this chapter, we will use EDIFACT as an example, but most of the mechanisms surrounding the BizTalk EDI capabilities will be the same, whether the standard used is X12, EDIFACT, or any other standard.

We will try and process an EDIFACT Order version D96A.

The order looks similar to the following screenshot:

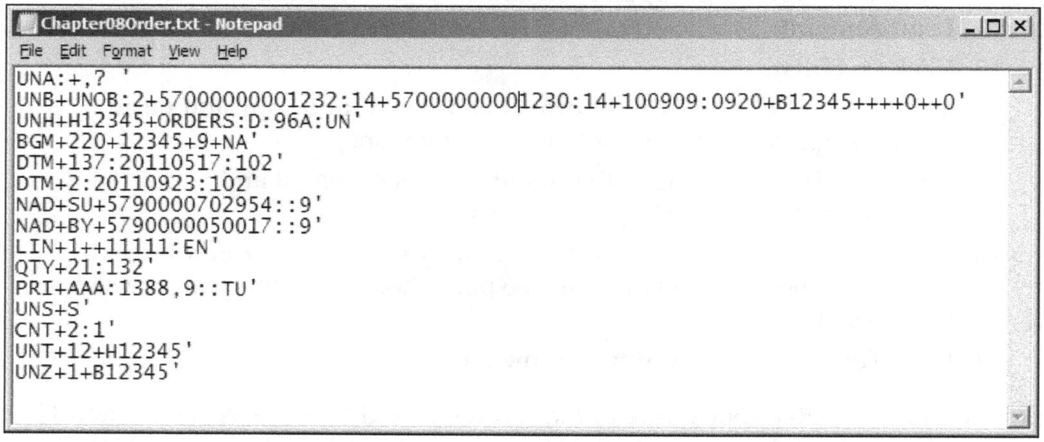

```
Chapter08Order.txt - Notepad                                    _ □ x
File  Edit  Format  View  Help
UNA:+,? '
UNB+UNOB:2+57000000001232:14+5700000000|1230:14+100909:0920+B12345++++0++0'
UNH+H12345+ORDERS:D:96A:UN'
BGM+220+12345+9+NA'
DTM+137:20110517:102'
DTM+2:20110923:102'
NAD+SU+5790000702954::9'
NAD+BY+5790000050017::9'
LIN+1++11111:EN'
QTY+21:132'
PRI+AAA:1388,9::TU'
UNS+S'
CNT+2:1'
UNT+12+H12345'
UNZ+1+B12345'
```

What we will do is receive the document in a Receive Location that uses the EdiReceive Pipeline, and by using the already created Schema for EDIFACT Order D96A, the Pipeline should be able to create an EDI XML message.

Finding and deploying the EDIFACT Schema

When starting an EDI Project, the first thing we need to do is get the Schemas needed for parsing/creating the documents we will receive and/or send. To find these Schemas, perform the following steps:

1. With developer tools installed on the BizTalk environment, go to the folder `%Program Files%\Microsoft BizTalk Server 2013\XSD_Schema\EDI`, and locate the self-extracting file named `MicrosoftEdiXSDTemplates.exe`.

2. Extract the file by double-clicking on it. This has to be done only once.

3. A new folder named `MicrosoftEdiXSDTemplates` is created. In this folder, locate the `EDIFACT\D96A\EFACT_D96A_ORDERS.xsd` file.

4. Create a BizTalk Visual Studio Project, and name it **Chapter08.Example02. Schemas**.

5. Add an existing item, and add the `EFACT_D96A_ORDERS.xsd` file located earlier.

6. Sign the assembly, and deploy it to a BizTalk Application named **BTS2013CertGuide-Ch08**.

Adding a reference to BizTalk EDI Application

With the EDIFACT Schema deployed, we now need to set up a Receive Port with a Receive Location that uses the EdiReceive Pipeline. The Pipeline is located in the BizTalk EDI Application, and therefore our **BTS2013CertGuide-Ch08** Application needs a reference to BizTalk EDI Application. In order to do this, let's perform the following steps:

1. Right-click on the **BTS2010CertGuide-Ch08** Application, and select **Properties**.

2. Select **References**, and click on **Add**, select **BizTalk EDI Application**, and click on **OK**.

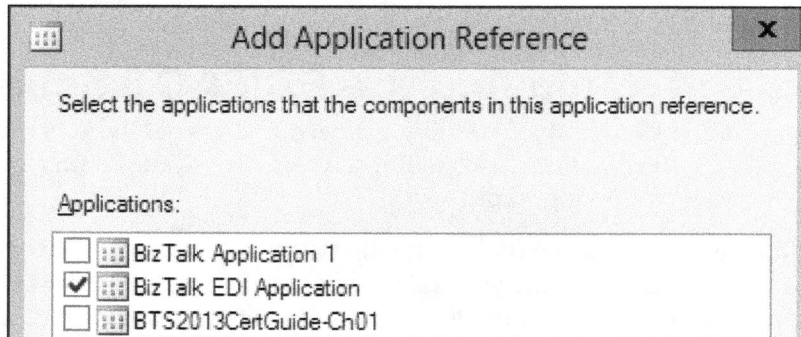

3. Refresh the Application.

Set up a Receive Port, Receive Location, and a Send Port

For the next step, we need to set up both a Receive and a Send Port so that we can monitor messages going through BizTalk and how the EDI functionality works:

1. Set up a new Receive Port (**CG0802_Receive**) and a Receive Location (**CG0802_Receive_File**) using the FILE Adapter that points to a new file folder, and select the EdiReceive Pipeline.

2. Set up a Send Port (**CG0802_Send_File**) that subscribes to all messages from the Receive Port (**BTS.ReceivePortName == CG0102_Receive**), use a FILE Adapter and point it to an output folder. This port should use the default **PassThruTransmit** Pipeline.

3. Start your Application (when the BizTalk EDI Application is referenced, starting the Application will suggest starting the EDI Application as well; this is not needed right now and should be unchecked).

4. Run the sample EDIFACT Order through the Application. The result should be a file sent through the Send Port.

5. Examine the XML sent from the Send Port as shown in the following screenshot:

```xml
<?xml version="1.0"?>
<ns0:EFACT_D96A_ORDERS xmlns:ns0="http://schemas.microsoft.com/BizTalk/EDI/EDIFACT/2006">
    <UNH>
        <UNH1>H12345</UNH1>
        <UNH2>
            <UNH2.1>ORDERS</UNH2.1>
            <UNH2.2>D</UNH2.2>
            <UNH2.3>96A</UNH2.3>
            <UNH2.4>UN</UNH2.4>
        </UNH2>
    </UNH>
    <ns0:BGM>
        <ns0:C002>
            <C00201>220</C00201>
        </ns0:C002>
        <BGM02>12345</BGM02>
        <BGM03>9</BGM03>
        <BGM04>NA</BGM04>
    </ns0:BGM>
    <ns0:DTM>
        <ns0:C507>
            <C50701>137</C50701>
            <C50702>20110517</C50702>
            <C50703>102</C50703>
        </ns0:C507>
    </ns0:DTM>
```

The top of the XML output should look similar to the preceding screenshot. Note the namespace and the root element and how they match the root element and the namespace of the EDIFACT Order Schema we deployed earlier from Visual Studio as shown in the following screenshot:

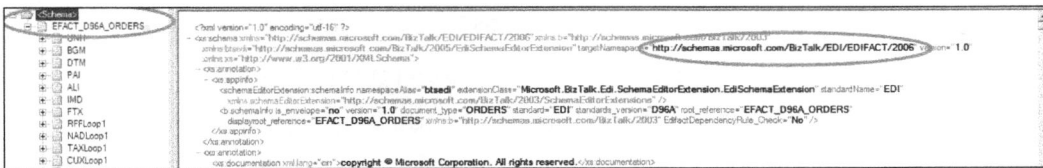

Setting up Parties and Agreements

As of now, BizTalk can process an incoming EDIFACT message and convert it to XML. The EDIFACT document is being accepted by the EdiReceive Pipeline and is transformed to XML so that further processing can take place.

At some point (especially when sending EDI documents), we might need to set up Parties so that the EdiReceive and EdiSend Pipelines know which trading partners the message came from or is being sent to.

Examine an unrecognized message

To set up Parties for receiving EDIFACT, we must tell the EdiReceive Pipeline how to identity who sent the document.

To do this, we use the UNB segment (ISA for X12 document), where information about the sender and receiver is stored as shown in the following screenshot:

```
Chapter08Order.txt - Notepad                                    _ |□| x|
File  Edit  Format  View  Help
UNA:+,? '
UNB+UNOB:2+57000000001232:14+57000000001230:14+100909:0920+B12345++++0++0'
UNH+H12345+ORDERS:D:96A:UN
BGM+220+12345+9+NA'
DTM+137:20110517:102'
DTM+2:20110923:102'
NAD+SU+5790000702954::9'
NAD+BY+5790000050017::9'
LIN+1++11111:EN'
QTY+21:132'
PRI+AAA:1388,9::TU'
UNS+S'
CNT+2:1'
UNT+12+H12345'
UNZ+1+B12345'
```

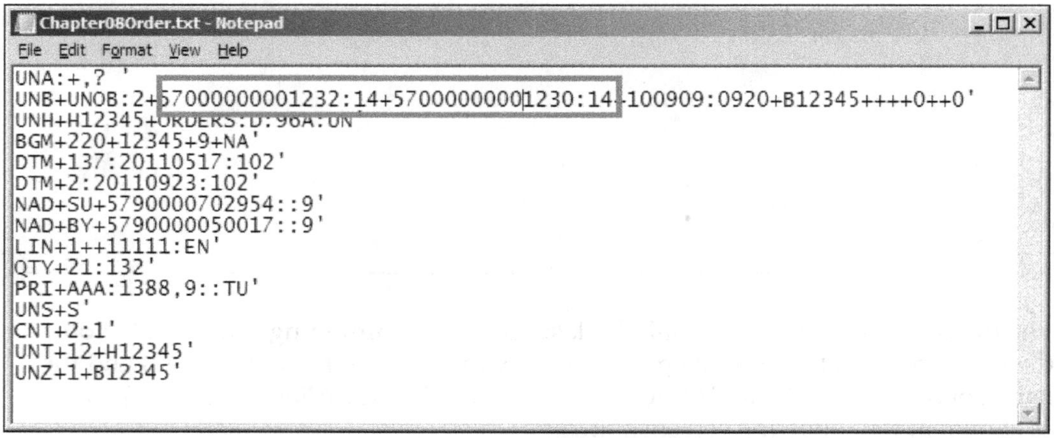

In the example file, the UNB segement contains the following two parties:

- **Sender**: 57000000001232 (EAN number code 14) (MyPartner)
- **Receiver**: 57000000001230 (EAN number code 14) (MySelf)

So, what we need to do now is set up two parties; the sender and the receiver.

The first thing we will do is examine how the Context of an EDI message appears when parties are not recognized:

1. Stop the Send Port (not Unenlist, just Stop).
2. Send an order through the Application.
3. Go to the **Group Hub** window in the BizTalk Administration Console, and click on **Suspended Items | Resumable**.
4. Examine the **Context Properties** of the message most recently suspended, as shown in the following screenshot:

Note that **ReceivePartyName** and **SenderPartyName** do not have any meaningful values. This indicates that the **EdiDisassembler** Pipeline Component did not find any matching Agreement between the two Parties in the UNB segment, so we need to set up such an Agreement.

Set up the Parties and the Agreement for receiving

For BizTalk to know which partner-specific properties should be applied for the incoming and outgoing EDI messages, we need to set up Parties and Agreements as follows:

1. In the BizTalk Administration Console, go to **Parties**.
2. Right-click and choose **New | Party**.
3. Name the Party as **MySelf**, and click on **OK**.
4. Expand the **MySelf** Party, and find the profile **MySelf_Profile**.
5. Double-click on the profile.

6. Under **Identities**, in the **Name** drop-down list, choose **EAN (European Article Numbering Association)**. Note that the **Qualifier 14** is automatically selected.

7. In **Value**, type in 57000000001230.

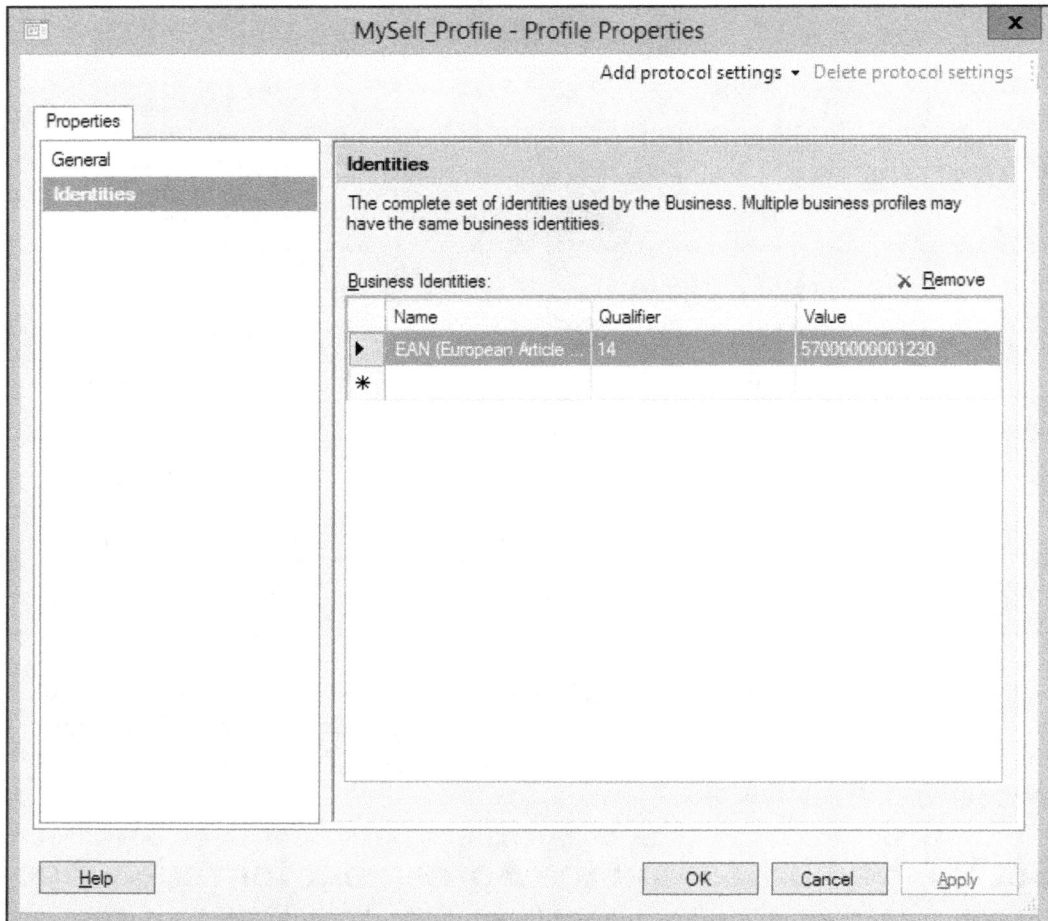

8. Click on **OK**, and do the same for party: **MyPartner** with EAN number: **57000000001232**. We now need to set up an Agreement between the two parties.

> Note that a Party can have several profiles if the Party has several identities and/or using different EDI formats (EDIFACT, X12, HIPAA, and so on).

9. Right-click on **MyPartner_Profile**, and choose **New | Agreement**.

10. Name the Agreement **AgreementWithMyPartner**.

11. Choose **EDIFACT** as **Protocol**.

12. Choose **MySelf** as **Second Party**.

13. Two new tabs, **MyPartner->MySelf** and **MySelf->MyPartner** (known as Agreement parts), should now appear as shown in the following screenshot:

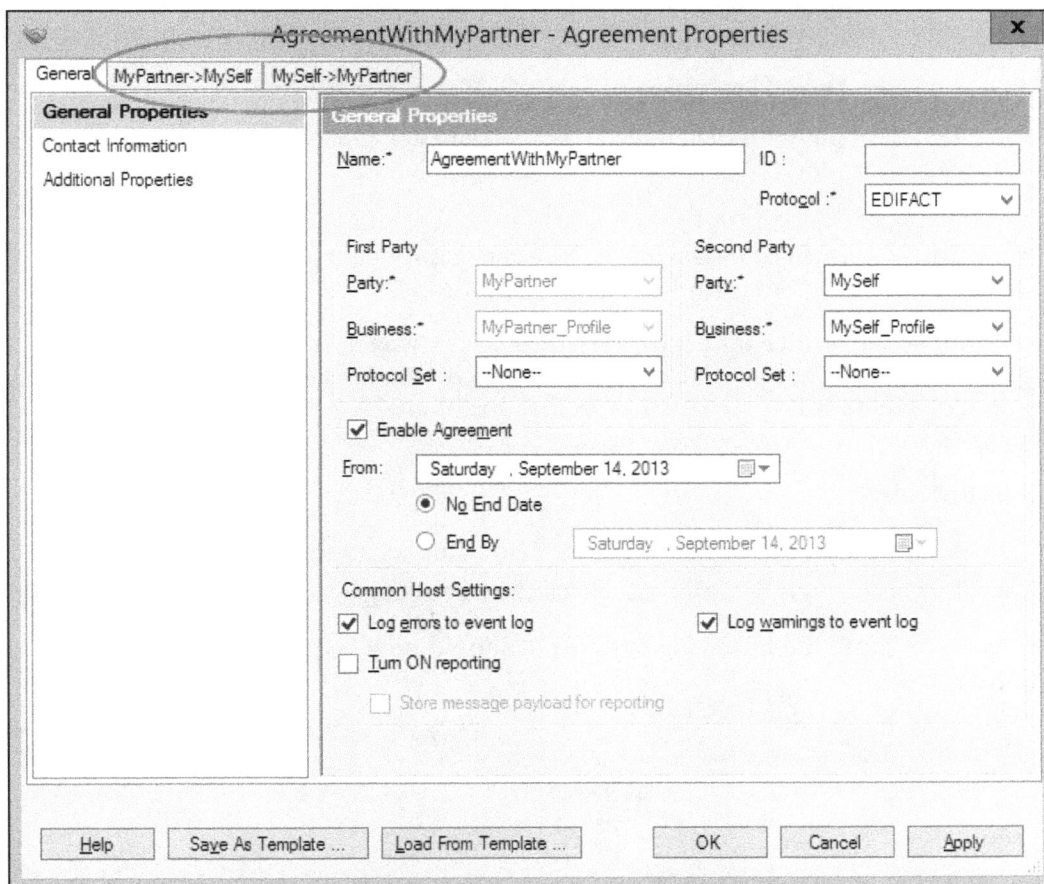

14. Click on the **MyPartner->MySelf** tab.

15. Click on **Interchange Settings | Identifiers**.

16. Verify that **UNB2.1** is the EAN number of the sender and **UNB3.1** is the EAN number of the receiver, and click on **OK**.

17. Restart your Host Instance(s). This needs to be done every time something changes in the Party section in BizTalk.

18. Send an EDIFACT Order through BizTalk; make sure that the Send Port is still in a **Stopped** state.

19. Examine the **Context**, the **AgreementName**, the **SenderPartyName**, and the **ReceiverPartyName** should now be populated with the correct data. This indicates that the Parties are now recognized on reception of the message.

20. Start the Send Port again.

Changing the Schema

Often when working with EDI, trading partners are going to send invalid EDI, which is EDI not conforming 100 percent to the standard.

All the Schemas available in BizTalk will, per default, only allow EDI documents to pass through the **EDIDisassembler** Pipeline Component and be transformed to XML, if the document complies with the standard.

For example, we receive orders as shown before; however, in the DTM (DateTime) segment, instead of code 137 (Document Date), the sender sends 70 as the code. This is not allowed according to the UN specification available at `http://www.unece.org/trade/untdid/d96a/uncl/uncl2005.htm`.

Let us test this:

1. Make a copy of the EDIFACT document, and change **DTM+137** to **DTM+70**.

2. Run it through BizTalk, and check the Event Log.

An error similar to the following screenshot should now be present in the Event Viewer:

```
Error encountered during parsing. The Edifact transaction set with id 'H12345' contained in interchange (without group) with id 'B12345', with sender id '57000000001232',
receiver id '57000000001230' is being suspended with following errors:
Error: 1 (Field level error)
        SegmentID: DTM
        Position in TS: 3
        Data Element ID: C50701
        Position in Segment: 2
        Position in Field: 1
        Data Value: 70
        12: Invalid value in data element
```

This is because 70 is not allowed in this field. If we are to allow **MyPartner** to send **DTM+70** in the documents (even though the preferred approach would be to ask the partner to send valid EDI, this is not always possible), we need to give the partner its own Schema representation of `EFACT_D96A_ORDERS`.

Now, since we cannot change the root element name of the Schema as that has to comply with certain patterns, the only way to create a new Schema is to change **TargetNamespace**.

Fortunately, this can be set up in Agreements as well.

Set up an alternate namespace for the Agreement

We now need to set up a new namespace to be used for the **MyPartner->MySelf** Agreement so that the messages being received with this Agreement will be given another namespace, and therefore, will be validated using an alternative Schema. We will do this using the following steps:

1. Under **Parties**, click on **MyPartner**, and double-click on **AgreementWithMyPartner**.

2. Go to the **MyPartner | MySelf** tab.

3. Under **Transaction Set Settings | Local Host Settings**, scroll to the right and locate **TargetNamespace**.

4. Change the **TargetNamespace** from `http://schemas.microsoft.com/BizTalk/EDI/EDIFACT/2006` to `http://schemas.microsoft.com/BizTalk/EDI/EDIFACT/2006/MyPartner`.

> Note that the **TargetNamespace** drop-down list suggests `http://schemas.microsoft.com/BizTalk/EDI/Edifact` without capitalized EDIFACT. This will NOT work, so make sure EDIFACT is capitalized.

5. Click on **OK**, and restart your Host Instance(s).

6. Run the **DTM+70** document through the application, and again check the Event Log.

You should now see the following error:

Finding the document specification by message type "http://schemas.microsoft.com/BizTalk/EDI/EDIFACT/2006/MyPartner#EFACT_D96A_ORDERS" failed.

So, we need to deploy such a Schema and allow the value 70 in the DTM segments.

Deploy an alternate Schema

Now, we need to create an alternate Schema with the new namespace and where **DTM+70** is allowed in the DTM segment. In order to do this, let's perform the following steps:

1. Go to the Visual Studio Project created earlier that contains the original order Schema.

2. Change the **TargetNamespace** of the Schema to the new namespace specified in the Agreement.

3. Go to the **DTM** record, and expand it.

4. Expand **C507**.

5. Select the **C50701** element, and choose **Enumeration** under **Properties**.

6. Add **70** to the list.

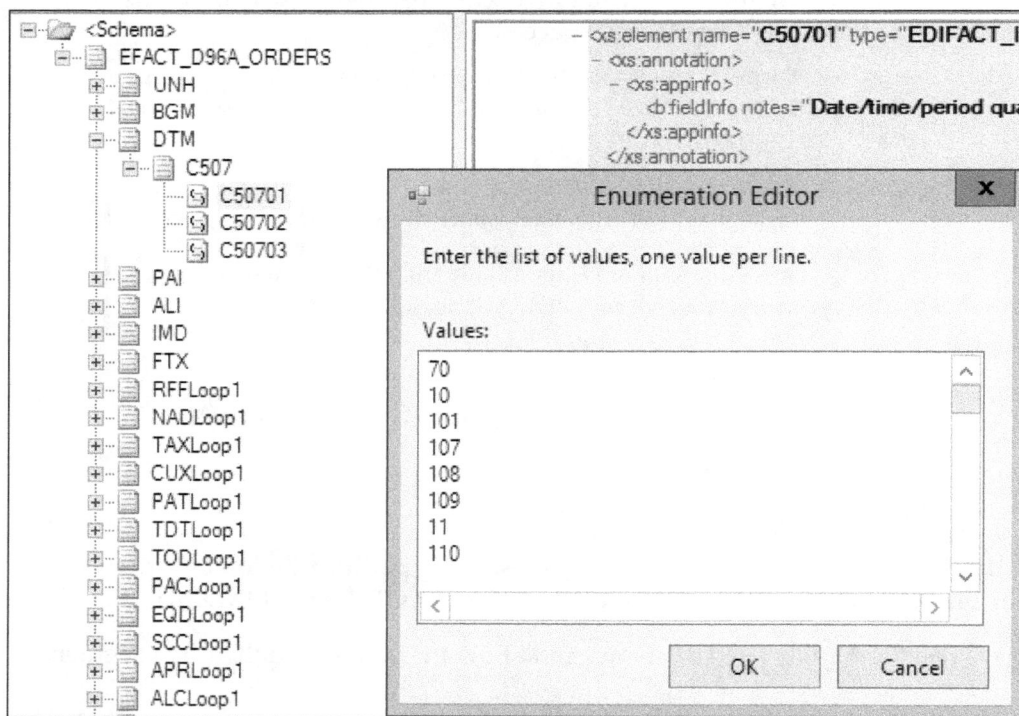

7. Rebuild the solution, click on **OK** to any information about clean up that might appear.

8. Deploy the solution, and restart the Host Instance(s).

9. Start your Send Port again (this might cause several old suspended items to be sent to your out folder).

10. Submit the new order with **DTM+70**.

11. Verify that a new XML file was submitted to the out folder without any problems. Examine the XML file as shown in the following screenshot:

```xml
<?xml version="1.0"?>
<ns0:EFACT_D96A_ORDERS xmlns:ns0="http://schemas.microsoft.com/BizTalk/EDI/EDIFACT/2006/MyPartner">
  <UNH>
    <UNH1>H12345</UNH1>
    <UNH2>
      <UNH2.1>ORDERS</UNH2.1>
      <UNH2.2>D</UNH2.2>
      <UNH2.3>96A</UNH2.3>
      <UNH2.4>UN</UNH2.4>
    </UNH2>
  </UNH>
  <ns0:BGM>
    <ns0:C002>
      <C00201>220</C00201>
    </ns0:C002>
    <BGM02>12345</BGM02>
    <BGM03>9</BGM03>
    <BGM04>NA</BGM04>
  </ns0:BGM>
  <ns0:DTM>
    <ns0:C507>
      <C50701>70</C50701>
      <C50702>20110517</C50702>
      <C50703>102</C50703>
    </ns0:C507>
  </ns0:DTM>
  <ns0:DTM>
    <ns0:C507>
      <C50701>2</C50701>
      <C50702>20110923</C50702>
      <C50703>102</C50703>
    </ns0:C507>
  </ns0:DTM>
  <ns0:NADLoop1>
```

As shown in the previous screenshot, the XML now has a custom namespace (.../MyPartner), and we have allowed DTM to hold the qualifying value of 70.

Debatching and Error handling

EDI documents are envelopes of, potentially, several different messages of the same or even different types.

When receiving EDI, the user needs to take into consideration if these documents should be split (debatched) into individual messages or the whole batch should continue onwards in BizTalk as one batched document.

In the Agreement part, there are four different options (found under the **Interchange Settings | Local Host Settings | Inbound batch processing** option).

Here are the four different options:

Name	Description
Split Interchange as Transaction Sets – suspend Transaction Sets on Error (Default)	Debatch the document and suspend only the messages that fail validation
Split Interchange as Transaction Sets – suspend Interchange on Error	Debatch the document and suspend the whole document if just one message fails validation
Preserve Interchange – suspend Interchange on Error	Keep the document as a whole and suspend the whole thing if messages fail validation
Preserve Interchange – suspend Transaction Sets on Error	Keep the document as a whole but suspend individual messages that fail validation, and remove them from the Interchange that is passed onward

Setting up a Party and Agreement for sending

When sending EDIFACT, more information must be provided to BizTalk through the Parties and Agreements in order for BizTalk to know how the partner expects the EDI to be structured.

The way EDI really differs here from XML, Flat Files, and so on is that the metadata structure and envelope of an EDI document cannot be determined, neither from the XML message entering the Assembler Pipeline Component (EdiAssembler) nor from the Schema.

If we take our previous example where we received an EDIFACT Order and transformed it to XML, we can now try and take the same XML, send it through the EdiSend Pipeline, and configure it to yet another party (**MyPartner2**).

Again have a look at our order example as shown in the following screenshot:

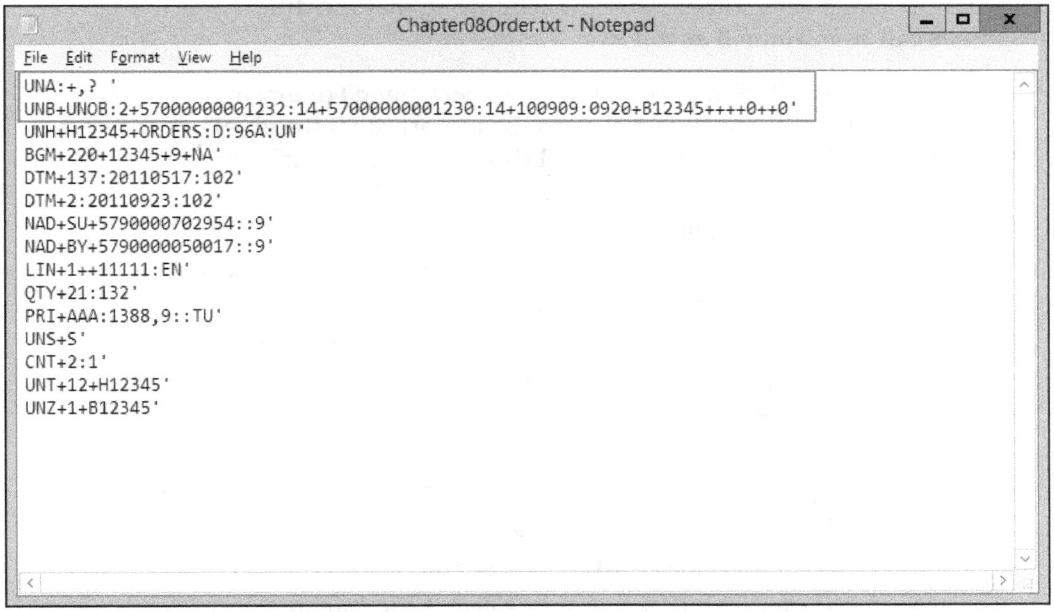

```
Chapter08Order.txt - Notepad                          —  □  x
File  Edit  Format  View  Help
UNA:+,? '
UNB+UNOB:2+57000000001232:14+57000000001230:14+100909:0920+B12345++++0++0 '
UNH+H12345+ORDERS:D:96A:UN'
BGM+220+12345+9+NA'
DTM+137:20110517:102'
DTM+2:20110923:102'
NAD+SU+5790000702954::9'
NAD+BY+5790000050017::9'
LIN+1++11111:EN'
QTY+21:132'
PRI+AAA:1388,9::TU'
UNS+S'
CNT+2:1'
UNT+12+H12345'
UNZ+1+B12345'
```

The UNA segment is metadata about how the document is delimited, how decimal numbers are presented, and how to escape a reserved character.

The UNB segment tells the encoding of the document, the sender and the receiver, and several other document metadata.

None of these metadata can be created from the EDI Schema or the XML being sent to the Send Port because they will be partner-specific.

So, what must be done is that these properties must be set up in a **Partner Agreement**, and then the Send Port must be connected to that Agreement (as opposed to when receiving EDI, the Send Pipeline will have no way of knowing which Party to use without being explicitly told).

Setting up a new Party for sending

We will now make yet another Party for sending so that the differences in EDI properties can be examined as follows:

1. Make a new File Send Port named **CG0802_SendToPartner2_File**. Make a subscription identical with the first Send Port (**BTS.ReceivePortName == CG0802_Receive**), and select the **EdiSend** Pipeline. Make the file extension `%MessageID%.txt` instead of `%MessageID%.xml`.

2. Make a new Party called **MyPartner2**.

3. Give the Party profile the EAN number **57000000001233**, the same way it was done in the previous exercise.

4. Right-click on **MyPartner2_Profile**, and select **New | Agreement**.

5. Name it as **AgreementWithMyPartner2**, choose **EDIFACT**, and select **Myself** as **Second Party**.

6. Select the **MySelf->MyPartner2** tab.

7. Check the **Identifiers**, both **UNB2** and **UNB3** should be filled out with EAN numbers, and **Code Qualifiers** as **14**.

8. In **Envelopes**, check the **Apply UNA Segment**.

9. Under **Character set and separators**, select the following (UNA5 holds a space):

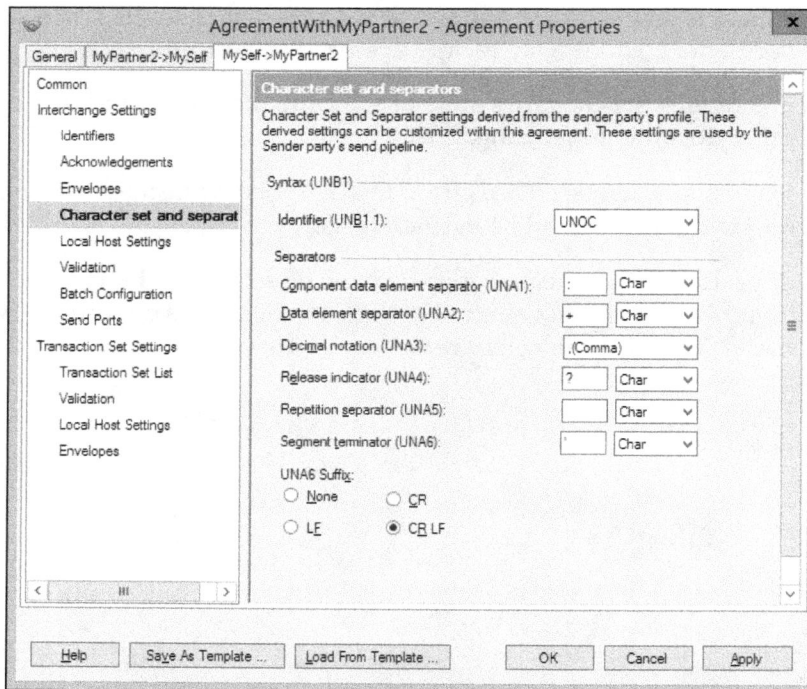

10. Most of the values are left as default, but choosing **UNOC** for **Identifier** will encode the document with western European character set (ISO-8859 -1). Most EDIFACT partners use a space in UNA5, so make sure to put a space instead of *, and we will also set **Suffix** to **CR LF**, which will make the EDIFACT more readable because this will present each segment as a separate line.

11. Go to Send Port, and choose **CG0802_SendToPartner2_File**.

12. Click on **OK**, and restart the Host Instance(s).

13. Submit a new message in the Application. Examine the output from **SendToPartner2 Send Port** which is as follows:

```
{DBA9B019-C8DC-46C8-A2C9-166C3AB2F2FB}.txt - Notepad
File  Edit  Format  View  Help
UNA:+,? '
UNB+UNOC:1+57000000001230:14+57000000001233:14+130914:2114+1++++0++0'
UNH+1+ORDERS:D:96A:UN'
BGM+220+12345+9+NA'
DTM+70:20110517:102'
DTM+2:20110923:102'
NAD+SU+5790000702954::9'
NAD+BY+5790000050017::9'
LIN+1++11111:EN'
QTY+21:132'
PRI+AAA:1388,9::TU'
UNS+S'
CNT+2:1'
UNT+12+1'
UNZ+1+1'
```

Note that the UNA segment has a comma (,), which indicates that decimal numbers should be presented with commas. Also, note that PRI+AAA:1388,9 is a decimal number with commas. If we change the Agreement UNA3 from comma to decimal, all decimal numbers in the document will be presented using decimals instead.

Also, note that the UNB segment is using the correct sender and receiver EANs, and that each segment is separated by carriage returns, as specified in the Agreement.

Send Port control

In the previous exercise, we made a link between the Agreement and the Send Port used for sending the EDIFACT. This hardcoded link does not always meet our business requirement since the Agreement resolution might happen because of the data from within the message or the Context, and also, there is the possibility that the same Send Port is sending to many different Agreements.

Instead of setting up a Send Port in an Agreement, we have the ability, using the Context Properties, to manipulate and configure what Agreement an **EdiAssembler** Pipeline Component will use. Here are the three options:

- Write to the **AgreementPartIDForSend** Context Property in the `http://schemas.microsoft.com/Edi/PropertySchema` namespace with the Agreement Part ID you want the Assembler to use. This is mostly used internally because getting the ID requires some selection from the database tables inside the `Management` database.

- Write to the three Context Properties, **AgreementNameForSend**, **SenderPartyNameForSend**, and **ReceiverPartyNameForSend**, in the `http://schemas.microsoft.com/Edi/PropertySchema` namespace, where the first is the Agreement name, the second is the name of the sender Party, and the third is the receiver Party name. The reason that the name of the Agreement is not sufficient is because the Agreement holds two parts; one for each direction.

- Write to the **DestinationPartyName** Context Property in the `http://schemas.microsoft.com/Edi/PropertySchema` namespace. This is for legacy support before Agreements were introduced to Parties in BizTalk, and this will only work in BizTalk Server 2010 and in versions earlier to this. In 2010, it also requires the same Party name set up in the Agreement part under **Identifiers | Additional Agreement Resolvers | DestinationPartyName**.

> Even though the **DestinationPartyName** set up in the Agreement is still available in BizTalk Server 2013, it has no function. The **DestinationPartyName** Context Property has been removed for the Property Schema and **EdiAssembler** will not use it.
>
> When using one of the templates listed earlier, it is important that the Context Properties are written to the Context of the message before the message enters **EdiAssemble** stage of the Send Port.

Batching

When sending EDI, batching is often a requirement, meaning a specific Party might require that messages meant for him should be gathered into a large document and sent once every night, or once every 2 hours, and so on.

The EDI capabilities in BizTalk provide out of the box batching capabilities, and batching can be set up in the Agreement parts under **Interchange Settings | Batch Configuration**. When batching is set up for an Agreement, an Orchestration will be started, picking up all messages with certain properties set in Context, and then release the whole batch in the interval selected in the Agreement.

These Context Properties are typically set by the **Batch Marker** Pipeline Component, in the EdiReceive Pipeline.

The **Batch Marker** Component can also be used for non EDI messages, if other XML documents are mapped to EDI XML later on in the process but still require the batching Properties to be set. To do this, the Component has a Property named **IgnoreMessageEncoding** that, if set to true, will allow the Component to set the batching Properties and not try to resolve the EDI message type.

Business Activity Monitoring

BAM is typically used for bringing BizTalk to the world, in the sense that it is often somewhat transparent to the outside world what goes on inside BizTalk. If errors occur in BizTalk, these will be handled both by BizTalk and the operators, but what about all the stuff that did not fail? BAM is typically used to show just that.

Here are some examples of questions that BAM could provide answers to:

- How many orders did we receive last month?
- Was the order with ID 1005 ever received, and when did BizTalk send it to the ERP system?

Out of the box, there is no easy way of supplying these answers to the business outside BizTalk. By using the built-in tracking, we could give the answers, but that would both be very tedious, and would require a field, such as **OrderID**, to be promoted (see *Chapter 2, Developing BizTalk Artifacts – Creating Schemas and Pipelines*, for more information about promotions).

BAM, on the other hand, can do all this easily without requiring certain features, such as Promotion, to be present in the BizTalk Solution.

BAM is non-intrusive, which means we can apply BAM to an existing BizTalk Application without BAM making any changes or performance impact to that solution. This means that BAM can easily be applied after a solution is already deployed and running in production. Also, even if BAM is failing, if it had been developed with errors or the BAM databases were unavailable, and so on, the BAM solution would not cause the actual BizTalk Solution to fail.

When using BAM together with BizTalk, we are able to receive information from the following places in the BizTalk flow:

- Receive Pipelines
- Orchestration shapes
- Send Pipelines

Each time a message enters one of the previously mentioned items inside BizTalk, BAM is able to collect data from this event. The examples of data from such events could be:

- Time of event
- Data from the actual message
- Data from the Context of the message
- Various message properties such as `MessageID` and `InstanceID`

The information collected will be stored in SQL tables (when working with BAM known as Activities).

Creating Activities

A BAM Activity is somewhat similar to an SQL table. The examples of Activities inside BAM could be:

- Order Received
- Order Processed
- Invoice Processed
- Order Sent
- Invoice Sent

If we have a BizTalk setup where orders are received and processed and maybe sent to multiple applications or systems we could have a one-to-many relationship between processing an order and sending it, because processing it could result in sending it to three systems and we want to track all the three events. In that case, we would need two BAM Activities (two tables), an Order Processed Activity and an Order Sent Activity.

As mentioned earlier, each Activity will be represented by SQL tables. If an Activity named TestBAM is created, the following five Activity tables will be created in the primary BAM database named BAMPrimaryImport:

- bam_TestBAM_Active
- bam_TestBAM_ActiveRelationships
- bam_TestBAM_Completed
- bam_TestBAM_CompletedRelationships
- bam_TestBAM_Continuations

Along with the tables, each Activity also implements a package, called BAM_DM_TestBAM, in Integration Services. This package should be scheduled to run frequently to maintain and archive the Activity data. When this package is run, the Completed and CompletedRelationships tables will be split into subtables with internal unique names. So, as time goes by, more and more tables will appear, but the applications reading the BAM Activity data will not notice this because they should only access the data through views, and the views are updated each time a new subtable is created using the SQL Union statement.

Here is an example of how a BAM Activity would be represented in the BAMPrimaryImport database after the maintenance package has run for the first time:

```
⊞ 🗔  dbo.bam_TestBAM_A88BA880_2B85_4C7C_8AAB_061A0B3D579E
⊞ 🗔  dbo.bam_TestBAM_A88BA880_2B85_4C7C_8AAB_061A0B3D579E_Relationships
⊞ 🗔  dbo.bam_TestBAM_Active
⊞ 🗔  dbo.bam_TestBAM_ActiveRelationships
⊞ 🗔  dbo.bam_TestBAM_Completed
⊞ 🗔  dbo.bam_TestBAM_CompletedRelationships
⊞ 🗔  dbo.bam_TestBAM_Continuations
```

The tables we will pay the closest attention to are _Active and _Completed. The _Active table is where Activity instances reside before the Activity profile has completed, where they will be moved to the _Completed table.

Activities are created by using Microsoft Excel.

Setting up the BAM Add inside Excel

Microsoft Excel needs to be installed on a BizTalk Development machine in order to create Activities. It is only necessary to have Excel installed on development servers, and it should not be installed on production or test environments.

BAM Client, found under **Additional Software** when installing BizTalk, should also be installed on the developing machine; this will result in an **Add-Ins** menu being installed in Excel, and this **Add-Ins** can now be activated by selecting **File | Options | Add Ins | Go** as shown in the following screenshot:

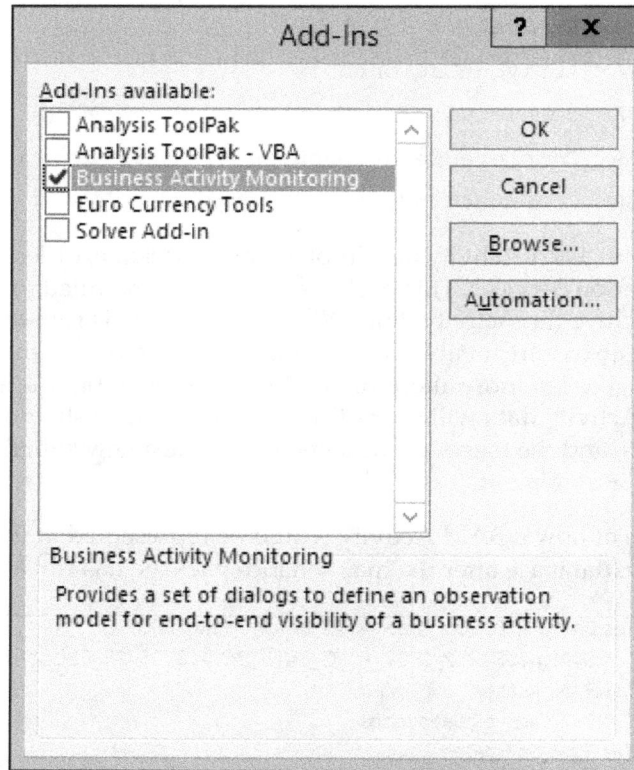

Make sure that **Business Activity Monitoring** is selected.

Now, BAM should be visible under the menu **Add-Ins**.

Creating an Activity inside Excel

We are going to make an Activity that extracts both the internal BizTalk metadata and the data from the actual XML message sent through BizTalk. For that, we will need to deploy a Schema and set up a Receive Port receiving the messages and a Send Port that subscribes to all the messages coming from the Receive Port.

The Schema should look as shown in the following screenshot (note that no Promotion of any kind is needed):

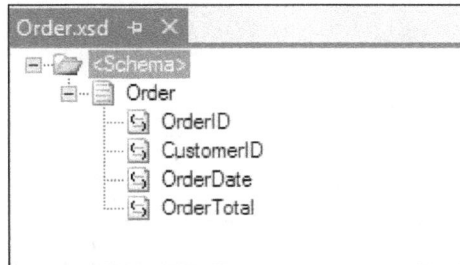

The Schema and XML documents used in this example do not have to be identical with the previous Schema. The two elements we will be working with are, **OrderID** and **OrderTotal**, both of which we want to collect to the BAM Activity we create.

Deploy the Schema and generate an instance of an XML document that matches the Schema. Set up a Receive Port and Send Port flow in BizTalk, use the **XMLReceive** Pipeline on the receive side, and verify that the flow is working.

Now, we will make an Activity called **ReceiveOrder** as follows:

1. Open Excel, and create a new Activity by clicking on **Add Ins | BAM | BAM Activity** as shown in the following screenshot:

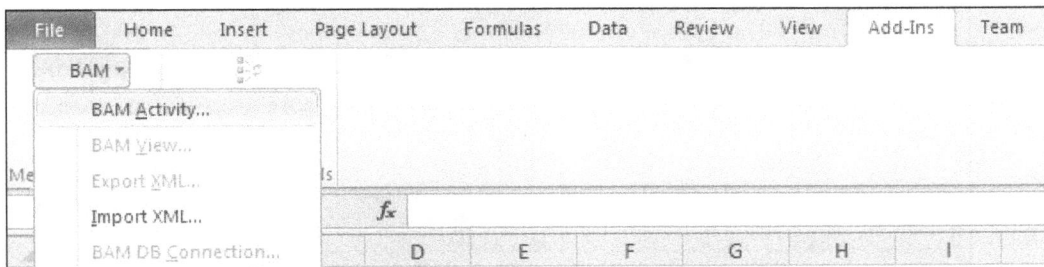

2. Select **New Activity**.

3. In **Activity** name, write `ReceiveOrder`.

4. Click on **New Item**, and create **OrderID** as shown in the following screenshot:

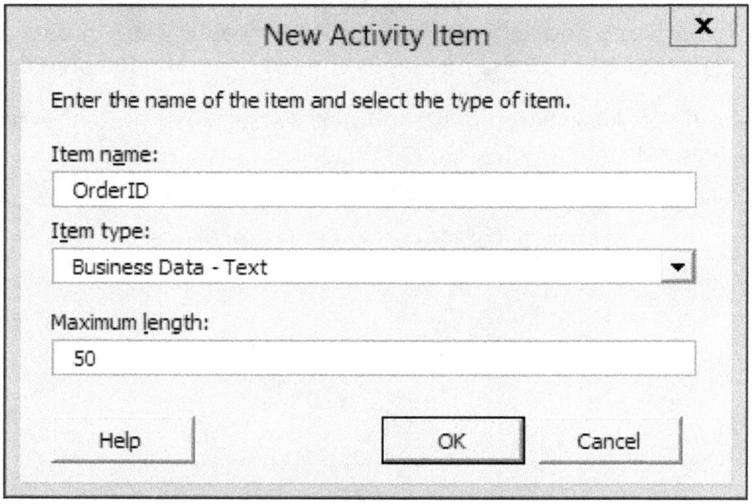

5. Create three more items as shown in the following screenshot:

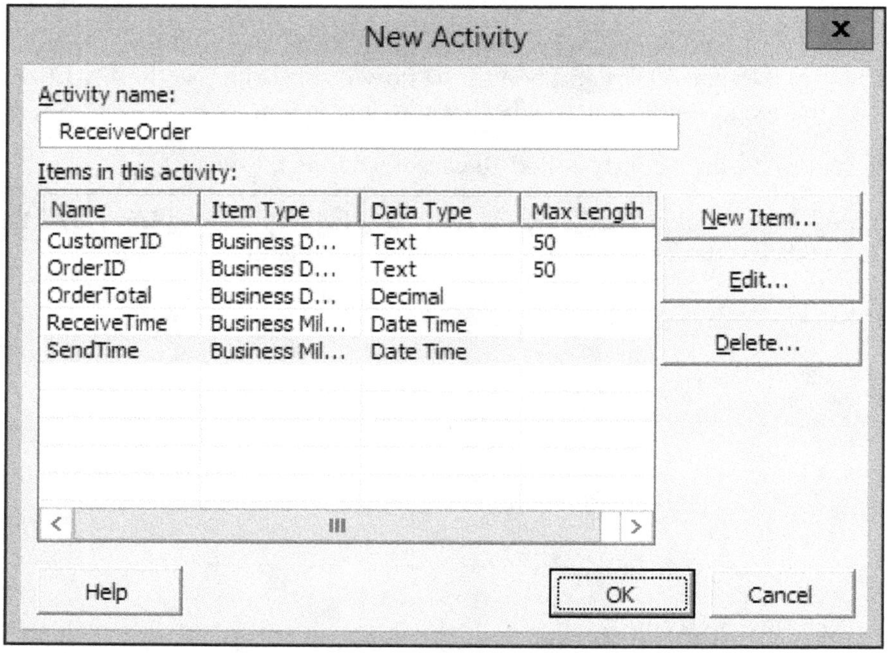

6. Click on **OK** twice.

7. A welcome screen for creating views is now shown. If no views are needed, we can click on **Cancel** at this time, but often at least one view per Activity is needed if the data is to be used in the BAM Portal.

8. Click on **Next**.

9. Click on **Next** again (**Create a new view** should be selected).

10. Enter a view name (vwReceiveOrder), and select the **ReceiveOrder** Activity.

11. Click on **Next**.

12. Select all items to be present in the view.

13. Click on **New Duration**. Since our Activity has two milestones (**ReceiveTime** and **SendTime**), we can create a duration called **TimeInBizTalk** which will be the difference between the two milestones. Make sure that **Time resolution** is **Second** as shown in the following screenshot:

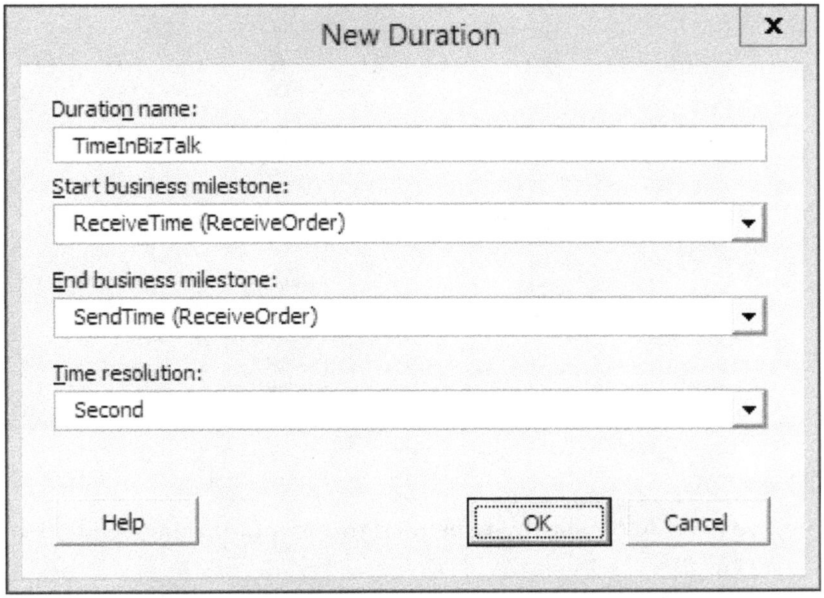

14. Click on **OK** and then **Next**.

15. In the **Aggregation Dimensions and Measures** window, we will create a pivot table that shows the number of orders received, grouped by the **CustomerID** and also the average order total per customer.

16. First, we will create the customer as a dimension. Select **New Dimension**.

17. Name the dimension as **Customer**, select **Data dimension**, and add **CustomerID**, as shown in the following screenshot:

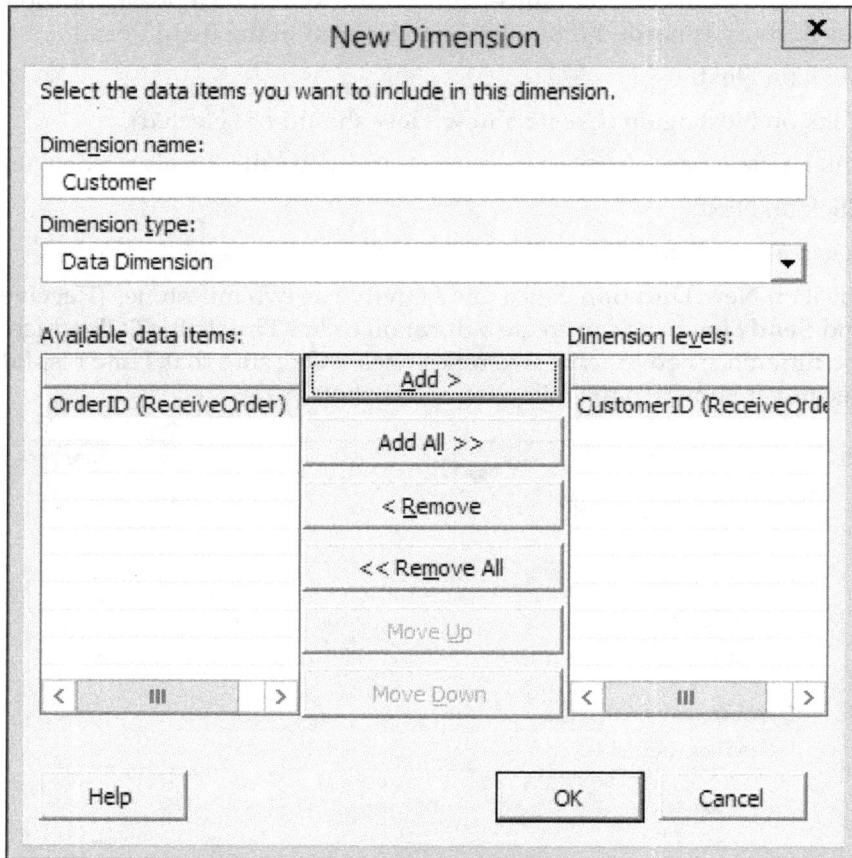

18. Click on **OK**.

19. Now, we need two measures: the total number of orders received and the average order total.

20. Click on **New Measure**.

21. In **Measure name**, type in `TotalReceived`, select **Count**, and set **Base activity** to **ReceiveOrder** as shown in the following screenshot:

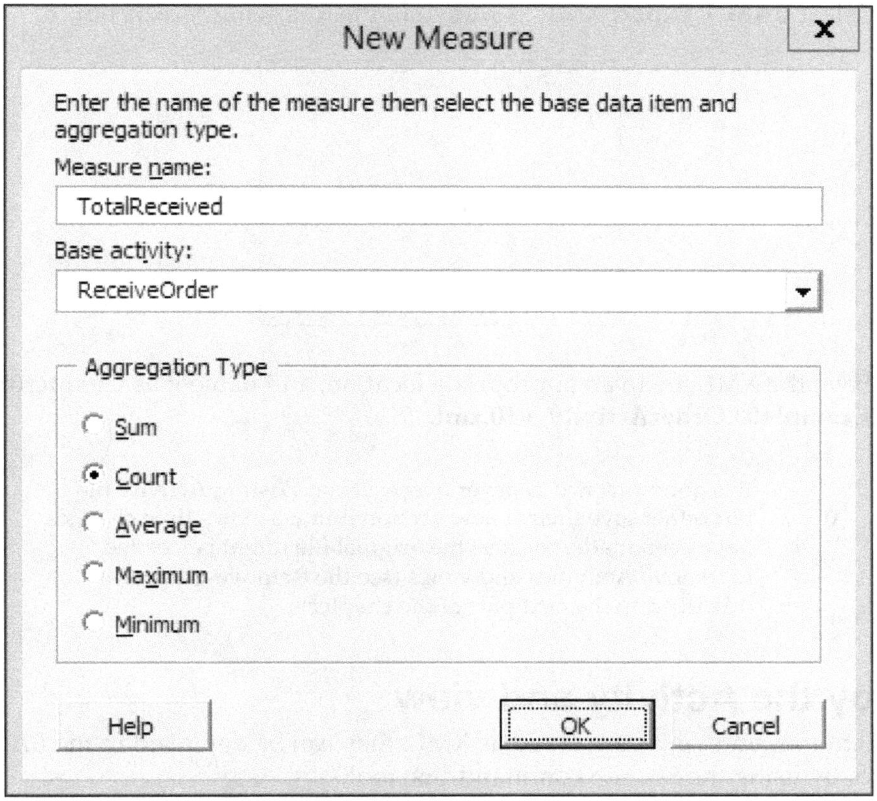

New Measure   X

Enter the name of the measure then select the base data item and aggregation type.

Measure name:

TotalReceived

Base activity:

ReceiveOrder ▼

Aggregation Type

○ Sum

◉ Count

○ Average

○ Maximum

○ Minimum

Help   OK   Cancel

22. Click on **OK**.

23. Now, create another measure for the order total average. Select **New Measure**.

24. Name the measure as **AverageTotal**. Choose **Aggregation Type** as **Average** and **Base data item** as **OrderTotal (ReceiveOrder)**.

25. Click on **OK**.

26. Click on **Next**, **Next**, and **Finish**.

27. The pivot table now needs to be dimensioned.

28. On the right-hand side, under **PivotTable Field List**, check **Customer**, **TotalReceived**, and then **AverageTotal**.

29. Select **BAM | Export XML** as shown in the following screenshot:

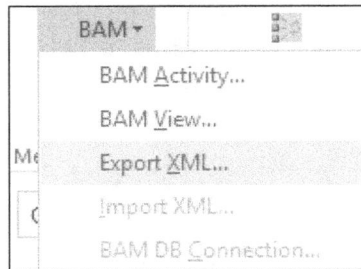

30. Save the XML file in an appropriate location, and name it as **Chapter08. Example03.OrderActivity_v10.xml**.

> It is good practice to never overwrite an existing Activity file but rather give them a new version number every time changes have been made, because the original file might be needed to remove Activities and views (see the **Remove-all** option described in the next part of the chapter).

Deploy the Activity and view

When Activities and views are saved as XML, they can be deployed in the BAM databases by using the bm.exe command-line tool.

If the BAM client tools are installed, the bm.exe tool can be located in the following folder %Program Files%\Microsoft BizTalk Server 2013\Tracking.

If we need to work with the tool a lot, it is recommended that the path is made into a system path so that it can be accessed by the command line, no matter where you are located.

The bm.exe command-line tool has three main options which are as follows:

- Deploy-all (deploy all Activities and views from scratch)
- Update-all (only deploy new Activities and/or views; updating existing Activities and/or views are only allowed if no existing items are updated or deleted)
- Remove-all (removes all Activities and views previously deployed; the XML file used must match the Activities and views in the database)

1. For deploying the Activity and view created earlier, locate the XML file that was exported from Excel, and run the following command (remember that the Tracking folder needs to be in the system path for easy access):

```
Administrator: C:\Windows\system32\cmd.exe                          _  □  x

C:\BTS2013CertGuide\Chapter08\Chapter08-Example03\BAM>bm.exe deploy-all -definit
ionFile:Chapter08.Example03.OrderActivity_v10.xml
Microsoft (R) Business Activity Monitoring Utility Version 3.10.229.0
Copyright (C) Microsoft Corporation. All rights reserved.

Using 'BAMPrimaryImport' BAM Primary Import database on server 'WIN-3959LG7QODF'
...

Deploying Activity... Done.
Deploying View... Done.
Deploying Security... Done.

C:\BTS2013CertGuide\Chapter08\Chapter08-Example03\BAM>_
```

2. Once the Activity and view have been created, go to the `BAMPrimaryImport` database, and verify that five tables were created starting with the name `bam_ReceiveOrder`, and that five to seven views exist starting with `bam_vwReceiveOrder`.

3. With the Activity created, we now need to map the Activity items to the events and data inside our BizTalk flow so that BAM will pick up data and write it to our tables at certain points inside BizTalk.

Creating a Tracking Profile

To map the Activity to the events inside BizTalk, we use the **Tracking Profile Editor** tool that ships with BizTalk as follows:

1. Open the **Tracking Profile Editor**.

2. Select **Click here to import a BAM Activity Definition**.

3. Find the **ReceiveOrder** Activity in the list, use **Filter** if needed as shown in the following screenshot:

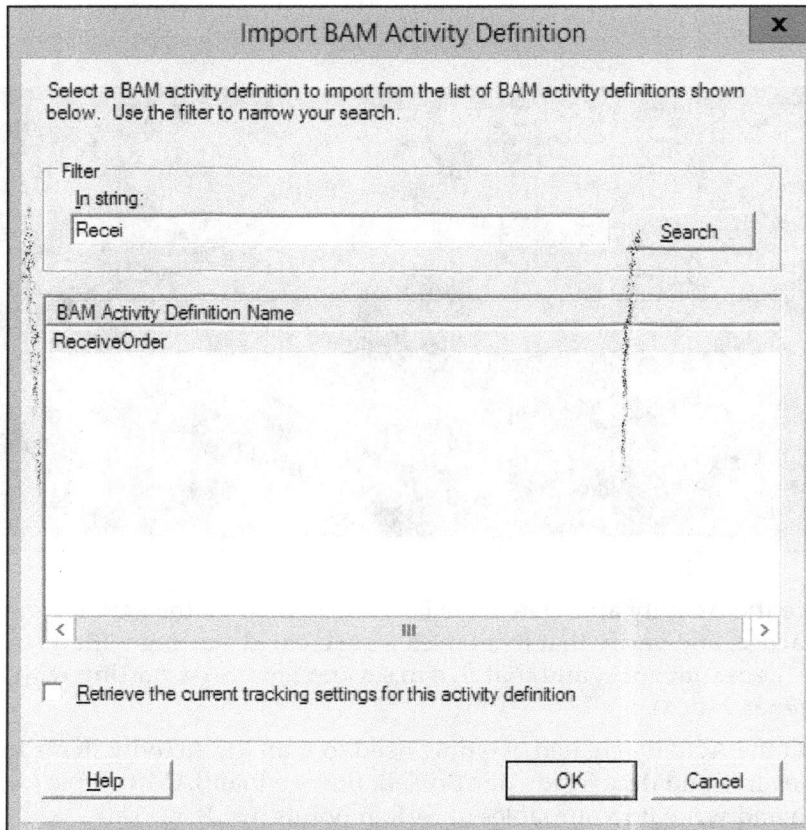

4. Select **ReceiveOrder**, and click on **OK**. We are now back in the **Tracking Profile Editors** main page, and the left-hand side should now contain our **ReceiveOrder** Activity with the items that need to be mapped. (Note that the **ActivityID** item is not required for what we are doing right now. It is primarily used for performing BAM relationships which are out of scope for this book). For now, we will map the following four items (all of them from the Receive Port):

    ○ **CustomerID** (taken from the message)

    ○ **OrderID** (taken from the message)

    ○ **OrderTotal** (taken from the message)

○   **ReceiveTime** (taken from the Receive port)

We will not map the SendTime milestone for now.

The first step will be to map the three items that are taken from the message. To do this, we will perform the following steps:

1. Click on **Select Event Source**, and select **Select Messaging Payload**.

2. A list of all deployed BizTalk assemblies that contain Schemas are now shown. Find the assembly previously deployed with the Order Schema, and click on **Next**.

3. Now, a list of Schemas inside the assembly is listed. In this case, there should be only one Schema; select the **Schema** and then click on **OK**.

4. The **Tracking Profile Editor** page should now look similar to the screen in the following screenshot:

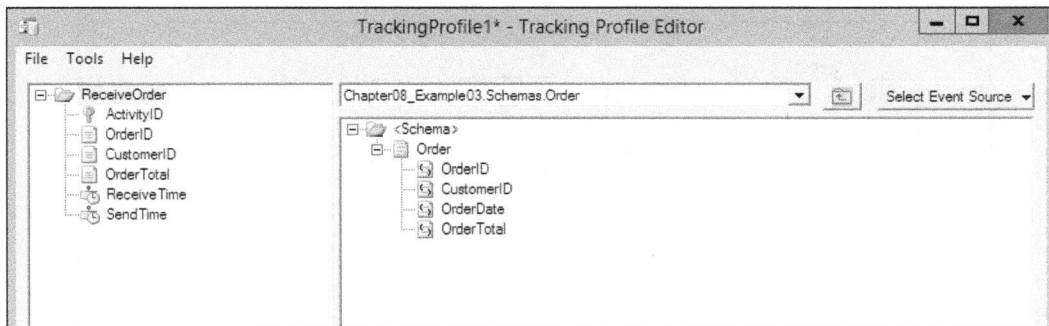

5. Three items, **OrderID**, **OrderTotal** and **CustomerID**, can now be mapped to the correct elements in the Schema. Carry out the following steps for all three items:

    a. Drag **OrderID** from the right-hand side (the Schema) to **OrderID** on the left-hand side (the Activity).

    b. Right-click on **OrderID** in the Activity, and select **Set Port Mappings** as shown in the following screenshot:

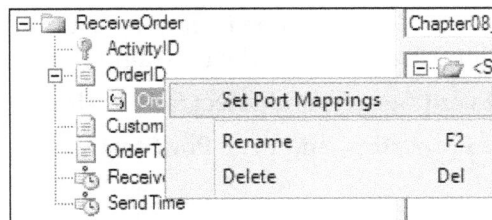

> c. In the **Select Ports** window, find the Receive Port created earlier and add it to the right-hand side, as shown in the following screenshot:

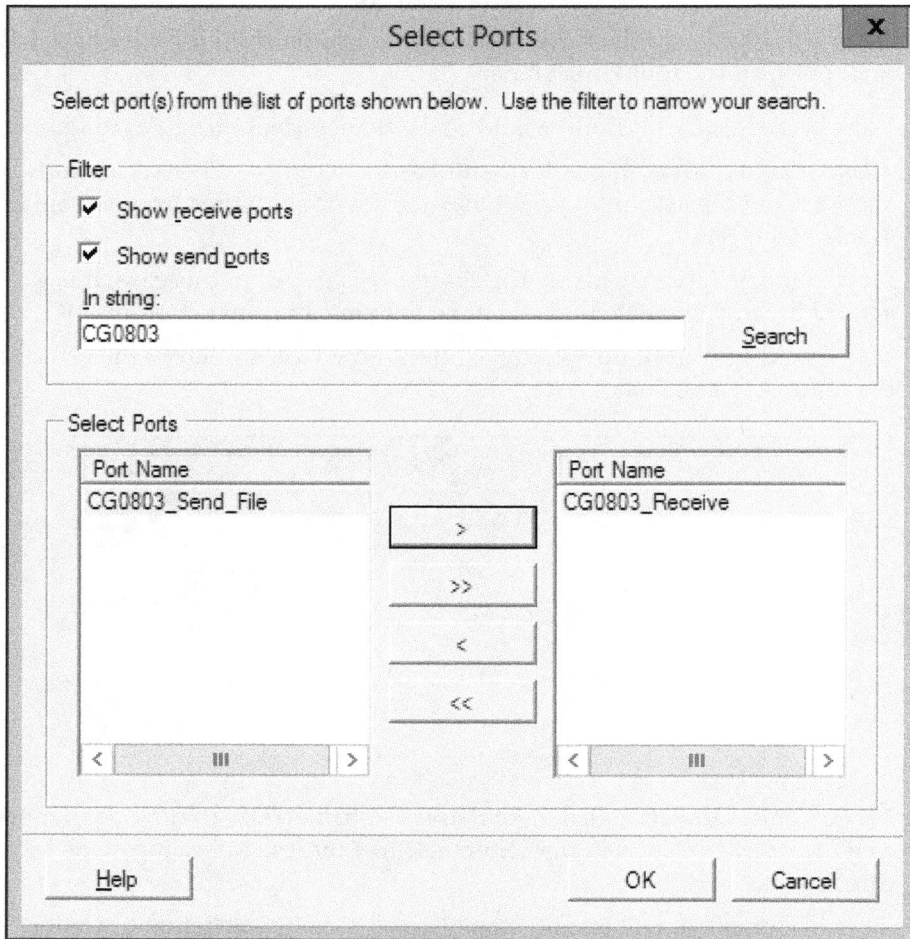

> d. Click on OK.
>
> e. Do the same for **OrderTotal** and **CustomerID**.

6. Now, we need to map **ReceiveTime** from the Port. This information is not found in the Order Schema but on the messaging properties in BizTalk.

7. Click on **Select Event Source**, and select **Select Messaging Property**.

8. Expand **MessageProperties**, and drag **PortStartTime** to **ReceiveTime** on the Activity.

9. Map the Port as we did with the previous three items. The **Tracking Profile Activity** window should now look similar to the following screenshot.

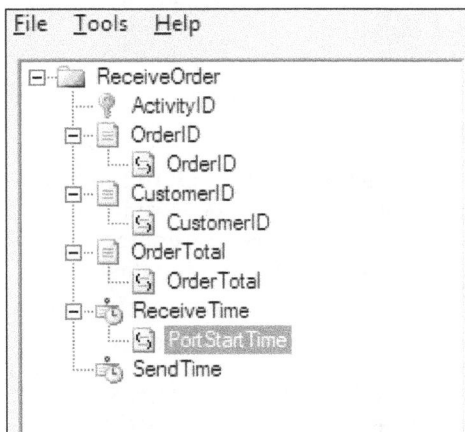

10. Save the Tracking Profile in the same folder where the Activity was exported to and name it `Chapter08.Example03.ReceiveOrder_Tracking_v10.btt`.

11. Go to the command line, and execute the following statement in the folder where the `.btt` file was saved:

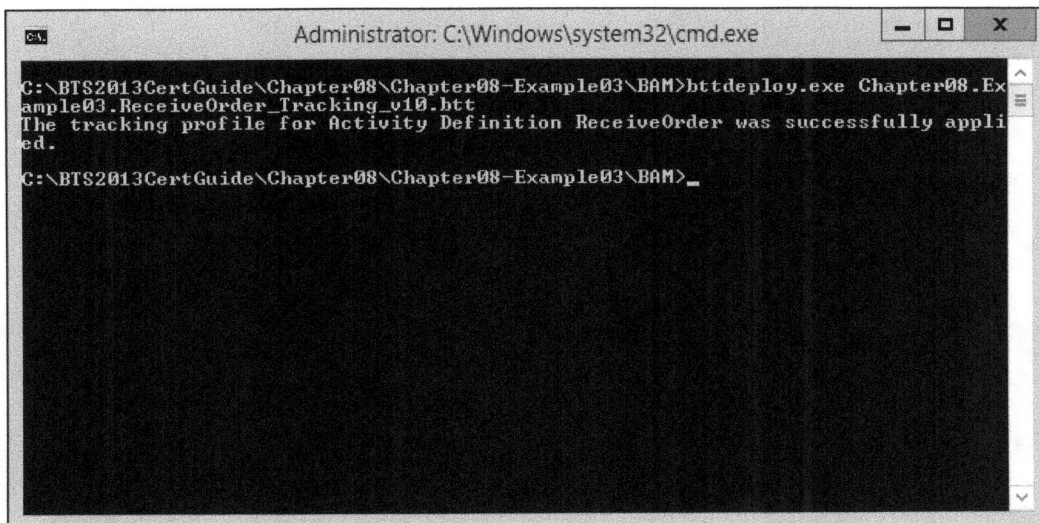

12. We are now ready to test the solution. Before sending messages through our BizTalk Application, verify that all Activity tables are empty by opening SQL Server Management Studio, and execute the following query in the `BAMPrimaryImport` database:

```
select * from
dbo.bam_ReceiveOrder_AllInstances
```

> The `select` statement should return zero rows. Before starting this test, ensure that at least one Host Instance of a Host with Allow Host Tracking enabled is running because a Tracking Host Instance is required to move data to the BAM tables.

The `_AllInstances` view is a union of the `_Active` and `_Completed` tables.

13. Submit a message through the Receive Port, and verify that a single row was inserted in our Activity table by executing the previously mentioned SQL again. Now, we need to map the last item, **SendTime**, in our Activity. Start by removing the Tracking Profile so that we can edit it and redeploy it. When removing a Tracking Profile in a production environment, all Receive Locations running in the affected applications should be disabled so that no BAM data will be lost.

14. Remove the Tracking Profile by typing the following command in the command prompt, as shown in the following screenshot:

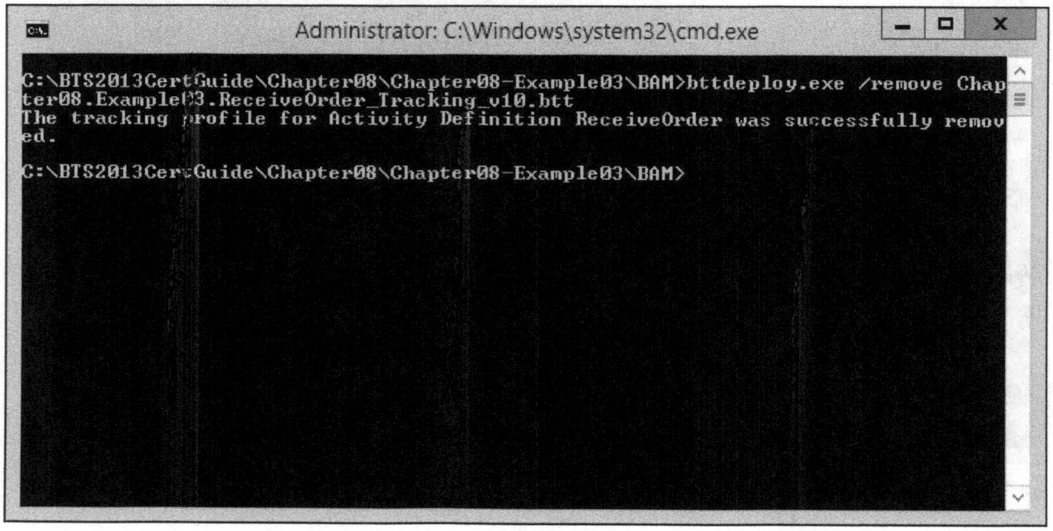

```
C:\BTS2013CertGuide\Chapter08\Chapter08-Example03\BAM>bttdeploy.exe /remove Chap
ter08.Example03.ReceiveOrder_Tracking_v10.btt
The tracking profile for Activity Definition ReceiveOrder was successfully remov
ed.

C:\BTS2013CertGuide\Chapter08\Chapter08-Example03\BAM>
```

Now that the Tracking Profile is removed, we can change the existing profile file.

1. Open the **Tracking Profile Editor** application again, and open the tracking file (.btt) saved before.

2. Open **Messaging Properties**, and drag **PortEndTime** to **SendTime** on the Activity.

3. Map **PortEndTime** to the Send Port of our Application.

4. Save the profile, and deploy it using bttdeploy just as we did earlier.

Now, test the solution again by submitting another message through BizTalk. Note that two rows are now inserted; one when the message went through the Receive Port, which also holds the data from the actual message, and another from the Send Port, which only holds **SendTime** and some internal data.

This is not what we wanted. The purpose of the Activity was to create one row every time an order entered our system and have some data written in the Receive Port and some data in the Send Port.

The reason this is happening is because the Receive and the Send Ports are different instances inside BizTalk, and BAM will see a new instance as a new row unless we tell it otherwise. What we need to do is to set up a Continuation.

Creating Continuations

What we will do now is tell BAM that the two instances (Receive and Send Ports) should be considered as one Activity entry, by using **OrderID** for correlating between the two instances as follows:

1. Remove the Tracking Profile created earlier.

2. Clear the Activity table by executing the following SQL statement in the BAMPrimaryImport database:

   ```
   delete from
   dbo.bam_ReceiveOrder_Completed
   ```

3. Open the **Tracking Profile Editor** application.

4. Right-click on the **ReceiveOrder** folder in the top left-hand side, and add a new **Continuation** and a new **ContinuationID**.

5. Rename both, and give them identical names as shown in the following screenshot:

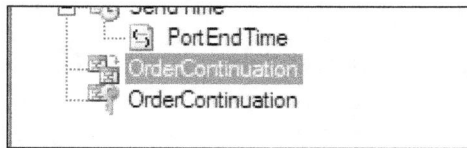

6. On the right-hand side, select the Order Schema (if not already chosen). Select the **OrderID** element.

7. Right-click on **Continuation,** and select **Associate Selected Data**. The **OrderID** should now appear as a child.

8. Do the same for the **ContinuationID** as shown in the following screenshot:

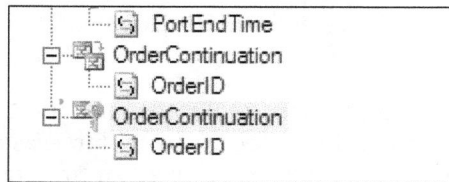

9. Map **OrderID** inside **Continuation** (icon with no key) to the Receive Port.

10. Map **OrderID** inside the **ContinuationID** (icon with a key) to the Send Port.

11. Save and deploy the Tracking Profile.

When testing the solution now, we should get a result with only one row being inserted in the Activity table with all five items populated. Verify that this is the case.

We can also check the view created earlier to see the duration (**TimeInBizTalk**).

Run the following SQL statement in the `BAMPrimaryImport` database:

```
select * from
dbo.bam_vwReceiveOrder_ViewReceiveOrder_View
```

There should now be a new column **TimeInBizTalk,** which should hold a very small number in seconds.

BAM Portal

Once the data starts being populated in the Activity tables, the BAM Portal can be used to track the data and view aggregations.

The BAM Portal ships with the BizTalk installation, and when set up correctly, should be accessible from a web browser by typing `http://BizTalkServerName/BAM/default.aspx`.

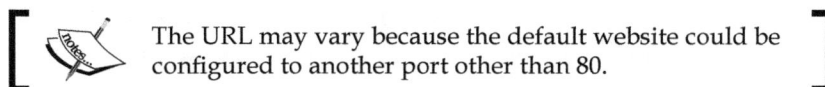

> The URL may vary because the default website could be configured to another port other than 80.

In the Portal, only created views (with or without aggregations) will be shown. The BAM Activities are not intended to have its data utilized directly but only through the views created in Excel.

The main reason for creating and using views are so that different business people can view the data relevant for them and also be given aliases for item names, and so on.

It is also possible to restrict the view of views to certain Windows Groups.

When opening the Portal, the user should be presented with the views that the user currently has access to.

The views are located on the left-hand side under **My Views** as shown in the following screenshot:

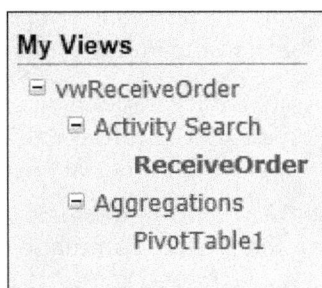

My Views
- vwReceiveOrder
  - Activity Search
    - **ReceiveOrder**
  - Aggregations
    - PivotTable1

Testing your knowledge

1. You have two customers, Customer1 and Customer2, who both receive EDI invoices. Both of them have agreed to receive invoices in a format decided by your company, so the same Map can be applied to each of their Send Ports. However, they do have different requirements concerning the metadata and envelope of the documents. What should you do?

   a. Make a new Schema and a new Map for Customer2. Deploy the Schema and Map, and use it on the Customer2 Send Port.

   b. Set up Agreements for Customer1 and Customer2 under BizTalk Parties, and link the Agreements to each Send Port.

   c. Create a Pipeline Component that can change the structure of the messages, and deploy it in a Pipeline before the **EdiAssembler** Pipeline has executed.

   d. Set up a Send Port Group, and add both Send Ports to the Group.

2. You have deployed a Policy in the Business Rule Composer that is being used by several BizTalk Orchestrations. You now need to change the Policy, and use some different values and boundaries. What should you do?

   a. In the Rule Composer, un-deploy, then un-publish the Policy, change it to the new values and boundaries, and republish and redeploy it.

   b. Make a new version of the Policy and publish it.

   c. Make a new version of the Policy and deploy it.

   d. Make a new version of the Policy and publish it. Make all Orchestrations that call the Policy point to the new version.

3. You need to create a BAM Activity for receiving invoices. The Business Managers have given you a list of required fields from the invoice messages they would like to extract. How should you create the Activity?

   a. In Excel, use the BAM Add-in to create an Activity file. Deploy the Activity by using the `bm.exe` command-line tool.

   b. In Excel, use the BAM Add-in to create an Activity file. Deploy the Activity by using the `bttdeploy.exe` command-line tool.

   c. In the **Tracking Profile Editor** application, select an Activity, and deploy it using the `bttdeploy.exe` command-line tool.

   d. In the **Tracking Profile Editor** application, select an Activity, and deploy it using the `bm.exe` command-line tool.

4. You have created and deployed a BAM Activity but no data is being inserted when messages runs through BizTalk. What should you do?

    a. In Excel, use the BAM Add-in to create a new Activity, and deploy it using the `bm.exe` command-line tool.

    b. In the **Tracking Profile Editor** application, link the Activity to the events and messages in BizTalk, and deploy the profile by using the `bm.exe` command-line tool.

    c. In Excel, use the BAM Add-in to create a new Activity, and deploy it using the `bttdeploy.exe` command-line tool.

    d. In the **Tracking Profile Editor** application, link the Activity to the events and messages in BizTalk, and deploy the profile by using the `bttdeploy.exe` command-line tool.

5. One of your customers is sending X12 EDI documents. You want BizTalk to process the documents. How should you approach this?

    a. Use the **EdiSend** Pipeline, EDI Schemas, and the Party/Agreement setup.

    b. Create a Flat File Schema for processing the X12 documents. Create a Flat File Pipeline and deploy both.

    c. Use the EdiReceive Pipeline, EDI Schemas and the Party/Agreement setup.

    d. Create a Custom X12 Assembler Pipeline Component.

Summary

This chapter has dealt with some of the extended capabilities of BizTalk by looking at Business Activity Monitoring, Business Rules Engine, and the EDI capabilities in BizTalk Server. This chapter should prepare the reader for the questions that might be asked regarding these topics.

Using Azure BizTalk Features

9

This chapter covers the *Identify the processes used to run a BizTalk Server environment as a Windows Azure Virtual Machine* and *Identify the processes used to enable integration using Windows Azure BizTalk Services* part of the Assessment. It will introduce the reader to some basic concepts of Microsoft Windows Azure as well as cover both running BizTalk in a virtual image on Azure and using the new **Windows Azure BizTalk Services (WABS)**. Using the new mapper, XML, and Flat File bridges as well as using the EDI Portal for receiving X12 documents will also be covered.

The following topics will be discussed:

- Setting up WABS
- Creating Bridges and Maps
- Sources and destinations in WABS
- The WABS Portal
- Using Virtual Machines
- Setting up BizTalk in a virtual environment (both single-server and multi-server farm)
- The EDI Portal

Understanding the Windows Azure BizTalk Services

WABS is not a new BizTalk Server in the cloud. It does, however, bear a lot of resemblance to the classic BizTalk Server Product and, as we shall see in this chapter, many of the BizTalk Server mechanisms have been ported to this new integration tool residing purely in the Cloud (Azure).

The product consists of the following main artifacts:

Artifact	Description
WABS Portal	A portal used for receiving and sending EDI documents from/to trading partners. As of now only X12 is supported, but support for EDIFACT has been announced by Microsoft. The Portal is also used for Tracking and maintenance of other artifacts.
Itinerary	Surface or canvas inside Visual Studio used for placing Bridges, Sources, Destinations, and connections between these.
Bridges	Used for receiving messages in Azure, processing them, transforming them, promoting properties, and routing the messages onwards.
Sources	Entry points for receiving messages. FTP, SFTP, and HTTP(S) are currently supported.
Destinations	Targets for delivering messages. Bridges, Services, FTP, SFTP, Topics/Queues (**Azure Service Bus**), Azure Blobs and on-premise systems (**LOB Services**) can be targets.
BizTalk Adapter Services	Used for targeting on-premise systems from WABS.
Schemas	Used the same way as in BizTalk Server; XML, Flat Files, and EDI is supported out of the box.
Maps	Used for transforming one Schema structure to another. As used in BizTalk, but heavily changed with many new features.

Let us first have a look at how to set up a BizTalk Service in Windows Azure.

Setting up a Windows Azure BizTalk Service

For setting up and using WABS, a Windows Azure account is required. It is out of scope for this chapter to discuss how this is obtained, so from here on it is assumed that the reader has such an account.

When setting up a BizTalk Service, the following underlying Windows Azure services are used by WABS:

- A SQL Azure Database for storing Tracking information
- An Azure Storage Account for Tracking messages and so on
- An Access Control Namespace used for security for accessing the BizTalk Service

> The SQL Azure Database and the Azure Storage Account can either be created up front, or you can have the BizTalk Service Setup Wizard create them for you.

Running the setup wizard in Windows Azure

As mentioned earlier, before running the setup, you will need an existing SQL Azure Database and an Azure Storage account, or you can have the setup wizard create this for you. This chapter will not go into details about these Azure Services. Also note that the use of these will result in the account being charged fees for using them.

1. In the Windows Azure Portal, choose **BIZTALK SERVICES** and click on **NEW**.

2. Navigate to **APP SERVICES | BIZTALK SERVICE | CUSTOM CREATE**.

NEW BIZTALK SERVICE – CUSTOM CREATE

Create BizTalk Service

BIZTALK SERVICE NAME

certguide2013   .biztalk.windows.net

DOMAIN URL

certguide2013.biztalk.windows.net

EDITION

Developer

REGION

North Europe

TRACKING DATABASE

Create a new SQL Database instance

SUBSCRIPTION

Pay-As-You-Go

3. Enter a unique name in the **BIZTALK SERVICE NAME** block and verify that this name is not already in use (the green check mark). Leave the **DOMAIN URL** as it is and choose **EDITION, REGION**, and whether you are using an existing **TRACKING DATABASE** or creating a new. Also select the appropriate **SUBSCRIPTION**.

Please note that the different editions are charged per month. Please refer to the pricing details for further information at the following site:

`http://www.windowsazure.com/en-us/pricing/details/biztalk-services/`

Also, it is possible to use custom domain names if needed, read more at the following site:

`http://blogs.msdn.com/b/biztalk_server_team_blog/archive/2013/07/11/custom-domain-names-with-biztalk-services.aspx`

4. Click on **Next**. Choose either an existing Database Server or a new. Provide a **SERVER LOGIN NAME** and **SERVER LOGIN PASSWORD**, and click on **Next** again, as shown in the following screenshot:

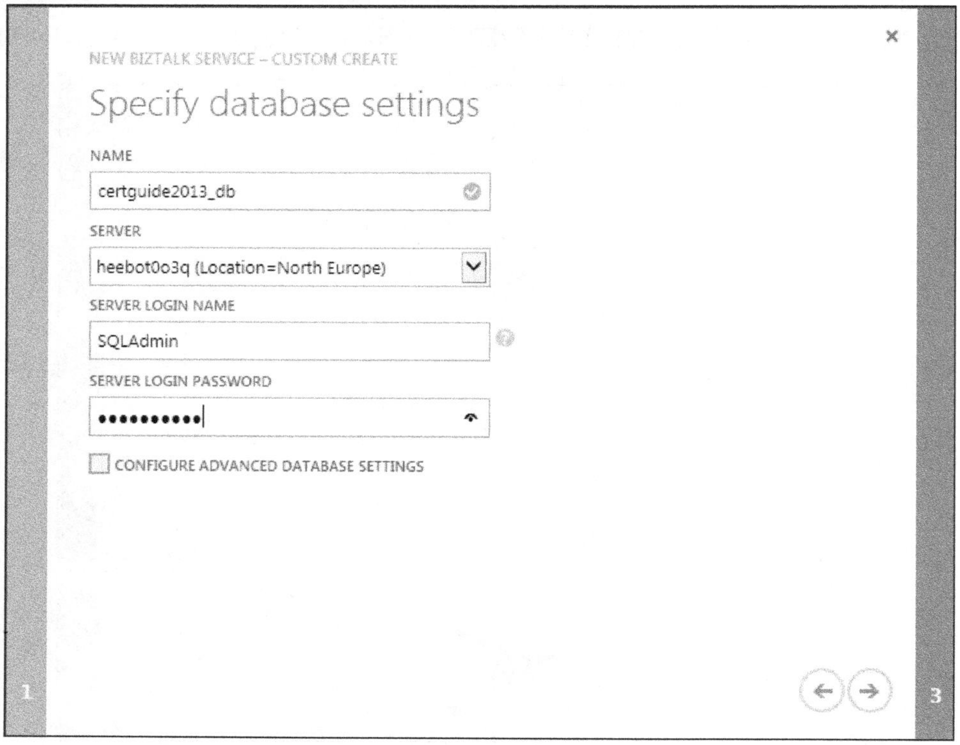

NEW BIZTALK SERVICE – CUSTOM CREATE

Specify database settings

NAME

certguide2013_db

SERVER

heebot0o3q (Location=North Europe)

SERVER LOGIN NAME

SQLAdmin

SERVER LOGIN PASSWORD

•••••••••

☐ CONFIGURE ADVANCED DATABASE SETTINGS

5. Choose either an existing storage account or create a new one, and then click on **Complete**.

After completion of the setup wizard, the BizTalk Service will be created. It might take a few minutes before the service creation is completed.

Exporting the WABS root certificate

The creation wizard has automatically created a self-signed certificate used for the SSL traffic (HTTPS) between developers, partners, and the WABS. For communicating with our BizTalk Service, we will now need to export a public version of this certificate and place it in the root certificate store of all machines needing to communicate with our WABS using HTTPS. To do this, perform the following steps:

1. In the Windows Azure Portal, choose **BIZTALK SERVICES** and select the newly created service.

2. The **DASHBOARD** dialog box should now appear (you may have to scroll down a bit):

quick glance

→ Update Tracking Database credentials

→ Update SSL Certificate

⊕ Download SSL Certificate

STATUS	CREATED
Active	2013/12/14 10:12:03

SERVICE URL	TRACKING DATABASE
certguide2013.biztalk.windows.net	certguide2013_db

PUBLIC VIRTUAL IP (VIP) ADDRESS	MONITORING/ARCHIVING STORAGE
137.135.245.163	ACCOUNT
	certguide2013bs

ACCESS CONTROL NAMESPACE
certguide20139003-bts

SUBSCRIPTION NAME
Pay-As-You-Go

EDITION
Developer

SUBSCRIPTION ID
0f4dd0dd-3278-47c3-9e2e-4f5fa2fa9b3e

LOCATION
North Europe

3. Take a note of the **ACCESS CONTROL NAMESPACE** generated while setting up the WABS, you will need it later.

4. Click on **Download SSL Certificate** and store the certificate for later usage.

5. Click on **CONNECTION INFORMATION** at the bottom of the Portal.

6. Copy the **DEFAULT ISSUER** (should be owner) and **DEFAULT KEY** and save them for later usage.

Installing Windows Azure BizTalk Services SDK

For developing artifacts in WABS, Visual Studio and the **Windows Azure BizTalk Services SDK** are required. To download the SDK, go to the following website:

`http://www.microsoft.com/en-us/download/details.aspx?id=39087`

Here you will find the SDK setup needed for your development environment:

- WindowsAzureBizTalkServicesSetup-x64.exe (for 64 bit environment)
- WindowsAzureBizTalkServicesSetup-x86.exe (for 32 bit environment)

Download the appropriate setup file for your environment. Notice that apart from the setup files, there are some additional migration tools and EDI Schemas.

Tool	File	Description
MicrosoftEdiXSDTemplates	MicrosoftEdiXSDTemplates. zip	Contains all X12 Schemas from version 204 to 503
BTMMigrationTool	Tools.zip	Migration tool used for migrating BizTalk Maps to the new WABS Maps
TPMMigrationTool	Tools.zip	Migration tool used for migrating existing Partners and EDI setup to the new WABS EDI Portal

Download these two zip files also, as we will need EDI Schemas later on in this chapter.

We will now run the setup wizard for setting up the SDK.

The SDK contains the following features:

- Microsoft WCF LOB Adapter SDK
- Microsoft BizTalk Adapter Pack (Both 32 and 64 bit will be installed if running on a 64 bit environment)
- Windows Azure BizTalk Services ASK
- Microsoft BizTalk Adapter Service
- PowerShell extensions for Microsoft BizTalk Adapter Service and Windows Azure BizTalk Service

Before installing the SDK, you also need to make sure that **.NET Framework 3.5.1** features are enabled and that **.NET Framework 4.5** is installed. As we will also examine the use of the LOB Adapters later on, a local SQL Server 2012 is required.

The latest SDK requires Visual Studio 2012; this is likely to change, and support for 2013 should be expected soon.

If you already have a previous version of the WABS SDK installed, you will first need to uninstall it.

Install the SDK by taking the following steps:

1. Extract the appropriate setup file.
2. The setup file should start automatically, otherwise start it manually (`WindowsAzureBizTalkServicesSetup.exe`).
3. Accept the license terms and click on **Next**.
4. Select all three features (**Developer SDK**, **Runtime**, **Tools**).
5. Click on **Install**.
6. After installation has completed, we will be prompted to configure a Management Service. (If you had installed a previous version of the SDK, the Management Service might already be configured, and you will therefore not be prompted for these next steps, just click on **Finish**).
7. For the identity of the Application Pool used by this service, choose **Network Service** and click on **Next**.
8. Specify your local SQL Server name and leave **Windows Authentication** enabled if your user has permissions to create a database, otherwise specify a user that has.

9. Click on **Next** and choose a **Master key password** for recovering the key used for encrypting sensitive data stored in the local configuration database (such as passwords). Click on **Next**.

10. Leave the **Port** at 8080 and uncheck **Use SSL to secure the management service**. Click on **Next**.

11. Configure the Management Service; the configuration wizard should now be completed.

To verify that the SDK is installed and working properly, open Visual Studio and make sure that you are able to choose the new **BizTalk Service** project type and perform the following steps:

1. Open **Visual Studio 2012** and select **New Project ...**.

2. Navigate to **Installed | Templates | Visual C#** and verify that the **BizTalk Services** category is present, as shown in the following screenshot:

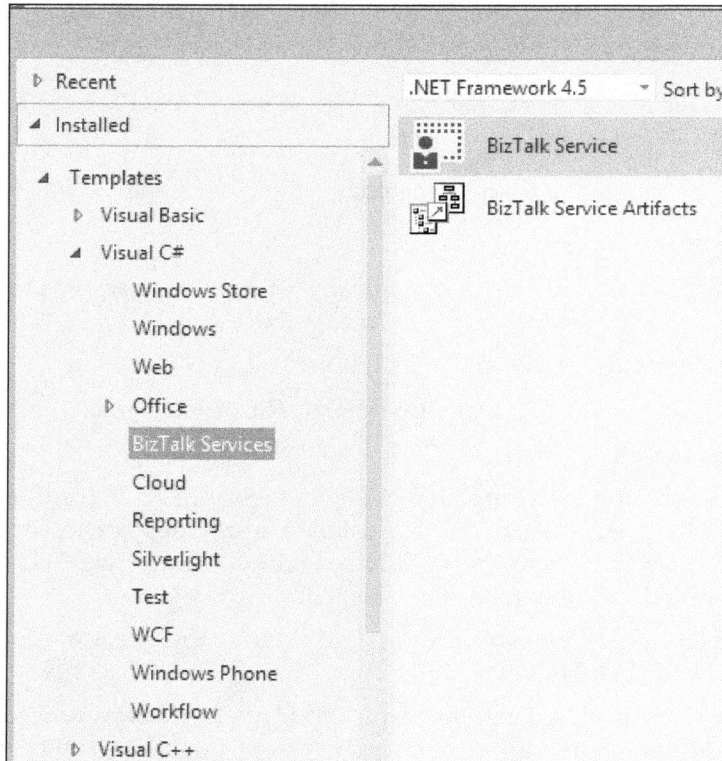

Creating a Bridge

In WABS, a bridge is used for transporting a message from one place to another. Unlike BizTalk Server, a message entering a bridge will always be routed to one destination only.

All bridges have an HTTPS entry point. Additional entry points, such as FTP and SFTP, can be added.

The following is a list of what can happen in a bridge:

- Receiving a message (message format could be XML, Flat File, or any custom format such as JSON, since custom Message Inspectors can be created). Message Inspectors are not covered in this book, but several examples can be found on the Internet. Refer to the following link on how to include custom code in bridges:

  http://msdn.microsoft.com/en-us/library/windowsazure/dn232389. aspx

- Decode the message to XML (from Flat File or custom formats).

- Validate the message with the Schemas specified in the bridge.

- Enrich the message by writing metadata to the message (similar to Property Promotion in BizTalk Server).

- Transform the message using Maps.

- **Encode** the message from XML to the target format (Flat File or custom format).

A bridge can also send messages to another bridge for further processing. A bridge will always act as one whole step, meaning that if a bridge cannot submit to its destination, the message will not be removed from the source.

Let us create a very simple bridge that picks up a text message from an FTP folder and drops the file in another FTP location.

For this example you will need an FTP site and three folders:

- In: This is used for submitting files to the bridge
- Out: This is used for dropping files from the bridge
- AltOut: This is used as an alternative file drop from the bridge

Also, a username that has full access to these folders and a corresponding password will be required.

1. Open Visual Studio, create a new project, and choose **Visual C# | BizTalk Services | BizTalk Service**.

2. Choose the Location C:\BTS2013CertGuide\Chapter09\Projects, name the Solution **Chapter09.Example01**, and name the Project **Chapter09. Example01.SimpleBridge**.

3. Click on **OK**.

4. You should now have a project with a blank canvas where a text reads **Drag a bridge to this diagram...**, and a toolbox that resembles the following screenshot:

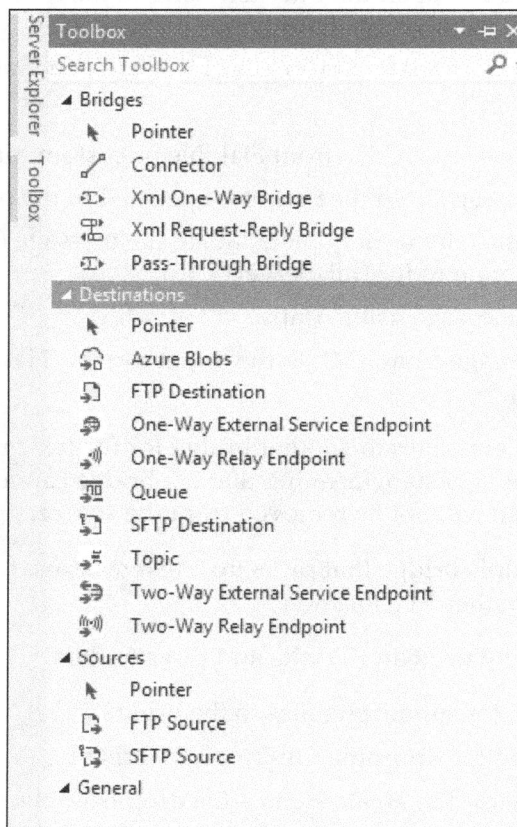

5. Drag a **Pass-Through Bridge** from the toolbox to the empty canvas.

6. Check the Properties for the created bridge and notice that the default **Entity Name** and **Relative Address** have been given the name **PassThroughBridge1**.

7. Change both names to **MySimpleBridge**.

8. We now need to create an FTP source so that the bridge will automatically pick up messages, whenever they are submitted from this source. In the toolbox, choose **Sources | FTP Source** and drag it onto the canvas to the left of your bridge.

9. Once dragged onto the canvas, notice that the source has a yellow exclamation mark, indicating that the source needs to be connected to a bridge. To do this, choose **Bridges | Connector** in the toolbox.

10. The connector is not used by dragging it to the canvas, but rather just selecting it and then dragging and connecting from the FTP Source to the bridge. You need to be precise when doing this, connecting from the red dot to the other red dot, as shown in the following screenshot:

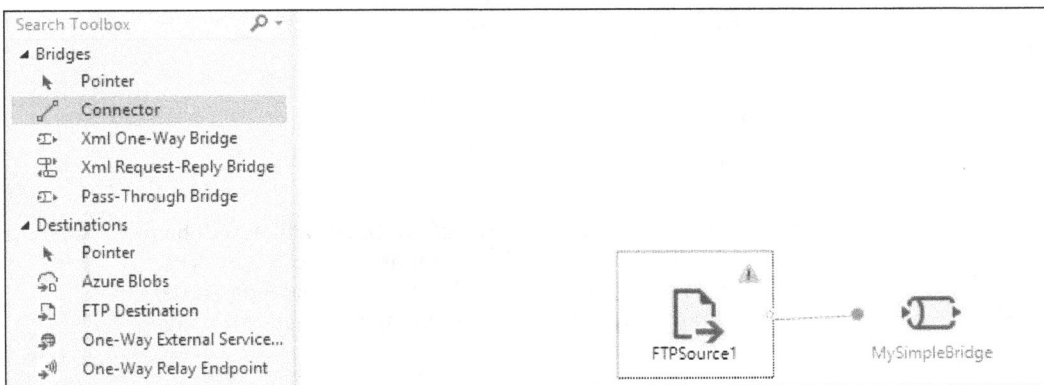

11. Rename the **FTPSource1** by selecting it, and change **FTPSource1** to **MySimpleFTPPickup** under **Properties | Entity Name**.

12. We now need to configure the FTP Source; select the source and configure the following properties.

Parameter	Value
File Mask	*.*
Folder Path	In
Initial Status	Stop
Password	[The FTP User's password]
Server Address	[The FTP Server address]

Parameter	Value
Use SSL	False
Username	[The FTP Username]

13. Your FTP Source properties should now look somewhat similar to this:

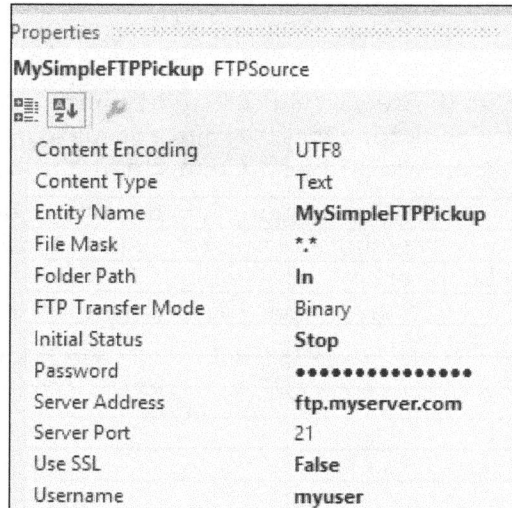

Properties	
MySimpleFTPPickup FTPSource	
Content Encoding	UTF8
Content Type	Text
Entity Name	**MySimpleFTPPickup**
File Mask	*.*
Folder Path	**In**
FTP Transfer Mode	Binary
Initial Status	**Stop**
Password	••••••••••••••
Server Address	**ftp.myserver.com**
Server Port	21
Use SSL	**False**
Username	**myuser**

> Note that the **Initial Status** is by default **Start**, which will have the source polling from the FTP folder as soon as the project is deployed. To gain better control of when the polling starts, we will set it to **Stop** instead and then manually start it using a PowerShell command.

14. In the toolbox, choose **Destinations | FTP Destination** and drag it onto the canvas on the right side of the bridge.

15. Connect the bridge to the destination.

16. Change the name of the FTP Destination from **FTPDestination1** to **MySimpleMainFTPDest**.

17. Set the appropriate properties, making it point to the Out folder; with a few variations your properties should resemble the following:

Properties

MySimpleMainFTPDest FTPDestination

Entity Name	**MySimpleMainFTPDest**
Folder Path	**Out**
Password	•••••••••••••••
Server Address	**ftp.myserver.com**
Server Port	21
Transfer Mode	ASCII
Use SSL	**False**
Username	**myuser**

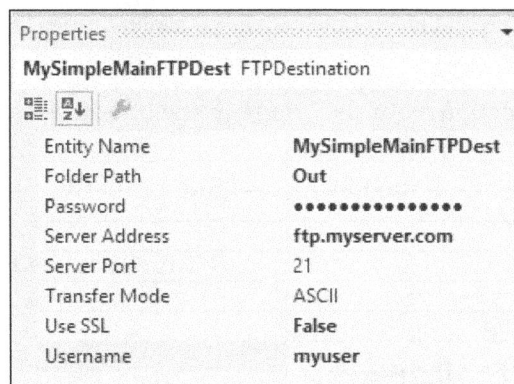

> As of now, the only place we can configure the FTP properties are in Visual Studio. In the future, other configuration options in the Azure Portal might be possible. This also means that, for now, if a password changes, you will need to change this in the Visual Studio project, and then redeploy the project.

18. Try building your project. You should receive a warning about the FTP destination name not being set and two errors stating something about filter conditions. Let's fix these issues.

Filter Condition and Route Ordering

A bridge can have from one to many destinations. Unlike a publish-subscribe engine, the message will only be routed to one of these destinations. This is done by setting a filter condition on each connection to the destinations and then prioritizing the destinations in the bridge's Route Ordering Table property.

All destination connections need a filter condition (which is also the reason we received the two errors before), and a bridge will always have each of its destinations in a prioritized **Route Ordering Table**.

When a message leaves the bridge, the filter condition for the destination connections will be evaluated in the order they appear in the Route Ordering Table. The first positive match will get the message, and the algorithm will stop, so that no more than one destination will get the message.

In our rather simple example from before, all we have is one destination, and we naturally want all messages to evaluate to that destination's Filter Condition.

1. Select the connection from the bridge to the FTP destination and locate the `Filter Condition` property.

2. Click on the ellipsis of the Filter Condition property, and click on the **Match All** radio button.

3. Click on **OK**. Notice that the **Filter Condition** now reads **1 = 1**, which will naturally always evaluate to true!

Setting the FTP filename

We are now left with a single warning message when building the project:

FTP Filename property needs to be specified at the Route Action stage

Although this is only a warning and the project will build and deploy, the solution would not work since the FTP destination will not have any name to assign to the file it is writing to the `Out` folder.

For now, we will just hardcode the `output.txt` filename. Later, we will change the solution so that the original filename is used, by using the Enrich feature in the bridge.

To set the FTP filename used by the FTP destination, we need to create a Route Action on the connection to the destination, by using the following steps:

1. Select the connection from the bridge to the FTP destination and locate the **Route Action** property.

2. Click on the ellipsis, and then click on **Add**.

3. In **Property (Read From)**, select **Expression** and type `'output.txt'`. Notice that single quotes are needed around the name.

4. In **Property (Write To)**, choose **Ftp** and **FileName**.

Add Route Action   x

Property (Read From)

○   Property **N**ame: ▼

●   E**x**pression: 'output.txt'

Destination (Write To)

Type: Ftp ▼

I**d**entifier: FileName ▼

O**K**   **C**ancel

5. Click on **OK** twice.

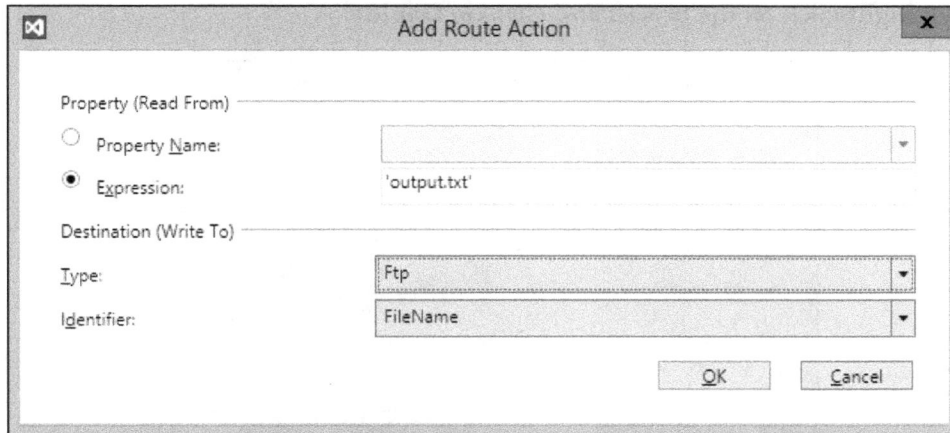

6. Build the project again, and verify that we are left with no warnings.

Deploying a Bridge

To deploy a project to the BizTalk Service in Azure, we need the following:

- The name of the BizTalk Service
- The name of the Access Control Namespace gathered earlier
- The Default Issuer
- The Default Key

To deploy, perform the following steps:

1. Click somewhere on an empty space on the canvas where the bridge, FTP source, and destination reside.

2. Under **Properties**, locate the **BizTalk Service URL**.

3. Replace **servicename** with the name of your BizTalk Service.

4. Right-click on the project and click on **Deploy**.

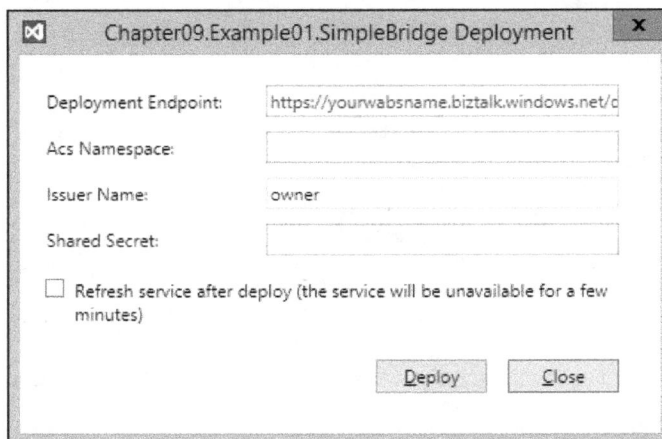

```
Chapter09.Example01.SimpleBridge Deployment      x

Deployment Endpoint:   https://yourwabsname.biztalk.windows.net/d

Acs Namespace:

Issuer Name:           owner

Shared Secret:

☐  Refresh service after deploy (the service will be unavailable for a few
   minutes)

                                         Deploy        Close
```

5. In **Acs Namespace**, type the namespace of the Acs.

6. Set **Shared Secret** to the token fetched previously from the Azure Portal.

7. Leave the **Refresh server after...** checkbox unchecked, as we will refresh the service manually from PowerShell if needed.

8. Click on **Deploy**.

> The certificate we downloaded earlier needs to reside in the certificate store **Local Machine/Trusted Root Certification Authorities**, since it was a self-signed certificate. If the certificate is not imported to this store, you will receive an error about not being able to establish trust relationship. To do this, you can use the following PowerShell command:
>
> ```
> Import-Certificate -FilePath [The path of the .cer
> file] -CertStoreLocation Cert:\LocalMachine\root
> ```

9. Confirm that two items were successfully deployed (the bridge and the source).

Now we need to verify that the bridge and the source have been deployed in the WABS, and then start the source so that it will commence picking up files from the **In** FTP folder.

Using PowerShell with BizTalk Services

When the Windows Azure BizTalk Services SDK is installed, a **PowerShell** module is also installed. We will utilize this module now to list our bridges and the source of these bridges. We will then check the source state and see how to start and stop the sources, by using the following steps:

1. Open **PowerShell** as administrator and import the BizTalk Service module, by executing the following syntax:

   ```
   import-module "C:\Program Files\Windows Azure BizTalk Services
   Tools\Microsoft.BizTalk.Services.Powershell.dll"
   ```

2. Verify that you now have several BizTalk Services commands by typing:

   ```
   Get-Command -Module Microsoft.BizTalk.Services.Powershell
   ```

We will be looking at several of these commands in this chapter. The first command we will use is **Get-AzureBizTalkBridge** to get a list of all bridges deployed in the BizTalk Service.

First, let us set a couple of variables that we will re-use several times:

```
$acsns = '[Name of the ACS Namespace]'

$in = '[The default issuer (owner)]'

$ik = '[The default key]'

$du = 'https://[The Biztalk Service name].biztalk.windows.net/
default'
```

> The loading of the module and the setting of these variables is only in scope as long as the PowerShell window is open. They will need to be executed again whenever PowerShell is started.

With all the parameters in place, we should now be able to list the bridges deployed.

```
Get-AzureBizTalkBridge –AcsNamespace $acsns -IssuerName $in -IssuerKey
$ik -DeploymentUri $du
```

Verify that the bridge **MYSIMPLEBRIDGE** is listed.

Now, let's list the sources of the bridge; in our case we just have one, namely, **MySimpleFTPPickup**.

```
Get-AzureBizTalkBridgeSource –AcsNamespace $acsns -IssuerName $in
-IssuerKey $ik -DeploymentUri $du -bridgepath MYSIMPLEBRIDGE
```

Verify that the source was listed and **Status** is **False (Stop)**.

Starting the bridge source

Now start the source by running the following command:

```
Start-AzureBizTalkBridgeSource –AcsNamespace $acsns -IssuerName $in
-IssuerKey $ik -DeploymentUri $du –BridgePath MYSIMPLEBRIDGE
```

You should receive a status saying:

All the sources in the pipeline '......' have been started.

Verify that the status is now **True (Start)** by running the
Get-AzureBizTalkBridgeSource command from before.

> To stop the source(s) again, run the following command:
> ```
> Stop-AzureBizTalkBridgeSource –AcsNamespace $acsns
> -IssuerName $in -IssuerKey $ik -DeploymentUri $du –
> BridgePath MYSIMPLEBRIDGE
> ```

Restarting the BizTalk Service

After redeploying existing artifacts (bridges, schemas, maps, and so on) to a BizTalk Service, a restart may be required for the changes to take place. To do this run the following command:

```
Restart-AzureBizTalkService –AcsNamespace $acsns -IssuerName $in
-IssuerKey $ik -DeploymentUri $d
```

Restarting the Service takes a while and is not always required. Therefore, first try to validate if the changes have taken effect before doing a restart.

Testing the bridge

Now that the source has started, we are ready to submit a file to the `In` folder and verify that the file is sent to the `Out` folder. Place a file in the `In` folder and verify that the file is removed and another file (`output.txt`) is placed in the `Out` folder.

> If the file is not removed within approx. one minute, then it is likely that something is wrong (wrong credentials or some misspelling when configuring either the source or destination FTP in Visual Studio). To debug this, we need the WABS Portal associated with the BizTalk Service (refer to *Using the WABS Portal | Tracking* for further details).

If you don't want the source to keep polling from the `In` folder continuously, stop it by using the PowerShell command described earlier.

Enriching data

Now let us write the incoming filename to a metadata property on the message, and use this property both for the destination filename and for routing.

1. If not already open, open your project created before. On the canvas, double-click on the bridge and select the inner **Enrich**.
2. Under **Properties**, click on the ellipsis of the **Property Definitions**.
3. Click on **Add**.
4. Fill in the **Add Property** screen as follows (this will fetch the filename from the FTP source and place it in a custom property named `OriginalFileName`):

5. Click on **OK** twice.

6. Build the project.

> This is only an example used to show how the various aspects of the bridge work. It might not be the best choice to assume that a message came from an FTP source, since other means of transportation (for example, HTTPS) could have been delivering the message. In that case we would not get anything written to the OriginalFileName property.

7. Back at the canvas, select the destination connection, and choose **Route Action**.

8. Edit the existing route action and change **Property (Write To)** from **Expression** to **Property Name**, and choose **OriginalFileName**.

9. Click on **OK** twice.

10. Make sure the source is in a stopped state.

11. Redeploy the project to Azure, start the source again.

12. Delete the output.txt file in the Out folder and submit a new file named Hello.txt.

13. Verify that the file is picked up (within a minute) and that the Out folder now contains a file named Hello.txt.

Bridge Routing

As mentioned earlier, it is possible to have several destinations from a single bridge, and based upon routing conditions, route the message to one of these destinations.

Let us now create a second destination on our already created bridge. Make that destination point to the AltOut folder, and route all files named Alt.txt to this folder and all others to the original Out folder.

1. Create a second FTP destination called **MySimpleSecondFTPDest**.

2. Give the new destination the same properties as the first destination created, but use the FTP AltOut folder instead of Out.

3. Connect the bridge to the new destination.

4. In the connection's **Route Action**, write to the FTP filename from the OriginalFileName metadata property just as we did with the first destination.

5. In the connection's Filter Condition, specify the following:

    OriginalFileName = 'Alt.txt'

6. Click the bridge and choose the **Route Ordering Table** property.

7. Make sure that `MySimpleSecondFTPDest` is placed first in the table so that it will be evaluated first.

8. Build the project.

9. Stop the source in PowerShell.

10. Redeploy (remember that restarting the BizTalk Service might sometimes be required for the changes to take effect, but not always).

11. Start the source again.

12. Clear the `Out` folder if any files are present.

13. Drop a file (`Hello.txt`) to the `In` folder and verify that it is picked up and sent to the `Out` folder.

14. Now drop a file (`Alt.txt`) to the `In` folder and verify that this time it is sent to the `AltOut` folder instead.

15. Stop the source again so that it doesn't poll continuously.

Working with XML in bridges

Let us now turn the attention onto working with XML. We will be working with the following XML and Schema. Refer to *Chapter 2, Developing BizTalk Artifacts – Creating Schemas and Pipelines*, for more information about working with XML and creating Schemas based on XML.

```xml
<?xml version="1.0"?>
<LoanApp xmlns="http://Chapter09_Example02.Schemas">
    <ApplicationID>12345</ApplicationID>
    <CustomerID>665</CustomerID>
    <Amount>3000</Amount>
</LoanApp>
```

Creating a new Schema

We will now add a Schema to the existing BizTalk Service project for receiving XML messages in an Xml bridge by using the following steps:

1. In your BizTalk Service project, add a new Item and choose **Schema**.

2. Give your Schema an appropriate name and make it match the XML shown in the previous screenshot. Note that the **Amount** element should have a numeric type, int, or decimal.

3. Build your project.

Your Schema should resemble the following structure and types:

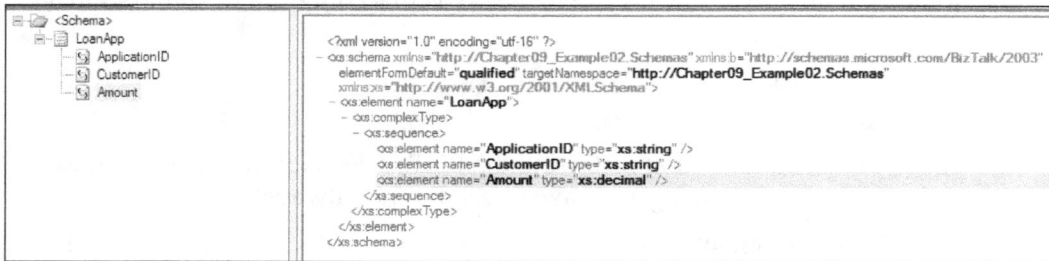

With a Schema in the project, we can now introduce an **Xml One-Way Bridge**. An Xml bridge typically takes either XML or Flat File as input and requires that the Schema representation for the messages received is configured in the bridge.

We now need to add an Xml bridge, associate the newly created Schema with the bridge, make sure that the bridge only picks up XML files from our In folder, and that the existing bridge only picks up text files.

1. From the toolbox, drag an **Xml One-Way Bridge** onto the canvas.
2. Change both **Entity Name** and **Relative Address** to **MyXmlBridge**.
3. Make a connection from the new bridge to **MySimpleMainFTPDest**, and choose **Match All** for **Filter Condition**.
4. In **Route Action**, set the FTP filename to `'output.xml'`.
5. Double-click on the **Xml Bridge**. Click on the big plus-sign inside **Message Types**.
6. Select the **LoanApp** Schema and click on the right arrow to add the Schema.
7. Click on **OK**.
8. Create a new FTP Source and name it `MyXmlFTPPickup`.
9. Connect the Source to the Xml Bridge.
10. Change the existing **MySimpleFTPPickup's** File Mask from ***.*** to ***.txt**.
11. Configure the new Source with the same properties as the original one, change the **File Mask** from ***.txt** to ***.xml**. Also change the **Content Type** from **Text** to **Xml**.

Your canvas should appear similar to the following diagram:

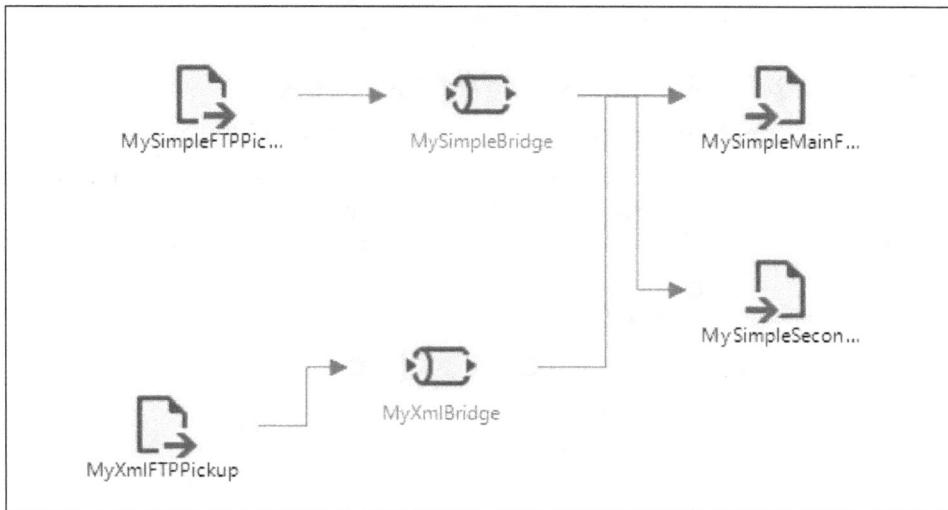

12. Redeploy the project.
13. Start the new Source and drop a valid XML file matching the Schema in the In folder.
14. Verify that the file is processed and dropped in the Out folder.
15. Delete all files from the Out folder.

Using the BizTalk Adapter Services

The BizTalk Service introduces the ability to connect from Azure onto local on-premise systems by using the following components:

- The BizTalk Adapter Pack (5 Adapter types are available, which are exposed as a local service and can therefore be used to send message to the system(s)).
  - ° SQL Server
  - ° Siebel
  - ° SAP
  - ° Oracle DB
  - ° Oracle EBS

- Azure Service Bus Relay Service (used for exposing an on-premise service in Azure, used for the bridge to communicate with the local LOB Service when using the LOB Services in BizTalk Services).

To do the following exercise, you will need the following:

- A **Service Bus Namespace** in your Azure account and the owner's token.
- A local SQL Server with a database containing a table for submitting Loan Applications. Also, a SQL user with db_owner rights for the database and the password for the user. The table we will be working with can be created as follows:

```
create table dbo.LoanApp
(
  ID int identity(1,1) primary key,
  ApplicationID varchar(50),
  CustomerID varchar(50),
  Amount decimal(18,2),
  Inserted DateTime
)
```

Creating a Service Bus Namespace

In the following walk-through, we will create a Service Bus Namespace and fetch the owner's token.

1. In the Windows Azure Portal, select **SERVICE BUS** and click on **CREATE**.
2. In **NAMESPACE NAME,** type a new unique namespace and verify that it is indeed unique.
3. Select an appropriate **REGION**, and click on the check mark.
4. The namespace might take a second or two to complete.
5. Once completed, click on the newly created namespace.
6. Select **CONNECTION INFORMATION**.
7. Copy the **DEFAULT KEY** for later use.
8. Close the popup again.

> Everything created in Azure has a price model and will cause the account owner charges.

Adding an LOB Target

To add an LOB Target, do the following:

1. In the previously created project, open the **Server Explorer**.

2. Right-click on **BizTalk Adapter Services** and choose **Add BizTalk Adapter Service**.

3. Change **[host]** to your local computer name.

4. Click on **OK**.

5. Expand the newly created service and locate **SQL** under **LOB Types**.

6. Right-click on **SQL** and choose **Add SQL Target**.

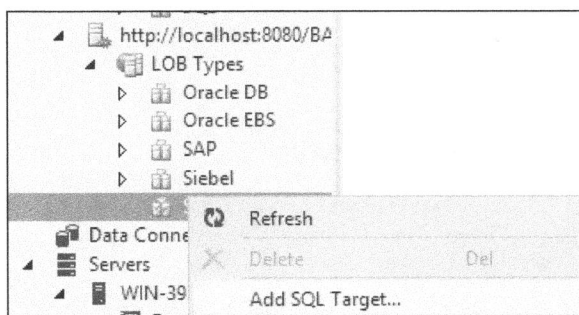

7. Click on **Next>** on the welcome screen.

8. Specify the name of the SQL Server, the **Instance** if needed, and the **Catalog** (Database).

9. Select **Use the following username and password** and specify the db_owner user and password.

10. Click on **Next>**.

11. Expand the icon under **Select operations** and expand **Tables**.

12. Select **[dbo].[LoanApp]** and click on the right arrow to select the table.

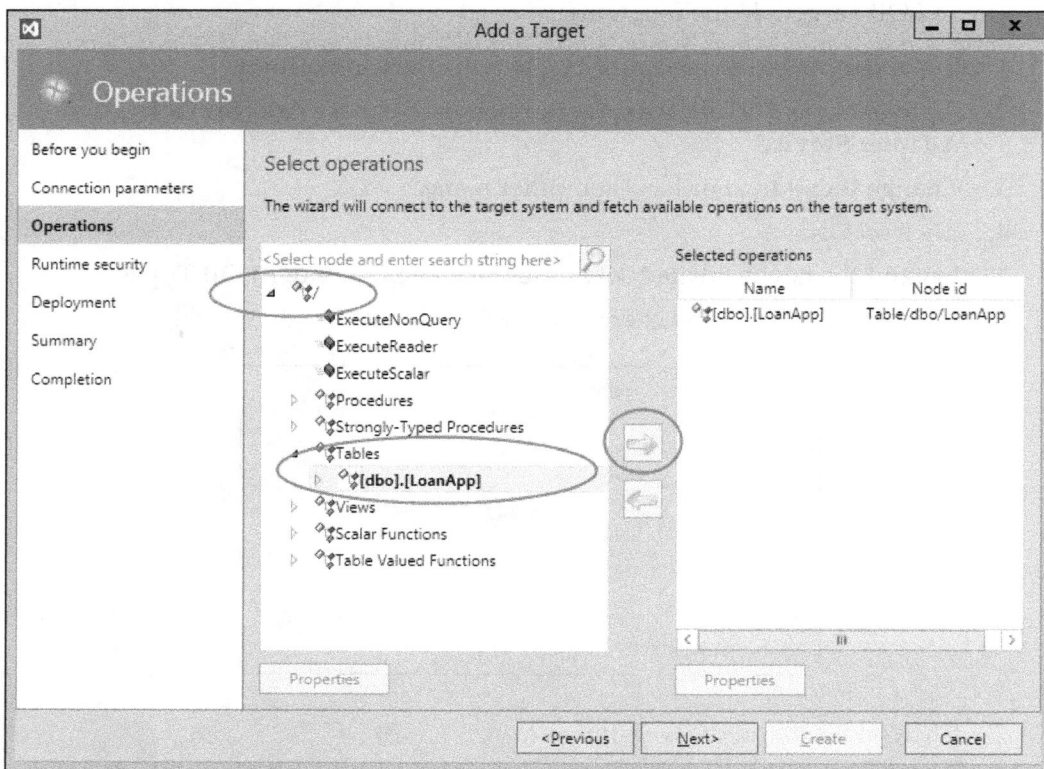

13. Click on **Next>** twice.

14. Under **Deployment**, create a new relay target and specify your service bus account and the owner and token created earlier. Also specify a path and sub-path, as shown in the following screenshot:

15. Click on **Next>** and then click on **Create**.

16. When completed, click on **Finish**.

17. In the **Server Explorer** under the **SQL LOB Type**, there should now be a Enabled icon (green arrow) with the name **servicebus_namespace/lobsql/loanapp**.

18. Drag the newly created type onto the canvas to the right of **MyXmlBridge**.

19. In the Solution Explorer, expand the **MessageFlowItinerary.bcs** file and locate the **lobsql_loanapp.config** file.

20. Double-click on the **config** file.

21. The XML configuration should now appear. Locate **[Specify issuer name]** and replace it with owner.

22. Locate **[Specify issuer secret]** and replace with the service bus owner token.

23. Save the `config` file and close it again.

We now want to connect the Xml Bridge (MyXmlBridge) to the AppLoan LOB Service, route all loan application with an amount less than 1000 directly to the SQL table, and all others will need to still be routed to our Out FTP folder.

24. Double-click on the Xml bridge. Select the inner **Enrich** between **Validate** and **Transform**.

25. Under **Properties**, select **Property Definitions** and click on **Add**.

26. Select Xpath as Type. In Identifier, specify the following Xpath (or similar if your Schema does not match this):

```
/*[local-name()='LoanApp' and namespace-uri()='http://
Chapter09_Example02.Schemas']/*[local-name()='Amount' and
namespace-uri()='http://Chapter09_Example02.Schemas']
```

27. Select the **LoanApp Message Type** and **Write To** of the LoanAmount property of the **Double** type.

What we have done now is made sure that the bridge will write the Amount element taken from the LoanApp XML into the metadata property of LoanAmount. We will then use this property to decide whether to send the message directly to our SQL Server, or to send it to the FTP folder. When sending to the LOB Service, we will need to convert the LoanApp XML into XML understood by the SQL LOB Service. We will do this by creating a new SQL Bridge, and applying a transformation (Map) to this bridge, map from our LoanApp format to the SQL Service format.

28. Drag a new Xml One-Way Bridge onto the canvas to the right of **MyXmlBridge**.

29. Name both **Entity Name** and **Relative Address** as MySqlBridge.

30. Make a connection between **MySqlBridge** and **lobsql_loanapp**.

31. Select **Filter Condition** for the connection and choose **Match All**.

32. Make a connection between **MyXmlBridge** to **MySqlBridge**.

33. Select **Filter Condition** for the newly created connection and specify the `LoanAmount < 1000` condition.

34. In the **Route Ordering Table** of **MyXmlBridge,** make sure that the **Endpoint Alias** of **lobsql_loanapp** is evaluated first by moving it to the top of the list.

Creating a Map

We now need a map that transforms a LoanApp to the XML expected by the **LOB Service** to insert data into the LoanApp table.

First we need a Schema representation of the XML expected by the SQL Service.

1. In **Server Explorer,** right-click on the SQL Service created earlier and select **Add schemas to…**.

2. Click on **OK.** Your project should now have a folder named **LOB Schemas**.

3. Locate the Schema that contains the phrase **TableOperation** and examine it.

4. Notice that we have a **Delete, Insert, Select,** and Update operation that we can utilize for manipulating data in the **LoanApp** table. We will be using the Insert operation.

5. Add a new Map to your existing project and name it `LoanApp_to_InsertSQLLoanApp.trfm`.

6. Click on **Open Source Schema,** and select the **LoanApp Schema** created previously.

7. Click on **Open Destination Schema,** and select the **LOB Schema** containing **TableOperation**.

8. Select **Insert** and click on **OK.**

9. Expand both Schemas.

10. Map **ApplicationID** from the Source to the same element in the destination Schema by dragging it.

11. Do the same for **CustomerID** and **Amount**.

12. For the element Inserted, we will need a Functoid for inserting today's date and time.

13. In the toolbox, locate **Date / Time Operations** and select the **Generate Date Time** Functoid, dragging it onto the canvas between the source and destination Schema.

14. Double-click on the Functoid on the canvas and type the following in **Format**: yyyy-MM-ddThh:mm:ss

15. Connect the Functoid to the **Inserted** element on the target Schema.

16. Close the Map and build the project.

> Notice that we left the ID element on the target side blank. This is because it is an identity column and will be seeded automatically by SQL Server.

New Functoids

Although the new mapper bears a lot of resemblance to the classic BizTalk mapper, the Functoid toolbox has been changed quite a bit. We will not go into details with all the new tools introduced, but merely describe a few of the quite innovative new Functoids.

Before starting work with the new mapper, there are a few things to bear in mind:

- The new mapper is not backward compatible; new maps will, therefore, not work with BizTalk Server.

- There is still the possibility to drop the mapper altogether and use custom XSLT. Here you also have the ability to select Compiled Transformation for better performance (something that was also introduced in BizTalk Server 2013, but here the developer can control whether it should be used or not).

- Reusing existing BizTalk Server maps is possible, and a migration tool has been introduced (BTMMigrationTool).

Here is a list of some of the new Functoids introduced with the new mapper. The functiods mentioned here are by no means all of the new Functoids introduced, but just a few of the interesting new ones. This chapter will not go into details about the usage of these.

Functoid	Category	Description
DateTime Reformat	Date/Time Operations	Converts from one date time syntax to another. For example, 31/01/2013 to 2013-01-31.
Generate Id	Misc Operations	Inserts a random generated ID into an element on the target side. The length can vary from 12 to 32 characters.
Get Context Property	Misc Operations	Retrieves a metadata (context) property from the message.
MapEach Loop	Loop Operations	Iterates through a multioccurence record and gives the user the ability to filter (hence, only maps records that meet certain conditions).
If-Then-Else-Expression	Expressions	The much-needed Functoid that never made it to the BizTalk mapper. Gives the user the ability to map something if a certain criteria is met, otherwise maps something else.

Applying the map and testing the solution

For applying the map and testing the solution, go through the following steps:

1. Go back to the itinerary canvas and double-click on the MySqlBridge.
2. In **Message Types**, select the **LoanApp** Schema.
3. Click on **Xml Transform** inside the **Transform** shape.
4. Under **Properties**, select **Maps**.
5. Select the **LoanApp_to...** map and click on **OK**.

Your itinerary should now look like the following diagram:

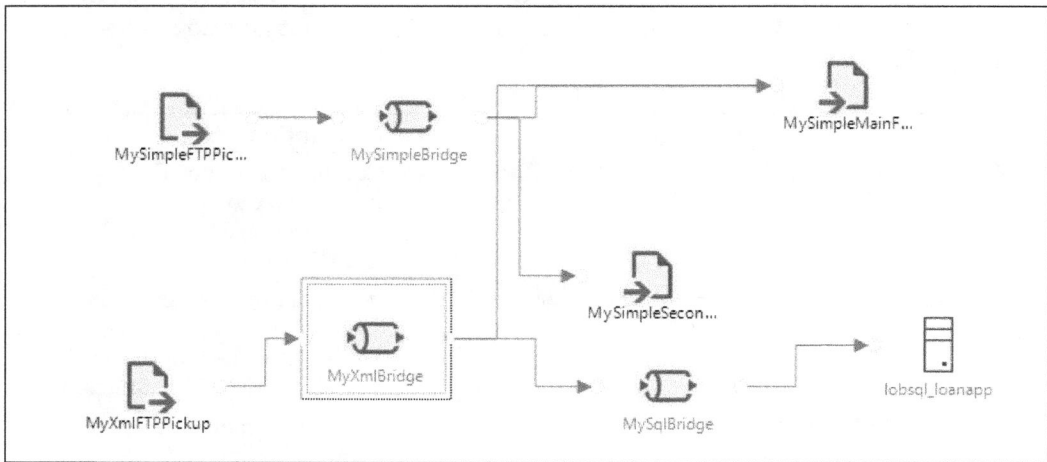

6. Before deploying, we also need to set the SOAP Action property when calling the LOB Service. Click on the connection from **MySqlBridge** to **lobsql_loanapp** and choose **Route Action**.

7. Add a new action and set the action as follows (again notice that single quotes are needed surrounding the action):

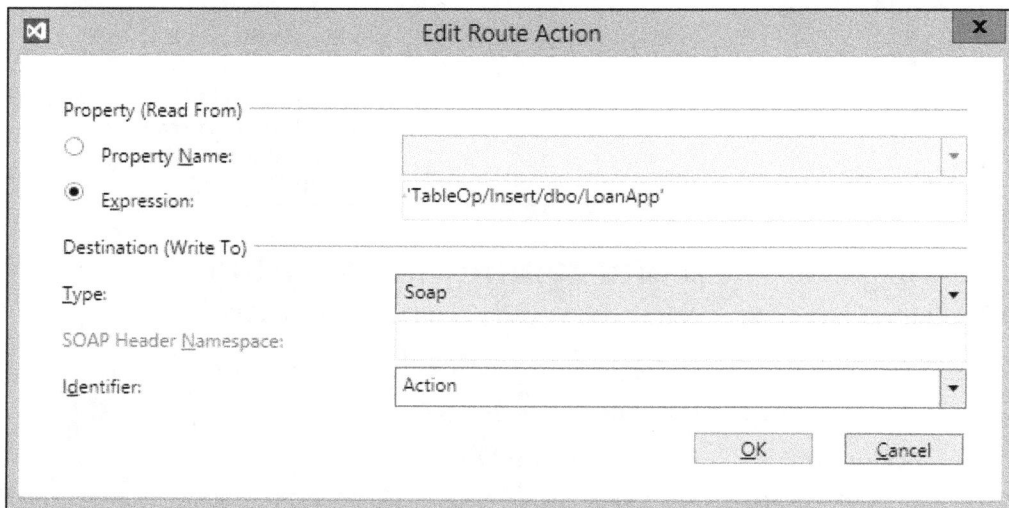

8. Save everything.

9. Deploy the project.

10. Make sure your Out folder is empty.

11. Start the **MyXmlFTPPickup** source.

12. Submit a loan application with an amount larger than 1000. This file should be transmitted to the Out folder with the name of Output.xml.

13. Now submit an application with a loan amount smaller than 1000. The result should be an inserted row in the LoanApp table.

Using the WABS Portal

The Windows Azure Portal also comes with a BizTalk Service Portal, where additional setup and information can be done and gathered.

To open the portal, select your BizTalk Service in the Windows Azure Portal, and select **MANAGE**.

When using it for the first time, you will be required to register your BizTalk Service account to the portal. To do this, type in the name of the BizTalk Service owner as ACS Issuer name and the token used when creating the WABS.

> As default, the owner and ManagementClient have the same token in ACS.

Once inside the Portal, we have the following options:

• Managing EDI Partners and Agreements

• Adding and deleting resources (Schema, Maps, Certificates, and so on)

• Viewing and deleting existing bridges

• Viewing Tracking

Setting up EDI partners

When working with EDI (as of now, the North American format X12 is the only supported format, but EDIFACT is likely to follow), we need to set up the partners we are exchanging EDI documents with (including ourselves). For each of the partners, we then need to set up an agreement between them and us and specify message formats, mapping (if needed), and Receive and Send Pipelines (entry/exit points).

To create and use EDI using WABS, do the following:

1. Download the MicrosoftEdiXSDTemplates zip file from the Windows Azure BizTalk Services SDK download page.

2. Extract the file and locate the X12_00501_840.XSD file.

3. In the Portal, select **PARTNERS** and create two partners (**Partner name MySelf**, and **MyPartner**). Create the partners by selecting **ADD**. **Partner name** is the only required field and the rest can be left blank.

4. Choose **AGREEMENTS** and click on **ADD**.

5. Fill in the page as follows:

new agreement (x12)

GENERAL SETTINGS

| *Name: | MyPartnerAgreement |
| *Description: | |

Hosted Partner		Guest Partner	
*Partner:	MySelf ▼	*Partner:	MyPartner ▼
*Profile:	MySelf Profile ▼	*Profile:	MyPartner Profile ▼

Identities

| *Qualifier: | ZZ - Mutually Defined (X1 ▼ | *Qualifier: | ZZ - Mutually Defined (X1 ▼ |
| *Value: | US | *Value: | THEM |

Tracking

- ☑ Track Send side message properties
  - ☑ Archive Send side message
- ☑ Track Receive side message properties
  - ☑ Archive Receive side message

6. Click on **Continue**.

7. In **Receive Settings | Transport**, set up an appropriate FTP receive folder, use *.txt as **File mask**.

8. In **Receive Settings | Protocol,** click on **UPLOAD** to upload the X12 Schema located earlier.

9. In **Receive Settings | Route,** click on **ADD** to add a Route Setting.

10. Select **Use advanced definitions** and specify **1=1** to have all successful processed messages routed to the same place. Name the rule **Everything.**

11. Under **Route destination,** choose **Azure BizTalk Bridge** and type `mysimplebridge` in the URL text box.

12. Click on **SAVE.**

13. Under **Message Suspension Settings,** again choose **Azure BizTalk Bridge** and specify **mysimplebridge.**

    This means that we will now send both successful and failed messages to our MySimpleBridge bridge and forward them to our `AltOut` FTP folder.

14. Under **SEND SETTINGS,** all we will set up is our partner's two destinations (successful and failed). For now, we will just use **mysimplebridge** for both of these.

15. We also need to specify a Schema under **SEND SETTINGS | Protocol.** Click on the plus sign and select the Schema uploaded previously.

16. Click on **DEPLOY.**

> To re-use our **MySimpleBridge,** for this purpose, we need to remove the Enrichment of the FTP filename, since the message will now come from an EDI Agreement and not directly from an FTP Source. You will also need to remove the `OriginalFileName = 'Alt.txt'` from the connection to **MySimpleSecondFTPDest.** Replace this with `1=1 / Match All.` Also, the Route Action on each of the outgoing connections from the bridge needs to use the expression **EDI.XML** instead of the `MyFileName` metadata property. Redeploy your project after these changes.

17. Use the `EDI.txt` file that ships with this chapter and submit it to your Agreement FTP Receive source.

18. Confirm that the `AltOut` folder now contains an EDI XML document.

What we have done here is set up an Agreement that receives EDI documents from a trading partner. In our example, we just dropped the raw EDI XML into an FTP folder. In real life we would process it in a bridge, maybe route it based upon certain values, and then send it onwards to our ERP system, using different techniques (maybe using the LOB Services).

Tracking

All tracking in WABS is stored in the Azure SQL Server in several tables, and the actual message bodies (if tracked) are stored in the Azure Storage account associated with the WABS.

> Out of the box only EDI messages have their bodies tracked.

Viewing these data can be done by querying these tables and storage, but the WABS Portal also contains a Tracking view that shows a lot of these data.

To view the Tracking part of the Portal, select the **TRACKING** option on the left pane.

Check the events created when we submitted an X12 document through an Agreement and onto a bridge (**mysimplebridge**).

> In my example, my created agreement was assigned an ID of 2. This may vary on your setup. Since my ID is 2, my agreement has an endpoint URL of /agreements/2/receive.

The highest entries show what happened when we submitted an X12 document. We have one error and three information entries. Let us examine the error by using the following steps:

1. Select the error reading **EDI Disassembler Activity: CustomRecord**.

2. At the bottom of the Portal, click on **DETAILS**.

3. Notice that the **message info** holds information about the **Event Level**, **End Point**, **RequestId**, and **TrackId**, and in what stage the error occurred. It does not, however, tell us what the error was. For this we need to look into the **PROTOCOL** tab.

4. Close the message info and select the **PROTOCOL** tab.

5. Select **SEARCH** to refresh the board.

6. Select the top entry and click on **DETAILS**.

7. The error description should read **Invalid Segment Terminator**.

8. Let us download the actual message received and examine it (this is possible because we choose Archive messages when setting up the Agreement).

9. In the **Select an entry** drop-down list, select **incoming X12 Message** and click on **Download**.

10. Choose an appropriate location and give your file a valid name and save it.

11. Locate the file and change the extension to `.txt` so that it can easily be opened.

12. Verify that WABS did archive your actual incoming message and allowed you to retrieve it again.

13. The reason we received the error was that the last line was not ended with a carriage return. Delete the file in the `AltOut` folder, alter your X12 document with the extra carriage return, and resubmit the file.

14. You should now see information entries in Tracking without any errors. (Click on **Search** to refresh the tracking board).

Running BizTalk on a Windows Azure Virtual Machine

As of BizTalk Server 2013, we can now choose to either run our BizTalk Server(s) on-premise as before, or run them on a virtual server in Azure.

Running your BizTalk environment in the cloud has several advantages:

- You can access your servers from anywhere, if you have Internet access.
- Your images are backed up by Microsoft.
- No hardware is needed, therefore no hardware maintenance is required.
- Fast deployment of new servers. In about an hour, you can have a brand new BizTalk environment installed, configured, and ready for use.

Besides the actual benefits of hosting your BizTalk Server(s) in the cloud, it is also possible to connect your cloud servers to your on-premise network or domain by setting up a Virtual Network in Azure.

Setting up a single BizTalk Server

We will now set up a standalone BizTalk Server evaluation edition that also has SQL Server evaluation edition installed, as follows:

> The evaluation edition will only work for 120 days.

1. In the Windows Azure Portal, navigate to **NEW | COMPUTE | VIRTUAL MACHINE | FROM GALLERY**.

2. In **Choose an Image**, select **BIZTALK SERVER**.

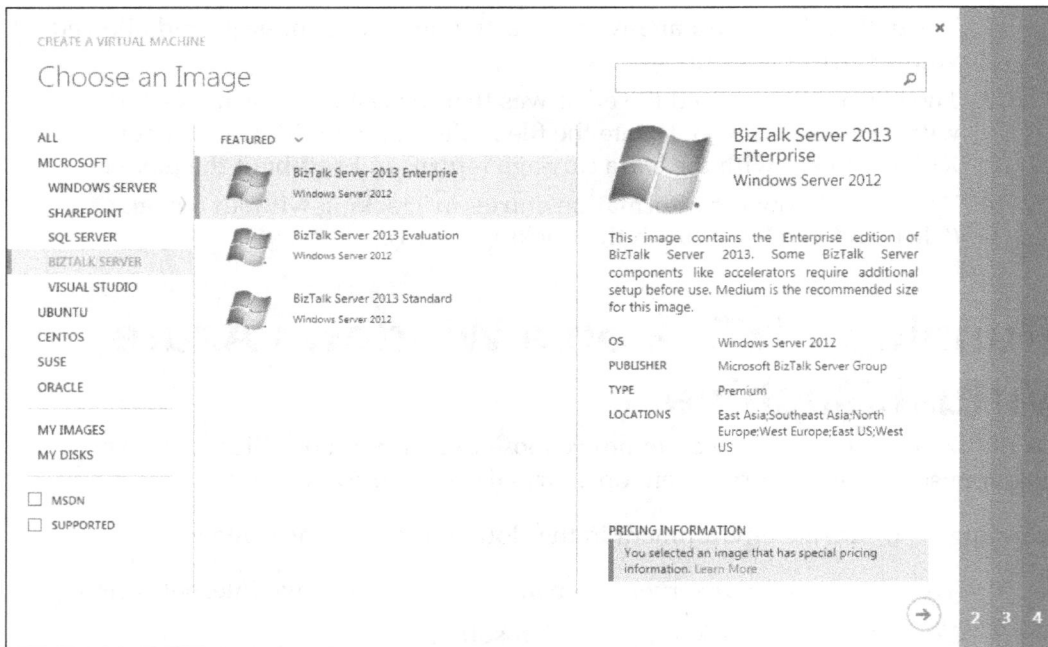

> A developer image with both Visual Studio 2012 and BizTalk Server 2013 is due to be added in the future, but it is not yet here as this chapter is being written.

3. Under **FEATURED**, select **BizTalk Server 2013 Evaluation**.

4. Click on the next arrow.

5. Give the Virtual Machine an appropriate name, set the **Size** required, and create a new Administrator user (The username **Administrator** is not allowed).

6. Click on the next arrow.

7. Choose an appropriate **REGION** and leave the rest of the parameters as they are.

8. Click on the next arrow.

9. Note the TCP Ports assigned to Remote Desktop and PowerShell.

10. Click on **Complete**.

    The Server will now take a few minutes to complete. Once completed, we can access it using Remote Desktop.

11. Click the newly created Server, and select **CONNECT**.

12. Click on **OK** and open the .rdp file.

13. Click on **Connect** if a warning is received.

14. Enter your credentials ServerName\Your Administrator created in the Wizard, and then the password.

15. You should now be able to access the remote virtual machine. BizTalk can be configured on the local SQL Server, just as you would a local BizTalk Server.

Installing a multi-Server Virtual Machine

To install a multi-Server environment in Azure, you will need multiple servers that can communicate with each other. A **SQL Server** and x number of **BizTalk Server(s) Enterprise** editions (images that do not contain SQL Server).

To do this, you need to either create a Domain Controller hosted in Windows Azure or use an on-premise Domain Controller before you create the virtual machines. The latter requires your BizTalk Servers to be joined to the local networks and domain. Refer to the following link for more information:

http://msdn.microsoft.com/library/windowsazure/jj156090.aspx

> Windows Azure does not currently support Windows Clustering, sometimes used together with BizTalk Hosts.

If you need to join your on-premise Domain, you will need to create Virtual Network. Refer to the following link for more information:

```
https://www.windowsazure.com/en-us/manage/services/networking/create-
a-virtual-network/
```

Configuring multiple BizTalk Servers

When needing to configure multiple BizTalk Servers in Azure the same way, a new tool, BizTalk Provisioning tool, can be used. The tool is automatically installed on all BizTalk Server 2013 virtual machines and can be used locally, giving the user a fast way to configure the Servers remotely.

This approach is done by creating local users and groups on each server, and then creating a configuration XML file that contains all information needed for setting up the BizTalk Group.

When this is done, the Provisioning tool can be executed; the tool can be found in any of the virtual BizTalk Servers in the folder `C:\BizTalk_Provisioning`.

Refer to the following link for more information:

```
http://msdn.microsoft.com/en-us/library/dn133605(v=bts.80).aspx
```

Testing your knowledge

1. You want to create a Windows Azure BizTalk Service in the Windows Azure Portal. Which of the following components are used by WABS (choose all that apply):

    a. A local SQL Server

    b. An Azure SQL Server

    c. A local BizTalk Server

    d. A virtual machine BizTalk Server in Azure

    e. An Azure Storage Account

    f. An Access Control Namespace

2. You receive messages through an **Xml one-way bridge**. You want to write the Receiver ID from the message to the context of the message for routing purposes. Where should you do this:

    a. In the **Validate** Stage

b. In the **Transform** Stage

c. In the **Decode** Stage

d. In the **Enrich** Stage

3. You need to route everything from a bridge to an FTP destination. You have created the bridge and the destination, what should you do:

a. Create a **Pass-Through Bridge** between your bridge and the FTP destination.

b. Connect your bridge to the FTP destination and create a **Route Action**. Set **FTP | ServerAddress** to **All**.

c. Connect your bridge to the FTP destination and create a **Filter Condition**. Set the **Filter** to **Message = All**.

d. Connect your bridge to the FTP destination and create a **Filter Condition**. Select **Match All**.

4. What types of LOB Adapters are available in the **BizTalk Adapter Pack** (choose all that apply):

a. FTP

b. SQL Server

c. DB2

d. Oracle

e. Siebel

f. SAP

g. SOAP

5. You need to track an EDI message sent through a bridge, where is the tracking information stored?

a. In the Windows Azure Portal

b. In the bridge used for transporting the message

c. In SQL Azure

d. In Azure Storage

Summary

This chapter has dealt with some of the basics of BizTalk Server and BizTalk Services in Azure. We have seen how to create accounts and Servers in Azure, how to use them, how to set up an EDI agreement for exchanging messages with partners in the cloud, and even how to route messages from Azure to your local on-premise applications.

10
Test-taking – Tips and Tricks

Since the second edition of this book targets both the *Exam 70-595: MCTS: Developing Business Process and Integration Solutions by Using Microsoft BizTalk Server 2010* and the *Microsoft Partner Network Technical Assessment for Application Integration (BizTalk Server 2013)*, this chapter uses the word **Test** when discussing topics that are relevant to both. It only uses the terms **Exam** or **Assessment** when the content truly only applies to that.

This chapter intends to go beyond providing content that educates you, the reader, on important technical information, concepts, and techniques, and provide you with a better understanding of what the process of taking a test is like, starting with preparation, what to expect through the actual test itself, and the follow-up once done. Due to this, while the other chapters of the book are to the point and technical, this chapter is less so. The following areas are discussed in this chapter:

- Understanding the difference between the exam and the assessment
- Preparing for taking a test
- At the test center (BizTalk Server 2010)
- Test structure
- Time management
- Answering questions

Understanding the difference between the exam and the assessment

This section will explain how the exam and assessment are alike, and how they differ.

Historically, there has not been an exam available for every version of BizTalk Server. For example, BizTalk Server 2009 never got an associated exam. There is an exam for BizTalk Server 2010. The exam is available to all professionals, partners as well as customers or otherwise, to take. This exam was the focus for the first edition of this book, and for the most part still is for the second edition. Since writing the first edition of this book, BizTalk Server 2013 has become available. There is no associated exam for BizTalk Server 2013. There is however a Microsoft Partner Network Technical Assessment, a requirement for professionals employed at partners who wish to pursue the Application Integration competency. The assessment is targeted at and accessible to Microsoft Partners only.

Both tests test an individual's skill in BizTalk Server. Both tests follow the Microsoft exam question and answer multiple choice formats. Both tests require the same basic skills and knowledge, although the BizTalk Server 2013 assessment has a slightly wider target area than the exam, including Windows Azure Virtual Machines and BizTalk Services, as well as other 2013 news in the skills measured.

The exam is taken on-site at a test center where you book a seat for a specific time. You need to show up on time, identify yourself, and enter a room together with others where you access the exam under controlled forms through a locked down PC with access only to the test software.

The assessment, however, can be accessed at any time and from any computer by following the link available in the Microsoft Partner Network web portal. Also, unlike the exam, you have access to anything and everything that you normally have access to from your PC.

The exam has a retake policy, which means you cannot try again immediately (after your first attempt the wait is a minimum of 24 hours, and after the second and consecutive attempts it is 14 days). With the assessment you can just try again if you fail.

Since the rules around the assessment are different from those for the exam, the approach to studying for it will likely be different in reality. For both the exam and the assessment, as a rule, you can always try taking the test even if you are not sure that you are a hundred percent ready. Failing an exam is not a total failure. It is part of the learning process and often gives you great feedback to continue with focused studies. While the exam enforces retake policies and infers cost, the assessment does not. It is free to take and you can retake it immediately. For this reason it is likely, and wise, not to study as much for it in comparison to the exam.

The exam is still, in this book's opinion, the primary and most up-to-date test available for all individual BizTalk Server professionals that wish to prove their worth. However, if you are a Microsoft Partner, the assessment is a must have if you are aspiring to achieve the Application Integration competency. Therefore, it is crucially important to partner companies to have employees pass the assessment; likely more so than have them pass the certification.

As explained in this section, the assessment is a different entity from the exam. For the most part however, the concepts, ideas, and information in this chapter apply equally to both, although they were mostly written with the exam in mind.

Preparing for taking a test

We all learn in different ways. The preparation that works best for one of us does not necessarily work for someone else. You need to find the way that you learn the best, and learn the way you learn. At the same time, it is a proven fact that while we are different, we all learn best when we get information through more than one channel and more than one experience. Reading, hearing, seeing, trying, perhaps even showing or teaching, all adds to your understanding of a topic. There is simply nothing that measures up to the experience built up by different kinds of exposure over time, but being prepared and knowing what will happen and being aware of the process as well as the technology might just be the thing that tips the scale in your favor.

Preparation sources

The following are examples of different kinds of material you can use to prepare:

- Literature
- Classes
- Webcasts
- Labs

- Training kits
- Sample code
- Practice tests
- Colleagues and peers
- Forums, blogs, and other online sources such as **Microsoft Developer Network (MSDN)** documentation and TechNet Wiki

We will go through these and try to highlight what and when each of these is good to use.

Literature

If reading is your thing, read this book from cover to cover. Having been written specifically to help you pass the certification, it covers the topics needed to get you up to date on the certification objectives. However, it is not written for the BizTalk beginner. Should you crave more basic and introductory content, as well as simply more, there are a lot of good BizTalk books out there.

You can, of course, also read the BizTalk documentation, although it is not meant to be read cover to cover as a book. It serves as a good reference, but is little like a book. You can turn to the documentation once you have closely narrowed down the topics on which you lack knowledge or need improvement.

For most of us, having read something does not lend expertise, but it does help to strengthen the knowledge that is already there, store new knowledge to be recollected, and tickle the senses at the right time.

Classes

Although Microsoft has not released a **Microsoft Official Curriculum (MOC)** course for BizTalk Server since BizTalk was in its 2006 version, there are many training providers that have kept up to date with BizTalk Server versions. You should be able to find at least one training provider in your area that has training for BizTalk Server 2010 or 2013. If you cannot, there is BizTalk Server 2010 or 2013 training available online from companies such as *Pluralsight* and *Quicklearn*, among others.

Classes will give you different kinds of exposure to BizTalk. You will hear the trainer talk about it, you will see him demonstrate it, and you will get a chance to try it on your own, under controlled and well-prepared circumstances during labs. You will probably not get as effective and well-rounded training elsewhere as the hours spent in class while doing it on your own.

Classes tend to be most effective for beginners or less-experienced BizTalk developers. Experienced developers will most likely find classes to contain things they already know well, mixed with new and previously forgotten knowledge. For experienced developers, other sources to prepare for certification are often more effective.

Webcasts

Webcasts often have a shorter format and are made to cover a specific topic. Some webcasts are very general in nature and do not provide much value as certification preparation, but there are also webcasts that are made specifically to cover a part of BizTalk in more detail. These webcasts are great, if they cover an area you need improvement in. Many BizTalk developers are not closely accustomed to all parts of BizTalk; most often, the extended capabilities such as **Business Activity Monitoring (BAM)**, **Business Rules Engine (BRE)**, **Electronic Data Interchange (EDI)**, and **Radio Frequency Identification (RFID)** are areas where there are gaps in exposure. For those specific areas, getting up to date with a targeted webcast is very useful. The places that contain or link to BizTalk Server webcasts and videos include the following:

- BizTalk Server Developer Center webcasts: `http://msdn.microsoft.com/en-us/biztalk/aa937645`

- BizTalk Server Developeztalk/dd849956.aspx

- Cloudcasts BizTalk community webcasts: `http://www.cloudcasts.net/Default.aspx?category=BizTalk`

- Cloudcasts BizTalk community webcasts, the Light and Easy series: `http://www.cloudcasts.net/Default.aspx?category=BizTalk+Light+and+Easy`

- Cloudcasts BizTalk community webcasts, ESB Toolkit: `http://www.cloudcasts.net/Default.aspx?category=BizTalk+ESB+Toolkit`

- BizTalk247 BizTalk Server webcasts: `http://www.biztalk247.com/webcasts.aspx`

- BizTalk247 BizTalk Server videos: `http://www.biztalk247.com/videos.aspx`

> Although many new features have been added and much improvement has been made, much of the BizTalk Server still remains relatively unchanged since BizTalk Server 2004. This means that any content that covers earlier versions of BizTalk may very well still be valid. However, some specifics such as EDI have changed dramatically, so be alert when viewing webcasts made for previous versions.

There are also quite a few websites around that try to keep updated lists of BizTalk presentations and recordings, examples of such are as follows:

- Technet Wiki: `http://social.technet.microsoft.com/wiki/contents/articles/18829.biztalk-server-webcasts-and-videos.aspx`

- BizTalk Events: `http://biztalkevents.com/presentations/`

> The resources linked to can contain material around topics not required by the exam or the assessment. Be mindful of the objectives as you study. For example, the ESB Toolkit is not one of the objectives for the exam or the assessment.

Training kits

If you have a machine and want more time to play around with the topics than you are given in the virtual lab, and if you want to be able to come back to the content more than once and not lose your progress, you might be better off downloading and installing one of the available training kits. Most of these do not come as a bunch of word documents alone, but include a complete virtual machine for you to use. Some of them are as follows:

- What's new in BizTalk Server 2010 Training Kit: `http://www.microsoft.com/download/en/details.aspx?id=17956`

- BizTalk Server 2010 VHD (with the What's new in BizTalk Server 2010 Training Kit preinstalled): `http://www.microsoft.com/download/en/details.aspx?id=13624`

- BizTalk Server 2010 Developer Training Kit (including VHD): `http://www.microsoft.com/download/en/details.aspx?id=14865`

- BizTalk Server 2010 Administrator Training Kit (including VHD): `http://www.microsoft.com/download/en/details.aspx?id=27148`

- BizTalk Server 2009 BAM Training Kit: `http://www.microsoft.com/en-us/download/details.aspx?id=5416`

- BizTalk Server 2010 ESB Training Kit (including. VHD): `http://www.microsoft.com/download/en/details.aspx?id=27151`

> The ESB Toolkit is not one of the objectives for the exam or the assessment. However, familiarizing yourself with it serves both to better understand BizTalk Server and to better prepare yourself for the exam, the assessment, and work scenarios.

You could also download the required software and build a virtual machine yourself. You will gain additional insight into the BizTalk Server by going through the installation and configuration required. If you have the required access to MSDN, you can download and install a full non-expiring version of the software. If you don't have any such subscription, you can still download trial versions that usually have a limited amount of time that you are allowed to use them for.

> BizTalk Server 2010 had a Developer Edition that was free for everyone. With BizTalk Server 2013, this version is free for MSDN subscribers, but for everyone else there is a small cost (the exact amount still depends on the agreement type and level but is below the $50 mark).

Windows Azure virtual machines

You may have noticed that most of the links in the prior section were for previous versions of BizTalk Server rather than BizTalk Server 2013. The reason is that, so far, the amount of available downloadable images and samples for BizTalk Server 2013 has been few. To a large extent the explanation for this is Windows Azure and the possibility to use BizTalk Server in the Windows Azure **Infrastructure as a Service (IaaS)** virtual machines environment. You can easily activate your Windows Azure MSDN benefit or start a free trial that will allow you to provision a BizTalk Server 2013 server in Windows Azure that you can log in to and try out. At the moment, the Windows Azure gallery virtual machine images do not contain Visual Studio, so these machines are not development ready, although a trial of Visual Studio can be freely and easily installed. This topic is covered in more depth in *Chapter 9, Using Azure BizTalk Features*.

Sample code

If you don't want a full training kit but just want to get your hands on code that shows some specific feature, there are a lot of samples available for download:

- BizTalk Server 2010 SDK samples (also available in your BizTalk install folder): `http://msdn.microsoft.com/en-us/library/aa560186(v=bts.70).aspx`
- BizTalk Server 2013 SDK samples (also available in your BizTalk install folder): `http://msdn.microsoft.com/en-us/library/aa560186(v=bts.80).aspx`
- BizTalk Server code samples: `http://msdn.microsoft.com/en-us/biztalk/aa937647.aspx`

- BizTalk Server 2010 Adapter Pack samples: `http://msdn.microsoft.com/en-us/biztalk/gg491395.aspx`

> The BizTalk Server adapter pack is not one of the objectives for the exam, but it is a small part of the assessment.

Blogs are also a great resource for samples, but there are too many of them to point out, and since the content varies greatly in quality and quantity over time and is not something that has been verified as part of the process of this book, no links will be added to point to blogs.

Besides sample code that is limited to showing specific features, there are also tutorials and scenarios that show complete architectures, as follows:

- BizTalk Server 2010 Tutorials: `http://msdn.microsoft.com/en-us/library/aa560270(v=bts.70).aspx`

- BizTalk Server 2013 Tutorials: `http://msdn.microsoft.com/en-us/library/aa560270(v=bts.80).aspx`

- BizTalk Server 2010 Scenarios for Business Solutions: `http://msdn.microsoft.com/en-us/library/aa561965(v=bts.70).aspx`

- BizTalk Server 2013 Scenarios for Business Solutions: `http://msdn.microsoft.com/en-us/library/aa561965(v=bts.80).aspx`

Again, there are more places than this. A simple search on any search engine using words such as "BizTalk Server Tutorials" will turn up a number of hits.

Practice tests

Practice tests are useful as they make you comfortable with the functionality and working of the test engine. Recommended practice test providers are those that have a good spread of questions that are not copies of the exam itself, but cover similar topics. They also have explanations of which answers are correct and which are incorrect, and why, similar to the *Testing your knowledge* section in this book. At the time of writing this book, no practice tests are currently available for the BizTalk Server 2010 Exam or for the BizTalk Server 2013 Assessment. However, there are practice tests available for previous versions of BizTalk and the exams that cover those versions, for example, the BizTalk Server 2006 Exam. Those tests will serve the purpose of making you comfortable with the format to a large extent, and at the same time the content they cover is mostly viable for BizTalk Server 2010 and BizTalk Server 2013 as well. They will, however, not cover all the topics.

This book is also a very good source of practice with the type and style of questions, although you will not get them framed in a test engine similar to the live one.

Colleagues and peers

If you know someone who is experienced in BizTalk, take the opportunity to pick their brain on the topics that you feel hesitant about. Even if they have taken the tests themselves, they would not be able to give you direct insight into the questions or the topics covered, since they will have committed themselves to an NDA when taking the exam. However, they will be able to give you general directions and help. No such NDA is explicitly presented for acceptance for the assessment.

Forums, blogs, and other online sources

BizTalk Server, in its current core architecture, has been around for many years and has a large user base. As such, there is a large community out there that writes articles and blogs and staffs many forums. You are almost guaranteed to find someone out there who has had the same or similar problem or questions. One place that allows the community to contribute to the documentation provided by Microsoft is the TechNet Wiki; the page at `http://social.technet.microsoft.com/wiki/contents/articles/2240.biztalk-server-resources-on-the-technet-wiki.aspx` summarizes the articles that focus on BizTalk Server.

If you do not find what you are looking for, there are places you can ask your questions and get them answered, for example, the MSDN BizTalk Server forums: `http://social.msdn.microsoft.com/Forums/en-US/category/biztalkserver`.

Getting familiar with the objectives

One of the main things about studying for the exam is of course to know what the exam covers. If the exam is your objective, do not overstudy. Learning is fun, and the risk of learning too much is virtually non-existent. However, the possibility that you will end up learning more than you need to pass the exam is equally large. Often, if you study towards a goal, you can be more focused, get a learning path, and be more selective in what you need to learn right now. You should study the exam objectives which can be found at `http://www.microsoft.com/learning/en/us/exam.aspx?ID=70-595#tab2`.

There is currently no web page that details the objectives for the assessment in the same way. They are, however, more or less the same.

Finding time to study

Set aside time to study. Many of us are lucky enough to be able to work and study at once, since what we do all day is architecting, developing, or administrating BizTalk Server solutions. Usually though, even in those situations, our daily routines and what we do does not touch each and every part of BizTalk Server. Since feeling confident about ourselves when taking the tests helps, even though it might not be altogether necessary to get a passing score, try to find time to at least briefly look at the topics that you are not that familiar with, to build that confidence.

Depending on the way you study best, here are a few suggestions on how you can sneak that study time into your daily routines:

- **Commute**: If reading is your choice, the time that you are commuting — using public transportation (not while driving!) — is prime time. Many of us can easily find an hour or more each day, during which we would not be doing much anyway. Some, even more.

- **As part of your work role**: If you can find time at work, you will easily get many hours of study done daily during paid work time. Perhaps you can enforce concepts or incorporate techniques from this book or ideas brought forward in the test objectives as part of your solutions. Hands-on is a good way to learn!

- **Expanding your horizons at work**: If it does not fit your daily routine, perhaps volunteer to take part in an EDI prestudy, or a PoC, on how to allow business users to best interact with your BizTalk Server solutions by define rules in the **Business Rules Composer**, or how you should configure your solution using the new settings dashboard to best handle your combination of integrations. This combines research with hands-on learning!

- **Before or after work**: Take the first 20 minutes when you get to work to look at something new, or re-enforce a lesser-known topic. Getting to work 20 minutes early can usually be worked into a new routine, and if you are there 20 minutes before the others, it is also usually a very quiet and focused time of the day.

- **At home**: Instead of channel zapping or viewing that useless TV show that neither educates nor enriches you, do a lab!

- **Before bed**: Although you should not do this if you are tired, if you spend the last 30 minutes before going to bed with BizTalk topics, not only will you be able to wind down, you will also think BizTalk when you go to sleep.

As you learn how you can best fit time to study into your schedule and your routines, set goals. Decide what you need to learn before taking the exam or assessment, and plan that across the days leading up to it. Leave enough room in the schedule to make sure you have time for everything that you feel you need to. Better to look at some things twice, rather than finding that the day of the test is upon you and that you have not had time to finish your studies. Remember, build confidence.

Incentives

Many of us work better with a good incentive—find yours. It could be anything. Here are a few common ones.

Knowledge

Here are some points that cover knowledge:

- To know more
- To become a better (more knowledgeable) developer or architect or consultant or employee

Money

Here are some points that cover money:

- To earn more—to be able to bill more or get a better salary
- An employer-supplied gratification or gift

Opportunities

Here are some points that cover opportunities:

- To get a new job, a more fun job, or more challenging work
- To be more sought after and have more choices
- To get new opportunities or new roles

If you cannot find a goal, or one does not really fit your situation, give yourself an incentive, perhaps something along the lines of "When I pass the test, I will…

- …go out to a really nice dinner at restaurant X."
- …go to see X play the Y at the Z."
- …go to the city of AABC over the weekend."
- …visit that spa I pass when I drive to work for a new treatment."

Vouchers and offers

Take advantage of offers and vouchers for test takers. Microsoft and Prometric (the exam provider) will often have valid offers for you to take advantage of, for example:

- Second chance free
- Discounted exam costs
- Two-for-one

Current offers are listed at the following link: `http://www.microsoft.com/learning/en-us/offers.aspx`

There are also Microsoft Partner Network discounts from time to time, but no relevant ones are available at the time of writing, so there is no URL, but it is worth checking when it's time for you to book an appointment.

Finally, you can also turn to your **Microsoft Certified Trainer (MCT)** and ask them for a voucher that will get you a discount on the certification.

Learn more

Microsoft maintains Exam policies and FAQ section at `http://www.microsoft.com/learning/en-us/certification-exam-policies.aspx#faq`.

If you are a Microsoft partner, the Microsoft partner learning paths are available at `https://mspartnerlp.mspartner.microsoft.com/LearningPath`.

At the test center

Prometric is the current exam provider for Microsoft certifications at the time of writing this book. Usually, your **Certified Provider of Learning Solutions (CPLS)** or Learning Partner will be a Prometric test center where you take the exam. You can usually contact either the test center or Prometric. The test center can add a handling fee on top of the certification fee. On the other hand, it will often be able to bill your company or employer directly, while you will have to supply a credit card when registering directly with Prometric. Some test centers require you to contact them directly or you will find yourself without a seat once you arrive to take the exam.

On the day of the certification, these are the most important points that you should keep in mind when arriving at and taking the exam at the test center:

- Be on time. However, if you are not, most of the time this will not be an issue; you are still allowed to take the exam, should you arrive late.

- Bring photo ID. You will need to be able to prove who you are. You should bring two ID proofs (though they need not be two photo ID proofs).

- You will not be allowed to bring anything into the test room. No phones, no books, and no notes.

- You will be supplied a scratch pad on which you can make notes on anything you want during the exam. This will have to be turned in once you are done.

- You will be monitored during the exam through video surveillance.

- The computer on which you do the exam has very limited functionality — you will only have access to the test itself, no Internet, no help files, and no development environment.

- You are allowed to take breaks (though the time does not stop counting down).

Prometric maintains a FAQ section at the following link:

```
https://www.prometric.com/en-us/for-test-takers/prepare-for-test-day/
frequently-asked-questions/pages/default.aspx.
```

Examining the exam structure

The exam itself has a simple structure that is divided into three parts.

Before the exam

Before starting the exam, you will go through a series of informational screens, including information on how much time you have, in all, to complete the exam and information on the **Non-disclosure Agreement** (**NDA**) that you must agree to before being allowed to take the exam. This agreement prohibits you from discussing the content of the exam or the questions. Reviewing the agreement is not included in the time you have to complete the exam.

Questions

A Microsoft exam will have somewhere between 35 and 80 questions. The norm is 40 to 50, but part of the NDA is the exact number of questions for this particular exam, so this book will not disclose it.

A question screen of the exam will have the following general appearance:

```
☐ Mark for review           Question 23/XX                    2:15

        Question content, questions content,
        questions content, Question content,
        questions content, questions content,
        Question content, questions?

     ○ a.    Aaa
     ○ b.    Bbb
     ○ c.    Ccc
     ○ d.    Ddd

   [ Previous ]   [   Next   ]
```

Questions are single- or multiple-choice questions.

You will always be able to keep track of the time you have left, and which question you are on, out of the total number of questions. You will also be able to mark the question for review and navigate between questions, either by going to the next or previous questions.

After the last question, you will come to a review screen where you will see which questions you have marked for review and will be able to return to them, or any other question you choose, easily.

After the exam

Whenever you decide you are done with answering and reviewing questions, you can choose to end the exam. At this point, you will get a chance to give comments on the certification material or any of the questions. You will also get your score immediately, once done, and learn whether you passed or not.

With it, you will get a report on how you did on the different areas. You will get it printed and can take it home regardless of the fact you passed or failed. This will help you understand which areas you were strong in and which need development. If you passed, you passed; there is no coming back to take the exam again to improve your score. But, if you did not pass, take careful note of this report. The certification report will generally look something like this:

Once done, you leave the exam room and need to hand in the scratch pad and sign out.

The assessment does not offer an equally helpful report. You need to guess (or have a feeling for) which areas you need improvement in and which you were strong in.

Managing your time

For most certification test takers, having too little time to complete the test is not an issue. The total time for the exam is around three hours. However, if the exam is not available in your native language, you will get additional time added to your exam time to compensate for that fact.

Even so, managing your time during the certification can help you reduce the feeling that time is running out.

The assessment is simply one and a half hours; roughly half the time.

Do not spend too much time on any one question. If you feel you cannot answer a question after reading the questions and the suggested answers, mark it for review. Do not overthink on it. Do not turn it every other way, and do not feel bad. Very few will ace them all.

For example, say that we have 50 questions and three hours. That means an average of 3.6 minutes per question. You will, without a doubt, find some questions easy. Those will be answered quickly, leaving time for the ones where you need to think more.

Do not spend too little time on any question. Do not speed through. Be thorough. There will be no bonus points given out if you complete in record time.

Take advantage of the fact that you are allowed to take breaks. If you feel your concentration is failing you or you are feeling tired, take a break. Many test centers provide free drinks and snacks.

> Interviewing experienced BizTalk developers that have taken the exam shows that they typically need between about 45 and 90 minutes.

However, you should not benchmark yourself against others.

If your colleague, who has taken the exam, did it in 60 minutes and you are in your 70th minute and are only on question 32, do not worry. You will probably score better than they did.

If the other eight people who were in the room doing exams at the same time as you are done and have left, and you are still in your 140th minute and on question 40, do not worry. They are probably not even taking the same exam that you are.

Answering questions

There are a few cardinal rules to answering exam questions. The foremost one is answer the question. You will get no reduction in score for incorrect answers, but you will absolutely get no points if you do not answer. Always answer.

Besides that, consider these points as you address questions:

- Always make sure you have read the question thoroughly
- Do not assume that you know the question before you have read it all through
- Do not assume you know the answer before you have read the question
- Make sure that you have read and understood all requirements
- There is no trickery
- There are no hidden requirements
- Only take into account what is stated
- Take into account all that is stated
- Do not read other things into the question than stated
- Do not make assumptions about circumstances not stated
- Do not try to put your own requirements or preferences into the question

There is also a set of rules that applies to the answers in the exam that is good to keep in mind:

- Only one answer is correct
- Only one answer can solve all the requirements
- No second answer can fulfill the requirements or solve the problem even if it presents a really silly and stupid way to do it
- You will not be asked what the quickest or most direct answer is (since only one answer is allowed to solve the problem)
- You will not be asked which answer is the best answer (since only one answer is allowed to solve the problem)
- All answers are real and possible to perform
- No answer is impossible or illegal
- No answer may present a series of steps, properties, settings, concepts, or otherwise, that cannot be found or done in BizTalk Server
- No answer may present an illegal combination or faulty context (goes back to "no answer is impossible or illegal")

Keeping in mind the time management, if you feel that after having read the question as stated and looking at the answers that you do not know the answer, mark the question for review and move on.

If, on the other hand, you think that two answers are equally possible, read the question and review the answers again, perhaps there is a requirement in an aspect of the answer that you missed. If you still feel that two answers are equally plausible, choose the one that makes the most sense, based on what you know of BizTalk Server best practice, technology, and services.

Not all questions have the same style. A team of experts have been involved in making sure that the questions cover topics that are important and have the right combination of answers. However, they are written by different people, and different people have slightly different styles. So there are some guidelines that apply to most questions.

Most questions will have four alternative answers. Out of those four, two can often be discounted without deep knowledge and using common sense, for example:

1. Mooremountain Motors is a big dealership that offers many different kinds of brands. As a result, they are receiving invoices from many different car manufacturers. Jill, a developer at Mooremountain Motors, has developed an Orchestration that handles a canonical version of an invoice. She has also developed Maps from each of the manufacturers' Invoice Schemas to the Canonical Schema. What must she do to ensure that the Orchestration receives the canonical message and not the manufacturers' formats?

    a. In the Orchestration, after the initiating Receive shape, configure a Transform shape with the Maps.

    b. Create a Send Port Group and a Send Port for each of the manufacturers. Configure the Send Ports with the Maps.

    c. Create a Receive Port and Receive Location. Configure the Receive Port with the Maps.

    d. Configure a Receive Port and Receive Location. Configure the Receive Pipeline to be the Xml Receive Pipeline and set the `Validate document` structure property to `true`.

In the preceding question, based on very basic knowledge about how BizTalk Server works, you will be able to rule out configuring Send Port Group and Send Ports, since the requirement is that the Orchestration should get the canonical formatted invoices. Also, for that same reason, the transformation cannot occur in the Orchestration, since that is too late. The two remaining options both talk about the Receive side. Configuring a Pipeline and the XML Disassemblers Validate document structure property has very little to do with canonical formats and transformations. So, you can rule that out. Finally, you are down to receiving and Maps, which is the only option that fits.

However, sometimes it might not be that easy, and sometimes you might not have the knowledge necessary to decide which of the last two is correct. When you are down to two options, it is a matter of knowing or having had enough exposure to BizTalk to have a feeling or hunch about the correct answer.

Knowing which answers are incorrect is often as useful in these situations as knowing which is correct.

You can also find help in unexpected places. One question can contain the answer to a previous question.

2. HWLC Motors is receiving XML documents in a Receive Port. The Port is configured with a map to transform the incoming documents to a canonical format before triggering the correct Orchestration, based on the content of the document. Once in a while, a document arrives that cannot be routed to a subscribing Orchestration. Roger, an administrator, is tasked to set up a Send Port that outputs the failing incoming documents from this port in their original format. What must he do?

    a. Enable Failed Message Routing on the Receive Port. Create a second Receive Port to receive the failed messages.

    b. Enable Failed Message Routing on the Receive Port. Create a Send Port to receive the failed messages.

    c. Enable Failed Message Routing on the Receive Port. Create a Send Port to receive the failed messages, and configure it to Map from the canonical format to the original format.

    d. Create a Send Port to subscribe to all messages so that a subscriber can always be found to get rid of the routing errors.

Now, obviously, if you read this question once you have read the previous one, had you been ever so slightly hesitant on whether having Maps on the Receive Port was the correct choice, you will now know and can return to the previous question and easily supply the correct answer.

Test makers do their best to avoid this from happening, but subtle references can still be found, and even though they might not always contain the answer, they might jog your memory enough to make a difference.

Once you are done, you will reach the review screen and can make a pass over the questions again, perhaps even all questions, and not just the questions marked for review. This can help finding cross-references between questions that will help you solve those final questions.

Summary

In this chapter, we examined what you need to know about taking any of the tests themselves. We talked about how the exam and the assessment differ. We also talked about preparing for the test, including giving tips about additional resources outside of this book as well as strategies during the test.

The following appendices hold answers to the questions that appear at the end of each chapter as well as additional questions and answers on top of those provided in the chapters.

A
Sample Certification Test Questions

This chapter holds additional sample exam questions. They are categorized to align to their exam skill area. This allows you to measure your skill in the areas most relevant to you, so that you can pinpoint where you need improvement.

Answers to the questions in this chapter are in *Appendix B, Sample Certification Test Questions – Answers*.

Configuring a Messaging Architecture

1. You have two Send Ports, both of which wish to subscribe to all the Order messages from the ERP system. What should you do?

   a. Create two Receive Locations in one Receive Port and make both Receive Locations receive orders from the ERP system. Create one Send Port and make the Send Port subscribe to all orders.

   b. Create two Receive Ports with one Receive Location in each and make both Receive Locations receive orders from the ERP system. Create one Send Port and make the Send Port subscribe to all orders.

   c. Create one Send Port. Configure transport options for one of the destinations and backup transport for the other destination. Set the filter to BTS.MessageType == Order.

   d. Create one Receive Port with one Receive Location in it and make the location receive orders from the ERP system. Create a Send Port Group. Make the Group subscribe to orders. Create two Send Ports and add the Send Ports to the Group.

2. You need to send invoices to a partner using the FTP Adapter. The partner has requested a special XML format that differs in structure from the canonical invoice format that you use in your Application. What should you do (choose all that apply)?

    a. Use the `PassThruReceive` Pipeline on the Receive Port

    b. Use the `PassThruTransmit` Pipeline on the Send Port

    c. Create a Map from the partner format to the Canonical invoice

    d. Create a Map from the Canonical invoice format to the desired partner format

    e. Apply a Map on the Send Port

3. HWLC Motors uses two BizTalk Servers, but only one Host (HostA) and one Host Instance per Server. High Availability is a requirement and this is the reason that two BizTalk Servers were set up. We want to ensure that FTP Receive only happens on one of the servers. What should you do (choose all that apply)?

    a. Turn off the Host Instance for HostA on one of the servers

    b. Create a new Host (HostB)

    c. Cluster HostB

    d. Create a Receive Handler for the FTP Adapter for HostB, and delete the Receive Handler for HostA

    e. Make all Receive Locations using the FTP Handler run under HostB

4. You have several Pipelines, both Receive and Send, deployed in a BizTalk Application **Common**. The Pipelines will be needed in several Applications. You create a new Application **ApplicationA**, and start to create Receive Ports and Receive Locations. When choosing a Pipeline for your Receive Location, you notice that the Pipelines deployed in the **Common** Application do not appear in the drop-down list of available Receive Pipelines. What should you do?

    a. Make a reference to the default BizTalk Application in **ApplicationA**

    b. Redeploy all the Pipelines in the **ApplicationA** Application

    c. Make a reference to the **Common** Application in **ApplicationA**

    d. Make a reference to **ApplicationA** in **Common**

5. You want to make sure that all Receive Locations in the entire BizTalk Group are disabled. What should you do?

    a. Stop all running Host Instances.

    b. In the BizTalk Administration Console, open the **Group Hub** and choose **New Query**. Query the **Running Service Instances** and make sure that the query doesn't return any rows.

    c. In the BizTalk Administration Console, open the **Group Hub** and select **Applications**. Check that all Applications are in a stopped state.

    d. In the BizTalk Administration Console, choose the **All Artifacts Application** and open **Receive Locations**. Check that all locations are disabled.

6. You are deploying a Receive Port in your production environment. You do not want it to automatically start processing messages until June 5, 2014. How do you enable this?

    a. In the **Receive Port**, enable the **Service Window** and set it to stop at 05:00 (5 am) and start at 20:14 (8:14 pm)

    b. In the **Receive Port**, configure the **Schedule Stop date** to June 5, 2014

    c. In the **Receive Port**, configure the **Schedule Start date** to June 5, 2014

    d. In the **Receive Port**, enable the **Service Window** and set it to start at 05:00 (5 am) and stop at 20:14 (8:14 pm)

Developing BizTalk Artifacts

1. HWLC Motors is receiving shipment content details from their suppliers. They receive many each day. They need to manually audit some of them. You need to make sure that they can separate out all shipments that have a TotalSum value of $1 million or more. You set up a Send Port to receive shipments. What must you do before you can subscribe to orders equal to or greater than a TotalSum value of $1 million?

    a. Make TotalSum a distinguished field

    b. Promote the TotalSum field

    c. On the root node of the Schema, configure Body XPath to point to the TotalSum field

    d. On the file properties of the Schema, set the **Default Property Schema Name** value to **GreaterThanOrEqualTo**

2. As part of the integration with a major investment bank, HWLC Motors needs to exchange data with an old legacy system. Unfortunately, the system creates incorrect XML, which would cause the disassemble and validation exceptions. A component has been developed to correct the XML on arrival to mitigate errors in later processing. In what Pipeline stage must the component be placed?

    a. The Pre-assemble stage

    b. The Assemble stage

    c. The Disassemble stage

    d. The Decode stage

3. Mooremountain Motors is a big dealership that offers different kinds of brands. As a result, they receive invoices from many different car manufacturers. Jill, a developer at Mooremountain Motors, has developed an Orchestration that handles a Canonical version of an invoice. She has also developed Maps from each of the manufacturer's invoice Schemas to the Canonical Schema. What must she do to ensure that the Orchestration receives the Canonical message?

    a. Create a Receive Port and Receive Location. Configure the Receive Port with Maps that transform from the Canonical format to the manufacturer formats.

    b. Create a Send Port for each of the manufacturers. Configure the Send Ports with Maps that transform from the Canonical format to each of the manufacturer formats.

    c. Create a Receive Port and Receive Location. Configure the Receive Port with Maps that transform from the manufacturer formats to the Canonical formats.

    d. Configure a Receive Port and Receive Location. Configure the Receive Pipeline to be the XmlReceive Pipeline and set the **Validate document structure** property to **True**.

4. HWLC Motors is having problems with an Orchestration in the production. The Orchestration has plenty of trace statements that can be turned on or off to output meaningful information that would help the troubleshooting process. The server processes must remain active at all times; Host Instances cannot be restarted. What would be a suitable location to store the state of the trace output flag?

    a. Create an external .NET component to store the value. Update the .NET component in the GAC to change the value when needed.

b. Create a configuration value in BizTalk's configuration file to store the value. Update the value in the `config` file whenever needed.

c. Create an Orchestration variable to hold the value. Re-deploy the Orchestration to change the value when needed.

d. Create an SSO Application to hold the value. Update the value in the SSO application to change the value when needed.

5. Bo, a developer for HWLC Motors, is developing an integration that will exchange purchase-order messages in an asynchronous request-response pattern over MSMQ. The request is sent out on one queue and the response arrives at another queue. The `OrderId` is unique and included in both the request and response messages. Requirements dictate that the response must be handled by the same Orchestration that sent the request. What must you do in the Orchestration to enable this scenario?

a. Create a Correlation Set. Configure the Send shape to initialize the Correlation Set and the Receive shape to follow the Correlation Set.

b. Set **Ordered Delivery** to **True** on the Orchestrations Receive Port.

c. Create a Correlation Set. Configure the Receive shape to initialize the Correlation Set and the Send shape to follow the Correlation Set.

d. Place the Receive and Send shapes in a scope. Make sure that the scope's **Synchronized** property is set to **True**.

6. HWLC Motors are receiving batched information about cars. They need to design an Envelope Schema to enable the batch to be split. The envelope has the conceptual structure `ManufacturingReport/Cars` under which many `Car` nodes, whose definitions are in another Schema, will be received. What configuration must be present for the Envelope Schema?

a. In the Envelope Schema, set the **Envelope** property of the Schema to `Yes` and then set **Body XPath** of the root node to point to `ManufacturingReport/Cars`

b. In the Envelope Schema set the **Envelope** property of the schema to `Yes` and then set **Body XPath** of the root node to point to `ManufacturingReport/Cars/Car`

c. In the Envelope Schema set the **Root Reference** property to `ManufacturingReport`

d. In the `Car` Schema set the **Root Reference** property to `Car`

Debugging and exception handling

1. Elisa is an administrator for HWLC's BizTalk Server 2010 platform. She is receiving messages through the `ReceiveNewCustomer` Receive Port. She wants to route any message that fails processing to the `SendFailureNotification` Send Port that is configured to use SMTP to send the failed messages by mail to her. How must she configure the `SendFailureNotification` Send Port to receive failures that occurred on the `ReceiveNewCustomer` Receive Port?

    a. Enable Failed Message Routing for the `ReceiveNewCustomer` port. Configure the `SendFailureNotification` Send Port to have a filter on `BTS.ReceivePortName` = `ReceiveNewCustomer`.

    b. Enable Failed Message Routing for the `SendFailureNotification` port. Configure the `SendFailureNotification` port to filter on `BTS.ReceivePortName` = `ReceiveNewCustomer`.

    c. Enable Failed Message Routing for the `SendFailureNotification` port. Configure the `SendFailureNotification` Send Port to have a filter on `ErrorReport.ReceivePortName` = `ReceiveNewCustomer`.

    d. Enable Failed Message Routing for the `ReceiveNewCustomer` port. Configure the `SendFailureNotification` Send Port to have a filter on `ErrorReport.ReceivePortName` = `ReceiveNewCustomer`.

2. HWLC have nightly batch loads of customer information from a legacy system into a new RDMS system. The new system has very strict rules set up, and does not allow null values for vital fields or strings in integer fields. The Schema used to receive data from the legacy system in BizTalk Server 2010 has implemented those rules. The legacy system has not implemented these rules and HWLC is experiencing customers arriving with incorrect data. The customer batch is de-batched in the Receive Pipeline's `XmlDisassembler` component and entered into the new system one by one. HWLC wants all correctly formatted customers to be entered into the new system and wants only the incorrectly-formatted customers to be suspended, and not the whole batch. What must be done to allow the correct messages to proceed?

    a. On the Receive Port from the legacy system, enable Ordered Delivery and make sure that Stop sending subsequent messages on current message failure is not enabled

    b. On the Send Port to the RDMS system, enable Ordered Delivery and make sure that Stop sending subsequent messages on current message failure is not enabled

    c. On the Receive Port from the legacy system, set `RecoverableInterchangeProcessing` to `True` on the `XMLDisassembler` component

    d. On the Send Port to the RDMS system, set `ProcessingInstructionsOptions` to `1` on the `XMLAssembler` component

3. Carly, a developer at HWLC, has been tasked with creating unit tests for a BizTalk Server 2010 solution. A senior developer has told her to use the `ValidateInstance` method to unit test Schemas. She instantiates the Schema class, but can find no such method. What must she do to be able to use the `ValidateInstance` method?

    a. Manually add references to `Microsoft.BizTalk.TestTools` and `Microsoft.XLANGs.BaseTypes`

    b. Set the project's **Enable Unit Testing** option to **True**

    c. Cast the Schema class to a `TestableSchemaBase` class

    d. Configure the `Input Instance Filename` property of the Schema file to point to the instance to validate

4. HWLC has implemented an Orchestration that processes the sensor data. The sensor data is delivered once every second. The next message to arrive makes the previous message obsolete. Suspending the instance in case of failure is not meaningful. The requirement is that a warning needs to be logged to the `EventLog` and then the Orchestration should end without leaving any suspended instances. What must be done to the Orchestration to allow this behavior?

    a. Implement the Orchestration without using any scopes. Ensure that the **Report to Analyst** property of the Orchestration is set to **True**.

    b. Implement the Orchestration using a scope to encapsulate all the logic. Ensure that the **Report to Analyst** property of the scope is set to **True**.

    c. Implement the Orchestration using a scope to encapsulate all logic. Add an exception block to catch the exception. Use the `EventLog` class to write to the `EventLog`. Use the Throw Exception shape to re-throw the exception and end the Orchestration.

    d. On the Receive Port where the sensor data message is first received by BizTalk, select **Enable routing** for failed messages.

5. HWLC has implemented a process that receives sensor data from an engine performance test bench system. The data is sent to a downstream service for further processing through a solicit-response port. At occasions the service is unavailable. The Orchestration has encapsulated all its logic inside a scope and has implemented an exception block to catch the exception and use a Terminate shape to end gracefully without suspending the Orchestration instance. When the Orchestration terminates, there are still suspended messages left on the Send Port. What must you do so there are no messages suspended on the port when errors occur?

   a. Enable Failed Message Routing on the Send port. Configure an Orchestration to filter on the `ErrorReport.SendPortName` property.

   b. Enable Failed Message Routing on the Send port. Configure an Orchestration to Filter on `BTS.AckType` = `NACK` and `BTS.AckSendPortName`.

   c. Configure an Orchestration to Filter on `BTS.AckType` = `NACK` and `BTS.AckSendPortName`.

   d. Configure the logical port in the Orchestration with Delivery Notification so that the Orchestration waits for the port processing to complete and throws a `DeliveryFailureException` if there are failures.

6. HWLC is currently considering implementing unit testing. Which BizTalk artifacts have unit testing APIs?

   a. Schemas, Maps, and Pipeline components

   b. Schemas, Maps, and Pipelines

   c. Schemas Maps, and Orchestrations

   d. Orchestrations

Deploying, tracking, and supporting a BizTalk Solution

1. Nicki has just optimized HWLC's QA environment by setting Messaging and Orchestration polling settings that will improve performance of the environment. She now needs to get these settings into a Production environment. What should she do?

   a. Request a database backup of `BizTalkMgmtDB` and have it restored in the Production environment.

   b. Copy the `BTSNTSVC.exe.config` file from the QA server and place it in the correct folder on the Production server.

   c. Launch the BizTalk settings dashboard and export settings from the QA environment. Import these settings into the Production environment using the BizTalk settings dashboard.

   d. Export the `SSOConfig` database from the QA environment and restore this database in Production.

2. HWLC has just built a two-node BizTalk farm. Juan, who is new to the company, is ready to deploy his first application. What steps must he take to ensure that his application can run on both the BizTalk nodes?

   a. He must first create a Clustered Host Instance and then import his MSI package on both the nodes.

   b. He must run the installation program of his application on the first node, so his assemblies are installed in the GAC. He only needs to import his MSI package using the BizTalk Administration Console on the second node.

   c. He must run the installation program of his application on both nodes so that his assemblies are installed in the GAC. He must then import his MSI package on either node.

   d. He must run the installation program of his application on the first node. He must then import his MSI package using the BizTalk Administration Console on the first node.

3. HWLC's Human Resources department has asked that no messages be sent to their Payroll system until 10 tonight due to system maintenance. At 10 pm, all outstanding messages need to be sent. Jose is planning on attending the big game tonight. What steps can Jose perform to solve this problem?

   a. Jose can stop the Send Port that is used to communicate with the Payroll system before he leaves work. When he arrives in the morning, he can start the Send Port.

   b. In the Send Port, that is used to communicate with the Payroll system, Jose can enable a service window that won't send any messages until 10 pm.

   c. Jose can do nothing and let BizTalk's retry mechanism take care of resubmitting messages that need to be sent. The Send Port that is used to communicate with the Payroll system currently is using the default Retry count and Retry interval settings.

   d. Jose should stop his application using the **Partial Stop - Allow running instances to continue** option. The next morning, he can just start his application.

4. Nick is working in his local development environment. He has a bug that has resulted in 10 suspended messages. Nick has addressed the bug and now wants to re-deploy his application, but can't. What step must he take before he can re-deploy it successfully?

   a. Stop his application with the **Partial Stop - Suspend running instances** option

   b. Restart his Host Instances

   c. Stop his application with the **Full Stop - Terminate instances** option

   d. Stop his Host Instances

5. HWLC has an Orchestration deployed that uses a Direct bound port for receiving messages. Erin would like to track message bodies for these incoming messages. Where should she enable tracking message bodies for these messages?

   a. In the Direct Bound Receive Port, she should enable **Track Message bodies Request before Port Processing**

   b. In the **Orchestration's Tracking** options, she should enable **Track Message Bodies – Before Orchestration processing**

   c. In the **Orchestration's Tracking** options, she should enable **Track Message Bodies – After Orchestration processing**

   d. In the Direct Bound Receive Port, she should enable **Track Message bodies Request after Port Processing**

6. As per the recommendations of the BizTalk Server Administrator, HWLC's BizTalk Server environment is configured with a single host that has **Allow Host Tracking** set to `true`. What is one of the tasks performed by this host?

   a. Move configuration data from the `BizTalkMgmtDb` database to the `BizTalkMsgBoxDb` database

   b. Move BAM tracking data from the `BAMPrimaryImport` database to the `BizTalkDTADb` database

   c. Move protected data from the `SSODB` database to the `BizTalkMgmtDb` database

   d. Move tracking data from the `BizTalkMsgBoxDb` database to the `BizTalkDTADb` database

Integrating Web Services and Windows Communication Foundation (WCF) Services

1. Stephen has just deployed a new application in HWLC's Production environment. This particular application uses a Custom Behavior to authenticate the service requests from a third-party **Customer Relationship System (CRM)**. He needs to specify this endpoint behavior for this service, but is unable to modify the server's `machine.config` file. Where else can he register this endpoint behavior?

    a. Registry

    b. `BTSNTSvc.exe.config`

    c. WCF Send Handler

    d. `Web.config`

2. Kim, an HWLC BizTalk developer, has been asked to consume a third-party Web Service over the Internet that is written in Java hosted on the Unix platform. Which WCF binding do you suggest her to use?

    a. `BasicHttpBinding`

    b. `NetTcpBinding`

    c. `NetNamedPipeBinding`

    d. `NetPeerTcpBinding`

3. Alan has just developed a BizTalk Application that will communicate with a third-party financing WCF Service. At the last minute, the third-party financing company added a new root node to their existing Request Schema. Alan's application has just gone live and he is receiving errors due to a mismatch between the message that he is sending, and the message that the third-party financing application is expecting. What should Alan do to solve this problem without deploying any application(s)?

    a. Re-consume the WCF Service from Visual Studio, recompile, and deploy the application

    b. In the Send Port, specify an Outbound WCF Message Body Template and include this new root node

    c. Change the existing Send Port to use the `PassThruTransmit` Pipeline

    d. Build another WCF Service to intercept the BizTalk request and then pass through a request that conforms to the third-party financing application's specification

4. You have just exposed a BizTalk Orchestration as a WCF Service to IIS and have enabled anonymous access to the service. You have started the application in the BizTalk Administration Console and all the required Host Instances have been started. When you browse to your WCF Service's URL in a Web Browser, you are presented with an error. What could the problem be? Here are few options:

    a. You have not restarted IIS.

    b. You need to add your username to the authorization section of the service's `Web.config`.

    c. The Default Application Pool's identity does not have sufficient permissions. You need to create and use an Application Pool that uses the same identity as the BizTalk Isolated Host Instance.

    d. WCF Services cannot have anonymous access enabled.

5. Javid has just finished exposing his BizTalk Orchestration as a WCF Service using the BizTalk WCF Service Publishing Wizard. He has also deployed his application to his BizTalk Server and ensured all related assemblies have been added to the Global Assembly Cache. Calvin, a business analyst with HWLC, has just informed Javid that he needs to add another field to his Web Service Request Schema called `DateRequiredBy`. Javid has added this field to his Web Service Request Schema, compiled his BizTalk Solution, and has then re-run the BizTalk WCF Service Publishing Wizard. When prompted, he selects the updated BizTalk assembly that includes his Web Service Request Schema and new `DateRequiredBy` field. In Javid's test application, he consumes his updated Web Service to discover that his `DateRequiredBy` field has not been published. What must he do in order to have the `DateRequiredBy` field published?

    a. Before re-running the BizTalk WCF Service Publishing Wizard, he needs to restart his Host Instance that he has configured his Orchestration to use

    b. He must restart Internet Information Services (IIS) after re-publishing his WCF Service

    c. Before re-running the BizTalk WCF Service Publishing Wizard, Javid must add his updated assembly that contains his Schema to the GAC

    d. In order to update a WCF Service that has been exposed by the BizTalk WCF Service Publishing Wizard, he must delete the original Virtual Directory from IIS

6. Fred needs to expose a web service from BizTalk Server 2013 that must be securely accessible to partners using the service from the Internet. The service must be using the most interoperable binding. How should Fred accomplish this?

    a. He should use `WCF-BasicHttp`

    b. He should use `WCF-NetTcpRelay`

    c. He should use `WCF-BasicHttpRelay`

    d. He should use `WCF-WebHttpRelay`

Implementing extended capabilities

1. You want to remove a BAM Activity `act1`, which is already deployed. What should you do?

    a. Go to the `BAMPrimaryImport` database and delete all the tables and views that contain the name `act1`.

    b. Use the command-line tool `bm.exe` with the **Remove all** option.

    c. Use the command-line tool `bttdeploy.exe` with the **Remove** option.

    d. Create an empty Activity in Excel with the name **act1**. Export the Activity to XML. Use the `bm.exe` tool with the update all option and the newly created xml file to delete the Activity.

2. You have set up a BizTalk RFID Server that receives the RFID tags from your warehouse. The BizTalk Server team already has an existing BizTalk Application where FILE, FTP, WCF-SQL, and HTTP Adapters are used. You would like to have the tag information submitted to BizTalk. What should you do?

    a. Write an RFID WCF binding and use the WCF-Custom Receive Adapter in BizTalk to receive the tags.

    b. Write a custom processing Pipeline that writes files to a shared folder and deploy it to the RFID server. Make the BizTalk Server poll the files by using a FILE Receive Adapter.

    c. Set up the `SqlServerSink` Event Handler in RFID. Create a WCF-SQL Receive Location in BizTalk and poll from the `rfidsink` database created by the Event Handler.

    d. Set up the `SqlServerSink` Event Handler in RFID. Create a trigger on the relevant `rfidsink` tables that pushes data from the tables to a file share. Use the FILE Adapter in BizTalk to pick up the messages.

3. The managers want to know what is happening in BizTalk on a weekly basis. How many orders we received, what the average order size was, and so on. How should you implement this capability?

   a. Set up an additional Send Port that subscribes to all messages, use the SMTP Adapter, and mail the messages to the managers

   b. Use BAM Activities and tracking profiles to populate BAM Activities, extract the required information from the orders, and build reports on top of the Activities

   c. Use the Rules Engine to set up `RuleSets`, where a condition is met every time an order is received

   d. Enable Tracking on the Receive Ports and have the managers use the Group Hub to query **Tracked Service Instances**

4. You have set up several rules for your BizTalk Application inside the Rules Engine Composer. These rules need to be altered several times a year, and this process should be handled by the non-IT staff. What should you do to make the rules appear more human-readable when the users update the Rules?

   a. Create new Schemas inside BizTalk that uses non-IT terms

   b. Create a vocabulary inside the Rules Engine Composer using non-technical phrases

   c. Create a new rule and apply synonyms for each rule term

   d. Create a new version of the existing rules and apply synonyms for all technical phrases

5. You receive EDIFACT Orders from several partners through the same FTP Receive Location. When receiving an order 96A EDIFACT message from a partner, you realize that the message does not conform to the EDIFACT standard, and a segment that allows only numbers one to five contains the number six. You talk to the business and you agree that the partner should continue to send a six in that segment, as you don't use the value for anything. You agree that only this partner and only this particular extra rule will be allowed. How should you make BizTalk accept the particular field to allow one to six instead of one to five?

   a. In the Party Agreement for the partner, deselect **Perform EDI Data Type Validation**.

   b. On the Receive Locations **EDIReceive** Pipeline, set **Validate document** to **False**.

   c. Alter the order 96A Schema and extend the Enumeration for the segment with a six.

d. Create a new Order 96A Schema and extend the Enumeration for the Segment with a six. Give the Schema a new Namespace and set up the Namespace on the specific partners Agreement.

e. Write a custom Pipeline Component that replaces the six with a five.

6. You have developed and deployed an Orchestration that makes the use of a Business Rule Policy. When you submit a message to the Orchestration, you get a runtime error caused by the Policy not being available to the Orchestration. What must you do?

a. Ensure that the Policy is published

b. Ensure that the Policy is deployed

c. Ensure that the Orchestration is started

d. Ensure that the Policy is in the same Application as the Orchestration

Using Azure BizTalk features

1. You want to exchange X12 documents with partners using **Windows Azure BizTalk Services**. What would be the minimum requirement of the setup (choose all that apply)?

a. A BizTalk Service Map

b. An X12 Schema

c. A BizTalk Service Bridge

d. Partners

e. Agreements

f. An FTP Source

g. A destination

2. You need to check the message content of messages sent through your WABS. Where is the message content stored?

a. In the Windows Azure Portal

b. In the bridge used for transporting the message

c. In SQL Server Azure

d. In Azure Storage

3. When using the Mapper in WABS, you want to map only order lines with a quantity element larger than 100. Which Functoid should you use?

   a. ForEach

   b. MapEach

   c. If-then-Else

   d. CSharp Scripting

4. You want to receive **Json** format through an **XML** bridge. How would you accomplish this?

   a. Create a custom **Flat File** Schema matching the **Json** format

   b. Create a Message Inspector that transforms **Json** to **XML**

   c. Create a Message Inspector that transforms **XML** to **Json**

   d. Create a Map that maps from Json to XML

5. You are using the **LOB Adapter Services** for communication between a bridge and your local database. You realize that you also need a **Windows Azure Service Bus Namespace** for this to work. What part of the **Service Bus** is used together with the **LOB Services**?

   a. Queues

   b. Topics

   c. Relay

   d. Notification

6. You want to connect your BizTalk Server running in a virtual machine on Azure to your local domain. What technique should you use?

   a. Access Control Service

   b. Virtual Network

   c. Azure Domain Controller

   d. FTP

B
Sample Certification Test Questions – Answers

In order to allow the reader to consider the answers to the questions in *Appendix A, Sample Certification Test Questions*, the answers are separated from the questions. This appendix holds the answers. Also, *Appendix C, Testing Your Knowledge Answers*, holds the answers to the additional *Testing your knowledge* section of the chapters.

In order to help to have better understanding of the answers, a very brief explanation is given as to why the answer is correct and in cases where it's relevant, why the other options are not.

Configuring a messaging architecture

1. Answer: d

    If multiple Ports need to implement the same subscription, Send Port Groups should be used so that the subscription only needs to be implemented once and any changes to the subscription can be maintained in one place.

2. Answers: b, d, e

    `PassThruReceive` on the receive side will cause BizTalk to not recognize the `MessageType` and therefore, we will not be able to Map on the Send Port. The Map should be from the canonical format to the partner format.

3. Answers: b, c, d, e

    We need a new Host so that HostA will still do all the work except receiving FTP. The new Host needs to be clustered so that if one server fails, a Host Instance will start on the other Server.

4. Answer: c

    This should be done using references and it is in the Application, which needs to access artifacts from another Application, the reference needs to be made. The same Pipelines cannot be redeployed in another Application in BizTalk when already residing in another Application.

5. Answer: d

    By choosing **All artifacts**, we can get an overview of everything inside BizTalk, not limited to a certain Application. The other answers either stops too much or otherwise doesn't fulfill the requirement of disabling all the locations.

6. Answer: c

    You should use the **Schedule Start Date** to allow the Port to start at a later date. Setting the stop date does not allow you to control the start date. Setting the service window controls what time of the day the Port runs but says nothing about which day it should start.

Developing BizTalk Artifacts

1. Answer: b

    A distinguished field is used only to create an alias for xpath statements for expressions in Orchestrations. The Body xpath property of the root node is used with Envelope Schemas to point out the node that contains the body of the document. Changing the **Default Property Schema Name** property on the Schema file only affects what the filename of the created Property Schema will be, when you do a Quick Promotion.

2. Answer: d

    The Pre-assemble and Assemble stages are stages in a Send Pipeline and would do nothing to affect the XML in a Receive Pipeline. Therefore the Decode stage, the Receive Pipeline stage before the Disassemble stage, which throws the exception, is correct.

3. Answer: c

    Maps are configured on Receive Ports. As the Orchestration needs the canonical format, you need a Map that transforms to the canonical format. As the files are received into BizTalk, configuring a Send Port is pointless. Pipelines in general, the XMLReceive Pipeline or the **Validate document structure** property of the XML Disassembler, have nothing to do with Maps.

4. Answer: d

   As both, the external component and the Orchestration, are the .NET components, they will load into the Host Instances memory. When they are updated on disk or in the GAC, they will not be refreshed unless the Host Instances are restarted (or a sufficient amount of time passes for the assemblies to unload). Storing the value in BizTalk's configuration file also requires a Host Instance restart for the BizTalk Server to retrieve the new value as the `config` file is read only when the service starts.

5. Answer: a

   Scope and their **Synchronized** property ensure that data being read is not simultaneously written to by other branches of a Parallel shape. It has nothing to do with this scenario. As we are sending a message out and receiving a response, we need to initialize the correlation set on the Receive shape and follow it on the Send shape. The **Ordered Delivery** property makes sure that messages are delivered to the Orchestration in the same order that they were written to the `MessageBox`.

6. Answer: a

   You need to set **Envelope** to `Yes` and point out the node that will contain the nodes to be split; that is, you need to point out the `Cars` node. Specifying the **Root Reference** does not hurt but it does not help.

Debugging and exception handling

1. Answer: d

   You must enable Failed Message Routing on the Receive Port where processing fails and you must add a filter on `ErrorReport`. `ReceivePortName` to the `SendFailureNotification` Port. The `BTS`. `ReceivePortName` property is available but will not be promoted in a failed message and cannot be used for routing.

2. Answer: c

   `RecoverableInterchangeProcessing` is a property on the `XMLDisassembler` component. When configured to `True`, it allows successfully processed messages from a batch to pass through while suspending only the incorrect ones. By default the property is `False`, which means that one incorrectly formatted message fails the entire batch. Ordered Delivery does not help with this nor does processing instructions.

3. Answer: b

   You need to set Enable Unit Testing to `True`. References to `Microsoft.BizTalk.TestTools` and `Microsoft.XLANGs.BaseTypes` are needed, but you do not need to add them manually. Also, when setting **Enable Unit Testing** to **True**, the Schema will get the `TestableSchemaBase` as its base class, which surfaces the `ValidateInstance` method on the Schema class. You cannot cast a Schema that does not inherit from the `TestableSchemaBase` class to that class and use the `ValidateInstance` method.

4. Answer: d

   You need to use a scope with an exception block to be able to catch the exception. Once caught, the Orchestration will terminate without suspending. The Throw Exception shape will rethrow the exception and cause the Orchestration to become suspended. The **Report to Analyst** option is connected to the **Orchestration Designer for Business Analysts (ODBA)** and has nothing to do with exception handling.

5. Answer: a

   In order to get rid of suspended messages on a Send Port that fails processing, you must enable Failed Message Routing and create a subscription that matches any of the `ErrorReport` properties, for example `SendPortName`. Subscribing to `BTS.AckType` and `BTS.AckSendPortName` will get you the NACK message (the exception), but you will not avoid the suspended message. Also, Delivery Notification does not help you avoid suspended messages either.

6. Answer: b

   You can unit test Schemas, Maps and Pipelines. You cannot easily unit test the Pipeline components by themselves, only inside a Pipeline, since they require the context of a Pipeline. Orchestrations must be deployed to be run and tested.

Deploying, tracking, and supporting a BizTalk Solution

1. Answer: c

   The BizTalk Settings Dashboard provides us with the ability to import and export our settings allowing for a very portable solution between BizTalk environments.

2. Answer: c

   When dealing with multiple BizTalk nodes, all related assemblies must be installed in the Global Assembly Cache. Our MSI package only needs to be imported on one node.

3. Answer: b

   The best solution is to take advantage of the service window of the Send Port. This way, we will have our messages queued and in a Scheduled service instances state. When the clock strikes 10 p.m., our messages will automatically be delivered. We also will not be actively communicating with the Payroll system, as this was one of the requirements of the solution.

4. Answer: c

   If we have suspended instances, we cannot redeploy an Application. As this is just a development environment, it is safe just to terminate them. Of the options listed, the only way to terminate these messages is through stopping the Application using the **Terminate instances** option.

5. Answer: b

   As Direct Bound Ports do not show up as physical Ports in the BizTalk Administration Console, we must rely upon using Orchestration tracking. As we want to track the message body as it is received, then we need to use the **Track Message Bodies - Before Orchestration processing**.

6. Answer: d

   Tracking information is temporarily stored in the `BizTalkMsgBoxDb` database while waiting to be transferred to either the `BAMPrimaryImportDb` or `BizTalkDTADb` database. No tracking data is moved in the other direction or between the `BAMPrimaryImportDb` and `BizTalkDTADb` databases. The `BizTalkMgmtDb` database contains only configuration data.

Integrating Web Services and Windows Communication Foundation (WCF) Services

1. Answer: c

   The WCF Send Handler provides the ability to import a WCF Extension/ Custom Behavior. We can access this function by clicking on the **Properties** button inside the WCF Custom Send Handler.

2. Answer: a

   Of the answers available for this question, the BasicHttpBinding is the most interoperable binding.

3. Answer: b

   WCF-based Send Ports provide the ability to alter an outbound message by specifying an XML template. By using this template, we can wrap our message with additional XML tags that will conform to the third party financing the company's specification.

4. Answer: c

   When the BizTalk WCF Service Publishing Wizard runs, it will create a Web Application inside IIS. The problem is that the Web Application will use the Default Application pool. Unless this Default Application pool has been modified to use the identity of the BizTalk Isolated Host Instance account, the Application Pool will not have sufficient BizTalk rights to launch our Web Service in a browser.

5. Answer: c

   The BizTalk WCF Service Publishing Wizard will use the latest version of our Schema's assembly that is in the GAC. It is not enough to just recompile our Application and then select the most recent assembly.

6. Answer: d

   He needs to create a relay Port since he needs to use Windows Azure Service Bus to securely expose his service to the Internet. Although BasicHttp is fairly interoperable, the WebHttp binding or REST is even more so.

Implementing extended capabilities

1. Answer: b

   Bm.exe is the tool used for deploying, updating, and removing activities. The commands are:

   ° Deploy-all

   ° Update-all

   ° Remove-all

2. Answer: c

   Out of the box, the RFID server ships with a SQL Server Event Handler, which will automatically create a Database and polling Stored Procedures and submit data to the tables.

3. Answer: b

   For exposing business data to the rest of the business, BAM is used. The Rules Engine will not work for this and tracking and sending mail will not give the ability to view averages, and so on.

4. Answer: b

   Vocabularies inside the Rules Engine Composer are used for giving the rules a more human-readable language.

5. Answer: d

   We should not disable the validation altogether, because there could be other problems with the documents received, which we do not want to allow. Writing a custom Pipeline component will work, but it will work for all partners, so will changing the original Order 96A Schema.

6. Answer: b

   A Policy must be (at least) published to be visible and usable inside an Orchestration in Visual Studio. However, for it to be able to execute in runtime, it must be Deployed. The Policy does not have to reside in the same BizTalk application. Although the Orchestration must be started for it to be able to execute at all, it has nothing to do with the solution.

Using Azure BizTalk features

1. Answers: b, d, e

    For making the reception of X12 documents work, all that is needed are partners, **Agreements**, a Schema, and a destination where to send the **X12 XML**. An FTP Source could be needed but is not required since all Agreements has an HTTP(S) **endpoint url** as default.

2. Answer: d

    The message body is stored in the Azure Storage account.

3. Answer: b

    The MapEach Functoid is used for conditional mapping of a repeating record and will be the optimal choice here.

4. Answer: b

    When processing custom formats in a bridge, **Message Inspectors** are used. As we are receiving **Json**, we want to convert from **Json** to **XML**. **Json** is not **Flat File** and a Map can only convert from **XML** to **XML**.

5. Answer: c

    The communication between **Azure** and the on-premise **LOB services** requires relaying.

6. Answer: b

    For connecting your virtual machines to local domains, **Virtual Networks** are used.

C

Testing Your Knowledge – Answers

To allow the reader to consider the answers to the questions in the *Testing Your Knowledge* section of the chapters, the answers are separated from the questions. This appendix holds the answers. A second appendix holds the answers to the additional *Sample Certification Test Questions* chapter.

In order to have better understanding of the answers, a very brief explanation is given as to why the answer is correct, and in cases where it's relevant why the other options are not.

Chapter 1: Configuring a Messaging Architecture

1. Answers: b, d, f

   When using the same **Filter** for multiple Send Ports, a Send Port Group should be used so that maintaining the **Filter** only needs to be done at one place. The actual Send Ports should have no **Filter** themselves since that will cause the messages to be sent more than once.

2. Answers: b, d

   In this case, routing for failed messages needs to be set up on the Receive Port (there will be no Send Port activity when a message fails on the receive side). When failed message routing is enabled, all normal Context Properties such as **BTS.ReceivePortName** are **Unpromoted** (written), and only Context Properties in the **ErrorReport** namespace can be used for routing.

3. Answer: b

    Receive Locations should still be enabled and the BizTalk service(s) should still be running so that others subscribers will still get their messages. Setting a Send Port state to the Unenlisted state will cause the Send Port to stop subscribing to the messages and will, therefore, never receive the messages received in BizTalk while the state was Unenlisted. Setting the Port to a stopped state will allow the Port to receive all the messages intended for the Port and not send them, until the Port is started again.

4. Answer: a

    Only option a will work. We cannot use the Send Port since the requirement clearly states that the transformation should happen before the message enters the `MessageBox`. Also option b doesn't work since no chained mapping is allowed in BizTalk.

5. Answer: c

    POP3 is the the only out of the box adapter that has the capabilities of receiving emails from an exchange server. Also the **Body Part Index** should be **0**, because the actual mail body is required as the message part.

Chapter 2: Developing BizTalk Artifacts – Creating Schemas and Pipelines

1. Answer: a

    Rob needs to import the Customer Schema to Supplier Schema since it has a different namespace and the Customer Schema holds the type that he wants to use in the Supplier Schema. Include should be used if it is the same namespace. Defining a new Schema will not help us re-use the existing type.

2. Answer: d

    In a Public Key Infrastructure (PKI), the partner will distribute his public key to allow the signature created using the private key to be validated. The MIME/SMIME Decoder component is used to validate signed messages in a Receive Pipeline.

Chapter 3: Developing BizTalk Artifacts – Creating Maps

1. Answer: c

    The Scripting Functoid should be used to call a .NET component from within a Map. It should be configured to call an external assembly. Although inline C# can technically be used to call a method in an external assembly that violates the statement that no additional code should be written. The Expression shape cannot be used in maps since it is an Orchestration shape. Activities are Windows Workflow artifacts, not BizTalk.

2. Answer: b

    The Greater Than Functoid should be used since you want to output the nodes with value greater than $70000, not equal to or less than this. Conditional Mapping using Logical Functoids can be used to control the output of a node. Although a Value Mapping Functoid is also capable of that, it takes a Boolean as its first input and the value as its second input.

Chapter 4: Developing BizTalk Artifacts – Creating Orchestrations

1. Answer: c

    The `Microsoft.XLANGs.BaseTypes.Address` is a property that must be set on the Port for a Port with Dynamic binding. It cannot be set on the message. Whether you do it in a Message Assignment shape or an Expression shape is not important. There is no `BTS.ReceivedFileName` property.

2. Answer: b

    To configure a block of logic so that either everything commits or nothing commits, you should place the logic within an Atomic scope. To be able to use an Atomic scope, the Orchestration must be configured to have a Long Running transaction type. Although configuring the Orchestration as Atomic, will treat the logic as a unit; it will also treat the entire Orchestration as a unit which was not the goal, and might not be possible.

Chapter 5: Testing, Debugging, and Exception Handling

1. Answers: b, d

   A scope is needed to handle an exception within an Orchestration. To be able to catch an exception, the scope does not have to be transactional, but it must have an exception block. Transactional scopes cause additional persistence points and should be avoided if they are not needed.

2. Answer: a

   If no exception handler is implemented, the default exception handler will trigger. The default exception handler will trigger the compensation block of any nested scopes, if they have one; therefore, a compensation block must be added to the scope to allow compensation to be made. Compensation for what happened inside the scope should be done in that scope's compensation block, not in a parent scope or an Orchestration's compensation block. Also compensating the logic should be placed in the compensation block, not an exception block.

3. Answer: c

   Port processing halts while delivering to the MessageBox only. What happens after a physical Send Port processes messages matching its subscription is, by default, nothing the Orchestration is aware of. **Delivery Notification** can be configured to **Transmitted** on a logical Send Port in the Orchestration to halt the processing until the Physical Send Ports processing is successful before completing a Scope. If the physical Port fails, DeliveryFailureException will be raised. Failed message routing routes the message in case of Port failure but does nothing to affect Orchestration processing. The **Synchronized** property has nothing to do with this behavior.

4. Answer: b

   For a Port to fail processing on its first attempt (immediately), the **Retry Count** on the **Transport Advanced Options** pane must be set to **0**. It will then try to use the backup transport. Configuring the **Retry Count** or **Priority** of the backup transport does not affect the primary transport behavior. This scenario has nothing to do with **Ordered Delivery**.

5. Answer: c

Although there are several things that could potentially be wrong, of the possible answers only option c will affect how the message is interpreted or how it is routed and potentially solves the problem. Messages cannot be edited in the Administration Console and reconfiguring Send Port does not affect how the message is processed by the Receive Port and Pipeline.

Chapter 6: Deploying, Tracking, and Administrating a BizTalk Server 2010 Solution

1. Answer: d

We need to let our application drain by not allowing any new message instances to be received while any existing messages can complete. By stopping all Receive Locations we cannot receive any new messages and by waiting for any active instances to complete, we can safely perform a Full stop once we know there are no messages currently being processed.

2. Answer: b

Since we are interested in tracking just the Flat File that BizTalk received, we want to enable **Track Message Bodies – Request message** before Port processing. By doing so, we are capturing a copy of the message before our flat file reaches our custom Pipeline that will include our flat file disassembler.

3. Answer: b

Whenever we configure a new Host in an environment, we need to be sensitive to the Adapters that will be using this new Host. When this occurs, we need to add this Host as a Send and/or Receive handler depending upon whether we will use our Host in a Send Port or Receive Location.

4. Answer: c

In this scenario, we want to see how many message instances are currently retrying. In order to discover this, we need to run **Running service instances – Retrying** and idle Ports query from BizTalk Group Hub.

5. Answer: d

When we need to export an MSI file from a BizTalk application, we have the ability to add Binding Files as resources. We can tag these binding files with a **Target Environment** that will allow us to distinguish one binding file from another. If we do not provide a binding file with a Target Environment, this binding file will be treated as the default binding file. So when we go to use this MSI package in another environment, we will only see the default binding file.

Chapter 7: Integrating Web Services and Windows Communication Foundation (WCF) Services

1. Answer: c

When a service is taking a longer time than we expect to complete, we need to increase the Send timeout property, which will allow our Send Port to wait longer before throwing a timeout exception.

2. Answer: d

Since we changed our logical Port's **Operation** name inside of our Orchestration and deployed it, our only option is to update the Physical Send Port's SOAP Action header so that it matches the value that we specified inside our Orchestration.

3. Answer: a

We need to configure our Send Port to pass on the exception that we received from the **Custom Paint** service. In order to do this, we need to enable the **Propagate fault** message inside our Send Port's configuration.

4. Answer: b

Our only option in this case is to actually rerun the BizTalk WCF **Service Publishing** wizard. The reason for this is that when this wizard generates our WCF Service and the related folder in the `c:\inetpub` folder, references to the Adapter we selected in the wizard exist.

5. Answer: c

The default message size that a WCF Receive Location can handle is 65,536 bytes. If we are planning on receiving a message that is larger than this value, we need to increase the Maximum received message size value.

Chapter 8: Implementing Extended Capabilities

1. Answer: b

   Agreements is what is used to set up various customer specific EDI properties.

2. Answer: c

   We cannot unpublish an existing rule, and for a new rule to take effect in BizTalk, it needs to be deployed. Changes in the Orchestrations are not needed, because they will always use the highest version deployed.

3. Answer: a

   Excel and `bm.exe` are the tools used for creating Activities. `Bttdeploy.exe` is the tool used for deploying the Tracking Profiles.

4. Answer: d

   After deploying an activity, a tracking profile needs to be set up so that BAM can map the activity items to items/events in BizTalk. `Bttdeploy.exe` is the tool used to deploy the tracking profile created in the tracking profile editor.

5. Answer: c

   It is on the receive side (Disassemble) that BizTalk needs to process the incoming EDI messages.

Chapter 9: Using Azure BizTalk Features

1. Answers: b, e, f

   When creating a WABS, an Azure SQL Server, an Azure Storage account, and an ACS are required. Neither a BizTalk Server nor any other on-premise prerequisites are required.

2. Answer: d

   Writing to the Context (Metadata) of a message in a bridge is done in the **Enrich** Stage.

3. Answer: d

   To make the connection match everything, we choose **Match All**, which is equivalent to **1=1**.

4. Answers: b, d, e, f

    The Adapter pack contains a **SQL Server** Adapter, **Oracle** (both **DB** and **EBS**), **Siebel,** and **SAP**.

5. Answer: c

    Tracking information is stored in the **Azure SQL Server** associated with the **WABS**. The actual messages are stored in the **Storage** account.

Index

[PACKT] PUBLISHING   enterprise
professional expertise distilled

Thank you for buying
(MCTS) Microsoft BizTalk Server (70-595) Certification and Assessment Guide *Second Edition*

About Packt Publishing

Packt, pronounced 'packed', published its first book "Mastering phpMyAdmin for Effective MySQL Management" in April 2004 and subsequently continued to specialize in publishing highly focused books on specific technologies and solutions.

Our books and publications share the experiences of your fellow IT professionals in adapting and customizing today's systems, applications, and frameworks. Our solution based books give you the knowledge and power to customize the software and technologies you're using to get the job done. Packt books are more specific and less general than the IT books you have seen in the past. Our unique business model allows us to bring you more focused information, giving you more of what you need to know, and less of what you don't.

Packt is a modern, yet unique publishing company, which focuses on producing quality, cutting-edge books for communities of developers, administrators, and newbies alike. For more information, please visit our website: www.packtpub.com.

About Packt Enterprise

In 2010, Packt launched two new brands, Packt Enterprise and Packt Open Source, in order to continue its focus on specialization. This book is part of the Packt Enterprise brand, home to books published on enterprise software – software created by major vendors, including (but not limited to) IBM, Microsoft and Oracle, often for use in other corporations. Its titles will offer information relevant to a range of users of this software, including administrators, developers, architects, and end users.

Writing for Packt

We welcome all inquiries from people who are interested in authoring. Book proposals should be sent to author@packtpub.com. If your book idea is still at an early stage and you would like to discuss it first before writing a formal book proposal, contact us; one of our commissioning editors will get in touch with you.

We're not just looking for published authors; if you have strong technical skills but no writing experience, our experienced editors can help you develop a writing career, or simply get some additional reward for your expertise.

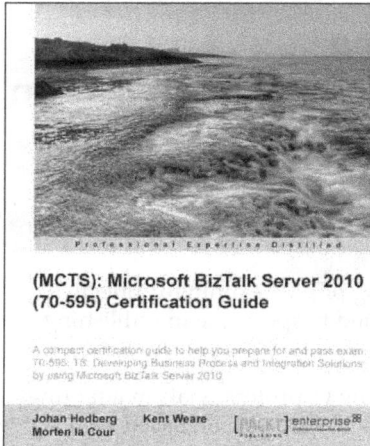

(MCTS): Microsoft BizTalk Server 2010 (70-595) Certification Guide

ISBN: 978-1-84968-492-7   Paperback: 476 pages

A compact certification guide to help you prepare for and pass exam 70-595: TS: Developing Business Process and Integration Solutions by using Microsoft BizTalk Server 2010

1. This book and e-book will provide all that you need to know in order to pass the (70-595) Developing Business Process and Integration Solutions exam by Using Microsoft BizTalk Server 2010 book.

2. Includes a comprehensive set of test questions and answers that will prepare you for the actual exam.

3. The layout and content of the book closely matches that of the skills measured by the exam, which makes it easy to focus your learning and maximize your study time in areas where you need improvement.

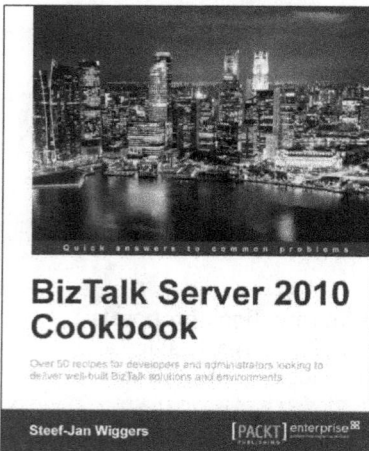

BizTalk Server 2010 Cookbook

ISBN: 978-1-84968-434-7   Paperback: 368 pages

Over 50 recipes for developers and administrators looking to deliver well-built BizTalk solutions and environments

1. Enhance your implementation skills with practically proven patterns.

2. Written by a BizTalk expert and MVP, Steef-Jan Wiggers, the book is filled with practical advice.

3. Learn best practices for deploying BizTalk 2010 solutions.

Please check **www.PacktPub.com** for information on our titles

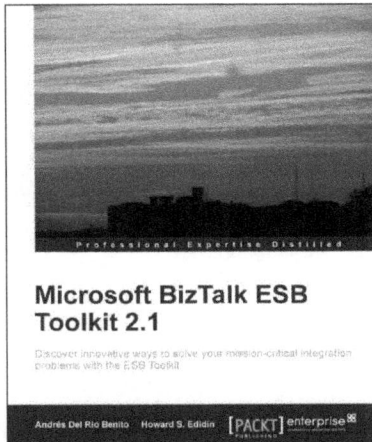

Microsoft BizTalk ESB Toolkit 2.1

ISBN: 978-1-84968-864-2 Paperback: 130 pages

Discover innovative ways to solve your mission-critical integration problems with the ESB Toolkit

1. A comprehensive guide to implementing quality integration solutions.

2. Instructs you about the best practices for the ESB and also advises you on what not to do with this tool.

3. A sneak view of what's new in the ESB Toolkit 2.2.

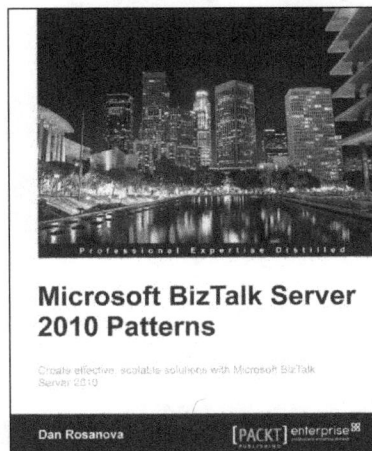

Microsoft BizTalk Server 2010 Patterns

ISBN: 978-1-84968-460-6 Paperback: 396 pages

Create effective, scalable solutions with Microsoft BizTalk Server 2010

1. Provides a unified example from the beginning to end of a real world solution.

2. A starter guide expecting little or no previous BizTalk experience, but offering advanced concepts and techniques.

3. Provides in-depth background and introduction to the platform and technology.

4. Written by a Biztalk architecture MVP.

Please check **www.PacktPub.com** for information on our titles